PAGE 38

ON THE ROAD

YOUR COMPLETE DESTINATION GUIDE
In-depth reviews, detailed listings and insider tips

TOP EXPERIENCES MAP NEXT PAGE

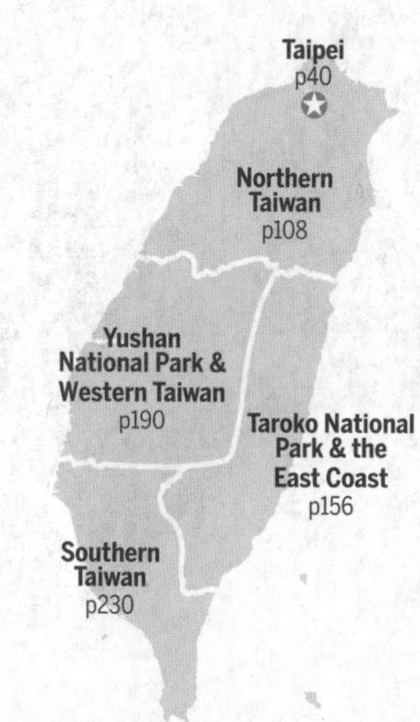

PAGE 363

SURVIVAL GUIDE

YOUR AT-A-GLANCE REFERENCE
How to get around, get a room, stay safe, say hello

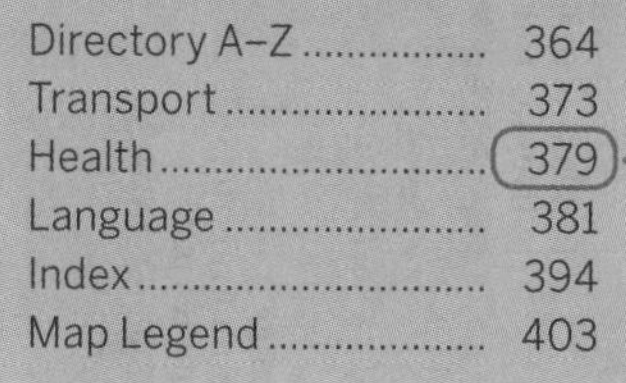

THIS EDITION WRITTEN AND RESEARCHED BY

Robert Kelly

Joshua Samuel Brown

Taiwan

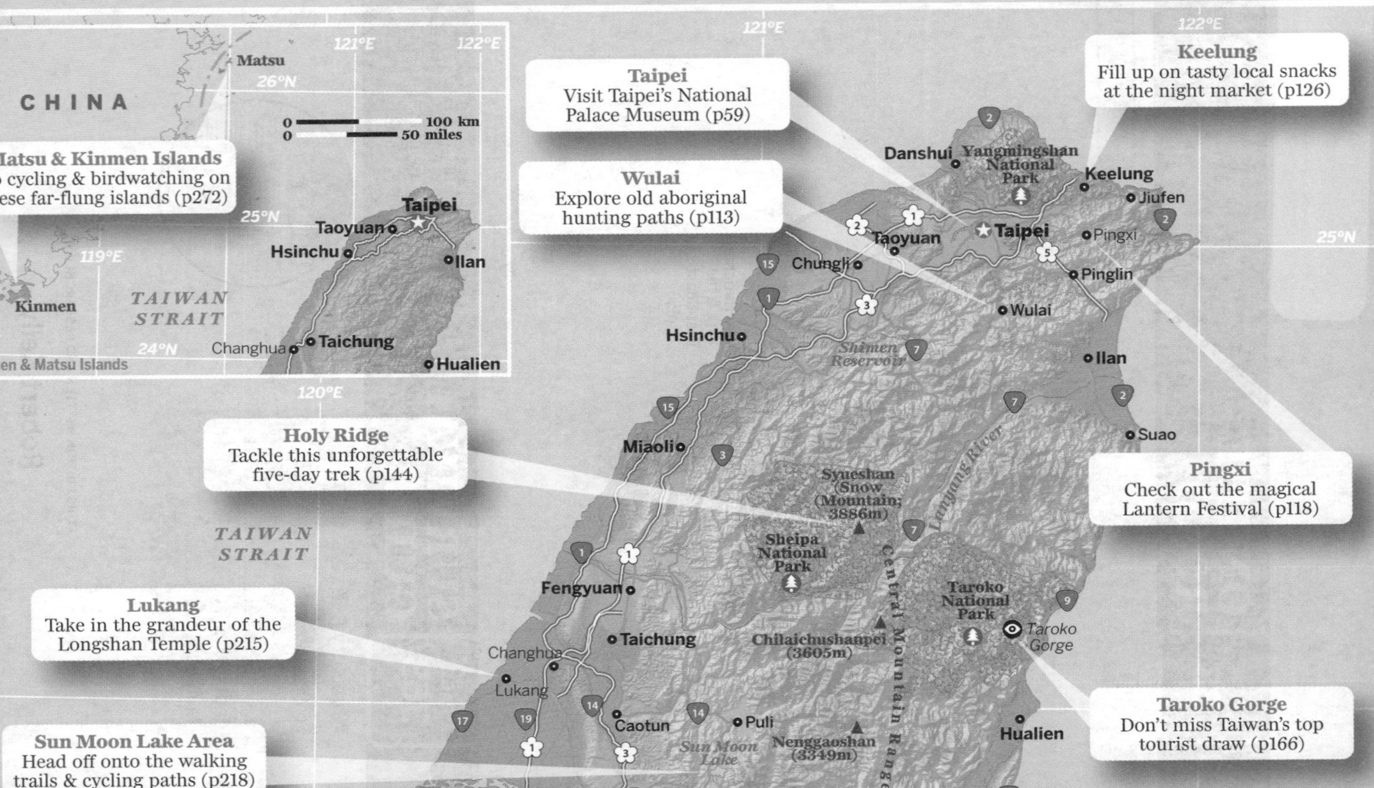

Keelung
Fill up on tasty local snacks at the night market (p126)

Taipei
Visit Taipei's National Palace Museum (p59)

Matsu & Kinmen Islands
Go cycling & birdwatching on these far-flung islands (p272)

Wulai
Explore old aboriginal hunting paths (p113)

Holy Ridge
Tackle this unforgettable five-day trek (p144)

Pingxi
Check out the magical Lantern Festival (p118)

Lukang
Take in the grandeur of the Longshan Temple (p215)

Taroko Gorge
Don't miss Taiwan's top tourist draw (p166)

Sun Moon Lake Area
Head off onto the walking trails & cycling paths (p218)

East Coast Cycling
Cycle along the Hwy 11 coastline (p171)
Walami Trail
Hike the brilliant Walami Trail (p180)
Dulan
Get your groove on at a live-music performance (p173)
Penghu Archipelago
Go swimming, snorkelling & windsurfing (p291)
Alishan
Find remote villages, forests & a historic railway (p202)
ELEVATION
3000m
2500m
2000m
1500m
1000m
500m
200m
100m
0
0
50 km
0
25 miles
Makung
Penghu
Tropic of Cancer
Chiayi
Baihe
Sinying
Tainan
Kaohsiung
Fengshan
Pingtung
Donggang
Little Liuchiu Island
Fangliao
Fengkang
Kenting National Park
Kenting
Eluanbi
Alishan National Scenic Area
Chushan (2489m)
Yushan (3997m)
Yushan National Park
Guanshan (3666m)
Central Mountain Range
Nan-tsu-hsien Chi
Laonung River
Kaoping River
Peinan River
Rueisui
Shihtiping
Yuli
Walami Trail
Litao
Sixty Stone Mountain (952m)
Dulan
Taitung
Chihpen
Tawu
Green Island
Lanyu
PACIFIC OCEAN
SOUTH CHINA SEA
23°N
22°N

20 TOP EXPERIENCES

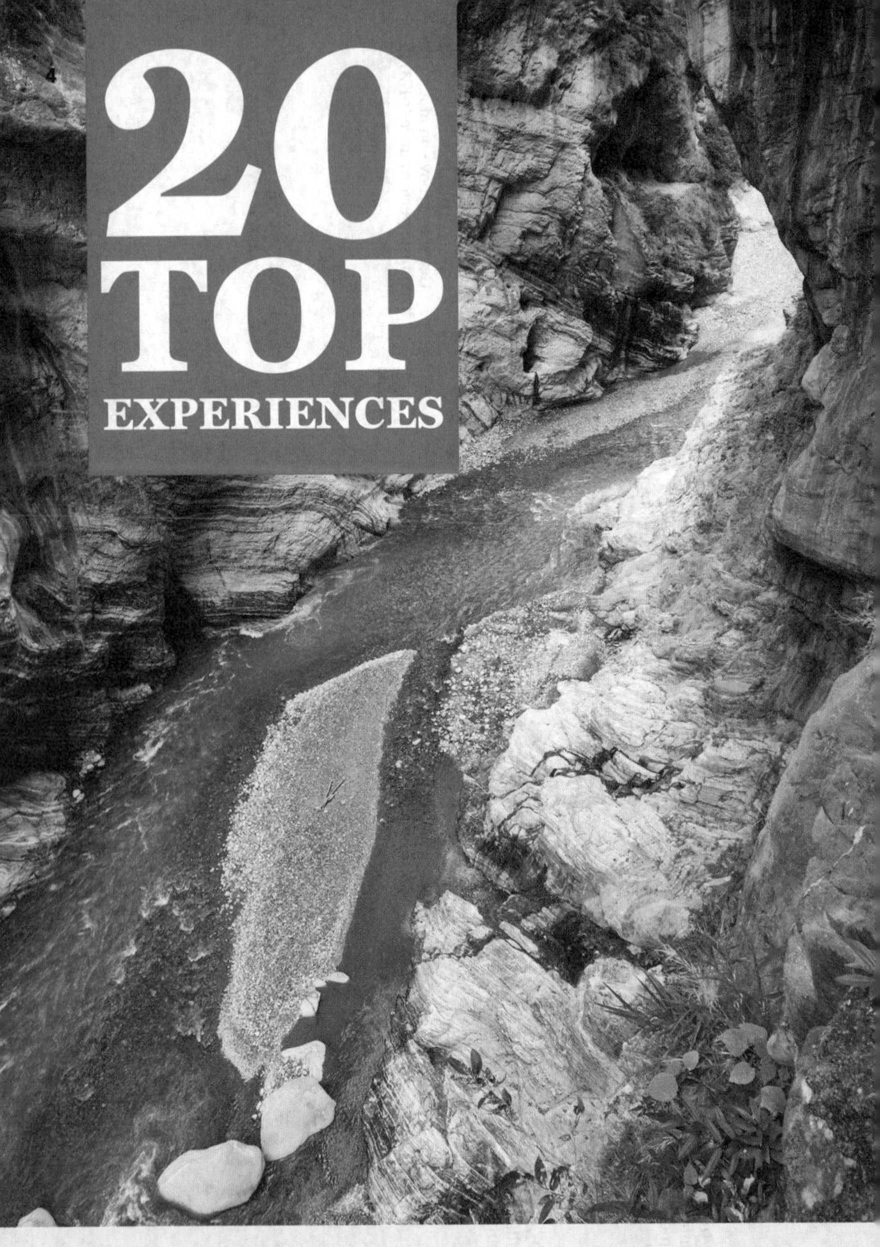

Taroko Gorge

1 Taiwan's top tourist draw is a walk-in Chinese painting. Rising above the froth of the blue-green Liwu River, the marble walls (yes, marble!) of Taroko Gorge (p166) swirl with the colours of a master's palette. Add in grey mist, lush vegetation and waterfalls seemingly tumbling down from heaven, and you truly have a classic landscape. Walk along the Tunnel of Nine Turns to see the gorge at its most sublime, or brave the Jhuilu Old Trail, a vertigo-inducing 500m above the canyon floor.

Hiking the High Mountains

2 Don't forget your boots, because two thirds of Taiwan's terrain is mountainous – and what mountains they are. Hundreds soar above 3000m, and well-established hiking routes run everywhere. These are the real deal (no shops, no restaurants) and on remote trails you might just find yourself alone for several days. Everyone wants to tackle Yushan (p194), the highest peak in Northeast Asia, but the second highest, Snow Mountain, is a more scenic climb, and leads to the sublime Holy Ridge (p144), a 5-day walk on an exposed ridgeline that never drops below 3000m.

CRAIG FERGUSON

The National Palace Museum

3 By a pure accident of history, Taiwan houses the greatest collection of Chinese art in the world (take that Beijing!). With ancient pottery, bronzes and jade, Ming vases, Song landscape paintings and calligraphy even a foreign eye can appreciate, Taipei's National Palace Museum (p59) isn't merely a must-visit; it's a must-repeat-visit. Why? Out of the estimated 60,000 pieces in the museum's collection – pieces spanning every Chinese dynasty – only a tiny fraction are ever on display at the one time.

The Temple Towns: Tainan & Lukang

4 There are 15,000 official temples in Taiwan; three times the number of 30 years ago. Still the focus of local culture, temples play the role of community centres as much as houses of worship. Both Tainan and Lukang boast a wealth of old buildings, from understated Confucius temples to Matsu temples rich in examples of the decorative arts. If you can only visit one, make it the Buddhist Longshan Temple (p215) in Lukang, a showcase of traditional design and woodcarving.

ROBERT KELLY

Cycling the East Coast

5 Cycling fever has taken over the island, and the unspoiled and sparsely populated east coast has emerged as the top destination for multiday trips. Fans of the sea should ride Hwy 11 (p171), with its stunning coastline, beaches, fishing harbours and art villages. Those with a love of mountains should head to the Rift Valley (p175), bounded on each side by lush green ranges. On both routes there are enough roadside cafes, campgrounds, homestays and hot springs to ensure your cycling trip won't be an exercise in logistics.

ANDY TSAI

Underwater Delights

6 With hundreds of types of soft and hard corals, intact reefs brimming with tropical sea creatures and year-round good visibility, Taiwan offers some fantastic venues for snorkelling and scuba diving. Probably the only thing keeping the international buzz down is the lack of trendy bars to relax in at the end of the day. If that doesn't bother you head to Penghu, Kenting, Lanyu, or visit Green Island (p306) where you can check out the 200-plus species of coral and the hammerhead shark migration in winter. Worth more than a few cocktails, don't you think?

Sun Moon Lake National Scenic Area

7 Sun Moon Lake (p218) is the largest body of water in Taiwan and boasts a watercolour background ever changing with the season and light. Although the area is packed with Chinese tourists these days it's still remarkably easy to get away from the crowds on the many trails and cycling paths. Loop down to the old train depot at Checheng to explore 1950s Taiwan, or head to Shuili to see the last working snake kiln. No matter what, don't miss the region's high-mountain oolong tea: it's some of the finest in the world.

Alishan National Scenic Area

8 The remains of the logging days are the top draw at Alishan (p202), and include a rare narrow-gauge rail line that hauls passengers from sea level to 2800m in 3½ hours. But there's so much more to this 33,000-hectare mountainous region, including quiet tea-growing villages, old-growth forests, hiking trails and stunning sunrises and sunsets. There are Zhou aboriginal villages in some of the most remote parts; an overnight in a local homestay will introduce you to a way of life far removed from the city ways down on the plains.

PHILIP GAME

The Teas of Taiwan

9 Boasting good soil, humid conditions and sunny weather, Taiwan is a prime tea-growing area. High-mountain oolongs will blow your taste buds away with their creamy texture and honey flavours (and that's without sugar or milk of course). The ruby colour and sweet aroma of Oriental Beauty tea might just convince you to make it your new morning 'coffee'. Whether you brew it old-man style, or in Song dynasty bowls, you'll find a tea house to your tastes in scenic areas such as Taipei's Maokong (p103) or the old gold-mining town of Jiufen (p128).

ROBERT KELLY

The Walami Trail

10 Part of a system of 'Pacifying the Natives' mountain routes under Japanese colonial rule, the Walami Trail (p180) runs deep into the heart of one of the best-preserved subtropical environments on the island. Monkeys battle in the trees, barking deer peek out from the underbrush and a host of native birds and butterflies flitter about. Just do be careful of whatever slithers past your feet. A brilliant day hike, the Walami continues as the Batongguan Traversing Route for another seven days to reach the main peak of Yushan.

Jungle Treks & River Swims

11 Taiwan is 50% forested and the urban jungle gives way to the real thing astonishingly quickly. In the mountainous Wulai township (p111), 30 minutes from Taipei, old aboriginal hunting paths cut through intensely green tropical forests. Trailside you can count more species of fern than you have fingers and toes. Take a break from your trek to enjoy crystal-clear streams and deep swimming pools. Paradise? You bet, and you can rinse (don't lather, you'll spoil the water) and repeat this experience all over the island.

ROBERT KELLY

ROBERT KELLY

The Birds & the Butterflies

12 Taiwan is a special place for the winged creatures of the world. More than 500 species of birds and an almost equal numbers of butterflies can be seen here, with a very high percentage found nowhere else. Habitats are well preserved and you don't need to trek days into the jungle for a fleeting glimpse. Indigenous species like the Blue Magpie can be spotted in any forest park; raptor migrations can be enjoyed from grassy fields in Kenting National Park (p266); and in this Kingdom of Butterflies, the Lepidoptera will probably find you first.

ROBERT KELLY

The Dulan Arts Scene

13 It all began with a small cafe offering live music on Saturday nights on the grounds of a former sugar factory. Now, the tiny aboriginal town of Dulan (p173) is starting to pull in artists, craftspeople, drifters and real-estate speculators from around the island. They all want the same thing: to tap into the unmistakable groove of the place. Don't miss the regular Saturday night live concerts. Performances mix modern, folk, Western and aboriginal elements, and the audience, drawn from around East Asia, is equally diverse.

The Magic Lights of Lantern Festival

14 One of the oldest of the lunar festivals, the Lantern Festival celebrates the end of the New Year's festivities. The focus of course is light, and everywhere streets and riversides are lined with glowing lanterns, while giant neon and laser displays fill public squares. Making the mundane surreal and the commonplace magical, the little mountain village of Pingxi takes simple paper lanterns and releases them en masse into the night sky (p118). There are few sights more mesmerising.

CRAIG FERGUSON

ORIEN HARVEY

A Stationary Feast: Night Markets

15 Taiwan's night markets are as numerous as they are varied. Fulfilling the need for both food and entertainment (to say nothing of socialising), the markets bring happy crowds almost every night of the week to gorge on a bewildering array of snacks and dishes. Check out the Keelung Night Market (p126), in many ways the granddaddy of them all, for the quintessential experience of food and people. The night market snacks in Tainan (p239) are copied everywhere but still best enjoyed on their home turf.

The Matsu Pilgrimage

16 This mother of all walks across Taiwan is, appropriately enough, dedicated to Matsu ('old granny'), the maternal patron deity of the island (p200). For eight days and 350km, hundreds of thousands of the faithful follow a revered statue of Matsu across Taiwan, while several million more participate in local events. This is Taiwan's folk culture at its most exuberant and festive, with crowds, wild displays of devotion, theatrical performances and a whole lot of fireworks.

ROBERT KELLY

IMAGEMORE CO., LTD. / ALAMY

Penghu Archipelago: Little Jewels in the Crown

17 One of East Asia's best kept secrets, the Penghu Archipelago (p291) includes some of Taiwan's finest beaches, best snorkelling sites and most temple-laden towns. Need more? How about a top windsurfing venue in the winter with wind speeds of 40 knots? But it's all pricey top-end resorts here, right? Nope. On Penghu you're more likely to see a traditional fishing village beside that flawless beach than anything else. For now, the archipelago's over-the-top charms are distinctly under the radar.

Hot Springs: Wild & Tamed

18 Formed by the collision of two major tectonic plates, Taiwan's surface has plenty of cracks and fissures and the abundance of spring sources is hard to match anywhere else in the world. The waters boil and bubble but cause no trouble, instead being effective for everything from soothing muscles to conceiving male offspring (we can only vouch for the former). Nature lovers will find spas a double happiness: stone, wood and marble are in these days, as are mountain views. And if you're willing to walk in, many pristine wild springs still lie deep in the valleys. See p33 for more.

PATRICK LIN/AFP/GETTY IMAGES

JOSHUA SAMUEL BROWN

The Cold War Frontiers: Matsu & Kinmen Islands

19 Close enough to see the other side (China) on even a hazy day, Matsu (p284) and Kinmen (p274) Islands were long the front lines in the propaganda (and occasional real) wars between the nationalists and communists. These days with the military presence scaling down, travellers are discovering islands whose rich history is not limited to recent times – Matsu and Kinmen are treasure troves of preserved old villages. Visitors will also find some fine cycling and birdwatching among the varied landscapes.

Succulent Fruit

20 Blessed with an astonishing range of climates and soils, and a populace that's in the know when it comes to fruit, Taiwan is the perfect place to indulge your sweet tooth naturally. Start with something familiar: cut up pineapple, honeydew melon, or a little guava (often served with salt to bring out the flavour), before moving on to starfruit, wax apple, tangerine or custard apple (better known as the Buddha head fruit because of its odd, lumpy appearance). For a straight injection of sweet, succulent, addictive goodness, however, nothing beats a Taiwanese mango. See p162 for more.

MARTIN MOOS

welcome to Taiwan

With a pulsating modern capital, temple towns, hot-springs villages and adventures in both shopping malls and wooded mountains, Taiwan cuts a figure as one of Asia's most diverse destinations.

The Beautiful Isle

Famed for centuries as *Ihla Formosa,* the Beautiful Isle, this is a land with more sides than the 11-headed Guanyin. Sandy beaches, marble-walled gorges and tropical forests are just the start of your journey, which could take you as far as Yushan, Taiwan's 3952m alpine roof.

The activities possible in this landscape are equally diverse. Criss-cross Yushan National Park (p192) on colonial-era hiking trails. River trace up to the Golden Canyon (p168). Windsurf the fastest conditions in Asia, or cycle Hwy 11 (p171) with the blue Pacific on one side and green volcanic arcs on the other. Along the way you'll find plenty of locals to keep you company. And not just the sporting people. Taiwan is the Kingdom of Butterflies, and home to a host of other endemic flying, crawling and swimming things. When you step away from the urban jungle into the real thing be prepared to say 'I've never seen that before' very often.

Have You Eaten?

These words are a greeting here, like 'Hello', and your answer will always be 'Yes', because there's just too much nibbling to be done. Taiwan offers travellers the gamut of Chinese cuisines (p344) – Sichuanese, Cantonese, Beijing-style, Fujianese, hot pot and heavenly vegetarian. But that's just the beginning. Taipei's got the best Japanese outside Tokyo and night markets around the island offer endless feasts of local snacks. Try stewed spare ribs, oyster omelettes, beef noodles, coffin cake, shrimp rolls and slack-season noodles.

In the countryside, sample hearty staples of the Hakka people, such as fried ginger intestine, or try some leaner, lighter aboriginal fare including wild chicken, mountain vegetables and rice steamed in bamboo shells. If you need a drink there's local beer, potent firewater like Kaoliang, and some of the finest oolong teas in the world.

It doesn't matter if you're a Southeast Asian out to compare Taipei's street food with your own, or a Western traveller looking to expand your taste buds with stinky tofu, you'll find Taiwan consistently delivers on variety, flavour and pure culinary adventure.

The Tao of Today

Who's coming to Taiwan to check out the religious life? Overseas Chinese for one, looking to connect with roots that have been lost elsewhere. Taiwan is heir to the entire Chinese tradition of Buddhism, Taoism, Confucianism, and that amorphous collection of ancestors, gods, goddesses, local heroes and plague demons worshipped under the moniker of folk faith. All thrive here as nowhere else, and over the centuries the Taiwanese have mixed and matched their way to a unique religious culture that's sometimes as ritual heavy as Catholicism, as opened-minded as Methodism, or as wild as Santeria.

Taiwanese temples (all 15,000 of them) combine art house, worship hall, community centre and festival venue under one roof. Watch a ritual plague boat burn to the ground at Donglong Temple (p260). March with the Empress of Heaven from Chenlan Temple (p201) across half of Taiwan. Bathe the Buddha on his birthday or *bwah bwey* (cast moon blocks) at any folk temple to answer your deepest questions.

need to know

Currency

» New Taiwanese dollar (NT$)

Language

» Mandarin and Taiwanese

When to Go

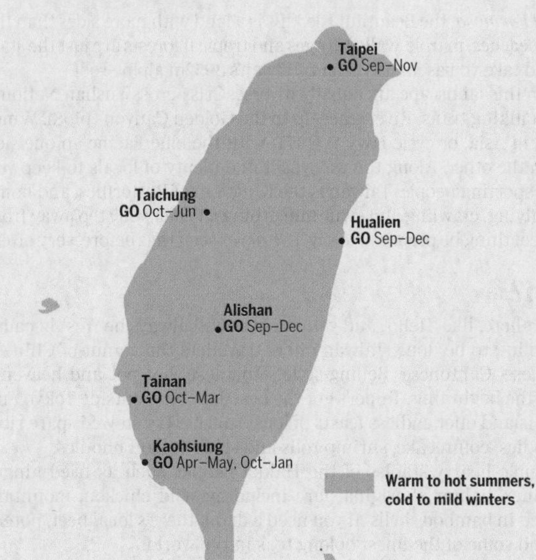

High Season
(Jul–Aug)

» Accommodation costs increase 30% to 50% in tourist areas

» Saturday nights and Chinese New Year also see increases

» Heavy crowds at major tourist sights and beaches

Shoulder
(Sep–Oct, Apr–Jun)

» Good discounts on accommodation midweek

» Crowds at major sights on weekends

» Best time to visit outer islands

» Nontourist areas see no price increase or decrease

Low Season
(Nov–Mar)

» Crowds are low except during Chinese New Year

» Big discounts on accommodation at major tourist sights (up to 50%)

» Saturday-night rates may still be higher

Your Daily Budget

Budget NT$1500–2500

» Dorm bed NT$300–500

» Cheap hotel NT$500–1200

» Eat at convenience stores, noodle stands, night markets

» Take late-night intercity buses for cheapest rates

Midrange NT$3000–5000

» Double room in B&B NT$1500–2400

» At this price range B&Bs usually offer superior rooms to hotels

» Lunch and dinner at a decent local restaurant NT$250–400

» Go to popular destinations midweek for discounts on better accommodation

Top end more than NT$6000

» Double room at 4-star hotel NT$4000–6000

» Hotel restaurant meals NT$600–1200

Money

» ATMs widely available. Credit cards accepted in most mid- to top-range hotels (but few B&Bs) and better restaurants.

Visas

» Generally not required for stays of up to 30 days.

Mobile Phones

» Local SIM cards can be used in mobile phones from most countries. Purchase SIM cards at the airport. Cheap mobile-phone rentals are also available at the airport.

Driving

» Drive on right side of road; steering wheel is on the left side of the car. Most visitors rent scooters or use the bus and train.

Websites

» **Forumosa** (www.forumosa.com) Informative expat community site.

» **Information For Foreigners** (http://iff.immigration.gov.tw/enfront) Visa regulations and daily life matters.

» **Lonely Planet** (www.lonelyplanet.com) Visit the Thorn Tree forum for updates from fellow Lonely Planet readers.

» **The View From Taiwan** (http://michaelturton.blogspot.com) Unparalleled local political and cultural coverage with a major bike trip recorded each week.

Exchange Rates

Australia	A$1	NT$28.30
Europe	€1	NT$41.30
Japan	¥100	NT$37.00
Malaysia	MYR1	NT$10.00
Singapore	SGD1	NT$23.40
UK	UK£1	NT$49.00
USA	US$1	NT$32.20

For current exchange rates see www.xe.com.

Important Numbers

When calling local long-distance numbers, the '0' in the area codes is used. When dialling from overseas it's dropped.

Emergency	☎119
Country code	☎886
International access code	☎002
Taipei area code	☎02
24-hour tourism hot line	☎0800-011 765

Arriving in Taiwan

» **Taiwan Taoyuan International Airport** (www.taoyuanairport.gov.tw)
Buses – every 15 minutes to centre of city (NT$85–140) from 5am to 1am.
Taxis – NT$1200–1500, around 40 to 60 minutes to the city
See p90

» **Kaohsiung International Airport** (www.kia.gov.tw)
MRT – every six minutes from 5.55am to 11.40pm (NT$35)
Taxis – NT$300
See p255

Can I Get By Without Mandarin?

Thousands of people get by without being able to speak Mandarin every year. It's relatively easy in Taipei, Tainan and Kaohsiung, and challenging but doable in rural areas and the east coast outside Hualien. It helps if you at least learn your numbers, basic phrases such as 'How much?' and some common dishes.

There is a **24-hour tourism hot line** (☎0800 011 765) with English-/Japanese-/Chinese-speaking operators. Visitor information centres at most tourist sights, train stations and High Speed Rail have English-language materials available and sometimes English-speaking staff. If staff don't speak English, look lost and they will call for help. See also the National Youth Commission (p366).

Transportation signs are usually bilingual. Hotels usually have room types and prices in English. Streets have numbered addresses (except in very rural areas and offshore islands). English menus are common in midrange/top-end restaurants. Most Taiwanese are very friendly and will help any traveller who looks lost.

if you like...

Outdoor Activities

As a large mountainous island, Taiwan has both the land and sea for a host of outdoor activities. Hiking is outstanding and scenic cycling routes are endless. As for water sports, there's scuba diving, surfing and one gusty archipelago for world-class windsurfing.

Wulai Just a short ride from Taipei, this expanse of tropical forest and wild rivers is one of the north's top spots for hiking, cycling and river tracing (p111)

Yushan National Park 105,000 hectares of high mountains and deep valleys crossed by hiking trails (p192)

Hwy 11 This coastal highway backed by steep, green mountains is Taiwan's premier biking destination (p171)

Penghu One of the windiest places in the world in autumn, Penghu offers Asia's finest windsurfing (p291)

Lanyu Unspoiled reefs, an abundance of fish life and a unique island culture make this a mecca for scuba and snorkelling fans (p301)

Hot Springs

Taiwan's got the quantity and the quality: over 100 hot springs ranging from common sulphur springs to rare seawater springs on an offshore volcanic isle. There's even a cold spring or two for the summer heat. Facilities are equally diverse, with Japanese and Western designs, and many left as nature intended them.

Taian A favourite with Japanese police on R&R in the 1920s, Taian's stylish modern spas overlook rugged wilderness (p152)

Beitou The closest springs to Taipei are reachable by a quick Mass Rapid Transit (MRT) ride. A soak in the public pools at the old museum is one of the best uses of NT$20 you can find (p91)

Guanziling There are only three mud springs in the world and this is one of them (p244)

Lisong This wild spring deep in a remote river valley sprays down on you from a multicolored cliff face (p182)

Beaches

Taiwan's beaches vary from short crescent beaches with tropical blue waters, to long stretches of black sand, to pebbly shorelines, to some exceptionally fine coral-sand beaches on the outer islands. What's more, most are free and not overrun with resorts.

Shanshui Swim, surf, snorkel, or just hang out at this superb beach next to a pretty little village (p299)

Baisha Clear blue tropical waters, coconut palms and a white crescent beach make this the south's top beach (p267)

Nanao This wide crescent bay has a black-sand beach and looks down a stunning coastline of high steep cliffs (p135)

Chipei Sand Tail The finest white-sand beach in Taiwan with an ever-changing shape (p301)

Taimali No swimming, but camping and bonfires are encouraged (p189)

Fulong Not the most stunning of beaches but a water-sport hot spot in the summer months (p131)

» Lantern Festival, Kaohsiung (p246)

TOM COCKREM

Temples

With 15,000 and counting there is a temple for every god and even one for a dog. Storehouses of history, display rooms for traditional art, and of course vibrant houses of worship, temples are a quintessential part of Taiwan's living folk culture.

Lukang Longshan One of the last walled compound temples and a treasure house of woodcarving and design (p215)

Makung Matsu This temple has been altered little since its masterful 1920s restoration (p293)

Tzushr Miao The temple's post-WII reconstruction was overseen by an art professor – and it shows (p122)

Tainan Confucius Temple Taiwan's first Confucius temple and a model of graceful design and dignified atmosphere (p233)

Chung Tai Chan Monastery Designed by the same architect as Taipei 101, the rocket-ship-meets-mosque exterior belies an interior filled with traditional decorative arts (p221)

Traditional Festivals

Rising living standards and economic prosperity didn't kill folk culture in Taiwan: it just means there is more money than ever to hold extravagant and sometimes outlandish festivals.

Matsu Pilgrimage Taiwan's largest religious festival is a nine-day 350km walk around the island for Matsu believers – which is almost everyone (p200)

Burning of the Wang Yeh Boats A sublime weeklong religious festival that concludes with the torching of a 'plague ship' on a beach (p260)

Lantern Festival High-tech lantern shows are held in every city, but the most beautiful spectacles are the hanging lanterns along Kaohsiung's Love River (p250) and Pingxi's sky lantern release (p118)

Yenshui Fireworks Festival Like Spain's Running of the Bulls, only they let fireworks loose here and you're not supposed to run from them. Loads of fun and games and sometimes people do lose an eye (p243)

Night Markets

Taiwan's reputation as a culinary hot spot is spreading; even food-obsessed Singapore grudgingly admits that Taipei may at least be the challenger that robs them of their long-standing 'best street food in Asia' crown.

Shilin The popular king of Taipei's night markets, this carnival of snacking and shopping is packed to the gills (which you can eat) every night (p59)

Raohe The cognoscenti's night market, Raohe is Taipei's oldest, and unrivalled in snacking opportunities (p55)

Liuhe Every night 100 stalls line the market road, offering everything from squid-on-a-stick to fresh chicken wraps (p254)

Tainan It seems half the city and every temple square is a night market – the unique local snacks like coffin cakes and shrimp rolls are well worth the trip down south (p239)

Keelung Miaokou Nightly offerings from the bounty of the sea; afterwards pray at the temple that gives the market its name to atone for your gluttony (p126)

If you like...challenging your taste buds, try stinky tofu (think of it as Taiwanese blue cheese; p345) or aboriginal food: fried bees, fermented pork, bacon-wrapped baby corn. Yum (p345)

Unique Wildlife

Taiwan has a rate of endemism far higher than the world average. Which means lots of critters and plants you won't find anywhere else. Birds and butterflies are easiest to spot, but with conservation efforts well entrenched even larger mammals are making a comeback.

Birds Taiwan's range of habitats supports over 500 species, of which at least 15 are endemic and 69 are endemic subspecies (p356)

Butterflies Taiwan isn't known as the 'Kingdom of Butterflies' for nothing. Over 400 species (56 endemic), numerous reproductive valleys and yearly mass migrations are a few highlights (p357)

Fish Check out the Formosan salmon; it never leaves the rivers of its birth (p141)

Mammals Seventeen endemic species are here, including the Formosan rock monkey and giant flying squirrel, one of the world's largest (p356)

Mountain Retreats

With the land over two thirds mountainous there's lots of space to get away from the crowds and the heat in summer. Small villages dot the foothills of major mountain ranges, forest reserves and national parks. A few even offer splashy hot-spring facilities.

Taipingshan This mist-shrouded high-mountain reserve features a small village with outstanding views over the Snow Mountains, and hot springs are nearby (p140)

Alishan Wows travellers with its rare alpine railway, ancient cedars and phenomenal sea of clouds (p202)

Dasyueshan In the heart of Taiwan's pine-and-hemlock belt, this high-mountain reserve is a prime birding venue (p199)

Nanzhuang In the stunning foothills of the Snow Mountains, the villages here have an enticing mix of Hakka, Taiwanese and aboriginal people (p151)

Mingchih On the remote North Cross-Island Hwy, Mingchih lies near wild hot springs and two forests of ancient cedars (p139)

Tea

Taiwan has ideal conditions for growing tea, and not surprisingly it has the goods to satisfy the novice looking for a flavourful brew, as well as the connoisseur willing to pay thousands of dollars for a few ounces of dry leaves – *if* they are of high enough quality.

High Mountain Oolong Grown above 1000m in moist but sunny conditions, this tea has a honey flavour that must be experienced to be believed (p221)

Bao chung A national favourite with a slightly floral fragrance; a good tea to start your explorations (p119)

Oriental Beauty Unique to Taiwan, this sweet reddish-coloured tea lacks all astringency (p151)

Lei Cha A field-worker's drink; rich and hearty with puffed rice and pounded nuts added (p155)

Black Tea Sun Moon Lake black-tea growers spent a decade reviving their industry; drink this tea straight without sugar or milk (p221)

month by month

Top Events

1 **Matsu Pilgrimage,** April

2 **Lantern Festival,** January or February

3 **Hiking & Biking,** Autumn (September–December)

4 **Aboriginal Festivals,** Summer (July–August)

5 **Start of Mango Season,** May

January

Weather patterns vary across the island. Generally wet and cool in the north, dry and sunny in the south. Few people other than students travelling unless the week of Chinese New Year (CNY) falls in this month.

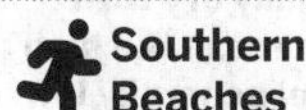

Southern Beaches

If you want to swim in the winter months, head south to Kenting National Park (www.ktnp.gov.tw). Beaches in the north, the east and on Penghu will be closed and the waters choppy and chilly.

February

Weather patterns vary. Generally very wet and cool in the north, dry and sunny in the south. Possibility of cold fronts and sand storms. Travel during the week of CNY is difficult but usually easy before and after.

Lantern Festival

One of the most popular traditional festivals, with concerts and light shows across Taiwan. However, the simplest of all, the Pingxi sky lantern release (p118), is the most spectacular. On the same day, Yenshui holds a massive fireworks festival.

April

Weather patterns vary. Usually very wet and warm in the north, wet and hot in the south. Generally low season for travel.

Spring Scream

Taiwan's largest and longest-running outdoor music event (www.springscream.com) is held in the bright sunshine of Kenting National Park.

Matsu Pilgrimage

This annual religious pilgrimage is Taiwan's premier folk event. Hundreds of thousands of believers follow a revered Matsu statue on a weeklong, 350km journey, with a million more participating in local events (www.dajiamazu.org.tw).

Youtong Flowers

The tall branching youtong tree is found all over the north and blooms in spring. The large white flowers make entire mountainsides appear dusted with snow. Check them out at Sanxia, Sanyi, Taian Hot Springs and Sun Moon Lake.

May

Weather patterns vary. Start of plum rain; expect heavy afternoon showers. Travel picking up across the island and on outer islands.

Start of Mango Season

Taiwan's mangoes are rated number one in Japan for good reason: they are sweet, succulent, fleshy and nearly sublime. Prices vary each year depending on the rains. Season lasts till about August.

Welcoming the City God

A smaller-scale pilgrimage than the Matsu, but with unique and colourful parades across the charming landscape of Kinmen. The festival was injected with new life (and funding) in 2010.

June

Getting warmer everywhere – already low 30s in the south. Heavy showers possible. Travel to major destinations crowded on weekends.

Dragon Boat Festival

Honouring the sacrifice of the poet-official Qu Yuan, the Dragon Boat Festival is celebrated all over Taiwan with flashy boat races on the local rivers and tasty sticky rice dumplings.

July

Hot and humid across the island. Heavy afternoon showers in the north but not in the south or east. Possibility of typhoons. Many student groups travelling. Major destinations very busy especially on weekends.

Aboriginal Festivals

Every July and August a number of traditional aboriginal festivals are held down the east coast (see p174). Themes include coming of age, ancestor worship, courting, harvest and good old-fashioned displays of martial and hunting skills.

August

Hot and humid. Heavy afternoon showers in the north but not in the south or east. High possibility of typhoons. Many student and family groups travelling. Major destinations very busy especially on weekends.

Day Lily Season

Orange day lilies are grown for food in the mountains of the east coast, and their blooming in late August and early September is an enchanting sight that attracts flower lovers and photographers from all over the island (see p182).

September

Weather cooling but still hot during the day. Possibility of typhoons high but conditions generally very dry and windy. Local travel dropping.

Hiking & Biking

You can hike and bike year-round but the weather is most stable, dry and pleasant in autumn. It's the best time to plan a trip if coming from abroad though there is the possibility of typhoons.

Windsurfing in Penghu

There's world-class windsurfing from September to March across the Penghu archipelago (see p299). Wind speeds can reach 40 to 50 knots, and windsurfers from all over the world can be found here.

October

The most stable weather across the island if there's no typhoon – dry, warm and windy. Best time of year in the north. Few travellers except for tour groups.

Grey-faced Buzzard Migration

Tens of thousands of buzzards, and other raptors, appear over the Hengchun Peninsula during autumn in what is described as one of the world's great avian migrations (see p267). The birds appear in Taiwan again in the spring over Changhua (www.birdingintaiwan.com/gray-faced buzzard.htm).

December

Cooling in the north but still warm to hot during the day; possibility of cold fronts and wet, humid weather. In the south usually dry with temperatures in the high 20s. Travel generally low except for tour groups to major destinations.

Purple Butterfly Valleys

Mass overwintering of purple butterflies in the valleys stretching across southern Taiwan (see p358). Can be seen in Maolin Recreation Area in small public areas from December to March during the morning hours after sunrise.

Hot Springing

You can, of course, hot spring all year round but the days are cooling, especially in the mountains where many springs are located. It's a good chance to avoid the big crowds in January and February at outdoor pools.

Whether you've got six days or 60, these itineraries provide a starting point for the trip of a lifetime. Want more inspiration? Head online to lonelyplanet.com/thorntree to chat with other travellers.

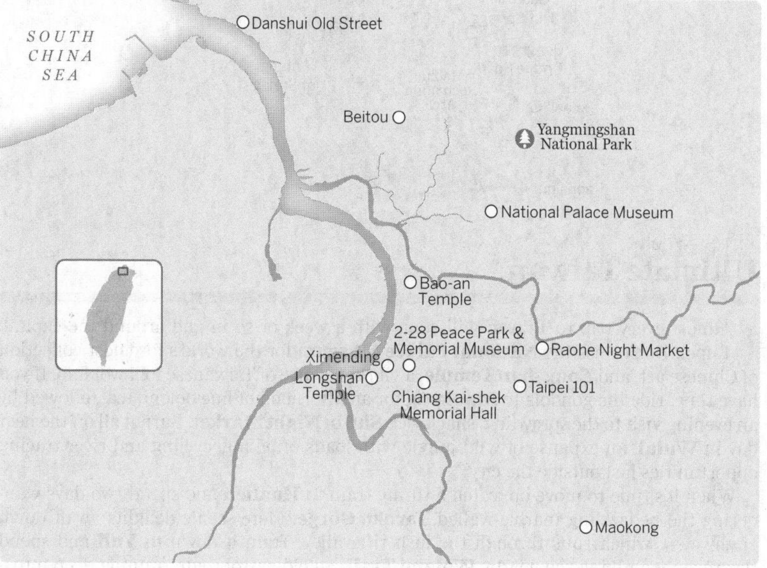

One Week

Taipei & Around

Spend the first two days museum-hopping in the capital; with the world's greatest collection of Chinese art, **National Palace Museum** takes a day on its own. At night, hit the city's myriad **night markets** before or after the clubs and bars. They're all open late.

On day three, spend the morning exploring different perspectives on Taiwan's past in the **2-28 Peace Park & Memorial Museum** and at the **Chiang Kai-shek Memorial Hall**, then blast into the neon future with a visit to **Ximending**, Taipei's youth central. Head south the next day for an afternoon sipping tea in **Maokong**, followed by a ride to the top of **Taipei 101** to take in the whole city as the sun goes down. That night head to **Raohe Night Market** for a late dinner at one of the best snacking venues in town.

If it's sunny on day five, rent a bicycle and ride the river trails to **Danshui**, followed by strolling and snacking along the **Old Street**. The next day you can go hiking on **Yangmingshan** followed by a hot spring in nearby **Beitou**. On the final day explore the city's old temples, **Longshan** and **Bao-an**, centres of both folk faith and folk art.

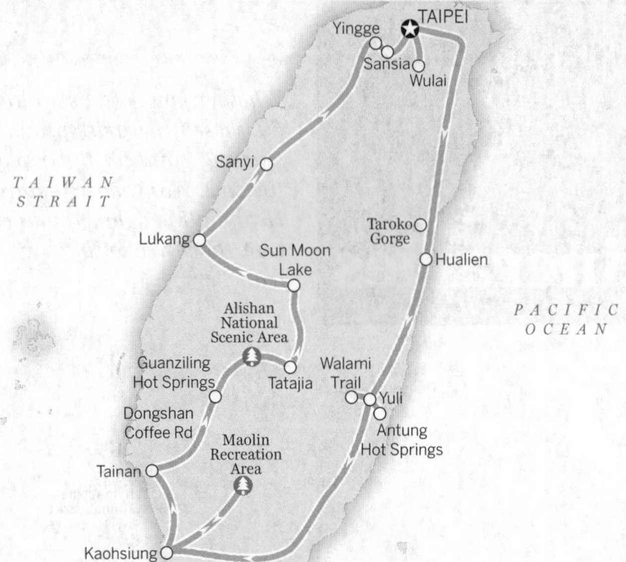

Three Weeks
Ultimate Taiwan

Almost every trip to Taiwan will start with a week or so in and around the capital, Taipei. Don't miss the **National Palace Museum** for the world's foremost collection of Chinese art, and **Longshan Temple**, a vibrant centre of Taiwanese folk worship. If you have time, ride the gondola to **Maokong** for an afternoon of fine oolong tea, followed by an evening visit to the sprawling, snack-rich **Shilin Night Market**. Burn it all off the next day in **Wulai**, an expanse of wild jungle with loads of biking, cycling and river tracing opportunities just outside the city.

When it's time to move on, catch a tilting train to **Hualien** and spend two days wandering the bedazzling marble-walled **Taroko Gorge**. More scenic delights await down Highway 9, which runs through the lush rift valley. Train it down to **Yuli** and spend the afternoon hiking the nearby **Walami Trail**, an old patrol route running deep into a subtropical rainforest. Rest and recuperate that night at nearby **Antung Hot Springs**.

Another train ride – this time across Taiwan's fertile southern tip – takes you over to **Kaohsiung**, Taiwan's second-largest city, for two days of seafood and urban adventures in the old harbour district. In winter take a two-day side trip to **Maolin Recreation Area**, home of Rukai aborigines, and the overwintering site of millions of purple butterflies.

Continue by train up the coast to the old capital of **Tainan** for a couple of days of temple and relic touring. Rent a car now for the drive up the **Dongshan Coffee Road**. At **Guanziling** that evening indulge yourself in rare mud hot springs. The following day continue up into a wild expanse of mountain ranges in the **Alishan National Scenic Area**. The next day ride the Alishan Forest Train up to the sunrise viewing platform and then hike around **Tatajia** in the shadow of Yushan, Taiwan's highest mountain.

The drive from Yushan to **Sun Moon Lake** the following morning passes some sublime high-mountain scenery and should be taken slowly. At the lake itself, stop to sample oolong tea and maybe catch a boat tour. Heading north, fans of traditional arts and crafts will enjoy the next two days with stops in **Lukang**, home to master lantern, fan and tin craftsmen; in **Sanyi**, Taiwan's woodcarving capital; and in **Yingge**, a town devoted to ceramics.

Finally, on that home stretch to Taipei, drop in on the Tzushr Temple in **Sansia**, a top example of traditional design and decorative arts.

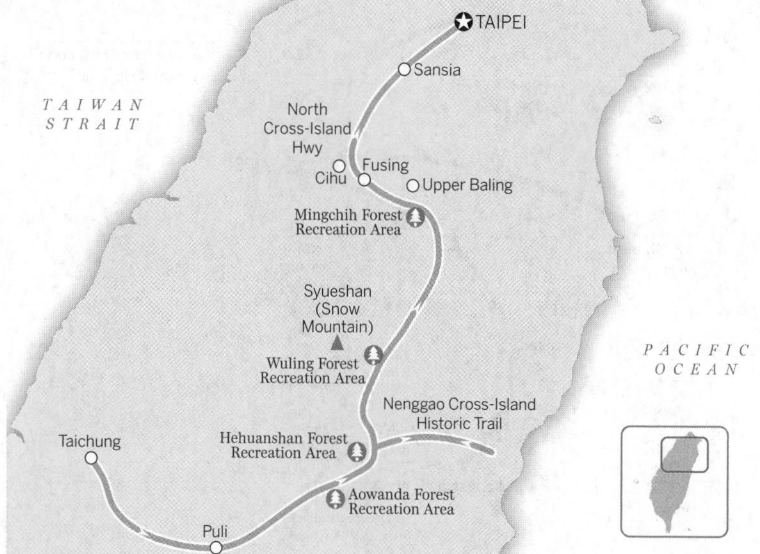

Two Weeks

A Cross-Island Tour

After **Taichung** your first stop is the Chung Tai Chan Temple in **Puli**, an amazing centre of Buddhist art and research. After Puli the highway starts to rise into the Central Mountains, and from here on in it's just one gorgeous landscape after the other begging for a photo. For a side trip, head down to **Aowanda Forest Recreation Area** and spend the night in little cabins among cherry and plum trees. Keep an eye out for the birds: this is a top birdwatching venue.

Returning to Hwy 14, continue to the end to find the **Nenggao Cross-Island Historic Trail**. You don't need to do the whole thing, but consider hiking in and spending a night in the cabin. Retrace your route, and head north up Hwy 14甲. Prepare for an endless windy road and numerous washouts. Also prepare for a stunning landscape of receding blue-tinged mountain ranges.

After Wuling Pass (3275m), the highest bit of road in Northeast Asia, stop in **Hehuanshan Forest Recreation Area** to photograph (and maybe stroll over) the treeless hills of mustard-coloured Yushan cane. Then head up Hwy 8 to Hwy 7甲 and follow this north to **Wuling Forest Recreation Area**, an area of thick forests, high waterfalls and cool mountain streams, some of which are home to the endangered Formosan landlocked salmon. If you have a couple of days to spare, climb **Snow Mountain**, Taiwan's second-highest mountain.

Past Wuling the road winds down the mountains past quaint aboriginal villages, with their trademark churches and steeples, until it reaches the Lanyang River plains and one very large cabbage patch.

From here it's a seamless connection with the **North Cross-Island Highway**. First stop: **Mingchih Forest Recreation Area** and its nearby forest of ancient trees. More ancient trees can be found a couple of hours later at **Upper Baling** or you can just continue on to enjoy stunning views of high forested mountains and rugged canyons. Stop for lunch at **Fusing** and then explore Chiang Kai-shek's legacy at nearby **Cihu**. At Daxi head north towards **Sansia** and perhaps stop to look at the masterful Tzushr Temple before connecting with National Fwy 3 for the 30-minute ride to **Taipei** – and the crowds.

Two Weeks
The East Coast Loop

From **Hualien**, it's but a quick hop to **Taroko Gorge**, Taiwan's premier natural attraction since the '30s. After a few days exploring this treasure, head down **Highway 11**. If you can manage the ride, it's three great days on a bike alongside some of Taiwan's best coastal and mountain scenery.

South of Taitung, stop at **Chihpen Hot Springs**, first opened during the Japanese colonial era. Nearby **Chihpen Forest Recreation Area** offers quiet trails through monkey-filled banyan forests.

When you're ready to head back north, remember to take **Highway 9**. You're between two mountain ranges here, in the rice belt of Taiwan. At **Luye** get a bird's-eye view of the valley at Taiwan's top parasailing venue. The next day, stop at **Yuli** to cycle out to the historic **Walami Trail**, once a Japanese patrol route. On the way up the valley you'll have many opportunities to soak weary muscles in hot springs. To indulge the tastebuds, head to aboriginal **Mataian**, a wetland area with some unique local dishes on offer.

Three Weeks
Island-Hopping

Start with **Matsu** to get a taste of maritime Fujian culture that you can't find in Taiwan proper. A night in the traditional houses of Beigan, a walk through old military tunnels and a meal of fresh-off-the-boat seafood are considered obligatory.

From Matsu, fly to **Kinmen** via Taipei and explore the island's ancient villages and Cold War history. Birdwatchers will want to include an extra day for walking around the saltwater lakes, home to a mixture of waterfowl you can't find in Taiwan proper.

Next, get in some beach time (or windsurfing) on **Penghu** via Taipei, and explore the archipelago's myriad temples. The Makung Matsu may be Taiwan's first. Moving on from Penghu, fly to Kaohsiung and catch a train across southern Taiwan to Taitung. Take a boat or fly to **Green Island** and **Lanyu**, both top diving and snorkelling venues. Lanyu is home to the Yami, an aboriginal people with close ties to the sea, while Green Island boasts a rare seawater hot spring best enjoyed with the stars overhead, at night.

Taiwan Outdoors

Hiking
There are hundreds of well-maintained natural trails in Taiwan, with no guide needed for most of them. The best low-altitude trails are all located within an hour of Taipei, and the best high-mountain trails can be found in Yushan and Sheipa National Parks.

Cycling
Taiwan has good roads with wide shoulders in popular biking areas, with hundreds of kilometres of bike-only routes around cities. Bikes are allowed on Mass Rapid Transit (MRT), trains and buses, and there are many day and multiday rental programs widely available.

Hot Springs
Springs are located all over the island, ranging from five-star resorts to wild mountain springs. The most accessible springs are in Beitou, reachable by Taipei MRT. Don't miss Taian hot springs in Miaoli County.

Water Sports
Taiwan offers rich coral reefs for diving around the offshore islands. Hundreds of clean mountain streams make the island an ideal river-tracing destination. There is beginner to advanced surfing around northern Taiwan, the east coast and Kenting National Park. In winter head to Penghu for world-class windsurfing.

Hiking

Why Hike Taiwan?
Taiwan has a striking landscape that is still heavily forested. With climatic zones ranging from tropical to alpine, the country's flora and fauna range widely (see p354). It is possible to hike year round on a well-developed trail network from sea level to 3952m. You don't need a guide for most hikes, and many trails are quiet – it's possible to hike for days without seeing others, and when you do, most other hikers are locals. There is also a free cabin system on national-park trails.

National Parks & Other Hiking Venues
Over 50% of Taiwan is mountainous and heavily forested. About 20% is protected land divided between national parks, forest recreation areas, reserves and various state forests.

National parks and forest recreation areas (FRAs) have excellent-quality trails. Within the boundaries of each you'll find a visitor centre and often a small village with basic accommodation and food. If the FRA does not have a village you'll still usually find basic facilities to support day trippers. Paved trails are available to scenic spots, while unspoiled areas with natural paths may be further in the park. Forestry reserves may have good trails but offer few facilities for hikers.

LOCATION	TYPE OF HIKE	TYPE OF TERRAIN	WORTH CHECKING OUT
northern Taiwan	low altitude, vast network all over the north, most developed trails in Taiwan	tropical and mixed forests, river valleys, coastal bluffs, narrow ridges	Yangmingshan NP Wulai Shihting Caoling Historic Trail Manyueyuan FRA
northern Taiwan	high altitude, plenty of trails	rugged high-mountain conditions; narrow ridgelines; mixed and evergreen forests, grasslands and tundra	Snow Mountain Wuling Quadruple Holy Ridge Dabajianshan
western Taiwan	low altitude	mixed and coniferous forests in rugged mountainous areas	Daxueshan FRA Yushan NP
western Taiwan	high altitude, plenty of trails	rugged high-mountain conditions; mixed and evergreen forests, grasslands and tundra; alpine lakes in many areas	Yushan peaks Japanese Occupation Era Batonguan Traversing Route Nenggao-Andongjun
eastern Taiwan	low altitude, few trails but outstanding	rugged river valleys, steep gorges, jungle and mixed forest	Taroko NP Walami Trail
eastern Taiwan	high altitude, few trails but outstanding	rugged high-mountain conditions; evergreen forests and grasslands	Jiaming Lake
southern Taiwan	low altitude, few trails but worth doing	tropical and mixed forests, rocky coastline	Kenting NP Jin-shui Yin Old Trail Maolin Recreational Area
southern Taiwan	high altitude, plenty of trails but many closed for repairs	steep high-mountain conditions; very thin ridgelines; evergreen forests; ancient trees	Beidawushan
islands	low altitude, few trails	tropical forest	Green Island Lanyu

Lower-Altitude Trails (Under 3000m)

There are low-altitude trails all over Taiwan. Trails run through subtropical and tropical jungles, broadleaf forests, temperate woodlands and along coastal bluffs. Some are just a few hours long while others go on for days. All three major cities – Taipei, Kaohsiung and Taichung – have mountains and trails either within the city limits or just outside.

Planning Your Hike

The best times to hike lower-altitude trails are from September to December and March to May. Midweek is best for popular trails but many are never busy. Avoid hiking during or after typhoons, heavy rains or earthquakes. The weather can vary from 37°C and 100% humidity to just above zero (and usually high humidity too). Always be \prepared for a change of weather and for the weather in the mountains to be different from the city.

Permits are not needed for most low-altitude hikes, except for areas that restrict the number of hikers who can enter per day. For these areas you may need to register on the spot at a police checkpoint on the way into the area – this is a simple process.

What to Pack

» Lightweight moisture-wicking material is best – Gortex is not much use at lower altitudes because of the humidity and heat (a small umbrella is more useful if it rains)

» Running shoes are better on jungle trails and ridge walks because of their superior grip

» Plenty of water (at least 3L to 4L if hiking in the warmer months)

» Torch (flashlight; trails are notorious for taking longer than you think)

Trail Conditions

Trails conditions vary greatly. Although few are flat, most of them now have signposts and map boards. Note that many trails are so steep that ropes or ladders are needed to climb. These are usually already fixed in place. Some ridge walks are so narrow that metal posts and ropes are in place along the most dangerous sections.

There are a variety of different trail types that you may encounter. It may be a foot-wide slice through dense jungle, possibly overgrown in parts or even washed out, or you may come across a good footpath with bridges (could just be bamboo) over streams. Some trails are a steep path up the side of a slope that uses roots and rocks as hand- and footholds. Trails in Yangmingshan National Park are largely cement paths and stairs. Other national parks have natural paths. While it is common in most parts of the world to hike 3km to 4km an hour, on Taiwan's trails 1km an hour progress is not unusual because of the extremely steep conditions and the need to often climb ladders and ropes.

Water

Water sources are usually natural streams and springs, but it is advisable to bring what you need for the day.

Sleeping

Camping on the trail is mostly a DIY thing (there are few established sites on trails). Some forest recreations areas and national parks forbid it at lower elevations. Water sources are usually available but should be treated first.

Transport

Public transport (usually bus) is available to the majority of lower-altitude trails but there are often few daily buses. This may improve, as the Taiwanese government is committed to re-introducing a comprehensive rural bus system.

High-Mountain Trails (Above 3000m)

Taiwan has some genuinely world-class high-mountain hikes and anyone in decent shape can conquer them. Few demand any technical skills (in part because rougher sections already have ropes and ladders in place). Many routes are closed in the winter months. Note that you need permits for most high-mountain trails.

Trails have been improved in recent years. They are wider or at least clear of overgrowth, there are good bridges over streams, and paths have frequent distance and direction markers. For sleeping there are A-frame shelters and campsites.

High-altitude trails are found in national parks, forest recreation areas and forestry reserves. Paths generally begin in a dense mixed forest turning coniferous higher up. The treeline ends around 3300m to 3600m. After this short Yushan cane spreads across the highlands until the very highest elevations. Alpine lakes are surprisingly rare. High-altitude terrain tends to be strikingly rugged with deep V-shaped valleys and steeply sloped mountain ranges. Long exposed ridgelines are common obstacles to cross.

Planning Your Hike

The best times to hike in Taiwan's high-altitude areas are from September to December and from March to May. July to August is good if the weather cooperates (the sun can be fierce), as there are fewer hikers about.

Avoid high-altitude hiking during or after typhoons, plum rains in May and June, and earthquakes.

THE NATIONAL TRAIL SYSTEM

The National Trail System (http://trail.forest.gov.tw) was established in 2001 by the Forestry Bureau to create an islandwide network of hiking paths. National trails usually exist outside national-park and forest-recreation-area boundaries.

Hikers can expect to find wide, clear and well-signposted trails at both lower and higher altitudes. Maps on the National Trail website will be of little use (for proper maps, see p30) and permits, when needed, will be police permits only.

National trails to check out are the **Fu-Ba National Trail** (p113), the **Jin-shui Yin Old Trail** (p266) and the **Nanao Historic Trail** (p136).

What to Pack

» Wet- and cold-weather gear is essential even in summer – because of altitude gains of 2000m to 3000m, most hikes take you through a range of climatic conditions

» All the food you will need – most cabins offer nothing but bedding and water

Trail Conditions

In general, high-mountain trails are well made and clear to follow. Solid metal or wood bridges will be in place where needed. Almost all trails require a great deal of steep uphill climbing, often more than 1000m of elevation gain a day. Many trails require at least some rope or chain climbs (these will be fixed in place and are generally not especially demanding).

Water

Most high-altitude trails will have water sources, which are available from streams or rainwater-collecting tanks at cabins. Maps show water sources, but always ask at the national-park headquarters for the latest; sources do sometimes dry up in winter. Water should be filtered or chemically treated.

Sleeping

Cabins and campsites are available on most trails. Cabins can range from boxy cement structures to stylish wood A-frames. There is often bunk bedding with thick mats, solar lighting and ecotoilets. Water sources are usually available at the cabin or nearby. With the exception of Paiyun Cabin on Yushan, cabins are usually unmanned and do not provide meals or snacks. Campsites are flat clearings in for-

HIGH-MOUNTAIN PERMITS

Permits are largely a holdover from martial-law days, but they do prevent overcrowding on the trails, and let authorities know who is in the mountains in case of an emergency (such as an approaching typhoon). Restrictions have eased in recent years (eg you no longer need a guide and solo hikers can apply) but if you are caught without one you will be fined. If a rescue is required you will have to pay the full costs.

Everyone needs permits to hike the high mountains. Anyone can apply (foreigners, locals, groups or individuals) but the process is complicated. Most people pay to have the permits done for them; they are nontransferable and they are valid only for the date you apply for. If a typhoon cancels your hike, permits cannot be changed to another date (you have to reapply). Note that Taroko National Park only allows Taiwanese to apply for permits (though foreigners can join a local hiking group).

There are two kinds of permits depending on where you hike – **National park permits** (入園; rù yuán), for entering restricted areas in a national park and **Police permits** (入山; rù shān), for entering a restricted high-mountain area. Hiking in national parks requires both kinds of permits.

National park permits must be applied for at least seven days in advance (for Yushan main route, at least a month in advance). It is best to apply online but you'll need a valid Republic of China (ROC) ID number. Passport and Alien Resident Card (ARC), numbers do not work online. Online forms are in Chinese but English forms can be printed and mailed to the national park. National parks will also usually process police permits for you. Shei-pa National Park website (www.spnp.gov.tw) has a sample of a completed form in English.

Police permits can be applied for at the **Ministry of the Interior** (☎02-2321 9011; 7 Zhongxiao E Rd, Sec 1, Taipei) or at a police station in the same county as hike or at the police squad within the national park. You'll need triplicate copies of your itinerary written out, the trail map, a name list of group members (including their dates of birth and emergency contacts) and a national park permit (you must have this before applying for a police permit). Make sure you have ID and/or your passport. Free printable English sample police permits are available online from **Barking Deer Adventures** (http://barkingdeernews.blogspot.com) for almost all major hike itineraries. Non-national-park hikes usually only require a police permit. See p193 for a list of some of these hikes.

PRACTICAL TIPS

Hikers are often tempted to head to the top of a peak in light clothing and with only a few supplies if the weather looks good at the cabin they spent the night in. Don't. Always be prepared with wet- and cold-weather gear and plenty of food and water. Deaths are not uncommon on Taiwan's high mountains and they are often related to hikers being unprepared for fast-changing conditions.

When it comes to a good night's sleep in a cabin, be aware that snoring can be a terrible nuisance, as can Taiwanese hikers' habit of getting up at 3am so they can catch the sunrise on the peak. Bring earplugs!

Ribbons are placed on trails by hiking clubs to indicate the correct path to take on a complicated or easily overgrown system. If you aren't sure where to go, following the ribbons is usually sound advice.

est (sometimes the sites of former police outposts). Water sources are sometimes available.

Transport

Outside of northern Taiwan you will need your own vehicle to get to most high-mountain trailheads.

Further Information

Safety

Weather

Afternoon fogs are common in autumn and winter, and thunderstorms are common in spring and summer. Typhoons affect the island from summer to late autumn. Do not go outside when they are raging, and avoid going to the mountains in the few days after as landslides, swollen rivers and streams can wash out roads and trails. Many mountainous areas have microclimates. It may be clear in the city but thundershowers could occur in the mountains.

Natural Disasters

Earthquakes are common all over the island and are especially strong along the east coast – don't hike for a few days after a big earthquake. Taiwan is prone to massive landslides. Sections of trail are often washed out after earthquakes and typhoons. Trails can be closed for months or even years (sometimes forever) – don't attempt trails that have been closed.

Plants & Animals

Dogs See the information contained within the Cycling section (p32)

Māo yào rén (貓咬人; cat bite people) Taiwan's version of poison ivy. Grows at mid-elevations.

Snakes You won't find snakes at higher elevations. Most are harmless but Taiwan has its share of deadly venomous snakes, which often have triangular-shaped heads, very distinctive patterns, thin necks and tapered tails. Large, fat python-like snakes are usually harmless rodent eaters. The most comprehensive English site on Taiwan's snakes is www.snakesoftaiwan.com, run by a passionate German snake-watcher.

Ticks A possible problem at lower altitudes, even around cities. Be careful in summer. Check yourself after hiking.

Wasps These dangerous insects kill and put people in the hospital every year. In danger areas you will often see warning signs. Most active in autumn. Avoid wearing perfumes and bright clothing.

Getting Lost

It's easy to get lost in Taiwan if you are not on a good trail. The forest is extremely thick in places, and trails are sometimes little more than foot-wide cuts across a steep mountainside with many unmarked branches. Trails also quickly become overgrown (some need teams to come in every year with machetes just to make them passible). Never leave a trail and if you hike alone let someone know where you will be.

Emergency Numbers

Even in high mountains it's often possible to get mobile-phone reception. Hiking maps often highlight good reception areas. If you can't communicate by voice, try texting.

» Basic emergency numbers ☎119 or 112

» ☎112 connects you to available signals even if your mobile phone doesn't have a SIM card

» National Rescue Command Center ☎0800 077 795

» Ministry of Defence Rescue Centre ☎02-2737 3395

» Emergency radio frequencies: 145MHz, 149.25MHz, 148.74MHz or 148.77MHz

Books

Good titles to whet your appetite for the region's great hikes include *Taipei Day Trips 1* and *2* and *Yangmingshan, the Guide,* both by Richard Saunders. *Taiwan Forest Vacation Guide,* published by the Forestry Bureau, covers 21 forest recreation areas around the country.

Maps

GPS devices are of limited use in Taiwan; it is best to learn to use a compass and map. For northern Taiwan maps, **Taiwan Jiaotong Press** (台北縣市近郊山圖) publishes a series of 14 maps at a scale of 1:25,000 that covers the north only (from Sansia/Wulai up). These are available at stores that are mountain-equipment, around the Taipei train station. National trails have waterproof foldable maps with a 1:25,000 scale available at equipment shops or **San Min** (三民網路書店) bookstores. Itineraries in Chinese are included. National-parks maps are available at park visitor centres or mountain equipment shops. **Sunriver** (上河文化) publishes 1:25,000 topographic maps of most of the 100 Top Peaks and the main hiking trails. Itineraries are included in Chinese. Most national-park websites have basic maps (in English) of the climbing routes. Topographical maps may be available at national-park bookstores.

Top 100 Peaks

The Top 100 (百岳; Bǎiyuè) are all peaks over 3000m and considered special or significant because of elevation, beauty, geology or prominence. Taiwanese hikers dream of completing the full list (available at Wikipedia).

Clubs

Richard Saunders (richard0428@yahoo.com), author of *Taipei Day Trips 1* and *2*, runs a free weekend-hiking club. Check out the Events and Hiking threads on **Forumosa** (www.forumosa.com). **523 Mountaineering Association** (http://523.org.tw) runs a couple of free day hikes a month as well as reasonably priced longer hikes.

Hiking Companies & Guides

523 Mountaineering Association (http://523.org.tw) Nonprofit organisation with a good reputation. Mix of locals and foreigners. Also offers free day hikes around Taipei

Barking Deer (www.barking-deer.com) Foreign-run company with reasonable rates. Also provides permit and transport-only packages.

Cloud Leopard Hiking Association (www.go837.com.tw) Bunun cooperative focusing on portering and guiding services. Japanese and Chinese language services.

Websites & Blogs

Forest Recreation Areas (www.forest.gov.tw)

Hiking Taiwan (http://hikingtaiwan.blogspot.com)

Kenting National Park (www.ktnp.gov.tw)

National Trail System (www.forest.gov.tw)

Off the Beaten Track (http://taiwandiscovery.wordpress.com)

Pashan (http://hikingintaiwan.blogspot.com)

Sheipa National Park (www.spnp.gov.tw)

Taroko National Park (www.taroko.gov.tw)

Yushan National Park (www.ysnp.gov.tw/en)

Cycling

As little as five years ago, cycling in Taiwan was for lonely adventurers. Now it's a national obsession that has reached every generation and income level. Politicians routinely promise the construction of bike paths as part of their campaign pledges and cities boast of how many kilometres of bike-only paths they have built and plan to build. This obsession is also cultivating a friendly local bike culture.

This great institutional support, combined with public enthusiasm, is quickly turning Taiwan into one of Asia's top cycling destinations. Much of the focus is on the more sparsely populated east coast but there are excellent routes everywhere.

In addition to world-class road cycling minutes from urban centres, Taiwan has challenging high-mountain, cross-island routes, leisurely paths through rice and tea fields and dramatic mountain and coastal scenery to enjoy.

WHERE TO CYCLE?

Taiwan has three types of cycling venues: **bike-only paths**, **roads**, and **mountain-biking trails**. Mountain biking seems a lot quieter than years ago but there are still popular routes around Taipei. Bike-only paths are concentrated in Taipei, Kaohsiung and small towns down the east coast. To date there is about 1000km of such paths and the network is growing. Roads in Taiwan are generally in good condition, with wide shoulders (often marked as exclusively for bikes and scooters) on many popular routes.

LOCATION	CYCLING OPPORTUNITIES	DESCRIPTION	CYCLING ROUTES
northern Taiwan	plenty	road cycling either along steep mountain or flat coastal routes; hundreds of kilometres of riverside paths in Taipei; some mountain-biking trails.	North Cross Island Hwy Wulai Hwy 9 Hwy 2 Taipei riverside paths
western Taiwan	plenty	mostly road cycling on mountain routes in the interior; challenging grade in many areas	Sun Moon Lake circuit Hwy 21 Daxueshan FRA road
eastern Taiwan	plenty	range of routes along the coast, inland valley and up rugged gorges; some exceptionally challenging rides up to the high mountains	Hwy 11 Hwy 9 Taroko Gorge Hwy 14 (Mugua River Gorge) Liyu Lake
southern Taiwan	plenty	mostly gentle road riding on quiet country routes; some coastal riding and mountain biking on old trails	County Rd 199 Dongshan Coffee Rd Jin-shui Yin Old Trail
islands	fair	mostly flat coastal ring roads; often windy conditions; difficult to get bike to islands but some have free rentals	See individual islands

Planning Your Bike Trip

The best time to cycle in Taiwan is from September to December for generally good weather islandwide. Winter (December to February) in the south and coastal west sees warm and dry conditions. Riding after a typhoon (assuming there has been no road damage) is usually a good way to ensure clear weather. Other than directly during a typhoon or sand storm, you can ride all year.

Sleeping & Eating

An explosion of B&Bs islandwide means quality (and reasonably priced) accommodation is easy to find everywhere. B&Bs and hotels are used to cyclists and will find a place to store your bike safely. There are plenty of campsites on the east coast. Cheap restaurants are everywhere in rural areas. Only on the cross-island highways would you ride more than a few hours without finding food or lodging.

Convenience stores are ubiquitous, except on cross-island roads. They provide drinks, decent food and washrooms. On popular cycling routes, they often have bicycle pumps and repair kits. Cyclists can ship items from one 7-Eleven store to another: for example, a change of clothes for the end of the trip or a bike bag for shipping your bike back on a train or bus.

On many popular cycling routes the local police station functions as a rest stop for cyclists. Inside you are welcome to use the bicycle pump, repair kit, water and rest area. Some stations even allow camping out back.

Bikes on Public Transport

Public buses in rural areas are experimenting with front racks for carrying bikes. If the bus is not full (usually they are not) you can often take a bagged bike on the bus.

Some private intercity bus companies will take bagged bikes as luggage (for half fare).

When travelling on trains, be aware that the train policy on bikes is confusing and evolving. It's best to ship a bagged bike to your destination train station one day before. You only need to give your phone number and the destination in Chinese. Note that you cannot ship from Taipei Main Station – go to Wanhua or Songshan. Usually you can take a bagged bike on slow non-reserved trains in rural areas. Some fast Tze-chiang trains have a 12th car with bike racks (few now but more are expected). Look for the bike symbol next to the schedule on the website. The high-speed rail allows you to take bagged bikes on trains as luggage.

Work is proceeding on refitting stations all along the east coast. By 2011 you will be able to wheel bikes up on special ramps to platforms, and some stations will have showers, storage and possibly accommodation. More trains are also being refitted with bike carriages for roll-on roll-off capabilities. You will be able to roll your bike into the carriage and ride the same train. Also expect special night sleeper trains from Taipei to the east for cyclists.

Renting Bikes

Bike-rental outlets are widely available and growing. Good city bike-rental programs are available in Taipei and Kaoshiung, with rentals all down the east coast. For multiday rentals **Giant Bicycles** (www.giant-bicycles.com/zh-TW) has the best program: three days for NT$1200, with NT$200 for each additional day. Good-quality road bikes include saddle bags and repair kits. Not all outlets do multiday rentals, so email first. For mountain bikes (and weekend rides) check out **Alan's Mountain Bike** (www.alansmountainbike.com) in Taipei. Be warned that most shops do not carry larger-frame bikes for taller riders.

Tours

Most cycling companies are used to local customers only. Conditions of tours are unlikely to appeal to Western travellers. Routes are often chosen for convenience and speed and may not be particularly scenic. If a tour involves much riding on Provincial Hwy 1, avoid it. **In Motion Asia** (www.inmotionasia) is a foreign-run company focusing on mountain- and road-biking tours into remote areas.

Taiwan Hot Springs

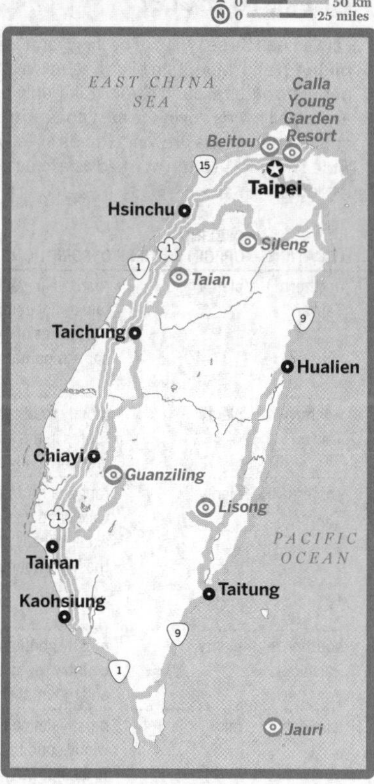

Websites & Blogs

Rank (http://rank.blogspot.com) Great information on long and more obscure routes.

Taiwan in Cycles (http://taiwanincycles.blogspot.com) A serious rider with interesting commentary.

The Forgetful (www.bikingintaiwan.theforgetful.com) Detailed writing and pics on routes around Taiwan.

The View from Taiwan (http://michaelturton.blogspot.com) Politics during the week and cycling on the weekend.

Dangers & Annoyances

Feral dogs are common in the mountains. The best approach if they run after you is simply to stop, place your bike in front of you, and remain calm or indifferent. Dogs may snarl and bark but they will quickly grow tired if you don't give them any reason

HOT SPRINGS

Taiwan is ranked among the world's top 15 hot-spring sites and harbours a great variety of springs including sulphur springs, cold springs, mud springs and even seabed hot springs. Hot springing was first popularised under Japanese rule and many of the most famous resort areas were first developed in the early 20th century. In the late 1990s and early 21st century hot-spring fever struck Taiwan a second time and most of the hotels and resorts you'll find today are of recent vintage.

What's in the Water?

Water bubbling up from underground picks up a variety of minerals that offer a veritable bouquet of health benefits (some more believable than others) according to aficionados.

WATER TYPE	BENEFICIAL FOR	WHERE TO FIND
alkaloid carbonic	nervousness, improving skin tone	Taian
sodium bicarbonate	general feelings of malaise, broken bones	Jiaoshi
alkaline	making good coffee	Antung
sodium carbonate	skin tone	Wulai
ferrous	conceiving a male child	Rueisui
sulphurous	arthritis, sore muscles	Beitou
mud spring	improving skin tone	Guanziling

Hotels & Resorts

The best-developed springs are set in forested valleys, meadows or overlooking the ocean. Private rooms and public spas are usually both available. Private rooms feature wood or stone tubs and can be basic or very luxurious. They are available by the night or hour – the average hourly rate is NT$800 to NT$1200, and the average nightly rate is NT$2400 to NT$6000. Public spas are usually a whole bathing complex, with multiple pools, jets and showers. They can be outdoors or indoors and have an average cost (unlimited time) of NT$300 to NT$500.

Hotel and resort hot springs worth checking out are in Beitou, Taian, Yangmingshan, Green Island and Guanziling.

Wild Springs

There are still probably a hundred or more wild springs deep in the mountains. Some can be hiked into relatively easily while others require several days. Wild springs worth checking out are in Sileng and Lisong.

Random health checks show overuse at many resort areas. Hotels and resorts in fact often dilute natural hot-spring water, and even recycle water between bathers. This is common around the world, even in Japan; if you want to avoid it, remember that in general the less developed the area, the purer the water quality. In popular spots go midweek when there are fewer bathers.

Before entering public hot springs, shower thoroughly using soap and shampoo. Mixed pools require a bathing suit (there are no nude mixed pools in Taiwan). Bathing caps must be worn in all public pools.

to get excited. Throwing rocks or squirting dogs with water is counterproductive.

Drivers are very used to scooters so you won't encounter aggression for being a two-wheeled vehicle on the road. However, general driving skills are poor and vehicles cutting across lanes when rounding bends, passing on the outside lane on blind corners and driving too fast and carelessly are all common and potential hazards for cyclists.

Water Sports

Water sports have boomed in the past 10 years. The Japanese influence has spawned interest in river tracing and **surfing** (see p133). Scuba, snorkelling and windsurfing are less popular but top notch.

General dangers to be aware of include the fact that Taiwan has no continental shelf. The deep blue sea is just offshore and dangerous currents and riptides flow around the island. Do not go out further than you can stand on your tiptoes and don't swim at a beach unless you know for certain it is safe.

River Tracing

River tracing (*sùoxī*) is the sport of walking and climbing up a riverbed. At the beginning stages it involves merely walking on slippery rocks. At advanced stages it can involve climbing up and down waterfalls. Taiwan has hundreds of fast clean streams and rivers, some just minutes from the cities. There are no dangerous animals in the water and the landscape is exotic.

The general season for tracing is June to September. On the hottest days of summer many people simply trace up to deep waterfall-fed pools for swimming. Afternoon thundershowers in summer are common in the north and central mountains; water levels can rise fast.

River-tracing sites worth checking out include Wulai, which is one of the best venues for amateurs (it has deep river pools for swimming, endless waterfalls and a jungle landscape), and the Golden Canyon, a full-day trip into a marble canyon organised by local aboriginals.

Equipment required for river tracing includes a life jacket, helmet, ropes or climbing slings and a waterproof bag. Felt-bottomed rubber shoes are necessary for gripping the slippery rock – you can pick up a pair for NT$300 to NT$400 in mountain-equipment shops. Neoprene can be useful even in summer as it can get chilly in higher mountain streams, especially when you've been in the water all day.

Scuba & Snorkelling

Taiwan has an excellent range of venues for scuba and snorkelling with good visibility and warm waters year-round in the south. There are well-preserved deep- and shallow-water coral reefs off Lanyu, Green Island, Kenting and the east coast around Dulan. Green Island alone has 200 types of soft and hard corals and plenty of tropical reef fish. It also has a yearly hammerhead shark migration during the winter months (for advanced divers only).

In the north there's good diving from Yeliu down to Ilan, including off Turtle Island. With the Kuroshio Current running close to shore you'll find an intriguing mix of tropical and temperate sea life, including some gorgeous soft coral patches. See p131.

In Taiwan, currents are strong and have been known to sweep divers out to sea. Exits on shore can be hard. The biggest problem is usually sunburn, so wear a shirt with SPF protection even when snorkelling. Sharks and jellyfish are not usually a problem but caution is advised.

The best time to scuba is the shoulder season, which runs before and after summer. Winter is also a good time to escape the crowds, with visibility in the south and the east still very good (20m).

Green Island Adventures (www.greenislandadventures.com) is a foreign-run dive company, specialising in tours in the east. **John Boo** (www.udive.com.tw) has a good reputation among divers for his skill and knowledge.

Windsurfing

Taiwan has two main windsurfing venues: Penghu and the west coast of Hsinchu and Miaoli Counties. Penghu is Asia's top-rated windsurfing destination and the windiest place in the northern hemisphere during the autumn. The unique topography of the archipelago keeps the waves down and advanced windsurfers can reach some impressive speeds.

Lessons from experienced windsurfers and rentals are available at both venues. See p147.

regions at a glance

Taipei lies in a basin surrounded by lush hills. Within the city limits are world-class museums, ancient temples and never-ending opportunities for snacking. Heading out towards the coast or the hills puts the traveller in northern Taiwan, a cycling, biking and hot-spring mecca. The dusty plains of western Taiwan hold some of the best temple towns, while heading east the unspoiled Central Mountains rise quickly to over 3000m. Over the mountains completely lies eastern Taiwan, the least developed region of the country, with a landscape that's pure eye candy. In tropical southern Taiwan, ecotourists brush against culture vultures taking in traditional festivals and night markets. Finally, scattered on both sides of the mainland are Taiwan's islands, boasting a Cold War legacy, timeless seaside villages and a top windsurfing destination.

Taipei

Cuisine ✓✓✓
History ✓✓✓
Shopping ✓✓✓

Eating

With hundreds of restaurants incorporating flavours and culinary influences from every corner of China, scores of equally good eateries serving top-rate Asian and Western fare, and a night-market-snack scene rivalled only by Singapore's, Taipei definitely has it all foodwise.

History

Beneath Taipei's ultra-modern and flashily consumerist exterior you'll find temples dating back hundreds of years and neighbourhoods little changed since the days of the Japanese occupation.

Shopping

Need a new laptop, portable hard drive, MP3 player or an assortment of new lenses? When it comes to shopping for high tech, Taipei can't be beat. And if it's more-traditional items you're after, from jade to fine teas, Taipei won't let you down either.

p40

Northern Taiwan

Outdoor Activities ✓✓✓
Hot Springs ✓✓✓
Museums ✓✓✓

Hiking & Cycling

The north's network of trails cross landscapes that vary from tropical jungles to alpine meadows above 3000m. The roads offer some first-class cycling, with day and multiday options along coastal routes, riverside paths and cross-island highways.

Hot Springs

With dozens of hot springs dotting the north, there's always a place for a dip somewhere close by. And with facilities ranging from five-star resorts to natural pools deep in the mountains, there's something for every taste and style.

Museums

Once a centre for traditional cottage industries such as tea, pottery and woodcarving, the north now boasts a rich little collection of museums highlighting each. Master woodcarver Juming and his internationally acclaimed works have their own outdoor park overlooking the sea.

p108

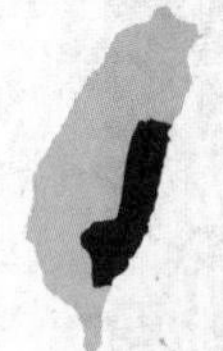

Taroko National Park & the East Coast

Landscapes ✓✓✓
Cycling ✓✓✓
Culture ✓✓✓

Gorges, the Coast & the Rift Valley

Earning the name Ilha Formosa (Beautiful Island), the east has hardly changed its face for modern times. It's still a land of 1000m seaside cliffs, river gorges, tropical forests and vast yellow rice fields nestled between blue-tinged mountain ranges.

Cycling

The scenery that makes the east a mecca for nature lovers is best viewed at cycling speeds. The premier challenge is an 86km route from sea level to 3275m through Taroko Gorge, but most opt for all or part of the 400km ride down the coastline and back through the Rift Valley.

Aboriginal Festivals & Art

Hunting, fishing and coming-of-age festivals dot the summer calendar. Woodcarvers operate small studios up and down the driftwood-rich coastline, while Dulan's weekly bash at a former sugar factory is keeping the music alive.

p156

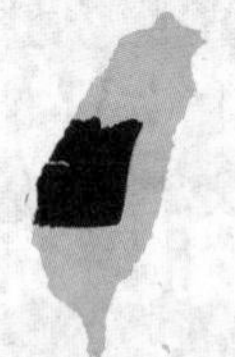

Yushan National Park & Western Taiwan

Mountains ✓✓✓
Culture ✓✓✓
Wildlife ✓✓✓

Hiking & Landscapes

The 3000m+ spine of Taiwan runs through the west with three ranges competing for scenic supremacy. The highest mountain in Taiwan, Yushan (3952m) acts as a talisman for hikers around the world, but it's just one of many worthies.

Temples & Traditional Festivals

As one of the first areas settled by Chinese immigrants, the west is home to some of Taiwan's oldest temples. Exuberant yearly festivals such as the weeklong Matsu Pilgrimage honour a pantheon of traditional folk gods.

Bird- & Butterfly-Watching

With its wealth of protected reserves and national parks, the west is a haven for endemic species such as the Mikado pheasant. Several hundred butterfly species also call the region home, with purple milkweed butterflies passing through each year in vast numbers as they migrate north to south.

p190

Southern Taiwan

Culture ✓✓✓
Wildlife ✓✓✓
Food ✓✓✓

Temples & Traditional Festivals

Early immigrants to Taiwan faced a hostile environment. In the south, the legacy of the faith that sustained them is evident in a wealth of old temples and the spectacular boat-burning festival in Donggang.

Bird- & Butterfly-Watching

The warm, sheltered valleys of the south provide a safe winter haven for millions of butterflies. The ponds, forests, grasslands and lakes of Kenting National Park support hundreds of species of birds year-round, making the region one of Taiwan's top twitching venues.

Night Markets & Traditional Snacks

Tainan's traditional snacks are famous throughout Taiwan: *dànzǎi miàn* (noodle dish) and coffin cake are just a couple of quirky, mouthwatering highlights. Kaohsiung's night markets serve anything, but specialise in fresh-off-the-boat seafood.

p230

Taiwan's Islands

Landscapes ✓✓✓
Activities ✓✓✓
History ✓✓

Beaches & Coastal Scenery

Penghu's beaches are Taiwan's finest, and the traditional villages are a nice backdrop. The volcanic origins of Lanyu, Green Island and Penghu have left coastal formations such as towering basalt columns. Kinmen's landscape includes lakes, mudflats and fine beaches.

Windsurfing & Snorkelling

As the windiest place in the northern hemisphere in late autumn, Penghu attracts windsurfers from all over the world. For snorkellers, the easily accessed coral reefs off Lanyu and Green Island burst with marine life and colour year-round.

History

Former frontiers of the civil war, Matsu and Kinmen have a rich legacy of old military tunnels, memorials and museums. More interesting to many are the traditional villages, wonderfully preserved because of their frontier status.

p272

Look out for these icons:

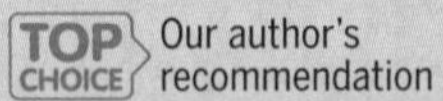
Our author's recommendation

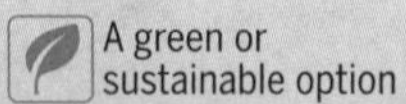
A green or sustainable option

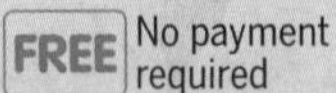
No payment required

See the Index for a full list of destinations covered in this book.

On the Road

Taipei

☎02 / POP 2.6 MILLION

Includes »

Best Places to Eat

» #21 Goose & Seafood (p74)

» Shilin Night Market (p59)

» Xiangyi Vegetarian Heaven (p71)

» Wu Hua Ma Dumpling House (p77)

» Celestial Restaurant (p75)

Best Places to Stay

» $$$: Grand Hotel (p68)

» $$: Dandy Hotel (p67)

» $ Holo Family House (p66)

Why Go?

Once the ugly duckling of East Asia, Taipei (台北) has undergone a transformation over the last two decades that has turned the city into one of the region's most dynamic, sophisticated, exciting – and yes, even beautiful – metropolises. Taipei offers a huge variety of sights and attractions, from temples dating back to the Qing dynasty to wide, noisy neon-lit avenues that offer shopping malls as gaudy and exclusive as any you'll find in Shanghai or Tokyo. The city's restaurants and street-food scene are second to none (save perhaps Singapore, whose famously food-obsessed citizens flock to Taipei for a taste of something different). With places to go, culture to experience and things to eat, Taipei is particularly well suited to exploration, so make sure you leave yourself some time to investigate this truly dense and often unexpectedly strange city.

When to Go

Taipei

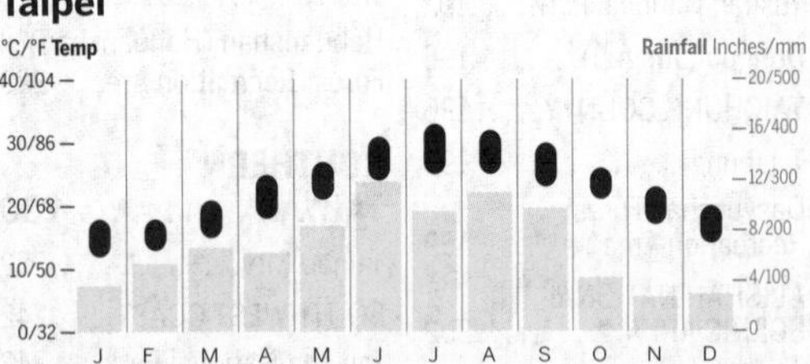

January/February Though often chilly, the weeks around Lunar New Year are a great time to visit Taipei.

June Xindian's riverside park is a prime spot for watching the Dragon Boat Festival races.

October/November Hot summer gone and winter chill yet to begin: the perfect time to explore Taipei.

Orientation

Central Taipei is constructed on a grid, with major streets running east–west and north–south. These streets are named according to direction and broken up further into sections, numbered according to the distance from the central axis (roughly speaking, Taipei Main Station). The lower the section number, the closer to the centre of the city the address tends to be; Zhongshan N Rd Sec 1 is close to Taipei Main Station; Sec 7 is in the wilds of Tianmu, 25 minutes by taxi in good traffic.

But wait, it gets more complicated. Taipei also has numbered 'lanes', which generally run perpendicular to the main streets. Major sights, hotels and restaurants are located along the main streets, but many addresses include lanes. So if you're looking for, say, Grandma Nitti's restaurant (p73), at 8 Lane 93, Shida Rd, you need to first find Shida Rd, then look for where number 93 would be. But instead of finding a building, you'll find the lane where you'll find Nitti's.

Then there are alleys, which are to lanes as lanes are to streets. Though the system's a bit complicated, it's actually quite logical. But before you head out, there's one more thing you should know: though Taipei is an increasingly English-friendly city, with all street signs featuring both Chinese and English lettering, over the past few years there have been a number of, er, interesting developments concerning the spellings of nearly every street name in the city. But visitors to the city should be aware that the Taiwanese approach to English translation is in no way rigidly dogmatic. As a result, don't be surprised to find a restaurant whose business card address reads Chunghsiao East Rd under a street sign reading Zhongxiao E Rd.

Sights

OLD TOWN CENTRE, DA'AN & SHIDA
萬華區、大安區、師大區

The first part of the city to be developed, this proto-Taipei (also known as Wanhua) was once encircled by a wall (the last Qing-era city to get one). Though the wall is gone, four of its five gates still stand, adding to the historic character of this district. It's in and around this area where you'll find sights traditional (Longshan Temple), contemporary (Ximending) and historically edifying (2-28 Memorial Museum). It's in the Old Town Centre where you'll find the government district. Da'an and Shida, meanwhile, are home to Da'an Park, the Shida Night Market, and the weekend jade and flower markets.

Ximending NEIGHBOURHOOD
(西門町; Xīméndīng; Map p44; MXimen) Like Tokyo's Ginza, Ximending is the ultra-consumerist heart of Taipei's mainstream youth culture. This eight-branched intersection dates from the Japanese era and is now chock-full of shops selling fashion, fast food, sneakers, sunglasses, scarves, Sanrio, Sony and spaghetti. If it's young and trendy, it's here. The pedestrian streets northwest of the main intersection (between Chengdu Rd and Wuchang St) is more or less the epicentre, but for the full Ximending experience you'll really want to explore the smaller alleys. It's here you'll find the edgier side of Taiwan's youth culture, the places they hang out and the stores in which they work and shop.

There are restaurants for all tastes in Ximending, from coffee shops and steakhouses to sushi bars both cheap and expensive, and plenty more. Though there are gift shops aplenty in Ximending, you may want to bring home something a bit more permanent to remember your Taiwan trip. Hanzhong Lane 50 is where you'll find your tattoo parlours and piercing joints. If it can be inked, pierced or otherwise modified, chances are good you can get it done in Ximending.

While it's busy most of the time, nights and weekends are prime time, especially Friday and Saturday nights. You might catch a musical act on a temporary stage set up on the streets and if you want to see a film, Wuchang St is home to many cinemas, as well as some fine examples of Japanese-period architecture, notably the **Red Pavilion Theatre** (紅樓劇場; Hónglóu Jùchǎng; Map p44; ☎2311 9380; 10 Chengdu Rd; admission free except during events; ⏰1-10pm Mon-Fri,

TAIPEI TRAVEL ONLINE

The Taipei city government has really tried to make a couple of fun and usable websites to help people find their way around the city. Typically, they've sacrificed some usability (at least for English speakers) in the name of adorability. Still, if you can figure your way around the interface, www.taipeibus.taipei.gov.tw can be helpful in trip planning.

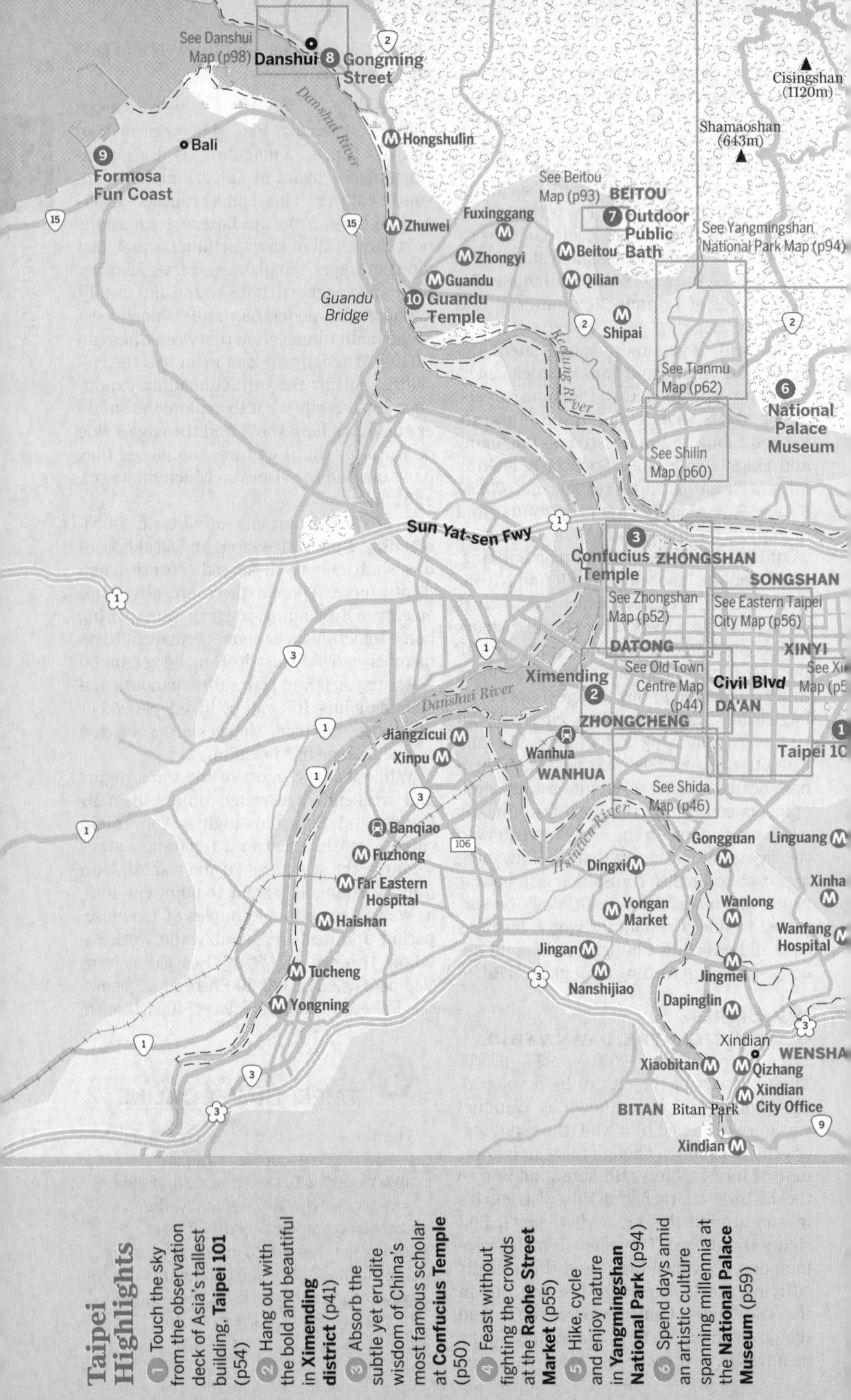

Taipei Highlights

1. Touch the sky from the observation deck of Asia's tallest building, **Taipei 101** (p54)
2. Hang out with the bold and beautiful in **Ximending district** (p41)
3. Absorb the subtle yet erudite wisdom of China's most famous scholar at **Confucius Temple** (p50)
4. Feast without fighting the crowds at the **Raohe Street Market** (p55)
5. Hike, cycle and enjoy nature in **Yangmingshan National Park** (p94)
6. Spend days amid an artistic culture spanning millennia at the **National Palace Museum** (p59)

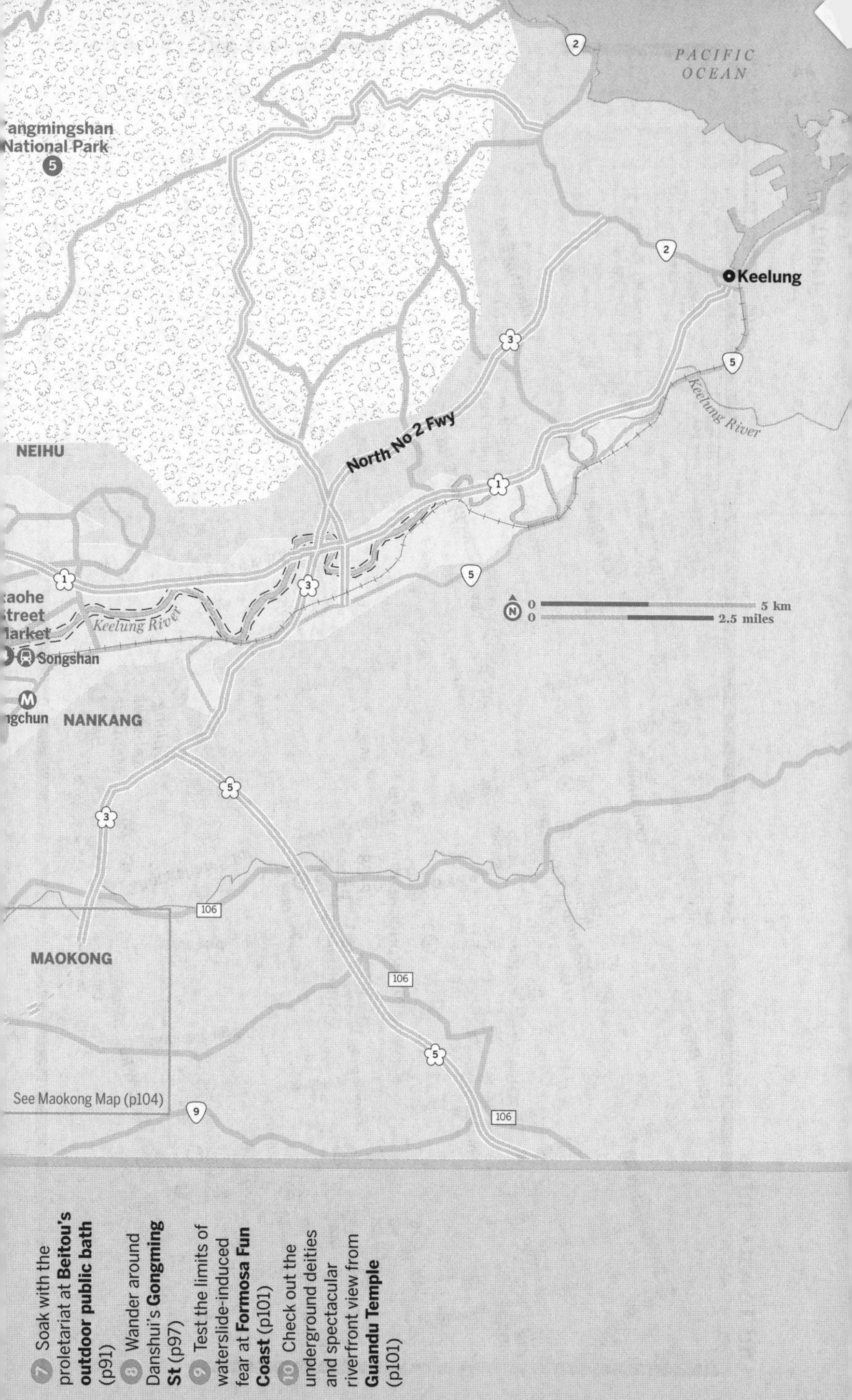

7 Soak with the proletariat at **Beitou's outdoor public bath** (p91)

8 Wander around Danshui's **Gongming St** (p97)

9 Test the limits of waterslide-induced fear at **Formosa Fun Coast** (p101)

10 Check out the underground deities and spectacular riverfront view from **Guandu Temple** (p101)

Old Town Centre

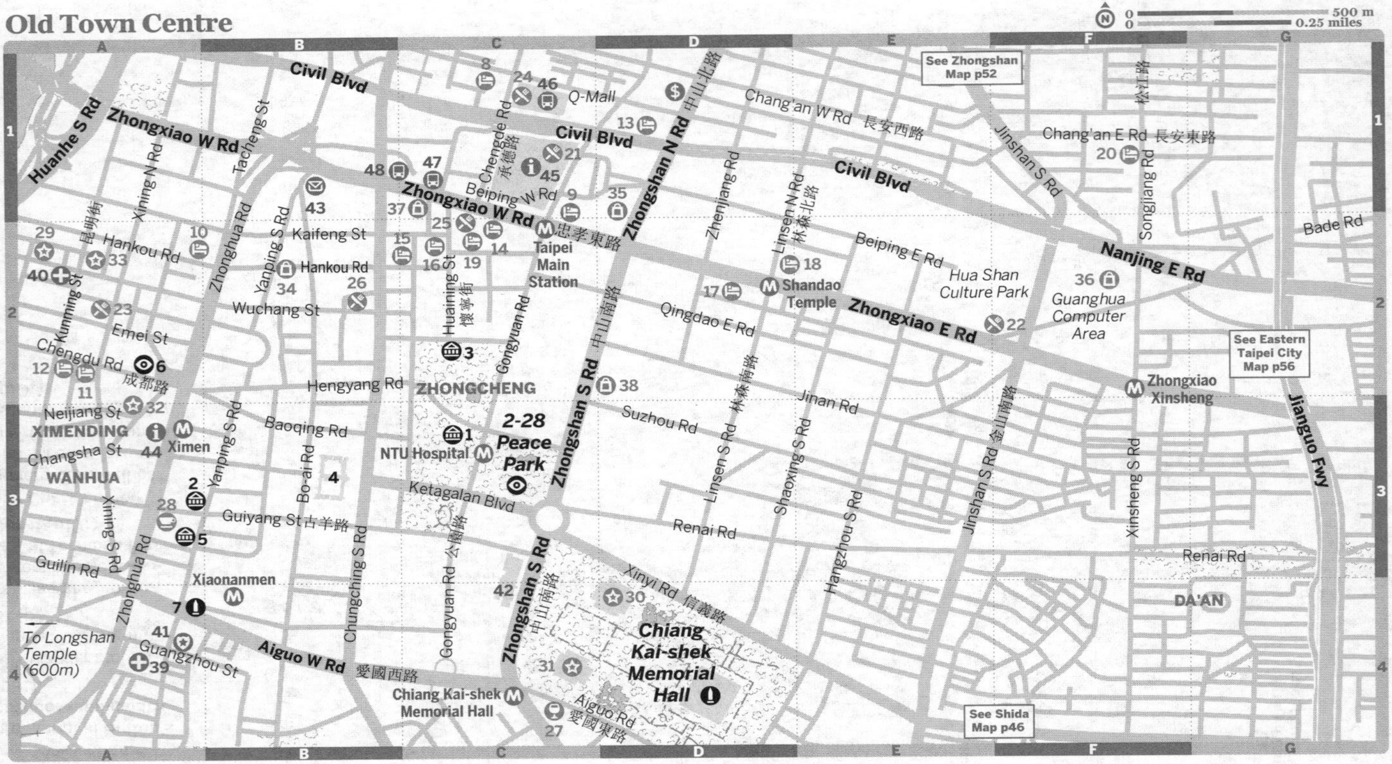

0 — 500 m
0 — 0.25 miles

See Zhongshan Map p52
See Eastern Taipei City Map p56
See Shida Map p46
To Longshan Temple (600m)

Civil Blvd
Zhongxiao W Rd
Huanhe S Rd
Xining N Rd
Tacheng St
Zhonghua Rd
Yanping S Rd
Kaifeng St
Hankou Rd
昆明街
Kunming St
Emei St
Chengdu Rd
成都路
Wuchang St
Neijiang St
XIMENDING
Ximen
Changsha St
WANHUA
Xining S Rd
Guilin Rd
Guiyang St 古羊路
Bo-ai Rd
Baoqing Rd
Hengyang Rd
Xiaonanmen
Guangzhou St
Aiguo W Rd 愛國西路
Chungching S Rd
Gongyuan Rd 公園路
Chiang Kai-shek Memorial Hall
Huaining St 懷寧街
ZHONGCHENG
NTU Hospital
2-28 Peace Park
Ketagalan Blvd
Chengde Rd 承德路
Q-Mall
Beiping W Rd
Zhongxiao W Rd 忠孝東路
Taipei Main Station
Zhongshan N Rd 中山北路
Zhongshan S Rd 中山南路
Chang'an W Rd 長安西路
Zhenjiang Rd
Linsen N Rd 林森北路
Linsen S Rd 林森南路
Qingdao E Rd
Shandao Temple
Beiping E Rd
Zhongxiao E Rd
Suzhou Rd
Jinan Rd
Renai Rd
Shaoxing S Rd
Hangzhou S Rd
Xinyi Rd 信義路
Chiang Kai-shek Memorial Hall
Aiguo Rd 愛國東路
Hua Shan Culture Park
Jinshan S Rd
Jinshan S Rd 金山南路
Chang'an E Rd 長安東路
Songjiang Rd 松江路
Nanjing E Rd
Guanghua Computer Area
Zhongxiao Xinsheng
Xinsheng S Rd
Bade Rd
Jianguo Fwy
DA'AN

Old Town Centre

Top Sights
- 2-28 Peace Park ... C3
- Chiang Kai-shek Memorial Hall ... D4

Sights
- 1 2-28 Memorial Museum ... C3
- 2 Armed Forces Museum ... A3
- 3 National Taiwan Museum ... C2
- 4 Presidential Building ... B3
- 5 Taipei Contemporary Art Center ... A3
- 6 Tien-ho Temple ... A2
- 7 Xiaonanmen (Little South Gate) ... A4

Sleeping
- 8 City Inn ... C1
- 9 Cosmos Hotel ... C1
- 10 East Dragon Hotel ... A2
- 11 Good Ground Hotel ... A2
- 12 Han She Business Hotel ... A2
- 13 Happy Family Hostel ... D1
- 14 Holo Family House ... C2
- 15 Hotel Flowers ... C2
- 16 Keyman's Hotel ... C2
- 17 Sheraton Taipei ... D2
- 18 Taipei Hostel ... D2
- 19 Taipei YMCA International Guest House ... C2
- 20 World Scholar House ... F1

Eating
- 21 Breeze ... C1
- 22 Ching Ye Shin Le Yuan ... F2
- L'air Rouge ... (see 24)
- 23 Modern Toilet ... A2
- 24 Q Mall ... C1
- 25 Shingong Tower Food Court ... C2
- 26 Xiangyi Vegetarian Heaven ... B2
- Yun Thai ... (see 32)

Drinking
- 27 Source ... C4
- 28 Urban Core Café & Bookshelf ... A3

Entertainment
- 29 Movie Theatres ... A2
- 30 National Concert Hall ... D4
- 31 National Theatre ... C4
- 32 Red Pavilion Theatre ... A3
- 33 Velvet Underground ... A2

Shopping
- 34 Camera Stores ... B2
- 35 Camping Stores ... D1
- 36 Guanghua Market ... F2
- 37 NOVA Computer Arcade ... C1
- 38 Taiwan Handicraft Mart ... D2

Information
- 39 Heping Hospital ... A4
- 40 Hospital of Traditional Chinese Medicine ... A2
- 41 Ministry of Foreign Affairs ... A4
- 42 National Central Library ... C3
- National Immigration Agency ... (see 41)
- 43 North Gate Post Office ... B1
- 44 Tourist Information Booth ... A3
- 45 Tourist Information Booth ... C1

Transport
- 46 Taipei North Bus Terminal/Q Mall ... C1
- 47 Western Terminal A ... C1
- 48 Western Terminal B ... C1

10am-10pm Sat & Sun; MXimen), one of Taipei's older buildings. The wooden, octagonal structure was originally a public market, then a theatre for Chinese opera as well as a second-run cinema. Since beginning life anew as a multipurpose centre for vocal and visual arts it has hosted a variety of performers and performances. The Red Pavilion Theatre is surrounded by excellent bars and restaurants, and has in recent years become something of a magnet for Taipei's gay and lesbian population.

Ximending is also home to the **Tien-Ho temple** (天后宮; Tiānhòu Gōng; Map p44; 51 Chengdu Rd, Ximending; MXimen). A narrow (though exceptionally ornate) storefront in the otherwise distinctly commercial district leads you into one of central Taipei's most beautiful Buddhist temples, complete with statues of Matsu, ancient Chinese generals, a bell tower and a small dragon-shaped pond filled with huge carp. The original temple was built during the mid-Qing period and demolished during the last years of Japanese rule to make way for a road. The current temple was built in 1948 and holds several ancient statues brought over from mainland China hundreds of years ago.

2-28 Peace Park MEMORIAL PARK

(二二八和平公園; Èrèrbā Hépíng Gōngyuán; Map p44; MNTU Hospital) At first glance the lovely 2-28 Peace Park doesn't seem more significant than any of the other dozen or

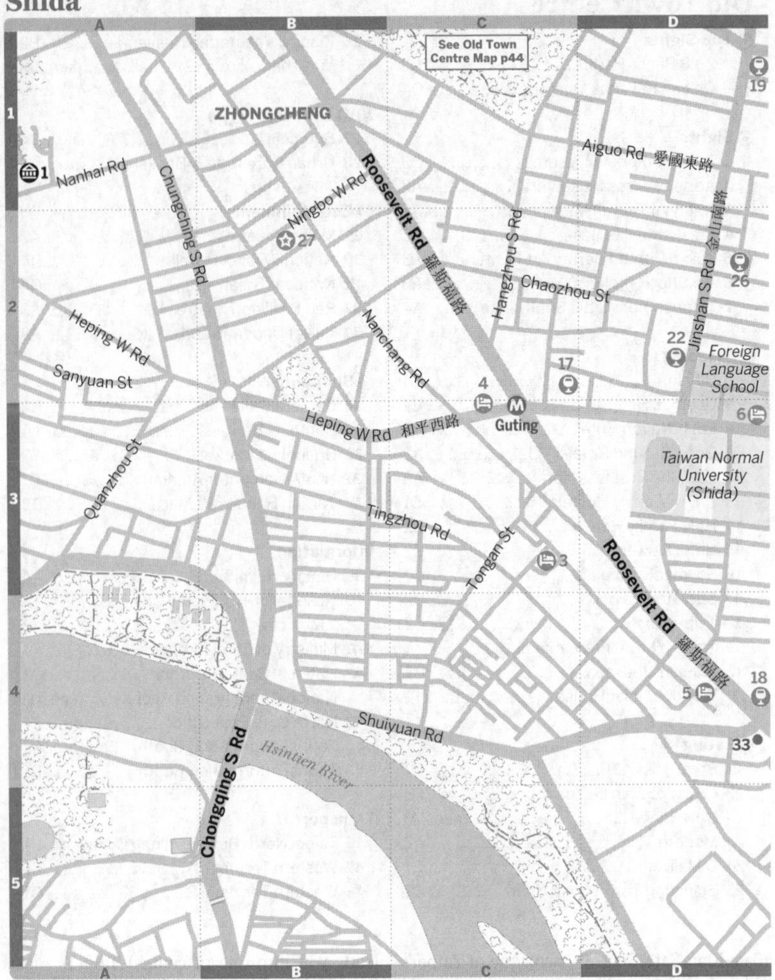

so parks in Taipei. There's a band performance stage, some lovely shrines and pavilions, paths and playgrounds. But there is a certain air of solemnity to this place, for it is dedicated to the memory of a massacre that began on 28 February 1947 (hence the 2-28), an event that heralded the start of Taiwan's martial-law era. In the centre of the park stands the memorial itself, a steepled sculpture surrounded by three enormous cubes turned on their corners.

If the monument is the soul of the park, then the **2-28 Memorial Museum** (二二八紀念館; Èrèrbā Jìniànguǎn; Map p44; adult/concession NT$20/10; ⏲10am-5pm Tue-Sun; Ⓜ NTU Hospital), which offers an explanation of the events and repercussions of the 28 February 1947 massacre, can be considered its memory. Though there is little in the way of English signage in the museum, a multilingual walking tour device is available for NT$50, plus NT$1000 rental deposit. However, there are generally bilingual volunteers on hand willing to walk you through the displays. The building itself is significant, for it was from this, the former Kuomintang (KMT) radio station, that officials tried to calm the masses as panic swept the island.

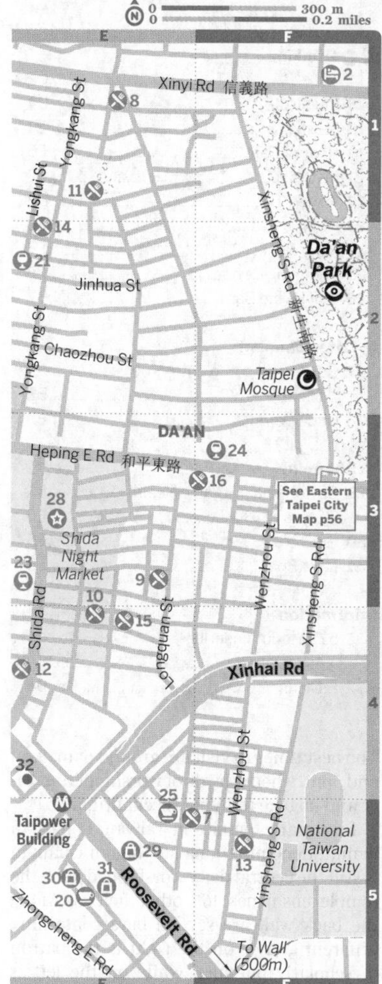

Solemn origins aside, the vibe of the park is cheerful and vibrant. In the early mornings, the park is a good place to watch people practising taichi and you can join in if you're so inclined. Farmers markets are often held on the weekends. And it's said that the park is a popular cruising ground for gay men at night.

Just north of the museum (by the park's northern gate) is the **National Taiwan Museum** (國立台灣博物館; Guólì Táiwān Bówùguǎn), with displays on the flora and fauna of the island, as well as special exhibits.

FREE Chiang Kai-shek Memorial Hall

MONUMENT/MUSEUM

(中正紀念堂; Zhōngzhèng Jìniàn Táng; Map p44; 21 Zhongshan S Rd; 9am-5pm; M Chiang Kai-shek Memorial Hall) This iconic monument with its white walls and blue octagonal roof still stands as a grandiose, ostentatious and perhaps fitting memorial to the man who, in life, was known in some circles as 'General Cash-my-check'. On the ground floor you'll find a museum dedicated to Chiang's life, with an assortment of military uniforms, medals, paintings and manuscripts, along with two humungous black, bulletproof Cadillacs he used. You'll also find in this museum an interesting version of history in which Chiang's Kuomintang (KMT, Nationalist Party) forces nearly single-handedly defeated the Japanese empire, and the Chinese communist revolution is reduced to a mere speed bump in history.

The sculpture of the man himself is equally ostentatious. To get to it, visitors ascend a flight of 89 steps (representing Chiang's age when he died), where the gigantic bronze sculpture occupies a cavernous hall, and looks out over the gate and towards China. The statue is flanked by two motionless guards with bayoneted rifles and, behind him, carved into the white marble walls, are Chinese characters reading 'ethics', 'democracy' and 'science', the 'Three Principles of the People'. The hall, opened in 1980, five years after Chiang's death, has a sign out the front stating that those with slippers or slovenly dress shall not be admitted.

The grounds (250,000 sq metres) also include the **National Theatre** (國家戲劇院) and **National Concert Hall** (國家音樂廳); it's here that the Taipei City Classical Chinese Orchestra often performs. The plazas and gardens around the three buildings are among Taipei's grandest and best used, and on weekends you'll often find anything from outdoor art exhibitions to hip-hop concerts.

In 2007, the memorial was ground zero in a tug of war between Taiwan's two main political parties, and at one point it was conceivable that the sculpture itself might be removed. As of 2010, a semi-truce between those who see themselves as political descendants of the General and those who would see him relegated to the ash-heap of history seems to have taken hold. While the monument is still called 'Chiang Kai-shek Memorial Hall', the park in which it stands is now known as 'Liberty Plaza'.

Shida

Top Sights
Da'an Park F2

Sights
1 National Museum of History A1

Sleeping
2 Dandy Hotel F1
3 Eight Elephants Hostel C3
4 Friends Star Hotel C3
5 Li-Yuan Hotel D4
6 NTNU Guesthouse D3

Eating
7 Bongos E5
8 Dintaifung E1
9 Fruit Auntie E3
10 Grandma Nitti's E4
11 Hui Liu E1
12 KGB E4
13 Maryjane Pizza F5
14 Oma Ursel's German Bakery & Restaurant E2
15 Salt Peanuts E4
16 Vegetarian Paradise F3

Drinking
17 45 ..... C2
18 Blue Note D4
19 Fresh D1
20 H*ours Cafe E5
21 Maussac E2
22 Roxy 99 ..... D2
23 Roxy Jr E3
24 Roxy Rocker F3
25 Tongjong Coffee E5
26 Vinyl Wine Bar D2

Entertainment
27 Gu Ling Street Avant-garde Theatre B2
28 Underworld E3

Shopping
29 Cottonfields Organic Health Store E5
30 GinGin's E5
31 Love Boat E5

Information
32 523 Mountaineering Association E4
33 E-Clean D4

FREE **Longshan Temple** BUDDHIST TEMPLE
(龍山寺; Lóngshān Sì; 211 Guangzhou St; 6am-10.20pm; Longshan Temple) Religious life in Taiwan is alive and kicking seven days a week at Longshan Temple. Though not the biggest temple in the city, there is something unique and beautiful about the vibe at Longshan that keeps people coming back.

The temple dates back to 1738. As the story goes, a passer-by left an amulet of Guanyin (goddess of mercy) hanging on a tree on the site of the present temple, and the amulet shone so brightly, even after dark, that all who passed by knew the site was blessed. Nearly three centuries later, the spot still exudes a certain warmth. The stones that line the courtyard of the temple were originally ballast on the ships that ferried immigrants from Fujian province across the often treacherous Taiwan Strait, and the waterfall inside the courtyard is a favourite spot for shutterbugs. Once you enter the main building, expect a riot of scarlet and gold in the form of enormous bronze incense burners and carved-stone columns. The best times to visit are around 6am, 8am and 5pm, when crowds of worshippers gather and engage in hypnotic chanting.

Like many temples in Taiwan, Longshan is multidenominational. Although Guanyin is still the central deity worshipped here, the temple enshrines 165 other deities. Along the back wall are several bays containing different gods – on the right is the patron of scholarly pursuits, while on the left is the god of military pursuits and business people. The goddess Matsu (p201) is in the centre, and provides for the safe return of travellers by sea or land (air travellers pay their respects to Guanyin).

The lights on columns at the back of the temple represent a person whose family has made a donation in his or her honour.

Outside the front gate of the temple, old monks sit selling cedar-wood beads, and old women sell magnolias. The number of vendors increases markedly on weekends. Across the street from the temple is an underground market and the entire neighbourhood is good for shopping for religious items and trinkets of all sorts.

Da'an Park PARK
(大安公園; Dàān Gōngyuán; Map p46; MDa'An) This is Taipei's central park, where the city comes to play. And play it does, from kiddies rollerblading and playing tag to teens playing basketball and ultimate frisbee to old men whomping each other in *xiàngqí* (Chinese chess). The park is a great place to hang out on sunny afternoons; take off your shoes and walk barefoot on the foot-massage path or just stop and smell the flowers. In the early mornings, you'll see folks practising taichi. Perhaps more incongruous for visitors expecting Asian-themed pursuits are the ad hoc ballroom-dancing classes that often occur on cool summer evenings. Find a partner and join in. On big holidays, especially Christmas, New Year and Chinese New Year, the amphitheatre hosts free stage shows featuring some of the biggest names in Taiwanese entertainment. There's also a row of restaurants with outdoor seating across the street from the park's northwest corner.

FREE **Botanical Gardens** GARDEN
(植物園; Zhíwùyuán; 53 Nanhai Rd; 4am-10pm; MXiaonanmen) A beautiful oasis

TAIPEI IN A DAY FOR THE...

Spiritual Traveller

Rise at dawn and head to **2-28 Peace Park** for some taichi and morning contemplation, followed by walking 200 steps along the stone foot-massage path to build inner resilience. Go to **Longshan Temple** to mingle with morning devotees and fellow travellers. After that, head over to the **Museum of World Religions** and check out exhibits until noon, then head back downtown to have lunch with the monks at **Xiangyi Vegetarian Heaven**. Afterwards, visit the compact yet beautiful **Tien-Ho Temple**, located in the heart of ultrachic Ximending. The walk from the MRT will test your resolve against a variety of forms of sin. Travel north to the Yuanshan neighbourhood to check out **Confucius Temple** and the surrounding temples in the area. If you've still got an hour or two left, take the MRT north to contemplate the sunset from the balcony of **Guandu Temple**. After the sun sets, head to **Beitou** for a soak in the hot spring. You've earned it.

Culture Vulture

Spend the morning in the government district getting your historical bearings. To glean two very different versions of Taiwanese history, visit the **Chiang Kai-shek Memorial Hall** and the **2-28 Memorial Museum**. Walk to Taipei Main Station and catch a quick lunch upstairs, before heading north to the **Museum of Contemporary Art Taipei** to see what's being exhibited. Afterwards, head up to Shilin and divide the rest of the afternoon between the **Shung Ye Museum of Formosan Aborigines** and the **National Palace Museum**, as they're close to each other. When the museums close, head up to **Danshui** for the evening, checking out the old shops and eating on Danshui's Gongming St (also known as Danshui Old St).

Glutton

Get up whenever. If it's before 10am, find a breakfast shop and get yourself two *qǐ sī dàn bǐng* (rolled cheese and egg omelettes), a side of *luóbógāo* (turnip cake – trust us, they taste better than they sound), and maybe a *wēn dòujiāng* (warm soymilk) to settle your stomach. If it's after 10am, go to the new **Q Mall food court** just across from Taipei Main Station for lunch in the flashy basement food court. After lunch, head back to your hotel, crank up the air-con and rest up for a long night. For dinner, head out to the **Shida neighbourhood**. Eat liberally from any of the stalls that appeal to you and don't forget to buy some fruit (to aid digestion). Hit the nearest 7-Eleven for a bottle of Whisbih, Red Bull or maybe an evening coffee before taxiing up to the **Shilin Night Market**. If your driver offers you betel nut, don't forget to spit politely into a plastic cup. Spend a few hours eating light snacks such as *zhū xiě gāo* (congealed pig's blood) and *chòu dòufǔ* (stinky tofu). If you're still a bit peckish, **#21 Goose & Seafood** is open until 2am.

in Taipei's funky west side, this park has greenhouses featuring a vast variety of lush plants, literature- and Chinese-zodiac-themed gardens and a marvellous lotus pond. Taipei's Botanical Gardens are also considered one of the best places in the world to see the rare Malaysian night heron, making the park a major stop on foreign birding tours. That such a rare bird can be seen so close to, let alone inside, a major urban centre is quite amazing, or so our twitcher friends tell us. The Botanical Gardens are where you'll find the **National Museum of History** (國立歷史博物館; Guólì Lìshǐ Bówùguǎn; adult/child NT$20/10; ⏲10am-6pm Tue-Sun). Housed in an elegant Japanese-era building, Taiwan's first museum is still an anchor of local arts and culture, housing thousands of Chinese artefacts from the Tang, Shang and other dynasties. The tearoom on the 3rd floor has views of the Botanical Gardens' lotus pond. A tour in English takes place at 3pm each afternoon.

FREE **Presidential Building** HISTORICAL BUILDING

(總統府; Zǒngtǒng Fǔ; Map p44; www.president.gov.tw; 122 Chungching S Rd, Sec 1; free with pasport; ⏲9-11.30am Mon-Fri; Ⓜ Ximen) Built in 1919 as the headquarters of the then-occupying Japanese forces, this building has housed the offices of the president since 1949. Its ornate brickwork is typical of the Japanese era, and at 85m it was the tallest building in town for decades.

Exhibits include documents from Taiwanese history (both originals and copies) and artefacts such as lacquerware and statues from the Japanese occupation. Although most signage is in Chinese, there is usually an English speaker on hand to guide you through.

Snake Alley NIGHT MARKET

(華西街夜市; Huáxījiē Yèshì; Huaxi St; ⏲7pm-midnight; Ⓜ Longshan Temple) Once considered a Taipei must-see, nowadays Snake Alley (aka Huaxi St Night Market) is more of a window into Taiwan's less enlightened past, when the live skinning of reptiles for the benefit of passing tourists was considered an appropriate form of cultural expression. In decades past, Taipei dwellers might bring their visitors from abroad to Snake Alley and express mild amusement as their foreign guests squirmed at the sight of a local merchant baiting a cobra with a hooked metal rod before slitting its belly and offering the foreigners a shot glass of snake bile mixed with Kaoliang liquor. These days, Snake Alley is considered somewhat passé and cruel by many.

Taipei Contemporary Art Center MUSEUM

(TCAC; 台北當代藝術中心; Táiběi dāngdài yìshù zhōngxīn; Map p44; www.tcac.tw; 160-6 Yanping S Rd; ⏲1-7pm Thu-Sun; Ⓜ Xiaonanmen) The sort of spot you'd expect to come across in Berkeley or Melbourne, TCAC's existence in Taipei is yet another sign of how cool the city is becoming. The small, privately run museum and gallery space offers a wide and rather eclectic variety of exhibits, both of local and international artists, as well as hosting parties, international DJs and other hipster-attracting club-type events.

Armed Forces Museum MUSEUM

(國軍歷史文物館; Guójūn Lìshǐ Wénwùguǎn; Map p44; 243 Guiyang St; ⏲9am-4pm Mon-Sat; Ⓜ Xiaonanmen) Like weapons and selective retellings of 20th-century military history? Then this museum might be for you. Focusing on the military history of the Republic of China (ROC), the three-storey museum houses artefacts and items ranging from the early days of warlord pacification and the struggle against Japanese invasion to the battle between the Nationalists and communists, and finally into the ROC government's temporary movement to Taiwan. Laminated placards on the wall offer translations into English and Japanese.

ZHONGSHAN 中山區

This area north of the Zhongshan (Zhōngshān) train station and south of the Keelung River features museums (large and small, and even a miniature one), beautiful parks and some of Taipei's most important temples. The western part of this district, near the Danshui River, is sometimes known as Dadaocheng or Datong. In general, most of the major sights listed are within walking distance of the Xindian/Danshui MRT line.

FREE **Confucius Temple** CONFUCIUS TEMPLE

(孔廟; Kǒng Miào; Map p52; 275 Dalong St; ⏲8.30am-9pm Tue-Sat, 8.30am-5pm Sun; Ⓜ Yuanshan) Modelled after the temple in Confucius' native town of Shandong, this temple is based on classical Chinese temple architecture. Confucius (551–479 BC) is generally acknowledged as China's greatest educator and scholar. In his day, education was exclusive to nobility but Confucius successfully promoted popular education.

Confucius valued simplicity, a trait seen in the temple's architecture and relatively muted adornments. Inscriptions that might be found on columns, doors and windows in other temples are banned here; who would have the temerity to think his or her writing could compare with that of the great master? Do take note of the detailed carvings of dragons on the temple's Ling Xing Gate and the fired pottery on the Yi Gate. The central Ta Cheng hall is one of the few traditional wooden buildings in Taiwan and contains a Confucius tablet. A seven-storey pagoda in the centre of the roof is said to drive away evil spirits. A total of 186 tablets representing the Confucian disciples are located on the premises.

The temple at this site (13,935 sq metres) dates back to 1928, replacing the original 1879 temple that was damaged beyond repair during a rebellion under Japanese occupation.

The temple's biggest day of the year is Confucius' birthday, celebrated on 28 September. Events begin at 6am with a ceremony presided over by the mayor of Taipei and officiated by rafts of attendants, supervisors and officers, all dressed in elaborate costumes. Confucius' spirit is welcomed with drumming, music, bowing, incense, chanting, a sacrificial feast and the burning of spirit money. Tickets go on sale at the temple about five days in advance and always sell out.

Fine Arts Museum MUSEUM

(市立美術館; Shìlì Měishùguǎn; Map p52; 181 Zhongshan N Rd, Sec 3; adult/student NT$30/15; ⌚9.30am-5.30pm Tue-Sun; Ⓜ Yuanshan) Constructed in the 1980s, this airy, four-storey box of marble, glass and concrete showcases contemporary art, with a particular focus on Taiwanese artists. These include pieces by Taiwanese painters and sculptors from the Japanese period to the present. Right next door to the Fine Arts Museum and keeping roughly the same hours is the **Taipei Story House** (台北故事館; Táiběi Gùshìguǎn; adult/student NT$30/20, child & senior free; ⌚10.30am-6pm Tue-Sun). Built in 1914 by an aristocratic tea trader, the house is an exhibition space for Taipei nostalgia and history. Exhibits change frequently and might include goodies such as toys, matchboxes and comic books. The gift shop features the work of a dozen local artists and the tearoom serves afternoon tea and French-style cuisine. Although the Taipei Story House was closed for renovation at the time of writing, we are told that it should be open by the time you read this.

Museum of Contemporary Art Taipei MUSEUM

(MOCA Taipei; 台北當代藝術館; Táiběi Dāngdài Yìshùguǎn; Map p52; www.mocataipei.org.tw; 39 Chang'an W Rd; admission NT$50; ⌚10am-6pm Tue-Sun; Ⓜ Zhongshan) Demonstrating Taipei's determination to be taken seriously as a city with a taste for art, Taiwan's first museum dedicated explicitly to contemporary art occupies an important Japanese-era building that was once Taipei's city hall. Shows are all special exhibits and fill anything from one gallery to the entire museum; at press time, MOCA Taipei was featuring an exhibit by cutting-edge American artist David LaChapelle, whose apocalyptic themes (as well as nudity) managed to raise few eyebrows in this once artistically conservative culture. Multilingual MP3 players designed to guide visitors through the museum are available with a deposit of either NT$1000 or a passport. The museum also has a very cool cafe with reasonably priced lunch specials.

Dihua Market TRADITIONAL MARKET

(迪化街; Díhuà Jiē; Map p52; Ⓜ Zhongshan) The several blocks that make up this market are Taipei's best-preserved examples of historic architecture. Building styles range from Fujianese to baroque to modernist. The area is sometimes called 'Grocery St', and for most of the year it's thought of as a good place for buying traditional Chinese medicines and herbs, bolts of cloth and sundries. If you're lucky enough to be in Taipei for the weeks leading up to the Lunar New Year celebrations, Dihua Market's true colours shine, as the area is considered Taipei's best for traditional New Year foods, party supplies and gifts of all kinds. During these weeks, a festive spirit of bonhomie descends on the market, manifesting itself in a veritable orgy of giving as merchants offer samples of their edible wares to all passers-by. Should you come during this period, be prepared to be fed.

No matter when you come, be sure not to miss the nearby **Hsiahai City God Temple** (霞海城隍廟; Xiáhǎi Chénghuáng Miào; Map p52; 61 Dihua St, Sec 1), one of the best-preserved temples in the city. Visit on the city god's birthday (the 13th day of the fifth lunar month) for one of Taipei's biggest, loudest and most lively celebrations.

Zhongshan

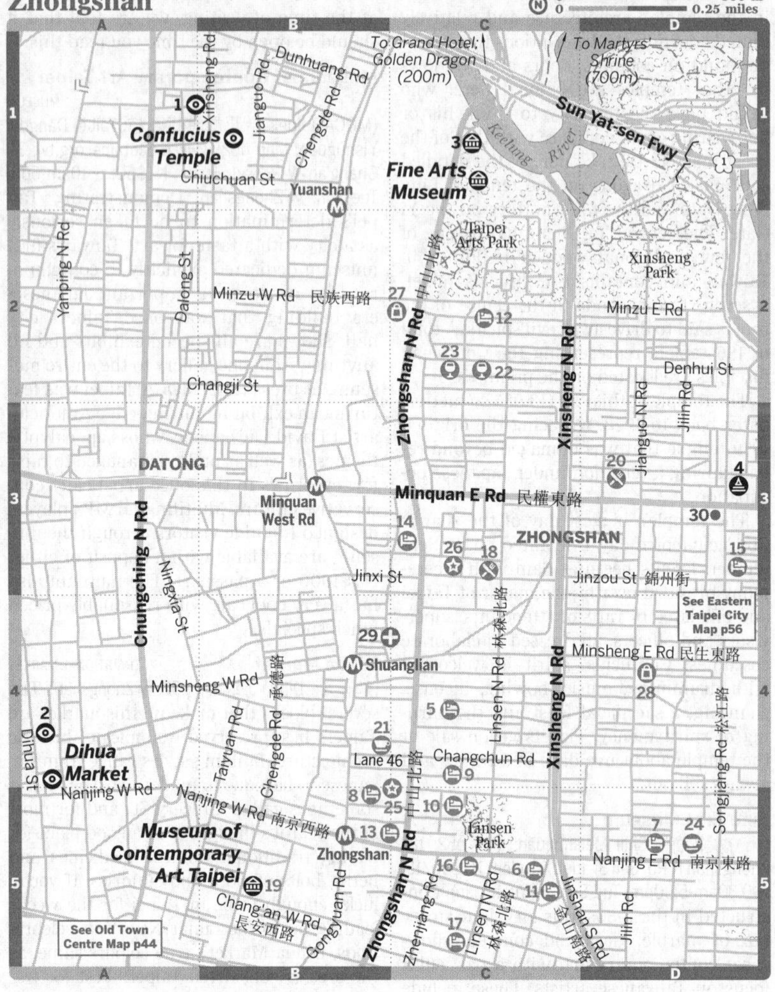

FREE **Martyrs' Shrine** HISTORICAL BUILDING (忠烈祠; Zōngliècí; 139 Beian Rd; ⏲9am-5pm) Against a backdrop of mountains across the Keelung River from the city centre, the monumental National Revolutionary Martyrs' Shrine enshrines the dead of the wars fought on behalf of the ROC. The complex covers around 5000 sq metres and the main sanctuary was modelled after the Taiho Palace in Beijing. Plaques, paintings and friezes in the arcade surrounding the main sanctuary describe the details of various 20th-century rebellions and battles. A bell tower and drum tower are used during memorial ceremonies.

The main reason most people come here, however, is to see the hourly changing of the guards. Blue-uniformed, silver-helmeted, implacable and silent, they wield and spin their bayoneted rifles with the precision of a drill team. The public is able to march along with the guards as they tread the path from the sanctuary to the main gate hundreds of metres away. The shrine is about 10 minutes' walk east of the Grand Hotel (p68).

Zhongshan

Top Sights
Confucius Temple B1
Dihua Market A4
Fine Arts Museum C1
Museum of Contemporary Art Taipei B5

Sights
1 Bao-an Temple A1
2 Hsiahai City God Temple A4
3 Taipei Story House C1
4 Xingtian Temple D3

Sleeping
5 Ambassador Hotel C4
6 Emperor Hotel C5
7 First Hotel D5
8 Formosa Hostel B5
9 Grand Formosa Regent C4
10 Hôtel Royal Taipei C5
11 Moon Hotel C5
12 Riviera Hotel C2
13 Royal Inn Taipei B5
14 Taipei Fortuna Hotel C3
15 Taipei House International Youth Hostel D3
16 Taipei International Hotel C5
17 Tango Hotel C5

Eating
18 #21 Goose & Seafood C3
19 Artco De Cafe B5
Celestial Restaurant (see 13)
20 Paris 1930 D3

Drinking
21 Dance Cafe B4
22 Malibu West C2
23 My Place C2
24 Rose House D5

Entertainment
25 SPOT – Taipei Film House C5
26 Taipei Eye C3

Shopping
27 Caves Books C2
28 Ten Shang's Tea Company D4

Information
29 Mackay Hospital B4
30 Shabon Coin Laundry D3

FREE **Xingtian Temple** TAOIST TEMPLE
(行天宮; Xíngtiān Gōng; Map p52; 109 Minquan E Rd, Sec 2; ⏲5am-11pm) This temple is one of the city's busiest. It's dedicated to Guangong (AD 162–219), a famous red-faced general who became deified and is worshipped as the god of war, patron of knights and those who live by a righteous code. Business people also flock here as Guangong was said to be adept at finance.

Although it does not have the long history of other temples (the present building dates from 1967), it has heft. One distinctive feature is the large shed that covers the central courtyard. This is where supplicants leave their daily offerings on tables. Temple officials wear handsome royal-blue robes.

Xingtian Temple is also popular for fortune-telling. Within the temple grounds you'll hear, and then see, visitors dropping oracle blocks *(bwah bwey)*. Fortune-tellers can often be found even in the pedestrian underpass outside the temple.

The temple god is celebrated on the 24th day of the sixth lunar month, and at smaller festivals during the third and ninth lunar months.

FREE **Bao-an Temple** TAOIST TEMPLE
(保安宮; Bǎoān Gōng; Map p52; 61 Hami St; ⏲7am-10pm; ⓂYuanshan) One of the city's leading religious sites, the original, wooden structure was completed in 1760 by immigrants from Fujian province using materials brought from the home country. The current temple, dating from 1805, took 25 years to build.

The temple deity is the emperor Bao-shen, famous as a doctor and great healer. As such, the temple gets many visitors who come to pray for good health. Enshrined in the bell tower is the goddess of birth. She is flanked by 12 female aides, each of whom assists with childbirth during a particular month. So naturally it's long been popular with pregnant women. Other gods commemorated here are patrons of business and good fortune.

The two open-mouthed lions (one male, the other female) are said to be an appeal for the rule of law and good government.

EASTERN TAIPEI 東台北市

With rivers and established subcities to the north and west, and mountains to the south, when it came time for Taipei to expand

Xinyi

Top Sights
- Sun Yat-sen Memorial Hall A2
- Taipei 101 .... B3

Sights
- Core Pacific City .... (see 9)
- 1 Taipei World Trade Centre A3

Sleeping
- 2 Grand Hyatt Hotel A3

Eating
- 3 Taipei 101 Food Court B3

Drinking
- 4 Marquee B3

Entertainment
- 5 Brown Sugar B3
- 6 Puppetry Art Centre of Taipei A1
- 7 Roxy Roots B3
- 8 Taipei Comedy Club B2

Shopping
- 9 Core Pacific City A1
- 10 Shin Kong Mitsukoshi Department Store B3
- 11 Warner Village B3

there was but one direction left. Encompassing Songshan, Xinyi and pretty much everything east of Fuxing Rd, eastern Taipei is fast becoming a second city centre of Taipei. While central Taipei is characterised by its older neighbourhoods and winding lanes, neighbourhoods in the eastern districts are laid out in a grid, and feature spiffy new high-rise office blocks, five-star hotels, city hall as well as some of Taipei's trendiest nightspots and restaurants. And of course, there's one edifice that sticks out, both literally and figuratively: the world's second-tallest (sigh...curse you, Dubai!) building, Taipei 101.

Taipei 101 TOWER

(台北101; Táiběi Yīlíngyī; Map p54; www.taipei101tower.com; M Taipei City Hall) Towering above the city like the gigantic bamboo stalk it was designed to resemble, Taipei 101 is impossible to miss. At 508m, Taipei 101 held the title 'world's tallest building' for a number of years, though it now must be content with second-place status. The pressure-controlled lift is quite a rush; at 1010m per minute it takes a mere 40 seconds to get from ground level to the 89th-floor observation deck.

Buy a ticket (NT$400) to the indoor and outdoor observation decks on floors 89 to 91, where you'll also be able to see the massive gold-coloured iron ball that keeps the tower stable through typhoons and earthquakes. In the basement of the structure is an excellent food court, and the lower five floors are taken up by one of Taipei's swankiest malls.

Some folks wonder what sits between the mall and the observation decks. The answer: office space, some of the city's priciest. But don't get any bright ideas about pretending to work on the 80th floor just to sneak up and catch the view from a bathroom window without paying the observation deck fee, business-floor elevators are strictly monitored and controlled.

FREE **Sun Yat-sen Memorial Hall** HISTORICAL SITE

(國父紀念館; Guófù Jìniànguǎn; Map p54; 9am-5pm; M Sun Yat-sen Memorial Hall) Occupying an entire city block, this hall serves as a cultural centre (concerts, performances and special events), a large public park and a museum of the life of the man considered the founder of modern China. A huge statue of Dr Sun sits in a cavernous lobby facing the park to the south. It's guarded by two implacable sentries – watch the changing of the guards (twice a day), an intricate choreography with much spinning of bayoneted rifles and precision stepping. Morning visitors practising taichi on the grounds provide another kind of choreography.

Core Pacific City NOTEWORTHY BUILDING

(京華城; Jīnguáchéng; Map p54; 138 Bade Rd, Sec 4; Ⓜ Taipei City Hall) Some people call it Core Pacific City, we like to think of it as the Great Golf Ball of Taipei. Designed by Jon Jerde, the Pablo Picasso of the architecture world, Core Pacific City is quite probably the weirdest shopping mall in Asia. A building that is inspired (by MC Escher or perhaps LSD) to say the least, from the outside CPC looks like a gigantic golf ball being embraced by a stone sarcophagus. Though you can get in through the basement, for maximum weirdness take the escalator from the street into the main lobby, which is somewhat reminiscent of the Death Star from the first Star Wars trilogy.

Since the initial rush of publicity over its grand opening in 2001, Core Pacific City seems to have had a bit of a mixed ride, and if it's mostly empty shops are anything to go by, business is not booming inside the wonderfully strange, egg-shaped behemoth. Although the mall boasts restaurants, shops and a world-class movie theatre, as a shopping destination Core Pacific City has been completely eclipsed by the malls in and around nearby Taipei 101. Although it's still fairly unthinkable that the Living Mall will go belly-up anytime soon (though it would make a spectacular paintball arena in some future incarnation), exactly how much life is left in the Living Mall is anybody's guess.

Su Ho Paper Museum MUSEUM

(樹火紀念紙博物館; Shùhuǒ Jìniàn Zhǐ Bówùguǎn; Map p56; ☎2507 5539; www.suhopaper.org.tw; 68 Chang'an E Rd, Sec 2, 長安東路二段68號; admission NT$100, with paper-making session NT$180; ⏲by appointment 9.30am-4.30pm Mon-Sat; Ⓜ Nanjing East Rd) Don't blink or you might walk right past the storefront housing this four-storey museum. Fulfilling the lifelong dream of Taiwanese paper-maker Mr Chen Su Ho, this museum features special exhibits of ultracreative uses of paper (such as paper sculpture or installation art). Exhibits change two or three times a year, and there's a beautiful spot on the 2nd floor with pillows surrounding a book-filled tree (made of paper, of course) tailor-made for relaxing.

The museum shop sells cards, elegant kites and other trinkets constructed from handmade paper. Paper-making classes take about 15 minutes and happen daily at 10am, 11am, 2pm and 3pm. On the roof of the museum is a beautiful chill-out spot consisting of an outdoor area and an enclosed bamboo dome. The roof is often used to host parties, readings and musical happenings. Check with the staff to find out what's going on during the time of your visit.

Raohe St Market NIGHT MARKET

(饒河街觀光夜市; Ráohéjiē guānguāng yèshì; Ⓜ Houshanpi) The Shilin Night Market may get all the press, but if feasting while fighting crowds isn't your scene, set your sights east and head to Raohe. Claiming to hold Taipei's oldest night market, Raohe St is a single pedestrian street stretching between two ornate gates, in between which you'll find an amazing assortment of Taiwanese eats, treats, and sometimes even seats (unlike the always packed and mazelike Shilin Night Market). At the eastern end of Raohe St sits the fantastically ornate **Ciyou Temple** (慈祐宮; Cíyòu Gōng), dedicated to the goddess Matsu and one of the oldest in the city. For a real treat, come to Ciyou Temple on the day of Matsu's birthday (p201), when the temple holds the loudest, most colourful birthday celebrations in Taiwan.

Museum of Jade Art MUSEUM

(瑩瑋藝術翡翠 文化博物館; Yíngwěi yìshù Fěicuì Wénhuà Bówùguǎn; Map p56; ☎2509 8166; www.museumofjadeart.com; 96 Jianguo N Rd, Sec 1; adult/student & child NT$250/180; ⏲10am-6pm Wed-Mon; Ⓜ Zhongshan Junior High School) Offering a variety of jade exhibits that nearly rivals the National Palace Museum (in beauty, though of course not in volume), this newly opened museum displays work designed by master jade artist Hu Soofeen, whose family has been involved in the jade trade for several generations. In addition to dozens of beautiful small and medium-sized jade objects, the front of the museum is taken up by an imposingly massive, movable wheel crafted of brass and jade, which can be turned to display the 12 animals and five elements of the Chinese zodiac. For a small charge (NT$50), visitors can have a photo printed of themselves standing before the wheel, customised to indicate their Chinese zodiac animal, element and fortune.

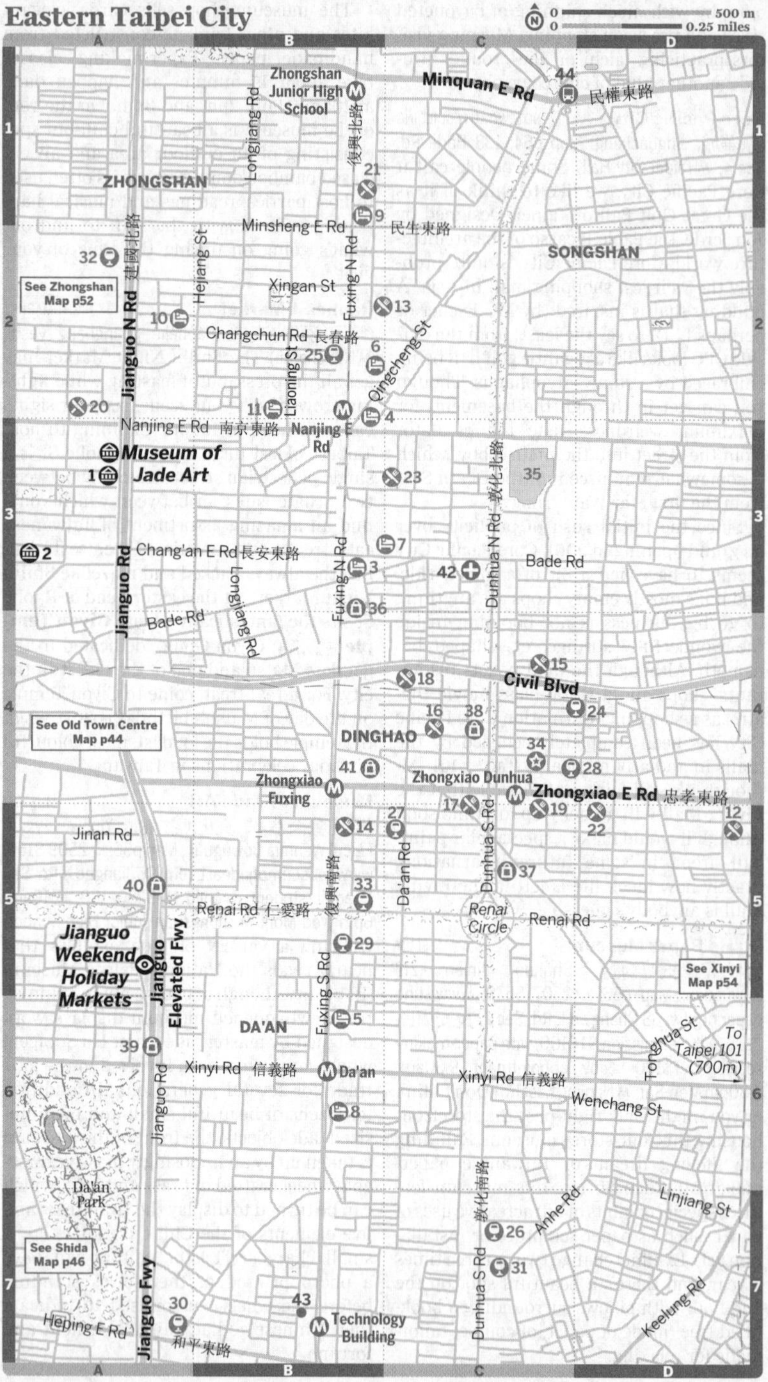

Eastern Taipei City

See Zhongshan Map p52
See Old Town Centre Map p44
See Xinyi Map p54
See Shida Map p46

Eastern Taipei City

Miniatures Museum of Taiwan MUSEUM
(袖珍博物館; Xiù Zhēn Bówùguǎn; Map p56; ☎2515 0583; 96 Jianguo N Rd, Sec 1; adult/student/child NT$180/150/100; ⊙10am-6pm Tue-Sun; MZhongshan Junior High School) Bigger is better, so some say; but not at the Miniatures Museum of Taiwan, where quite the opposite is true. This small, private museum is dedicated to the exhibition of the minuscule, the tiny, the 'I can't believe someone had the patience and steadiness of hand to create something so small and intricate!'. Among the items on display are dollhouse-sized replications of some of Europe's most classic structures, as well as dolls in full period regalia. The gift shop, though small (naturally) is also fairly impressive.

SHILIN & TIANMU 士林區、天母區

North of the city centre and south of Tianmu (Tiānmǔ), Shilin (Shìlín) is home to some of Taipei's best-known cultural attractions, such as the National Palace Museum, the CKS Shilin Residence Park and, of course, the Shilin Night Market. Shilin is also where you'll find some of Taipei's most kid-friendly venues, including the Astronomical Museum and the National Taiwan Science Education Centre. Bustling, crowded and usually noisy, Shilin is a must to visit.

Just north of Shilin, in many ways Tianmu is its diametrical opposite. Whereas Shilin is usually crowded and noisy, Tianmu tends to be quieter, less crowded, with wider avenues and more spread-out neighbourhoods. Shilin is where you go for street food and Tianmu is the place for sit-down restau-

JADE BUYING TIPS FROM AN EXPERT

Valued throughout Asia for its beauty and elegance, jade is a desired keepsake for visitors to Taipei. But how do you distinguish the high quality from the low? Roxanne Tu, Gemmologist at the Museum of Jade Art, gave the author, Joshua, and his family some pointers.

Roxanne Tu brings out a velvet-lined box containing nine jade bracelets and announces that we'll be starting with a test. 'Only three of these are real jade. The others are fake. Can you tell them apart?' The bracelets pass from hand to hand, and are held to the light, examined by five pairs of eyes. We separate them using little more than beginners' instinct. Smiling, Roxanne does not tell us whether we've chosen wisely.

'Now you're ready to learn about jade,' she says. 'In the jade world, we use a special machine to scan a piece, a machine that measures the spectrum of light as it goes through the jade.' Roxanne shows us two documents of jade authenticity, each containing a line graph representing light passing through the stones. One line is a smooth arc, the other jagged like a steak knife's edge.

'The first graph is the spectrograph of a piece of true jade, and the second of a fake. It's the first line that you want to see when looking at a certificate of authenticity.'

'Fair enough,' I say. 'But what should the casual shopper be looking for?'

Roxanne takes out a second black velvet-lined box, this one containing several pieces of translucent jade of different shapes, colours and sizes. She takes one jade bangle and dangles it from a string.

'Listen.' She strikes it gently with a coin. We hear a light 'plink'. She strikes a second dangled bangle. We hear a dull thud, and assume the first bangle, with its lighter sound, must be the better-quality one.

'This is a common trap. The fact is that neither of these pieces is of very good quality. It isn't the pitch you need to listen for, but the length of the sound itself. This is what real jade sounds like.' Roxanne picks up a third bangle by its thread and strikes it. The resulting sound, while only slightly longer, resonates. 'It's not that the tone is high or low. It's the last second that you want to listen for. You should be able to hear the vibration at the end.'

But not all jade bracelets resonate – only translucent jade, which comes from the water, will produce a vibrational frequency. For jade bracelets made from mountain stones, another method must be used.

Roxanne takes two similar-looking bracelets, both containing varying shades of light- and dark-green. When she shines the light through the bracelets from behind, the difference becomes apparent. On one, the light causes the line between the varying shades of green to become more distinct. On the other, the line becomes blurred.

'Light heightens the difference between the shades of green on real jade, while blurring it on fake jade,' she tells us. 'This method is useful for different articles of mountain jade, not only bracelets.'

Roxanne offers other sensible tips as well. Always buy from a licensed dealer who'll provide a certificate of authenticity. (The Jade Market, in her opinion, is best suited for trinket shopping rather than high-end purchases.)

Our group is now ready for the examination. The box is brought back out, and using the methods that we've been taught, we get two out of three correct. We're about to consider the possibility of actually buying some real jade for ourselves when Roxanne tells us how much the real article goes for.

Holding a dark-green bracelet we'd correctly identified as real, she says 'this one is worth around 30,000.'

'That's a lot,' I say. 'Most casual tourists aren't going to spend 30,000 Taiwan dollars on a keepsake.'

'Taiwan dollars? No. I mean American dollars. A real jade bracelet such as this can cost that much, or even more.'

Duly schooled in the value, complexity and nature of this very precious stone, we thank our teacher and exit the museum to shop for what we now know will be mere baubles at the Jade Market.

rants. Though once thought of as kind of a foreigner ghetto, a nice place to live without much to draw the casual visitor, Tianmu has an excellent mountain park complete with temples and pavilions, as well as some of Taipei's posher malls. Tianmu is also a great place to start or finish a hike into the volcanic wilds of Yangmingshan (p94).

Shilin Night Market NIGHT MARKET
(士林夜市; Shìlín Yèshì; Map p60; Ⓜ Jiantan) Considered by many to be the king of Taipei's night markets, the sprawling Shilin Night Market is a nightly carnival of snacking and shopping offering the latest in trendy clothing (from shoes to hats and everything in between), games of skill and chance and much, much more. Quiet during the day, once the sun goes down the Shilin Night Market becomes a frenetic buzz of food carts offering tasty Taiwanese treats such as grass jelly soup, stinky tofu, beef-noodle soup, fresh-cut fruit and more meat-on-a-stick than you can shake a stick at. Once upon a time, the centre of the night market had a food court with teppanyaki booths, noodle stalls and milk-tea joints, but after many artery-clogging decades, city elders deemed the place a fire risk, and moved most of the food court's purveyors of tasty grease to their new home in the **Shilin (formerly Chiantan) food court**, located just across from the Jiantan station.

While food and entertainment are what brings folks to the night market, there's a good bit of cultural heritage to be seen if you know where to look. The cobblestone streets in the northern end of the market contain excellent examples of early-20th-century Japanese-influenced architecture. It's in this area that you'll find one unsung cultural gem, **Cixian Temple** (慈誠宮; Cíchéng gōng; Map p60). Dedicated to the worship of the goddess Matsu, the original temple was built in 1796 in Tianmu, and moved in 1864 by a group of devotees to provide a guardian deity for the current area. The temple was rebuilt again in 1927. Sharp-eyed visitors may note differing styles of architecture on the two wings of the temple – the northern one acts as a general house of worship, while the south one is a pavilion for performances from puppetry to opera to open-air movies. Exquisite carvings and the cochin ceramic art in the main hall are worth taking a break from snacking for.

FREE **CKS Shilin Residence Park** PARK/GARDENS
(士林官邸; Shìlín Guāndǐ; Map p60; 60 Fulin Rd; ⏲8am-5pm Mon-Fri, 8am-7pm Sat & Sun; Ⓜ Shilin) Once upon a time this multifaceted botanical garden was part of the sprawling estate of Generalissimo and Mrs Chiang Kai-shek. They ruled the gardens with an iron hand, overseeing the pruning, weeding and other daily gardening tasks from their palatial home overlooking the estates, all the while dreaming of their inevitable triumphant retaking of mainland China. When the Generalissimo died, Madame Chiang (who never cared much for Taiwan), wasted no time in moving her official residence to America. For decades the estate and the surrounding gardens were closed to the public.

In the late 1990s, then-mayor (later president, later still prisoner) Chen Shui-bian decided to turn the whole area into a park. This did not please Chiang's widow, who, though in her late nineties, still claimed title to the property. Eventually a compromise was reached and the gardens were opened to the public while the house remained closed.

The main features of this sprawling estate, one of 15 of Chiang's estates still left over around the country, are its fabulous Chinese- and Western-style gardens. There is also a horticultural exhibition hall often filled with artistic displays of flowers and plants. Rafts of gardeners take care of them all.

The estate is just off Zhongshan N Rd, Sec 5. The main entrance is about 10 minutes' walk from the Shilin MRT station. If at all possible, time your visit to coincide with one of the two major annual horticultural events; the chrysanthemums bloom throughout November and the roses come up in February.

The cafe and gift shop serves up an interesting variety of snacks and Chiang Kai-shek–themed souvenirs, so if you feel like taking home an Andy Warhol–esque pastel postcard of the late dictator smiling and wearing sunglasses, this may well be one of the few places to acquire just such an item.

National Palace Museum MUSEUM
(故宮博物院; Gùgōng Bówùyuàn; ☎2881 2021; 221 Zhishan Rd, Sec 2; adult/student NT$100/50; ⏲9am-5pm; Ⓜ Shilin) Considered by many a must-visit, this museum is home to what could quite easily be termed the world's largest and finest collection of Chinese art. This vast collection (much of it liberated from mainland China during the last retreat of the KMT) is far too large to exhibit

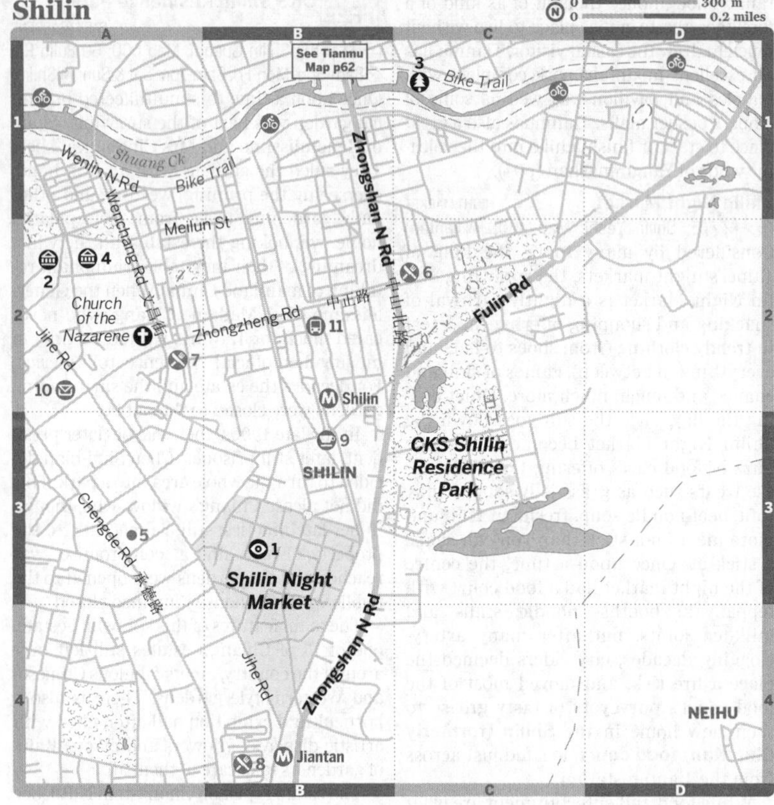

at any given time, so most of the museum's treasures are on rotation.

Among the treasures to be seen at the National Palace Museum are painting, calligraphy, statues and ceramic and jade. Some pieces date back thousands of years into Chinese history and even prehistory. The museum also has an amazing collection of Buddhist artefacts inherited from the Forbidden City. Some of the most popular items are always on display – check with the front desk to find out where they are during your visit.

The museum offers free guided tours in English at 10am and 3pm. Tour contents vary with each guide, but all offer a good overview. If you prefer to move about at your own pace, there's an English headphone guide (NT$200).

To reach the museum, take the MRT to Shilin, exit to Zhongzheng Rd (north exit), and catch bus 304, 255, red 30, minibus 18 or 19 or culture bus 101.

Shung Ye Museum of Formosan Aborigines MUSEUM

(順益台灣原住民博物館; Shùnyì Táiwān Yuánzhùmín Bówùguǎn; www.museum.org.tw; 282 Jishan Rd, Sec 2; adult NT$150; ⌚9am-5pm Tue-Sun, closed 20 Jan–20 Feb) Featuring the history and artefacts of Taiwan's indigenous peoples (of which there are currently 14 recognised tribes), this tastefully put-together museum features soft lighting and an interesting array of exhibits. Fine examples of Taiwanese aboriginal handicrafts are displayed and video footage offers an educational summary of the histories of the tribes themselves.

While the culture of Taiwan's aboriginal people was nearly subsumed as Han Chinese overtook the island both culturally and demographically, in the past decade there's been a remarkable upswing of interest among Taiwanese people towards their aboriginal brethren, due perhaps in part to the

Shilin

wishes of many in Taiwan to establish a cultural identity distinct from that of mainland China. The museum is about 200m past the bus stop for the National Palace Museum, across the street. Combination tickets allowing admission to both museums at a reduced cost are available at either.

Zhishan Garden PARK/GARDEN

(芝山花園; Zhīshān Huāyuán; Map p62; Ⓜ Zhishan) Just south of Tianmu's Yangming Hospital and a few blocks east of the Zhishan MRT station sits one of our favourite Taipei parks, a jungle-filled mountain just north of the Shuangxi River (also a lovely park in its own right). It's filled with gardens and shrines and the top of the mountain has a temple dedicated to a much-revered sage and general called Chen Yuan Kwang, who lived 1500 years ago. Though the temple itself is lovely enough, more interesting still are the statues surrounding it – carved stone representations of characters well known to anyone familiar with the Chinese classic *Romance of the Three Kingdoms*. And what really makes the climb worth it is the view, a sweeping panorama of the whole of Taipei city. The park itself offers a wide variety of hikes, on dirt trails as well as wooden boardwalks that skirt sections of the mountain.

There is no admission charge to hang out in the park, but there is a NT$50 charge on weekdays to visit the **Zhishan Cultural & Ecological Garden** (芝山文化生態綠園; zhīshān wénhuà shēngtài lǜyuán; www.zcegarden.org.tw; ⏲9am-5pm), which takes up a small portion of the park – its entrance is across from Yangming Hospital. As this area is home to a decent archaeological exhibit, a fantastic greenhouse and a wild-bird rehabilitation centre, it's a small sum well spent.

Taipei Astronomical Museum MUSEUM

(天文科學教育館; Tiānwén Kēxué Jiàoyùguǎn; Map p60; www.tam.gov.tw; 363 Jihe Rd; adult/child NT$40/20; ⏲8.50am-5pm, Tue-Sun; Ⓜ Shilin) Opened in 1997, this museum houses four floors of constellations, ancient astronomy, space science and technology, telescopes and observatories. Though a good place to while away an hour with the kids, what keeps this otherwise excellent museum from being a must-visit is a dearth of English content. Although every exhibit features English and Chinese, most of the actual information is in the latter language only. A recorded English-language guide is available, though the information is fairly basic. More English-friendly attractions (at an extra charge) are an IMAX theatre, a 3-D theatre (presentations change frequently) and the 'Cosmic Adventure', an amusement-park ride through 'outer space'.

Out behind the Astronomical Museum is a very peaceful – though slightly baffling – sculpture garden, featuring a dozen or so water-filled steel-and-glass sculptures that whirl and gurgle in different ways when buttons are pushed and levers depressed. What these are supposed to demonstrate is a mystery.

National Taiwan Science Education Centre MUSEUM

(NTSEC; 國立台灣科學教育中心; Guólì Táiwān Kēxué Jiàoyù Zhōngxīn; Map p60; 189 Shihshang Rd; admission NT$100; ⏲9am-5pm Tue-Fri, 9am-6pm Sat & Sun; Ⓜ Shilin) Interactive exhibits at this children's museum cover the gamut of scientific knowledge, from anatomy (a walk-through digestive tract!) to zoology (a cat-head-shaped helmet that gives the wearer feline hearing powers). Though the NTSEC is not fully bilingual, museum staff have gone to great lengths to include enough English content to make the whole museum accessible to non-Chinese speakers.

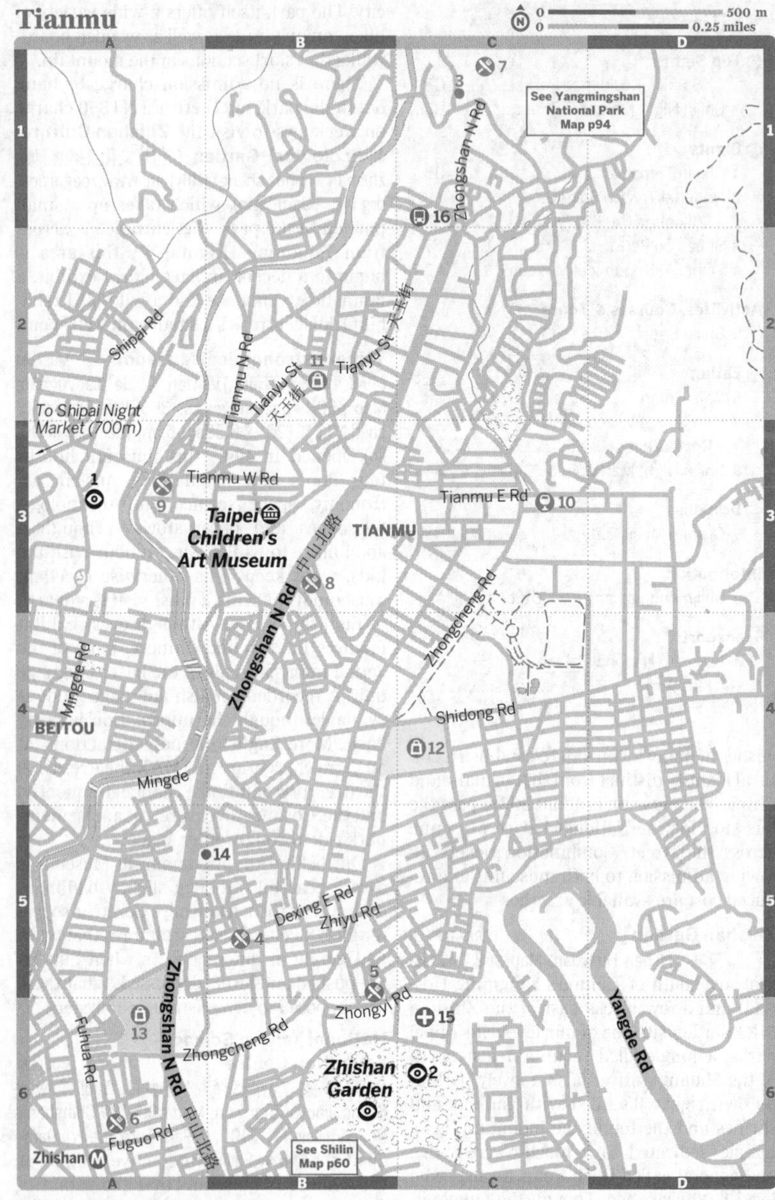

Taipei Children's Art Museum MUSEUM
(蘇荷兒童美術館; Sūhé Értóng Měishùguǎn; Map p62; ☎2872 1366; www.artart.com.tw; 20 Alley 50, Tianmu W Rd; admission NT$100; ⏲10am-5.30pm Tue-Sun, open Mon holidays, closed Tue after holidays; Ⓜ Shipai, then Red bus 12 or 19, or 5km walk east) Opened in 2003, this highly interactive children's museum was designed specifically to encourage children to participate in the creation of art. The museum features life-sized walk-through panoramas painted in the styles of various

Tianmu

Top Sights
Taipei Children's Art Museum B3
Zhishan Garden B6

Sights
1 Carol Young Clayart Workshop A3
2 Zhishan Cultural & Ecological Garden C6

Activities, Courses & Tours
3 Bottom of Tianmu/Yangmingshan Trail C1

Eating
4 Beitou Squid B5
5 Escargot B5
6 He Xiang Delicious Food A6
7 Lavender Garden C1
8 Maison Alexandria B3
Tianmu Sogo Food Court .... (see 13)
Tianmu Takashimaya Food Court (see 12)
9 Wu Hua Ma Dumpling House A3

Drinking
10 8898 Bar C3

Shopping
Carol Young Clayart Workshop ...... (see 1)
11 Caves Books B2
12 Dayeh Takashimaya C4
13 Sogo Department Store (Tianmu) A6

Information
14 Community Services Centre A5
15 Yangming Hospital C6

Transport
16 Tianmu Bus Circle C1

famous artists, as well as galleries featuring artwork done by children themselves.

Carol Young Clayart Workshop GALLERY
(蘿漾手作藝術坊; Luóyàng Shǒuzuò Yìshù Fǎng; Map p62; ☎2826 2247; www.carol-young.com; 31 Zhenxing St, 台北市振興街31號B1; ⏰10am-6pm Mon-Thu, Sat by apt; Ⓜ Shipai, then Red bus 12 or 19, or 400m walk east) Carol Young is a local artist who works with clay and specialises in creating three-dimensional clay figures that are, quite frankly, charmingly cute. Her shop in Tianmu is part gallery, part studio and part store, so you can drop in to look around, buy pre-made sculptures, or even arrange to have yourself or a loved one made immortally adorable.

Activities

Cycling

At the risk of veering into hyperbole, Taipei may well be the best major metropolis for cycling in Asia. In recent years, cycling has transformed from fringe activity to genuine craze, and on any given day you'll see respectable-looking 40-, 50- and 60-somethings decked out immaculately in the latest spandex and lycra wear, riding state-of-the-art road bikes up Quanyuan Rd (which leads from Beitou to Yangmingshan), along Taipei's many bike trails and even on the city's traffic-congested avenues. At the opposite end of the spectrum, the sight of teens and 20-something's riding fixed-gear track bikes (unheard of in these parts a decade ago) has now become almost passé. Whether you like winding mountain roads, riverside bicycle trails or urban riding, Taipei has what you're looking for.

The free *Taipei City Cycling Map* (available at any Taipei Visitor's Information Centre) shows some great trails running along the banks of Taipei's rivers. The booklet also lists seven city-run bike-rental stalls where you can pick bikes up at one and leave them at another. Charges vary depending on bike quality and you'll be asked to leave a deposit and show your passport. Call the **Taipei Cycling Lifestyle Foundation** (☎2719 2025) to get English directions to the nearest bike-rental place. The trails range from 9km to 18km in length and you can easily get from one end of the city to the other along the rivers.

Serious cyclists looking to rent mountain bikes will want to know about **Alan's Mountain Bike** (☎2933 4319; www.alansmountainbike.com.tw; 38 Roosevelt Rd, Sec 5; ⏰noon-9.30pm Mon-Sat), which rents good-quality bikes for NT$1000 per day, with discounts for rentals of a week or more.

Bicycles are allowed on all lines of the MRT except for the Brown (Muzha to Neihu) line on the weekends, though there is a NT$80 charge (which also covers the passenger); furthermore, bikes are allowed on and off only at certain stations as marked on station maps. Folding bicycles are allowed on any train at any time free of charge, but only if they are fully disassembled and placed in a bag. Two popular blogs describing

TWO GREAT TAIPEI RIDES

Riverside Ride (2 hours; easy)

Beginning in Xindian, follow the riverside path as it curves and meanders, forming Taipei proper's western edge. It's a popular trail, especially on weekends (when your biggest danger is accidental collision with inexperienced cyclists), and along the way you'll pass through greenery, wetland and public parks. North of the Dadaocheng wharf, other cycle traffic thins as the path reaches the juncture of the Danshui and Keelung Rivers. (If you want to continue all the way north to Danshui, you need to cross over the Zhoumei Expressway bridge just north of Yanping Riverside Park.)

Taipei Urban Pedal Mash (1.5 hours; hectic)

Perhaps scenic views and riverside trails packed with weekenders fail to excite you. If you, like a certain co-author of the book you now hold in your hands, also happen to be a former bicycle courier, you may crave the sort of life-and-death adrenalin rush that only racing through traffic offers. If so, a fine ride that will allow you to say that you've ridden along Taipei's spine and through its very heart stretches from Xindian station, where you'll want to take Beixin Rd north until it crosses the Jingmei River and becomes Roosevelt Rd. Following this takes you through the student areas of Gongguan and Shida, past the government district, and then to Taipei Main, where the road becomes Zhongshan N Rd. This road stretches all the way through the city, past Shilin, and into the northernmost reaches of Tianmu, where it becomes a mountain trail; however, at Minquan Rd you'll need to duck one block west to cross the Keelung River over the Chengde Bridge.

all sorts of wonderful rides in Taipei and Taiwan are http://bikingintaiwan.theforgetful.com/taipei and www.danielcarruthers.com.

Hiking

First-time visitors will be astounded by just how thin the line between Taipei's urban jungle and jungle-jungle can be. Head south at either end of the MRT blue line and before long you're hiking through mountain foothills with only the occasional glimpse of Taipei 101 to remind you of how close to the city you still are. Head east out of the Xinbeitou MRT station and before long you'll be walking through jungle that's dotted with sulphur-spewing steam vents.

One good hike is the Tianmu Trail, beginning at the very top end of Zhongshan N Rd, Sec 7. It's here that Taipei's longest street becomes a dirt trail and later a stone staircase that pretty much leads to the front gate of Yangmingshan National Park (p94). Expect to pass by mountain streams and dense jungle on the way in. Though we can neither confirm nor deny tales of monkeys prowling the upper sections of the trail, looking to waylay travellers, signs warn of the dangers of monkey-feeding and help lend such rumours official credence.

Birdwatching

For a city, Taipei sure has a lot of birdwatching opportunities. **Shuangxi park** (Map p60) is a great place to spot cormorants and herons, and the **Botanical Gardens** is said to be a good place to spot the rare Malaysian night heron. The serious twitcher will want to contact the **Wild Bird Society of Taipei** (台北市野鳥學會; Táiběi Shì Yěniǎo Xuéhuì; Map p56; ☎2325 9190; www.wbst.org.tw; 3 Lane 160, Fuxing S Rd, Sec 2; Ⓜ Technology Building), which arranges birdwatching tours around Taipei and Taiwan and stocks a number of English books for visiting birdwatchers. See the Taiwan Wildlife Guide (p354) for more info on birdwatching.

Gyms & Swimming

While there are a number of private clubs with hefty per-use fees (NT$400 or more), you'd be silly to shell out the dough as there are two great public gyms in northern Taipei. The **Beitou Sports Center** (北投運動中心; Běitóu yùndòng zhōngxīn; www.btsc.org; 100 Lane 39, Shipai Rd, Sec 1, 北投區石牌路一段39巷100號; Ⓜ Shipai) and the **Shilin Sport Centre** (Map p60; 士林運動中心; Shìlín yùndòng zhōngxīn; www.slsc-taipei.org/big5; 1 Shishang Rd; Ⓜ Jiantan) both have huge lap pools and fully stocked workout rooms.

Pools cost NT$110 to use and the exercise rooms are NT$50 per hour.

There are a few public outdoor swimming pools around town and some hotels have arrangements where you can use their pools for a fee. We've noted hotels with pools under Sleeping (p66). However, outdoor swimming is a seasonal thing in Taipei and is usually reserved for warmer months. People do swim in the river up in Wulai (p111) and there are a number of good beaches on the northeast coast. For a serious water-park experience, head up to Bali and check out Formosa Fun Coast (p101).

Photography

Taipei is a photo-mad town, and whether you're shooting with your mobile phone or the newest top-of-the-line DSLR you'll be competing with your fellow shutterbugs to capture the perfect shot. One Taipei-based organisation comprised primarily of local expatriates is **Taiwan Photographers** (http://taiwanphotographers.com). Their regularly scheduled Taipei Photo Walks are a great way to simultaneously socialise and photograph the sights of Taipei. If you need to upgrade your gear, Hankou St, southwest of Taipei Main Station, is the place to go.

Tours

You won't have any trouble finding an organisation to take you on a bus tour of Taipei. The companies listed in the Transport chapter (p376) all offer them. Three-hour city tours (adult/child NT$700/600) take in the Martyrs' Shrine, National Palace Museum, Chiang Kai-shek Memorial Hall, a temple visit and some shopping, although at three hours you won't get more than a taste of any one sight. Other options include a Taipei-by-night tour (NT$1200, 3½ hours) and a culture tour that takes in Chinese opera (NT$1200, three hours).

523 Mountaineering Association MOUNTAINEERING
(523 Dēngshān Huì; Map p46; ☎2365 1143; www.523.org.tw; 7th fl, 189 Roosevelt Rd, Sec 3; Ⓜ Taipower Building) A government-approved non-profit organisation since 1999, the 523 can help travellers obtain mountain permits for a small fee as well as arranging transport to and from trailheads. The office is sporadically staffed, so your best bet

FAMILY FRIENDLY TAIWAN *EVE BROWN-WAITE*

Our trip to Taiwan might have been the best family vacation ever! We visited monuments, temples and museums. We shopped at chaotic markets and luxurious malls. And that was just in Taipei. Outside of the city, we hiked, biked, snorkelled and swam, soaked in hot springs, visited water parks, played in arcades, and had a blast. Through it all, we were immersed in a fascinating culture, language, history and tradition. What more could you want in a satisfying vacation?

Well, there's always food. And as every parent knows, food – or finding something your kids will eat – can make or break a vacation. So good news: Taiwan is basically one gigantic buffet. Even if your kids turn out not to be great fans of fried squid, garlic snails or stinky tofu, you'd be surprised how much of the Taiwanese 'street' diet consists of hot-dog-looking items (including tiny hot dogs on sticks, sausages of every ilk and corn dogs). There are also abundant teahouses that make tapioca bubble teas in all sorts of variations, including fruit smoothies and good old chocolate milk.

Practical Tips for Happy Family Travels in Taiwan

» With a little orientation, older children and teenagers can be fairly independent in Taipei. All maps, signs and announcements on public transport are made in English as well as several local languages. And wherever they go, there will be no shortage of local folks willing to help them.

» Aside from prescription medications, don't worry about forgetting things back home. If you need it, Taiwan has it – probably at a place that's open all night, too!

Eve Brown-Waite is the author of First Comes Love, Then Comes Malaria *(2009), a memoir dealing with (among other things) travelling with children in remotest Africa. She's also the sister of Lonely Planet author Joshua Samuel Brown.*

in contacting someone at 523 is via email through its website.

Formosa Dive Academy DIVING, TOURS
(☎0917647351; www.formosadiveacademy.com; formosadiveacademy@gmail.com) A dive training and travel company based in Taipei but foreign-owned and -managed, Formosa Dive Academy runs diving and hiking trips throughout Taiwan. PADI Open Water Diver courses (three to four days) are NT$12,900, inclusive of equipment and transport. The company also leads other trips, both land and sea, throughout Taiwan.

Festivals & Events

In addition to national festivals, interesting events include the celebration of the birthdays of the city god at the Hsiahai City God Temple (p51) and Confucius at the Confucius Temple (p50). Christmas Eve has become a de facto holiday, too, with bars and restaurants throwing big parties. The weeks leading up to the Lunar New Year's festivities are a great time to visit the Dihua Market (p51) and if you're around during the Lantern Festival be sure to hit both Chiang Kai-shek Memorial Hall for the official festivities and Xindian's Bitan Park for ad hoc pyrotechnics.

Trade shows are big business in Taiwan, with dozens taking place each year. While usually the domain of the business and not the casual traveller, trade shows are actually pretty cool if you're interested in the wares being traded. And what wares indeed, ranging from orchids to motorcycles to every high-tech gadget you can imagine. Trade shows are a great place to get cool samples, make connections and often buy things at rock-bottom prices (especially on the last day when vendors are looking to lighten their take-home loads). Most trade shows take place in or around the **Taipei World Trade Centre** (台北世貿中心; Map p54), which sits in the shadow of Taipei 101 (p54). Smaller ones tend to be held elsewhere. To check out what trade fairs are happening and when, check out www.taipeitradeshows.com.tw.

Sleeping

Budget lodgings have basic rates of up to about NT$1600 per room and dorm beds in hostels start at about NT$400. Midrange rates are up to about NT$4000 and anything above that is considered top end. Top-end accommodation in Taipei is easy to locate, so we've just culled our favourites from that end of the pool. (On the subject of pools, you'll generally only find swimming pools in a few of the top-end hotels and indoor pools are scarce).

Note that when Taipei hotels list rates for a 'single' room, it often refers to a room with one queen-size bed that most travellers will find big enough for two. Many hotels also throw in breakfast, though you may have to ask when you make reservations. Upmarket hotels tend to charge a 10% service fee and 5% value-added tax (VAT) on top of their rates.

The rates listed here are rack rates, the base rate charged at peak times. However, most midrange and top-end hotels offer reductions of up to 30% on weekdays as well as during nonpeak periods. Further, we've made note where hotels offer deep discounts on their websites. With various discounts factored in, some top-end hotels can be booked for midrange rates, and midrange for close to budget, so plan your trip wisely. Another option for cheaper lodgings are 'love hotels'; just specify that you're renting for the night and not to 'take a rest'.

Also note that some hostels charge between NT$20 and NT$50 for air-con use during summer.

OLD TOWN CENTRE, DA'AN & SHIDA
萬華區、大安區、師大區

Holo Family House HOSTEL $
(阿羅住宿接待家庭; Āluó Zhùsù jiēdài jiātíng; Map p44; ☎2331 7272; http://tw.myblog.yahoo.com/traveler_hostel; 22nd fl, 50 Chungxiao W Rd, Sec 1; d/s/ste incl breakfast 690/790/1500; @📶 Ⓜ Taipei Main Station) For central location, you can't beat Holo's. Its 28 rooms range from multibed dorms to small single rooms to apartment-sized family rooms with en suite bathrooms. The 22nd-floor hotel is always a lively spot, with a fair-sized communal area with computers, books, maps and posters, and everything you'd need in general to plan your trip around Taiwan. Perhaps the most interesting room is Holo's 'VIP Room', a three-bed tatami room, built with floor-to-ceiling windows offering spectacular views of Taipei city and Yangmingshan to the north, which goes for NT$1200. Holo is also connected with other hostels around Taiwan, making it a good place to plan your island-wide journey.

Eight Elephants Hostel HOSTEL $
(八隻大象青年之家; Bāzhīdàxiàng Qīngniánzhījiā; Map p46; ☎0968-484 614; 1st fl,

Alley 4, Lane 48, 6 Jin-Jiang St, 晉江街48巷4弄6號1樓; dm/r 490/780 @📶ⓂGuting) Opened in 2007, Eight Elephants has 13 dorm beds and four private rooms, a relaxed basement spot with stereo, TV, DVD player, cool couches, guitars and public computer. Bathrooms and showers are separated, minimising waiting time, and there's a communal kitchen fully stocked with stove, microwave, fridge and all appliances. Located on a quiet back lane not far from Shida, this clean and serene hostel is definitely a chilled-out addition to the sometimes overly boisterous Taipei hostel scene.

Han She Business Hotel BOUTIQUE HOTEL **$$**

(函舍商務旅店; Hánshè Shāngwù Lǚdiàn; Map p44; ☎2371 8812; www.handsomehotel.tw; 4th fl, 68 Chengdu Rd, 成都路68號4樓; r from NT$1880; @ⓂXimen) Museum-lit objets d'art in the corridors, clean, handsomely furnished rooms and kind staff are just a few reasons that make finding this 55-room business hotel worthwhile. While the address is on Chengdu Rd, the entrance is on a small side street. Look for the sign reading 'hotel' and you've found the place.

Sheraton Taipei HOTEL **$$$**

(台北喜來登大飯店; Táiběi Xǐláidēng Dàfàndiàn; Map p44; ☎2321 5511; www.sheraton-taipei.com; 12 Zhongxiao E Rd, Sec 1, 忠孝東路1段12號; r from NT$9000; @🏊ⓂTaipei Main Station) Smack in the centre of Taipei's government district, the Sheraton is the height of luxury. If you're hoping to run into ambassadors and trade ministers, this is the place to be. The hotel offers a number of excellent restaurants, a great gym and beautifully decorated rooms fit for diplomats. But be prepared to pay; in Taiwan, neither luxury nor diplomacy is cheap.

Taipei Hostel HOSTEL **$**

(台北青年旅社; Táiběi Qīngnían Lǚshè Map p44; ☎2395 2950; www.taipeihostel.com; 6th fl, 11 Lane 5, Linsen N Rd, 林森北路5巷11號6樓; dm/s/d NT$300/500/550; @📶ⓂShandao Temple) This aged dame may be a bit frayed around the edges, but she still attracts guests from all points on the map with the cheapest dorm beds in town. On a quiet backstreet, the hostel has a large room for socialising, kitchen facilities, washer/dryer, free ADSL use for laptop users and a rooftop garden. Long-term rates are available, and as the hostel is a nexus of sorts for early-stage Taiwan expats, there's always a buzz about jobs, visas and what-have-you on Taipei life. The website has tips and links to information on Taipei and teaching English.

Dandy Hotel BOUTIQUE HOTEL **$$**

(單迪旅店-大安店; Dāndí Lǚdiàn-Dàān diàn; Map p46; ☎2707 6899; www.dandyhotel.com.tw; 33 Xinyi Rd, Sec 3, 信義路3段33號; r incl breakfast from 1920; @📶ⓂDa'an) With a cool jazz vibe, this very nice boutique hotel across from Da'an Park offers a good choice for travellers looking for someplace at the lower end of the midrange scale. Though the cheapest rooms lack windows, they manage not to feel claustrophobic thanks to the judicious use of interior design elements, which include white walls, glassed-in bathrooms and large, wall-mounted LCD screens. The room price includes a full Western-style buffet breakfast.

Cosmos Hotel HOTEL **$$**

(天成大飯店; Tiānchéng Dàfàndiàn; Map p44; ☎2361 7856; www.cosmos-hotel.com.tw; 43 Zhongxiao W Rd, Sec 1, 忠孝西路1段43號; d/tw from NT$2600/3500; @ⓂTaipei Main Station) Ah, the Cosmos; if it were any closer to Taipei Main Station it would be inside it – it even gets its own sign on exit 3! This is where visiting midlevel businessmen on expense accounts, working for companies with tight-fisted accountants, come to stay. The decor is a bit mismatched, but overall the hotel is immaculately kept. The cheapest rooms, however, are windowless.

East Dragon Hotel HOTEL **$$**

(東龍大飯店; Dōnglóng Dàfàndiàn; Map p44; ☎2311 6969; www.east-dragon.com.tw; 23 Hankou St, Sec 2, 漢口街2段23號; s/tw NT$1920/2400; @ⓂXimen) The East Dragon is a comfortable 70-room hotel on the far and quiet end of Ximending's pedestrian plaza, making it an ideal place to rest and heal up from any gruelling 12-hour, liquor-fuelled piercing-and-tattoo session. Popular with tourists from around Asia, it's a good place to practise your Korean and Japanese. Breakfast and internet access included.

Hotel Flowers HOTEL **$$**

(華華大飯店; Huáhuá Dàfàndiàn; Map p44; ☎2312 3811; 19 Hankou Rd, Sec 1, 漢口街1段19號; s/d incl breakfast NT$1920/2400; ⓂTaipei Main Station) Two hotels run by the same management, with one building on the north and a slightly newer annexe on the south side of the street. Hardly a quiet location, but you won't have to change out of your flip-flops (thongs) to get great snacks, as it's just a few minutes' walk to either Taipei Main Station or Ximending.

NTNU Guesthouse GUESTHOUSE $$
(臺師大迎賓會館; Táishīdà Yíngbīn Huìguǎn; Map p46; ☎7734 5800; 129 Heping Rd, Sec 1; r incl breakfast from NT$2800; @ⓦⓜTaipower Building) On the campus of Shida University, the NTNU Guesthouse has large enough rooms that four people would be comfortable in a double room (if two of 'em brought their own sleeping bags). Rooms include use of the school gym, and discounts are available for NTNU students or friends of students.

Friends Star Hotel HOTEL $$
(友星大飯店; Yǒuxīng Dàfàndiàn; Map p46; ☎2394 3121; 11 Heping Rd, Sec 1; r incl breakfast from NT$1800; @ⓦⓜGuting) Fairly popular for its budget range, this newish hotel next to the Guting MRT is a quick hop to both the Shida nightlife and the cultural attractions of downtown Taipei. Small, windowless rooms cost the least and are good if you like things quiet.

Also recommended:

World Scholar House HOSTEL $
(台北國際學舍; Map p44; ☎2541 8113; www.worldscholarhouse.com; 8th fl, 2 Lane 38, Songjiang Rd, 松江路38巷2號8樓; dm/d NT$350/650; ❄@ⓦ) Offers both dorms and double rooms, cable TV, laundry and ironing facilities, and wi-fi. Weekly and monthly rates make this a popular spot for expat English teachers.

City Inn BOUTIQUE HOTEL $
(新驛旅店; Xīnyì Lǚdiàn; Map p44; ☎2555-5577; www.gocityinn.com; 81 Chang An West Rd, 長安西路81號; r from NT$1560; @ⓦⓜTaipei Main Station) A member of the Taipei Inn Group, City Inn offers the amenities of a mid-price hotel at near-budget prices.

Happy Family Hostel HOSTEL $
(快樂家庭; Kuàilè Jiātíng; Map p44; ☎2581 0716; www.taiwan-hostel.com; 2 Lane 56, Zhongshan N Rd, Sec 1, 中山北路1段56巷2號; dm/s/d from NT$400/500/800; @ⓦⓜTaipei Main Station) Happy Family Hostel enjoys a good reputation among travellers and long-term Taipei expat residents alike, with discounts for longer-term stays. Owner John Lee is an old travel hand and a fount of local knowledge.

Good Ground Hotel HOTEL $$
(國光大飯店; Guó guāng Dàfàndiàn; Map p44; ☎2371 8616; www.goodground.com.tw; 6 Lane 27, Chengdu Rd, 成都路27巷6號; r from NT$2200, f NT$4800; @ⓜTaipei Main Station) The faux-jade stone-pattern lobby floor makes the hotel feel like something out of the Flintstones, but rooms are clean and comfortable.

Li-Yuan Hotel HOTEL $$
(儷園飯店; Lìyuán Fàndiàn; Map p46; ☎2365 7367; 98 Roosevelt Rd, Sec 3; r incl breakfast from NT$1960; @ⓦⓜTaipower Building) Small, comfortable and clean, the Li-Yuan is on the south side of the Shida Night Market, and popular with friends and families who are visiting students at the local university.

Taipei YMCA International Guest House HOTEL $$
(台北青年國際旅社; Táiběi Qīngnían Guójì Lǚshè; Map p44; ☎2311 3201; 19 Xuchang St, 許昌街19號; s/tw from NT$1800/2800, f NT$4500; @ⓜTaipei Main Station) Rooms are plain, furnishing a bit spartan, but the location is good and there's a laundry on site for guests.

Keyman's Hotel HOTEL $$
(懷寧旅店; Huáiníng Lǚdiàn; Map p44; ☎2311 4811; www.keymans.com.tw; 1 Huaining St, 懷寧街1號; r from NT$2080; ⓜTaipei Main Station) The rooms are a bit small, but the hotel is well kept, and as far as location goes the place is a good deal.

ZHONGSHAN 中山區

Grand Hotel HISTORIC HOTEL $$$
(圓山大飯店; Yuánshān Dàfàndiàn; ☎2886 8888; 1 Lane 1, Zhongshan N Rd, Sec 4; r from NT$4800; @ⓦ≋) It's the big Kahuna of Taiwan's hotels and a tourist attraction in itself. Since the opening of cross-Strait tourism ties, this 1970s reconstruction of the original 1952 Chinese-style high-rise has become a serious magnet for mainland tourists. With red columns and painted beams, the lobby is resplendent of 'Old Chinese Money'. Suitably spacious and decorated in old-style Chinese, rooms offering both city and mountain views are available. Recreation includes a golf driving range, tennis courts, year-round swimming, a fitness centre and sauna, and there are eight in-house restaurants.

Moon Hotel BOUTIQUE HOTEL $$
(新月商旅; xīnyuè shānglǚ; Map p52; ☎2521 3301; 122 Xinsheng N Rd, Sec 1, 新生北路1段122號; s incl breakfast from NT$1680; ⓜZhongxiao Xinsheng) 'A lovely place for lovers', reads the business card, and if it's a real Taipei 'love hotel' experience you're looking for, well, you've found it. Conversation with the con-

cierge is kept at a minimum; a softly glowing board in the back of the lobby shows pictures and prices of available rooms – all you need do is ask for your room of choice by number and pay the lady behind the desk. Go ahead, we know you want to check it out. We won't tell a soul.

Royal Inn Taipei HOTEL $$
(老爺商務會館; lǎoyé Shāngwù huìguǎn; Map p52; ☎2351 6171; www.royal-inn-taipei.com.tw; 8th-11th fl, 1 Nanjing W Rd, 南京西路1號8–11樓; s/d incl breakfast NT$3400/4000; MZhongshan) This unpretentious little inn-cum-business-hotel takes up the 8th to 11th floors of a building in Taipei's Zhongshan district. Rooms are quite nice, boasting 26-inch LED screens with ready-to-go DVD hook-ups, as well as full bathrooms with heated toilet seats. The Royal offers free wireless, breakfast and undergarment laundering. Discounts are available through online booking. The Royal is in the same building as the Celestial Restaurant, so you won't have far to go for your Peking duck fix.

Grand Formosa Regent HOTEL $$$
(台北晶華酒店; Táiběi Jīnghuá Jiǔdiàn; Map p52; ☎2523 8000; www.grandformosa.com.tw; 41 Zhongshan N Rd, Sec 2; r from NT$8400; MZhongshan) Set back from busy Zhongshan Rd, the Regent is tops in every way, from the gold-leaf accents and exclusive shopping to the mountain views from the rooftop pool. Standard rooms are large and well furnished, complete with lovely deep-soaking tubs. If you want to pamper yourself further, the 20th-floor Wellspring Spa is among the city's loveliest.

Riviera Hotel HOTEL $$$
(歐華酒店; uhuá Jiǔdiàn; Map p52; ☎2585 3258; www.rivierataipei.com; 646 Linsen N Rd, 林森北路646號; d/tw from NT$6000/7000; MYuanshan) With its European exterior and comfortable rooms, the Riviera is a favourite with business travellers and those looking for a quiet oasis within walking distance of some of Taipei's busiest nightlife districts, not to mention the Fine Arts Museum. The health centre is excellent and the rooftop jogging track is a unique topping for this high-class hotel.

Formosa Hostel HOSTEL $
(Map p52; ☎2511 9625, 0910 015 449; 3rd fl, 16 Lane 20, Zhongshan N Rd, Sec 2, 中山北路2段20巷16號3樓; dm/s/tw NT$300/400/500; MZhongshan) An extremely basic hostel with simple cooking and laundry facilities. The dorm rooms are dark and a bit cell-like. Far better are the two full apartments rented out by the proprietors in a building a few blocks north that once housed a second hostel. They are fully furnished and go for NT$800-900 per day, with deep discounts available for long-term (weekly or monthly) rentals.

Tango Hotel BOUTIQUE HOTEL $$
(柯旅天閣; Kēlǚ Tiāngé; Map p52; ☎2531 9999; www.thetango.com.tw; 15 Lane 83, Zhongshan N Rd, Sec 1, 中山北路1段83巷15號; r incl breakfast from NT$3600; MZhongshan) Part of the Tango Hotel chain (there are now four in Taiwan), this small hotel gives more expensive hotels a run for their money. Rooms feature flat-screen TVs, DVD players, silk bedspreads and a Jacuzzi bathtub. Although the address is a lane off Zhongshan N Rd, the hotel is actually closer to Linsen N Rd.

Taipei International Hotel HOTEL $$
(台北國際飯店; Táiběi Guójì Fàndiàn; Map p52; ☎2562 7569; 66 Nanjing E Rd, Sec 1, 南京東路1段66號; r incl breakfast from NT$3960; MZhongshan) Eurasian in feel and well located at the corner of Linsen N Rd, the International has well-decorated (though somewhat small) rooms with dark wood trim and cool bathroom faucets. Other amenities include a gym, free wi-fi and daily newspaper delivery.

Hôtel Royal Taipei HOTEL $$$
(老爺大酒店; Lǎoyé Dàjiǔdiàn; Map p52; ☎2542 3266; www.royal-taipei.com.tw; 37-1 Zhongshan N Rd, Sec 2, 中山北路2段37之1號; r from NT$8000; MZhongshan) This contemporary hotel features a subtly understated French design (dark wood and white linen) that goes well with its overall quality of service. It offers a gym and sauna, and each of the 202 rooms has bathrobes, a safe and a minibar.

Ambassador Hotel HOTEL $$$
(國賓大飯店; Guóbīn Dàfàndiàn; Map p52; ☎2551 1111; www.ambassadorhotel.com.tw; 63 Zhongshan N Rd, Sec 2, 中山北路2段63號; r incl breakfast from NT$4500; MShuanglian) Crisp, contemporary and international in style, the 430-room Ambassador is a beautiful hotel that's popular with business travellers and flight crews. There's blonde wood and marble throughout and a spa with massage services.

Also recommended:

First Hotel HOTEL $$
(第一大飯店; Dìyī Dàfàndiàn; Map p52; ☎2551 2277; www.firsthoteltaipei.com; 63 Nanjing E Rd, Sec 2, 南京東路2段63號; s/tw incl breakfast

from NT$2700; @ wi-fi M Zhongshan) The First makes the most of its four-decade-old shell and smallish rooms with renovated facilities, free wi-fi and several restaurant options. For friendliness, the staff can't be beat.

Emperor Hotel HOTEL $$

(國王大飯店; Guówáng Dàfàndiàn; Map p52; ☎2581 1111; emperhtl@ms9.hinet.net; 118 Nanjing E Rd, Sec 1, 南京東路1段118號; r incl breakfast from NT$3400; @ M Zhongshan) Its decor is a little dated and the rooms are a bit musty. However, its location is excellent: near shopping and surrounded by dining (with lots of Japanese restaurants nearby).

Taipei Fortuna Hotel HOTEL $$

(富都大飯店; Fùdū Dàfàndiàn; Map p52; ☎2563 1111; www.taipei-fortuna.com.tw; 122 Zhongshan N Rd, Sec 2, 中山北路2段122號; r from NT$3400; @ wi-fi M Minquan W Rd) Often busy with tour groups, this ageing hotel offers decent-sized rooms for the price. There's a health club with a sauna on the premises. Book online for deep (up to 40%) discounts.

Taipei House International Youth Hostel HOSTEL $

(台北之家; Táiběi Zhījiā; Map p52; ☎2503-5819; www.taipeiyh.com; F11-1 293 Songjiang Rd; dm from NT$610; @ M Xingtian Temple) This travellers hostel offers clean and comfortable dorm beds in a fun part of town.

EASTERN TAIPEI 東台北市

Taipei Fullerton 315 Hotel HOTEL $$

(台北馥敦飯店; Táiběi Fùdūn Fàndiàn; Map p56; ☎2703 1234; www.taipeifullerton.com.tw; 315 Fuxing N Rd, Sec 2; r incl breakfast from NT$2900; @ swimming M Zhongshan Junior High School) This is one of a pair of boutique hotels on Fuxing Rd. The Fullerton 315 has a lobby furnished like a classical British sitting room, comfortable rooms and pretty much anything the business traveller might want. It's also slightly cheaper than its sister hotel, the Fullerton 41. A very nice rooftop garden with a small exercise room equipped with running machines, dumbbells and even a sauna allows guests to work out with a view. Rooms are well appointed, with desks and chaise longues. Rooms at the back are quieter.

Grand Hyatt Hotel HOTEL $$$

(台北君悅大飯店; Táiběi Jūnyuè Dàfàndiàn; Map p54; ☎2720 1234; www.taipei.grand.hyatt.com; 2 Songshou Rd; r from NT$6800; @ wi-fi swimming M Taipei City Hall) The Grand Hyatt is huge (more than 850 rooms) and looms like a massive stone hawk, wings outspread in the shadow of nearby Taipei 101. Rooms have three phone lines, there's a business centre, health club and the very upmarket Ziga Zaga nightclub. Rooms are as lovely as you'd expect for the price, and all have views of either the city or the mountains. This is where the company sends you when the shareholders are very happy.

Hotel Delight HOTEL $$

(大來飯店; Dàlái Fàndiàn; Map p56; ☎2716 0011; 432 Changchun Rd; s/d incl breakfast from NT$2727; @ wi-fi M Nanjing East Rd) This delightful little hotel has a classy, subdued feel, free wi-fi and an excellent free breakfast. The overall package gives more expensive hotels a run for their money. There's a little lounge area on the 1st floor with a small business centre.

One-Star Hotel BOUTIQUE HOTEL $

(萬事達旅店; Wànshìdá Lǚdiàn; Map p56; ☎2752 8168; www.onestartaipei.com.tw; 12th fl, 219 Chang'an E Rd, Sec 2, 長安東路2段219號12樓; r incl breakfast from NT$1580; non-smoking M Nanjing East Rd) This cool little boutique hotel is clean and well furnished. There's free breakfast and a fruit basket on the bed when you arrive just to say 'thank you' for staying. The only catch is that the place is a bit tricky to find. Follow the blue One-Star sign just off Chang'an Rd. Rates are slightly higher on weekends and holidays.

Waikoloa Hotel BOUTIQUE HOTEL $$

(首都唯客樂飯店; Shǒudū Wéikèlè Fàndiàn; Map p56; ☎2507 0168; www.waikoloa.com.tw; 187 Changchun Rd; r incl breakfast from NT$2640; @ wi-fi M Nanjing East Rd) Located in an interesting neighbourhood, the Waikoloa is decorated in Japanese-and-Chinese-via-Versailles styles. Rooms are furnished in a traditional Chinese style not easily found in a midrange hotel, making the Waikoloa a worthy place for your Taipei stay.

Taipei Fullerton 41 Hotel HOTEL $$$

(台北馥敦飯店-復南館; Táiběi Fùdūn Fàndiàn-Fùnán Guǎn; Map p56; ☎2703 1234; www.taipeifullerton.com.tw; 41 Fuxing S Rd, Sec 2; r incl breakfast from NT$5500; @ swimming M Technology Building) The Fullerton 41 has 95 rooms offering slick, contemporary decor that you'd expect in the best hotels in San Francisco or Tokyo. Rates include use of the business centre, sauna and fitness centre. Internet discounts can often make the 41 almost as inexpensive as its sister hotel, Taipei Fullerton 315.

Hope City Fuxing Hotel HOTEL $$

(豪城大飯店; Háochéng Dàfàndiàn; Map p56; 2703 9999; 275 Fuxing S Rd Sec 1; s/d 1800/3700; Technology Building) This mid-priced business hotel keeps you on the Fuxing main drag, right next to the MRT line. There's free wireless access and coffee and snacks available all day in the 1st-floor lounge. All rooms have tubs with showers.

Baguio Hotel HOTEL $$

(碧瑤大飯店; Bìyáo Dàfàndiàn; Map p56; 2781 3121; www.baguio-hotel.com.tw; 367 Bade Rd, Sec 2; d/tw from NT$2300/2600; Nanjing East Rd) Some might say the Baguio Hotel is a bit long in the tooth, but we prefer to use the phrase 'old-school Taipei'. Expect Chinese art on the walls and a well-kept interior. Rooms are clean and comfortable and the staff are quite friendly. Seasonal discounts are available.

Also recommended:

Brother Hotel HOTEL $$$

(兄弟大飯店; Xiōngdì Dàfàndiàn; Map p56; 2712 3456; www.brotherhotel.com.tw; 255 Nanjing E Rd, Sec 3; r incl breakfast from NT$4300; Nanjing East Rd) Well situated on the corner of Nanjing and Fuxing Rds, the Brother becomes a midrange hotel when the 20% discount (often available) is factored in. The hotel is popular with business travellers.

Westin Taipei HOTEL $$$

(六福皇宮; Liùfú Huánggōng; Map p56; 8770 6565; www.westin.com; 133 Nanjing E Rd, Sec 3; r from NT$12,500; Nanjing East Rd) If high-priced American-style hotels are what you like, then the high-rise Westin, with its 288 rooms, piano bar and a dozen food and beverage outlets, won't disappoint. An indoor pool means that you can swim all year.

Eating

Beijing has its duck and Shanghai its dumplings. Singapore has its fish-head curries and Hong Kong its dim sum. But Taipei has it all and more, and goes toe-to-toe with any of Asia's culinary capitals.

OLD TOWN CENTRE 萬華區

The Old Town Centre offers myriad eating opportunities for diners of all tastes and budgets. The warren of roads stretching southwest from Taipei Main Station to Ximending is popular with students and has scores of coffee shops, cheap noodle joints and mid-priced restaurants. The crowd in this neighbourhood tends to skew towards the young side, though there are also a number of wallet-lightening fancy restaurants in the hotels by Taipei Main Station. Very politically incorrect on a number of levels, Huaxi St Night Market, otherwise known as Snake Alley, has a few restaurants worth visiting. If you're on a budget or in a hurry, this area also offers a plethora of food courts.

Xiangyi Vegetarian Heaven VEGETARIAN BUFFET $

(祥意素食天地; Xiángyì Sùshí Tiāndì; Map p44; 15 Wuchang St, Sec 1; meals from NT$100; lunch & dinner; Taipei Main Station) Easily one of the best vegetarian buffets in Taipei, this narrow two-storey restaurant is usually crowded, with the ground-floor seating generally taken by the monks who eat here daily. A beautiful assortment of Taiwanese vegetarian cuisine is cooked fresh and served to the lilting sounds of Buddhist songs coming from an overhead boom box. The restaurant has no English signboard, just look for a yellow sign above the door or follow the sounds of soft Buddhist chanting.

Ching Ye Shin Le Yuan TAIWANESE $$$

(青葉新樂園; Qīngyè Xīnlèyuán; Map p44; 3322 2009; 1 Ba De Rd, Sec 1; meals from NT$600; lunch & dinner Mon-Fri; Zhongxiao Xinsheng) Located inside the Hua Shan Culture Park complex, this beautiful, high-ceilinged, converted factory space serves an exquisite all-you-can-eat buffet comprised of Chinese favourites such as roasted pork, traditional soups infused with Chinese vegetables, various dumpling, vegetable and meat dishes, as well as cooked-before-your-eyes Taiwanese classics such as oyster pancakes. As if this wasn't enough to bring you in, there's a full dessert bar including cakes, coffees and teas. Dinner is more expensive, but includes a fully stocked seafood bar of raw oysters, peel-and-eat shrimp and baby octopus.

L'air Rouge WESTERN FUSION $$

(紅色檳氛; Hóngsè Bīnfēn; Map p44; Q Mall; dishes NT$250-500; lunch & dinner; Taipei Main Station) With its jet-black walls, Victorian chairs and tables (also black), high red ceilings and curtains, the decor at this place comes right out of an Anne Rice novel. A soundtrack of light piano and violin concertos only enhances the illusion. Though portion-wise the grilled beef salad (NT$280) is only adequate, the use of high-

A (FOOD) COURTING WE WILL GO!

So you're a vegetarian and your date has a thing for Korean BBQ? Or perhaps you're travelling with a nine-year-old with a hankering for a three-course meal of beef-noodle soup, French fries and freshly baked mini doughnuts? Fret not, hungry traveller; Taipei's fabulous food courts have you covered. Here are a few worth visiting:

» **Q Mall, basement** (Map p44; ⏲breakfast, lunch & dinner; Ⓜ Taipei Main Station) Just north of Taipei Main Station, Q Mall (aka the new bus station) has a great selection of stalls serving everything from Chinese to Western to Indian food. There's also a small branch of the upmarket Jason's Supermarket.

» **Breeze, 2nd fl Taipei Main Station** (Map p44; ⏲breakfast, lunch & dinner; Ⓜ Taipei Main Station) Totally renovated in 2008, the 2nd floor of Taipei Main Station now boasts a slightly higher class of fast-food joints alongside old favourites such as conveyer-belt sushi and Mr Brown Coffee.

» **Shingong Tower, basement** (Map p44; ⏲breakfast, lunch & dinner; Ⓜ Taipei Main Station) Two floors of food stalls to choose from, including hard-to-find items such as duck-meat sandwiches and fish-ball soup. Many of the shops on the lower level offer samples, making the Shingong food court a moocher's paradise.

» **Taipei 101, basement** (Map p54; ⏲breakfast, lunch & dinner; Ⓜ Taipei City Hall) Though most people are drawn to Asia's tallest building by its height, some folks never leave the basement. Expect sandwiches, sushi, pasta, prime rib and more. Freeloaders take note: Jason's – a very upmarket supermarket in the basement – doles out free samples liberally.

» **Tianmu Takashimaya, basement** (Map p62; 55 Zhongcheng Rd, Sec 2; ⏲breakfast, lunch & dinner; Ⓜ Zhishan) Sashimi, Indian, bratwurst and doughnuts. What more could you ask for in the basement of an upmarket department store? Also home to one of the best Korean hot-pot places in town.

» **Tianmu Sogo, basement** (Map p62; 77 Zhongshan N Rd, Sec 6; ⏲breakfast, lunch & dinner; Ⓜ Zhishan) New on the food court scene, what this one lacks in size (there are only a dozen or so stalls, far fewer than at nearby Takashimaya) it makes up for in quality and excellent ice-cream crêpes.

quality beef as well as rocket and other high-end greens is a pleasant surprise. Pasta dishes are also acceptable, and soups – particularly the pumpkin – are quite good.

Yun Thai THAI **$$**
(雲泰; Yún Tài; Map p44; 25 Lane 10, Chengdu Rd; dishes from NT$150; ⏲lunch & dinner; Ⓜ Ximen) Ximending's Red Pavilion Theatre boasts a dozen or so restaurants, any of which are worth a visit. But you might overlook this unassuming Thai place in the corner, which would be a shame. Though plain in ambience, Yuan Thai serves excellent Thai dishes like pad thai and *tom yum* (spicy seafood soup), and you'll have no problem finding places in Ximending to spend the bucks you'll save eating at one of the cheaper Thai places in town.

Modern Toilet ASIAN FUSION **$$**
(便所主題; Biànsuǒ Zhǔtí; Map p44; www.moderntoilet.com.tw; 2nd fl, 7 Lane 50, Xining S Rd, 西寧南路50巷7號; meals from NT$180; ⏲lunch & dinner; Ⓜ Ximen) Where do we even begin with this one? OK, it's a theme restaurant, the theme being *everybody poops*. Patrons, sitting on toilets, are served food out of toilet-shaped dishes. The food – curries mostly – are about as good as you'd expect to eat out of a toilet bowl. Still, Modern Toilet is worth a visit for the novelty factor, especially if you're travelling with young children.

DA'AN & SHIDA 大安區、師大區

For the student crowd, the grid of roads south of Shida University, in between Heping and Roosevelt Rds, is the place for a feed. It's an excellent choice for the traveller with an appetite as well. At night the main drag is packed, as are most of the alleys, side streets and restaurants. You can buy everything from meat skewers to oyster omelettes to stinky tofu, and the stalls in the area tend to be pretty cheap. There are also a number of self-serve buffets in the

Shida neighbourhood that charge by weight (the food weight, not yours), and a meal at any of these shouldn't set you back more than NT$150. The best time to hit a buffet is between 11.30am and 12.30pm for lunch and 4.30pm and 6pm for dinner, as that's when the dishes are freshest.

Hui Liu VEGETARIAN **$$**

(回留茶藝素食; Huíliú Cháyì Sùshí; Map p46; 9 Lane 31, Yong Kang St, 永康街31巷9號; set meals from NT$250; ⏲lunch & dinner; 📄Ⓜ Guting) This exquisitely quirky restaurant has been serving vegetarian fare a cut above the buffets that line the streets of Taipei since 1990. An imaginative chef (and imaginative decor) are the hallmarks of Hui Liu. They will happily help you choose what teas go best with what meals. 'Marco Polo Comes to Taiwan' is a set meal consisting of soup, three side dishes and fresh pasta with tomato crème sauce and vegetables (NT$480). All with pleasant and calming classical music in this traditional Chinese teahouse setting.

Salt Peanuts FUSION **$$**

(鹹花生; XíanHuāShēng; Map p46; 23 Lane 60, Taishun St, 泰順街60巷23號; set meals from NT$220; ⏲lunch & dinner; 📶📄Ⓜ Taipower Building) This unique cafe and restaurant (it even has a small art gallery in the back) offers a great selection of mixed Western and Chinese fare. At NT$220 for a small dish, roasted Italian sausage with tomatoes is more than enough to fill an average eater. We absolutely went crazy for the lightly grilled duck breast, served with pasta, bread and homemade jam (NT$320). Salt Peanuts also has great desserts and a wide selection of beers.

Grandma Nitti's WESTERN **$$**

(中西美食; Zhōngxī Měishí; Map p46; 8 Lane 93, Shida Rd; dishes NT$150-400; ⏲breakfast, lunch & dinner; 📶📄Ⓜ Taipower Building) A mainstay of Taipei's Western community, Nitti's serves comfort food such as waffles, burgers, Philly-cheese steaks, Mexican dishes and family-sized pastas. Best bang for your buck are Nitti's all-day breakfasts, served from 9am to 5pm. At NT$180 for the usual eggs, pancakes, bacon, ham, hash browns and bottomless tea or coffee, it's the best deal in the house. There's a comfy streetside terrace and the windowed space upstairs is a great place to mull over newspapers. Animal lovers take note: Rainbow (aka Grandma Nitti) is a mainstay in Taiwan's animal-protection community, so if you wind up adopting a pet and want to know how to go about bringing it back home with you (this happens more often than you might think – Taiwanese dogs are exceptionally adorable), she's the one to ask about pet-export regulations.

Nitti's sister business, **My Sweetie Pie** (3 Lane 93, Shida Rd; cakes from NT$80; ⏲noon-midnight Mon-Fri, 11am-midnight Sat & Sun; 📶📄) is on the same alley, has a less frantic atmosphere than the always-busy Nitti's, and serves some of the best cakes and pies to be had this side of the Taiwan Strait.

Vegetarian Paradise VEGETARIAN BUFFET **$**

(素食天地; Sùshí Tiāndì; Map p46; 182 Heping E Rd; meals from NT$100; ⏲lunch & dinner; Ⓜ Taipower Building) Because of its location (right across from Shida University), this is usually the first vegetarian buffet many newly arrived students visit. The owners haven't let success go to their heads, though, and they still serve the same sublime vegetarian cuisine they did when some of us came here as students, way back when. Price is by weight, and unless your eyes are far bigger than your stomach, shouldn't ever exceed NT$160.

Dintaifung SHANGHAINESE **$$**

(鼎泰豐; Dǐngtàifēng; Map p46; ☎2321 8928; 194 Xinyi Rd, Sec 2, 信義路2段194號; dumplings NT$190-320; ⏲lunch & dinner; 📄Ⓜ Zhongxiao Xinsheng) With Taipei's most celebrated dumplings, Dintaifung is deservedly popular for Shanghai-style treats made fresh to order. Try the classic *xiǎolóng bāo* (steamed pork dumplings). Very popular with locals and visitors alike, so either phone in reservations (they speak enough English) or prepare to queue up.

Oma Ursel's German Bakery & Restaurant GERMAN **$$**

(歐嬤烏蘇拉; Ōumā Wūsūlā; Map p46; 9 Lane 6, Yongkang St, 永康街6巷9號; set meals from NT$280; ⏲lunch & dinner; 📄Ⓜ Guting) This newly remodelled German restaurant boasts a family-friendly atmosphere (kids' menu) as well as some excellent German local cuisine. The menu is in German and English, with family multicourse meals (for six) for NT$2500. There's wine and beer, delicious cakes and bread. Best value is the lunch special: sausage vegetable risotto for NT$280 includes soup, salad, fresh-baked German bread and coffee. Best of all, there's heavenly cakes.

KGB WESTERN $

(KGB紐西蘭漢堡; Nĭuxīlán Hànbăo; Map p46; ☎2363 6015; 5 Lane 114, Shida Rd, 師大路114巷5號; burgers NT$140-330; ⊙lunch & dinner; ; MTaipower Building) Opened in 2007 by a gregarious Kiwi named Antony, KGB (short for Kiwi Gourmet Burger) has developed quite the cult following among locals and expats alike, both because of its chilled-out atmosphere and its amazing burgers (including a number of vegetarian selections that are out of this world). Check the board for daily specials. Located on a tiny alley just off Shida Rd about three blocks north of the MRT station, KGB is a difficult first find but worth the search.

Bongos WESTERN $$

(Map p46; 3 Alley 5, Lane 74, Wenzhou St; dishes NT$150-300; ⊙lunch & dinner; MTaipower Building) Have a hankering for *poutine* (French fries topped with cheese curds and gravy) and pasta, or perhaps some salad served with a secondhand science-fiction paperback? In addition to serving good Western-style lunches and dinners, including the aforementioned Canadian favourite, Bongos has a comfortable reading area, outdoor seating and a huge collection of used books for sale.

Maryjane Pizza PIZZA $$

(瑪莉珍披薩; Mălìzhēn Pīsà; Map p46; 89 Wenzhou St; www.maryjanepizza.com; pizzas from NT$150; ⊙lunch & dinner; MGongguan) With a menu filled with sly stoner references, Maryjane offers some of the best pizza in Taipei. But don't get your hopes up. The only greens you'll get here are in Maryjane's salads, which are actually pretty good (proper greens and vegies as opposed to the usual iceberg, tomato and canned corn).

ZHONGSHAN 中山區

This is the neighbourhood that stretches north from the city centre, roughly encompassing the neighbourhoods along the Danshui line from the train station until the point that the subway becomes an elevated train line. Located in this area is Taipei's once-infamous bar and brothel zone, aka the Combat Zone, now more noteworthy for the Shuangcheng Street Night Market to the south (a great place for late-night eats and livelier than the Zone, in our opinion). Linsen Rd and the surrounding alleyways are popular among Japanese businessmen and tourists, so if you're looking for sake, teppanyaki, Kobe beef or tekka maki, you'll find it there.

#21 Goose & Seafood TAIWANESE $

(21號鵝肉海鮮; 21 hào éròu hăixiān; Map p52; 21 Jinzou St; dishes NT$100-400; ⊙4.30pm-4.30am; MMinquan W Rd) This is it, your for-real local dining experience – great food in a genuine Taiwanese environment (sometimes there's a guy wandering around selling betel nut, and you can't get much more Taiwanese than that). The place gets its name from its two specialities, roasted goose meat (hanging on a hook behind a window by the front of the restaurant) and fish so fresh that a

NIGHT MARKETS WE LOVE

» **Shilin** (Map p60; MJiantan) If you can eat it, wear it or give it a name and bring it home with you (stalls selling puppies are big here, though we question the ethics of a spur-of-the-moment puppy purchase), you'll find it here. If you're squeamish about crowds, stick to the edges!

» **Shida** (Map p46; MTaipower Building) If Shilin is king, then Shida is queen. It's almost as crowded as Shilin; you'll be met with a mind-boggling array of stuff to eat here as well as some very cool shops. Check out the stall run by a lady known as Fruit Auntie *(shuĭguŏ āyí)*, on Longquan Rd just a block down from Hoping Rd. Her freshly cut fruit must be tasted to be believed.

» **Jingmei** (MJingmei) Though a bit on the dark and grotty side, there's something about the realism of this night market on the southern end of the city that we respect. The market is also a good place to shop for cheap T-shirts.

» **Raohe** (MHoushanpi) Taipei's oldest and definitely one of the best; check out the sautéed-crab vendor at the eastern end of the street for a real treat.

» **Shipai** (MShipai) Where people in Tianmu go for night-market food when they can't stand the crowds at the Shilin Market. It's a good place to hit after soaking at Beitou Hot Springs, and the chicken soup at Tai-G will cure what ails ya.

few will be staring at you as you stand on the sidewalk waiting for a table. And wait you might – the place is very popular with locals and Japanese tourists alike – the food is just that good. Some specialities besides goose and fish include fresh shrimp served grilled or sautéed, excellent clam soup made with shredded ginger, and some of the best Kung Pao chicken we've ever had. There's no English menu, but its not a big problem as much of what's being served is also on display, and, in a pinch, a few of the waitresses speak a smidgen of English.

Artco De Cafe FUSION **$**

(典藏咖啡館; Diǎncángkāfēiguǎn; Map p52; http://artouch.com/food; 39 Chang An W Rd, 長安西路39號; meals from NT$100; ⏲lunch & dinner; 🅼Zhongshan) It's no surprise that the food at this cafe connected to the Museum of Contemporary Art Taipei is creative. That it's also well done, especially for the price, is pleasantly unexpected. In addition to serving standard coffee-shop sandwiches, Artco serves up a rotating daily menu of regional specialities, such as Hakka squid.

Golden Dragon CANTONESE **$$**

(金龍餐廳; Jīnlóng CānTīng; ☎2886 8888, ext 1262; Grand Hotel, 1 Lane 1, Zhongshan N Rd, Sec 4; dishes NT$150-500; ⏲lunch & dinner; 🅼Jiantan) Popular with politicos and visitors alike, the Golden Dragon is the gorgeous Hong Kong–style restaurant inside the Grand Hotel (one of Taipei's best-known landmarks). Excellent dim sum and other Cantonese favourites are served in style. Diners have a panoramic view of the Keelung River.

Celestial Restaurant TRADITIONAL CHINESE **$$**

(天廚菜館; Tiānchú Càiguǎn; Map p52; ☎2521 1097; 3rd fl, 1 Nanjing W Rd, 南京西路1號3樓; dishes NT$165-380, Peking duck from NT$750; ⏲lunch & dinner; 🅼Zhongshan) Lovers of Beijing-style cooking have been coming to this restaurant for generations. In addition to Peking duck (expensive but meant for sharing), try the elegant, comforting 'green beans (actually peas) with shredded chicken'. Reservations are recommended, and the Celestial is in the same building as the Royal Inn Taipei should your meal make you sleepy.

Paris 1930 FRENCH **$$$**

(巴黎廳; Bālítīng; Map p52; ☎2597 1234; 41 Minquan E Rd, Sec 2; meals NT$1800-3500; ⏲dinner Mon-Sat; 🅼Zhongsan Junior High School) This restaurant in the Landis Hotel is consistently rated as having the best French food in town. Dinners will often run over six courses. There's piano music and a refined atmosphere, and the hotel's art-deco setting provides a suitably sophisticated backdrop. Reservations are definitely recommended.

EASTERN TAIPEI 東台北市

Taipei city east of Fuxing Rd is vast and offers a plethora of flavours. While some of the city's most expensive restaurants are located here, there's no shortage of budget and mid-priced places. If street eats are your thing, have a walk up Da'an Rd just north of the Zhongxiao Fuxing MRT station, where you'll find a bunch of noodle shops and stalls selling everything from roast corn to stinky tofu. Just to the south, the stretch of Zhongxiao E Rd between the Zhongxiao Fuxing and Zhongxiao Dunhua stations are chock-full of eateries for all budgets.

Pho Hoa VIETNAMESE **$**

(美越; Měi Yuè; Map p56; http://noodle.zeelive.com.tw; 43 Lane 190, Dunhua S Rd, Sec 1; mains from NT$120; ⏲lunch & dinner; 🅼Zhongxiao Dunhua) Taipei is loaded with Vietnamese restaurants, but this one – favourite of local salary people and some noted Taipei bloggers – can be considered among the best. Its Pho Bo (beef noodles) is excellent, served with beef so rare it practically leaps from the bowl, but what really sets Pho Hoa apart is its spring rolls, crammed full of tasty shrimp and fresh salad greens. The lane that Pho Hoa is on – just behind SOGO – is a particularly good one for restaurants.

Yong Ming THAI, TAIWANESE **$**

(永明; Yǒng Míng; Map p56; ☎2752 6142; 36 Lane 256, Nanjing E Rd, Sec 3; dishes NT$100-200; ⏲11am-2pm & 5.30pm-2am) This kitschy little place on a small alley off the main Nanjing E Rd hub is a rare find indeed. Traditional Thai dishes such as lemon fish share the menu with more traditional Chinese fare such as Kung Pao chicken and hybrid items such as dragon balls *(long zhu)*, a dry deep-fried squid mouth served with green onion, garlic and hot pepper. Alas, there's no English menu, though courteous staff will be happy to help you choose your food. We've saved the best for last: self-serve all-you-can-drink Taiwan beer on tap; NT$199 buys you three hours of unlimited refills of the local brew.

Ninja JAPANESE **$$**

(忍者餐廳; Rěnzhě cāntīng; Map p56; ☎2577-3300; www.ninja-tw.com; 129 Civil Blvd, Sec 4; dishes from NT$250; ⏲6pm-2am; 🅼Zhongxiao

Dunhua) Equal parts eatery and experience, the newly opened Ninja restaurant offers the chance to dine in a faux-classical Japanese-style stone fortress and be served by sword-wielding waitresses. From the moment you enter, you'll know you're in for a themed experience. If the ninjas climbing up the building's exterior don't tip you off, the stairs leading to the upstairs dining area, which are artfully hidden behind an artificial waterfall that stops flowing on command, surely will. In between courses (acceptable Japanese fare, though nothing spectacular) a wandering multilingual ninja-magician performs card tricks to the delight of all. Only two things may mar an otherwise excellent family dining experience: a lack of English menus, and the fact that the ninjas in charge seem to turn a blind eye to the city's nonsmoking regulations.

Sweet Dynasty CANTONESE **$**
(糖朝甜品專門店; Tángcháo Tiánpǐn Zhuānméndiàn; Map p56; ☎2772 2889; 160 Zhongxiao E Rd, Sec 4; dishes from NT$80; ⏰lunch & dinner; Ⓜ Zhongxiao Dunhua) Though specialising in Chinese desserts, Sweet Dynasty also serves a wide variety of mouth-watering dishes such as Shanghai prawns, braised beef ribs with bitter melon and other Chinese classics. Desserts, of course, are amazing, so top off your meal with a slice of taro cake or a dish of mango pudding. Come during teatime (2pm to 5pm), when dim-sum specials bring dish prices down as low as NT$49, making feasting cheaper.

G'day Café WESTERN **$$**
(晴西餐廳; Qíngxī Cāntīng; Map p56; 180 Xingan St, 興安街180號; dishes NT$180-320; ⏰10am-10pm Mon-Sat, 10am-5pm Sun, closed last Mon of month; 📋Ⓜ Zhongshan Junior High School) Though no longer the popular expat hangout of yore, the G'day is still serving exactly the same Western fare to a primarily local clientele. Come here for burgers, tacos and Western-style brunches served all day with bottomless cups of coffee. Home-away-from-home remnants – an English bulletin board advertising jobs, a few dozen old paperbacks for trade – still exist.

Capone's Lounge Bar ITALIAN **$$**
(卡邦義大利餐廳; Kǎbāng Xīnyìshì Měishí; Map p56; 312 Zhongxiao E Rd, Sec 4; dishes NT$350; ⏰11.30am-1.30am; 📋Ⓜ Zhongxiao Dunhua) Named after the noted Italian-American gourmand, merrymaker and racketeer, Capone's serves some of the area's best Italian food. In the evenings, Capone's is popular with upmarket expats, especially after 9pm when the house band plays. Also popular is Capone's weekend brunch, which, at NT$499 for all you can eat ($350 for the kids) is truly an offer you can't refuse.

Qimin From Farm To Table ORGANIC HOT POT **$$$**
(齊民有機中國火鍋; QímínYǒujī Zhōngguó Huǒguō; Map p56; 2nd fl, 128 Zhongxiao Rd, Sec 4; meals from NT$600; ⏰lunch & dinner; 📋Ⓜ Zhongxiao Dunhua) Health-conscious diners rejoice! This lovely hot-pot restaurant offers 100% organic food, meats free of growth hormones, and non-GMO vegies certified pesticide- and heavy-metal-free. One of the priciest hot-pot places in town, true…but what good is money if you don't have your health?

Also recommended:

Umeko TAIWANESE **$$**
(梅子餐廳; Méizǐ Cāntīng; Map p56; 206 Nanjing E Rd, Sec 2; dishes from NT$250; ⏰lunch & dinner; Ⓜ Zhongshan Junior High School) A very traditional Taiwanese banquet-style restaurant, from the seafood-filled glass

CULINARY COURSES & MORE

Those looking to take more than memories of great Taiwanese cuisine back home will be glad to know that the **Community Services Centre** (☎2836 8134; www.community.com.tw) in Taipei conducts cooking courses where visitors to Taiwan can learn all the secrets to preparing amazing traditional Chinese and Taiwanese dishes. Call or visit the website for information on current courses, prices and scheduling. The Community Services Centre also has regularly scheduled tours, outings and even classes in Mandarin Chinese!

Located in Taipei, the **Lu-Yu Tea Culture Institute** (☎2331 6636) offers basic, intermediate and advanced courses in tea arts, culture and lore. All courses are in English. Course length and schedules vary; call for more information or email Steven R Jones at icetea8@gmail.com and check out his blog (http://teaarts.blogspot.com).

AFTER-HOURS EATS

The stretch of Fuxing Rd just beneath the Muzha elevated train line on the west side, right between the Technology Building and Da'an stations, has a number of typical Taiwanese restaurants serving stomach-soothing Taiwanese items such as *wēn dòujiāng* (warm soymilk) and *qīngzhòu* (thin rice porridge served with chunks of sweet potato). Most of these restaurants are open very late, and are quite popular with the post-libation bar crowd.

counter to the huge round tables (complete with lazy Susans).

Very Thai THAI $$
(非常泰; Fēicháng Tài; Map p56; ☎2546 6745; 319 Fuxing N Rd; dishes NT$220-450; ⏰lunch & dinner; Ⓜ Zhongsan Junior High School) Dark and cool Thai with black-on-black decor and lovely dishes.

Hello Kitty Sweets FUSION $$
(Map p56; ☎2772 5123; 90 Da'an Rd, Sec 1, 大安路一段90號; dishes from NT$230; ⏰11.30am-10pm; Ⓜ Zhongxiao Fuxing) Waitresses dressed in frilly pink and white outfits; pink, white and purple couches; and Japanese pop music, all under the watchful gaze of Hello Kitty.

Yogurt Art DESSERT $
(Map p56; www.yogurtart.com.tw; 14 Alley 8, Lane 216, Zhongxiao E Rd, Sec 4; per 100gm NT$50; ⏰noon-10pm; Ⓜ Zhongxiao Dunhua) Heavenly frozen yoghurt with self-serve toppings!

SHILIN & TIANMU 士林區、天母區

Avoiding food in Shilin is a bit like avoiding casinos in Las Vegas; you can do it, but you really need to be committed. Indeed, the very name 'Shilin' is synonymous with Taipei's most celebrated night market (p59).

Though the two neighbourhoods border one another, culinary-wise Tianmu is Shilin's diametric opposite. While Shilin is the place for crowded night markets and street food, Tianmu is generally more upmarket, offering a wide variety of sit-down restaurants.

Wu Hua Ma Dumpling House DUMPLINGS $
(五花馬水餃館; Wǔhuāmǎ Shuǐjiǎoguǎn; Map p62; 60 Tianmu W Rd; dishes from NT$80; ⏰lunch & dinner; Ⓜ Shipai) Taipei is rich with restaurants serving dumplings, and this one is among the best. Dumpling choices include a variety of pork/vegetable mixtures, beef, shrimp and even the less common scallop. Dumplings go for a fixed price of NT$8 per dumpling, with a minimum order of 10 per type. One of the main joys of a meal here is making mix-and-match condiments using ingredients from the well-stocked condiment bar. For those who aren't dumpling fans, a variety of soups and noodle dishes are also available for between NT$50 and NT$100.

Café Onion WESTERN $$$
(洋葱; Yángcōng; Map p60; ☎8866 3081; www.cafe-onion.com; 124 Zhongzheng Rd, 中正路124號; full meals from NT$550; ⏰lunch & dinner; Ⓜ Shilin) Getting a good steak dinner for under a grand in Taipei is difficult; there are plenty of bargain steakhouses, but most of these places tend to deal in chunks of cheap meat cooked to an unappetising grey on iron plates before being slathered with peppery gravy and served with a raw egg. Café Onion is a welcome relief from the Taiwan beefsteak norm, serving flame-broiled steaks from Australia, New Zealand and the US – well cooked and well priced. In addition to excellent appetisers (full meals come with soup, salad, appetisers, beverage and dessert, all of which are quite good), Café Onion is one of the few places in town where you can get roast beef (NT$1350 for a full meal for two to three people; one-hour advance notice recommended.)

Haw Kuang Vegetarian Restaurant VEGETARIAN BUFFET $
(毫光素食; Háoguāng Sùshí; Map p60; 357 Zhongzheng Rd; meals from NT$100; ⏰lunch & dinner Fri-Wed; Ⓜ Shilin) At the other end of the spectrum is this amazing vegetarian buffet just down the block from the Onion and a few blocks northwest of the Shilin Night Market. Why is this among Taipei's best vegetarian buffets? Simply put, the chef is a genius, with an eye for both colour and flavour. Arrange your meal from dozens of beautifully prepared vegetarian dishes and enjoy. Imagine yourself a painter and the white cardboard tray your canvas.

ORGANIC MARKETS

Need something to balance out the night markets' stick-meat, fried tofu and assorted artery-clogging goodness? Taipei has a number of places to get organic fruits, vegetables and other healthy products. **Cottonfields Organic Health Store** (花田生機園地; huātián shēngjī yuán dì; Map p46; ☎2364 8899; 273 Roosevelt Rd, Sec 3) sells the sort of stuff you'd find at a farmers market in San Francisco, as well as salads and fresh juices. It also has upstairs seating.

Santa Cruz (聖德科斯天然有機; shèng dékēsī tiānrán yǒujī; Map p56; www.santacruz.com.tw) is another organic chain, with branches all over the city, including eastern Taipei city and another just east of the Shipai MRT station. Santa Cruz is a good place to stock up on vitamins, though they tend to be pricier than those you'd find in North America and Australia.

He Xiang Delicious Food TAIWANESE $

(荷香美食; Hé Xiāng Měishí; Map p62; 60 Fuguo Rd; dishes NT$50; ⏲lunch & dinner; ⓂZhishan) A long-standing favourite streetside eatery in Tianmu, He Xiang has kept the same tiny menu for decades (the picture menu on the wall behind the counter has almost totally faded). The speciality of the house, and a local must-try, is the bamboo-steamed sticky rice with red pork and vegetables, wrapped in a lotus leaf and served with hot sauce. Look for the faded picture of this dish above the entrance. The restaurant is on the north side of the street, just east of the Zhishan MRT. Another excellent dish is the shrimp-ball soup. Nothing fancy, just cheap, good and very Taiwanese.

Lavender Garden VEGETARIAN $$

(天母古道森林花園; Tiānmǔ Gǔdào Sēnlín Huāyuán; Map p62; ☎2873 7581; 4 Alley 1, Lane 232, Zhongshan N Rd, Sec 7; dishes NT$250-350; ⏲lunch & dinner Tue-Sun) At the bottom of a long, steep stairway that (eventually) leads up into Yangming Mountain lies this excellent restaurant set inside a two-storey home surrounded by an aquatic garden. Amazing health-oriented Chinese dishes such as 'health-tonic hot pot with 10 Chinese herbs' will give you strength for the climb ahead. Then again, as Lavender Garden's desserts are delicious as well, you might want to save the meal as a reward for the climb down.

Beitou Squid TAIWANESE $

(北投魷魚; Běitóu Yóuyú; Map p62; 96 Dexing E Rd; dishes NT$30-50; ⏲lunch & dinner; ⓂZhishan) This funky little eatery in Tianmu serves excellent traditional Taiwanese dishes such as pork and seafood dumpling, cold cucumber salad and tofu with thousand-year eggs. But the coolest part is the decor. Old 1960s Taiwanese movie posters adorn the wall (they're for sale) and the shop sells kitsch nostalgia items including wind-up cars and candy cigarettes. John Waters would just love this place.

Also recommended:

Maison Alexandria FRENCH DELI & CAFE $

(Map p62; 756 Zhongshan N Rd, Sec 6; sandwiches/set meals from NT$100/220; ⏲breakfast, lunch & dinner; 📋ⓂZhisan) This small European-style deli sells great sandwiches, decent salads (don't expect rocket) and good coffee and pie. Lunch specials are a good deal and take-away food is available.

Tai G MEDICINAL BROTH $

(台G; Shipai Night Market; dishes NT$100-150; ⏲lunch & dinner; ⓂShipai) The Shipai Night Market has a plethora of spots to eat, but Tai G (a pun meaning 'Taiwan Chicken') may trump them all in health benefits, serving a variety of medicinal chicken soups. For maximum benefit, bring a Chinese speaker with you to explain what ails you (lethargy...cold...allergies) and ask to be served the appropriate remedy.

Escargot PASTRY $

(Map p62; www.escargot.com.tw; 24 Zhongyi St, 忠義街24號; ⏲11am-9pm Sat, noon-7pm Sun; ⓂZhishan) Just north of Zhishan Garden, this take-away place serves some of the best cakes in the neighbourhood.

Drinking

Cafes

Once hard to find, coffee shops now abound throughout Taipei. Typical opening times are 7.30am to 10pm and you might find folks, particularly students, camped out at them for hours studying or chatting over a coffee, pastry or light meal. As finding a coffee shop in Taipei has become as easy as, well, finding a coffee shop in Taipei, we've skipped the chain shops and listed some of our favourite unique spots. Many of these are as much 'chill-out and event' spots as they are places to get coffee.

Vinyl Wine Bar WINE BAR

(凡諾; Fánnùo; Map p46; 140 Jinhua St; meals from NT$150; 1pm-1am Tue-Sun; Taipower Building) This quirky and mellow little wine bar is just north of Shida University in a quiet neighbourhood. The walls are covered with old album covers, primarily Asian jazz bands and the menu itself (available in English and Chinese) is a recycled vinyl LP. Vinyl offers a relaxed spot, jazz on tap and an excellent selection of fine wines imported from vineyards from Europe to Australia to North America. There is a fair selection of edibles, with coffee also available. It's home to more than 10,000 records, everything from Taiwanese to jazz. Double and triple espressos cost NT$90.

Dance Cafe CAFE

(跳舞咖啡廳; tiàowǔkāfēitīng; Map p52; 1 Lane 46, Zhongshan N Rd, Sec 2, 中山北路2段46巷1號; coffees NT$80; 11.30am-9.30pm; Shuanglian) Located in a historic wooden house that once housed a dance troupe (hence the name), this lovely, low-slung cafe serves good coffee, sandwiches, snacks and a wide variety of teas and other beverages in a quiet setting just off the main drag.

Orange Music Cafe CAFE

(看電車; Kàn Diànchē; Map p60; 302 Wen Lin Rd; 11.30am-1am Sun-Thu, 11.30am-3am Fri & Sat; Shilin) This very cool coffee shop is just a quick hop south from Shilin station's exit 2. While food and libations are on the menu, Orange is best known for it's long-standing 'fire dance' performances, which begin every Friday night at 10.50pm. Admission for the performance is NT$150, but if you come in costume it drops to NT$80. The cafe plays cool music and has an excellent rooftop chill-out spot, a good place to retreat from the noise and chaos of nearby Shilin Night Market.

Tongjong Coffee CAFE

(統將咖啡; Tǒngjiàng Kāfēi; Map p46; 2366 1594; 12 Lane 74, Wenzhou St, 溫州街74巷12號; 7.30am-8pm; Taipower Building) The aroma of roasting coffee beans will tell you that you've arrived. When you enter the shop – much of which is taken up by huge burlap bags filled with beans from around the globe – you'll realise you've entered a place catering to the aficionado. Though there are a few tables set up, best not to tarry; Tongjong's business is done on a to-go basis.

Also recommended:

H*ours Cafe CAFE

(奧爾斯咖啡; àoěrsī kāfēi; Map p46; 12 Alley 8, Lane 210, Roosevelt Rd, Sec 3, 羅斯福路三段210巷8弄12號; 2-11pm Mon-Fri, noon-11pm Sat & Sun; Taipower Building) Lovely little gay-owned cafe and bookstore serving food and beverages.

Urban Core Café & Bookshelf CAFE

(Map p44; 2389 6971; 89-6 Zhonghua Rd, Sec 1; coffees NT$80; noon-10pm; Ximen) This chic little coffee shop has an art-gallery feel, excellent espresso, tea and desserts, as well as free wireless and a small selection of art periodicals free for the browsing.

Teahouses

Tea is an institution in Taiwan, in addition to being a major export, and Taipei has a

IN THE ZONE

The Combat Zone got its name back when Taiwan was still known in some circles as 'Free China'. Then, American soldiers came here in droves. They were either stationed in Taiwan or on R&R leave from Vietnam. The neighbourhood was a major red-light district, a little slice of Bangkok, or perhaps of Amsterdam.

Times have changed and nowadays it's difficult to say exactly who the habitués of these few grungy alleys really are. Japanese businessmen perhaps, though the section of alleys across Linsen Rd to the southwest seems more geared towards such clientele. Shuangcheng St, the main road from which the alleys branch off, is a night market to the south, not much different from many of Taipei's other small night-market streets. North of the night market on the main drag are a few respectable pubs such as Malibu West or My Place. As for the girlie bars, nowadays only one alley in the Combat Zone is still dedicated to them. While we're reluctant to advertise it by name, it isn't too hard to either find or avoid.

great variety of shops that serve it. You'll find teahouses in places as varied as atop serene mountains down to stands in crowded markets.

Though eschewed by tea purists, *zhēnzhū nǎichá* (pearl milk tea) is way popular with everyone from kids to secretaries. This sweetened tea with chewy black balls of tapioca is served in a plastic cup with a seal as tight as a bongo head and drunk through a straw thick enough to suck up marbles. Order yours *rè* (hot) or *bīng* (cold). Another favourite is *paòmò hóngchá* (bubble black tea), which is tea frothed until it has a head not unlike that of beer. Both are available at tea stands and stalls citywide for about NT$25.

Rose House TEAHOUSE
(古典玫瑰園; Gǔdiǎn Méiguī Yuán; Map p52; 95 Nanjing E Rd, Sec 2; ⏲11am-10pm; Ⓜ Zhongshan) Readers have written in praise of this teahouse, which, despite its normal storefront, looks like it could have been decorated by Laura Ashley inside. Among its dozens of varieties are Earl Grey and mango. Teas are sold by the cup, the set and the tin.

Maussac EUROPEAN
(摩賽卡法式茶館餐廳; Mósàikǎ Fàshì Cháguǎn; Map p46; www.maussac.com.tw; 24 Lishui St, Sec 1; dishes NT$280-500; ⏲11.30am-10pm; Ⓜ Taipower Building) Maussac is an upmarket teahouse, complete with a bookshelf's worth of jars featuring teas from around the world. In addition to tea, set-meal specials, including pasta, meat and seafood dishes, are all served with a haute-European flair. Maussac's charming atmosphere makes it a popular spot for Taipei's chic looking to unwind with a meal, tea or both.

☆ Entertainment

Bars & Clubs

Ah, where to begin? Taipei is a city where the young heading home from a night of hard clubbing pass through parks where the old have been practising taichi since dawn. There is no lack of clubs, pubs, bars, musical venues or other places to drink, hear music or, if you're drunk enough, to make music of your own. Typically, beers sell for between NT$100 and NT$150. Hard liquor might set you back NT$250. Ask around for happy hours or drink specials.

Clubs come and go, but we've done our best to list ones that should still be around when this book goes to print. A loose affiliation of pubs have come together to promote their latest menus and events. Check out their website, www.taipeipubs.com. Another excellent site to find out which bands are playing and where is www.waakao.com.

45 BAR
(Map p46; 45 Heping E Rd, Sec 1; Ⓜ Guting) Go up the narrow stairs and join the huge crowd (which includes many foreigners), especially on Friday and Saturday nights. It's festooned with Americana, from licence plates to movie-star photos, and the food is American-style, too.

Brass Monkey CLUB
(Map p56; 166 Fuxing N Rd; 復興北路166號; ⏲4pm-1am Mon-Wed, 5pm-4am Thu, 5pm-2am Fri & Sat; Ⓜ Nanjing E Rd) A smoking-hot bar and club with a definite reputation as the in spot for hooking up (especially on Thursday – Ladies Night). The Brass Monkey is also known for its Pub Quiz Night (second Wednesday of the month).

Carnegie's BAR
(Map p56; 100 Anhe Rd, Sec 2; dishes NT$260-780; Ⓜ Technology Building) Carnegie's caused quite a stir when it first opened in 2001, what with patrons dancing on the bar and all, but even if it has calmed down a notch, it's still one of the liveliest nightspots in Xinyi. It's a popular meeting place for afterwork drinks. The menu includes steaks, halibut and lamb.

Luxy CLUB
(Map p56; www.luxy-taipei.com; 5th fl, 201 Zhongxiao E Rd, Sec 4; Ⓜ Zhongxiao Dunhua) A massive club that often features international bands, DJs and some of the hippest live entertainment in Taipei. Check the website for the latest offerings.

Malibu West SPORTS BAR
(Map p52; 9 Lane 25, Shuangcheng St; ⏲3pm-2am Mon-Sat, noon-3am Sun; Ⓦ Ⓜ Minquan W Rd) Located in the Combat Zone, Malibu West has a pool table and a menu with dishes including burgers, pastas, pizzas and snacks. Happy hour is between 4pm and 9pm. It has a tropical feel and one of the most competitive pool tables in town. Best of all, Malibu is fully wireless, meaning laptop-toters can spend their evenings there, er, working. Sure. We believe you.

My Place PUB
(Map p52; 3-1 Lane 32, Shuangcheng St; ⏲6.30pm-3.30am; Ⓜ Minquan W Rd) Also in the Zone, My Place bills itself as Taiwan's first pub (established 1975) and is still go-

ing strong. This Brit-owned establishment boasts friendly hostesses, a pool table and a huge 100-inch-screen TV for sport broadcasts. Happy hour – all beers for NT$100 – runs from 6.30pm to 9.30pm weekdays, and to 8.30pm on weekends, and Warsteiner draught is NT$100 all night. Also has wireless.

8898 Bar PUB
(Map p62; 78 Tianmu E Rd; dishes NT$250-425) Once known as the Pig, this Tianmu pub has changed its name but retained the British feel and menu. It serves steaks, chops and chicken, and Guinness by the pint.

Roxy 99 BAR
(Map p46; ☎2358 2813; 69 Jinshan S Rd, Sec 2; ⏲9pm-4am Mon-Fri, to dawn Sat & Sun; Ⓜ Taipower Building) Popular with students, workers and assorted 20- and 30-somethings, Roxy 99 has a great CD collection and a food menu that includes pastas, fried rice and more adventurous fare. It's in the basement, yet manages not to feel claustrophobic.

Saints & Sinners BAR
(Map p56; 114 Anhe Rd, Sec 2; dishes NT$150-550; Ⓜ Liuzhangli) This bar attracts Taiwanese and foreigners alike. Expect a pool table, foosball, darts and a couple of big screens to watch sport broadcasts. Menu choices include Thai, Chinese and British pub food. The house drink, the 'upside down', includes, among other things, vodka, honey, plum powder and cherry brandy.

Wall LIVE MUSIC
(www.thewall.com.tw; 200 Roosevelt Rd, Sec 4; ⏲8pm-late; Ⓜ Gongguan) Easily Taipei's premier venue for alternative music, the cavernous Wall is tucked into the end of a grunge-and-punk-focused mini-mall. Live bands play Wednesday to Saturday.

Underworld LIVE MUSIC
(Map p46; 45 Shida Rd; admission NT$250; ⏲8pm-late; Ⓜ Taipower Building) A little bit psychedelic, a little bit smoky and very friendly, this cosy, graffiti-painted basement pub pours lots of beer and Long Island Iced Teas.

KNOW YOUR ROXIES

The origins of the original Taipei Roxy club are shrouded in drunken legend and mystery, told by boozy long-term Taiwan expatriates along with fanciful tales of days when Taipei had no Subway (of either the transit or sandwich-franchise kind) and a plucky lawyer surnamed Chen was but a mere mayoral hopeful. What is known is that the first Roxy club, opened in 1989, is now long gone. But the Roxy name has lived on and, like some determined mutant amoeba, the Roxies have divided, spawning new and different Roxies and Roxy-ettes.

Probably most well known is **Roxy 99** (Map p46; ☎2358 2813; 69 Jinshan S Rd, Sec 2; ⏲9pm-4am Mon-Fri, to dawn Sat & Sun; Ⓜ Taipower Building). Popular with foreign students and English teachers, the basement club became a mainstay of Taipei's club scene. Not far from 99 sits **Roxy Rocker** (Map p46; 177 Heping E Rd, Sec 1; ⏲8pm-4am; Ⓜ Taipower Building), whose CD-and-record-covered walls (10,000 of each, so it's claimed – and who are we to argue) makes it clear that music, as well as booze and food, is on the menu. Over on the east side of town, the slightly more upmarket **Roxy Roots** (Map p54; ☎2351 8177; ⏲10am-4am; Ⓜ Taipei City Hall) bills itself as Taipei's first reggae and blues bar, and is a great place to see live music.

And then there are the little Roxies, **Roxy Jr** (Map p46; ☎2366 1799; 1 Lane 80, Shida Rd; ⏲24hr; Ⓜ Taipower Building) and **Roxy Mini** (Map p56; ☎2709 1108; 2 Lane 53, Heping E Rd, Sec 2; ⏲24hr; Ⓜ Taipower Building). The former serves drinks and meals 24/7, boasts both pool and foosball tables, and has a massive TV screen showing sport around the clock. The latter is mini in every way – a mini dance lounge, a mini bar, and mini chill-out spot, perfect for intimate moments. (Alas, its time on the scene may be truncated as well, as rumours of its coming demise are in the air).

But as with life itself, Taiwan's club scene can often be transitory, and today's hot venue may well be tomorrow's warehouse space (or vice versa, as is sometimes the case). Will all of these Roxies be in business by the time you read this? Will there be even more Roxy choices? Only time will tell, but one thing is fairly certain: if you're in town and need a venue to drink, dance, party or just relax, Taipei should have a Roxy to suit your tastes. Check out www.roxy.com.tw to find the Roxy nearest you.

Come here after having dinner at nearby Shida Night Market and stay for DJs spinning house music, or watch a live band on weekends.

Maybe Pub BAR
(台北搖滾音樂Pub; Táiběi Yáogǔn Yīnyùe Pub; Map p56; ☎2705 7399; 15 Lane 253, Fuxing S Rd, Sec 1, 復興南路一段253巷15號; ⏰8pm-3am Mon-Fri, 8pm-4am Sat & Sun; Ⓜ Zhongxiao Fuxing) A flag-bedecked rock bar with decently priced beer and cocktails, and boasting a wall-mounted LCD screen big enough to drive a Volkswagen through. What makes Maybe unique on the scene is what goes on the screen (except during major sporting

(VERY) GAY-FRIENDLY TAIPEI

Foreign-born gay and lesbian travellers will find Taipei friendly and exciting. An open-minded city, Taipei hosts Asia's finest Gay Pride parades every autumn, with the 2009 Pride attracting 25,000 participants (www.twpride.info). Gay life here is well documented in film and literature. You'll find dozens of gay bars in the area behind the Red Pavilion Theatre in Ximending and there's no lack of bookshops, bars, saunas and social options scattered around town to choose from.

Love Boat (愛之船拉拉時尚概念館; Map p46; Aizhīchuán lālā shíshànggài niànguǎn; www.lesloveboat.com; 7-14 Alley 8, Lane 210, Roosevelt Rd, Sec 3; Ⓜ Taipower Building) is Taipei's only shop catering exclusively to lesbians. It has videos, books, jewellery, clothes, binders, toys, finger condoms and more, with upstairs tarot readings and community events in English and Mandarin. The shop staff and owners speak English and are very friendly. For lesbian travellers, **Lady Emperor** (www.ladyemperor.com) has all the goods on the famous Miss/Mr drag king competitions.

As for nightlife, Taipei definitely has it going on. Like the rest of the city's nightlife scene, the hot club when we go to press may not even exist by the time you read this, but the establishments listed here have been around for a while. *G-spot* magazine puts out an informative little Taipei map listing some of the city's hot spots and you can usually pick up a copy at some of the venues listed below. Visitors should check out www.fridae.com, and of course, the folks at **Utopia** (www.utopia-asia.com) keep the data fresh for those looking to hook up in Taipei and elsewhere.

Men's Saunas

Rainbow Sauna (☎2370 2899; 2nd fl, 142 Kunming St; Ⓜ Ximen), **Garden of Eden** (☎2311 8681; 2nd fl, 120 Xining St; Ⓜ Ximen) and **24 Men's Sauna** (☎2361 1069; 5th fl, 72 Zhongxiao W Rd, Sec 1; Ⓜ Taipei Main Station) are three popular men's saunas in Taipei.

Though not a sauna per se, the men's section of the **Chuantang hot spring** (川湯; Chuāntāng; 10 Lane 300, Xingyi Rd), one of the many hot-spring places located on Xingyi Rd (just north of Tianmu) is definitely a cruising spot, especially on weekends.

GLBT Venues

» **Taboo** (Map p56; www.wretch.cc/blog/taboo126; 90 Jianguo N Rd, Sec 2; Ⓜ Zhongshan Junior High School) Open Wednesday to Saturday, but Friday and Saturday are usually the biggest nights. There's a dance floor and DJ. For women, it's NT$300 to NT$500 to get in, with free drinks all night. For men, entry is NT$700 or more, depending on the event. Taboo often has theme parties: those who dress up get in cheaper. Be sure to bring your ID!

» **Fresh** (Map p46; ☎2358 7701; 2nd fl, 7 Jinshan S Rd; Ⓜ Guting) Taipei's gay club *du jour* has three floors of fun: a bar floor, a dance floor and a chill room. In addition, there's a roof garden. It's friendly and the crowd is international.

» **Source** (Map p44; ☎3393 1678; 1-2 Roosevelt Rd, Sec 1; Ⓜ Chiang Kai-shek Memorial Hall) There's a small bar downstairs, a dance floor upstairs and the handsome top floor is reminiscent of an old-world Chinese salon. Foreigners aren't just welcome here, they're encouraged.

» **GinGin's** (Map p46; Jīngjīng Shūkù Jīngpǐndiàn; ☎2364 2006; 8 Alley 8, Lane 210, Roosevelt Rd, Sec 3; Ⓜ Taipower Building) Gay and lesbian bookshop and cafe.

LOCAL KNOWLEDGE

MARCUS AURELIUS: DJ, MUSICIAN, CREATOR OF WWW.WAAKAO.COM

Why Taipei?

While we may not have the diverse population of Tokyo or Hong Kong, Taipei is still very cool, and getting exponentially better every year. As far as nightlife, Taipei is definitely Asia's undiscovered gem.

Who Plays Here?

Jay-Z, Pitbull, 50 Cent, and the Black Eyed Peas have all played here, as have Deep Purple, Linkin Park and Guns N' Roses. On the DJ loop, Taipei is an important stopover, with big names like Tiësto and Armin van Buuren showing up multiple times over the last few years.

Live Music Spot?

The Wall is a great midsize venue for rock and DJs.

Good Sports Bars?

Brass Monkey shows nearly every sporting event known to mankind, ranging from rugby to F1 to UFC events. Forget about finding a seat during big events like the World Cup. The Tavern has big screens as well as personalised TVs at every table.

Pick-up Joint?

Since Roxy Vibe closed in 2009, Roxy 99 has taken its place as the undisputed place where a smile and some small talk can lead to a no-strings-attached romp in the hay. Brass Monkey has a reputation as the hot spot for hook-ups on Ladies Night.

What is Waakao?

A website (www.waakao.com) that'll tell you what's going on in Taiwan, with event listings, party pictures and in-depth interviews with DJs, bands, musicians and articles on anyone else that is doing something cool in Taiwan. A one-stop site to learn all about Taiwan's nightlife activities, Waakao in Taiwanese means, roughly translated, 'amazing'.

events like the World Cup, naturally), for Maybe is a rock 'n' roll singalong bar with a full complement of English-language rock standards. Just don't call it karaoke!

Velvet Underground LIVE MUSIC
(地下絲絨; Dixià Sīróng; Map p44; www.velvet-underground.com.tw; 77 Wuchang St, Sec 2, 台北市武昌街二段77號; Ⓜ Ximen) New location, same cool underground rock club hosting pop, rock, electronic and metal bands from Taiwan and around the world. Draught Taiwan beer is two for NT$100, shots of mescal are NT$100 and some interestingly named cocktails are definitely among the cheapest drinks in town. Try a Kiss of Death – we don't know what's in it, but it's like being kissed by death. The owner, Jeff, is a definite rock 'n' roll dude. A very, very cool place to rock out and get very drunk.

Darts One SPORTS BAR
(Map p56; Lane 84, 19 Da'an Rd; ⏲7.30pm-2.30am; Ⓜ Zhongxiao Fuxing) Darts One gets its name from its five dartboards (NT$25 per game), but you don't need to be a darts fan to enjoy this chic Japanese-feeling bar. The house special, mojitos (NT$260), should help your aim.

W Bar LOUNGE
(Map p56; 15 Renai Rd, Sec 4; Ⓜ Zhongxiao Fuxing) Part of a three-storey lounge/restaurant cafe opened in 2005 by Taiwanese fashion designer Isabelle Wen, this 3rd-floor bar lounge oozes chic, with beaded glass curtains, high-backed wooden chairs and soft lighting. The 1st-floor cafe has a more casual, feminine vibe and a definite light safari theme. There's also a small clothing shop on the 1st floor selling Ms Wen's clothing and accessories. There's no cover charge, but there is a NT$350 spending minimum.

Bed SHISHA BAR
(水煙館; Shŭiyānguăn; Map p56; ☎2711-3733; 29 Alley 35, Lane 181, Zhongxiao E Rd, Sec 4, 台北市忠孝東路四段181巷35弄29號1樓; Ⓜ Zhongxiao

Dunhua) Lush couches, bumping techno music, imported hookahs and towers of alcohol all make you feel like you're in Bangkok or Saigon rather than just behind the main shopping drag that is Zhongxiao E Rd. Be sure not to miss the almost hourly go go dancing show staged just above the bar. Unisex bathrooms are a classy touch!

Brown Sugar JAZZ CLUB

(黑糖; Map p54; www.brownsugarlive.com; 101 Sungren Rd; ⏲noon-3am Sun-Thu, noon-4am Fri & Sat; Ⓜ Taipei City Hall) Taipei's pre-eminent club for jazz and soul, Brown Sugar hosts both local house musicians and guest musicians from around the world. Wednesday is Ladies Night, with free champagne from 9pm to 11pm.

Taipei Comedy Club COMEDY

(卡米地喜劇俱樂部; KămìdìXǐjù Jūlèbù; Map p54; ☎2764 5529; www.comedy.com.tw; 20 Lane 553, Zhongxiao E Rd, Sec 4; ⏲6pm-1am; Ⓜ Taipei City Hall) Taipei's only comedy club has a new location. Shows here can be a mixed bag of Chinese and English, funny and not so. But a night here is usually good for a few laughs. Admission is typically NT$250 and includes a free drink.

Marquee LOUNGE

(Map p54; ☎2729 5409; 16-1 Xinyi Rd, Sec 5; Ⓜ Taipei City Hall) High ceilings and lush lighting make this upper-end club just south of Taipei 101 the place to meet and greet the movers and shakers of Taiwan's young financial community, expat and native born. Opened in 2009, the Marquee also has a restaurant serving organic pasta dishes, burgers and salads, from 5.30pm to 1am (to 2am weekends).

Blue Note JAZZ CLUB

(藍調; lándiào; Map p46; 4F 171 Roosevelt Rd, Sec 3; ⏲7pm-1am; Ⓜ Taipower Building) Taipei's longest-running jazz club, Blue Note has been in the same location since 1978. The intimate lounge has live piano music on Friday and Saturday night. Drink choices run the gamut from beer (local and imported) to single malts and cocktails.

Chinese Opera & Theatre Venues

While some venues around town host touring Chinese-opera companies, there are regularly scheduled performances at the following places. Call or check websites for schedules.

Taipei Eye PERFORMANCE

(台北戲棚; Táiběi Xìpéng; Map p52; ☎2568 2677; www.taipeieye.com; 113 Zhongshan N Rd, Sec 2; tickets NT$880; ⏲8pm Thu-Sat; Ⓜ Shuanglian) Taipei Eye showcases Chinese opera together with other rotating performances, including puppet theatre and aboriginal dance. Audience members have the unique opportunity to watch the actors as they rehearse and put on make-up, wigs and costumes.

Puppetry Art Centre of Taipei PUPPETRY

(台北偶戲館; Táiběi Ǒuxìguǎn; Map p54; ☎2528 7955; www.pact.org.tw; 2-4 fl, 99 Civic Blvd, Sec 5; tickets NT$100; ⏲10am-5pm Tue-Sun; Ⓜ Sun Yat-Sen Memorial Hall) This theatre sits in the shadow of the extraterrestrial-looking Core Pacific Mall. Born of a love of puppetry, the puppets on display and those used for performances all come from the vast collection donated by Lin Jung-fu, chairman of the board of the Tai-Yuan Art & Culture Foundation.

Gu Ling Street Avant-garde Theatre PERFORMANCE

(Gūlǐngjiē Xiǎojùchǎng; Map p46; ☎2391 9393; www.glt.org.tw; 2 Lane 5, Guling St; Ⓜ Chiang Kai-shek Memorial Hall) This grassroots, community-based, avant-garde company presents music, drama, dance and children's theatre. The majority of the shows are not culturally specific, meaning that even those without Chinese-language skills will be able to follow. The building, which dates from 1906, was

DON'T MISS

TRADITIONAL ENTERTAINMENT, TAIWANESE STYLE

One of the greatest theatrical pleasures in Taiwan is found not in any theatre venue, but at adhoc performances given in temples, parks and courtyards from Keelung to Kenting. Sometimes opera, sometimes puppetry, sometimes a mix with other elements thrown in for good measure, these neighbourhood shows (usually performed in the Taiwanese dialect) are a great way to experience the flavour of Taiwan. They're generally held after sundown, but we can't tell you where to find these hidden cultural gems. If you're wandering in the early evening and come across a few dozen people gathered in front of a temple with a stage set-up, stick around.

NOT THE MTV YOU EXPECTED

Another interesting choice for watching films are the once-ubiquitous MTV houses. These have nothing to do with the music channel of the same name. Rather, a Taiwanese MTV is a place where, for about the same cost as a normal movie ticket, you can rent a DVD and watch it in a private room complete with a wide-screen TV, comfy couch and your choice of beverages. Favoured by teens looking for a quiet spot to make out on the cheap, most MTVs have a pretty decent collection of movies and are open 24 hours. Once found all over Taipei, there seem to be fewer and fewer every year. There are a few still open around Taipei and we know of at least two in Ximending. To find one, look for big signs with the words 'MTV'.

originally a police station, and during some performances the audience can see all the way through to the former jail cells. Check the website for upcoming performances.

National Theatre Concert Hall PERFORMANCE SPACE
(國立中正文化中心; guólì zhōng/zhòng zhēngwén huà zhōngxīn; Map p44; ☎3393 9888; www.ntch.edu.tw; Ⓜ Chiang Kai-shek Memorial Hall) Located inside Liberty Plaza (aka Chiang Kai-shek Memorial), the National Theatre Concert Hall hosts large-scale concerts and cultural events including dances, musicals, Chinese and Western opera and concerts of Chinese and Western classical and popular music. Renowned Taiwanese dance company Cloud Gate performs here several times a year.

Taipei Arena PERFORMANCE SPACE
(台北體育館; Táiběi Tǐyùguǎn; Map p56; www.taipeiarena.com.tw; Ⓜ Nanjing East Rd) Vast, cavernous and shaped like a flying saucer, the Taipei Arena hosts concerts, sporting events and noteworthy performances. Check out the website for the latest schedule.

Cinemas

Ximending is the place to head for a large variety of movies, where there's a cluster of movie theatres along Wucheng St. Other leading multiplexes are at Warner Village, the Core Pacific Living Mall and Breeze Center. Ticket prices tend to be between NT$220 and NT$280, but expect to pay more for 3-D or IMAX shows.

Taipei's most respected art-house cinema is **SPOT – Taipei Film House** (光點台北之家電影主題館; GuāngdiǎnTáiběi Diànyǐng Zhǔtíguǎn; Map p52; ☎2511 7786; www.spot.org.tw; 18 Zhongshan N Rd, Sec 2; tickets nonmember/member NT$220/170; Ⓜ Zhongshan), an excellent cinema with a bookshop and an indoor/outdoor cafe. The building, a landmark that dates back to 1925, was once the home of the US Ambassador.

Shopping

Taipei is a paradise for shoppers of all stripes. For those who like their shopping old school, the city has a plethora of streets and alleys chock-full of stores selling everything from antiques to religious items, herbal medicines to high-tech gadgetry. If you like your shopping new school, have we got malls for you. There are big malls, small malls, tall malls and even a mall shaped like a golf ball. As a general rule of thumb, bargaining is fine in outdoor places (the Jade Market, for example).

Taiwan Handicraft Mart CHINESE HANDICRAFTS
(台灣手工業推廣中心; Táiwān Shǒuyè Tuīguǎng Zhōngxīn; Map p44; ☎2393 3655; www.handicraft.org.tw; 1 Suzhou Rd; ⏲9am-5.30pm; Ⓜ NTU Hospital) Four storeys of clothing, jade, porcelain, ceramics, teasets, jewellery, scrolls, aboriginal artwork, paintings and prints are just highlights of the variety on offer here.

Jianguo Weekend Holiday Jade Market JADE, JEWELLERY
(建國假日玉市; Jiàrì Yùshì; Map p56; Ⓜ Da'An) Just north of Renai Rd, this is perhaps the largest market for jade and other semiprecious stones in Asia. The Jade Market is also a great place to buy jewellery, objets d'art both small and large, religious items and everything you might need to set up your own feng-shui practice back home (outside of actual knowledge of Chinese geomancy, of course).

Jianguo Weekend Holiday Flower Market FLOWERS, PLANTS, HANDICRAFTS
(建國假日花市; Jiàrì Huāshì; Map p56; Ⓜ Da'An) South of Renai Rd the Jade Market becomes the Holiday Flower Market, a veritable

cornucopia of plants, flowers and incredibly impressive bonsai trees. This market is also a good place to buy tea and tea supplies, as well as dried fruits, nuts and some locally grown organic produce.

Wu Fen Pu CLOTHING
(五分埔; Wǔfēnpǔ; Ⓜ Houshanpi) Easily the largest outdoor clothing market in Taipei, Wu Fen Pu encompasses several square blocks of lanes and alleys in eastern Taipei (not far from the Songshan Train Station). Here you'll find everything from the latest fashions to shoes to T-shirts with comically bad Chinglish slogans. Stores here tend to open around noon and stay open until 11pm or so, making it a good place to combine

SHOPPING MALLS, DISTRICTS & SPECIALITY STREETS

You'll have no difficulty finding cool places to spend your money as well as interesting stuff to spend it on. Here are just some of the places we recommend.

» **Sogo Department Store (Tianmu)** (太平洋崇光; tàipíngyáng chóng guāng; Map p62; ☎2834 5000; 77 Zhongshan N Road, Sec 6; Ⓜ Zhishan) Tianmu's newest department store offers a wide and very swank range of places to shop (you can even exchange foreign for local currency at the information counter if you've brought your passport). Brands like Gucci and Anna Sui fill the top floors, while the basement caters to the moneyed and hungry with a Godiva Chocolate, Cold Stone Creamery and Momi & Toy's Creperie. A local branch of the Citysuper Supermarket is just the place to sate your afternoon take-away caviar and foie gras craving.

» **Sogo Department Store (Dinghao)** (太平洋 Sogo 百貨; Tàipíngyáng SOGO Bǎihuò; Map p56; ☎7713 5555; 45 Zhongxiao E Rd, Sec 4; Ⓜ Zhongxiao Fuxing) Two branches of this department store anchor Taiwan's most famous shopping street in the Dinghao District (頂好商圈; Dǐnghǎo Shāngjuān). Zhongxiao E Rd is complete with shops both big and small, restaurants, cafes and nightspots.

» **Breeze Center** (微風廣場; Wéifēng Guǎngchǎng; Map p56; ☎6600 8888; 39 Fuxing N Rd, Sec 1; Ⓜ Zhongxiao Fuxing) Nine floors above ground and three below, the Breeze Center houses worldwide brands including Ralph Lauren, Coach, Marc Jacobs, Omega and Prada...and that's just on the ground floor. The top floors feature the Ambassador cinemas.

» **Warner Village** (華納威秀影城; Huá'nà Wēixiù Yǐngchéng; Map p54; 124 Songshou Rd; Ⓜ Taipei City Hall) The centrepiece of this mall is the 18-screen Warner Village cinema. The centre is busy all day (especially so on weekends). The food court is also popular.

» **Shin Kong Mitsukoshi Department Store** (Xīnguāng Sānyuè Bǎihuò; Map p54; ☎8780 1000; 11 Songshou Rd; Ⓜ Taipei City Hall) This is a ritzy shopping centre not far from Warner Village.

» **Dayeh Takashimaya** (大葉高島屋; Dàyè Gāodǎowū; Map p62; ☎2831 2345; 55 Zhongcheng Rd, Sec 2; Ⓜ Zhishan) Braving competition from nearby (and newer) Tianmu Sogo, Takashimaya is still the grand dame of Tianmu's department store scene. Just between us, its food court is still tops!

» **Miramar Entertainment Park** (Měilìhuá Bǎilèyuán; ☎2175 3456; 20 Jingye 3rd Rd, Neihu; Ⓜ Jiannan Rd) Part mall, part amusement park, all fun. This entertainment facility in the Neihu suburb northeast of the city boasts the world's second-largest Ferris wheel, located on its top floor. There are panoramic views, and of course, plenty of things to eat in Miramar's fine food court.

Some other speciality streets in Taipei are Aiguo E Rd, across from the Chiang Kai-shek Memorial Hall, where you'll find wedding dresses and other items matrimonial. Xiuan Rd, west of Longshan Temple is – naturally – a hot spot for religious items. If it's great deals on cameras you're looking for, check out Hankou St, southwest of Taipei Main Station. And if you're planning to do any camping, river tracing or other outdoor activities, there's a cluster of **camping stores** (Map p44) on the west side of Zhongshan N Rd, Sec 1, just north of the intersection of Zhongxiao E Rd.

with a visit to the Raohe Street Market just up the road.

Guanghua Market COMPUTERS, ELECTRONICS

(光華電腦市場; Guānghuá Diànnǎo Shìchǎng; Map p44; cnr Civic Blvd & Jinshan Rd; Ⓜ Zhongxiao Xinsheng) This is a cyberpunk's paradise: numerous blocks of stores, alleys and underground malls that are to electronics what a night market is to clothing and foods. It has software, hardware, laptops, peripherals, mobile phones and gadgets of all kinds. Though the area still retains its old-school street-shop flavour, the new four-storey indoor mall on the corner of Civic Blvd and Jinshan Rd is a bit less chaotic than the outdoor shops surrounding it.

Nova Computer Arcade COMPUTERS, ELECTRONICS

(NOVA 資訊廣場; NOVA Zīxùn Guǎngchǎng; Map p44; ☎2381 4833; 100 Guangjian Rd; Ⓜ Taipei Main Station) Across from Taipei Main Station, this arcade has about 130 shops and booths dealing in computers, components, digital cameras, mobile phones and just about any electronic peripherals you can imagine.

Ten Shang's Tea Company TEA

(天样茗茶; Tiānsháng Míngchá; Map p52; ☎2542 6542; 156 Jilin Rd, 吉林路156號; ⏰9.30am-10.30pm Mon-Fri, 10.30am-10.30pm Sat & Sun; Ⓜ Zhongshan) Hailing from a tea-growing mountain community in central Taiwan's Nantou, Mr and Mrs Chang have been selling organically grown oolong teas from all over Taiwan for a quarter of a century. Visitors are welcome to come in and chat over a pot or two of their exquisite high-mountain tea while shopping for tea and supplies. The Changs' new location is around the corner from their previous one on Nanjing E Rd, Sec 2.

Jame May KITSCH

(津美外銷藝品; jīnměi wàixiāo yìpǐn; Map p56; ☎2741 6632; 41 Lane 190, Dunhua S Rd, Sec 1, 敦化南路一段190巷41號1樓; ⏰10.30am-10.30pm; Ⓜ Zhongxiao Fuxing) Weird and wonderful best describes this cluttered basement knick-knack store just down the block from Pho Hoa Vietnamese restaurant. Selling everything from porcelain dolls to kites to fake fossilised dragon bones, this shop is worth a visit if you're in the neighbourhood.

Caves Books BOOKS

(敦煌書局; Dūnhuáng Shūjú) Tianmu (Map p62; ☎2874 2199; 5 Lane 38, Tianyu St; Bus 220); Zhongshan (Map p52; ☎2599 1169; 54-3 Zhongshan N Rd, Sec 3; Ⓜ Yuanshan) Frayed and fading like a long-owned paperback, Caves was once one of the only places in Taipei where Westerners could find a decent selection of English books. Nowadays, although Caves is still among the best places to find books on both teaching English and on learning Chinese, selection-wise Caves has been well outdone by Taipei's newer and flashier generation of booksellers.

Eslite BOOKS

(誠品; Chéngpǐn; Map p56; ☎2775 5977; 245 Dunhua S Rd; Ⓜ Zhongxiao Dunhua) Eslite is Taipei's most renowned bookshop, with locations all over town. The flagship Dunhua S Rd location is the first place most locals look for foreign-language books, particularly on travel. Students at NTNU or Shida might find the branch at **Gongguan** (☎2362 6312; cnr Roosevelt & Xinsheng Rds; Ⓜ Gongguan) more convenient. Lonely Planet guides (in Chinese and English) are definitely in stock.

ℹ Information

Emergency

Police ☎110

Central District police station (☎2556 6007; 33 Chengde Rd, Sec 2) Has dedicated English-speaking staff.

Fire & Ambulance ☎119

English-language directory assistance ☎106

National Immigration Agency (Map p44; ☎2388 9393; www.immigration.gov.tw; 15 Guangzhou St; Ⓜ Xiaonanmen) For visa extensions and other immigration-related enquiries. You can also dial '1999' for bilingual service and general enquiries.

Internet Access

It should come as no surprise that the capital city of an island whose main export is semiconductors is pretty much totally wired when it comes to internet access. Nearly all hotel rooms in the city have in-room broadband, and many have wi-fi in the lobby. Internet cafes are around, but as Taipeiers become more wired and the city becomes more wireless, these seem to be a dying breed. Neighbourhoods surrounding universities are good places to find internet cafes (they'll mostly be filled with kids playing games). Expect to pay around NT$60 per hour. If you happen to be travelling with a laptop or another wireless device, you're pretty well set; when it comes to wi-fi access, cities don't get much friendlier than Taipei. We've noted bars and restaurants offering free wi-fi. For paid wi-fi, you can buy stored-value wireless cards at 7-Eleven. The **National Central Library** (NCL; 中央國家圖書館; Guójiā Túshūguǎn; Map p44; 20 Zhongshan S Rd; ⌚9am-9pm Tue-Fri, 9am-5pm Sat & Sun; Ⓜ Chiang Kai-shek Memorial Hall) across from Chiang Kai-shek Memorial is a good place to check your email for free.

Internet Resources & Blogs

http://taiwan.net.tw Taiwan Tourism Bureau

http://forumosa.com/taiwan & www.tealit.com Websites for expats living in Taiwan

www.culture.tw Taiwan Culture Portal

www.cwb.gov.tw/eng/index.htm Central Weather Bureau

www.taiwanderful.net General website for visitors and residents in English

http://a-gu.blogspot.com/index.html That's Impossible! political blog from Taiwan

http://blog.taiwan-guide.org A plethora of essays and articles about Taiwan, from David on Formosa

http://hungryintaipei.blogspot.com Restaurant reviews galore from a hungry girl

www.waakao.com Information on nightlife around the island

http://taiwanreview.nat.gov.tw Website of popular magazine covering Taiwanese issues

Left Luggage

The basement floor of Taipei Main Station has several rows of coin-operated lockers, and so does the food court in the Shingong Tower across the street and the SOGO department store. Taipei International Airport has small/large lockers for NT$80/120 per 24 hours, with a six-day limit. Most hostels also offer a left-luggage service.

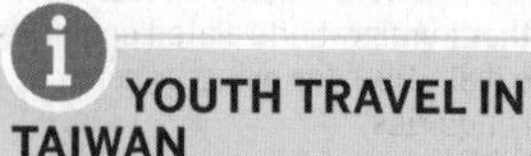

YOUTH TRAVEL IN TAIWAN

Youth Travel in Taiwan is a government-run organisation whose mission is to attract international travellers from 15 to 30 and create a user-friendly environment for them. Among the ways it facilitates youth travel is by providing discount cards to young travellers, budget rail tickets, advice on trekking and discount accommodations. It even offers loaner mobile phones. Check out http://youthtravel.tw or visit the **Taipei Youth Volunteer Centre** (1st fl, 31 Zhongxiao E Rd, Sec 1; Ⓜ Shandao Temple) for more details.

Media

Taiwan has 2½ daily English-language newspapers. The *Taipei Times* tends to lean towards the Democratic Progressive Party (DPP), while the *China Post* tends to lean towards the Kuomintang (KMT). Both papers are available at any convenience store. Formerly known as the *China News*, the *Taiwan News* is still published on paper, but it's rarely seen outside the libraries.

If you're after a steady stream of nonthreatening English-language pop tunes punctuated with light banter, traffic reports and news on the hour, then Taiwan's International Community Radio Taipei (ICRT; 100.7FM, 576AM) is the station for you. ICRT is Taiwan's only English-language radio station and may be single-handedly responsible for making Taiwan's youth think that people in the West are actually still listening to ABBA and Hootie and the Blowfish.

Several free magazines published in English have loads of useful Taipei-specific information. These include *Wow Taipei* (published by the city government) and *Taiwan Fun* (www.taiwanfun.com), which has a great city map.

Medical Services

Almost every hospital in Taipei has English speakers on staff; most also have an English-speaking information-booth attendant close to the entrance.

Heping Hospital (Map p44; ☎2192 6068; 33 Zhonghua Rd, Sec 2; Ⓜ Xiaonanmen)

Mackay Hospital (馬偕醫院; Mǎjiē Yīyuàn; Map p52; ☎2543 3535; 92 Zhongshan N Rd, Sec 2; Ⓜ Shuanglian)

Veterans General Hospital (榮民總醫院; Róngmín Zǒng Yīyuàn; ☎2875 7346; 201 Shipai Rd, Sec 2; Ⓜ Shipai)

Adventist Hospital (臺安醫院; Táiān Yīyuàn; Map p56; ☎2771 8151; 424 Bade Rd, Sec 2; Ⓜ Zhongxiao Fuxing)

Hospital of Traditional Chinese Medicine (臺北市立聯合醫院中醫門診中心; Táiběi Shìlì Liánhé Yīyuàn Zhōngyī Ménzhěn Zhōngxīn; Map p44; ☎2388 7088; 100 Kunming St; ⌚8-11.30am & 1-4.30pm Mon-Fri, 5-8.30pm Tue-Fri, 8-11.30am Sat; Ⓜ Ximen) If you're interested in checking out traditional medicine, this hospital has English-speaking doctors.

STD Clinic (Táiběi Shìlì Xìngbìng Fángzhì Sǔo; ☎2370 3739) Located in the same building as the Hospital of Traditional Chinese Medicine.

MEDICAL TOURISM IN TAIWAN

While Taiwan isn't quite the medical tourism mecca that Bangkok is, an increasing number of travellers are choosing to stick around for the excellent-quality (and inexpensive, relative to many Western countries) medical and dental care available. The government-sponsored website www.medicaltravel.org.tw lists a number of hospitals, practitioners and costs.

Money

Most Taiwanese banks are connected to either the Cirrus or Plus network and usually accept foreign cards from aligned banks. Many McDonald's and 7-Elevens also have ATMs. The ATM on the ground floor of the Nova Computer Arcade (p87) across from Taipei Main Station accepts foreign cards, as do all HSBC branches (there's one right next to exit 8 at Taipei Main Station). Most Taiwanese ATMs ask you to choose a language before entering your PIN. See p369 for further information. Your best bet for exchanging money is to do so in the airport, as unlike Hong Kong, Taipei lacks currency-exchange kiosks.

Post

North Gate Post Office (台北郵局; Map p44; Zhongxiao W Rd; Ⓜ Taipei Main Station) Taipei's main post office is southwest of Taipei Main Station. Come here to claim poste restante packages. There are post offices throughout the city, easy to find because of their bright-green facades and large signs in English. Post-office workers can generally understand a bit of English and are overall pretty helpful.

Tourist Information

There are seven Taipei Visitor's Information Centre booths scattered around the city, all with the usual assortment of maps and pamphlets, stacks of free magazines and generally helpful English-speaking staff. The four centres that are easiest to find are located on the main floor of Taipei Main Station, by the exits of the Beitou and Ximen stations, and inside the East Metro Mall that runs under Chunghsiao Rd. Check out http://taipeitravel.net for the locations of other centres, plus loads of useful tips.

Travel Agencies

There are a number of travel agencies located just south of the Taipei Songshan Airport by the junction of Minquan E and Dunhua N Rds and English-speaking agents advertise in all of the English-language newspapers. Low advertised prices without taxes and fees are often quoted, so clarify the total price before you buy any tickets. If you need to make a visa trip to avoid overstaying a landing or 60-day visa, the three cheapest spots to fly to are generally Manila, Okinawa and Hong Kong.

ℹ Getting There & Away

Air

International flights leave from Taoyuan Airport (www.taoyuanairport.gov.tw), 40km from downtown Taipei. Domestic flights (and some flights to China and Japan) leave from Taipei Songshan Airport (www.tsa.gov), located in the city itself.

One service that can help you arrange flights and travel within Taiwan and to China is **ezTravel** (☎2501 0808; www.eztravel.com.tw), which has offices all over the islands and one in Taipei Main Station, directly across from the information counter west of the TRA ticket counter. The following are sample prices and durations for one-way tickets to cities in China.

CITY	PRICE (NT$)	DURATION
Beijing	9900	3hr
Shanghai	8500	1hr 30min
Guangzhou	6199	1hr 45 min
Xian	9000	4hr

Bus

Taipei city is serviced by three major bus stations. Directly to the west of Taipei Main Station on Zhongxiao Rd is **Western Terminal A** (台北西站A棟; Táiběi xīzhàn A dòng; Map p44), which has buses to Taoyuan Airport, Taoyuan, Chungli, Keelung, Jinshan and other destinations (mostly) in northern Taiwan.

Next to this is **Western Terminal B** (台北西站B棟; Táiběi xīzhàn B dòng; Map p44). Serviced exclusively by Taiwan's government-run Kuo Kuang Bus Company (國光客運; Guóguāng kèyùn), this terminal offers buses to southern destinations like Taichung, Nantou, Sun Moon Lake, Tainan, Kaohsiung and Pingtung.

Directly to the north of the train station, the new multistorey **Taipei North Bus Terminal** (台北轉運站; Táiběi Zhuǎnyùnzhàn; Map p44) offers a wide variety of luxury buses to destinations around Taiwan, including Hsinchu and Taichung.

A fourth station in the east, next to Taipei City Hall, was being completed during the time of research, and should offer service around the island.

Bus schedules can change, and competition among companies on popular routes is fierce. The table below is for reference purposes only.

DESTINATION	FARE (NT$)	DURATION	STATION
Hsinchu	130	1hr 40min	North
Jinshan	120	1hr 30min	Western Terminal A
Kaohsiung	400	5hr	Western Terminal B, North
Keelung	90	1hr 10min	Western Terminal A
Sun Moon Lake	460	3hr 30min	Western Terminal B
Taichung	220	4hr 30min	Western Terminal B, North

High Speed Rail (HSR)

High Speed Rail trains begin at 6.30am and run until 10.12pm (11pm to Taichung). Fares below are for standard cars during peak hours. Prices are cheaper during discount hours – before 7am and after 7pm. Tickets can be purchased at the HSR counter and automated kiosk at Basement Level 1 of Taipei Main Station, and can also be purchased at automated kiosks at some convenience stores. Booking can also be done online at www.thsrc.com.tw/en.

DESTINATION	FARE (NT$)	DURATION
Chiayi	915	1hr 23min
Hsinchu	245	36min
Taichung	700	1hr
Tainan	1350	1hr 40min
Taoyuan	160	20min
Zuoying (Kaohsiung)	1490	1½-2hr

Standard Trains (TRA)

Taiwan's trains are clean, convenient and nearly always on schedule. Unlike the HSR, TRA train stations are usually in the centre of town. The following schedules represent prices and speeds for the local trains. TRA's website is www.railway.gov.tw.

DESTINATION	FARE (NT$)	DURATION
North/East Line		
Fulong	84	1hr 50min
Hualien	284	2hr 5min
Ilan	141	1hr 40min
Keelung	44	34min
Taitung	606	5hr 45min
West Line		
Chiayi	386	3hr 22min
Hsinchu	116	1hr 7min
Kaohsiung	651	4hr 55min
Taichung	141	1hr 40min
Tainan	475	4hr
Taoyuan	44	33min

Getting Around

To/From the Airport

Two airports serve Taipei. Taiwan Taoyuan International is about 50km west of the city centre and Songshan Airport is just north of the city centre. International flights are handled at the former, and domestic (as well as some flights to mainland China and Japan) at the latter.

A taxi from Taiwan Taoyuan International Airport to the city centre is about NT$1200, and a bus between NT$90 and NT$125. Songshan Airport now has its own MRT station.

If you're leaving Taiwan directly from Taipei, taking a bus to Taoyuan International Airport from the centre of town is probably your cheapest bet. Buses to Taoyuan International Airport leave from the bus terminal just west of Taipei Main Station; fares are between NT$90 and NT$140. The trip takes between 55 and 70 minutes depending on traffic. Taiwan's government-run **Kuo Guang Bus Company** (國光客運; Guóguāng kèyùn; ☎0800 010138) runs airport buses from 4.30am to 10.50pm. **Airbus** (大有巴士; Dàyǒu Bāshì; ☎0800 088626; www.airbus.com.tw) is a slightly more comfortable option.

Both of the above companies also pick up passengers from in front of the Sheraton Taipei, the Grand Formosa Regent and the Minquan W Rd MRT station. Kuo Kuang also offers an express service between Taoyuan and Songshan Airports.

Bus

Each MRT station has a map marking bus stops in its vicinity. If you can't find the map, just ask the attendant. Most buses have digital signs in Chinese and English. Fares are NT$15 on most routes within the city centre, double or triple on longer routes. If the sign over the fare box reads 上車 (*shàngchē*), that means you pay getting on and 下車 (*xiàchē*) means you pay getting off.

There are detailed maps by the exits of each station that show the surrounding neighbourhood. As with spelling, map orientation is not standardised in Taipei, so don't be surprised to see maps on which 'up' is east, west or even south.

Car

An international driver's licence is required to rent a car. One car-rental service with English-speaking staff is **VIP Car Rental** (☎2713-1111; www.vipcar.com.tw; 148 Minchuan E Rd, Sec 3; per day from NT$2000).

Subway (MRT)

Clean and convenient, trains run from 6am until 1am. Most places within the city centre are within about a 20-minute walk of an MRT station. Announcements and signs are in Chinese and English. Fares for each destination are noted in both English and Chinese on a map beside the machine. Coins and bills are accepted and change is provided.

Taxi

The base fare is NT$70 for the first 1.5km plus NT$5 for each 300m thereafter. After midnight, the base fare is NT$70 for the first 1.2km plus NT$5 for each 250m thereafter.

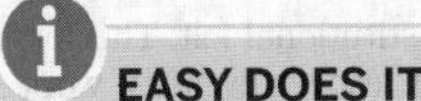

EASY DOES IT

If you're going to spend any length of time in Taipei, buy yourself an EasyCard, the stored-value card of the Taipei Rapid Transit Association (TRTA). Adult/child EasyCards sell for NT$500/300, of which NT$100 is a deposit. The rest is valid on both buses and subways, and will even get you on the train within Taipei County (to Keelung, for example). When you're done using your EasyCard, simply take it to an MRT ticket booth, where your deposit plus any remaining value will be refunded.

AROUND TAIPEI

Not to put too fine a point on it, but one of the many reasons for our boundless love of Taipei's MRT is that it has made once-difficult places a mere subway ride away. Even mountain spots such as Yangmingshan (p94), Maokong (p103) and Wulai (p111) are much easier to get to from the city centre thanks to the mass transit system.

Beitou 北投

Beneath the soil of Taiwan bubbles a veritable cauldron of sulphurous water, and though most hot-spring resorts are well away from major urban areas, Taipei's Beitou (Běitóu, sometimes spelled Peitou) is a welcome exception. Locals and travellers alike come here for a quick soak in the *wēnquán* (hot springs), whose sulphurous waters have lured pleasure-soakers for centuries.

Nowadays Beitou offers dozens of bathing options, from simply soaking your feet in the roadside creeks (cost: nothing) to glamorous private baths in ritzy high-rise resorts (cost: significantly more). The latter might include the use of several public pools, with optional massages and multicourse meals. Many places offer packages combining meals and hot-spring visits. There are also public hot springs with cheap admission and more downmarket private baths that won't set you back more than a few hundred NT$.

Orientation

Inside Beitou Park are the Hot Spring Museum and the newly built and ecofriendly **Beitou Library** (Map p93; admission free; ⏰8.30am-9pm Tue-Sat, 9am-5pm Sun & Mon), which is a great place to lounge around or check your email for free. Just past the library is where you'll find the public hot springs. The park is bordered to the north by Zhongshan Rd, where you'll find the Ketagalan Culture Centre and the route towards the Di-re Valley, the source of the many resorts' hot springs. Where Guangming and Zhongshan Rds converge at the far end of the park, you can continue along the mountain roads to some deluxe resorts. Most of these have shuttle buses to and from Xinbeitou MRT station.

Resorts and hotels are located in the streets and alleys around Beitou Park, with some of the more exclusive ones further up the mountainside away from town.

Sights & Activities

Outdoor Public Bath PUBLIC HOT SPRINGS

(公共露天溫泉; Gōnggòng Lùtiān Wēnquán; Map p93; ☎2893 7014; Zhongshan Rd; weekday/weekend NT$20/40; ⏰8.30-11.15am, noon-2.45pm, 3.30-6.15pm & 7-9.45pm) Next to soaking your feet on the side of the road, Beitou's co-ed outdoor public bath is one of the cheapest options in town. Bathing au naturel is not permitted, so bring a swimsuit or buy one there. This public hot spring boasts a number of pools ranging in temperature from comfortably warm to damn near scalding. There's also a frigid pool off to the side for those who enjoy a good constitutional jolt. The springs can get crowded, especially after work on chilly days, or on the weekends. If you want to have a bit more space, go during the day on a weekday, but even this is no guarantee.

An older gentleman is employed by the baths as some sort of 'hot-spring cop' – in addition to preventing horseplay, his job is to keep people from soaking only the lower half of their bodies in the pools. (According to Chinese medicine – or him, at least – this is unhealthy.) If you're standing in any of the pools, or – heaven forbid – sitting on the edge soaking only your feet, he'll come over and chastise you. (Seriously folks, you can't make this stuff up.)

Asia Pacific Resort RESORT

(北投亞太溫泉生活館; Běitóu Yǎtài Wēnquán Shēnghuóguǎn; Map p93; ☎2898 2088; www.apresort.com.tw; 21 Yinguang Lane; ⏲8.30am-1am Mon-Fri, 8.30am-2am Sat & Sun) At the other end of the soaking spectrum is the Asia Pacific Resort, a magnificent bathing/dining/meeting complex with Japanese raked-sand gardens and indoor and outdoor baths, including white-water mineral baths. Guests can rent private rooms with both indoor and outdoor hot-spring baths; some of these feature tea service and others have set-ups for hot-pot dining. Pricing begins at NT$500 for a three-hour soak, but there are other options available, laid out nicely on the trilingual website.

FREE **Di-re Valley** SCENIC AREA

(地熱谷; Dìrè Gǔ; Hell Valley; Map p93; ⏲9am-5pm Tue-Sun) Throughout the Japanese occupation this geothermal valley was considered one of the country's great scenic wonders and a visit by the Japanese crown prince sealed Beitou's reputation as the hot-spring destination of Taiwan. A walk through the valley's 3500 sq metres of bubbling waters and sulphurous gases leaves no question as to the origins of its name. These pools are the source of many of the hot springs used by the resorts in town, but don't try to soak in any of them here. In some spots they reach 90°C, and we'd prefer not to have to use your tragic death by scalding as a warning for future travellers.

FREE **Beitou Hot Spring Museum** MUSEUM

(北投溫泉博物館; Běitóu Wēnquán Bówùguǎn; Map p93; ☎2893 9981; 2 Zhongshan Rd; ⏲9am-5pm Tue-Sun) On the site of one of the original Japanese-era hot-spring baths, this handsome museum mixes a Victorian-style exterior with a variety of other architectural designs inside. Upstairs, wooden verandahs surround a large Japanese-style tatami room where bathers once took tea and relaxed after their baths. The former baths downstairs feel almost Roman in their construction. Don't let being asked to remove your shoes for admission fool you into getting your hopes up; there is no actual bathing allowed at this museum.

Taiwan Folk Arts Museum MUSEUM

(台灣民俗北投文物館; Táiwān Mínsú Běitóu Wénwùguǎn; Map p93; ☎2891 2318; www.folkartsm.org.tw; 32 Youya Rd; admission NT$120; ⏲10am-5.30pm Tue-Sun) Though the museum only opened in 2008, the building itself, an old wooden structure, has a history dating back to the Japanese occupation. Today the Taiwan Folk Arts Museum displays artwork from Taiwanese indigenous people as well as historical relics of traditional Taiwanese and Japanese folk culture. The museum also has a quaint Japanese-style restaurant offering tea and set meals from NT$580 to NT$880.

FREE **Ketagalan Culture Centre** MUSEUM

(凱達格蘭文化館; Kǎidágélán Wénhuàguǎn; Map p93; ☎2898 6500; 3-1 Zhongshan Rd; ⏲9am-5pm Tue-Sun) This multistorey centre explores Taiwan's aboriginal culture with exhibits, performances stages and various seasonal exhibits on other floors. Although signage is in Chinese, English-language leaflets explain Taiwan's tribes in detail.

Sleeping & Eating

All of Beitou's hotels have in-room hot-spring tubs.

Broadway Hotel HOTEL $$

(百樂匯溫泉飯店; Bǎilèhuì Wēnquán Fàndiàn; Map p93; ☎2895 6658; www.broadway-hotspring-hotel.com.tw; 99 Wenquan Rd, Beitou, 北投區溫泉路99號; d NT$3000) One of the newest of Beitou's hot-spring resorts, the gorgeous Broadway has a wide variety of room types, ranging from Japanese tatami rooms to Taiwanese to more Western-style rooms. There are a number of common areas furnished with mahogany Chinese tea tables, sculptures and other works of art. The Japanese-style rooms, with their stone hot tubs and beautiful mountain views, are especially lovely.

SweetMe Hot Spring Resort HOTEL $$$

(水美溫泉會館; Shuǐměi Wēnquán Huìguǎn; Map p93; ☎2898 3838; www.sweetme.com.

Beitou

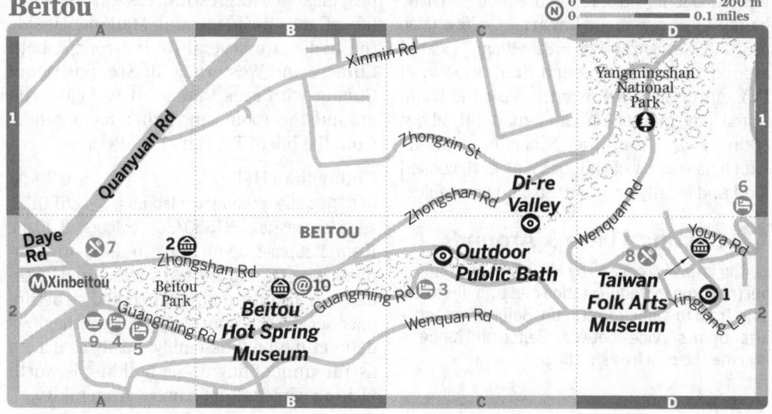

tw; 224 Guangming Rd; d/tw incl breakfast from NT$5600/6200) Across from Beitou Park and an easy walk from Xinbeitou MRT station, the SweetMe has an odd name but beautiful facilities. It opened in 2003 as the latest incarnation of an older, high-rise resort. There are indoor and outdoor baths, extensive spa and dining facilities and Japanese touches throughout. Even standard guest rooms have handsome bathtubs. The SweetMe also has public facilities, separated by gender.

Chyuan Du Spring Resort HOTEL $$
(泉都溫泉會館; Quándū Wēnquán Huìguǎn; Map p93; ☎2896 0077; www.cdhotel.com.tw; 220 Guangming Rd; d/tw incl breakfast from NT$2680/4140; wi-fi) A quick walk from the Xinbeitou station, the Chyuan Du is a decent midprice option for visiting fun-seekers, with free in-room Wii games, wi-fi, flat-screen TVs, and yes, in-room hot springs. Weekday discounts (NT$1940 for a double) almost drop this place into a lower budget category.

Whispering Pine Inn HISTORIC $$
(吟松閣溫泉旅館; Yíngsōnggé wēnquán Lǚguǎn; Map p93; ☎2895 1531; 21 Youya Rd, 北投區幽雅路21號; d NT$3600) More than 80 years old, this Japanese-style inn (once the last residence of pre-mission Kamikaze pilots) is a registered historic landmark. Beautiful, original woodwork, indoor stone baths and Japanese-style tatami rooms make it worth visiting, though for the price you'll get more luxury at a newer resort.

While Beitou is better known for relaxation than cuisine, there are plenty of places in the area to eat. In addition to the usual and easy-to-spot fast-food joints by the station, there's a fine **Sushi Express** (Zhēngxiān Guānxì; Map p93; 32 Zhongshan Rd; dishes NT$30; ⏲lunch & dinner) directly across from the station, where you can fill up on sushi cheaply. A more serene (and upmarket) choice is **Yuan Yuan Yuan** (緣源園; Yuán Yuán Yuán; Map p93; 2 Lane 5, Youya St, 北投區幽雅路5巷2號; meals from NT$400; ⏲10.30am-8pm), which offers a great traditional Taiwanese beef hot pot for NT$1000 (serves two to three). There's a Starbucks right under the Chyuan Du Spring

Beitou

Top Sights
- Beitou Hot Spring Museum ... B2
- Di-re Valley ... C2
- Outdoor Public Bath ... C2
- Taiwan Folk Arts Museum ... D2

Sights
1. Asia Pacific Resort ... D2
2. Ketagalan Cultural Centre ... A2

Sleeping
3. Broadway Hotel ... C2
4. Chyuan Du Spring Resort ... A2
5. SweetMe Hotspring Resort ... A2
6. Whispering Pine Inn ... D1

Eating
7. Sushi Express ... A2
8. Yuan Yuan Yuan ... D2

Drinking
9. Lavazza Coffee ... A2

Information
10. Beitou Library ... B2

Resort, but if you like good coffee you'll be happy to know about **Lavazza Coffee** (Map p93; 218 Guangming Rd; ⊙8am-10pm) located around the corner (behind Starbucks). And DIY enthusiasts will want to visit the traditional day market on Gongguan Rd (about 500m away from the Xinbeitou station), which has plenty of stalls serving both cooked food and locally grown fruits and vegetables.

Getting There & Around

Beitou is easily reached by MRT. Take the Danshui (red) line to Beitou station and transfer to a spur train to Xinbeitou station. Before 7am and after 9pm, services between Beitou and Xinbeitou may be by a free shuttle bus.

Yangmingshan National Park 陽明山國家公園

How fortunate Taipei is to have this national park (Yángmíngshān Guójiā Gōngyuán; www.ymsnp.gov.tw) at its doorstep, complete with majestic mountains, hot springs, tall grasses, forests of bamboo and broadleaf trees and some handsome lodgings and restaurants. Among its 1200-plus species of plants, the area is particularly known for rhododendrons, azaleas and Japanese cherry trees. An excellent escape from the city for hikers, hot-spring lovers, birdwatchers, or just about anyone getting away from it all.

The centrepiece of the park is **Cisingshan** (Qīxīngshān), northern Taiwan's tallest peak at 1120m. Yangmingshan bus station (陽明山國家公園公車站) is near the south entrance of the park, and from here you can catch a shuttle bus around the park. There are some cafes and convenience stores near the bus station and nearby Jianguo St turns into an adhoc food festival on nice days.

Yangmingshan tends to be a bit cooler than central Taipei, and afternoon thunderstorms are common, especially in summer. Roads further up and towards Jinshan can often be foggy, making for treacherous night driving conditions.

Sights

Yangming Shuwu HISTORICAL SITE
(陽明書屋; Yángmíng Shūwū; Yangming Villa; Map p94; ☎2861 1444; adult/concession NT$50/30; ⊙tours 9am & 1.30pm Tue-Sun) One of Chiang Kai-shek's 15 villas, Yangming Shuwu was the last and the grandest. Its valley setting makes for quite a sight, especially in March when its gardens are in full bloom. It also provides an interesting insight into the life of the president and Madame. Inside the house are several dining rooms, both Chinese and Western, a life-size portrait of Chiang with eyes that seem to follow you around the room, and other memorabilia from the life of Taiwan's last dictator.

Chungshan Hall HISTORICAL
(中山樓; zhōngshān lóu; Map p94; ☎2861 0123; adult/concession NT$50/30; ⊙tours 8.30am, 10am, 1.30pm & 3pm) Built in 1965 to commemorate Dr Sun Yat-sen's centennial birthday, this beautiful circular-roofed structure once served as a convention site for the now-defunct national assembly. Easily as ornate as Yangming Shuwu, the building is worth visiting while taking a break from hiking.

Activities

Hiking

Hiking is the main thing people do in Yangmingshan and no matter what else brings

you here (birdwatching, flower gazing, hot springing), it's more than likely it will take some hiking to get you there. Serious hikers can spend days exploring dozens of amazing trails here, some of which can be done in a couple of hours and others which can take up the day. Richard Saunders' *Yangmingshan The Guide,* available in bookstores in Taiwan, as well as through the **Community Service Centre** (Map p62; ☎2836 8134; www.community.com.tw; 25 Lane 290, Zhongshan N Rd, Sec 6; Ⓜ Mingde), outlines hikes both short and long in loving detail.

Casual visitors will have no problem finding trails. There are English signposts and maps with 'you are here' symbols all over the park, and you can pick up maps with trail instructions at the **National Park Visitor Centre** (陽明山遊客服務中心; Map p94). One popular hike on Cisingshan starts at Xiaoyoukeng, northwest of Cisingshan, and goes to the top of the mountain. The hike takes you past the brimstone-reeking sulphur pits for which the region is famous; it's really quite a sight (and aroma). There are high-plains buffalo (mind the cow pies!) and the panoramic view is stunning when the fog lifts.

Yangmingshan is also an excellent spot for cycling, both on- and off-road (though racing bikes seem more popular). The sight of cyclists climbing the roads leading to the park (often moving faster than the stop-and-go traffic) can be quite inspiring.

To get to the trailhead, take minibus 15 from the Shilin MRT station to the end of the line. From here, signs are clearly marked.

Birdwatching

Yangmingshan is definitely on the international birders circuit, being one of the best places to see endemic species such as the Taiwan blue magpie (an adorable bird with a tail almost twice its body length). The optimum time for birdwatching is early in the morning, with early autumn being the best season. The **Wild Bird Society of Taipei** (Map p56; ☎2325 9190; www.wbst.org.tw; 3 Lane 160, Fuxing S Rd, Sec 22; Ⓜ Technology Building) organises tours from its Taipei office.

Hot Springs

Ma Cao Hot Springs HOT SPRINGS
(馬槽花藝村; Măcáo Huāyìcūn; Map p94; ☎2861 6351; admission NT$150; ⏲24hr) Way over on the other side of Yangmingshan National Park close to Jinshan, this wonderful old-school hot-spring resort located down a windy road is difficult to find on a clear day, and even more difficult to find on a foggy, rainy night. Yet it is precisely on such a night that you'll appreciate soaking in pools ranging from scalding to warm to near ice, protected from the rain by a Japanese-style wooden canopy, as the lights from the nearby Taiwan Strait twinkle through the fog. Ma Cao brings relaxation to a new level with its mudbaths, beautiful woodwork and two electric hot-spring massage pools (yes, you read that right; small jolts piped into the water cause muscle contractions similar to those Bruce Lee used to train with).

The springs are au naturel and separated by sexes, but you can also rent your own small room with a tub.

Open 24/7, Ma Cao also has an on-site restaurant serving delicious hot-spring standards such as chicken hot pot, sautéed wild vegetables and other Taiwanese dishes.

The easiest way to get to Ma Cao is to bus it to Yangmingshan and then take a taxi for about NT$400. (If you've got a GPS unit, you'll find it at N25.11.338, E121.34.163). Alternatively, you could take a bus to Jinshan and taxi from there, but you'll only end up saving about NT$200.

Calla Young Garden Resort HOT SPRINGS RESORT
(陽明山水溫泉會館; Yángmíng Shānshuǐ Wēnquán Hùiguǎn; ☎2408 0001; www.calla.com.tw; Jinshan Township, Chonghe Village, Linkou 33, 金山鄉重和村林口33-3號; admission NT$400) This new hot-spring resort is tops in every way, from the outdoor co-ed pools offering varying temperatures for soaking (with amazing views of Yangmingshan to the south and Jinshan and the Taiwan Strait to the north), to the semi-enclosed sex-separated multi-temperature pools. All this makes Calla especially worth the trip, but what puts the resort over the top is its restaurant, with an excellent chef who excels at creating Japanese/Chinese/Western fusion dishes that may well be one of the culinary highlights of your Taiwan experience. Though you can come here just for a soak (or spend the night for that matter; check the website for Calla's various package deals), the best bet here is to come early evening for the meal-and-soak special (NT$800 per person, NT$900 on weekends), which entitles you to an amazing six-course meal and full bathing privileges. Calla is on the main Yangmingshan/Jinshan Rd, about 4km past the Ma Cao Hot Springs turn-off.

THE TIGERS OF DATUNSHAN *ROBERT KELLY*

Most of Taiwan's big cat species have unfortunately become extinct but one species of the genus *Parantica*, known casually as the Chestnut Tiger *(Parantica sita niphonica)*, can do something no feline ever could: fly all the way to Japan.

The 'tiger' in question is actually a mid-sized butterfly that lives in a well-studied colony on Yangmingshan National Park's Datunshan. In 2000, the lepidopterist world was rocked when one member of the colony, marked NTU1032C, was found in southern Japan – 1200km away. At first, researchers thought this was another instance of butterfly migration (see p358), but over the past decade only 12 other tigers have been found making that long ocean journey. Most likely dumb luck and strong winds account for the occasional long voyage. But it's still hard not to be impressed with such a feat.

The best time to see the tigers of Datunshan are June mornings when they swarm roadside. The butterflies, which are used to humans' presence, will often land right on you if you wear bright clothes.

FREE **Lengshuikeng** PUBLIC HOT SPRINGS
(冷水坑; Lěngshuǐkēng; Map p94; ☎2861 0036; ⏲6am-5pm Tue-Sun) The public bath on the park's eastern side has separate men's and women's indoor baths, although free admission means there can be long queues to enter. Its name means 'cold water valley', and compared with other local hot springs it's chilly, at 40°C. High iron content makes its waters reddish brown. Technically, Lengshuikeng is open to 5pm, but it's often open later, so phone ahead if you're considering an after-hours visit. The pools are closed for up to an hour at various times during the day for cleaning.

Sleeping

Yangming Sunrise Spring Hotel HOTEL $$
(日出陽明溫泉會館; Rìchū Yángmíng Wēnquán Huìguǎn; Map p94; ☎2862 0668; www.sunrise-spring.com.tw; 5 Lane 23, Yangming Rd, 北投區陽明路一段23之5號; r from NT$2500) Close to the entrance of the park, this cute hotel sits along a hot-spring river rolling down the mountain towards Beitou. Rooms are comfortable, but the main features in each are the deep, stone Japanese tubs for hot-spring soaking. The hotel's lower level is taken up by tub-only rooms, rented by the hour. Costs rise on the weekends (NT$800 for a 90-minute soak) but with a weekday 50% discount, the tubs alone make it worth the trip.

International Hotel HOTEL $$
(國際大旅館; Guójì Dàlǚguǎn; Map p94; ☎2861 7100; 7 Hushan Rd, Sec 1; r incl breakfast from NT$2310) Built in 1952 and maintaining its original character, the International has a rustic stone facade and charming rooms that are a great deal. The hotel is close to the hot-spring source and has both public and in-room hot-spring baths. Both Japanese- and Western-style rooms are available. Three-hour use of rooms (including hot springs) is NT$990.

Landis Resort Yangmingshan RESORT $$$
(陽明山中國麗緻大飯店; Yángmíngshān Zhōngguó Lìzhì Dàfàndiàn; Map p94; ☎2861 6661; www.landisresort.com.tw; 237 Gezhi Rd; r from NT$7000) With its low-slung profile, slate surfaces and lots of grainy wood and plate glass, this grand yet intimate resort feels inspired by Frank Lloyd Wright. Rooms in the deluxe category and up have hot-spring baths but any guest may use the spa and indoor pools. The Landis has an easy-to-use internet booking system that can get rooms down as low as NT$5000.

Eating

About a kilometre away from the entrance to Yangmingshan National Park sits Yangmingshan University, surrounding which is a plethora of student-type restaurants for quick and cheap eats. There's also a Subway shop if you'd like to carry a sandwich into the park with you. On weekends and most nice days during the high season, Jian Guo St (on the south side of the bus station) turns into an open-air food court serving Taiwanese favourites such as Hakka-style salt pork, seafood dumpling soup and a variety of noodle dishes.

Cao Shan TAIWANESE $$
(草山; Cǎoshān; Map p94; ☎2861 1501; 14 Hushan Rd, Sec 1; meals NT$180-450; ⏲breakfast, lunch & dinner; 📖) Wedged between the Starbucks and 7-Eleven on the road just before the entrance to the park itself, this eatery with

a charming hand-written English menu offers typical Taiwanese dishes. Chicken dishes are made with local free-range mountain chicken and tend to be the most expensive items on the menu.

Peak FUSION **$$**
(山頂; Shānding; Map p94; ☎2862 2358; www.thepeak.com.tw; 124 Gezhi Rd; meals NT$180-580; ⊙lunch & dinner;) This is one of the fancier restaurants in Yangmingshan. Its menu includes traditional Chinese dishes like stir-fried shrimp with broccoli alongside more esoteric dishes such as 'duck meat fried with XO paste'. The Peak is located between the university district and the Landis Resort.

Information

There are visitor centres at major tourist sights within the park and most usually have an English speaker on hand. All these centres have simple maps of the park that include basic information and hiking-trail details in English. You can pick up a detailed map of the park for NT$50 at the **National Park Visitor Centre** (Map p94; ☎2861 3601; www.ymsnp.gov.tw).

Getting There & Around

Catch bus 260 from Taipei Main Station, 5 from Shilin MRT, 230 or 9 from Beitou MRT or 15 from Jiantan MRT station. Buses run frequently between 5.40am and 10.30pm and cost between NT$20 and NT$35 one-way.

On weekends and holidays during flower season (late February to early March) a shuttle bus does the circuit around Yangmingshan's main road every 15 minutes from the Yangmingshan bus station (NT$60).

Danshui

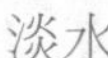

History

The long and storied history of this once-important fishing village, also known as Tamshui, has been shaped primarily by its geographical position at a place where the Danshui River meets the Taiwan Strait. Danshui was initially settled by the Ketagalan tribe, then at various times by the Spanish, Dutch, Japanese and of course, the Han Chinese. By the mid-19th century Danshui was a bustling port city thanks to its natural harbour, and it boasted a sizeable foreign population and even a British embassy.

By the end of the 19th century, Danshui's importance as a port had waned, and once Taiwan reverted to Chinese control after WWII the town slowly settled into a comfortable position as farthest suburb of a major metropolis. With the opening of the Danshui line of the Taipei MRT in 1998, Danshui suddenly found itself a popular weekend travel destination.

Orientation

Travelling from the Danshui MRT station towards the centre of town, the riverfront is on your left, while the town itself gradually slopes up the hills towards Tamkang University to the right. Directly north of the station is a great park for kite-flying and past this is Danshui's famous Gongming St and waterfront pedestrian plaza. Across the river is Guanyinshan and the town of Bali, both a quick ferry ride away.

Sights

A street filled with renovated colonial architecture, Danshui's **Gongming St** (Map p98; also known as Danshui Old St) is a favourite with visitors. Lined with shops and food stalls, the pedestrian street gets pretty crowded on the weekends, so if you're averse to crowds, weekdays are the best time to visit. In addition to the shops and stalls, Gongming St also has a branch of Taiwan's (no affiliation with Ripley's) **Believe it or Not** (Map p98; 67 Gongming St; ⊙11.30am-10pm), where, for a mere NT$50 entry, you can see a small collection of freak-show-type oddities of the animal kingdom, live and pickled.

Gongming St runs adjacent to a riverside promenade, which, though lacking an actual boardwalk, still manages to have a boardwalk vibe thanks to its seafood restaurants, outdoor seating and carnival amusements,

BUS RIDE TO BEAUTY

One good way to get a cheap tour of Yangmingshan and the surrounding area is to hop on Red bus 1717 from Taipei Main Station, which heads over the mountain on the way to the town of Jinshan on the northern coast. The trip costs a mere NT$130, and you'll catch some amazing views as the bus traverses the mountain range separating Taipei from the sea to the north. The bus also stops fairly close to both Ma Cao Hot Springs and Calla Young Garden Resort, which are far closer to Jinshan than to Taipei.

but with just a few shrines to let you know you're still in Taiwan. From here you can catch a ferry across the river to Bali and the Guanyinshan area (see p101), or upriver to Danshui's newly renovated Fisherman's Wharf, which is a great place to drink beer while watching the sun go down over the Taiwan Strait after you've exhausted yourself walking around Danshui all day. See p101 for details on how to get there.

Gongming St ends at Zhongzheng Rd, but keep walking north as there's still plenty to see. Right next to the **Longshan Temple** (龍山寺; Lóngshān Sì; Map p98) sits the Danshui **morning market** (朝市; Map p98; ⏲sunrise-noon), the traditional centre of town. Nestled in its alleys are a cacophony of shops and stalls selling fish, vegetables, meats and clothing and the like. About 100m further along Zhongzheng Rd is **Fuyou Temple** (福祐宮; Fúyòu Gōng; Map p98). Built in 1796, this beautiful low-lying structure is the oldest temple in Danshui. Naturally the temple is dedicated to Matsu, goddess of the sea. In bygone days, wives and families would come here to pray for the safe return, and sometimes the souls, of their menfolk. As of this writing, a wooden platform offering spectacular views of Guanyinshan across the river in Bali was very nearly built.

Hiking further up Zhongzheng Rd takes you past a plethora of shops, shrines and alleyways. Do you like bugs? Don't miss **Starbugs Insect Mall** (Map p98; 23 Lane 11, Zhongzheng Rd; ⏲3-9pm), a shop specialising in the care, breeding and raising of gigantic beetles. Browsers are welcome but a strict no-petting policy is enforced. But if you need tactile stimulation you can stick your hands inside puppets at the **Classical Chinese Puppet Art Center** (Map p98; 4 Lane 11, Zhongzheng Rd; ⏲10am-9pm). A giant bust of Dr George Mackay (a bearded, distinctly non-Chinese gentleman) stands watch over the eastern end of the otherwise difficult to locate Lane 11.

Further up the road sits Danshui's most famous sight, **Fort San Domingo** (紅毛城; Map p98; Hóngmáo Chéng; ☎2623 1001; ⏲9.30am-6pm Tue-Sun). The hill on which it sits has been home to a fort since the Spanish occupation of northern Taiwan from 1626 to 1641. The original fort no longer exists and there are two theories about its demise: either the Spanish destroyed it during their 1641 retreat from the Dutch, or the Dutch razed it in order to build a stronger structure. In any case, the basic structure of the current fort dates from 1642.

The fort was under Chinese control from 1683 to 1867 until the British took it over in 1868, painted it red and made it their

Danshui

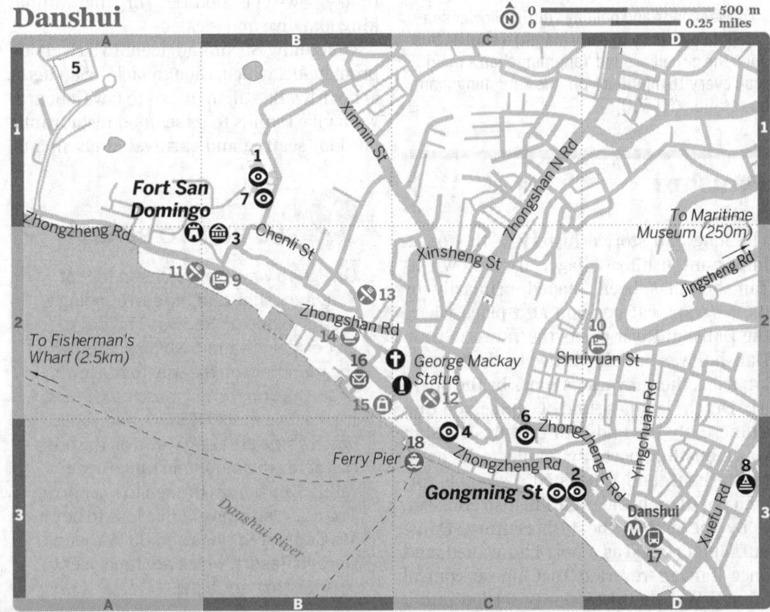

consulate. Adjacent to the fort is the 1891 **former British consular residence** (英國領事館; Map p98), a real throwback to the days of the British Raj in India, complete with original tiles from Java, ceiling fans and furnishings recreated from photographic records. The consulate was closed under Japanese occupation but reopened after WWII, and the British retained it until 1972 when diplomatic relations with Taiwan were severed.

The fort's present-day offices and ticket booth near the entrance were once guards' and servants' quarters. Inside you can view the jail cells they built for insubordinate sailors and businessmen. There are sweeping views from the fort itself. As of this writing, admission is free, but this may change.

Up the hill from the fort is **Alethia University** (真理大學; Zhēnlǐ Dàxué; Map p98), the first Western-style university in Taiwan. It was founded by a Canadian Presbyterian missionary, Dr George Leslie Mackay, who first came to Taiwan in 1872 and is revered in certain Taiwanese circles for introducing Western techniques of education and medicine. Thanks in no small part to Mackay's influence, Presbyterian is the most popular Christian denomination in Taiwan. The university's original building, **Oxford College** (牛津學堂; Map p98), was built in 1882 and fronts a Chinese-style pond and a large, more recent chapel.

About 1km beyond Fort San Domingo, **Huwei Fort** (滬尾砲台; Hùwěi Pàotái; Map p98; adult/student NT$25/15; ⏲9am-5pm Tue-Sun) is less flashy but no less interesting. This well-camouflaged fort dates from 1886. If Fort San Domingo is meant to convey authority, Huwei Fort was built for military action. It has thick walls, massive gates, four batteries and steep steps to its ramparts to deter intruders (try it and you'll see what we mean, but watch your step!). An inscription above the main entrance reads 'key to northern gate', denoting the fort's importance in the defence of the island. It was also used by the Japanese but never saw military action. In April and May, the fort's chinaberry trees are awash in purple flowers.

Back near the MRT station in town is **Yinshan Temple** (鄞山寺; Yínshān Sì; Map p98; ☎2625 2930; cnr Denggong & Xuefu Rds; admission free; ⏲6am-6pm May-Oct, 6am-4.30pm Nov-Apr), considered Taiwan's best-preserved example of temple architecture from the Qing dynasty. Although small, it's a riot of sculpture, especially obvious in the tiny glass and ceramic figurines and flowers among the roofing tiles. This is also the city-god temple for Danshui. Another unique feature is that the temple, founded 300 years ago, remains in the control of the 21 families who founded it. The current building dates to 1822 and it was most recently renovated in 1992.

From here, Xuefu Rd leads up to the campus of Tamkang University. As well as being one of the prettiest university campuses in Taiwan, boasting gardens and

Danshui

Top Sights
- Fort San Domingo ... A2
- Gongming St ... C3

Sights
- 1 Alethia University ... B1
- 2 Believe It or Not ... C3
- 3 Former British Consular Residence ... B2
- 4 Fuyou Temple ... C3
- 5 Huwei Fort ... A1
- 6 Longshan Temple ... C3
- Morning Market ... (see 6)
- 7 Oxford College ... B1
- 8 Yinshan Temple ... D3

Sleeping
- 9 La Flower Sea Resort ... B2
- 10 RegaLees Hotel ... D2

Eating
- 11 Bai Yun ... A2
- 12 Red Castle 1899 ... C2
- 13 Student Restaurants ... B2

Drinking
- 14 In Joy Chocolate ... B2

Shopping
- 15 Classical Chinese Puppet Art Center ... B2
- Starbugs Insect Mall ... (see 15)

Information
- 16 Post Office ... B2

Transport
- 17 Danshui Motor Transport Company ... D3
- 18 Suen Fung Ferry Company ... C3

STREET EATS IN DANSHUI

Dining on a budget is no problem in Danshui. Yingchuan Rd is chock-a-block with restaurants and food stalls. Chenli St, on the way to Alethia University, is filled with restaurants catering to local students.

If you want seafood, there are dozens of restaurants on Danshui's harbourfront promenade serving a 'catch of the day' probably caught just that day (though ask for the price first). And for Taiwanese favourites, Gongming St can't be beat as it's loaded with food stalls serving Taiwanese from-the-grill specialities such as squid, chicken and corn. There's even a stall selling a rather unique snack: a single spiralised potato, deep fried and served on a stick. Bet you can't eat just one.

One local dish you'll find in abundance is called 'iron eggs' – these are regular eggs that have been boiled, shelled and roasted until they turn black and leathery. If you don't like the flavour, you can always use them to play marbles. Another Danshui delicacy is *A-gi*, fist-sized pouches of fried tofu filled with bean-thread noodles, served in hot broth.

Qing-dynasty-style pavilions, Tamkang is the home of the **Maritime Museum** (海事博物館; Hǎishì Bówùguǎn; admission free; ⌚9am-5pm Tue-Sun), a four-storey museum shaped like an ocean liner – very appropriate, as it used to be a training centre for sailors and maritime engineers. The museum's collection is anchored by dozens of large model ships from around the world. Expect steamers, frigates, explorers' ships and aircraft carriers as well as an aboriginal canoe from Taiwan's Lanyu Island. You can learn about the treasure ship of Taiwanese admiral Cheng Ho, who was said to have navigated the Red Sea, Persian Gulf and East Africa 87 years before Columbus sailed. On the 4th floor, the 'ship's bridge' offers excellent views of distant buildings and Guanyinshan.

Sleeping & Eating

La Flower Sea Resort HOTEL **$$**
(淡水花間水岸; Dànshuǐ Huājiān Shuǐàn; Map p98; ☎2629 7890; www.searesort.com.tw; 241-1 Chung Cheng Rd; r from NT$3200) This lovely hotel sits on the banks of the Danshui River, just a few blocks north of Danshui's main action. Try to get a room in the rear so you can sit on the balcony and watch the sun set over the Taiwan Strait.

RegaLees Hotel HOTEL **$$$**
(福格大飯店; Fúgé Dàfàndiàn; Map p98; ☎2626 2929; www.regalees-hotel.com.tw; 89 Shie-fu Rd, 台北縣淡水鎮學府路89號; r from NT$4000) A few blocks east of the Ying Chuan Rd Night Market and within good walking distance of all Danshui's sights and smells. Located at the bottom of the hill leading up to the university, the hotel is popular with parents visiting students.

Bai Yun FUSION **$$**
(白雲; Báiyún; Map p98; ☎2623 5876; 1330 Zhongzheng Rd; ⌚11am-1am) The prices may be high, but the views are spectacular at this restaurant located right on the waterfront where the Danshui River meets the Taiwan Strait. Meals start at around NT$380, with full set meals going for NT$990. Locals say the restaurant is especially known for its grilled lamb chops with mint sauce (full set, NT$1380). The restaurant also has live music on weekends.

In Joy Chocolate CAFE **$$**
(巧克力音樂人文館; Qiaǒkèlì Yīnyùe Rénwénguǎn; Map p98; ☎2629 8549; 1330 Zhongzheng Rd; ⌚12.30pm-11pm Sun-Thu, 12.30pm-midnight Fri & Sat) Every now and again you run across something unexpected. This place, for example: a charmingly quirky little shop on Danshui's northern end, serving chocolate beverages and even fondue, imported from places as distant as Europe and Belize. Lo-fi ambient techno music plays lightly in the background as customers sip their beverages (moderately priced between NT$100 and NT$200). Two very docile cats are on the grounds, and the walls are covered with murals reminiscent of the beatnik era.

Red Castle 1899 CHINESE **$$$**
(紅樓; Hónglóu; Map p98; ☎8631 1168; 6 Lane 2, Sanmin St; dishes NT$280-680; ⌚lunch & dinner) Red Castle is a Victorian-style building and a well-known architectural landmark in Danshui, dating back to the late 19th century. Beautifully restored and reborn as a swank eatery, Red Castle serves both Western and Chinese dishes. Seafood, naturally, is a speciality – try the deep-fried soft-shell

crab with garlic (NT$680) or the steamed codfish with crispy soybeans (NT$460).

Getting There & Around

Take the MRT red line north until the end. All Danshui sights are within walking distance of the Danshui station. For trips along the northern coast, buses to Baishawan (p124), Keelung (p125) and points beyond are run by **Danshui Motor Transport Company** (淡水客運站; Map p98; 2621 3340). Red bus 26 from Danshui MRT station runs to Fisherman's Wharf, as does the ferry operated by **Suen Fung Ferry Company** (Map p98; Danshui Ferry Pier; adult/child NT$40/20; 9am-8pm Mon-Fri, 9am-10pm Sat & Sun).

Bali 八里

West of Danshui is the charming riverfront/seacoast town of Bali (no relation to the Indonesian paradise of the same name). Just across the wide mouth of the Danshui River where it meets the sea, Bali is quickly becoming a magnet for Taipeiers, especially families with children looking to get out of the big city for an afternoon. The entire bank of the river is taken up by the aptly named 'Left Bank Park', a waterfront park with 14km of biking and hiking trails and wooden boardwalks skirting wetlands teeming with plant and marine life. The area has also become a magnet for birdwatchers, as a number of species of birds either make their homes here or stop by for a quick feast on their migratory routes.

Sights & Activities

Bicycles can be rented for NT$50 per hour at a number of shops right off the boat dock from Danshui. Most of the bikes available are serviceable, but hardly in 'Tour de France' condition, so check to make sure yours has working brakes before you take off. A variety of four-wheeled 'family bikes' are also available. These are pedal-powered minicars. In addition to the park and bike trails, Bali is also home to the Guanyinshan scenic area, a water park and an excellent museum.

Shihsanheng Museum of Archaeology MUSEUM

(Shísānxíng Bówùguǎn; 2619 1313; www.sshm.tpc.gov.tw; 200 Bowuguan Rd, Bali Hsiang, Taipei County; admission NT$100; 9.30am-5pm Tue-Sun) This museum offers exhibits on the archaeological history of Taiwan's earliest residents. A variety of installations show the earliest evidence of aboriginal culture on the island, tracking the movements of the various tribes from prehistory to the present day. Highly interactive, the museum is surprisingly kid-friendly for a museum devoted to as scholarly a pursuit as archaeology; kids will especially like the aboriginal weaponry displays. English signage abounds and the museum staff will be happy to arrange a tour.

Formosa Fun Coast WATER PARK

(八仙樂園; Bāxiān Lèyúan; 2610 5200; www.formosafuncoast.com.tw; 200 Bowuguan Rd, Bali Hsiang, Taipei County; adult/child NT$590/490; 9am-5.30pm Jun & Sep, to 9.30pm Jul & Aug; M Guandu, bus R13/R22) In the shadow of Bali's Kuanyin Mountain sits this ancient park replete with cultural treasures dating back to the Ming...oh, who are we kidding? It's a water park, filled with rides, wave pools, and slides so hellishly steep that when you stand on the platform looking out over at Kuanyin Mountain in the distance (we didn't make that part up) you may say a short prayer to the goddess herself before throwing yourself over to gravity's tender mercies. Culturally significant? Not really. Hell of a lot of fun? Hell yes! Try to plan your trip on a weekday for maximum ride/minimum queue time.

Getting There & Around

From Danshui, take a ferry run by the **Suen Fung Ferry Company** (Map p98; Danshui Ferry Pier; adult/child NT$18/10; 6.15am-9pm), or follow signs for Bali buses from Guandu MRT station.

Guandu 關渡區

Sights & Activities

Guandu Temple TAOIST TEMPLE

(關渡宮; Guāndù Gōng; 360 Zhixing Rd) Dating back to 1661, this is one of Taiwan's oldest temples and is an absolute must-see. The multistorey temple is built right into the side of a mountain – in fact, among the most stunning areas of the complex is the 100m-plus tunnel that runs through the mountain itself. Lined with brightly painted deities enshrined in cases and exhibiting facial expressions ranging from blissful to downright frightening, the hall leads to a balcony offering a panoramic view of the Danshui riverscape. But don't let the view keep you from looking up; the balcony has a rich assortment of stone carvings, and an intricately carved and painted ceiling.

Around the marble facade of the back of the temple, there's a hillside park where you can contemplate an impressive frieze, and on the riverside sits a food court serving all manner of Taiwanese delicacies (salted duck and goose eggs seem to be the specialities of the area).

Guandu Nature Park PARK

(關渡自然公園; Guāndù Zìrán Gōngyuán; 55 Guandu Rd; adult/child NT$50/30; ⌚9am-5pm, closed 3rd Mon of month) Ten years in the planning, this nature reserve opened in 2001 under the control of the Wild Bird Society of Taipei. Over 100 species of birds, 150 species of plants and 800 species of animals live here on about 58 hectares of grass, mangroves, saltwater marsh and freshwater ponds at the confluence of the Danshui and Keelung Rivers (and their smaller tributaries). On weekdays it's rather busy with school groups, and with other tourists on weekends. Monday mornings are the least crowded.

Tittot Glass Art Museum MUSEUM

(琉園水晶博物館; Liúyuán Shuǐjīng Bówùguǎn; ☎2895 8861; www.tittot.com; 16 Lane 515, Zhong-Yang N Rd, Sec 4; admission NT$100; ⌚9am-5pm Tue-Sun; Ⓜ Guandu) From the outside, this museum just south of Guandu MRT station looks sort of like a factory. Inside, however, beautiful glassware objects are displayed on two levels. Glass-blowing demonstrations are held daily, and classes are given in glass-making.

ℹ Getting There & Around

Take the red line to Guandu MRT station, then leave by exit 1 and cross under the overpass to reach the nature park and temple. Both are about 15 minutes' walk from the station along Zhixing Rd. To reach the nature park, turn left when you see a playground. To reach the temple, continue on to the end of Zhixing Rd. Alternatively, bus 302 (NT$20) from Guandu station terminates at the temple. It's an easy walk (less than 15 minutes) between the nature park and temple.

South of City Centre

XINDIAN & BITAN 新店 碧潭

The Xindian station is the last stop on the red line (Danshui to Xindian) line or the first, depending on your perspective, which is fitting as Xindian is the far end of Taipei city, beyond which lies kilometres of mountainous splendour, bucolic scenery, and, if you take the right bus, a little town called Wulai (p111). The main attraction of Xindian is **Bitan Park**, which straddles both sides of the Xindian River as it rolls down the mountain. Should you be in town during the Lantern Festival (which caps the Lunar New Year's festivities), Bitan Park is a great place to come to see Taipei's 'unofficial' lantern festival. While CKS Shilin Residence Park is where folks go to see the floats, Bitan Park is where locals come to write out their wishes on paper lanterns before setting them alight and aloft. The burning lanterns usually sink slowly into the river, but occasionally they'll be carried by the wind into the surrounding neighbourhoods. The Lantern Festival can be a busy time for the local fire brigade.

Old Xindian St runs behind the station and stretches south along the river. The street boasts a small unspectacular night market that's good for a snack. Some stands sell grilled chicken, doughy octopus balls, and various other night-market fare. Nowadays, the area's main attraction is the newly built canopy-covered wooden deck along the eastern bank of the river, which contains stylish cafes and other eateries (slightly overpriced, in our opinion, but you can't beat the view). On weekends and holidays the area is positively packed with families and cyclists. You can also hang a right onto the pedestrian bridge and cross the river into Bitan. A marvel of low-tech engineering, the Bitan cable suspension bridge is extremely light. As a result, it has a peculiar tendency of bobbing and swaying in the near-constant breeze, offering the closest sensation you can get to seasickness without boarding a boat. Speaking of boats, small two-person pedal boats are available for rent at the river pier for NT$100 per hour. Either side of the river is a great place to be during the Dragon Boat Festival.

Bitan itself is increasingly becoming the main tourist attraction of the area. This small neighbourhood on the left bank of the river is home to the **Bi Ting** (Bì Tíng; ☎2212 9467; teas NT$200), a rustic, 50-year-old teahouse built on a rocky cliff overlooking the river (on the right side of the suspension bridge), where you can while away the afternoon or evening while brewing endless pots of tea.

On the Bitan side of the suspension bridge are a number of small restaurants and ice-cream stands, as well as a few stalls selling street food.

Taiping Temple (Tàipíng Sì), a multistorey Taoist temple, is just a few blocks north of the suspension bridge and worth a visit. Bitan is also the starting point for some excellent hikes.

Sleeping

There are a few cut-rate options in the area that shouldn't set you back more than NT$900 per night. Just look for the signs reading 'Hotel' hanging from the sides of run-down-looking buildings. Breakfast might be a banana; don't expect English service. We've listed two of the better options.

Beautiful Hotel BOUTIQUE HOTEL **$$**
(Měilì Chūntiān Dàfàndiàn; ☎8666 9999; www.beautifulhotel.com.tw; 8 Taiping Rd, Bitan, 北縣新店市太平路8號; r incl breakfast from NT$2666; @📶) Beautiful lobby decor and elegantly appointed (and fairly large) rooms with flat-screen TVs and large, soft beds. Rooms to the front have river views while those in the back gaze out over the mountains. For the price, you can't beat it. Book online to get discounts.

Bitan Hotel HOTEL **$**
(Bìtán Fàndiàn; ☎2211 6055; www.bitan.com.tw; 121 Bitan Rd, 臺北縣新店市碧潭路121號; d incl breakfast from NT$1490; @📶) Right next door to the Beautiful Hotel, the Bitan is slightly cheaper but a step down in quality. All rooms have flat-screen TVs, and some have swinging porch chairs (a nice, though somewhat odd, touch).

Getting There & Around

Xindian is the southernmost stop on the city's MRT line, as well as being at the end of bicycle paths leading from the city centre.

TAIPEI ZOO 木柵動物園

The **Taipei Zoo** (Mùzhà Dòngwùyuán; ☎2938 2300; http://english.zoo.taipei.gov.tw; 30 Xingguang Rd, Sec 2; adult/child NT$60/30; ⌚9am-5pm; Ⓜ Taipei Zoo) attracts five million visitors each year, making it one of Taiwan's top attractions. Its sprawling (165-hectare) grounds include a wide variety of simulated geographical regions, including a tropical rainforest zone, extensive gardens, and an aviary that rivals the one in Hong Kong Park in size. There's even an enclosed 'nocturnal world' section, kept dark during the day for the benefit of visitors.

Two of the zoo's most recent residents also happen to be their most famous – and to some, controversial. In 2008, the zoo accepted two pandas from mainland China, a gift that had been rejected by then-president Chen Shui-bian in 2005. The pandas are named Tuan Tuan and Yuan Yuan, names that together mean 'reunion'. The offering of pandas is a decades-old Chinese diplomatic tradition (spawning the phrase 'panda diplomacy'), and the gift is considered by supporters of Taiwan's independence as something of a Trojan horse. Regardless, Tuan Tuan and Yuan Yuan have proven a major draw for tourists and locals alike, and panda-themed souvenirs are ubiquitous throughout the zoo.

If you don't feel like walking around the entire zoo, there's a minitrain (adult/senior NT$5/3) that will take you around a circuit. If you really don't feel like walking at all but still want to see the zoo, the newly reopened gondola system (p105) actually goes over it, with a stop fore and aft, before climbing up to Maokong.

MAOKONG 貓空

The hilly region of southern Taipei, known as Maokong (Māokōng), has a history of tea growing that goes back to the 19th century. These days, however, the money is not in growing tea but selling a pleasing atmosphere for drinking it. The area is also popular with hikers and, increasingly, cyclists, who have discovered that Maokong is a quick, verdant retreat from the urban jungle below.

Sights & Activities

TEAHOUSES

Most teahouses are open from around noon to at least 10pm (later on weekends). Typically you pay for a small packet of tea (NT$300 to NT$800), which is enough for a group of four to enjoy for hours. You also pay a small 'water fee' of NT$100 per person. On weekdays you can bring your own leaves and just pay the water fee, though note that many teahouses close on Mondays.

Teahouse designs vary, allowing you to choose according to your mood and the weather: indoor or out, traditional or modern, city view or nature. Most serve food (and now coffee and flower drinks) and it's usually no problem just to have a meal.

Locally grown tea is a type of oolong called **Tieguanyin** (鐵觀音; TiěGuānyīn, Iron Goddess of Compassion). It's lightly oxidised, almost like a green tea, and has a delicate aroma. But you can find a wide variety of other teas for sale in Maokong.

Maokong

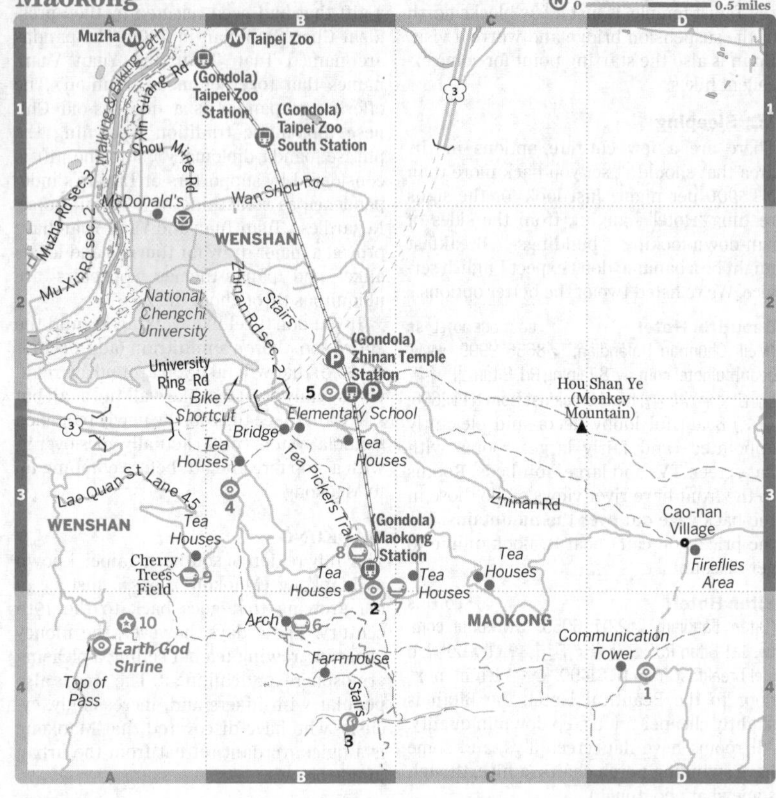

PLC Tea Tavern TEAHOUSE
(Hóngmùwū Xiūxián Cháguǎn; Map p104; 33 Lane 38, Zhinan Rd, Sec 3, 指南路3段38巷33號) One of our favourites for the old-style red-brick design and the verandahs with excellent views across the valley. The food here is quite good too, especially the chicken soup (great on a chilly, foggy evening). The tea tavern is down a flight of stairs to the left of a modern road-level cafe owned by the same family. There are at least five other teahouses in the immediate vicinity.

Zi Zai Tian TEAHOUSE
(Zìzài Tián; Map p104; 27 Lane 45, LaoQuan St, 老泉街45巷27號) Another gem with a traditional atmosphere inside (the building is a remodelled traditional stone house) and a lovely garden setting outside. This place is packed with old hikers in the mornings, but quiet during the rest of the day and at night.

Yuan Xu Yuan TEAHOUSE
(Yuán Xù Yuán; Map p104; 2nd fl, 16-2 Lane 38, Zhinan Rd, Sec 3, 指南路3段38巷16-2號2樓) Just a minute's walk from Maokong station, this fancy-looking place has one of the best city views in Maokong. It's also the only place with private booths where you can spread out on the floor with cushions and pillows.

Lioujisiang TEAHOUSE
(Liùjìxiāng; Map p104; 53 Lane 34, Zhinan Rd, Sec 3, 指南路3段34巷53號) The owners claim they run the oldest tea farm on Maokong. Try their namesake *liùjìxiāng* tea (six-seasons fragrant). The arch beside the teahouse leads to the network of trails around Maokong.

CYCLING

Maokong is the 'bee's knees' as one local rider described it. One minute you're in the grit and grime of Taipei's streets, the next you're rolling (slowly) up lanes that are virtually traffic-free and lined with spreading cam-

Maokong

Sights

1 Earth God Shrine D4
2 San Xuan Temple B3
3 Silver Stream Waterfall B4
4 Zhangshan Temple B3
5 Zhinan Temple B2

Drinking

6 Lioujisiang B4
7 PLC Tea Tavern C3
8 Yuan Xu Yuan B3
9 Zi Zai Tian A3

Entertainment

10 U-Theatre Performance Area A4

phor trees. There are no easy routes, but if you've gotten used to climbing hills (or want to) you won't find Maokong unmanageable. If you do want an intense challenge keep heading east from Cao-nan Village on the map. The road soon gets so steep your front tyre will pop up. The ride down on the other side is very pleasant and leads to Wenshan Rd (aka 106乙), which, if you turn left, takes you back to Taipei Zoo in 10 to 15 minutes.

The loop starting on Lane 34, Zhinan Rd, Sec 3 and finishing down Zhinan Rd, Sec 3 is a classic. To avoid traffic around the university area, head into the campus and follow the university ring road up to the lane marked 'Bike Shortcut'.

HIKING

Maokong is a fantastic area for getting away from it all: the trails are in good shape, natural (not staired like Yangmingshan), and many thickly wooded sections feel delightfully remote despite Taipei being just over the ridge. There are trail signs now in English and Chinese, so getting around is pretty safe.

One fun two- to three-hour return hike goes to the **Silver Stream Waterfall** (Yínhé Dòng Pùbù; Map p104), which you can climb behind via a cool old temple carved into the cliff. From Maokong gondola station follow the trail beside San Xuan Temple up to the ridge, then head straight down. At the bottom head downstream until you reach the falls. (An easier route starts beside Lioujisiang teahouse.)

OTHER SIGHTS & ACTIVITIES

Gondola — GONDOLA

(纜車; lǎnchē; Map p104; ride NT$50; 9am-10.30pm Tue-Sun) Closed for over a year for repairs, the gondola reopened in 2010 and is as popular as ever with residents and visitors alike. On clear days or nights the views across Taipei and up the lush Zhinan River Valley are great; on foggy days they are dreamy.

There are a number of teahouses within a short walking distance of the final station, as well as hiking trails into the mountains. This being Taiwan, if you walk for about five minutes you'll lose half the crowds. After 10 minutes you'll be practically alone.

Avoid taking the gondola on weekend mornings or afternoons. Take the bus up instead and catch the gondola down after 9pm or even 10pm. Most visitors are with family and don't linger long after dinner.

Zhinan Temple — TEMPLE

Stately Zhinan Temple (指南宮; Zhǐnán Gōng; Map p104) sits high above Wenshan district and on a clear day you can see across Taipei to Yangmingshan. The temple is dedicated to Lu Tung Pin, one of the eight immortals of classic Chinese mythology. It is said that, Lu, a jilted lover, often tries to break up couples who visit his temple before they are married. You'll find that many people still take this superstition seriously.

In the old days the only way to the top was by walking up 1200 steps. During the 1920s and '30s many miners from Jiufen and Jinguashi gladly made the effort as the temple's 'dream rooms' often told them of the location of gold deposits. Some of the old temple volunteers we've met can still recall being dragged up those 1200 steps every weekend by their fathers, who were anxious for a fresh lead.

The original temple was built in 1891 but very little of that remains.

U-Theatre — LIVE PERFORMANCE TROUPE

(優劇場; Yōu Jùchǎng; 2938 8188; www.utheatre.org.tw) One of Taiwan's most mesmerising performance groups, U-Theatre combines traditional drumming and music with dance inspired by Taoism, meditation and martial arts. As their very cool website states, 'The U-people believe that the combination of Tao and skill is the goal of their life and artistic creation.'

U-Theatre's unique outdoor night-time shows are held in a natural amphitheatre in Maokong usually in November or December. Check the website for the schedule.

Getting There & Around

In addition to the gondola, a bike, or your own two feet, you can take Brown bus 15 (NT$15)

OFF THE RAILS

Taipei's transformation from an ugly duckling of Asia to garden city has been nothing short of revolutionary. Though myriad are the factors involved in her rebirth, the greatest kudos probably goes to the Taipei MRT. Completed in 1999 (though 'completed' isn't quite appropriate, as the system is still expanding to connect ever-distant suburbs to the city centre), the Taipei MRT was instrumental in greatly reducing the capital city's once-noxious pollution. Of equal importance, the MRT turned travel in and around Taipei from hellish to pleasant, making for convenient exploration of neighbourhoods that might otherwise have been overlooked by the casual tourist. Here are some of our favourite, and often overlooked, stations and their neighbourhoods:

» **Yuanshan** The first above-ground station on the red line marks Taipei's change from claustrophobic to suburban, and from business to spiritual. The surrounding neighbourhood is good for temple-hopping, quiet meditation and drinking tea. In addition to being home to Taipei's well-known Confucius Temple, Yuanshan boasts a Buddhist temple and monastery (directly across from the station) built in the 1890s. Climbing the gnarled stone stairs that wrap around the complex's rear brings you past several shrines and statues, and eventually to a small grass park with old stone tablets and a few stone stools and tables. It's a good place to sit in silence, though your meditation may be punctuated with the regular sound of an airplane coming in for a landing at Songshan Airport, which lies directly east.

» **Xiaonanmen** Though in the city centre, this is another often overlooked station as it sits smack in the middle of a line with only three stops. Though there's only one cultural relic of serious note around here, the old 'little south gate' (小南門; Map p44) for which the station is named, it's well worth the 90-second ride from Chiang Kai-shek Memorial Hall station.

» **Kunyang** The eastern end of the blue line sees little tourist action. It's a shame, really, as Nankang Park is just a short walk south of Kunyang station. A wide expanse of green grass, trees, ponds, greenhouses, pavilions, with a lovely running track with a spectacular view of Taipei 101 to the west and mountains to the east, Nankang Park is an oasis on the city's edge.

» **Xindian** The red line's southernmost stop, Xindian station, reaches the last neighbourhood in Taipei proper. Beyond here lie mountains and rural splendour. Xindian is where the Danshui River comes down from the mountains, and sitting on both sides of the river is Bitan Park, home to various semiregular fairs and festivities that offer the requisite games of chance, and grilled meats. Xindian is also where you'll find the very cool, ever-swaying Bitan suspension bridge.

» **Shilin** Though the name Shilin is synonymous with Taipei's best-known night market, the Shilin station sits a few blocks north of the market itself and the area nearby is a great place to visit in its own right, especially during the day when the massive open-air street market north and west of the station (just cross Zhongzheng Rd; you can't miss it) is in full swing. South and west of the station are great places to wander around the warrens and alleys just north of the famous night market for a taste of traditional Taipei neighbourhood life.

» **Tucheng** Very nearly at the end of the western end of the blue line, Tucheng is a suburb of Taipei city that has a number of interesting temples, including the Buddhist Guang Cheng Yian and the Taoist Wugusiandi Temples. If you follow the main road westward towards the Yongning station, you'll pass a park on your left that's used for traditional Taiwanese funeral parties, with a massive statue of a black dog straddling the park's entrance. We don't know the canine's proper name, but we're told he's there to keep watch for wayward spirits. It's a bit spooky, to be honest. The area directly south of the station leads past some beautiful organic farms (volunteers welcome) and up into the hills.

WORTH A TRIP

IF YOU LOVE SHRIMP

Looking for a genuine Taiwanese eating experience? Love shrimp? Why not get serious and take the blue line to the last stop west? About 100m from Yongning MRT station you'll find an odd-looking spot that looks like a cross between a restaurant and an indoor fishing pond. This, friend, is **Shi Ho Shrimp Fishing** (溪湖釣蝦場; Qīhú Diàoxiāchǎng; ☎2269 4933; 134 Zhongying Rd, Sec 3, Tucheng City, 土城市中央路三段134號; ⏲12pm-3am; Ⓜ Yongning). Here's how it works: the ponds are filled with shrimp – really big, really tasty shrimp. Customers rent special shrimping poles (NT$500 for two hours) and commence shrimping. The attached restaurant will then cook your catch in a variety of tantalising ways (grilled with rock salt is a big favourite) for NT$150 per jīn (600g). The restaurant also serves beer, snacks and a variety of other dishes, and of course, plenty of shrimp dishes sold by weight (NT$600 per jīn) for customers unskilled, unlucky or just lazy.

Shi Ho Shrimp Fishing is definitely a social experience, and there are some real characters who hang out here spending their days and nights shrimping, eating and drinking beer. One of the women who works here, Su Fen, speaks pretty good English and is happy to give visiting Westerners tips on shrimping.

from the Taipei Zoo MRT station, or bus S10 (NT$15) from Wanfang Community MRT station. Buses run every hour on weekdays and every 30 minutes on weekends. Drivers know the teahouses, so show them the characters in Chinese if you want to go somewhere specific. You can get on or off anywhere.

A **tourist shuttle bus** (NT$15; ⏲9am-10.30pm) travels round Maokong every seven to 15 minutes on weekends and every 10 to 20 minutes on weekdays.

THE WILD WEST

The extension of the blue line out past the suburb of Tucheng has made convenient neighbourhoods that a few years back would have been too much bother to visit from the city.

We highly recommend the beautiful and unique **Museum of World Religions** (世界宗教博物館; Shìjiè Zōngjiào Bówùguǎn; ☎8231 6699; www.mwr.org.tw; 7th fl, 236 Zhongshan Rd, Sec 1, Yonghe City; adult/student NT$150/1100; ⏲10am-5pm Tue-Sun; Ⓜ Dingxi, then bus 706, 297 or 243), which incorporates symbols, art, ritual objects and ceremonies to illuminate 10 of the world's great religions. Though founded by a Buddhist order, the stated goal of the museum is not to promote Buddhism, but to build harmony by showing the communality of all religions. Highlights include scale models of various religious holy sites throughout the world; the insides of most can be viewed via tiny cameras. There are also a number of excellent multimedia presentations, a meditation room and a beautiful gift shop.

Signage in English is mostly good and there's a recorded English audio tour available for NT$50. Knowing the religious nature of the exhibits might prove a bit too solemn for the little ones, curators built a small but fun children's museum on the same floor called **Wonderland of Love** (NT$100).

Taiwan Nougat Museum (牛軋糖博物館; Niúgátáng Bówùguǎn; ☎2268 7222; 31 Zichang St; admission NT$50; ⏲9am-5pm; Ⓜ Yongning) is neither Taipei's biggest museum nor its best-known one, but one title that it surely wins hands-down is that of 'sweetest museum'. The family who run this museum and candy factory in Taipei's far-west suburb of Tucheng have been in the business of making nougat, a traditionally important confection for Taiwanese weddings, for over a century. After the family matriarch passed away, her son Chiu Yi-rong decided to transform parts of the newly expanded family factory into a place where families with children could come to learn about the history of nougat in Taiwan, watch sweets and wedding cakes being made, and even make the nougat themselves.

Though it's a bit out of the way, the museum is easy to find – just follow the large cow figurines set up along the side of the road from the MRT station exit to the museum's front door.

Northern Taiwan

Includes »

Best Places to Eat

- Keelung Miaokou (p126)
- City God Temple Market (p145)
- Shenlin Shui An (p137)
- Aux Cimes de la Fontaine (p154)
- Osmanthus Lane (p151)

Best Places to Stay

- Sunrise Hot Spring Hotel (p154)
- Full Moon Spa (p114)
- Chuanhua Tang (p150)
- Shi Shan Shui Chan (p130)
- Shui Yun Jian (p152)

Why Go?

For many travellers, heading outside Taipei gives them their first taste of what many consider to be the 'real Taiwan'. To some this means rural Nanzhuang, where hard-working tea farmers in straw hats sing under the midday sun. To others it's Smangus, a self-sufficient aboriginal hamlet a four-hour drive up a crumbling mountain road.

In the north, art lovers find their niche in temple-dotted towns devoted to traditional industries such as pottery, glass and woodcarving. Birdwatchers set goals for spotting endemic species, and as often as not reach them.

You'll find that the real Taiwan is a pretty diverse place. Like hiking? Like cycling? So do the locals, and if your idea of a fun weekend is climbing the Snow Mountains, or riding across the rugged North Cross-Island Hwy, you're going to find plenty of company. For real..

When to Go

Keelung

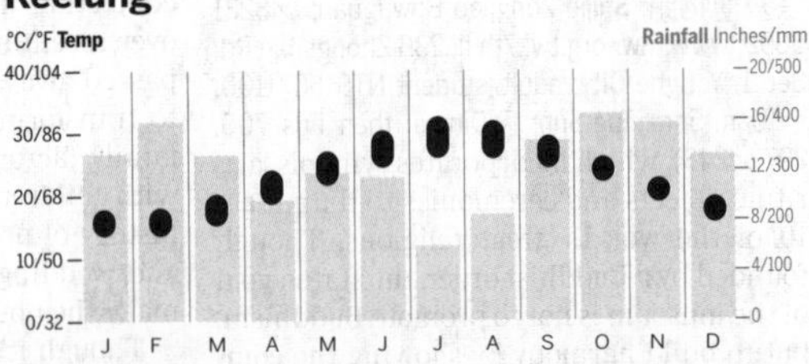

April Youtong flowers in bloom.

September–December Best months for cycling and hiking.

December Start of hot-spring season.

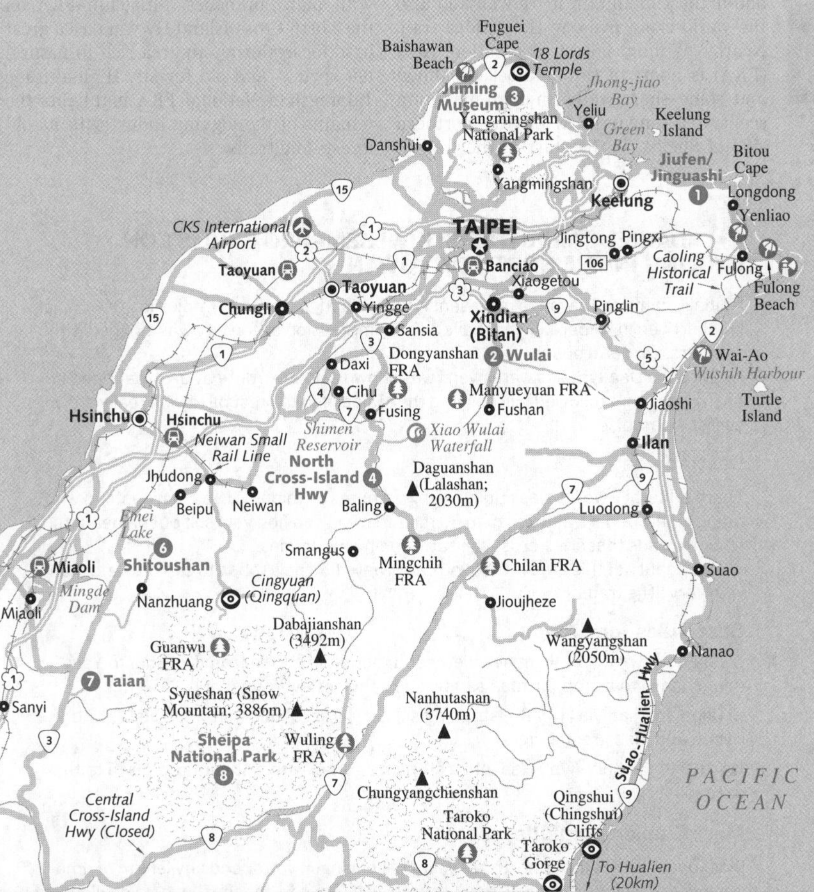

Highlights

1 Explore the quaint mining villages of **Jiufen** and **Jinguashi** (p128)

2 Hike, swim and cycle under a jungle canopy in **Wulai** (p111)

3 View the work of Taiwan's master carver at the **Juming Museum** (see boxed text, p125)

4 Enjoy wild vistas and natural hot springs on the **North Cross-Island Highway** (p136)

5 **Cycle** coastal and mountain routes all over the north of Taiwan

6 Spend the night in a temple on the slopes of **Shitoushan** (p150)

7 Soak in top-quality hot-spring water in **Taian** (p152)

8 Hike for days along the Holy Ridge's vertiginous paths in **Sheipa National Park** (p143)

National Parks & Forest Recreation Areas

The country's north has more than its fair share of parks and is a hikers' paradise, with trails literally beginning at Taipei's outer edges. Sheipa National Park (approximately 60km south of Taipei) has the second-highest mountain in Taiwan and also the world-class, five-day Holy Ridge trail. Nearby Wuling Forest Recreation Area (FRA) is home of the landlocked salmon and some short walks in high-mountain scenery. Guanwu FRA, on the northern side of Sheipa, is the start of the trail to Dabajianshan, one of the most magnificent peaks in Taiwan. Neidong FRA, near Taipei, has three beautiful waterfalls and is a popular birdwatching destination. Manyueyuan FRA is home to a stand of 2000-year-old cedars and is connected to Dongyanshan FRA by a 16km-long trail with many branches. Mingchih FRA on the North Cross-Island Hwy makes a great base for exploring an area rich in natural hot springs and old forests. High-altitude Taipingshan National FRA highlights the remains of the logging industry in its old forests and trails.

DANIEL CARRUTHERS: KIWI SEMI-PRO CYCLIST ON CYCLING IN THE NORTH OF TAIWAN

I initially came to Taiwan to represent New Zealand at the Deaflympics in 2009. When I first arrived in Taipei, I did not have a good impression as the city was clogged with scooters, cars and buses.

Once the Deaflympics were over, I was shown a nearby route by an expat rider. In the months that followed I discovered that Taipei and the rest of Taiwan really are a cyclist's paradise.

Best Advice

There is literally world-class riding within minutes of Taipei – if you can contend with riding in the Taipei traffic for 15 to 20 minutes, you can find yourself out on beautiful smooth roads that criss-cross the surrounding mountains.

The beauty of this area is that you can always find new roads to explore, and many with very little traffic.

Best Rides for Views

- Coastal Hwy 2 – brilliant sea views and mountains. Ride from Danshui to Yangmingshan with a stop for tuna sandwiches and coffee in Jinshan.
- Taipei to Yilan via Hwy 9 – stunning scenery. Panoramic mountain vistas and rivers, and lush green jungle.
- Wulai to Fushan – you ride into a stunning gorge, with a sheer drop down to the cascading river.

Most Challenging Ride

Most decent rides in the north are very challenging. If you spend any length of time here, your climbing skills will rapidly improve. If I have to choose the most challenging ride, I would say the **Balaka Climb** from Danshui up County Rd 101 to the top (over 1000m elevation gain). It finishes with a painful 3km to 4km, 18% grade climb to the peak. Speed demons can enjoy a screaming fast descent back to Taipei – reaching speeds in excess of 80km/h!

Best Quick Ride

Graveyard Ride – one moment you are riding in the hustle and bustle of busy Taipei and the next moment you are climbing a gradual mountain that winds its way through the world's biggest graveyard. You can try timing yourself to get to the top; the fastest time in 2009 was 8 minutes 37seconds.

For more on Dan's ride both in Taiwan and around the world check out his blog at www.danielcarruthers.com.

Climate

The weather in the north is generally warm and dry in autumn and wet and cool in winter, with possible sandstorms in spring. It can be hot and muggy in summer, though cool in the mountains.

Getting There & Around

There is excellent train and bus transport along the coastlines and between cities. Heading inland, bus routes dry up, and you need your own transport to visit many places. Traffic is light on weekdays, especially on mountain roads. The high-speed train stops in Taoyuan and Hsinchu, but this is of little use to most travellers.

CYCLING Northern Taiwan has been described as having some of the best road cycling in the world, and the list of good routes and regions is almost inexhaustible: you can thank a combination of mountainous terrain and political patronage (with a heavy emphasis on road building) for this. Add in the constant construction of faster routes and you have a wide network of quiet old roads, still maintained for the few residents who live off them, just waiting to be explored.

TAIPEI COUNTY (NEW TAIPEI CITY)

In many ways this county (新北市; Xīnběi Shì; http://tour.tpc.gov.tw/), likely to be called New Taipei City by the time you read this, is the poor cousin of Taipei, but transport is good, and there are some real treats for nature and culture lovers once you get away from the urban sprawl.

Wulai 烏來

02 / POP 7000

This mountainous township 25km directly south of Taipei is a world apart from its urban neighbour. In the thickness of jungle that covers most of the area you'll find spectacular waterfalls, deep river pools for swimming, endless hiking trails, and top birdwatching venues. Wulai (Wūlái, which means 'hot spring water') is a beautiful and largely untamed slice of Taiwan.

The main village in the township, also called Wulai, is a popular place for 'hot springing', though we wouldn't recommend that you come simply for that. The village area is a bit shabby but the tourist street is fun enough for sampling snacks and drinks you've never heard of (millet wine with bees, anyone?), and sitting down to a hearty meal after a long day in the wilds.

There's one main road through the township, Provincial Hwy 9甲, which terminates at Fushan (福山), the start of hiking trails running across to Ilan County and Baling on the North Cross-Island Hwy.

Dangers & Annoyances

If you go river tracing (*suòxī*; see p34), plan to be out of the water by 3pm or 4pm. Afternoon showers are a daily occurrence in late spring and summer, and rivers can become swollen very quickly. Also keep an eye open for snakes and leeches on the more-overgrown trails.

Sights & Activities

Neidong Forest Recreation Area

SCENIC AREA

(内洞森林遊樂區; Nèidòng Sēnlín Yóulè Qū; http://recreate.forest.gov.tw; admission NT$80; 8am-5pm) About 4km past Wulai Waterfall is this recreation area (popularly known as Wawagu, which translates as 'Valley of the Frogs'). This place is wonderful enough to make it worth a dedicated trip. It's particularly enchanting on a chilly winter's day.

The main attractions are the broadleaf and cedar forests, the bird and insect life (and the occasional monkey), and the three-tiered **Hsinhsian Waterfall** (Xìnxián Pùbù), one of the most gorgeous in the north.

There's only one main trail through the reserve, so you can't miss it. It starts near the first tier of the falls and leads up a series of steps and switchbacks through a broadleaf forest. At the top it connects to a dirt logging road that runs through thick cedar forests.

If you don't have a vehicle you can walk to Neidong from Wulai without much trouble in about an hour. Take the pedestrian walkway or the minitrain to the end of the line and then make your way to the main road. After you pass through a small tunnel, cross

FREE ADMISSION

At the time of writing, a number of Taipei County museums, including the Yingge Ceramics Museum, had stopped collecting admission fees. While this policy is likely to continue, there are no guarantees.

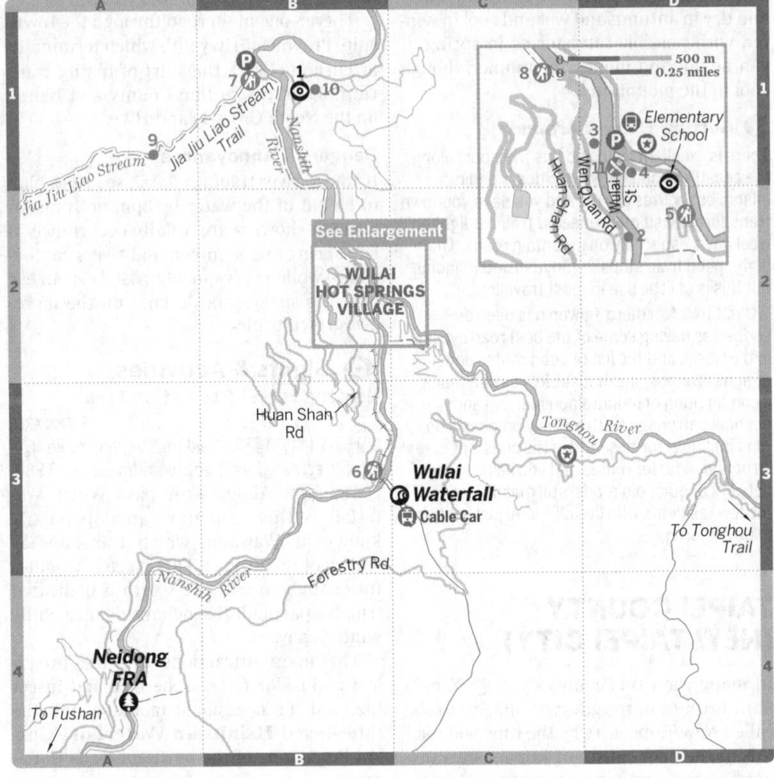

a bridge to the left and follow the almost unused road on the other side upstream to Neidong.

Wulai Waterfall WATERFALL

This 80m-high waterfall (烏來瀑布; Wūlái Pùbù) is a beauty, and the fact that you can float past it on a **gondola** (per person NT$220; ⏲8.30am-10pm) is one more reason to come to Wulai. There's a **minitrain** (per person NT$50; ⏲8am-6pm) to the base, or you can walk the pedestrian route beside the train line (about 1.5km). At the end of the line are lookouts and a pleasant strip of cafes.

Swimming & River Tracing

Every weekend in the hot summer months, river-tracing clubs or informal groups of friends flock to the rivers and streams around Wulai to practise river tracing, which combines scrambling, swimming and hiking (and true technical climbing and rappelling at higher levels).

Jia Jiu Liao Stream RIVER TRACING

A popular venue, the Jia Jiu Liao Stream (加九寮溪; Jiā Jiǔ Liáo Xī) features a jungle canopy worthy of a Tarzan film, an amazing natural **water slide** and a deep pool large enough for a group to swim in. The stream has no steep inclines and flows relatively gently, so it's pretty easy going but is still an absolute joy to trace up.

The best time to go is during summer, though on weekend afternoons you may find yourself sharing the river with organised groups. Follow one to find out where the natural slide is; the general location is about 100m downstream from the first big pool. An average person can reach the pool in less than an hour, though it takes most organised groups about two hours.

To get to the Jia Jiu Liao Stream, take a bus to Wulai and get off just past the 11.5km mark at Cheng Gong Village (成功) and then follow the side road down. Before the

Wulai

Top Sights

	Neidong FRA	A4
	Wulai Waterfall	C3

Sights

1	Cheng Gong Village	B1

Activities, Courses & Tours

2	Free Outdoor Pools	D2
3	Free Outdoor Pools	D1
4	Full Moon Spa	D1
5	Start of Birdwatching Route	D2
6	Start of Birdwatching Route	B3
7	Start of Jia Jiu Liao Stream Trail	B1
8	Start of Trail	C1
9	Waterslide	A1
10	Wulai Royal Resort	B1

Eating

11	Taiya Popo	D1

second bridge, head up the stairs on the left and then make your way to the stream. The first section is usually very crowded with picnickers and swimmers on summer weekends, but after five minutes you'll be alone.

Hiking

A simple but scenic trails runs for 5km along the Nanshih River, downstream from Wulai to its confluence with the Jia Jiu Liao Stream. The path starts near the old toll gate.

Jia Jiu Liao Stream Trail (Red River Gorge to Sanxia) HIKING TRAIL

Nothing conveys that lost-world feeling of Wulai like this 20km trail (加九寮溪步道; Jiā Jiǔ Liáo Xī Bùdào) running up the deep valley of the Jia Jiu Liao Stream. The trail is relatively straightforward these days, and while not signed, the main path is obvious. There are some fun rickety bridges (constructed out of bamboo and branches) on which it's always worth having your picture taken.

To get to the trailhead follow the directions for river tracing the Jia Jiu Liao Stream (see Jia Jiu Liao Stream, opposite), but instead of turning to the stream, head left up a series of wooden steps. From here just follow the main trail. In about two hours you'll reach a small cabin, which is a popular place for lunch.

Most hikers return to the trailhead at this point or go another hour to a small stream without a bridge, and then turn back. If you want to continue to the end, which drops you off just down from Manyueyuan FRA, pick up a copy of *Taipei Day Trips II* by Richard Saunders.

Fu-Ba National Trail HIKING TRAIL

This 18km national trail (福巴越嶺古道; Fú-bā Yuèlǐng Gǔdào) begins south of Wulai just before Fushan village. As the crow flies, Fushan isn't far from Wulai, but the landscape takes a noticeable turn to the wild along the road here as the Nanshih River valley narrows, and the sandstone cliffs drip with dark vegetation. Landslides are very common in this area and Fushan can be largely cut off from the rest of Taiwan for months at a time.

The name of the trail comes from the two villages connected by it: Fushan and Upper Baling on the North Cross-Island Hwy. Two hundred years ago the Atayal hacked the route up the mountains to facilitate trade and marriage (the trail is known as the Marriage Trail). Today it is still common to see Atayal hunting or fishing in the area.

Beginning in a dense broadleaf jungle, the trail ascends through forests of fir, beech and crepe myrtle to the mist-shrouded stands of ancient red cypress at Lalashan (2000m). Walking up takes about eight to 10 hours. It's possible to camp out on the trail or even call a B&B in Upper Baling (just down from Lalashan) to pick you up in Lalashan; you'll need to arrange this beforehand. The next day you can either hike back to Fushan or catch a bus in Upper Baling north to Taoyuan.

Note that on the way from Wulai to Fushan you need to stop and register at a police checkpoint. Bring your passport or Alien Resident Certificate (ARC).

Tonghou Trail HIKING/MOUNTAIN-BIKING TRAIL

One of several cross-island trails in the Wulai region, the Tonghou (桶後越嶺古道; Tǒnghòu Yuèlǐng Gǔdào) follows the eponymous river along a wide trail up to a watershed. After running along a grassy ridge for a spell, it then drops down onto dirt roads that eventually turn into pitched farm roads leading all the way to Jiaoshi on the coast.

It takes a little planning to get to the trailhead: taking a scooter or bike is best. From Wulai, head east on the road running along (and soon high above) the Tonghou

River. After a few kilometres you'll pass a police checkpoint where you must register using your passport or ARC if you want to go further. There is a daily limit on how many vehicles can enter past this point, so arrive early.

At the end of the road (20km from Wulai) you can continue on foot, or on mountain bike. It takes about three to four hours to the end of the trail, and another couple of hours down to Jiaoshi. The trail is marked and signposted to the end. After that, it can be tricky navigating down via farm roads.

Cycling

With its wild mountain scenery so close to the capital, Wulai is a popular biking destination. To get here, most cyclists ride Provincial Hwy 9 (and then Hwy 9甲) from Bitan to Wulai. There is a quieter route, however, that starts on the far side of the Bitan suspension bridge in Xindian and joins up with Hwy 9甲 a few kilometres north of Wulai. Both roads are winding and have some long climbs. Google Maps will show you the route, or pick up the Sunriver series of maps for the north.

Riding south of Wulai towards Fushan, the road hugs the Nanshih River gorge, a wild rugged canyon that is often closed because of landslides. The views here are superb.

The 20km to the start of the Tonghou trail is steep and winding. Riders on mountain bikes can take the Tonghou trail across to Jiaoshi.

Birdwatching

Wulai is renowned for its birdwatching areas and there are two main routes that birdwatchers take. One follows the road to Neidong FRA from the train; the other runs near the Tonghou River, starting from the car park in Wulai village.

For the latter route, head southeast, cross the first bridge and then take a left before Wulai St (the tourist street). Follow the road along the Tonghou River for a short distance, then turn right up a small road. The loop road/trail that eventually leads back to the road alongside the Tonghou River is said to be the best birdwatching area in Wulai.

Among the birds you can see in Wulai are common kingfishers, collared scops owls, and flocks of grey-chinned minivets. Winter is a particularly good viewing time as many mid-altitude species migrate to the lower river valleys. For more information pick up a copy of *Birdwatcher's Guide to the Taipei Region,* and see our Taiwan Wildlife Guide, p354).

Hot Springs

There are *wēnquán* (hot-spring hotels) starting a few kilometres from the main village; there are more along the tourist street; and there are even more spreading into the hills around the village. Undoubtedly there are too many competing for a limited resource, so it's best to come midweek and even during the warmer months if you want your water reasonably pure.

The easiest hotels to get to are along the tourist street in Wulai village. Prices range from NT$250 to NT$500 for unlimited time in the public pools, and around NT$600 to NT$1200 per hour for private tubs. Most hot-spring hotels on this street have pictures and prices outside.

Down along the river across from the tourist street is a ramshackle complex of **free outdoor pools**. Wash up at the entrance before heading in for a dip.

Full Moon Spa HOT-SPRING POOLS
(明月溫泉; Míngyuè Wēnquán; ☎2661 7678; www.fullmoonspa.net; 1 Lane 85, Wulai St; unlimited time public pools NT$490) One of the more stylish hotels along the tourist street, Full Moon has mixed and nude segregated pools with nice views over the Tongshi River. Its private rooms feature wooden tubs. The hotel also offers rooms for overnight stays from NT$2700. Go for the lower cheaper rooms as the views are surprisingly better than higher up.

Wulai Royal Resort HOT-SPRING POOLS
(御温泉養生會館; Yù Wēnquán Yǎngshēng Huìguǎn; unlimited time public pools NT$390; ⊙9am-10pm) The Royal looks like a community swimming centre, but it's inexpensive and in the perfect location for an after-hike dip if you've been on the Jia Jiu Liao trail. The resort is across the street from where the bus drops you off in Cheng Gong village.

Eating

Aboriginal cuisine is the standard fare in Wulai. A few mouth-watering selections that can be found at any number of shops along Wulai St include mountain vegetables, chicken and boar, *zhútǒng fàn* (竹桶飯; sticky rice steamed and served in bamboo tubes) and freshwater fish. Snacks and alcoholic drinks made from *xiǎomǐ* (小

THE GOOD-HEARTED MAMAS

Wulai may be a small paradise for hikers, cyclists and birdwatchers, but for dogs it can be a living hell. Remote in feel, but so close to the city, the area's quiet lanes and overgrown dead ends are, sadly, a favourite dumping ground for Taipei's unwanted pets.

But it's not just Wulai. According to Council of Agriculture statistics, 125,000 stray dogs were picked up last year all over Taiwan. The figure in England is similar, but in Taiwan the rate of euthanising is about 10 times higher. It's a terribly high number, and this, plus the practice of dumping pets, is something most Taiwanese are ashamed to admit still happens.

But as with all things in this remarkable society, for every action there is an equal reaction. When dumping started to become common (around 30 years ago, as Taiwan became increasing urbanised), some people stepped up to help. Helen Chang has been helping strays for 25 years. One of hundreds of women known island-wide as an *Àixīn māmā* (good-hearted mother), she currently takes care of 22 rescued dogs on her own property, and also goes out every day to nearby parks to feed strays and bring them medical care.

'I started helping animals because I couldn't bear to see them suffering,' Helen said. 'I also hoped that I can set an example for other people.'

Twenty-five years ago in Taiwan, animals were still largely treated as objects, or possessions, a holdover from the attitudes of agricultural society. Women like Helen were looked down upon as foolish, frivolous and sentimental. But the times have changed and dozens, if not hundreds, of animal welfare organisations have sprung up in recent years, including Taiwan's first Society for the Prevention of Cruelty to Animals. Wealthy philanthropists have also taken up the cause. Terry Gou, founder of Foxconn, sponsors several veterinarian hospitals where any dog or cat brought in will be spayed or neutered for free.

Taiwan's government has been slow to implement real changes but various municipalities are now starting to turn to alternative measures to deal with strays. Most of Taipei city, for example, now practises catch-neuter-release of stray cats rather than catch and euthanise. In 2010 the Taipei District Court handed down the first-ever jail sentence for animal abuse. The feeling among most in the animal welfare world is that in recent years the tide has genuinely turned.

As for Helen, no matter what happens she will continue to spend her own time and money to help where needed. 'In the future,' she said, 'I hope it's common knowledge among our children that respect for all beings is very important.'

For information on animal welfare organisations see Volunteering, p372.

米; millet) can be found at many shops and stalls in the village.

Taiya Popo ABORIGINAL **$**
(泰雅婆婆; Tàiyǎ Pópó; 14 Wulai St; dishes NT$50-150; ⊙10.30am-10pm, 📄) This long-running restaurant on the tourist street in Wulai village serves some great if obscure aboriginal dishes such as *déma miàn* (得麼面; fermented pork), betel-nut salad, and fried bees (they taste like popcorn chicken; NT$350).

 Getting There & Away

Bus 1061 to Wulai (NT$40, 40 minutes, every 15 to 30 minutes) runs frequently from near the Taipei Xindian MRT station (the last stop on the line) – to find the bus stop, head up the escalator, then walk to the main road in front of the station and turn right. Walk one block to the bus stop, which is just past the 7-Eleven.

Pingxi Branch Rail Line
平溪支線

☎02

Of the three small branch lines that have remained open for tourism, this 13km track (Píngxī Zhīxiàn) is the closest to Taipei, and our favourite by a long shot. For one thing, it's a highly scenic ride through a wild, wooded gorge. Furthermore, the stops are full of rewarding sights and activities, including thrilling hikes, high waterfalls, river pools in which to swim, and the remains of what was once a thriving coal industry. Pingxi town itself is the site of the annual sky lantern release during the Lantern Festival, an event not to be missed (see boxed text, p118).

The Pingxi line branches off from the main east-coast trunk line at Sandiaoling and extends to Jingtong, about a 30-minute ride east of Taipei Zoo. The most interesting stops are Sandiaoling, Shifen, Pingxi and Jingtong. The entire ride from Sandiaoling to Jingtong takes about 45 minutes.

At the **Shifen Scenic Administration Office** (☎2495 8409; ⏲8am-5.30pm), near Shifen station, you can pick up English-language brochures and consult the large maps on the 1st floor.

History

History is said to go in cycles, and that's certainly true for Pingxi township. Once a sleepy farming community whose residents grew yams and tea and harvested camphor, Pingxi was blasted into modern times with the discovery of 'black gold' in 1907: coal that is, not oil. By 1921, the Japanese Taiyang Mining Company had constructed the 13km Pingxi branch line from Sandiaoling to Jingtong and there was hardly a moment's rest for the next 60 years. At the height of operations, 18 mines were open, employing over 4000 miners. About 80% of the town's residents made their living directly from the mines.

Conditions were bad, even by the appalling standards of most coal mining. The mine veins ran deep underground, and the narrow pits forced miners to work lying down, often naked because of the oppressive heat and humidity. By the 1970s, cheaper foreign coal was already slowing down operations and by the mid-'80s mining ceased altogether in Pingxi. In 1992 the branch line was declared a scenic line, thus saving it from decay and closure.

And the people? Well, those who remained have gone back largely to sleepy farming, with a little pandering to the tourists who flock to their villages two days a week.

Getting There & Around

Bus Bus 1076 (NT$45) runs from Muzha MRT station to Jingtong and Pingxi every hour or so. The most useful morning times are probably 7.15am, 8.20am and 9.45am. Some buses go as far as Shifen.

Taxi The area can also be reached from Muzha in the south of Taipei. A 30-minute taxi ride from Muzha or Taipei Zoo MRT stations to Jingtong costs NT$500.

Train If starting your journey at Sandiaoling, catch a direct train from Taipei. There are two or three in the morning. If going to other stops first, take the train to Ruifang (fast/slow train NT$78/50, 40/50 minutes, every 30 minutes) and then transfer to the Pingxi line on the same platform. All-day train passes cost NT$54.

Sights & Activities

The following are presented in the order you will encounter them on the train starting from Riufang.

TOP CHOICE **Sandiaoling Waterfall Trail**
WATERFALL-VIEWING TRAIL

The upstream watersheds of the Keelung River receive more than 6000mm of rain a year and have more waterfalls than any other river system in Taiwan. On the wonderful Sandiaoling Waterfall Trail (三貂嶺瀑布步道; Sāndiāolǐng Pùbù Bùdào), once part of an important trade route between Ilan and Taipei, you can see half a dozen of the biggest and most beautiful falls in the north in their natural glory.

To get to the trailhead, exit Sandiaoling station and follow the tracks south until they split. Cross under and follow the tracks to the right (the Pingxi line). After a few minutes you will see the wooden signpost (in English) for the trailhead. The trail is simple and clear to follow, at least as far as the third fall (about an hour away).

The first waterfall encountered on the trail is **Hegu Falls** (合谷瀑布; Hégǔ Pùbù; Joining of the Valleys Falls). The trail runs over the streams that feed this and you can wade down to sit on top the rocky ledge and look down 40m to the base. Next up are two 30m falls that look almost identical and are in remarkably close succession: **Motian Falls** (摩天瀑布; Mótiān Pùbù) and **Pipa Dong Falls** (枇杷洞瀑布; Pípádòng Pùbù). You can get right in behind Motian via a cave formed by the overhang: it's like something out of *The Last of the Mohicans*.

If you have the afternoon or the whole day, continue up the trail until you reach a small paved lane. Turn left and follow this down into a small village (there are obvious shortcuts around bends in the road). Walk across the village and turn left after crossing a small bridge. Follow the road down (be on the lookout for an old pavilion that affords views of another fall) into a big car park beside the entrance to **Barbarian**

Valley (a famous old waterfall-laden valley largely destroyed in the 9-21 Earthquake of 1999).

On the other side of the car park is a trail. Follow it up and then down to the Keelung River, which is crossed via a large red pedestrian bridge. On the other side scramble up to the train tracks and turn right, following the line back to Shifen station. There are two more falls to see along the way (and also a long tunnel, so take care!). The 40m-wide **Shifen Waterfall** (十分瀑布; Shífēn Pùbù), the broadest fall in Taiwan, is a roaring beauty after heavy rain.

Just past this fall, after crossing a railway bridge, the **Eyeglasses Waterfall** (眼鏡洞瀑布; Yǎnjìngdòng Pùbù) pops into view. These are the last falls on the hike. From here it's a 15-minute walk to Shifen station. Along the way, watch for a large section along the river of rare **kettle holes**. The holes are formed by small pebbles that are spun around in the river current, wearing circles into the limestone riverbed.

Shifen SMALL VILLAGE

In little Shifen (十分; Shífēn), the train passes through the village just metres from the two- and three-storey houses running parallel to the tracks. It's the only place left in Taiwan where this occurs, and when the old steam engines are brought out once a month to ride the Pingxi line, the scene in Shifen will tug at your nostalgic heart no matter where you come from.

Photographers will keep themselves busy in Shifen for hours. Others may want to sample traditional snacks such as *mìfānshǔ* (蜜蕃薯; sweet potatoes cooked in wheat sugar) and *zhēngyùtóu* (蒸芋頭; steamed taro). A few restaurants serving locally grown food and even a couple of modern cafes have set themselves up in the village street where the trains slip past the houses.

If you didn't walk to Shifen from Sandiaoling, go take a look at Shifen Waterfall, about a 15-minute walk from the station. Head back along the tracks (east) and follow the signs and crowds.

Pingxi SMALL VILLAGE/HIKING

There are two reasons travellers step off the train in Pingxi (平溪; Píngxī): to climb the Pingxi crags and to release sky lanterns.

The highest crag is only 450m or so, but to reach the top you must scramble up metal ladders and steps that are carved into the rock face. No technical skill is required, but it's an adrenalin rush nonetheless.

To reach the trails, walk to the main road from the train station and go right. Just past the spiffy-looking red-brick school you'll see a set of stairs to the left and an English map. Head up the stairs, and then after a five-minute walk along the path look for the sign for **Cimu Feng** (慈母峰; Címǔfēng). Follow the path as it alternates running atop a ridge and hugging a steep grey limestone cliff. In one to 1½ hours you'll reach a set of cement stairs. You can take these down to Pingxi (essentially completing a loop) or begin the better loop up to the crags, which can take another couple of hours to complete depending on your route. There are signposts everywhere, and while you may get sidetracked, you won't get lost.

Jingtong SMALL VILLAGE/TRADITIONAL TRAIN STATION

The village of Jingtong (菁桐; Jīngtóng) marks the end of the line, and **Jingtong station** (菁桐站; Jīngtóng zhàn) is one of the best-preserved traditional train stations in Taiwan. With nearby coal carts, train engines, abandoned buildings strangled by roots, Japanese-era wood houses, and an obligatory 'Old Street', it's a fun place to explore and take pictures.

There's some great **hiking** around Jingtong and the excellent trails are never crowded, even on weekends. One favourite short hike is up to the pyramid-shaped **Shulong Point** (薯榔尖; Shǔláng Jiān). It's the highest mountain (622m) in the area and you can see Taipei 101 from the top. To get to the trailhead from the train station, walk to the main road, turn right and head uphill about 300m. There are English signs for the trailhead.

Eating & Drinking

Palace Restaurant SET-MEAL RESTAURANT $$

(皇宮咖啡簡餐; Huánggōng Kāfēi Jiǎncān; set meals NT$220; ⏲10.30am-9pm Wed-Sun) Set in a short row of Japanese-era houses, this restaurant has both an old-time wooden interior and good food. Guests can sit on the floor, Japanese style, or at tables. To reach the restaurant, cross the bridge over the Keelung River and turn right. Palace is 100m down the road. There are signs in Chinese.

Moca Cafe TRADITIONAL CAFE

(紅寶精典咖啡餐坊; Hóngbǎo Jīngdiǎn Kāfēi Cānfǎng; drinks NT30) Make sure you try the

LANTERN FESTIVAL

Over the past decade the **Lantern Festival** (元宵節; Yuánxiāo Jié) has emerged as one of the most popular holiday events in Taiwan. Of all the ancient Chinese festivals, it has best been re-imagined for the modern age, with spectacular light shows, live concerts and giant glowing mechanical lanterns showing across the island. Yet one of the best spectacles is still the simplest and most traditional: the sky lantern release in Pingxi.

A *tiāndēng* (sky lantern) is a large paper lantern with a combustible element attached to the underside. When the element is lit, hot air rises into the lantern sack and the lantern floats into the sky like a hot-air balloon.

In Pingxi people have been sending sky lanterns into the air for generations. Long ago, the remote mountainous villages were prone to attacks from bandits and marauders. Sky lanterns were used to signal to others, often women and children, to get packing and head into the high hills at the first sign of trouble. But today it's all about the sublime thrill of watching glowing colourful objects float up against a dark sky. Check out www.youtube.com for a teaser.

During the festival, which is spread out over two weekends (around February, but this varies with the lunar calendar), there are shuttle buses all day to the site. After dark, lanterns are released en masse every 20 minutes. Usually the participants in these events have been chosen beforehand, but if you hang around you may be asked to replace someone who didn't show up.

If you wish to light your own lantern, remember first to write some special wish on it. Then light the combustible element, wait till the paper sack has filled with hot air and made the skin taut, and let your lantern go. As it floats away to the heavens repeat your wishes to yourself...and pray your lantern doesn't burn up prematurely and crash down into the crowds, or light a tent on fire, as occasionally happens.

cafe's traditional and hearty *miànchá* (麵茶; sesame paste drink); it's great on a chilly day. When you exit the train station, turn right and follow the 'Old Street' 30m to this shop. You can't miss it as it has a blown-up photocopy of its Lonely Planet *Taiwan* entry plastered on the front with a caption about foreigners going crazy for their drinks (indulge them).

Pinglin 坪林

02 / POP 7000

Pinglin (Pínglín), which means 'forest on level ground', is famous nationwide for its honey-flavoured bao chung tea (a type of oolong). Only an hour from Taipei by bus (about 24km east of Xindian), or a couple of hours by bike, the region is well loved by day trippers for its emerald mountain landscape, picture-perfect tea fields, scenic mountain roads, and clear, swimmable rivers teeming with fish. The town also features a tea-theme museum that's worth visiting if you're in the area.

Pinglin village is quite small and easy to navigate. You can walk from the tea museum to the end of the dykes in 40 minutes. The township, however, is large and encompasses endless mountains, rivers, campgrounds and hiking trails. Pick up a copy of the Sunriver map for an overview.

Sights

Tea Museum MUSEUM

(茶葉博物館; Cháyè Bówùguǎn; admission NT$100; 9am-5pm, closed Mon) This place has everything you ever wanted to know about tea – and then some. The two floors of this classically designed museum feature all manner of displays, dioramas, charts, equipment and, of course, tea in all its forms. There are sections on the history of tea production in Taiwan and China, the culture of tea drinking, and tea-making methods over the centuries. All exhibits have complete English translations.

Activities

Cycling

Before Taipei's bike network really came together, and road cyclists starting discovering the wealth of back-mountain routes around the north, Pinglin's 20km bike path was considered pretty heady stuff. It's still a beautiful ride across the tea fields and up a lush river valley, and worth taking if you are passing through the area or have your own transport to carry your bikes out here.

Most cyclists now ride in to Pinglin from Taipei as a day trip or part of an extended journey to the coast. The routes are all pretty simple to follow and a couple of popular ones are outlined here.

Bitan to Xiaogetou CYCLING

This loop ride starts out at Bitan, at the end of the Red MRT line, climbs up Provincial Hwy 9 to **Xiaogetou** (小格頭) (about 14km from Bitan) and then drops back down towards Taipei on the winding 北47 or 北47-1. The latter roads run along steep mountainsides before dropping into Shihting (石碇; Shídìng). From there it's a flat ride back to Taipei on the 106乙 via Muzha and the city bike paths.

Instead of turning back at Xiaogetou you can also continue another 10km to Pinglin. It's all downhill just past Helen Coffee and the views over the green-blue Feicui Reservoir are spellbinding.

From Pinglin, riders sometimes continue to Jiaoshi on the coast. This is about 40km further, and consists of a long climb out of Pinglin followed by a long, steep, winding descent to the alluvial plains of Ilan County.

Muzha to Pinglin CYCLING

Here's another way to get to Pinglin (and beyond) from Taipei. This route is a little longer as you are going all the way to Pinglin. From the Muzha or Zoo MRT station, ride Wenshan Rd (aka 106乙, just south of the 106) to Shihting. At Shihting you have different choices for getting to Pinglin: stay on the 106乙, or take the 北47 and then connect with Provincial Hwy 9 to Pinglin. The 106乙 is not as steep as the 北47, although it's still challenging.

County Road CYCLING

The County Rd (北42) follows the contours of the Beishi River (the source of Taipei's drinking water) from a high perch, affording outstanding views of this natural landscape. A beautiful ride is to follow the above route from Muzha to Pinglin, connect to the 北42, and then ride all the way to where it connects with Provincial Hwy 2丙, heading towards Fulong Beach. This is a full-day outing for most cyclists. At the end, Fulong Beach, you can ship your bike back to Taipei on a train or bus.

Swimming

There are many sweet spots for a dip in the rivers around Pinglin. Head northeast on County Rd 北42 or follow the bike path to the end and walk upstream a short distance.

Hiking

In the hills just north of the village, along the rivers and through the tea fields there are short paths suitable for families and strolling couples. Children usually like watching the 'flashing fish' along the **Fish-Viewing Path** (觀魚步道; Guānyú Bùdào).

If you have your own vehicle (and map) there are numerous more-challenging trails in the Pinglin area. Look for the trail signs (in English and Chinese) around town to point you in the right direction.

Sleeping & Eating

There are a couple of campgrounds heading south along the bike path, and many off County Rd 北42. You need your own transport to reach these as they are quite far from the town centre. For simple, cheap fare there are noodle shops along the main road and a 7-Eleven that sells sandwiches.

Helen Coffee COFFEE SHOP

(www.helencoffee.com.tw, in Chinese; coffees NT$80; ⏲morning to dusk) Most cyclists stop here, just past Xiaogetou at the very top of the pass (around 15km from Bitan, or 10km from Pinglin). The coffee shop is unmistakable on the left and has a deck with a half-million-dollar view (there are some power lines) over a big forested valley. The turn-off for 北47 is just a few metres past Helen Coffee.

Shopping

On the main drag into town there's no end of stores selling tea and products made with tea. While tea jellies, ice lollies and *tǒngzǎi mǐgāo* (筒仔米糕; sticky rice) are inexpensive, a jar of decent *bāo zhǒng chá* (包種茶; bao chung tea), the local speciality, can cost NT$1000 or more. In our opinion, though, it is one of the most delicious teas in Taiwan and can be easily appreciated by the untrained palate.

Getting There & Away

In Taipei, take the MRT to Xindian station. From there, catch the free Orange Bus to the left when you exit the turnstiles. The bus leaves every hour and drops you off in the centre of Pinglin one hour later, from where it's a short walk to the museum; some buses may also take side tours into the tea-growing areas. The first bus to Pinglin leaves at 6.30am, and the last bus to Taipei leaves at 8.30pm.

Yingge 鶯歌

☎02 / POP 83,468

C is for Ceramics. C is for – Yingge? Well, not quite, but 'Yingge is for ceramics' is something almost any Taiwanese can chant. This little town in the very southern part of Taipei County lives by and for the production of high- and low-quality ceramic and pottery objects: everything from cupboard handles to Song-dynasty vases.

Pottery was introduced to Yingge (Yīnggē) in 1804, but it remained a cottage industry producing cheap earthenware until the Japanese ramped up production in the 1930s. In addition to daily-life items, the local kilns began to fire ceramic parts for mines and weapons. After WWII, ceramicists from all over Taiwan began to settle in Yingge and by the 1970s the town was the third-largest ceramic production centre in the world.

But as with so many other towns based on a single traditional industry, Yingge saw most of its production moved to China in the '90s. With the 1999 opening of the NT$6-billion Yingge Ceramics Museum and the creation of the 'Old Street', the town made a very successful leap from manufacturing base to cultural venue, putting itself on the map for lovers of traditional crafts.

Yingge makes an enjoyable, long day trip from Taipei and fits in naturally with a stopover at nearby Sansia for a look at the masterfully restored Tzushr Temple and the nearby blocks of Qing- and Japanese-era buildings.

Sights & Activities

Yingge Old Street OLD STREET

The Old Street (鶯歌老街; Yīnggē Lǎo Jiē), although not really old, is rather quaint, with its cobbled roads, traditional street lamps, red-brick facades and a walk-in kiln. Dozens of pottery shops and stalls, large and small, compete for your business, and you could spend hours just browsing. Prices start at around NT$30 for a cup or saucer, but these will most certainly be mass-produced in China. Quality handmade Yingge pieces can cost tens of thousands. A good compromise for the budget shopper (who still wants something nice) are teasets, coffee mugs, and earthenware jars and vases that can be purchased for NT$1000 to several thousand dollars. Most shops close between 6pm and 7pm.

To get to the Old Street from the train station, exit on the right side of the station and turn right when you're outside. Walk down the shop-lined street to a big four-way intersection. Turn right, pass through the tunnel (under the train tracks) and then head towards the arches on the left. The Old Street begins here.

FREE **Yingge Ceramics Museum** MUSEUM (鶯歌陶瓷博物館; Yīnggē Táocí Bówùguǎn; www.ceramics.tpc.gov.tw; 200 Wenhua Rd; 9.30am-5pm, closed Mon) Most people think that pottery and ceramics are the same thing, but they are actually quite different. They use different types of clay and are fired at very different temperatures: pottery under 1250°C, ceramics above 1260°C. Humans have been making pottery for around 8000 years, but only mastered the ceramic process around 3000 years ago.

If you didn't know this (as we didn't), then it's time to head to the very stylish and terrifically informative Yingge Ceramics Museum. Exhibits cover everything from 'snake kilns' (see p222) to the various woods used in firing, and influences on Taiwanese ceramics from China, Japan and the Netherlands. Special exhibitions of local artists show the direction modern ceramics is taking, and the flashy videos and occasional humorous exhibit help to keep interest high as you move around the three floors.

A **ceramic studio** (admission NT$50; 2-3pm & 3.40-4.40pm Sat & Sun, book a place 30min earlier) is open on weekends if you want to try your hand at making a pot (or something reasonably potlike). Instructions are in Chinese only, though it's common to have someone around who can speak English and help out.

To get to the museum from the Old Street, head up the pedestrian overpass that crosses the train tracks. On the other side just follow the alley down to the boardwalk and then follow that to the museum grounds. It's less than a five-minute walk and the way is completely obvious.

Eating

On the Old Street there are plenty of vendors, small restaurants and cafes to help you line your stomach. Next to the museum there's a street filled with the usual noodle shops.

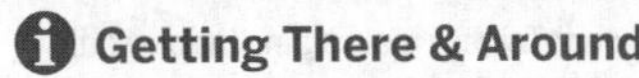

Getting There & Around

Trains from Taipei (NT$31, 30 minutes) run about every 30 minutes.

One branch of the Taipei riverside bike path network terminates in Yingge. A lazy ride

WORTH A TRIP

TWO RIDGE WALKS: BIJIA SHAN & HUANGDI DIAN

The little town of Shihting (石碇; Shídìng) sits in the foothills about 15km east of Taipei Zoo. There's not much to see in the town itself, but the valley it sits in cuts a long ridgeline in two, making the village the start of not just one, but two, of the best vertiginous walks in Taiwan. There's English signage on both trails now, and ropes and guide poles in the more-dangerous sections, but only go if you have a head for heights. Though not quite knife-edged, in many sections these ridgelines are narrow enough that two people can't pass.

Shihting is also the junction of several mountain routes to Pinglin that are very popular with cyclists.

Bijia Shan

(筆架山; Bǐjiàshān) The 18km Bijia Shan trail runs west of Shihting (back to Taipei) and is by far the safer of the two walks. Most of the ridgeline is wooded, which creates the illusion that you aren't so high or so precariously situated. From the bus stop in Shihting head downstream on the left bank of the river. You'll soon pass a primary school. Just past the last house look for a sign for the trail to the left. The trail climbs up to the ridgeline in about 40 minutes and then proceeds to run along that ridgeline all the way back to Maokong.

The way is obvious for the next three to four hours until you drop into a little saddle at the junction to **Ergeshan** (二格山). Follow the signs down towards Mt Hou-shan-yue and a few minutes later stay left at the sign for **Cao-nan** (草楠). Keep left on this trail all the way down to a road (about a 15-minute walk). Then simply follow that road down past the old banyan in Cao-nan vllage (an excellent spot to see the indigenous **blue magpie** up close, by the way) until you reach a major road. Buses go by here back to Taipei Zoo or Wanfang Community MRT station.

Huangdi Dian

(皇帝殿; Huángdìdiàn; the Emperor's Throne) Huangdi Dian runs east of Shihting and is by far the more sporting of the two hikes and the more dramatically scenic. From the bus stop head up the narrow road to the left of a convenience store (as you face it) and take the first left. Follow this road up to the arch and mapboard that start the trail.

After 30 to 40 minutes of climbing stairs you'll reach the ridgetop. Progress is slow from here on with numerous climbs up and down steel ladders and chains, scrambles over boulders and rock faces, and traverses across uneasily narrow and bare sections of ridge. Most exposed areas now have posts and ropes in place but there is at least one long stretch with no protection at all. Don't go on a windy day!

If you want to cut the hike short, a number of side trails lead off the ridge down to roads leading (eventually) back to Shihting. But try to give yourself all day to cover as much as possible; the entire walk is around six to eight hours. The stretch to the bare-crested **East Peak** (東峰; Dōngfēng) looks out over a beautiful range of forested hills and jagged peaks. It feels like the high mountains here though it is not quite 600m above sea level. Pick up a copy of *Taipei Day Trips I* for a full description of this hike and all its possibilities.

To get to Shihting take the bus of the beast, 666 (NT$30, 20 minutes), from Muzha MRT station – to find the bus, exit the station, walk to the main road and cross it to reach the bus stop. The bus runs on the hour on weekends and every 30 minutes on weekdays.

starting near Taipei's main train station would take about three hours.

Sansia (Sanxia) 三峽

☎02 / POP 86,958

Across National Hwy 3 from Yingge, this old town (Sānxiá) is most noted for a temple that has been described as an 'Eastern palace of art' and a couple of blocks of perfectly restored Qing- and Japanese-era buildings. In short, Sansia and Yingge go hand in hand, contrasting and complementing each other like peanut butter and chocolate.

Sights

TOP CHOICE Tzushr Temple TAOIST TEMPLE

The centre of religious life in Sansia, the Tzushr Temple (祖師廟; Zǔshī Miào) honors Qingshui Tsu-Sze, a Song-dynasty general worshipped by the people of Anxi, Fujian, for his power to protect their tea industry. First erected in 1769, the present structure hails from a late-1940s rebuilding that is still not finished.

In 1947, Tzushr Temple was in near total decay, as were many temples around Taiwan after WWII. Professor Li Mei-shu, scion of a wealthy and politically active family, was given the task of supervising the rebuilding. Li, a trained art professor, was the perfect man for the job. In addition to his formal training, which included a stint in Japan, Li had been a careful observer of temple crafts as a child.

Li supervised reconstruction with an obsessive attention to detail. He also changed the direction of temple arts in Taiwan by incorporating Western and Japanese aesthetics, and an assortment of unusual motifs, materials and carving techniques. The **bronze doors** at the gates are unique among temples in Taiwan. Other innovations, such as the blending of Western and Eastern styles in the **stone lions**, the use of gold foil over woodcarvings, and the bronze wall relief have been copied many times over.

Some standout features to look for include the 126 hand-carved **stone pillars** (the original design called for 156) and the astonishingly beautiful **plafond** (decorative ceiling), which recedes into a vortex. On every sculpted surface you'll find traditional motifs, auspicious symbols and illustrated stories from history. Buy a copy of the *Shan-hsia Tsu-sze Temple Tour Guide* (NT$200) booklet for more details, or call the temple (☎2671 1031) for a private tour (in Chinese only).

One last thing worth noting is the hideously out-of-place light-grey balustrade on the 2nd floor. After Professor Li's death in 1983, the temple committee attempted to go the cheap route with the rest of reconstruction. The master craftsmen were let go one by one, and a construction company was hired to oversee reconstruction. The ensuing public lambasting of such a move seems to have prevented worse abuses, if only by putting everything on hold.

Tzushr Temple is liveliest on the sixth day after Chinese New Year, during the infamous **Pigs of God Festival** (神豬; Shénzhū). It's an old ritual in which pigs are force-fed (sometimes with sand and metal) to the point where they can no longer move: in some years, winning swine have weighed over 900kg. It's a disturbing practice and many Taiwanese are ashamed that it still takes place (it's technically illegal). Animal-rights groups have been trying for years to force the festival to close or modernise.

Minchuan Old Street HISTORIC SITE

Sansia's name (Three Gorges) reflects the fact that it sits at the confluence of three rivers. Once an important transport hub for charcoal, camphor and indigo dye, the town's prosperity is evident in the old block of red-brick merchant houses and residences dating from the end of the Qing dynasty to the early years of the Japanese colonial era. Closed for two years for restoration work, the street now looks much like it did 100 years ago, and on weekends there's a lively market atmosphere as the little shops operating from behind dark-wood doors sell speciality snacks, tea, and souvenirs. Street performers also work the area, making this a fun venue to take in after the spiritual and aesthetic treasures of Tzushr Temple.

As you walk the **Old Street** (民權老街) look for the diversity of styles in the shop facades: they incorporate traditional Chinese, Japanese and Western baroque elements. Note that the mortar used for the bricks is a combination of sticky rice and crushed seashells.

To reach the Old Street turn right as you exit the temple and walk up the alley to Minquan (Minchuan) St.

Activities

Wuliao Jian HIKING TRAIL

On the outskirts of Sansia, the Wuliao Jian (五寮尖; Wǔliáo Jiān) trail doesn't cover much ground yet takes six hours to complete. But then you need to tread slowly on a ridge that's less than a hand's-breath wide in places. As with other crazy ridge walks in the north, these days you'll find secure ropes and guide poles in place, and they're a godsend. On one section, the trail is nothing but a bumpy slice of rock exposed on all sides. Years ago, when we first hiked the route, there was only a thin rope attached to the flat of the ridge and you had to straddle the rock and shimmy across. It was insane then; now it's just a good thrill.

Needless to say, don't go unless you have a good head for heights and are in the mood for a challenge.

Many people tackle Wuliao Jian without any more detail than above, as there are rough maps in place and it's tough to get lost. But if you want a full description of all the twists and turns, consult the *Taipei Day Trips II* guide.

The easiest way to get to Wuliao is to take the MRT to Yongning station (the last station on the blue line) and then a taxi to the trailhead (NT$300). At the temple at the end of the hike, ask for a taxi to come and pick you up.

Getting There & Away

From Yingge, the only sensible way to Sansia is by taxi (from Yingge Ceramics Museum to Tzushr Temple is NT$110). From Taipei, riverside bike paths should extend all the way to the Old Street by the time you read this.

Manyueyuan Forest Recreation Area

滿月圓森林遊樂區

This **recreation area** (Mǎnyuèyuán Sēnlín Yóulè Qū; www.forest.gov.tw; admission NT$100; ⏲8am-5pm) is truly a park for all seasons, and all people. The first section has paved or cobbled paths, scenic pavilions and short walks to a number of gorgeous waterfalls. It's perfect for families or strolling couples.

Once you get past this section, however, you're on natural trails that climb through sweet-smelling cedar forests up to **Beichatianshan** (北插天山; North Sky-Piercing Mountain, elevation 1727m), the highest peak in the north, and, further afield to a stand of **giant cedars** (神木; *shénmù*).

The trail starts up a short incline to the right of the toilets at the end of the paved route to Manyueyuan Waterfall. It's broad and clear and takes about four hours to hike. There are many side branches but the main route connects Manyueyuan with Dongyanshan FRA. However, there is no public transport to and from Dongyanshan, so if you walk there you must walk back.

The trail is straightforward, though the last stretch involves rope climbs and scrambles using roots as hand- and footholds. Follow the main trail through the park to its highest point and then turn left, following the English signs. It's a long day hike to the summit and back (expect 10 to 12 hours), so many people make it an overnight trip. There's a wild campground near the base, beside a rushing stream. Travellers with a vehicle can approach from Dongyanshan as the trail is much shorter from this direction.

The trail down to the old cedars follows the same path as to the base of Beichatianshan and then drops down a side trail, but this is not marked in English. Get a copy of *Taipei Day Trips II* for directions, or follow another hiking group.

Autumn is a nice time to visit the park, because the gum and soap-nut trees are changing colours. Fireflies come out in the spring and summer, though we have seen them as late as October. You can often spot monkeys further into the park during the day. Be aware that the park has its own microclimate, and while it may be sunny and dry in Taipei, it could be cool and wet here.

To get to the park take an infrequent **Taipei Bus Company** (☎2671 1914; NT$45) 807 bus from the station on Dayung Rd (台北客運三峽站 大勇路) in Sansia to Lele Valley (樂樂谷; Lèlè Gǔ). From Lele Valley it's about a 30- to 40-minute walk to the park gates. If you can get a few people together, take a taxi (NT$450) from Yongning MRT station to the park. You may be able to get a taxi back on a busy summer weekend, but don't count on it.

To return to Sansia, hitching back to town is an option, as is walking down to Lele Valley and catching the bus. The last bus leaves Lele Valley around 6pm (call the Taipei Bus Company to confirm).

HIGHWAY 2: THE NORTH & NORTHEAST COAST

02

The 166km coastal Provincial Hwy 2 winds along the top of the island from the mouth of the Danshui River to the alluvial plains of Ilan. It's a stunning route with a wide range of coastal landscapes: rolling grass hills, high rugged cliffs, sand beaches, pebble beaches, rocky terraces, and windswept peninsulas.

Most of the area falls under the auspices of either the **North Coast & Guanyinshan Scenic Administration** (www.northguan-nsa.gov.tw; 9am-5pm) at Baishawan Beach, or the **Northeast Coast Scenic Administration** (www.necoast-nsa.gov.tw; 9am-5pm), which is headquartered in Fulong. You'll find travel information centres at both offices.

Getting There & Around

There are public buses to almost every place we mention. There's also a good shoulder for cycling on most of the highway, and plans are in place for a dedicated bike path from Fulong down to Ilan (and possibly all the way to Taroko Gorge). There's great cycling off the highway around Sanzhi, Fulong and Daxi.

Baishawan Beach 白沙灣

One of the better beaches in Taipei County (this is not meant to be particularly high praise) is found at this little bay (Báishāwān), the name of which translates as 'white sand bay' – though these days it is definitely more of a yellow colour. The **North Coast & Guanyinshan Scenic Administration** (www.northguan-nsa.gov.tw; 9am-5pm) is based at the east corner of the beach and helps to keep the area clean and the vendors and shops organised.

The entrance to the beach is down a side road 100m or so off Hwy 2 (there are brown signs in English around the 23km mark). Swimming is permitted during summer (June to September) and in recent years a surfing scene of sorts has taken off. You'll find no end of shops offering boards and wetsuits, should you want to try your hand at the sport. You'll see many young Taiwanese paddling their boards in the shallows and not daring or caring to actually get on the waves.

Baishawan is formed by the stubby finger of rocky **Linshanbi Cape** (麟山鼻; Línshānbí) extending into the Taiwan Strait. This is a scenic part of the north coast and a several-kilometre-long **boardwalk** has recently been built along the shoreline as part of a 10km bike path from Sanzhi to Shimen.

To get to the beach, take the MRT to Danshui, then catch a **Tamshui (Danshui) Bus Company** (2621 3340) bus heading east to Jinshan/Keelung (NT$53, 20 minutes, every 20 to 30 minutes).

Fuguei Cape 富貴角

The cape (Fùguìjiǎo) is the most northerly point in Taiwan, and the constant sea winds make the local vegetation grow dwarfed and twisted. There's a small park here with good views and a large fisherman's wharf complex under construction. Years behind schedule, it most likely won't open until 2012.

About a 10-minute walk southeast from the cape is an area that is rather beautiful when the tide is low: the **Laomei Algal Reef** (老梅海岸; Lǎoméi Hǎiàn). Looking like a row of fallen monoliths carpeted with emerald moss (in reality layer upon layer of algae), the reef is a popular spot with photographers – check out Flickr for some amazing pictures.

18 Lords Temple 十八王公

People sometimes refer to this temple (Shíbā Wánggōng) as the 'dog temple'. According to one version of the legend, 17 fishermen went missing one day. A loyal dog pined for days for the return of his master until, unable to bear the suffering any longer, he leaped into the foaming sea and drowned himself. Local people were so impressed by this act of loyalty that they built a temple in honour of the dog.

Years later, the Kuomintang (KMT) constructed the first nuclear power plant behind the temple in their own kind of tribute. Both buildings are now just off Provincial Hwy 2.

Yeliu Geopark 野柳地質公園

Stretching far out into the East China Sea, this **limestone cape** (Yěliǔ Dìzhí Gōngyuán; admission NT$50; 8am-6pm) has long attracted people to its delightfully odd rock

WORTH A TRIP

JUMING MUSEUM

British art critic Ian Findlay has proclaimed Juming's work 'the most instantly recognisable of Taiwan's contemporary sculptors'. An afternoon spent at the **Juming Museum** (朱銘美術館; Zhūmíng Měishùguǎn; www.juming.org.tw; admission NT$250; ⌚10am-6pm, closed Mon) in Taipei County's Jinshan is kind of like an intensive course in short-story appreciation, with every tale created by a master of the genre, its text made of stone, metal and other mediums instead of words. Within the 15-hectare sculpture garden and museum, myriad tales are indeed told.

One painted bronze sculpture shows a man and woman sitting beneath an umbrella while behind them a third woman sits with arms folded, a dour, petulant expression creasing her face. The couple are lovers, that much seems certain, but is the third woman a jealous paramour or disapproving auntie? If the artist himself knows, he isn't saying. One of Juming's most oft-quoted traits is his belief that the interpretation of art is the domain of the viewer and not the artist. Visitors to the Juming Museum may well be struck by how few of his works bear titles besides the names of the series to which they belong. The artist has been quoted as saying that he feels that 'naming his sculptures would just get in the way' of the viewer's interpretation.

While many of his sculptures (most notably those in his most famous series, 'Tai Chi', which feature gigantic blocky stone monoliths in various martial-arts poses) have clearly Taiwanese – or at least Asian – themes, the majority of Juming's works are slice-of-life features, moments frozen in amber, scenes that could be taking place anywhere in the world.

It is fitting, we believe, to consider Juming's artwork as highly representative of modern Taiwanese art as a whole. The artist – and his personal artistic philosophy – seem to fit well with the spirit of 'strategic ambiguity' that Taiwan itself has used so well to navigate the potentially hazardous waters of being a political entity that, while clearly independent, dares not declare itself as such. Is Taiwan a nation or a province? Is the scowling woman a jealous suitor or an over-protective auntie? Different people have different interpretations, but the 'official' answer to both of these questions is roughly the same: 'Have a look. Draw your own conclusions.'

To get to the museum take a Kuo Kuang Hao bus heading to Jinshan from the Zhongxiao Fuxing MRT station (the bus stop is outside exit 2). Buses (NT$110) run every 15 minutes. From Jinshan it's a 10-minute taxi ride or you can try the free but infrequent museum shuttle bus (see the website for the schedule).

formations. It's a geologist's dreamland but also a fascinating place for the day tripper. Aeons of wind and sea erosion can be observed first-hand in hundreds of pitted and moulded rocks with quaint (but accurate) names such as **Fairy's Shoe** (仙女鞋; Xiānnǚ Xié) and **Queen's Head** (女王頭; Nǚwáng Tóu). The latter truly looks just like a silhouette of the famous Nefertiti bust, but sadly the delicate neck is eroding fast and this little treasure may not be with us much longer.

The **visitor information centre** (⌚8am-6pm) has an informative English brochure explaining the general conditions that created the cape and also the specific forces that formed different kinds of rock shapes, such as the mushroom rocks, marine potholes and honeycomb rocks. To get to the park, take a Kuo Kuang Hao bus heading to Jinshan from the Zhongxiao Fuxing MRT station, exit 2. Buses (NT$91) run every 15 minutes.

Keelung (Jilong) 基隆

☎02 / POP 387,000

Keelung (Jīlóng) is a port city, the second largest in Taiwan, and has a rough-around-the-edges, devil-may-care vibe. Though a modern city today, in the markets and alleys you'll catch a whiff of the city's long and storied history, which involves foreign invaders, pirates and intrigue by the barrelful.

Keelung is a quick trip from Taipei by either bus or train and offers a lot to the casual traveller who knows where to look. In

Keelung (Jilong)

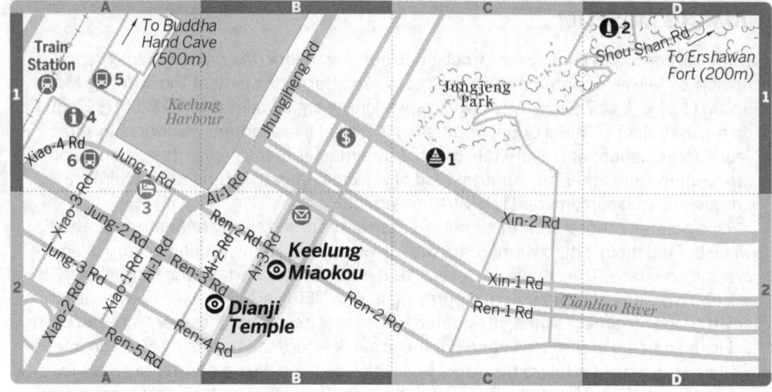

addition to its justly famous night market, the city has a number of beautiful old temples. Thanks to its strategic importance over the centuries, the area has a number of old forts. Befitting a coastal town, you'll also find ocean parks, scenic lookouts and, perhaps most germane to the gourmand, copious amounts of excellent seafood.

Weatherwise, Keelung has wet and drizzly winters and three other seasons in which it may well rain a bit on any given day. But something about the damp, mist-shrouded climate of Keelung suits its moody nautical feel to a T.

Keelung is a very wander-able town, with a small centre and plenty of winding alleyways that turn into quaint MC Escher-esque neighbourhoods (with houses built into the sides of hills, and steep alleyways that become staircases). You can visit most of the sights outside of the city by bus within 30 minutes.

The bus and train stations are adjacent to each other and located at the northern end of the city.

Sights

Keelung Miaokou NIGHT MARKET

(基隆廟口夜市; Jīlóng Miàokǒu Yèshì; hours vary) Encompassing several square blocks around the intersection of Ren-3 Rd and Ai-3 Rd, this area (famous throughout Taiwan) became known for its great food during the Japanese occupation, when a group of clever merchants started selling snacks at the mouth of the **Dianji Temple** (奠濟宮) – 'Miaokou' means 'temple entrance' and also 'temple mouth', which is a fine play on words, if you ask us. After the war, more shops opened up in both directions. Nowadays, Miaokou is considered the best place in Taiwan for street snacks, especially seafood. Though some shops are open during the day, it's after dark when the place really comes to life. Visit on a weekend evening and you'll understand the phrase 'people mountain, people sea', a Mandarin colloquialism meaning 'crowded'.

Stalls on the main street are all numbered and have signs in English, Japanese and Chinese explaining what's on the menu. If you can possibly make it past them all without falling over, the temple itself is worth visiting.

Buddha Hand Cave UNDERGROUND TEMPLE

(佛手洞; Fóshǒu Dòng) A few blocks northwest of Keelung Harbour you'll find a medium-sized **shrine** (admission free) built into a mountain. Entering this and following the signs leads deep into an underground cave, inside of which you'll find both a second shrine and an imprint on the ceiling that resembles nothing less than a giant hand. Locals say the underground temple dates back at least 400 years. Lending credence to this idea is barely decipherable graffiti in a variety of scripts etched into the cave walls.

Ershawan Fort HISTORICAL FORT

(二沙灣; Èrshāwān) Also known as Haiman Tienxian, this first-class historical relic was once used to defend Taiwan during the First Opium War. Its imposing main gate and five cannons, still tucked into their bat-

Keelung (Jilong)

Top Sights
Dianji Temple B2
Keelung Miaokou B2

Sights
1 Foguangshan Temple C1
2 Guanyin Statue D1

Sleeping
3 Harbourview Hotel A1

Information
4 Keelung Tourist Service Centre A1

Transport
5 City Bus Hub A1
6 Keelung Bus Company Station A1

tery emplacements, are a dramatic sight. To get here, take city bus 101 or 103 to Haimen Tianxian and walk up the footpath.

Jungjeng Park PARK

(中正公園; Zhōngzhèng Gōngyuán) This beautiful park, east of Keelung Harbour, overlooks the city and harbour. You can get here from the train station by bus 101, 103 or 105, but shouldn't you walk off that afternoon snack-fest at Miaokou? In any case, the park isn't hard to find. Let a Keelung icon, the bone-white, 22m-tall **Guanyin statue** (觀音佛像), flanked by two gigantic golden lions, be your guide. Note that while there's a main road leading up from the south side of the hill, the stairs and alleyways from the west side have more character.

Foguangshan Temple BUDDHIST TEMPLE

(佛光山極樂寺; Fóguāngshān Jílè Sì) Just south of Jungjeng Park is this beautiful and subdued Buddhist complex with an open meditation hall. There's an excellent vegetarian restaurant beside the temple.

Other Sights

If you have a bit more time to spend around Keelung, check out **Keelung Island** (基隆嶼; Jīlóng Yǔ), a tiny spot of land with an emerald peak and surprisingly high cliffs. Boats to Keelung Island (☎0910-091 043, per adult/child NT$450/350) leave from **Bisha Harbour** (碧砂漁港; Bìshā Yúgǎng), 10km east of the island and itself worth visiting. The return trip takes about 1½ hours and includes time on the island.

Boats leave when full, and on weekdays and in winter months you may find yourself waiting for a while. On the weekends it's a different story, so travellers are advised to reserve their seats in advance (the telephone number provided is for Mr Luo, the boat's captain).

To get to Bisha Harbour take bus 103 from Keelung's train station. Buses are frequent and the trip takes about 20 minutes (NT$15). Foreign travellers should bring their passport or ARC.

Festivals & Events

During the seventh lunar month, Keelung is host to Taiwan's most renowned **Ghost Festival** (Zhōngyuán Jié). The festival lasts the entire month (usually August), and each year a different Keelung clan is chosen to sponsor the events. Highlights include folk-art performances, the opening of the Gates of Hell and the release of burning water lanterns.

Sleeping

Most people treat Keelung as a day trip. If you want to stay a night there are cheap hotels close to the harbour.

Harbourview Hotel HOTEL $$

(華帥海景飯店; Huáshuài Hǎijǐng Fàndiàn; ☎2422 3131; harborview.hotel.com.tw; 109 Xiao-2 Rd; r incl breakfast from NT$1800; @) A mid-priced, chic, smartly furnished place in between the train station and the night market. The staff are friendly and helpful, though their English is limited.

Information

Keelung Tourist Service Centre (基隆遊客中心; ☎2428 7664; http://tour.klcg.gov.tw/; ⊙8am-5.30pm) Good English maps. Right next to the train station.

Getting There & Around

The train from Taipei costs NT$45 (40 minutes, every 20 minutes).

Keelung's local buses start at the city bus hub (基隆市公車總站) near the train station area and cost NT$15 for trips anywhere within the city. Buses to sights along the north coast start from the **Keelung Bus Company** (基隆客運; ☎2433 6111) station, also near the train station. Boats to Matsu Island leave from Keelung Harbour's Pier 2, but the schedule is not reliable.

Jiufen & Jinguashi 金瓜石 九份

☎02 / POP 2000

Nestled against the mountains and hemmed in by the sea are the small villages of Jiufen (Jiǔfèn) and Jinguashi (Jīnguāshí), two of the quaintest stops along the northeast coast. Both villages were centres of gold mining during the Japanese era. In the 1930s, Jiufen was so prosperous it was known as 'Little Shanghai'. Jinguashi later became notorious during WWII as the site of the prisoner-of-war camp Kinkaseki.

When the mining sources dried up, Jiufen and Jinguashi became backwaters just waiting to be rediscovered. Jiufen's discovery happened first. After the release of the 1989 film *City of Sadness,* set in Jiufen during the Japanese occupation, urban Taiwanese began to flock to the old village in search of a way of life that had been all but swept away in the rush to modernisation. The old village, rich in decorative old teahouses, Japanese-style homes and traditional narrow lanes, gave them exactly what they were looking for.

Jinguashi hit the travellers' radar more recently after a multiyear project to restore the old mining village (which includes the most beautiful Japanese-style house in Taiwan), the tunnels, and the general ecology of the area. The result is a small culture park that reflects almost completely the old atmosphere of 1930s Taiwan.

Any trip to the Juifen-Jinguashi area should leave time to wander the hills. If you can imagine a grassy emerald landscape, with a rugged topography dominated by jagged shale peaks and steep slopes dropping into the sea, then you've imagined something of this extraordinary bit of land.

Sights & Activities

JIUFEN

Orientating yourself in Juifen is fairly straightforward as there is only one main road and it winds up very steeply. The bus drops you off near the town's 7-Eleven, which is close to the sights.

Jishan Street (Juifen Old Street) OLD STREET

Narrow, covered Jishan St (基山街; Jīshān Jiē) often leaves lasting impressions. It's really just one long, narrow covered lane, but spending a few hours here browsing the knick-knack, curio and craft shops is a lot of fun.

One of the most popular activities on the street is snacking. Some distinctive snacks to look for include *yùyuán* (芋圓; taro balls), *yúwán* (魚丸; fish balls), *cǎozǐ gāo* (草仔糕; herbal cakes) and *hēitáng gāo* (黑糖糕; molasses cake).

Jishan St begins just to the right of the 7-Eleven on the main road.

Jilongshan SCENIC MOUNTAIN

You can't miss this emerald colossus for the way it dominates the skyline. At only 588m, Jilongshan (雞籠山; Jīlóngshān) may read like a rather puny giant, but it rises up so fast and steep, it's dizzying to stare at from below. You can climb the peak in about 40 minutes.

The trailhead is about 500m up the main road from the 7-Eleven.

Fushan Temple TAOIST TEMPLE

(福山宮; Fúshāngōng) The earth god (Tudigong) has one of the lowest rankings in the Chinese pantheon, but, not surprisingly in these old mining towns, he is among the most exalted. In the 1930s, miners crowded the 200-year old Fushan Temple daily, praying to the god to point them to a rich vein that would make them gentlemen overnight. After a decision to expand the temple caused panic ('What if it damages the efficacious feng shui?'), a larger structure was simply constructed over the original, giving Fushan the nickname 'the temple within a temple'. Alas, the damage appeared to have been done in any case (some claim that other gods were jealous to see Tudigong raised so high), and many blame the building of the larger temple for the decline of Jiufen not a decade later.

The temple is an interesting blend of Japanese, Chinese and Western elements. The outside features two old **toro shrines**, while the interior sports a beautiful post-and-beam structure (made without nails), and some gorgeous carved panels, including one over the main altar with two **nude angels**.

To reach the temple, walk up the main road to the top of the hill where the road splits. Left will take you to Jinguashi and right will take you to Fushan Temple about 1km from the split.

Jiufen Kite Museum MUSEUM
(九份風箏博物館; Jiǔfèn Fēngzhēng Bówùguǎn; 20 Kungwei Lane; admission NT$100; ⏲10am-5pm) This quirky private collection in the basement of a local B&B can seem underwhelming at first. But then, at some point it dawns on you: my God, these things can really fly! There are several hundred kites in the collection, from the tiniest butterfly-shaped kites, to a 3m-long phoenix with a fox in its mouth. Perhaps most astonishing are the kites with musical instruments built into them so that they drum or whistle when in the air.

The owner of the museum is rightfully proud of his collection and grows visibly happy when he sees visitors impressed.

Teahouses

Apart from shopping, strolling and snacking, the main attraction in Jiufen is spending a few hours in a stylish traditional teahouse sipping fine tea. This isn't everyone's – well – cup of tea, but for those of us who love it, Jiufen gets top marks as a place to indulge in a favourite pastime. The price for making your own tea *(pào chá)* is much the same everywhere: NT$250 to NT$900 for a packet of leaves and NT$100 for your water fee *(chá shuǐfèi)*.

TOP CHOICE **Jiufen Teahouse** TEAHOUSE
(九份茶坊; Jiǔfèn Cháfǎng; 142 Jishan St; ⏲10am-10pm) The owner claims his business, housed in a 90-year-old building at the far end of Jishan St, was the first teahouse in Jiufen. Certainly it has the best selection of teas, including some rarities such as roasted Oriental Beauty and a fruity Tieguanyin. There is indoor and outdoor seating, and it's hard to decide which to choose, though we usually sit inside as the wood and brick design has such a charming old-world feel to it. The teahouse only serves tea and snacks, but if you want a meal they will direct you to their sister restaurant down the street.

JINGUASHI

FREE **Gold Ecological Park** HISTORIC SIGHTS/MUSEUMS
(黃金博物園區; Huángjīn Bówùyuánqū; www.gep.tpc.gov.tw; ⏲9.30am-5pm, closed Mon) We could spend hours just wandering through this park, set high above the village in green, quiet hillsides. It's a slice of old Taiwan here, with pretty Japanese-era residential and office buildings, and narrow walkways bordered by aged brick walls.

The **Crown Prince Chalet** (太子賓館; Tàizǐ Bīngguǎn) at the back of the park was built to house the Japanese royal family on their visit to Taiwan (which alas, never came). It's the best-preserved Japanese-style wooden residence in Taiwan, and really quite a beautiful structure. However, at the time of writing you could only wander the gardens and look inside.

The former working **Beishan Fifth Tunnel** (本山五坑; Běnshān Wǔkēng; admission NT$50) allows visitors to go inside and glimpse mining conditions of the old days, while the **Gold Museum** (黃金博物館; Huángjīn Bówùguǎn) lets you touch

THERE'S *STILL* GOLD IN THEM THERE HILLS

In the 1890s, the construction of the Keelung to Taipei railway attracted Cantonese miners who had worked the fields in the great Californian gold rush. Among them were the Li family, who have long been credited with discovering the first gold deposits in Juifen.

In the following years, the Taiyang Mining Corporation was formed and began to exploit the deposit, using what were then the most advanced mining techniques. Mining continued until 1971, though the gold had not all been collected. Even today there remains a 250-metric-ton reserve estimated at more than NT$200 billion (US$6 billion) sitting under the Gold Ecological Museum. With the precious metal's value at an all-time high there has been talk of reopening the mines. Once again the most up-to-date mining methods would be applied and once again the good times would roll for Juifen and Jinguashi.

Unfortunately for Taiyang, its mining rights expired in 2008. Adding insult to injury, gold fever in Juifen has long cooled, and many locals are more concerned about environmental destruction than any profit that might be made. As one local businessman told us bluntly, 'We don't want mining. Tourism is our gold now'.

what is reportedly the largest gold bar in the world. Sitting high on the steep slopes above the park, the ruins of the **Gold Temple** (黃金神社; Huángjīn Shénshè) look like something out of Greek mythology.

Golden Waterfall WATERFALL

The water that forms this unusual fall (黃金瀑布; Huángjīn Pùbù) has a yellow hue from the copper and iron deposits it picks up as it passes through Jinguashi's old mines. You'll find the waterfall down from the Gold Ecological Park as you head towards the sea.

Remains of the 13 Levels HISTORIC SITE

Further towards the sea from the Golden Waterfall, the remains are a massive **copper-smelting refinery** (十三層; Shísāncéng). The refinery inspires such a heavy, dystopian industrial awe that it has been used as a background for music videos. There are signs in English to direct you here from the park.

Sleeping

There's no budget accommodation in the area, but a number of quaint B&Bs dot the hillsides, should you want to spend the night.

Shi Shan Shui Chan HOMESTAY $$

(石山水禪; Shí Shān Shuǐ Chán; ☎2424 9473; http://tw.myblog.yahoo.com/xzxz1019; d/tw NT$3000/4000) This three-storey red-brick residence hails back to the Japanese mining days and has retained most of its original character. Rooms have quaint architectural touches such as carved beams and window lattice, and are filled with old wood furnishings, statues and vases. Sleeping rooms look seaward and have balconies for watching the sunrise. There are 20% discounts midweek.

Shi Shan Shui Chan sits on the back side of Jinguashi as you head down to the sea, and it's very tricky to find. Ask for a pick-up when you make a reservation.

Information

Jinguashi Visitor Information Centre (金瓜石旅遊服務中心; ⏲9am-5pm) At the start of the Gold Ecological Park. An English brochure includes a good map, and information on sights inside and outside the park.

Juifen Visitor Information Centre (九份旅遊服務中心; ⏲9am-5pm) Just down the street on the opposite side from the Juifen Kite Museum, the centre is worth a visit for the informative history sections (in English).

Getting There & Around

From Taipei, catch a frequent **Keelung Bus Company** (www.klbus.com.tw; NT$95) bus at Zhongxiao Fuxing MRT (exit 1) to Jiufen/Jinguashi. Buses pass the Juifen bus stop near the 7-Eleven first and then proceed to Jinguashi (the final stop). The two towns are 3km apart and are served by buses every 10 minutes or so. By train from Taipei (fast/slow train NT$78/50, 40/50 minutes, every 30 minutes), exit at Ruifang, cross the road and catch a bus the last 15 minutes to Juifen/Jinguashi. Expect to stand on the train.

Bitou Cape 鼻頭角

One of three capes along the north coast, Bitou Cape (Bítóu Jiǎo) is of note for its beautiful sea-eroded cliffs, fantastic views along the coast, and the **Bitou Cape Trail** (鼻頭角步道; Bítóu Jiǎo Bùdào), which is like an easier version of the nearby and more majestic Caoling Historical Trail.

Interestingly, the rock formations on one part of the trail were formed six million years ago, while those at another, only 3km away, were formed 60 million years ago. For fun, make a bet with your companions to see who can tell which is which.

The trail starts near the cape's bus stop before the tunnel and takes a couple of hours to walk. There is a map available in English. To get here from Keelung, take a bus (NT$81, 20 minutes, hourly) from the **Keelung Bus Company** (基隆客運; ☎02-2433 6111) station.

Longdong 龍洞

Just through the tunnel past Bitou Cape is Longdong (Lóngdòng), a well-known diving and snorkelling spot. Within walking distance of the park is an area described as having the best **rock climbing** in Taiwan and some of the best coastal climbs anywhere. One standout feature of the area is the wealth of climbs at all levels. Pick up a copy of *Rock Climbing Taiwan* by Matt Robertson and see the brilliant website www.climbstone.com for more.

Keelung Bus Company buses stop outside the park every hour or so (NT$86, 20 minutes).

SCUBA OFF THE NORTHEAST COAST

Good diving spots can be found stretching from the limestone cape of Yeliu down to the high sea-cliff walls off Ilan. Visibility is generally good, averaging between 5m and 12m, while water temperature varies much more than down south: while it can be a comfy 25°C to 28°C in summer, in winter it can get down to 17°C. Bring a 5mm suit!

All entrances are shore based, and, frankly, are a bit tough, with rocky shores, swells and currents to contend with. However, those same currents mean you'll find a rich variety of tropical and temperate sea life. Divers rave about the soft coral patches along coastal walls, and the large numbers of beautiful sea fans that can be seen in areas with particularly strong currents.

If you go out, note that the seas off Yeliu, Bitou Cape and Longdong bay are very crowded with divers on summer weekends. However, during the week they can be delightfully empty (of people).

Yenliao 鹽寮

This is northern Taiwan's longest **beach** (Yánliáo; admission NT$60; 8am-6pm) and we're always surprised that it doesn't get the same buzz as Fulong Beach does. Facilities at the beach include a garden area as you enter, a children's water park, a cafe, showers and changing rooms.

To get to Yenliao beach, take a train to Fulong, 5km to the south, and then take a taxi. Alternatively, catch any bus heading up the coast.

Fulong Beach 福隆海水浴場

The most popular **beach** (Fúlóng Hǎishuǐ Yùchǎng; admission NT$90; May-Oct) in northern Taiwan is also one of the best and easiest to get to. Fulong has a long sandy beach and clear waters that are suitable for sailing, windsurfing, surfing and other sports. The coastline is a popular cycling destination.

In recent years the town of Fulong has seen some aesthetic improvements (some buildings have actually had a fresh coat of paint applied), and the beach area is getting new wooden boardwalks, pavilions, treed parks and open-air restaurants.

Note that there are two parts to the beach, divided by the Shuangshi River. The left beach, behind the **Northeast Coast Scenic Administration** (www.necoast-nsa.gov.tw; 9am-5pm) building is the paid area; you'll have to use this section if you want to do any water sports that require rentals, and it's a long and clean beach. If you head right and go through the YMCA grounds and continue towards a large temple on the end of a peninsula, you'll get to the free beach, which is a great place to swim or surf and is reasonably clean in summer.

Dangers & Annoyances

The beach is officially closed after October but people still come here to surf and swim. Note that the beach is usually pretty dirty at this time unless a crew has been in recently to clean it up.

The currents at Fulong can be treacherous in places, especially where the river flows into the sea.

The Environmental Protection Agency (EPA) recommends that people do not swim several days after a typhoon, as many contaminants get washed into the sea from the land. During summer, the EPA makes regular announcements about the water quality here and at other beaches.

Activities

Cycling

In addition to all the water activities, Fulong has bike routes suitable for families with kids, as well as for more-serious cyclists. Straight ahead from the train station a path crosses Hwy 2, runs to the visitor centre, goes over **Longmen Suspension Bridge**, and heads through a scrubby forest to Yenliao Beach, a few kilometres to the north.

To the right of the train station a bike path leads to the **Caoling Old Tunnel** (舊草嶺隧道; Jiù Cǎolǐng Suìdào), a 2km train tunnel built in 1924. The tunnel essentially cuts through the cape, dropping you off on the southeast side. At the time of writing construction was in place for a bike-only route to then follow Hwy 2 back up to Fulong, in all a 26km loop. You can rent cheap bikes all around the train station.

For a more challenging ride head north out of Fulong on Hwy 2 and take the first left at the petrol station. Follow the road to the town of **Shuangxi** (雙溪) and look for the bike signs just past a red bridge pointing to the **Shuangtai Industry Road** (雙泰產業道路; Shuāngtài Chǎnyè Dàolù). This 30km route runs through a quiet watershed area with superb views over densely wooded hills rolling down to the Pacific Ocean. The first section is very steep and seemingly endless, but is followed by a long, gentling rolling stretch with a final fast steep descent into Daxi.

Many cyclists ride the Shuangtai Industry Rd as part of a long day ride from Taipei to the coast.

Festivals & Events

Every July, Fulong hosts the **Hohaiyan Music Festival** (http://hohaiyan.com). Now in its eighth year, the festival has grown from a small indie event into the largest outdoor concert in Taiwan, attracting hundreds of thousands over a three-day period.

Sleeping & Eating

Fulong Bellevue Resort BEACH RESORT **$$$**
(福隆貝悅酒店; Fúlóng Bèiyuè Jiǔdiàn; ☎02-2499 2381; www.fulongbellevue.com.tw; d/tw NT$6000/8000; Ⓟ) This private garden resort sits just off the beach and offers for rent small cosy cabins with mountain or sea views. Though not a large resort, the access to bike paths through the forest and a long beachfront make it seem quite spacious. You're nicely removed from the madness on the rest of the beach as well. Rates drop midweek and during winter.

Longmen Riverside Camping Resort CAMPGROUND **$**
(龍門露營區; Lóngmén Lùyín Qū; ☎02-2499 1791; entrance fee NT$70, 4-person site incl tent from NT$800, 2-/4-person cabins NT$2300/3500) This 37-hectare campground by the Shuangshi River has accommodation for up to 1600 people. To get here from Fulong train station, exit the station and turn left at the main road (Hwy 2). Just past the visitor centre a dedicated lane runs along the highway to the campground. It takes about 10 minutes to walk here from the station.

There are cheap restaurants and convenience stores all around the train station area. **Fulong Biandang** (福隆便當; Fúlóng Biàndāng; lunchbox NT$55) is a bit of an institution in the area, having served cheap but tasty lunchboxes for decades. The rustic shop is just to the left of the train station as you exit. Just go to the back of the shop and shout 'Biàndāng' if no one is out the front.

Getting There & Away

Trains from Taipei to Fulong (fast/slow train NT$130/84, one hour/one hour and 20 minutes) leave every 30 minutes or so.

Caoling (Tsaoling) Historic Trail & Taoyuan Valley Trail

草嶺古道、桃園谷步道

If you can only do one hike in the north, make it this one. It runs along rugged coastal bluffs forming the very northeasterly extent of the Snow Mountain Range. The first sections of the trail take you through thick woodlands and scrub, which are pleasant enough, but it's the many, many kilometres along high grassy headlands overlooking the Pacific that make this hike such a treasure. To top things off, there are wild grazing buffalo to observe and a few boulder-sized historical tablets.

In 1807 the government in Taiwan built the Caoling Trail (Cǎolǐng Gǔdào) to provide transport between Danshui and Ilan. The 8.5km section that remains today is one of the few historical roads left in Taiwan.

In recent years, a long addition was made to the trail called the Taoyuan Valley Trail (Táoyuángǔ Bùdào). Taoyuan Valley is not a valley but is an emerald grassy bluff, kept trim by the water buffalo. It's stunningly beautiful up here and is a prime spot for picnicking. With the addition of the Taoyuan Valley Trail section, the entire Caoling trail is about 16km long and takes five to eight hours to complete.

The trail is broad and simple to follow, with signposts and maps (in English), though it certainly is strenuous in places. There is not the slightest danger of getting lost, but do save the walk for the autumn or spring months. You'll roast at the top during summer and during winter you'll understand exactly why there is a 10m-long boulder inscribed 'Boldly Quell the Wild Mists'.

There are many ways to tackle this trail, and several shortcuts, but the two most common starting and ending points are Fulong Beach and Daxi. Pick up a map at the Fulong visitor centre to plan which route is best for you. However, finishing in Daxi can mean having a fresh seafood dinner that you've picked out at the market.

Daxi (Miyuewan) 大溪

☎03 / POP 500

There's not much to recommend in the little coastal town of Daxi (Dàxī) itself, but its southern edge has a popular surfing beach known as Honeymoon Bay (蜜月灣; Mìyuè Wān). Waves are generally chest to head high, though during the summer typhoon months they can be over 3m high. Depending on the swells, conditions are suitable for beginner to advanced surfers.

As at other popular surfing venues you'll find board rental, and shops selling food and drink around the beach. One place where English is spoken is **Spider Surf Club** (www.spidersurfing.com; 96 Binghai Rd, Sec 5; 濱海路5段96號), which offers surfing lessons (including room and board, NT$3000) and dorm accommodation (NT$300) on weekends. When you exit the train station, the club is just to the left on the other side of the street.

Daxi is also the end (or start) of the Caoling (Tsaoling) Historic Trail & Taoyuan Valley Trail. The trailhead begins just north of town after you cross the bridge over the Daxi River.

Getting There & Away

There's a train from Taipei (NT$104, 1½ hours) every two hours. When you exit at Daxi, cross the road and walk south about 600m along the sea wall to reach the beach.

EVERYBODY'S GONE SURFING!

Or so it seems. So popular has the sport become these past few years that in the summer months you could probably walk from Baishawan all the way to Wushi Harbour. We mean on the water, or, rather, on the endless floating boards just offshore.

Baishawan has a nice safe sandy beach break and can accommodate the needs of beginner to advanced surfers. **Jhong-jiao bay** (中角灣; Zhōngjiǎo Wān), further east and just north of Jinshan, is one of the hottest surfing destinations these days. Depending on the swell the beach is suitable for beginner to advanced surfers but better surfers usually avoid the place. As at most popular venues, during peak season you will be sharing the waters with a lot of people who don't know what they are doing. We mean 'a lot' and there isn't much emphasis on skills or etiquette. To put it bluntly, as one veteran of the surf scene told us, the attitude on the water is basically, 'F-you, me first'.

Daxi hasn't suffered quite the fate of Jhong-jiao and can still be a chill-out place in the low season. Just a little further south is **Wai-Ao**, the least-crowded beach to date, largely because it lacks the number of guesthouses and rental shops found at the other beaches. Again, depending on the swell, conditions are suitable for beginner to advanced surfers.

The absolute craziest place to try to catch the waves is at **Wushih Harbour** (烏石港; Wūshí Gǎng), just south of Wai-Ao or just north of Toucheng. If you take the beach road from Wai-Ao you will start to hit the shops very quickly. A quiet beach just a few years ago, Wushih is now overrun with tents, rental shops, guesthouses, restaurants, and every wannabe surfer from Keelung to Pingtung. Avoid heading here on weekends unless this description appeals to you.

Surfboard rentals across the north are usually NT$500 to NT$600 per day. Wetsuits are available, though you can usually surf in the north in a swimsuit or shortie, with a wetsuit reserved for those cold snaps in January and February.

Those looking for a custom-made board should check out the services of **Master Hsieh** (☎04-2386 3558, 0955-198 368) in Taichung. He has been making custom boards (mostly for Japanese and Australian customers) for 28 years and has a great reputation.

For surfing in the south of Taiwan, see p267.

Wai-Ao 外澳

Wai-Ao (Wài-ào) is a small village on the coast that has become a popular **surfing** venue in recent years. The two most recognisable structures at Wai-Ao are a humungous yellow Mr Brown (a cafe chain shop) and what looks like a mosque but is actually the residence of a Taiwanese who has extensive business dealings in the Middle East.

There are a few B&Bs along the Wai-Ao beachfront, and some surf rental shops on the main road (Hwy 2).

Trains from Taipei (NT$117, one hour and 40 minutes) leave approximately every two hours.

Turtle Island (Kueishgan Island) 龜山島

This captivating volcanic islet (Gūishān Dǎo), 10km off the coast of Ilan, is less than 3km long yet rises up to 400m and supports 13 species of butterflies and 33 species of birds.

The island also has numerous quirky geological features. These include **underwater hot springs** that turn the offshore water into a bubbling cauldron, **volcanic fumaroles** that spout steam, and a **'turtle head'** that faces right or left depending on where you stand on shore.

Turtle Island is open from March to November. If you wish to land on the island you must apply at least two weeks in advance for a special permit. (If you simply wish to sail around it you don't need a permit.) You can download a copy of the application form, but only from the Chinese section of the **Northeast Coast Scenic Administration** (www.necoast-nsa.gov.tw) website. Once you get your permit, call a boat operator to make a reservation. Here's one with an English speaking guide: ☎03-955 8882.

Boats leave from Wushih Harbour. It costs NT$600 for a 1½-hour cruise to and around the island, and NT$1000 for a three-hour tour that includes a stop on the island. Combination tours involving stops on the island and **dolphin- and whale-watching** (April to September) are also available (NT$1600, 4½ hours).

To get to Wushih Harbour, take a train from Taipei to Toucheng (fast/slow train NT$189/122, 1½/two hours, every half-hour) and then a short taxi ride.

Call the **English Tourist Hotline** (☎0800-011 765) or **Northeast Coast Scenic Administration** (☎02-2499 1115) for more information.

Jiaoshi 礁溪

☎03 / POP 5000

This small coastal town is known for a three-layered waterfall (sadly reduced to two at the time of writing), hot springs and related cuisine (they grow vegetables in hot-spring water). As with many spa areas in Taiwan, Jiaoshi is overdeveloped, crowded and not terribly attractive but many cyclists riding from Taipei along Provincial Hwys 2 or 9 use it as an overnight stop. The hotels roadside are cheapest, while those further back towards the mountains have the best water and facilities.

For a cheap, fun place to soak try **Art Spa Hotel** (中冠礁溪大飯店; Zhōngguàn Jiāoxī Dàfàndiàn; 6 Deyang Rd; per person unlimited time NT$250; ⏲7.30am-11pm), which features the only hot-spring slide (that we know of) in Taiwan. To get here walk straight out of the train station, turn left on Zhongshan Rd and then right on Deyang Rd.

There's a **visitor information centre** (遊客中心; ☎987 2403; 16 Gongyuan Rd; ⏲9am-5pm; @) a 10-minute walk from the train station, with good brochures on Ilan County.

In addition to trains to Jiaoshi (fast/slow NT$200/129) there are fast direct buses from Taipei via the new tunnel. Catch these from the Taipei City Hall MRT station, exit 3 (NT$90, 50 minutes).

You can rent scooters outside the train station (NT$300 to NT$600) with an International Driver's Licence.

National Centre of Traditional Arts 國立傳統藝術中心

A must-see for anyone interested in folk art and customs, this **centre** (Guólì Chuántǒng Yìshù Zhōngxīn; www.ncfta.gov.tw; admission NT$150; ⏲9am-6pm; @) occupies 24 hectares along the scenic Tongshan River and is a venue for the research and performance of folk music, opera, dance, toy-making and even acrobatics. For visitors there is an exhibition hall loaded with prized artefacts and informative displays (in English) on everything from family shrines to the life

SHUTTLE BUSES AROUND ILAN COUNTY

At the time of writing, the Taiwan Tourism Bureau was experimenting with a shuttle bus system around Taiwan to encourage people to leave their cars at home. Some of these buses were going to popular routes such as Sun Moon Lake, but others were taking in more obscure sights, and those sights previously not served by public transport. There were several routes around Ilan County, starting at Jiaoshi train station. Buses were free at the time of going to press. See www.taiwantrip.com.tw (in Chinese).

of students under a Confucian education system. Along the river sits a genuine traditional scholar's house that was rescued from the wrecker's ball and reassembled on the centre grounds. The folk-art street shops sell good-quality glassware, paper cuttings and glove puppets in a recreated traditional township atmosphere.

Trains to Luodong (羅東; fast/slow train NT$239/154, 1½/2½ hours) leave Taipei about every half-hour. Once in Luodong, it's a short taxi ride to the arts centre.

Alternatively, take the bus to Jiaoshi and catch the tourism shuttle bus (see boxed text, above).

THE SU-HUA HIGHWAY: SUAO TO HUALIEN

Just past Luodong, Hwy 9 rejoins the coast and begins what is known as the Suao-Hualien Hwy. The road stretches for 118km along the coastline and is carved into sheer cliff walls. At one of the most breathtaking sections, the Qingshui (Chingshui) cliffs, the highway is literally cut into towering walls of marble and granite that loom 1000m above the rocky seashore.

The beginnings of the route go back to 1874, when the Qing government ordered a road to be built along the east coast to alleviate some of the region's isolation. The Japanese widened the road in 1920, battling with landslides and earthquakes the whole time. In fact, the road didn't officially reopen for public use until 1932.

Plans to turn the highway into a superfast freeway have been tossed about for decades but were finally scuttled in 2010 when the government announced that it would pay for an expansion of the existing highway, but not for a full freeway. The plan calls for widening the road, straightening it where possible using old tunnels, and most excitingly adding a dedicated **bike lane**.

Suao 蘇澳

☎03 / POP 44, 487

Suao is a grubby little port town noted only for the **Suao Cold Springs** (蘇澳冷泉; Sūaò Lěng Quán). The carbonated springs have an average temperature of 22°C and are completely odourless, making them a rare treasure in the world. Unfortunately you have a choice between cheap and grotty old facilities or swank but correspondingly pricey hotels that require an overnight stay. Unless you are a true aficionado, at this time they probably aren't worth visiting.

Many local photographers find the **harbour** to be a great subject.

Nanao 南澳

☎03 / POP 500

The small coastal town of **Nanao** (Nánào; www.nanao.e-land.gov.tw) has a pretty crescent bay with a dark sandy beach that's visible from the highway as you make your descent from the hills. It's a great spot for strolling along and taking in the gorgeous coastal scenery. Heading towards the hills, the scenery and the ethnography change completely, from alluvial plains and the Hakka to deep-cut river valleys and the Atayal.

Though it covers a large area, it's easy to find your bearings in Nanao. Highway 9 runs through the centre, you can clearly see the sea to the east and the mountains to the west.

History

Atayal aboriginals settled in the Nanao region about 250 years ago, and throughout the late Qing period were successful in repelling Taiwanese advancement. It was not until 1910, after a five-year campaign by the Japanese to 'pacify' aboriginal groups, that Taiwanese settlers were able to begin to develop the land for farming. These days the

Atayal presence is still strong, and much of their traditional way of life, including hunting for deer and pigs, is visible as soon as you head off the highway.

Sights & Activities

Cycling & Hiking

Despite being nestled between the sea and some very rugged mountains, Nanao's cycling is, for the most part, flat and leisurely. The alluvial plains on the east side of Hwy 9 offer hours of riding on empty roads through pretty farming fields. On the west side, a couple of roads head up the valleys formed by the North and South Nanao Rivers.

To reach the north river valley, head south out of town and at the 133km mark turn right onto **Township Rd 55**. A few kilometres past **Jin-yue Village** look for signs for the public **Four Parts Hot Springs** (四區溫泉; Sìqū Wēnquán) facilities. After a dip in the waters, continue to the end of the road. It's gorgeous up here.

To reach the south river valley road, head down Hwy 9 south out of town to the 136km mark and turn right on **Township Rd 57**. Ten kilometres up the valley, the road ends at the start of the **Nanao Historic Trail** (南澳古道; Nánào Gǔdào), an old Qing-dynasty cross-island road that recently had 3km restored. It's a beautiful walk up a deep river valley and the chances of hearing and spotting indigenous birds, monkeys, deer and even wild pigs are high.

You can rent cheap bikes (which should be fine for the conditions) just outside the train station.

Sleeping & Eating

There are many small noodle shops and restaurants in Nanao beside the highway, and a couple of lunchbox shops near the train station. There's also a 7-Eleven, a small grocery store and a night market near the town square.

Nan-Ao Recreation Farm CAMPGROUND $
(南澳農場; Nánào Nóngchǎng; ☎988 1114; http://nanao-farm.e-land.gov.tw/html/link2.htm, in Chinese; tent sites from NT$200) This large, clean and green campground is perfect when there's no one else around (locals can keep you up all night with karaoke). To reach the site from Nanao, turn left at the 134.5km mark just after crossing a bridge. Follow the road down about 1km to the obvious campground entrance (NT$60 entrance fee).

Getting There & Away

There are trains every hour or two to Nanao from Taipei (fast/slow NT$305/196; 2½ to three hours).

NORTH CROSS-ISLAND HIGHWAY

If you're looking for wild scenery but want a change of pace from coastal waters and rugged shorelines, try a journey down National Hwy 7, also known as the Běihéng or North Cross-Island Hwy (Běibù Héngguàn Gōnglù).

The highway starts in the old Taoyuan County town of Daxi (not to be confused with the Ilan County town on the north-east coast), famous for its excellent *dòugān* (firm tofu) and the Qing-dynasty facades on Heping St. At first the road winds through the countryside, passing flower farms and settlements, including the burial grounds of former leader Chiang Kai-shek. After passing above Shimen Reservoir, the largest body of water in northern Taiwan, the road narrows and starts to rise and wind its way along steep gorges, across precipitously high bridges and, in general, through some pretty fantastic mountain scenery.

At Chilan, the highway descends suddenly and an hour later enters the flood plains of the Lanyang River, which divides the Snow and Yushan Ranges and is home to the largest cabbage patch in Taiwan. The road then continues northeast to Ilan, with spur routes to Luodong and Wuling FRA.

You can drive the highway in four or five hours, but there are many great stops leading to waterfalls, caves, forest reserves, hot springs and stands of ancient trees. It's best to have your own transport, as buses are few and far between. Cycling the highway is popular these days, if challenging. In general, accommodation options are few and far between; if you're spending the night, stay in the Baling area, about halfway across.

The entire highway can literally become a car park during Chinese New Year and on hot summer weekends. Late autumn and winter are especially good times to go as the crowds are thin and the sights seem improved by the chill and mist in the air. If you drive, be very aware of both other drivers and the natural hazards. This road is curvy and treacherous, and some part of the surface is always under repair due to typhoons and landslides. While much of the road is being widened these days, in some places there is only enough room for one car.

Information

Cihu Visitor Information Centre (慈湖遊客中心; ☎03-388 3552; ⏰8.30am-5pm) Just off Hwy 7 at the back of a large car park, this centre covers Taoyuan County and sights along the North Cross-Island Hwy.

Getting There & Around

Bicycle

The highway usually takes two days by bike from Taipei, with an overnight stop in Baling or Mingchi. Bicycling is popular with bloggers, so there's lots of information online (see p32).

Bus

Taoyuan Bus Company (桃園客運; ☎03-388 2002; www.tybus.1968.com.tw) Has one daily bus to Lalashan (NT$203, three hours, 6.50am) leaving from Taoyuan, and one leaving from Chungli (NT$201, three hours, 10.30am). Both bus stations are close to the train stations in those cities.

Tourism bus (www.taiwantrip.com.tw) From the back of the Chungli train station to Cihuand Shimen Reservoir.

Car & Scooter

Rent a car in Taipei, or a scooter in Jiaoshi.

Cihu 慈湖

Cihu (Cíhú; Lake Kindness) is a quiet, scenic park where the remains of Chiang Kai-shek's body are entombed, awaiting an eventual return to China. It's also the site of one of Taiwan's oddest tourism attractions. No, not the mausoleum itself, but **Cihu Memorial Sculpture Park** (慈湖紀念雕像公園; Cíhú Jìniàn Diāoxiàng Gōngyuán; 8am-5pm), where 152 unwanted Chiang Kai-shek statues have been sent over the past decade to escape being melted down or smashed.

This sculpture safehouse is a hoot (surely unintentionally), with promenades of Chiang busts and clumps of Chiangs standing facing each other as if in conversation. There are storytime Chiangs reading books to shorter Chiangs, salesmen Chiangs bowed at the waist and hat removed, avuncular Chiangs always smiling, and martial Chiangs, sword in hand, ready to defend the nation. We have named the largest statue in the park (a 5m sheet-metal behemoth) Cheshire Chiang: you'll know why when you see it.

The sculpture park is free but if you want to see more of the area (including the mausoleum holding the remains of Chiang Kai-shek), apply ahead of time on the website of **Taoyuan County** (http://backcihu.tycg.gov.tw/Cihu/index.aspx, in Chinese) for the area called **Back Cihu** (後慈湖; Hòu Cíhú; admission NT$100), a former command centre only recently opened to the public.

Shimen Reservoir 石門水庫

In the past, when there were few areas for outdoor leisure in Taiwan, this reservoir (Shímén Shuǐkù; the largest body of water in the north) was deservedly popular for the beauty of its dark-green hills and green-blue water, as well as its numerous scenic pavilions and well-laid-out parks. There's no doubting its appeal, but today it's hardly a must-see destination.

Biking out to the reservoir from Taipei is a popular day trip for stronger cyclists. It's best to start by taking County Rd 110 from Bitan (p102), even if you have to ride through some ugly sprawl at the start. There are hotels at the lake if you wish to ride out, spend the night, and then ride back.

Fusing (Fuhsing, Fuxing) 復興

☎03 / POP 1000

The aboriginal village of Fusing (Fùxīng), 18km down Hwy 7 from Daxi, makes for an excellent pit stop, or an even better base from which to explore the whole area. You can stay (or at least have a coffee) at the Youth Activity Centre, or, in town, you can get solid, aboriginal-style food, such as *tǔ jī* (土雞; free-range chicken), *zhútǒng fàn* (竹筒飯; rice steamed in bamboo tubes) and a variety of noodle dishes served with the mushrooms for which Fusing is famous.

The **Youth Activity Centre** (青年活動中心; Qīngnián Huódòng Zhōngxīn; ☎382 2276; d/tw incl breakfast NT$2600/3200) sits in a pretty, landscaped park on a high ridge overlooking an arm of Shimen Reservoir. The land was formerly occupied by one of Chiang Kai-shek's summer villas (it burned

LOCAL KNOWLEDGE

CHRIS NELSON: GRAVER

My hobby is 'graving'; that is, I visit, research and document cemeteries around the world. It's not a hobby that endears me to superstitious locals here in Taiwan, but I think graving gives me insight into the history and culture of the places I visit.

Best Overall Gravesite

For an excellent introduction to the variety of Chinese graves, nothing beats the **Liuzhangli Cemeteries** in Taipei. There are Buddhist, Taoist, Christian and Muslim graveyards, as well as three White Terror cemeteries where people killed by the Kuomintang are buried.

Foreign Graves

At the **Tamsui Foreign Cemetery** in Danshui there are graves of dozens of foreign merchants, mariners and missionaries. Next to it is the **Mackay Cemetery**, where George Leslie Mackay and his family are buried.

The grave of Nelly O'Driscoll is the remotest one I know of. It's a lonely grave at the **Hsiyu Lighthouse** in Penghu. Nelly was the daughter of a lighthouse keeper, but little else is known about her. Kind of sad, to be buried in such a faraway place.

Don't Miss

Cihu where Chiang Kai-shek (CKS) is entombed. It's interesting: even though CKS is widely reviled now, people still look on his tomb with awe and respect.

Most Kitschy Grave

Up the road from the Juming Museum (see boxed text, p125) there's the tomb of singer Teresa Teng, at **Chin Pao San Cemetery**. Busloads of fans make pilgrimages here to pay homage to 'Taiwan's Sweetheart'. There are kitschy sculptures, piped-in music and even an oversized electronic keyboard you can play.

Best Time to Visit Graves

During the Qing Ming Festival when people return to their ancestors' graves for a once-a-year cleaning.

» For more cemetery information in Taiwan, and the locations of the places mentioned above, check out **Find a Grave** (www.tinyurl.com/taiwangraves).

down in 1992), which should clue you in to the fact that it's incredibly scenic here.

The centre has large, simply furnished rooms with balcony lookouts. Room 404 has one of the best views in the whole building. You can pick up a brochure in English at the centre that highlights attractions in the area.

On a small bluff to the right of the centre (head to the back of the car park and then down the wooden stairs) is **Shenlin Shui An** (森鄰水岸; Sēnlín Shuǐ Àn; Forest House Coffee; ☎382 2108; http://foresthouse.mmmtravel.com.tw, in Chinese; set meals NT$300; ⏲9am-8pm), a small wood-cabin restaurant and cafe run by an aboriginal family. The view here is even more incredible than at the Youth Activity Centre and the food and coffee are far superior. The owner speaks English and used to be a pub singer. If there are enough people around, or if he likes you, he will take out his guitar and play.

By the time you read this, Shenlin Shui An should also have **cabins** for overnight stays.

Dongyanshan Forest Recreation Area 東眼山森林遊樂區

About 1km past Fusing is the turn-off for this 916-hectare **forest recreation area** (Dōngyǎnshān Sēnlín Yóulèqū; www1.forest.gov.tw; admission NT$80; ⏲8am-5pm). There are no buses, but if you have your own vehicle it's a pretty 13km drive up a good road to the **visitor information centre** (遊客中心;

☎03-382 1506), where you can buy simple meals and maps for the area.

The park's altitude ranges from 650m to 1200m, making it a perfect cool retreat in summer. There are many trails, some of which are nature interpretation walks suitable for families, while many others involve two- to three-hour hikes up small mountains. The longest hike is along a 16km trail that actually connects Dongyanshan with neighbouring Manyueyuan FRA (p123). All trails start near the tourist centre and are well marked and easy to follow.

Xiao Wulai Waterfall 小烏來瀑布

Of the four big falls in northern Taiwan – Wufengchi, Shifen, Wulai and this one – we have to say that the 40m-high Xiao Wulai (Xiǎo Wūlái Pùbù) is our favourite. Like Wufengchi and Wulai, this fall is long and cascading, but unlike the other two you can view Xiao Wulai from a ridge almost half a kilometre away. The sweeping scene of steep mountain peaks and the long waterfall bears a remarkable likeness to the famous Song-dynasty landscape painting *Travellers in Mountains and Streams*.

If you are driving, the sign for the turn-off to the falls is just past the 20.5km mark. Two kilometres up County Rd 115 you'll run into a toll booth possibly charging entrance (NT$50) into the waterfall scenic area. The ridge lookout and the start of trails down to the falls are just a few metres past the toll booth.

Lower Baling 巴陵

This small pit stop (Bālíng) on the highway is the usual overnight stop for cyclists. The Youth Activity Centre was closed at the time of writing but you could stay at a couple of hotels on the roadside, including **Lower Baling Hot Spring Hotel** (下巴陵溫泉山莊; Xià Bālíng Wēnquán Shān Zhuāng; ☎03-391 2323; http://shabaling.mmmtravel.com.tw; d/tw NT$2500/4000), which has hot springs to soak in after a long day in the saddle.

Weekday prices are about 40% to 50% of weekend rates, and outside of summertime or holidays you should be able to negotiate lower rates at any time of the week. If the place isn't busy, see if they'll include breakfast and dinner in your room price.

Upper Baling 上巴陵

☎03 / POP 300

The imaginatively named Upper Baling (Shàng Bālíng) sits about 10km up the road from, you guessed it, Lower Baling. Perched on a high thin ridgeline, the village offers some splendid mountain views. More to the point for travellers, it's the site of the **Lalashan Forest Reserve** (拉拉山國有林自然保護區; Lālāshān Guóyǒ Lín Zìrán Bǎohùqū; ☎391 2761; admission NT$100; ⌚8am-5pm), a 6390-hectare expanse of mixed forest holding one of the largest stands of ancient red hinoki cypress trees left in Taiwan.

The most ancient of the ancients is over 2800 years old, but there are a hundred more that are not much younger. A 3.7km wooden boardwalk winds through the dense forest, and interpretative signs indicate the age, species, height and diameter of each giant.

To get to the reserve, exit Hwy 7 at Lower Baling onto County Rd 116. Pay your entrance fee at the toll booth and continue up a very steep road. Not long after passing Upper Baling you'll reach a car park at the end of the road (about 13km from the turn-off on Hwy 7). The trail begins just up from here and there's a small **exhibition hall** (⌚9am-6pm) at the start where you can pick up maps and information.

From the reserve it's possible to hike six hours all the way downhill to **Fushan** near Wulai on the Fu-Ba National Trail (p113). It's also possible to hike up (eight to 10 hours), spend the night in a nearby B&B and then hike back the next day. If you stay the night at **Magic World Country House** (富仙境鄉村渡假旅館; Fùxīanjìng Xiāngcūn Dùjià Lǚguǎn; ☎02-2880 5080; fax: ☎02-2883 7511; d incl breakfast NT$3000, 30% weekday discount), you can be picked up from Lalashan and returned the next day, if you request this in advance.

There is also one daily bus from Taoyuan and Chungli (see Bus, p137) to the reserve that gets you there early enough to explore and hike down to Fushan.

Mingchih Forest Recreation Area 明池森林遊憩區

This **forest recreation area** (Míngchí Sēnlín Yóuqì Qū; www.yeze.com.tw/mingchih/html/page002-1.htm; admission NT$120; ⌚8am-5pm) is a great base for exploration, and provides a retreat from the relentless heat of summer in the city. Lying at an altitude between 1000m and 1700m, even in July the average temperature is only 20°C.

There's not much in the reserve itself except pleasant little **Lake Mingchih** (明池湖; Míngchí Hú) across the highway. It's popular with ducks, and strolling around it when you first wake up is a great way to start the day. Nearby are wild hot springs and a stand of ancient trees (not the ones at Upper Baling).

Sights & Activities

TOP CHOICE Ma-Kou Ecological Park — ANCIENT FOREST

A few kilometres down Hwy 7 past Mingchih is the gated entrance to this ecological park (馬告生態公園; Mǎgào Shēntài Gōngyuán), with a stand of ancient red cypress trees easily the match of those at Lalashan.

Only 720 visitors a day can enter the park, and you need to be on a tour. Tours leave three times a day from Mingchih (guests staying at the forest recreation area pay NT$600; nonguests NT$800). There are also daily tours starting from Taipei (NT$1490). To make a reservation contact the front-desk staff at Mingchih or in Taipei call **Coconut Tree Company** (☎02-2507 1339; www.yeze.com.tw/index2.htm). Buses depart from Taipei around 7.45am to 8am from Sun Yat-Sen Memorial Hall MRT (exit 4) and return at around 8.30pm.

Hot Springs

There are numerous hot springs within a short drive of Mingchih, some developed, as at Jioujheze on the way up to Taipingshan, and Jiaoshi, but there are also some great natural ones for those willing to do a little hiking.

Sileng Hot Spring — WILD HOT SPRING

This beautifully set natural spring (四稜溫泉; Sìléng Wēnquán) lies at the bottom of a steep ravine. To get here, head west from Mingchih exactly 7.1km (to around the 59.5km mark). As you go around a sharp bend that juts out into the valley you'll see a small spot on the left to park. Park and then, standing back a bit and facing towards the valley, look for the faded signs for 'hot spring' (溫泉) on the cement barrier to your right. Cross the barrier here and look for a trail starting on the other side. Follow the trail down for 40 minutes or so till you reach the river. The springs are obvious on the other side, though you may get off track a few times on unmarked branch trails on the way down. Give yourself plenty of time.

Note that as you hike down, the trail seems to run flat for quite a while. Note also that you must cross the river at the end, so don't go after heavy rain. River shoes will be helpful.

Sleeping & Eating

Mingchih has rooms and cottages (from NT$3900) set among tall cedar trees. Try to get a room away from the highway, though, as trucks come by at all times of day or night and can disturb your sleep. An OK restaurant serves breakfast, lunch and dinner (average meal NT$250); it's the only restaurant here.

Getting There & Away

Guests who are staying overnight at Mingchih can take a daily shuttle (NT$600, around 8am) from Taipei MRT Sun Yat-Sen Memorial Hall station (exit 4). Otherwise, you need your own transport.

Taipingshan National Forest Recreation Area

太平山國家森林遊樂區

During the 20th century, Alishan (p205), Bashianshan (see boxed text, p223) and this 12,600-hectare **forest recreation area** (Tàipíngshān Guójiā Sēnlín Yóulè Qū; http://tps.forest.gov.tw; admission NT$200, per vehicle NT$100; ⏲6am-9pm) were the three top logging sites in Taiwan. Taipingshan only became a protected area in 1983 and has since transformed itself into one of the best mountain retreats in Taiwan. Around a small wooden village set on the forested slopes are endless lookouts over the Snow Mountains, as well as Japanese shrines, hiking trails through old forests, and informative displays on the old logging industry.

The 30km ride up to Taipingshan from Hwy 7 takes more than an hour on the very steep and tortuous road. Be aware that this area is often very foggy and at times you may not be able to reach the village. The best time to visit the park is from April to November, especially in late autumn when the leaves are changing color.

Sights & Activities

Hiking

Logging in the 20th century mostly stripped Taiwan of its ancient cypress forests, but left intact huge tracts of hemlock, pine, beech and maple. Which means that as you hike the many trails around Taiping village you're going to find yourself in some dense, beautiful old growth. A decent network of well-marked trails begins just up from the village but there are more trails starting off the road. Pick up a map at the visitor centre.

The tiny passenger **Bong Bong Train** (蹦蹦車; Bèngbèng Chē; NT$100), which leaves every half-hour, begins at the village and takes riders on a 20-minute trip through the forest. At the end two trails split, one through lush forest, the other to the **Sandie Waterfalls** (三疊瀑布; Sāndié Pùbù). The train's schedule is posted at the station.

Jioujhihze Hot Springs 鳩之澤溫泉 HOT SPRINGS

(Jiūzhīzé Wēnquán; unlimited time public pools NT$200; ⌚9am-8pm) Less than halfway up the road to Taipingshan (already at an altitude of 520m but with another 22km to go) are the mildly sulphurous and extremely hot Jioujhize Hot Springs. For fun before you head off for a dip, join others who are boiling eggs in a special pool.

The public facilities are simple rock-lined pools (and include two nude pools segregated by sex), while the private rooms feature nice wooden inset tubs (NT$400 to NT$800 per hour).

Lake Cuifeng SCENIC AREA

(翠峰湖; Cuìfēng Hú) This very scenic small lake is set at 1900m above sea level and is reportedly the largest alpine lake in Taiwan. Two trails offer a chance to get up close and personal with the 3.9km **Cuifeng Lake Circle Trail** (翠峰湖環山步道; Cuìfēng Hú Huánshān Bùdào), a favourite with those who want to get away from the crowds.

Lake Cuifeng is another 16km up the road from the villa area.

Sleeping & Eating

There's only one place at which to sleep and eat: in the lodge area called Taipingshan Villa. Here the **accommodation** (☎02-030 1176; tw/cottage from NT$2500, 20-30% weekday discount) includes dinner and breakfast. A huge lunch is an extra NT$200. You must make room reservations in advance.

Getting There & Around

It's best to have your own vehicle for Taipingshan, but **Kuo Kuang Motor Transport** (☎02-2311 9893; www.kingbus.com.tw) has buses from Ilan (NT$226, 9.30am) and Luodong (NT$200, 9.40am) only on Saturday, Sunday and holidays. Buses arrive at 12.20pm and leave the next day at 3.30pm. Note that buses don't run to Lake Cuifong.

Wuling Forest Recreation Area (Wuling Farm)

武陵農場

☎04

About 1½ hours further south down Hwy 7 from the turn-off is Wuling Forest Recreation Area, better known as **Wuling Farm** (Wǔlíng Nóngchǎng; admission NT$160). Originally established in 1963 as a fruit-growing area by retired soldiers, the farm (elevation 1740m to 2200m) became part of Sheipa National Park in 1992, and these days only a few show orchards remain.

Many travellers come to Wuling to climb Snow Mountain (see p144), Taiwan's second-highest mountain, but Wuling also makes for a nice weekend getaway, or a cool break from the heat of summer.

There's only one main road through the park, with an offshoot to the campground. The **visitor information centre** (旅遊客服務中心; www.wuling-farm.com.tw; ⌚9am-4.30pm) near the bus stop (公車站) is a good source of information about the park and offers maps, books and travel tips.

Activities

Hiking

For the average person, Wuling offers short walks down by the river or strolls along newly built paths beside the main road. The only longish hike is to **Taoshan Waterfall** (桃山瀑布; Táoshān Pùbù), 4.5km from the end of the road near Wuling Villa hostel and with an elevation of 2500m. The falls are 50m high and well worth the 1½-hour hike.

Salmon-Viewing

Wuling Farm is well known for its efforts to preserve the indigenous and endangered **Formosan landlocked salmon**

Wuling Farm

Wuling Farm

Sleeping

1 Camping Ground A2
2 Wuling National Hostel B5
3 Wuling Villa B1

Eating

4 Convenience Store B4

Information

Police Station .... (see 5)
5 Sheipa National Park Wuling Station B4
6 Visitor Information Centre B4

Transport

7 Bus Stop B4

(櫻花鉤吻鮭; Yīnghuā Gōuwěn Gūi), also known as the masu salmon. Unlike other salmon, these never leave the cool freshwater rivers they were born in. At the time of writing a new **ecocentre** was about to open in the riverside park area.

Sleeping & Eating

Wuling Villa HOSTEL $$
(武陵山莊; Wuling Mountain Hostel; Wŭlíng Shānzhuāng; ☎2590 1020; dm/s/d NT$690/2230/2480, 15% weekday discount) Despite the name, this is the hostel in the Wuling area. Rooms here have simple wooden interiors with a minimum of furniture. Breakfast (congee and salty eggs) is included and lunch/dinner costs NT$150/350. For dorm rooms ask for a *tongpu* (東埔).

Camping Ground CAMPGROUND $
(露營管理中心; Lùyíng Guănlĭ Zhōngxīn; ☎2590 1265; sites from NT$400) Set high on a gorgeous alpine meadow, this campground offers clean, modern facilities (including showers and a convenience store) with raised camping platforms and grass sites. The raised army-style tents are very cosy.

Wuling National Hostel HOTEL/CABINS $$
(武陵國民賓館; Wŭlíng Guómín Bīnguăn; ☎2590 1259; r & cabins from NT$3420) A pleasant place to stay. The cabins here offer decent comfort and nice scenery. Buffet-style meals (breakfast NT$150, lunch and dinner NT$350) are available for guests and non-guests at the hostel's restaurant.

For instant noodles and snack foods, there's a **convenience store** (便利商店; ⏲7am-8pm) near the visitor centre.

Getting There & Away

Two **Kuo Kuang Motor Transport** (☎02-2311 9893; www.kingbus.com.tw) buses leave each day from Ilan (NT$276, three hours, 7am and 12.40pm) – the bus station in Ilan is four to five blocks left of the train station (as you exit) on Yi Shin Rd. The return bus from Wuling leaves at 9.20am and 2.10pm. There are buses to/from Taichung via Lishan but these will take you all day. You can rent scooters in Jiaoshi (see p134).

Sheipa National Park

雪霸國家公園

Many rivers and one mountain range run through this 768-sq-km national park in northern Taiwan. Sheipa National Park (Xuěbà Guójiā Gōngyuán) is home to 51 mountain peaks of over 3000m each, and is the primary source of drinking water for northern and central Taiwan.

The park was established in 1992 and much of it remains inaccessible (in fact, prohibited) to ordinary travellers. The three sections you are permitted to enter are the forest recreation areas of Wuling, Guanwu and Syuejian near Taian hot springs. In the case of the first two, multiday trails from the recreation areas lead deep into the rugged interior of the park.

The park's main **headquarters** (037-996100; www.spnp.gov.tw; Dahu; 9am-4.30pm, closed Mon) are inconveniently placed on the road to Taian Hot Springs, though there is a branch in Wuling Farm (see p141), the starting place for most hikes.

Activities

Hiking

Trails in the park are well maintained, and usually clear to follow. Signs are in English and Chinese, and there are frequent distance posts. Before beginning a hike, make sure you drop into the Sheipa National Park Wuling Station (雪霸國家公園武陵管理處) to get your mountain permits in order (see boxed text, p28). At the trailhead for Snow Mountain the park's staff will check your park permit and afterwards ask you to watch a movie.

The best months for hiking in the park are October to December, and March and April. Winter hiking is becoming more popular, though you need to be prepared for snow and bitter cold. After April, seasonal heavy rains, including monsoons, are common but if you don't hit any typhoons,

Sheipa National Park

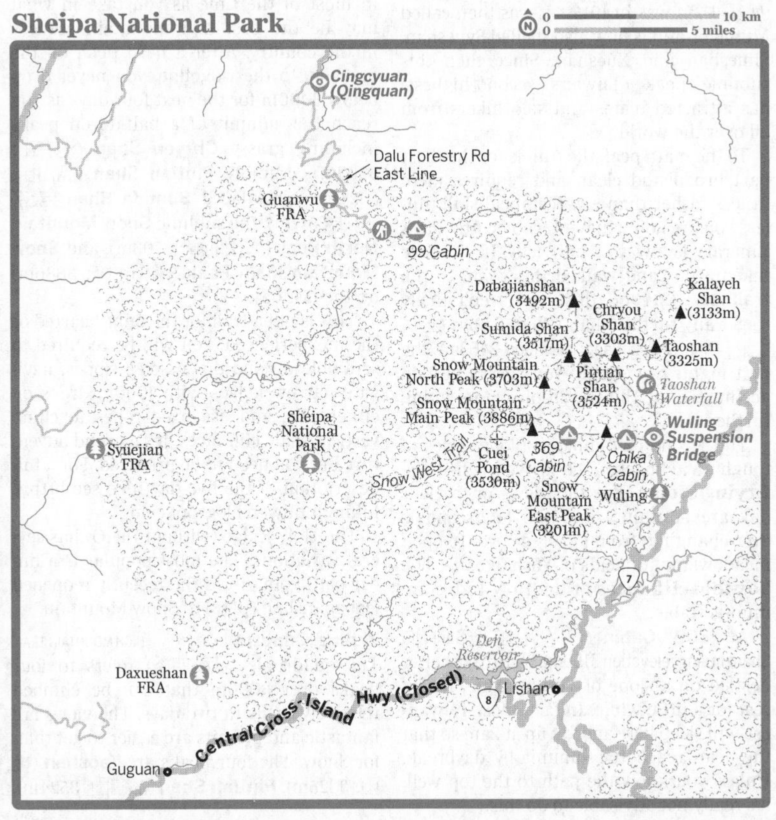

STANDARD SNOW MOUNTAIN ITINERARY

Trailhead to summit (10.9km, 8½ to 11½ hours)

» Trailhead to Chika Cabin: 2km, 1½ hours

» Chika Cabin to 369 Cabin: 5.1km, five to six hours

» 369 Cabin to Main Peak: 3.8km, three to four hours

Summit to trailhead (six hours)

» Main Peak to 369 Cabin: two hours

» 369 Cabin to trailhead: four hours

July and August are good months to avoid the crowds.

Snow Mountain Main Peak HIGH MOUNTAIN TRAIL

The first recorded climb of **Snow Mountain** (雪山主峰) was in 1915 – it was then called Mt Silvia, and is now also spelled Syueshan, Shueshan and Xueshan. Since then this sublime peak (Taiwan's second-highest) has attracted teams and solo hikers from all over the world.

To the main peak the trail is for the most part broad and clear, and requires mere fitness rather than any technical skill (unless you are going in winter). The first day's itinerary is always a bit tricky. If you have taken a bus and walked the 7.5km to the **trailhead** (2140m) then you aren't likely to get any further than **Chika Cabin** (七卡山莊; Qīkǎ Shānzhuāng; elevation 2463m) the first night. Nor should you, as it's best to acclimatise at this elevation before going further.

The second day's hike is a long series of tough switchbacks (one is even called the **Crying Slope**). But the views on a clear day are stunning, and the landscape is ever-changing: from forested cover to open meadowland, to fields of Yushan cane. The **box-fold cliff faces** of the Holy Ridge are unforgettable.

At **369 Cabin** (三六九山莊; Sānliùjiǔ Shānzhuāng; elevation 3150m), a sturdy shelter nestled on a slope of Yushan cane, hikers rest for a little while. In fact, most Taiwanese will sleep here and get up at 2am so that they can reach the summit by daybreak. Unless you know the path to the top well, it's really not advisable to do this.

So, assuming you get a reasonable start you'll soon be in the **Black Forest**, a sublime stand of Taiwan fir. At the edge of the forest be on the lookout for troops of **Formosan macaques**. Note that the giant hollow before you is a **glacial cirque** formed by retreating icefields.

It's another 1km from here to the summit along more switchbacks. Unlike Yushan, the summit of Snow is rounded and requires no effort to reach. But you'll want to linger here and take in the Holy Ridge and other surrounding peaks.

Hikers normally reach the summit of Snow and then return to the trailhead (and their vehicles) on the same day. You need to leave 369 Cabin no later than 6am to accomplish this before dark.

TOP CHOICE **'O' Holy Ridge** HIGH MOUNTAIN TRAIL

The O stands for the circular nature of this **hike** (聖稜線O型縱走), which begins and ends at Wuling Farm. It's also probably the shape your mouth will be in most of the time as you take in what may be the best high-mountain scenery in the country. After a hard push on the first day to the ridgeline, you never drop below 3000m for the next four days as you reach the summit of a half-dozen peaks including grassy **Chryou Shan** (池有山; 3303m), crumbly **Pintian Shan** (品田山; 3524m), black-faced **Sumida Shan** (素密達山; 3517m), the sublime **Snow Mountain North Peak** (雪山北峰; 3703m), and **Snow Mountain Main Peak** (雪山主峰; 3886m) on the last day.

This is not a trail for the faint-hearted or the inexperienced. You will be required to scramble up and down scree slopes, navigate narrow ledges with 1000m drops on either side, and use fixed ropes to climb vertical shale cliff faces. It's a grand adventure but you need to be prepared. For a full description of the five-day hike see http://hikingintaiwan.blogspot.com.

The Holy Ridge (without the O) has several variations. The most popular is a linear path going from the recently reopened Dabajianshan (p148) to Snow Mountain.

Wuling-Quadruple HIGH MOUNTAIN TRAIL

The quadruple (武陵四秀) refers to four peaks over 3000m that can be climbed relatively easily in two days. The views are fantastic and permits are easier to get than for Snow. The four peaks are **Taoshan** (桃山; 3325m), **Pintian Shan** (品田山; 3524m),

Chryou Shan (池有山; 3303m), and **Kalayeh Shan** (喀拉業山; 3113m). The clearly marked trailhead begins off the path to Taoshan Waterfall in Wuling Farm.

Sleeping & Eating

Before and after hikes you can sleep and eat at Wuling Farm (p142). On the trail there are cabins at the end of each day's hike with bunk bedding, ecotoilets, water, solar lighting and sometimes an outside deck. Cabins are unattended, so you must bring your own food supplies.

Getting There & Away

See Wuling Farm (p142).

HSINCHU & MIAOLI COUNTIES

The Hsinchu Science Park is by far the most famous site in this region, but most travellers come for the spectacular mountain scenery in the foothills of the Snow Range, the hot springs, and a small mist-shrouded mountain dotted with temples.

Ethnographically, Hsinchu and Miaoli Counties have a heavy concentration of Hakka, reflected in the food you'll find in many small towns. It's good to familiarise yourself with some of the staples before heading out (see p345). Atayal and Saisayat are also present in large numbers.

Getting around the area is pretty easy. Trains go up and down the coast all day, and there is inland bus service to most places.

Hsinchu 新竹

03 / POP 386,950

The oldest city in northern Taiwan, and long a base for traditional industries such as glass- and noodle-making, Hsinchu (Xīnzhú) sprang into the modern era in 1980 with the establishment of the Science Park. The park has often been described as the Silicon Valley of Taiwan and is the centre of the semiconductor industry. Though it's the most famous landmark of the city, the remains of Hsinchu's past is largely the key to a rewarding day trip.

The town centre is small and most sights can be reached on foot. Traffic is light during the day, there are snack and drink shops everywhere, and the constant wind (this is the Windy City) keeps air pollution down.

Sights

FREE Guqifeng (Guqi Mountain) ART COLLECTION

The Pu Tian Temple complex on the slopes of Guqifeng (古奇峰; Gǔqífēng), 5km south of the city centre, houses one of the most impressive private collections of artefacts and curios we have seen in Taiwan. A few standouts include a life-sized Chinese bed made out of pure jade, a 6m-long panel of pure jade high relief, ferocious carved dragon heads whose mouths you could step into, several miniature villages carved from wood, and a small taxidermy collection of rare Taiwanese mammals. The 40m-high statue of Kuang Kong that squats above the temple is quite a sight, too.

To get here take a taxi from downtown (NT$200) or an infrequent bus (NT$45) from the Hsinchu Bus Company station to Pu Tian Temple. There are nine buses a day, the most useful leaving at 8.20am, 9.50am and 12.40pm.

City God Temple TAOIST TEMPLE

First built in 1748, and masterfully restored in 1924, this Hsinchu landmark (城隍廟; Chénghuáng Miào) has the highest rank of all the city god temples in Taiwan. A sombre place (as you walk in, check out the figure holding an implement of torture), the temple is also a splendid example of the fine work local artisans were capable of in the early 20th century. Check out the shallow but vivid plafond, and the wealth of carved wooden brackets and beams. Most are covered in gold foil and if you take note you can find dragons, phoenixes and melons, as well as panels of birds and flowers (auspicious symbols when placed together). For an example of vivid *jiǎnniàn* (figurine decoration), check out the dragons on the roof.

The City God Temple is most lively during the seventh lunar month and on the 29th day of the 11th month, when the birthday of the temple god is celebrated. There's a lively food market around the temple selling all manner of traditional foods.

Municipal Glass Museum MUSEUM

(玻璃工藝博物館; Bōlí Gōngyì Bówùguǎn; www.hcgm.gov.tw; 2 Dongda Rd, Sec 1; admission NT$20; 9am-5pm Wed-Sun) A great little museum dedicated to the local history of glassmaking, which goes back to 1880. The 1st floor exhibits recent creative works, while the 2nd floor highlights the history

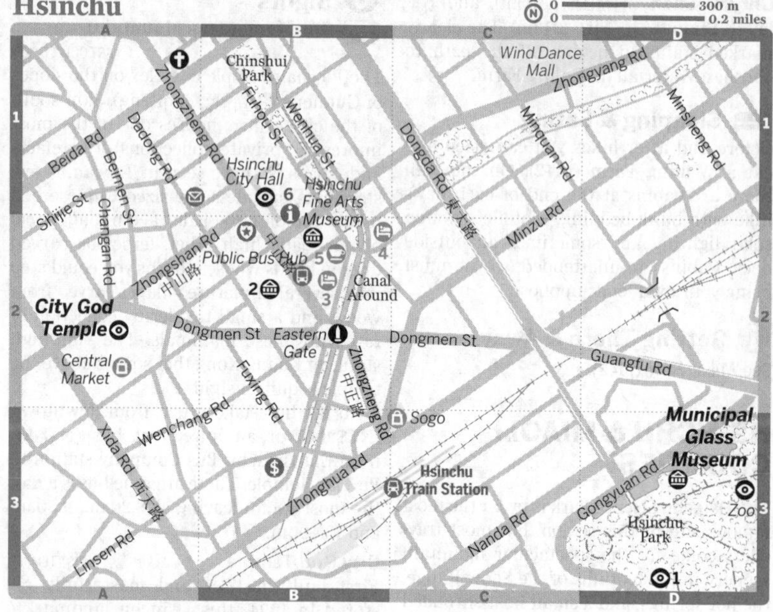

Hsinchu

Top Sights

City God Temple	A2
Municipal Glass Museum	D3

Sights

1 Confucius Temple	D3
2 Municipal Image Museum	B2

Sleeping

3 East City Hotel	B2
4 Sol Hotel	B2

Drinking

5 PAO	B2

Information

6 Hsinchu Foreigner Assistance Centre	B1

of glass (both in Taiwan and around the world) and the various techniques (with examples) used to produce glass art.

The museum is situated in Hsinchu Park (Xīnzhú Gōngyuán), a pleasant leafy area with a large and rather pretty pond backed by a cafe and a number of old buildings from the Japanese era. Some of these also display (and sell) glass-related works, so you can spend quite a few hours in this area.

On the other side of the park are a **Confucius Temple** (孔廟; Kǒng Miào; ⌚8.30am-4.30pm Wed-Sun) and zoo. You can easily walk to the park from the train station in 20 minutes.

Municipal Image Museum MUSEUM/MOVIE THEATRE

(影像博物館; Yǐnshàng Bówùguǎn; ☎528 5840; www.hmim.gov.tw; 65 Zhongzheng Rd; admission NT$20; ⌚9.30am-noon, 1.30-5pm & 6.30-9pm Wed-Sun) This museum occupies a stylish old building that was once the first air-conditioned movie theatre in Hsinchu – it now serves as a movie relics museum, educational centre and public movie theatre. Movies are shown around 7pm Wednesday to Friday and at 10am, 2pm and 7pm on Saturday and Sunday. Admission to the museum and movies is a low NT$20 unless a festival is on.

Relics

Hsinchu was called Hsinchang by the early Chinese settlers, who built a *hsinchang* (bamboo fence) around the city to protect themselves from Taiya, Saisha and Pingpu aborigines. In 1826 a solid brick wall was constructed around the city. Only one portion of the wall remains today, the **Eastern Gate** (東門; Dōngmén), but it is in fine shape and a great central landmark.

A number of buildings from the Japanese era dot the urban landscape and are worth a nod as you wander about, including the train station and city hall. Beimen St, just north of the City God Temple, also has a number of old dwellings that are worth checking out.

Sleeping

Hsinchu has lots of hotels that mostly serve the people working at the Science Park.

East City Hotel HOTEL $
(東城大旅社; Dōngchéng Dàlǚshè; ☎522 2648; 1 Lane 5, Fuhou St, 府後街5巷1號; d/tw incl simple breakfast NT$800/1200;) Sporting a recent upgrade, this hotel across from the canal and surrounded by restaurants and cafes is the obvious budget choice in Hsinchu.

Sol Hotel HOTEL $$
(迎曦大飯店; Yíngxī Dàfàndiàn; ☎534 7266; www.solhotel.com.tw; 10 Wenhua St, 文化街10號; d/tw incl breakfast NT$3250/5200;) A solid midrange business hotel, the Sol is also suitable for visitors looking for softer beds, better bathrooms, a higher thread count in their sheets, and English-speaking staff.

Eating & Drinking

The train station area is chock-a-block full of places to eat, both on the streets and in the shopping malls. The area around the City God Temple holds a lively and well-known food market. Two local dishes not to miss if you enjoy sampling local fare are meatballs (貢丸; *gòngwán*) and flat rice noodles (粄條; *bǎntiáo*). The latter are dried by wind, which means no one makes them like the Windy City makes them.

If you're looking for a quieter and more cosy atmosphere, head to the canal area. **PAO** (卡莎蕾義式餐廳; Kǎshāleí Yìshì Cāntīng; 30 Lane 96, Zhongzheng Rd; 11am-9.30pm), on the 2nd floor above one of the many Japanese restaurants in the area, is a relaxing place for a coffee. Despite the address you'll find PAO on the west side of the canal.

If you're looking for a beer or cocktail venue it's best to get a recommendation. Strangers aren't always welcome in Hsinchu's bars and clubs.

Shopping

For high-quality glass products, get the numbers and addresses of Hsinchu artisans at the glass museum or check out the small shops around the pond at Hsinchu Park.

Information

Bank of Taiwan (29 Linsen Rd) Has a 24hr ATM. ATMs are also found at 7-Elevens and other convenience stores.

Hsinchu City Website (www.hcccb.gov.tw) Excellent online guide to the city.

Hsinchu Foreigner Assistance Centre (新竹地區外國人協助中心; 107 Zhongyang Rd; ☎521 6121; http://foreigner.hccg.gov.tw; 8am-5pm Mon-Fri; @) Just like the name says. Travel, business, health and living information. There's also free computer usage with internet access. Staff speak English.

Getting There & Around

Roaming taxis are not numerous in Hsinchu. Get your hotel to call for a taxi before you head out, or keep the number of the driver you've found.

High Speed Rail (HSR)

Travel to/from Taipei costs NT$260 (35 minutes, every half-hour). Note that the HSR doesn't go directly to downtown Hsinchu. Shuttle buses connect the HSR and downtown (30 minutes, every 20 to 30 minutes), and drop you off at the public bus hub on Zhongzheng Rd. You can take a taxi from the HSR to downtown Hsinchu for NT$300.

Train

Fast/slow hourly trains from Taipei cost NT$180/116 and take one hour/1½ hours.

Around Hsinchu

Activities

Cycling

From Hsinchu Harbour at the northwest of the town centre, a 17km bike-only route winds its way down a pretty stretch of coastline. At the time of writing the path looked close to being connected to another 20km or so of routes along the Miaoli coastline.

To get to the harbour catch bus 15 (NT$15) from Hsinchu's public bus hub or beside Sogo on Minzu Rd just before the Cold Stone ice-cream shop. Bike rentals are available at the harbour and at other locations along the bike paths.

Windsurfing

The water is not the cleanest along the west coast but the conditions are great for windsurfing. Penghu's **Liquid Sport** (www.liquidsport.com.tw) organises summer lessons, and rentals, as does **Spot X-Sport** (www.spot.com.tw), which has a club with rentals and simple lodging in the **Jhunan Seashore Forest**

WORTH A TRIP

SMANGUS: TAIWAN'S MOST REMOTE VILLAGE

Deep in the forested mountains of Hsinchu County lies the Atayal settlement of **Smangus** (司馬庫斯; Címǎkùsī; www.smangus.org, in Chinese), the last village in Taiwan to be connected to the electric grid (in 1980). For centuries life went on pretty much as it always had, with hunting and farming for millet, taro, yams and bamboo forming the backbone of the local economy. In this tiny mountain community, possibly the most remote in Taiwan, when the old folks talked about walking four hours uphill to school, they weren't joking.

In the early 1990s a forest of ancient red cypress trees was discovered nearby and lowland Taiwanese began to flock to the little mountain village in numbers. In the coming years, there was intense competition between villagers for customers. Then in 2004 a cooperative (modelled on the Israeli kibbutz) was formed to manage lodging and also the area's resources. Fortunes could have been made selling out to developers but instead the village has admirably gone the local and sustainable route.

Directions to the village are posted on the website (in Chinese). It's a long drive – at least five hours from Taipei – but everyone knows the place once you get closer. **Homestay lodging** (☎03-584 7688) is booked through one office and ranges from NT$2000 for a four-bed dorm to some quite luxurious cabins for double that price. Meals are taken in the communal dining hall (NT$200 per meal).

The main attraction in the area, besides the chance to learn about Atayal life, is the old tree grove, which is reached by a clear 6km trail (about five hours return). The oldest tree is reported to be 2700 years old.

Park (假日之森; Jiàrì Zhī Sēn), 100m from the sea in a quaint little hamlet.

Neiwan Branch Rail Line 內灣支線

The Japanese originally built this line (Nèi-wān Zhīxiàn) to haul timber out of the mountains around Neiwan. Like the Jiji, Pingxi and Alishan lines, it has been kept open to promote tourism in the area. Neiwan village offers a cool, fresh summer retreat from the pollution and heat of the cities and retains much of its Japanese-era atmosphere. Hakka food and snacks are a perennial favourite with travellers here, and if you can make it in spring, stay till evening as the fireflies come out in numbers in the surrounding hills.

Neiwan is about 20km southeast of Hsinchu. The branch rail line trains leave from the Hsinchu train station and will also be connected to the High Speed Rail by 2011. At the time of writing the line was still closed awaiting this connection, but should be up and running in 2011 or 2012.

Cingcyuan (Qingquan) 清泉

County Rd 122 runs up a deep river valley in a rugged, chillingly beautiful part of the country that is too often completely cut off from the rest because of landslides. The last major village along the road before Guanwu FRA is Cingcyuan (Qīngquán).

Though the village is almost entirely Atayal, it's famous for once being the home of Taiwanese travel writer **San Mao** (三毛; Echo Chen) and the site of the long-term house arrest of **Zhang Xueliang** (張學良).

Zhang is famous in modern Chinese history as the man who kidnapped Chiang Kai-shek in 1936 in order to convince him to join with the Communists in their fight against the Japanese. Never one to hold a grudge, Chiang Kai-shek had Zhang held as a political prisoner for the next 50 years. In the 1950s, Zhang was held in Qingquan.

At the time of writing, a memorial hall for Zhang, and San Mao's former residence, were close to opening. Also check out the area's **hot springs**, and if you can find the Catholic priest who has lived in the area for decades, he'll most likely show you something of the Atayal accomplishments.

Not far from the village is the start of the **Syakaro Historic Trail** (霞喀羅古道; Xiákèluó Gǔdào) part of the National Trail System (see boxed text, p27).

Guanwu Forest Recreation Area & Dabajianshan 觀霧森林遊樂區、大霸尖山

If you're looking for a more-rugged experience compared with the tame resort atmosphere of a place like Alishan, **Guanwu**

(Guānwù Sēnlín Yóulè Qū; www1.forest.gov.tw; ⏲7am-5pm) is one of the better forest recreation areas. There are many trails from which to choose, most fewer than three hours long and leading to mountain peaks or scenic waterfalls. All trails are well marked and easy to follow.

If you wish to stay overnight in Guanwu contact the **visitor information centre** (☎037-272 917) for room bookings. All the accommodation was being rebuilt at the time of writing so we aren't sure what the end results or price will be (though it wasn't likely to be cheap).

To get to Guanwu you need your own vehicle.

DABAJIANSHAN 大霸尖山

The most famous climb in the area is to the recently reopened **Dabajianshan** (Dàbàjiān Shān; Big Chief Pointed Mountain, 3492m). The barrel-peaked Daba is one of the most iconic high mountain images in Taiwan and is a truly mesmerising sight up close. The mountain is sacred to the Atayal, who believe they originate from the rock.

The hike takes about three days to complete, including two overnight stays on the mountain in **99 Cabin** (Jiǔjiǔ Shānzhuāng) at 2800m.

The route from Guanwu is a 19.5km hike (four to six hours) along the forestry road to the old trailhead, followed by a 4km (three- to four-hour) hike to 99 Cabin. The next day, hikers leave 99 Cabin and hike another 7.5km (four to five hours) to the base of Dabajianshan peak (you can't climb to the very summit of the barrel anymore).

Most hikers return to 99 Cabin the same day, and then head back to Guanwu the following morning. But it is also possible to hike another three days from Dabajianshan to Snow Mountain (Syueshan) along what is known as the **Holy Ridge** (see p144).

Because Dabajianshan is within Sheipa National Park, police and national-park permits are required to climb it (see boxed text, p28).

Beipu 北埔

☎03 / POP 10,400

'I'm a little bit Lukang, I'm a little bit Meinong, too.'

With all due respect to Donnie and Marie, that's Beipu (Běipǔ), a small Hsinchu County town that in recent years has, like the others, tried to pull in visitors with its Hakka cultural heritage. Lest our little jingle makes it sound like Beipu hasn't been successful, note that it makes for an excellent morning or afternoon excursion. There's an authentic feel to the place, and it's one of the best places to try Hakka pounded tea.

There are almost no signs in English around town, but it's very small and most of what you'll want to see is close to each other. The bus drops you off in the heart of things.

Sights

The following is written as a short tour from the bus stop on Jhong Jheng Rd (中正路), across from an OK convenience store.

From the bus stop head towards the hill. In a minute or so you'll see old buildings on either side of the road. On the right is **Tian Shui Hall** (天水堂; Tiān Shuǐ Táng), the largest private traditional three-sided compound in Beipu. To the left is **Jinguangfu** (金廣福公館; Jīnguǎngfú Gōngguǎn), a heritage house from 1835. Unfortunately you can't go into the buildings, but if you continue up the narrow alley between them you'll reach a very quaint teahouse, the Well (see p150).

Facing Tian Shui Hall, go right. Shortly you'll pass **Jian Asin Mansion** (姜阿新故居; A-Hsin Jiang Residence; Jiāngāxīn Gù Jū) on the left. This two-storey Western-styled house was built by a rich tea merchant who, not surprisingly, had a lot of Western clients. Entry is by prior reservation only.

From the mansion it's just a hop to the **Zhitian (Citian) Temple** (慈天宮; Cítiān Gōng), a charming little temple (established in 1835) dedicated to the Guanyin. Some notable features to look for include the carved **stone pillars**, both out front and especially within the main hall, the painted beams, the assorted carved wood brackets, and the panels of excellent **cochin pottery** to the right and left of the main hall. On the roof look for an assortment of crustaceans (representing official promotion) and shaggy yellow lions in *jiǎnniàn*.

To the left of the temple (as you face it) is a small passageway; walk to its curvy end. Notice a few loose stones? That's not an accident. In the wilder days of Taiwan's history the narrow passageways into Beipu were lined with the occasional loose stone so that intruders (who, of course, wouldn't know this) could be heard approaching.

As you exit the temple the street directly in front of you is **Beipu Street** (北埔街).

There are a number of old buildings along the first few blocks and many pleasant snack shops, teahouses and cafes. There's also a tiny alley immediately to your left with a couple of old teahouses.

One block up Beipu St, at the intersection with Nansing Rd (南興街), turn right and walk back to the OK convenience store. This is where you got off the bus, and where you can catch it again back to Jhudong.

If you have a car, consider heading left down Nansing Rd and following the English signs 10km to the free outdoor **Beipu Cold Springs** (北埔冷泉; Běipǔ Lěngquán).

Eating & Drinking

Like Meinong in the south, Beipu (which means northern wild area) comprises over 90% Hakka people. In almost every restaurant you'll find Hakka staples including a variety of dried goods.

People don't linger in Beipu, so expect most shops to close by early evening.

Well TEAHOUSE **$$**
(水井茶堂; Shuǐjǐng Chátáng; ⏲10am-6pm) One of the best places to try *lei cha* (pounded tea; see boxed text, p155) is in this rustic Hakka house. You can sit inside at tables, or on wooden floors, or even outside on a wooden deck under the plum trees.

Getting There & Away

From Hsinchu, take a **Hsinchu Bus Company** (☎03-596 2018) bus to Jhudong (竹東; NT$45, 40 minutes, every 20 minutes). Buses leave from the station to the left of the train station. At Jhudong, transfer to a bus to Beipu (NT$23, 20 minutes, every 30 minutes). Buses run from early morning to evening. You may also be able to catch a tourism shuttle bus from Jhudong (see www.taiwantrip.com.tw).

Shitoushan 獅頭山

☎03 / ELEVATION 492M

Shitoushan (Shītóushān) is a foothill on the border of Miaoli and Hsinchu Counties. Beautiful dense forests and rugged rock faces define the topography, but if you ask anyone it is the temples tucked into sandstone caves and hugging the slopes that have given the place its fame. Shitoushan is sacred ground for the island's Buddhists and draws big weekend crowds, with people coming to worship or simply enjoy the beauty and tranquillity of the mountain. Over the years, Shitoushan has been consistently described by Lonely Planet travellers as a highlight of their trip to Taiwan.

Yuanguang Temple (元光寺; Yuánguāng Sì) was the first temple to be constructed in the area (in 1894). Many more buildings were added over the years, including **Chuanhua Tang** (勸化堂; Quànhuà Táng), the only Taoist temple on the mountain, and which today serves as a guesthouse. Also look for the **main gate**, built in 1940 by the Japanese to celebrate the 2600th anniversary of their royal court (that's one ancient royal line!). There are 11 temples, five on the front side of the mountain, six on the back, as well as numerous smaller shrines, arches and pagodas. Shitoushan is a veritable temple wonderland and a great hit with photographers, nature lovers and temple aficionados. Give yourself at least three hours to explore the area, or an overnight stay for the full effect.

On the other side of the mountain, connected by a walking trail, is the **Lion's Head Mountain Visitor Centre** (☎580 9296; ⏲9am-5pm). The centre is a pleasant place to grab a meal or a map. There are several good short hikes starting from the centre that follow old Qing-dynasty roads through dense forest cover. Along the way you can spot a freshwater crab species as old as Taiwan itself (five million years).

Visitors (including non-Buddhists) are allowed to stay overnight at **Chuanhua Tang** (Chuanhua Hall; ☎822 020, 823 859; dm/tw NT$800/1000). Excellent vegetarian meals are NT$60 each, but if that doesn't appeal to you there are stalls and shops lining the back car park and even a cafe on the way up the stairs to the hall. The old rules forbidding talk during meals or couples sleeping together are no longer enforced, but do be on your best behaviour.

From the car park it's a short walk up the stairs to Chuanhua Tang. The check-in counter is to the left, just before the temple. There's a large map (with some labels in English) on the right side of the car park to show you the way.

Getting There & Away

First catch a **Hsinchu Bus Company** (☎03-596 2018) bus heading to Jhudong (竹東; NT$45, 40 minutes, every 20 minutes). Buses leave from the station to the left of the Hsinchu train station. At Jhudong, transfer to a bus heading to Shitoushan (NT$23, 40 minutes, every two hours from 7.30am to 3.45pm). Ask the driver to let you off at Shitoushan Old Hiking Trail Arch (獅頭山舊登山口牌樓) at the 22km mark on

WORTH A TRIP

EMEI LAKE: HOME OF THE ORIENTAL BEAUTY

A short drive from Beipu, pretty **Emei Lake** (峨眉湖; Éméi Hú) serves as a reservoir for farmers growing Oriental Beauty tea. This highly oxidised oolong is renowned for several things: 1) Queen Elizabeth gave it its name; 2) it's completely lacking in astringency; and 3) it needs small crickets to bite the young shoots for the full flavour to come out.

The need for insect bites (which actually helps to oxidise the tea) means this is a completely organic product. When brewed the tea is red in colour, and has a natural sweet and slightly spicy flavour. Like high-mountain oolong it's one of those teas that is immediately appealing, and countries such as China and India are trying to imitate this home-grown Taiwanese product, with limited success.

While the tea is the lake area's claim to fame, visitors will most likely first notice an airport-terminal-sized (and -looking) monastery, and the **72m Maitreya Buddha Statue**, built by the World Maitreya Great Tao Organization (www.maitreya.org.tw). Both were almost completed at the time of writing and make for fabulous photos.

Township Rd 124; from here it's a 30-minute uphill walk to the car park. There are few buses a day to Shitoushan, so call to check the schedule. It may also be possible to catch a tourism shuttle bus from Jhudong (see www.taiwantrip.com.tw).

Nanzhuang 南庄

Off the travellers' radar until recent years, the Nanzhuang area is quickly emerging as one of the most popular retreats for Taiwan's expat population. One reason is that this former logging and coal-mining centre has changed little since Japanese times. Many streets and villages have retained their signature clapboard facades and the food reflects the diverse ethnic make-up of the residents: Hakka, Taiwanese, as well as aboriginal Taiya and Saisiyat.

Nanzhuang is set in the foothills of the Snow Mountains, with hardly an uninspiring scene anywhere. There are only a couple of roads running through the region, so orientating yourself is not hard, with a basic map. In essence, if you follow County Rd 124甲 as it makes a big loop off Provincial Hwy 3, you've covered most of Nanzhuang. If you take a side trip up Township Rd 21苗, you will have seen everything.

Nanzhuang is very close to Taian Hot Springs, Beipu and Shitoushan. Consider spending a week exploring the whole area.

Sights & Activities

The following appear in the order in which you would encounter them riding along County Rd 124甲 and Township Rd 21苗.

Nanzhuang Village OLD VILLAGE

After passing the side road up to Shitoushan, the 124甲 turns south and runs through a wide valley until it reaches the village of Nanzhuang (南庄), with its signature clapboard buildings on the Old Street.

A good place to start exploring is a little stone-stair alley called **Osmanthus Lane** (桂花巷; Guìhuā Xiàng), which winds up behind the main street. There are a dozen or more stalls and shops here selling local Hakka snacks, many flavored with sweet Osmanthus. At the start of the lane look for the **stone washing area**, still used by some older residents for cleaning their clothes. Almost across the street is Nanzhuang's new **visitor information centre** (⌚8.30am-5.30pm), which has some good maps and information on homestays and restaurants.

East River Spa Garden HOT SPRING

Past Nanzhuang village the road splits on the other side of a bridge. Going right takes you down a lovely green stretch of road that eventually swings back to join Provincial Hwy 3. Going left (Township Rd 21苗) takes you quickly to one of the most pleasant hot-spring resorts outside the Taipei area.

The **spa garden** (東江溫泉; Dōngjiāng Wēnquán; www.eastriver.com.tw; public baths unlimited time NT$350; ⌚9am-10pm) is nestled in the bend of a fast-flowing river with a design that makes use of traditional red bricks and lots of wood. It looks traditional, but there's no denying it's for urbanites who want *their* version of rural Taiwan: ie folksy but clean and comfortable.

FREE **Saisiyat Folklore Museum** MUSEUM

(賽夏族民俗文物館; Sàixiàzú Mínsú Wénwùguǎn; ⌚9am-5pm, closed Mon) A few kilometres past the hot springs, the road splits again. Left takes you up a winding uninhabited back road to Beipu, while right passes by some old clapboard villages. The latter route splits again with a side route to the right heading up **Xiang Tian Hu** (向天湖; Xiàngtiān Hú), which is a small lake with a large museum dedicated to the aboriginal **Saisiyat** (賽夏族) and their intriguing **Festival of the Short People** (The Pas-ta'ai Ritual; 賽夏族矮靈祭; Sàixiàzú Ǎilíngjì).

The Saisiyat ('the true people'), with just over 5000 members, are one of the smallest aboriginal groups in Taiwan. Every three years they hold a little-known festival in honor of the Ta'ai, a mythical pygmy race. According to legend, the Ta'ai and Saisiyat once lived in peace, but after the Ta'ai began molesting Saisiyat women they were killed off. Famine resulted and the festival arose as a way of appeasing the vengeful spirits who were clearly at the root of the disaster.

Luchang Village OLD VILLAGE

Retracing your way back from Saisiyat Folklore Museum to Township Rd 21苗, turn right and go up a deep rugged canyon to Luchang village (鹿場; Lù Chǎng) , one of the prettiest spots in the Nanzhuang area. Most houses are clapboard style, and perched on the sides of the slopes are a few cafes from where you can enjoy the mountain views.

A few kilometres further up the road is the trailhead to the 2220m-high **Jiali Mountain** (加里山; Jiālǐ Shān).

Sleeping & Eating

There are dozens of B&Bs scattered around Nanzhuang, most charging around NT$2000 to NT$3000 a night for a double. Many are set in old houses with grassy lawns and wood patios for enjoying the outdoors. Those on a budget can consider staying at nearby Shitoushan or the campground at Taian. There's also a simple free campground off Township Rd 21苗, not far past where the road splits to take you up to the lake.

Shui Yun Jian CABINS $$

(水雲間; Shuǐ Yún Jiān; ☎037-825 777; www.825777.com; d/tw incl breakfast NT$2500/4500) Your vehicle engine will whine in protest as you climb to this nicely landscaped wooden lodge set high above the Dadong River valley. The wood-panelled rooms are cosy, and heated during the winter months, and tasty Hakka-style homemade meals are available (set meal NT$350). Check out the website for an accurate look at what the high-mountain views are like from here.

To get to Shui Yun Jian look for the signs (in Chinese) not far past the East River Spa Garden as you head east.

For meals, head to the Old Street and Osmanthus Lane in Nanzhuang village, or one of dozens of obvious restaurants off the main roads. Locally raised trout is popular, as are Hakka staples (see p345).

Getting There & Around

You need your own vehicle to make it worthwhile to come here. Biking is good. Take a train to Jhudong and head straight out of the station. Ride 1km up to Provincial Hwy 3, turn right and follow until you reach the turn-off for County Rd 124甲, about 30km from Jhudong station.

Taian Hot Springs 泰安溫泉

☎037

There are hot springs all over Taiwan, and beautiful mountains for hiking, too, but we still think Taian (Tàiān Wēnquán) is special. For one thing, it has hot spring water so good that the Japanese built an officers' club here to take advantage of it 100 years ago.

In a remote mountainous corner of southeastern Miaoli County, just on the boundary of rugged Sheipa National Park, Taian is not precisely defined on maps, but is more or less the region that County Rd 62 runs through. Beginning just outside the town of Wenshui, County Rd 62 runs for 16km alongside the Wenshui River before ending in a car park just below the Japanese Police Officers' Club. Most visitors stay within the last 3km stretch, in an area known as Jinshui Village (Jǐnshǔi Cūn; population 200).

As you drive up County Rd 62, pay attention to the make-up of the people in the villages around you. At the start, they will be almost exclusively Hakka (evident both in the look of the people and the food on offer), while the further inland you go the more Atayal aboriginal they will become. This pattern is common in mountainous regions in Taiwan. As late immigrants to Taiwan, Hakka groups found the best land on the plains long settled and had to do with what was left over. What was left over was remote land still occupied by aboriginal groups. By purchase or pressure, Hakka groups acquired their share, forcing aboriginal groups even further into the hinterlands.

Dangers & Annoyances

Taian suffers frequent landslides, which can wash out roads and change the course and look of riverbeds. Avoid the area after heavy rains or earthquakes.

Sights & Activities

Hot Springs

Taian's alkaloid carbonic waters are clear, tasteless and almost odourless. Reputedly they are good for treating skin problems and nervousness. Your skin will certainly glow after a soak, and with three spring sources there's plenty of water to go around.

Cedarwood Villa HOT SPRINGS
(竹美山閣-溫泉會館; Zhúměi ShānGé Wēnquán Huìguǎn; ☎941 800; www.cedarwood-villa.com.tw; per 1½hr NT$1200) Though slate walled and not made of cedarwood at all, this quiet and stylish hotel offers large marble soaking rooms with huge windows overlooking a superb stretch of Taian's mountain. It's the kind of place you take someone special to. The hotel also has rooms for overnight stays.

The resort sits on its own on the side of a mountain up a rough side road.

Sunrise Hot Spring Hotel HOT SPRINGS
(日出溫泉渡假飯店; Rìchū Wēnquán Dùjià Fàndiàn; public pool unlimited time NT$350; ⏲9am-10pm) The wood and stone multipool outdoor complex is designed to let you take in the mountain views as you bathe.

Hiking

We mark a number of trails on our map but you should always check with locals about the conditions before heading out. This is a rough area. Try to finish higher trails before mid-afternoon, as fog can obscure the views and make it easy to get lost.

Shui Yun Waterfall WATERFALL
The path to the wide, thundering waterfall (水雲瀑布; Shuǐyún Pùbù) goes along a river, through a forest and up a canyon. Start at the car park at the end of County Rd 62 and follow the trail by the river for 1km until you reach a suspension bridge. Cross the bridge and climb the stairs on the other side.

The trail now enters the forest and splits. Take the lower path (the upper leads to Hushan). After a few minutes you'll come to a ledge. Climb down (there are ropes) and then follow the left bank of the river up the canyon until it narrows. The falls are just around the corner up a side channel. The whole return trip takes three to four hours and there are several deep and safe swimming holes for cooling off along the way.

Donggua Divine Tree Trail HIKING TRAIL
This popular trail (冬瓜山神木; Dōngguāshān Shénmù) begins at the campground and runs up a forested hill to a rather large and old tree. It's about 1½ hours one way.

Hushan HIKING TRAIL
The most difficult of Taian's hikes is up to Hushan (虎山; Hǔshān; 1492m), as it involves some climbing with ropes (the ropes are already in place). Start on the trail to Shui Yun Waterfall; when the path splits after the suspension bridge, take the upper route.

It's easy to lose the main trail on this hike so pay attention to the ribbons and markers. The return trip takes about five hours.

Sleeping

There are at least a dozen hotels in the area, the fancier charging NT$5000 to NT$6000 a night and the more basic charging NT$3000 a night.

Taian Hot Springs

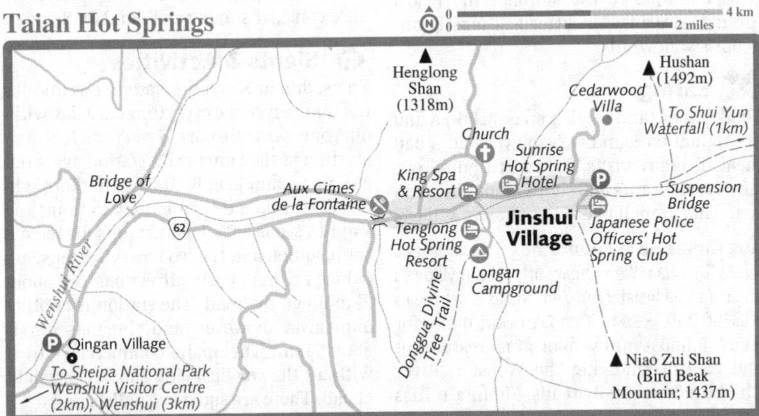

Longan Campground CAMPGROUND $
(龍安; Lóngān; ☎0933-733 728; sites NT$300) Grassy grounds with plenty of trees for shade. A high bluff setting with a ring of conical green peaks. Two rushing streams flowing nearby for river tracing and swimming. Put simply: one of the best camping spots in Taiwan.

To get here, take the side road into Tenglong Hot Spring Resort and head up a narrow rough lane to the left of a side stream pouring down into the Wenshui River. Follow this about 1km to the end.

Sunrise Hot Spring Hotel HOT-SPRING HOTEL $$$
(日出溫泉渡假飯店; ☎941 988; www.hotel.com.tw; d/tw from NT$5200/7500, 30% weekday discount) One of the more stylish hotels in Taian, the Sunrise makes liberal use of wood and stone and Southeast Asian decor in its public areas. Rooms are a little more staid, but they're cosy and feature large stone tubs (big enough for two Westerners) with open mountain views. Dinner and breakfast is included, as is free use of the outdoor hot spring complex.

Tenglong Hot Spring Resort HOT-SPRING HOTEL $$
(騰龍溫泉山莊; Ténglóng Wēnquán Shānzhuāng; ☎941 002; www.tenglong.com.tw/; 2-/4-person cabins NT$3300/4200) The cabins are fairly basic but the resort grounds are nicely cared for, and quiet when there aren't big student tour groups staying. Room price includes free use of the nude segregated hot-spring pools.

Tenglong (which looks like a little village as you drive past) is reached by a small side road and bridge across from the King Resort & Spa. In the summer the resort grounds swarm with butterflies, mostly gorgeous swallowtails.

Eating

Food is fresh and local, a mix of Hakka and aboriginal fare, and we've never had a bad meal in many visits. There are numerous small restaurants and shops along the main road, and a small market in Qingan Village.

Aux Cimes de la Fountaine ABORIGINAL $$
(山吻泉; Shān Wěn Quán; http://tw.myblog.yahoo.com/changsisters-mkf in Chinese; set meals NT$280-360; ⌚11am-10pm) An odd name for a cosy (almost funky) aboriginal restaurant and cafe overhanging the Wenshui River (the Chinese actually reads 'Mountain Kiss Spring'). The two Ami sisters who run the place whip up some fine meals (mostly hot pot and hot plates), and play good music, to boot. When you're there just be sure to give some attention to the two toy poodles lounging bar-side: they're family.

Information

Sheipa National Park Wenshui Visitor Centre (www.spnp.gov.tw; ⌚9am-4.30pm Tue-Sun) Sits at the start of County Rd 62. It doesn't have any information on travelling in Taian, but it does offer a good overview of the history of the Atayal and Hakka settlers in the area.

Getting There & Around

You need your own transport.

Sanyi 三義

☎037 / POP 5000

Over 100 years ago, a Japanese officer discovered that camphor grew in abundance in the hills around Sanyi (Sānyì), a small Miaoli County town. Since camphor makes for excellent wood products (it's aromatic, extremely heavy and can resist termites), the officer wisely established a wood business. Over time, Sanyi became *the* woodcarving region in Taiwan. Today, nearly half the population is engaged in the business in one way or another, with the other half probably wishing they were.

The best time to visit Sanyi is in April when the white flowers of the blooming Youtong trees *(Aleurites fordii)* give the surrounding mountains the appearance of being dusted with snow.

Most people visit on a day trip from Taipei or Taichung; if you have your own vehicle consider staying at Taian Hot Springs.

Sights & Activities

The sights in Sanyi are spread out and it's not that easy to see everything in a day without your own transport. If you're on foot, and starting at the Sanyi train station, walk out and up to Jungjeng Rd, the main thoroughfare in town, and turn left (everything you want to see is left). The turn-offs for the old train station and the woodcarving museum (which are in opposite directions) are about 2km down the road. The station is another 5km away, however, and the museum is about 1km. The main commercial street with all the woodcarving shops is straight ahead. There are signs in English.

LEI CHA

If you pronounce it incorrectly, *lei cha* (擂茶; *léi chá*) sounds like 'tired tea', but this hearty brew was designed to do anything but make you sleepy. It was a farmer's drink, rich and thick and full of nutrients and calories. In the old days, Hakka farmers would drink it both during and after work in the tobacco fields in order to fortify their bodies.

Or so the story goes.

Very likely, *lei cha* is a modern invention (like the Scottish tartan), or at best a family drink that has been cleverly promoted as an authentic part of Taiwan's Hakka heritage. In any case, it's everywhere now, and authentic or not, it's definitely part of the Taiwan experience.

Lei cha means pounded tea, and that's exactly what you must do before you can drink it. First you will be given a wooden pestle and a large porcelain bowl with a small amount of green tea leaves, sesame seeds, nuts and grains in the bottom. Using the pestle, you grind the ingredients in the bowl to a fine mush. Your host will then add hot water and dole out the 'tea' in cups. At this moment, or perhaps earlier, you will be given a small bowl of puffed rice. Add the rice to the drink and consume before the kernels get soggy.

If this sounds like your cuppa (and really, it is delicious), head to any teahouse at Sheng Shing station, or further afield at Beipu or Meinong.

Woodcarving

Woodcarving is the lifeblood of the town, and on Jungjeng Rd alone there are over 200 shops selling an array of carved items. We're not talking dull signposts here, but 3m cypress statues of savage-faced folk gods, delicate lattice windows, and beautiful traditional furniture. You can come here with the intention of buying, but if you just like to browse and enjoy the work of skilled artisans you won't be disappointed.

Most stores are clustered on a few blocks of Jungjeng Rd just down from the wood museum, and around the wood museum itself. Stores close around 6pm, though a few stay open until 10pm or later on weekends.

Miaoli Wood Sculpture Museum MUSEUM

(苗栗木雕博物館; Miáolì Mùdiāo Bówùguǎn; admission NT$80; ⏲9am-5pm, last ticket sale 4.30pm) Exhibits include informative displays on the origins of woodcarving in Sanyi, a knockout collection of Buddhas and Bodhisattvas, some gorgeous traditional household furniture and architectural features, and even a few pieces by Juming (see boxed text, p125).

Sheng Shing Train Station SCENIC AREA

Built during the Japanese era and without the use of nails, this charming train station (勝興火車站; Shèngxīng Huǒchēzhàn) was once the highest stop (at 480m) along the Western Trunk Line. When it was closed in 1997, walkers soon discovered that the 13.5km line made for a fine stroll through the countryside (though increased traffic on adjacent side roads has spoiled this for some). A small tourist village soon popped up around the station, filling the old brick houses with all manner of teahouses, cafes and Hakka restaurants.

Four kilometres past the station stands the picturesque ruins of the **Long Deng Viaduct** (Lóngténg Duàn Qiáo), destroyed in a 7.3-magnitude earthquake in 1930. The terracotta brick arches are held together with a sticky-rice and clam-shell mortar.

April Snow Trail HIKING TRAIL

This trail (四月雪步道; Sìyuè Xuě Bùdào) begins to the right of the Miaoli Wood Sculpture Museum and takes you through a forest of Youtong trees, whose white blossoms in April and early May give the trail its name.

Eating

There is no end of places to eat and drink traditional Hakka fare near Sheng Shing station and in Sanyi itself.

Directly across the old train station at Sheng Shing is **Mountain Legend** (山中傳奇; Shānzhōng Chuánqí; ⏲10.30am-7.30pm, later on weekends), a multidecked wooden-frame restaurant serving decent traditional fare such as *bǎntiáo* (NT$120) and set meals featuring mountain chicken or pig (NT$320 to NT$490). A picture menu is available.

Getting There & Away

There are two morning trains from Taipei (NT$193, 2½ hours, 6.30am and 9.56am), and many more from Taichung (30 minutes).

Taroko National Park & the East Coast

Includes »

Best Places to Eat

» Dou Sang (p162)
» Leader Village Taroko (p170)
» Cifadahan Cafe (p178)
» Mabanai (p186)

Best Places to Stay

» Amigos (p161)
» Rose Stone (p161)
» Taitung Sea Art Hostel (Motherland; p174)
» Leader Village Taroko (p170)
» Sea Fan Guesthouse (p172)
» Wisdom Garden (p179)

Why Go?

Much is made of the old Portuguese name for Taiwan, Ilha Formosa, which translates as 'the beautiful isle', but it's this part of the country that they gave it to, and it's this part to which it still applies best.

The eastern landscape is dominated by towering sea cliffs and marble gorges, as well as picture-perfect rice fields and wooded mountain ranges. There are no bad views here, and if you occasionally spot a worried look on a traveller's face, it means 'I hope they don't ever ruin the east'.

The east is Taiwan's premier outdoor playground, and cyclists in particular have discovered an ideal environment combining knockout scenery, good roads and plenty of cosy little B&Bs. Others have found that the high concentration of indigenous people gives the region an appealing distinction – and a less manic vibe than that of the west. Just look at the top speed limit: 70km/h! You don't rush through the east; you savour it.

When to Go

Hualien

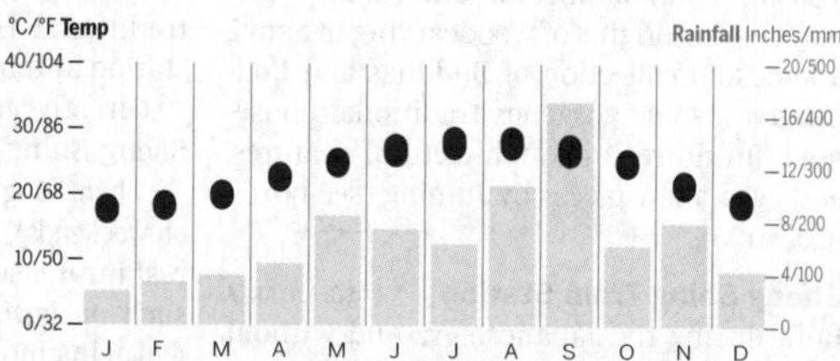

January Good time for beating the crowds at Taroko National Park.

July–August Aboriginal festivals all summer long.

September–December The best months for biking.

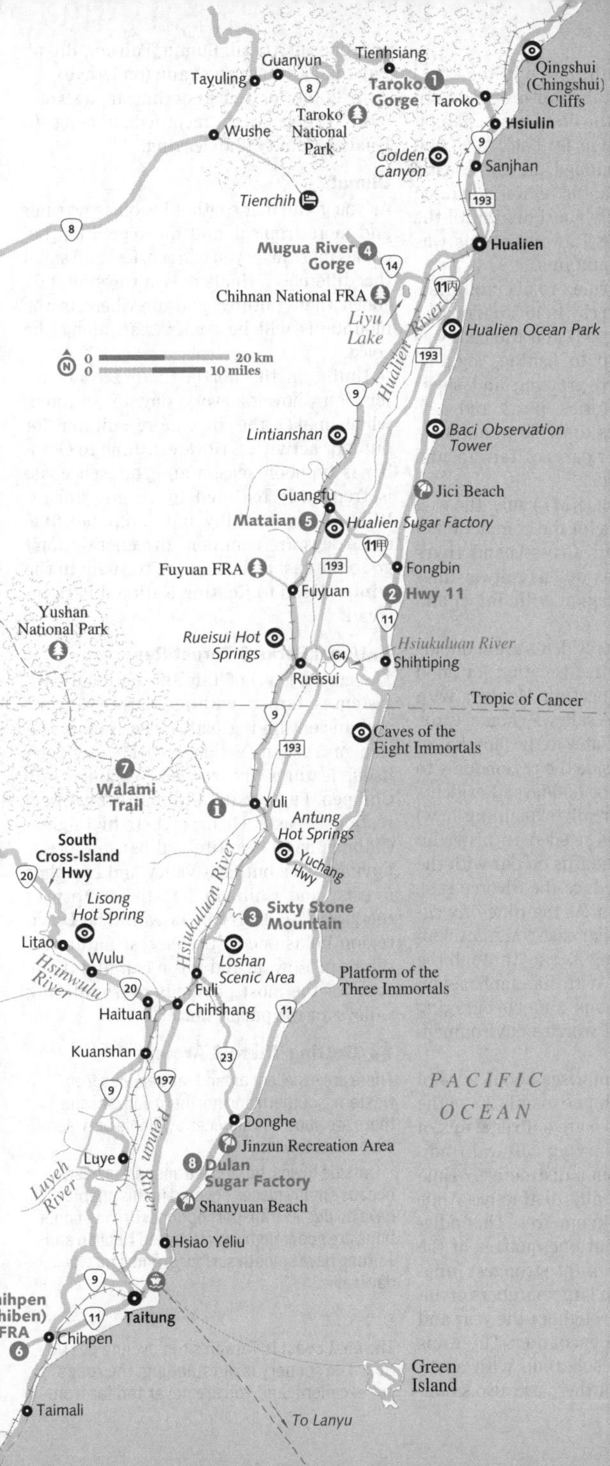

Highlights

1. Hike ancient hunting trails and patrol routes in **Taroko Gorge** (p166)
2. Cycle down the winding coastline on **Highway 11** (p171)
3. Photograph colourful fields of orange day lilies on **Sixty Stone Mountain** (p181)
4. Swim in pools of crystal-blue water in **Mugua River Gorge** (p176)
5. Visit the wetland classroom of **Mataian** (p178)
6. See monkeys and barking deer in a banyan forest in **Chihpen (Zhiben) Forest Recreation Area** (p188)
7. Retrace history and watch nature on the **Walami Trail** (p180)
8. Check out a thriving local music scene at **Dulan Sugar Factory** (p173)

History

Archaeological remains found in the Caves of the Eight Immortals, south of modern-day Shihtiping date the first human habitation on the east coast as far back as 25,000 years. However, hemmed in by coastal ranges and rough sea, the region remained isolated and primarily aboriginal until the late 19th century. To Taiwanese, this was the 'land over the mountains'.

Under Japanese rule, roads and rails lessened the isolation (by 1926 Hualien and Taitung were connected) and the east was gradually opened up to fishing, logging, gold mining, tobacco growing and sugar production. The factories, ports and new transportation routes drew large numbers of workers from other parts of Taiwan, and the population surged.

Under Kuomintang (KMT) rule, the east was opened further with the completion of the Central and South Cross-Island Hwys (now both defunct), as well as railway lines that connected the region with Taipei and Kaohsiung.

These days eastern residents are clamouring to end their relative isolation for good with a freeway connecting Hualien with Suao (Su-hua Hwy). 'A safe way home' is the catchphrase which relates to the fact that so many must work outside the region (only to return on weekends or holidays). Residents also argue (without really explaining how) that a faster route is needed to bring up wages and living standards on par with the north, and to help reduce the divorce rate, the highest in Taiwan. At the time of writing, a multibillion-dollar east-coast development plan was making its way through the legislative assembly. With its emphasis on easing land restrictions and encouraging development, the bill worries environmental groups.

The east coast comprises about 20% of Taiwan's land, but is home to only 3% of the population. The people are a diverse mix of ethnic groups with varying cultural traditions; one can go from a distinctively Hakka village to an equally distinctive Amis village within a few kilometres. The indigenous people, at about one-quarter of the population, have one of the strongest influences, reflected in the large numbers of annual festivals held throughout the year and the food visitors will encounter. The Amis make up the largest subgroup with about 140,000 members, but there are also smaller groups of Atayal, Bunun, Paiwan, Rukai, Puyuma, Kavalan and Yami (on Lanyu).

In 2009, for the first time in decades, more people were recorded moving to Hualien County than leaving.

Climate

As you go further south it becomes warmer and more tropical, and the vegetation becomes more lush; you can see, feel and smell the difference. Hualien is always slightly cooler than Taitung, and anywhere in the mountains will be cooler than along the coast.

Unlike in the north, there are not afternoon showers every day in summer, which makes the area more suitable for outdoor activities. However, June to October is typhoon season and the east coast is frequently battered by severe storms. Winters can be chilly and damp, but fine, clear days are common. In general, don't go to the east coast looking to swim in the winter. Head to Kenting National Park instead.

National Parks & Forest Reserves

The crown jewel of Taiwan's national-park system is Taroko, with its marble canyons and ancient hiking paths. The Nanan section of Yushan National Park, no slouch itself, features the rugged Walami Trail. Chihpen, Fuyuan and Chihnan Forest Recreation Areas each have their highlights: Chihpen has a beautiful old banyan forest; Fuyuan has a butterfly valley and camphor forests; and Chihnan has the history of the logging industry in Taiwan. The Dawu region holds one of the largest nature reserves in Taiwan, and if you can find them, some of the most populous overwintering valleys for the purple butterfly.

ℹ Getting There & Around

There are excellent air and rail services from western, southern and northern Taiwan, and there are good bus services available between east-coast towns.

Outside towns, personal transport is best, because many places covered in this chapter have no public-transport options. Driving conditions are good. Highways between Hualien and Taitung have smooth surfaces, and light weekday traffic.

BICYCLE

The east coast is Taiwan's top cycling destination. The scenery is outstanding, the roads are excellent, and you are never too far from

EAST-COAST CYCLING

Most Common Routes

» Hwy 9 or 11 between Hualien and Taitung

Don't Miss

» Highways connecting the 9 and 11

» County roads 193 and 197

Serious Challenges

» Taroko Gorge to Hehuanshan: a 0m to 3275m climb in 86km

» Audax Club Parisien (ACP) certified route: 200km from Jialulan (加路蘭), Taitung, to the Ruigang Hwy (瑞港公路) and back

a convenience store, restaurant or place to crash.

At the time of writing the maze of back-country roads west of Hwy 9 was being mapped and signed. Also, there was talk of building a bike path all the way from Ilan to Taroko Gorge as part of the Su-hua Hwy expansion.

Most small towns have cheap bike rentals. Good-quality long-distance rentals are available in Hualien and Taitung.

Hualien 花蓮

☎03 / POP 109,324

Hualien (Huālián) is eastern Taiwan's largest city and is the capital of Hualien County. Though much of the city's wealth comes from tourism, local deposits of limestone have also made Hualien the cement capital of Taiwan.

Hualien means 'eddies' in Hokkien (Taiwanese) and the story goes that Qing-dynasty immigrants gave the region this name after noticing the swirling waters off the coast.

Though blessed with few sites of interest, Hualien is arguably the most liveable small city in Taiwan, and traffic aside, a chill-out kind of place. Many travellers prefer to base themselves here even if Taroko Gorge is their main interest.

Hualien sprawls out but budget travellers will find everything they need near the train station. Head a few kilometres east to the Meilunshan Park (Měilúnshān Gōngyuán) and harbour area for wide streets, landscaped parks, bike lanes and ocean views in addition to boutique hotels and pricier restaurants. Downtown is clean and orderly for a Taiwanese town (again, traffic aside), with walkable pavements along which to stroll from cafe to restaurant to traditional snack shop.

Sights & Activities

Seaside Parks

Hualien has three seaside parks, all joined by a walking and bicycle path that continues to Chihsingtan Beach, and that passes the city garbage dump on the way through. The path starts at **Nan Bin Seaside Park** (南濱海濱公園; Nán Bīn Hǎibīn Gōngyuán), the southernmost park, which is a pleasant place for a stroll or a snack at the night market.

Chihsingtan (七星潭; Qīxīng Tán), about 3km north of Hualien, looks down a coastline of high cliffs and green mountains. The water is too rough for swimming but it's a great spot for biking, strolling or picnicking. At the south end sit a couple small fishing villages where a few modern B&Bs and restaurants have opened recently.

Cycling

The cycling path from Nan Bin Seaside Park to Chihsingtan begins well and ends well, but passes through a pretty dismal industrial area for a couple of kilometres in the middle. At the northern end of Chihsingtan, the path continues through a diverse coastal forest and then connects with quiet County Rd 193. From here it's an easy to ride to Sanjhan and Taroko Gorge. From Hualien to the base of Taroko Gorge the route is pretty much flat.

At the time of writing a new bicycle route from Nan Bin Seaside Park to Liyu Lake was close to completion. Another 10km-long route along the river in Hualien was ready to open from the train station area to the coast. As this passes within a few blocks of the train station, cyclists heading out to Hwy 11 or Hwy 9 can use it to avoid the downtown traffic.

Giant Bicycles (捷安特; Jié Ān Tè; ☎823 4057; giant.d21100@msa.hinet.net; ⏱8am-10pm) runs a shop inside the Parkview Hotel, about 1km northeast of the City Hall. Day (per hour NT$100 to NT$150) and multiday rentals (per three days NT$1200) are available – book in advance for the latter. For cheaper bikes ask at the information centre near the train station. Staff can call a local bicycle-rental shop, to deliver to you.

Hualien

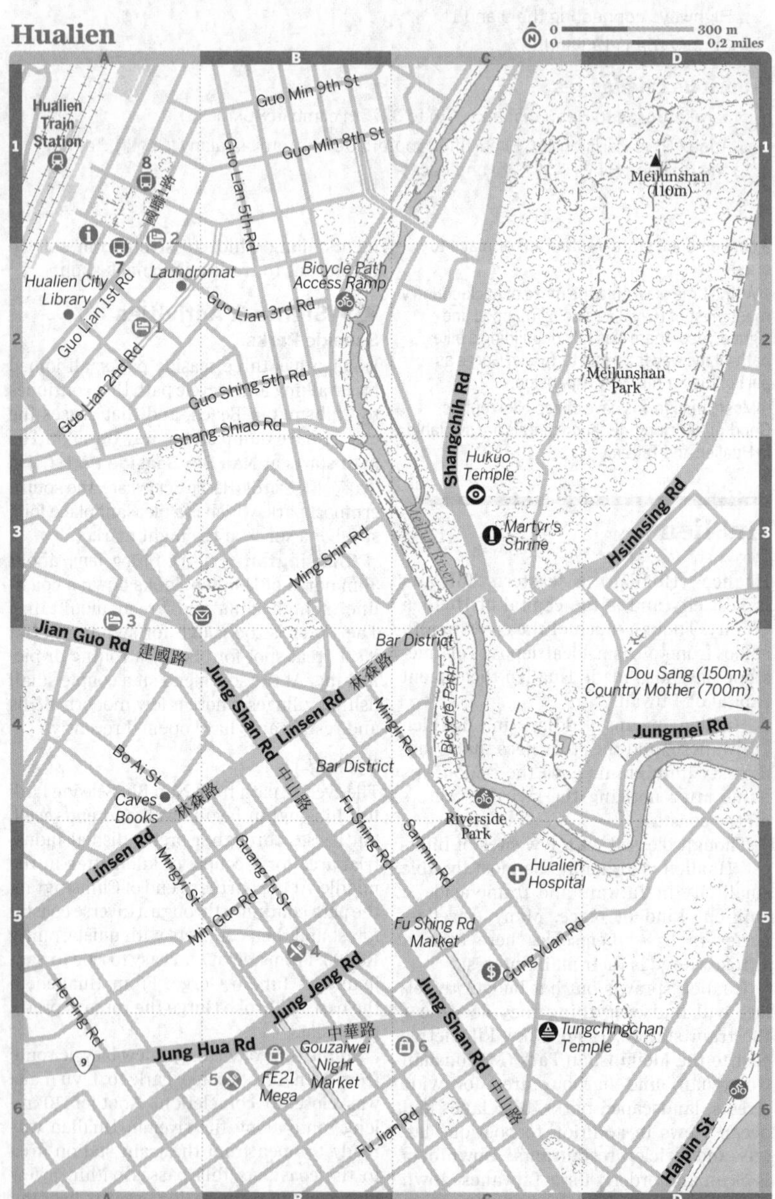

Hualien

Sleeping
1 Amigos A2
2 Ching Yeh Hotel A1
3 Formosa Backpackers Hostel A3

Eating
4 Kimamaya B5
5 Ye Hsiang Shi Dian B6

Shopping
6 Hui Pi Hsu Cake Shop C6

Transport
7 Dingdong Bus Company A2
8 Hualien Bus Company Kiosk A1

Other Sights

Chingszu Temple BUDDHIST TEMPLE
(靜思堂; Jìngsītáng; Chungyang Rd) The simple white and grey exterior of the 10-storey Chingszu Temple is striking. Inside, a large exhibition hall showcases the Tzu Chi Buddhist organisation's activities around the world. Exhibits are in English and Chinese. The temple is a couple of kilometres north of the train station. See also boxed text, p165.

Festivals & Events

For aboriginal festivals around Hualien County, see boxed text, p174.

Sleeping

In addition to basing themselves in Hualien, many travellers stay at Taroko Village, Liyutan, Chihsingtan, or even at one of the many B&Bs down Hwy 11.

Amigos HOSTEL $
(阿美客國際青年旅館; Ā Měi Kè Gúojì Chīngnián Lǚguǎn; ☎836 2756; http://amigos-68.myweb.hinet.net; 68 Guo Lian 2nd Rd; 國聯2路68號; dm incl breakfast NT$450; @) Everything you want in a hostel: bright, clean, inexpensive, run by a friendly, well-travelled local who speaks your language (English anyway), and just a five-minute walk from the train station. There's a shared kitchen, free ADSL, clean sheets and enough showers for everyone.

Amigos' owner can help with everything from scooter and bike rentals to tours. Reservations are recommended from July to September and for long weekends. Book online.

Rose Stone HOMESTAY $$
(福園古厝客棧; Fúyuán Gǔcuò Kèzhàn; ☎854 2317; www.rosestone.com; 48 Hai Bin Rd; 海濱路48號; d/tw NT$2300/3800, 20% weekday discount) Set in a beautifully preserved traditional brick mansion, the Rose is such a maze of corridors, courtyards, chambers and gardens that you'll need to be shown to your room. Despite the old-time atmosphere, rooms offer modern comforts. Home-cooked meals are served in an elaborately decorated tearoom.

To get to the Rose, drive south down Jung Shan Rd (中山路) to the end and turn right onto 193 (the last road at the coast). Continue down the 193 (also called Hai An and later Hai Bin Rd) until the Km19 mark. The turn-off for the Rose is just past this on the left. Note that you really can't see the place until you are on top of it and the nearby area does not look promising. A taxi from the train station will cost about NT$200.

Formosa Backpackers Hostel HOSTEL $
(青年民宿; ☎835 2515; formosahostels@yahoo.com; 206 Jian Guo Rd, 建國路206號; dm student/nonstudent NT$350/400, d with shared bath NT$1200; @) You might as well toss a coin to decide whether to stay here or at Amigos. Both are run by young, well-travelled, English-speaking Taiwanese women, and both offer great value for money. Formosa has laundry service, a full kitchen, a small cafe and bar, a 600-book English library, and free pick up from the train station. Each dorm room has its own bathroom, and if free shampoo and soap is what you need, you'll find it here. The hostel owner is a keen surfer and can arrange surf trips, rentals and lessons.

Ching Yeh Hotel HOTEL $
(青葉大飯店; Qīng Yè Dàfàndiàn; ☎833 0186; fax 833 0188; 83 Guo Lian 1st Rd; 國聯1路83號; d from NT$1500) The Ching Yeh is one of the best options by the train station. Rooms are small, simply furnished and very clean. Some have great views of the mountains.

Many visitors complain about Hualien's top-end accommodation. If service isn't bad, then the rooms have terrible sound insulation (a common complaint). If the rooms are good, then the food is lousy. If you must stay in a five-star, try **Parkview Hotel** (美崙大飯店; Měilún Dàfàndiàn; ☎822 2111; www.parkview-hotel.com; 1-1 Lin Yuan;

林園1-1號; d from NT$5800; @ ≋) out near the harbour. Amenities include golf course, tennis courts, restaurants, pool and everything else you can imagine.

Eating

Hualien cuisine is a mixture of typical Taiwanese cuisine (soup, dumplings and noodles) and the food of the aboriginal tribes who, for centuries, have sustained themselves on fish, wild game, and wild vegetables and flowers. One way to try the local food is to head to the night market at Nan Bin Seaside Park and sample what's on display. Some things to try include barbecued pork, stewed spareribs (燉排骨; *dùn páigǔ*), bitter gourd (苦瓜; *kǔguā*), coffin cake (棺材板; *guāncái bǎn* – different from the Tainan style) and fresh fruit drinks. Across from the train station on Guo Lian 1st Rd you can pick up lunchbox meals (NT$80).

Dou Sang TAIWANESE **$$**
(多桑; Duō Sāng; 2 Jungmei Rd; dishes from NT$180; ⏲5-10pm) You have to pronounce the name of this restaurant in Taiwanese, if you want to get it right. It's the least you can do, since it does such a good job with its dishes. Set in an old Japanese-era wood house, and serving ultra-orthodox Taiwanese dishes, Dou Sang is where locals take their visiting friends. Your stomach will love you afterwards, even if your arteries cry out in protest. No English menu.

Country Mother WESTERN **$**
(36 Fucian Rd; breakfast from NT$109; ⏲6.30am-2pm) Echoing its name nicely, Country Mother serves some of the best Western breakfasts and sandwiches in Taiwan in a cosy venue up from the harbour. Best of all, it's open very early for cyclists looking to fill up on something wholesome and hearty before the day's ride. Country Mother is just up from Dou Sang; head left when the road splits.

Kimamaya JAPANESE BBQ **$$**
(炭火燒肉工房; Tànhuǒ Shāoròu Gōngfáng; 144 Bo Ai Rd, dishes from NT$120; ⏲5-11pm) A laid-back Japanese barbecue place with sunken tables that serves handcrafted draft beer (per pint NT$140).

Ye Hsiang Shi Dian DUMPLINGS **$**
(液香扁食店; Yì Xiāng Biǎn Shí Diàn; 42 Shin Yi St; mains NT$40) 'Hualien dumplings' rings with brand-name cachet to the ears of most Taiwanese. Ye Hsiang Shi Dian has been serving steaming bowls of pork and seafood dumplings for over 70 years.

Drinking

Hualien has many trendy cafes and teahouses along its main streets. On Linsen

EAST-COAST EATING

Hualien and Taitung Counties have a diverse mix of aborigine, Hakka, Taiwanese and former mainland Chinese people, all contributing to the culinary traditions of the area. One of the most influential cuisines in Hualien is that prepared by the Amis people: the cooking tends to be simple and emphasises the natural flavours of fruits, flowers, taro and wild vegetables. Amis dishes made from betel-nut flowers, sorghum and rattan are common and can be seen in night markets and restaurants around Hualien and Taitung. For something very traditional head to Mataian for hot pot brought to boil with heated rocks.

Fruit grown in eastern Taiwan is often tastier and fresher than fruit grown elsewhere. Pineapples, mangoes and watermelons can be seen growing (or for sale) along the sides of the roads, and some orchards allow you to pick your own fruit and pay by weight. City markets have tables and carts heaped with a colourful assortment of common and exotic fruits, including star fruit, pomelos (the ones grown in Dulan are best), coconuts, durian, papaya and lychees. Taitung's custard apple (Buddha head fruit – so-called because the bumpy ridges on the fruit resemble the head of the Sakyamuni Buddha) has even garnered its own festival; sad to say, it's pretty lame. However, the fruit is pretty delicious and really does have the consistency of custard.

Other delicacies to try include the dumplings of Hualien, the dried fish of Chengkung and the sticky rice of Taitung. Fresh seafood is available all along the coast, and some of the best places to find it are in Chengkung, Shihtiping and Fukang Harbour, north of Taitung.

ODD THEME MUSEUMS IN TAIWAN

Taiwan has its share of themed museums, and more than its share of odd ones. Here are a few to keep in mind for a rainy day.

Chihsing Tan Katsuo Museum (七星柴魚博物館; Qīxīng Cháiyú Bówùguǎn; Chihsingtan Beach, Hualien; admission free) This museum near Chihsingtan Beach is dedicated to… dried bonito. All we can say is ???

Chunghwa Postal Museum (郵政博物館; Yóuzhèng Bówùguǎn; Taipei; admission NT$5) Stamps, uniforms and so, so, so much more for a token admission price.

Kite Museum (風箏博物館; Fēngzhēng Bówùguǎn; 20 Kungwei Lane, Juifen, Taipei County; admission NT$100; ⏲10am-5pm) Yep, these things can really fly.

TaiPower North Visitor Centre (台電核二廠北部展示館; Táidiàn Héèrchǎng Běibù Zhǎnshì Guǎn; Yeliu Village, Taipei County; admission free; ⏲9.30am-4.30pm) An exhibition hall for the second nuclear power plant. 'Excellent, Smithers'.

Taiwan Nougat Museum (p107) Come see the biggest piece of nougat in the world.

Taiwan Salt Museum (p243) Any country worth its sodium chloride should have one of these.

Some others we've noticed on our travels around the country include a Honey Museum, a Lunch Box Museum, a Furniture Museum, a Coffee Museum and a Sanitary Wares Museum.

Rd (林森路) east of Fu Shing Rd, and up Fu Hsing itself, is a small bar district with an obvious surfer section. Nan Bin Seaside Park has outdoor drinking venues.

Shopping

Hualien's main export, marble, is all over the city. Numerous souvenir shops sell marble carvings but be aware that the mining of marble is having a devastating effect on the local environment.

Hualien's delicious cakes and cookies are available at bakeries and gift shops around town. *Mochi*, a sticky rice treat, can be found elsewhere in Taiwan but many enjoy the Hualien variety most.

Hui Pi Hsu Cake Shop · TRADITIONAL SNACKS
(惠比須; Huì Bǐ Xū; 65 Jung Hua Rd; 中華路65號) This shop has been in business since 1899 and is well known for its delicious peanut and sesame cookies. Goodies are sold in bulk or in attractive tins that make good souvenirs.

Information

Internet Access

Hualien City Library (花蓮市立圖書館; 170 Guo Lian 1st Rd; ⏲10am-5pm Tue-Sun) Free internet access close to the train station. The Hualien County Information Centre also willingly acts as an internet station for travellers, with free computer access and wi-fi.

Laundry

Laundromat (洗衣店; 46 Guo Lian 2nd Rd; ⏲24hr) A DIY coin laundromat very close to Amigos hostel.

Medical Services

Tzu-chi Buddhist Hospital (慈濟醫院; Cíjì Yīyuàn; ☎856 1825; 707 Jung Yang Rd, Sec 3) A hospital known for its excellent facilities; it's northwest from the train station, at the intersection of Jung Shan and Jung Yang Rds.

Money

There are ATM machines all over town and in most 7-Elevens.

Bank of Taiwan (台灣銀行; 3 Gung Yuan Rd) Offers moneychanging in addition to ATM service.

Tourist Information

The informative and entertaining online magazine *Highway 11* (www.highway11.net) focuses on life on the east coast. Pick up a copy of the free *Highway 11* fold-out map (ringed with discount coupons) at the information centre to keep up with the latest bar and restaurant openings around town.

Hualien County Information Centre (花蓮縣旅遊服務中心; Huālián Xiàng Lǚyóu Fúwù Zhōngxīn; ☎836 0634; ⏲8am-8pm) An excellent visitor centre, on the right of the train-station exit. It has an abundance of information available in English – everything from bus schedules to tour prices and times. Staff are friendly and speak good English.

Websites

Hualien County (http://tour-hualien.hl.gov.tw) Good introduction to the attractions in the area.

Getting There & Away

Air

Hualien Airport (www.hulairport.gov.tw) Has daily flights to Taipei, Taichung and Kaohsiung with **Mandarin Airlines** (www.mandarin-airlines.com) and **Transasia Airways** (www.tna.com.tw).

Bus

The bus situation along the east coast is confusing (even to locals), with multiple companies operating out of multiple stations. The information centre at the train station has the most up-to-date information. Seek its help to confirm times and departure points.

Dingdong Bus Company (鼎東客運; http://diingdong.myweb.hinet.net; 138-6 Guo Lian 1st Rd) No station, just a small bus stop to the left of the Hualien County Information Centre. To Taitung: NT$475, 3½ hours, three times daily.

Hualien Bus Company (花蓮客運; www.hl.gov.tw/bus) The station to the left of the train station as you exit. To Taitung: NT$492, 3½ hours, twice daily.

Train

Frequent trains running north and south. To Taipei: fast/slow NT$441/284, two/3½ hours.

Getting Around

To/From the Airport

Hualien Bus Company runs buses to the airport (NT$25, 30 minutes, every 20 minutes).

Car & Scooter

Vehicles are available for rent around the train station. Rental prices: scooters NT$400 to NT$500 per day; and cars NT$1500 to NT$2000 per day (both exclude petrol). You need an International Driver's Permit and ID to rent a car. To rent a scooter, you need a Taiwanese driver's licence, except at **Pony Leasing and Rental Group** (小馬租車集團; www.ponyrent.com.tw; 國聯一路81號), to the left of the Ching Yeh Hotel, and the **Taroko National Park Headquarters** (ask the staff to call for a local shop to deliver a scooter for you; an International Driver's Permit could be useful).

Taxi

Drivers congregate around the train and bus stations. To travel to and around Taroko costs up to NT$3000 per day.

Taroko National Park

太魯閣國家公園

☎03

Just 15km north of Hualien sits **Taroko National Park** (Tàilǔgé Gúojiā Gōngyuán), Taiwan's top tourist destination. With its marble-walled canyons, lush vegetation and mountainous landscape, Taroko really puts the *formosa* (beautiful) in Ilha Formosa.

The park covers 120,000 hectares and rises from sea level in the east to over 3700m further west. In fact, Taroko is 90% mountainous with 27 peaks over 3000m. Almost all the biogeographical zones in Taiwan are represented here, providing a sanctuary for half the island's plant and animal species.

The blue-green Liwu River (called Yayung Paru – Great River – by the Taroko tribe) cuts through the centre, forging deep slitted valleys and ravines before emptying into the sea. In one stretch it forms Taroko Gorge, an 18km marble-walled canyon that many consider one of Asia's scenic wonders.

Most activities in the park take place within the gorge. Increasingly, however, people are exploring deeper, especially cyclists who have discovered a remarkable ride in the 86km from the base to Wuling Pass at 3275m.

You can visit Taroko any time of year, but be warned (with an extra-stern look) that during weekends and holidays the place is a madhouse, especially on the road. At times you may get stuck in traffic for a considerable time as two tour buses try to figure out a way to get past each other in some narrow, twisting tunnel. On the other hand, if you go on any of the longer trails, you will soon leave the crowds behind.

Summer is the best time to do any river tracing or swimming; unless a typhoon is coming, the weather is usually clear and warm. Winters are chilly, and there's often a drizzle, but that keeps the crowds away. May and June bring the monsoon rainy season.

There's only one road through the park (Hwy 8), and only one real village (Tienhsiang). Food and accommodation are limited here, so many people base themselves at the foot of the park in Taroko village, or even in Hualien.

THE MAVERICK

Her followers call her Shangren ('the exalted person') and consider her a living Bodhisattva. Business magazines think she is a powerful and effective CEO. If you listen in on one of her sermons you might think Cheng Yen is recycling plant owner. She isn't, but the head of the worldwide Tzu Chi organisation does have her own TV station on which she spends more time talking about doing good in the world (which includes recycling) rather than expounding on scriptures. What kind of Buddhist nun is this, you may ask? A maverick, an iconoclast, a Made in Taiwan special.

Cheng Yen was born in 1937 to a wealthy business family in Taichung. Beautiful and deeply compassionate, she began her journey to Bodhisattva-hood after the death of her father compelled her to seek comfort with the Buddhist nuns living nearby. At the age of 24, she made the extraordinary move of running away with another nun and spent the next several years wandering the island, living in huts and caves and studying scripture as a lay Buddhist.

Cheng Yen's potential was recognised early by the Venerable Yinshun, a major advocate of reformist humanitarian Buddhism. Yinshun took Cheng Yen on as his last student and helped her to become ordained. For the next year the nun meditated, endured hardship and, according to the small number of disciples, performed miracles.

More significantly, Cheng Yen began to display her genius for organising people (and being one step ahead of the times). With her own followers to lead, she set about restoring dignity and rationality to monastic orders. Disciples were, among other restrictions, forbidden to take money for alms but had to actually work for their living. Such changes would pay off in the 1980s, when Taiwan's spiritually void but progressive middle class began looking for a faith that didn't smack of superstition and backwardness.

Two chance events in 1966 set the stage for the most important phase in Cheng Yen's life: the formation of Tzu Chi. In the first incident, Cheng Yen witnessed a poor aboriginal woman die of a miscarriage. In the second one, not long after, Cheng Yen was challenged by three Catholic nuns over why Buddhists, with their concept of universal love, do no good work for the benefit of others.

Cheng Yen's response to the challenge came a few months later. Rather than accept a cushy position as a lecturer in Chiayi, she listened to her followers and stayed in Hualien. Once again, reading the times better than anyone else, Cheng Yen sensed the latent power of Taiwanese lay society to do good. In 1966, with a handful of housewives pledging 50c a day to charity, Cheng Yen started the Tzu Chi Buddhist Humanitarian Compassion Society.

The society (which is composed mostly of lay followers) grew slowly. By 1979, however, it was large enough to attempt to build a hospital in poor and mostly aboriginal Hualien. Again the odds, the Tzu Chi (Ciji) Buddhist Hospital opened in 1989 to islandwide acclaim.

The year 1989 was not long after the lifting of martial law, and Taiwanese, with their first taste of freedom, were forming civil associations with abandon. The established and well-respected Tzu Chi was well positioned to attract those whose humanitarian impulses had been stifled. Membership expanded rapidly, in particular among the middle class.

By 2000 Tzu Chi was the largest formal organisation in Taiwan, with hundreds of thousands of lay volunteers working on projects as diverse as rebuilding houses after disasters to recycling. Tzu Chi has also been a leader in the development of hospice care in Taiwan, and its medical university places a unique stress on the moral cultivation of physicians.

Today Tzu Chi is an international organisation with five million worldwide members and assets as high as US$9 billion. In Taiwan alone it runs four state-of-the-art hospitals, a recycling program, the medical university mentioned above, and a TV station.

For more on the remarkable story of both Tzu Chi and Cheng Yen, visit www.tzuchi.org or pick up a copy of Julia Huang's *Charisma and Compassion: Cheng Yen and the Buddhist Tzu Chi Movement*. Also see boxed text, p336.

Taroko National Park

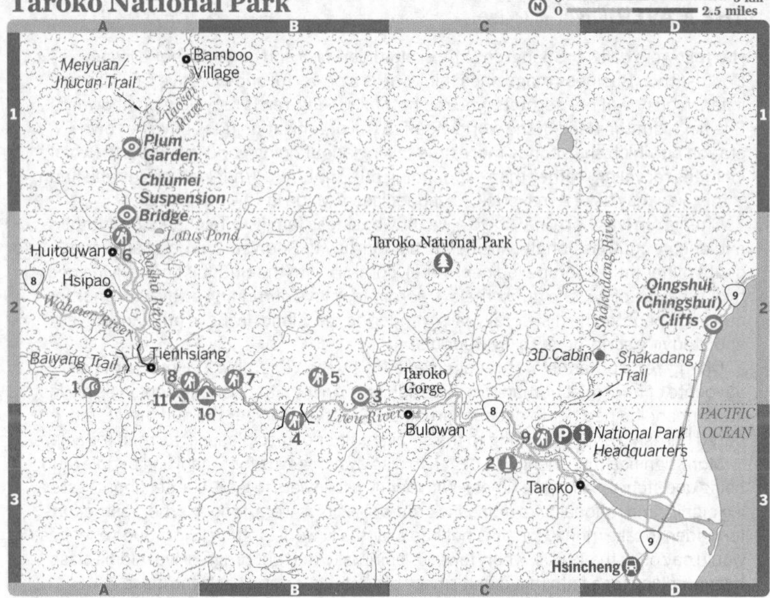

History

Although humans inhabited the park as long as 3000 years ago, the ancestors of today's Taroko tribe (a sub-branch of the Atayal, recognised in 2004) began to settle along the Liwu River in the 17th century. The Taroko were known for their hunting and weaving skills, the use of facial tattoos, and ritual headhunting.

The Taroko lived in isolation until 1874 when the Qing began to build a road from Suao to Hualien to help open the area to Chinese settlers. In 1896 the Japanese marched into the region looking to exploit the forestry and mineral resources. After an 18-year bloody struggle, they finally forced the outnumbered and outweaponed Taroko to submit, and most villages were relocated to the foothills or plains of Hualien.

The Japanese cut roads and widened existing trails (using Taroko labour) to form the 'Old Hehuan Mountain Rd' from the base of the gorge to Wushe in Nantou County. The road facilitated control over mountain aborigines and the extraction of the area's natural resources. It also spurred the first wave of tourism in the area, with hiking becoming a popular activity by the mid-1930s.

In the 1950s the KMT extended the road west as part of the first Cross-Island Hwy. Many of the road workers later settled in the area, often marrying Taroko women and becoming farmers. Plum Garden is one of the most well known of these settlements.

As with Yushan National Park, there were plans to turn the Taroko area into a national park in the 1930s. However, WWII scuttled that idea and it was not until the 1960s that the KMT government began to draft a national-park act. Taroko National Park is Taiwan's fourth such park, and it was officially established on 28 November 1986.

Dangers & Annoyances

Earthquakes, typhoons and landslides are having their effect on the strata of Taroko Gorge, and a small number of visitors have been killed in recent years from falling rocks. The park offers free helmets for visitors, although wearing them is optional.

Sights & Activities

Taroko Gorge SCENIC GORGE

This 18km marble-walled gorge (太魯閣; Tàilǔgé) began as coral deposits deep

Taroko National Park

Sights

1 Baiyang Waterfall ... A2
2 Eternal Springs Shrine ... C3
3 Swallow Grotto ... B2
4 Tunnel of Nine Turns ... B3
Zimu (Cimu) Bridge ... (see 7)

Activities, Courses & Tours

5 Jhuilu Old Trail ... B2
6 Meiyuan/Jhucun Trail ... A2
7 Start of Jhuilu Trail ... B2
8 Start of Lushui-Holiu Trail ... A2
9 Start of Shakadang Trail ... C3

Sleeping

10 Holiu Campground ... B2
11 Lushui Campground ... A2

under the sea. Under pressure from geological forces, the coral was transformed into limestone and then marble, schists and gneiss. Five million years ago, as Taiwan was lifted from the sea by the collision of the Philippine and Eurasian plates, the gorge began to be formed. In essence, the upward thrust of hard rock, combined with the erosion of the soft layers from water and landslides, left towering canyon walls that are so narrow in places that you could play catch with someone on the other side.

Taroko has been a popular walking and hiking destination since the 1930s. The park puts out an excellent guide in the *Trails of Taroko Gorge and Su-Hua Areas*. Pick up a copy (NT$220) at the National Park Headquarters. Useful trail maps are included with clear information on length, times, conditions, and things to observe along the way.

The following are presented in the order you would encounter them starting out from the base of the gorge.

Eternal Spring Shrine MEMORIAL

Not far from the park administration centre, overlooking the Liwu River from a cliff-side perch, sits this haunting shrine (長春祠; Cháng Chūn Cí), dedicated to the 450 workers who lost their lives building the highway. A gushing spring that never dries pours out onto the rocks below, gracing the shrine with what looks like a hoary old beard. It's a poignant memorial and can be reached by crossing a suspension bridge and hiking up a series of steps.

Shakadang Trail HIKING TRAIL

Formerly the Mysterious Valley Trail, this flat 4.4km hike (砂卡礑步道; Shākǎdāng Bùdào; one hour one way) follows the crystal-clear Shakadang River as it winds through marble canyons and boulder-strewn flats. The curving riverbed creates massive pools of bluish green water, and many outdoors groups from Hualien come here in summer to swim and river trace (although the park's board is not entirely happy about that).

Coming from the direction of the National Park Headquarters, the trailhead is to the right after emerging from the first tunnel. Follow the stairs down to the river to access the path.

The Shakadang Trail officially ends at 3D Cabin. However, if you have permits you can (theoretically) continue on the **Dali–Datung Trail** (大禮-大同步道; Dàlǐ-Dàtóng Bùdaò) to Dali and Datung, two isolated aboriginal villages. Apply for permits at the police station by the park headquarters. This trail should take about seven to eight hours, return.

DON'T MISS

TAROKO'S TOP NATURAL SIGHTS

» **The Gorge** – the marble-walled jewel in the national park's crown
» **Tunnel of Nine Turns** – how can rock make such magical patterns?
» **Swallow Grotto** – ditto to the above
» **Shakadang River** – a green-blue river tossed with even more colourful boulders
» **Baiyang Trail** – a Chinese landscape painting brought to life
» **Qingshui Cliffs** – classic towering sea cliffs
» **Golden Canyon** – a deep marble-walled pool in which you can swim
» **Eternal Spring Shrine** – poignant and picture perfect

Swallow Grotto SCENIC AREA

(燕子口步道; Yànzǐ Kǒu Bùdào) In this slice of the old highway, now closed to traffic, the gorge twists and towers in one of its most colorful and narrow sections. It's a superb location for taking pictures.

Jhuilu Old Trail HIKING TRAIL

One of the most spectacular (and easily accessible) hiking paths in Taiwan, the 10.3km Jhuilu Old Trail (錐麓古道; Zhuī Lù Gǔ Dào) follows the last long remaining section of the old Hehuan Mountain Rd. Justifiably famous in hiking circles, the trail gets its name from the section of the 1100m-high Jhuilu Cliff it traverses about 500m above the Liwu River. This exposed, airy ledge, 60cm wide at its narrowest and literally cut into the cliff face, affords a spellbinding (or possibly vertigo-inducing) bird's-eye view of the gorge. The trail begins at Zimu (Cihmu) Bridge and runs east along the north wall of the gorge before recrossing at Swallow Grotto. Hikers have been known to abandon their plans when they actually looked up and saw where they were going.

The path was closed after the 921 Earthquake of 1999, and reopened in 2008 on a permit-only basis. Applications must be made at least a week in advance and can be made online, though only on the Chinese section of the park's website (the park promises English applications will be available in the future).

Tunnels of Nine Turns SCENIC AREA

Like the Swallow Grotto, the tunnel (九曲洞; Jiǔ Qū Dòng) is an old section of the original highway. In the early '90s the highway was diverted to leave open to walkers this 2km slice of road.

Lushui-Holiu Trail HIKING TRAIL

Part of the Old Hehuan Mountain Rd, the 2km trail (綠水-合流步道; Lùshuǐ-Héliú Bùdào) runs above the highway along a cliff, with fantastic views of the Liwu River. Think of it as the Jhuilu Old Trail for the faint of heart. The trailhead starts behind the now-closed Lushui Information Centre.

Hsiangte Temple BUDDHIST TEMPLE

Just before Tienhsiang a suspension bridge leads to this temple (祥德寺; Xiángdé Sì), on a ledge overlooking the gorge. The temple is named after the Buddhist monk who prayed for the safety of the workmen as they built the Central Cross-Island Hwy.

Baiyang Trail HIKING TRAIL

This 2.1km trail (白楊步道; Báiyáng Bùdào) to the **Baiyang Waterfall** (白楊瀑布; Báiyáng Pùbù) is one of the most popular short walks in the park. The trail was recently blocked by a massive landslide. At the time of writing, the trail had reopened, but hikers should check at the visitor centre as it's a very different route and takes about six hours return with some rough sections and rope climbs.

Meiyuan/Jhucun Trail HIKING TRAIL

About 6km up the main road from Tienhsiang, at the KM164.5 mark on a switchback, this 12.4km trail (梅園竹村步道; Méiyuán Zhúcūn Bùdaò; Bamboo Village/Plum Garden Trail) begins its runs up the rugged Taosai River valley along a path chiselled into the valley walls. Though a popular hiking route (plan on eight hours for a return trip), it's also the only outside access for two tiny farming villages that are deep in the mountains. Once the site of Taroko aboriginal settlements, the villages were resettled after the construction of the Central Cross-Island Hwy.

At the Chiumei (Jiumei) suspension bridge, a 2.1km side trail leads to Lotus Pond (蓮花池步道; Liánhuā Chí Bùdaò), another farming area now reverting to a natural state. Should you take this diversion, plan on a good three-hour return workout up a steep, rough trail.

You can camp at Plum Garden and Bamboo Village, but get permission from the park first.

Qingshui (Chingshui) Cliffs SCENIC AREA

Towering coastal cliffs are a regular feature of Taiwan's east. The most spectacular examples, known as the Qingshui Cliffs (清水斷崖; Qīngshuǐ Duànyá), extend 21km from Chondge, just north of where the Liwu River enters the sea, to the town of Heren. The durable marble and schist walls, which rise 200m to 1000m above sea level, form the easternmost section of the Central Mountains, and reportedly are the oldest bit of rock in Taiwan.

The classic location for cliff viewing is a little pullover park at the KM174.2 mark on Hwy 9.

River Tracing

The Sanjhan North River (三棧北溪) flows through southern Taroko Park. A short 2km trail has been built along the river, following a canal built by the US government in

1952 (clean, clear water still flows down the canal). But the real reason to come is to river trace to the **Golden Canyon** (黃金峽谷; Huángjīn Xiágǔ). Those who have done the trip rave about the beauty of the gorge, the numerous waterfalls and the deep, blue-tinted swimming pools.

From spring to autumn, river-tracing outings are organised by the local aborigines in Sanjhan from the community **activity centre** (三棧社區發展協會; Sānzhàn Shèqū Fāzhǎn Xiéhuì; ☎826 9916, 0972-100 684; http://tw.myblog.yahoo.com/pratan-truku). The cost is NT$2000 per person, including all rental equipment. Trips take about eight hours return, and start from the activity centre, usually in the early morning. You should book at least three days in advance, and have at least three people in your group.

Sanjhan sits just south of Taroko National Park. If you are heading to Hualien from Taroko, turn right off Hwy 9 at the sign for Sanjhan (三棧; Sānzhàn; Sanchan). When you cross the bridge into the village, stay right along the river.

Cycling

Cycling the gorge grows in popularity each year, with the majority of riders making a day trip up to Tienhsiang (elevation 470m) and back. Bikes can be rented across from the Hsincheng train station at **Taroko Gorge Bike Rental** (太魯閣峽谷自行車行; Tàilǔgé Xiágǔ Zìxíngchē Háng; ☎0955-712 726; per 2/4hr NT$150/250) and also in Hualien and Chihsingtan. For a fee, the owner of the shop at Hsincheng will drive you up to Tienhsiang, allowing for an exertion-free descent.

A great deal more challenging is the 75km ride from the base to Dayuling and then, for the brave, on to Lishan (another 29km) and, for the heroic, to Hehuanshan (another 11km): the latter takes you from sea level to 3275m at Wuling Pass, the highest section of road in east Asia. Buses at both Lishan and Hehuanshan connect to Taichung, Ilan or back to Taroko.

It's a gruelling ride up switchback after switchback, with the air cooling and thinning considerably at higher levels. The rewards, beyond the physical accomplishment, include world-class mountain vistas as your constant companion, and an ever-changing forest cover that eventually gives way to rolling fields of dwarf bamboo at the highest levels.

The ascent is not particularly steep up to Tienhsiang but afterwards it becomes more relentless. Most riders spend the first night in the hostel at Guanyun (altitude 2374m), about 71km up from the base. A complete cross-island ride from Taroko to Taichung covers 200km of road and typically takes three days, with the second night's stop in Wushe (p226).

Tours

All travel agencies in Hualien and Taipei can arrange full- or half-day tours of the gorge. Taking a tour is a convenient way to see Taroko but it doesn't leave enough time for exploring.

Taiwan Tour Bus TOUR BUS
(www.taiwantourbus.com.tw; half-/full-day tours NT$600/988) Leaves from Hualien train station visitor centre. Staff at the visitor centre can help with ticket purchases.

Festivals & Events

Taroko International Marathon MARATHON
The park has been the venue for this autumn event since 2000. Organisers like to stress that it's the only canyon marathon in the world. The event attracts runners from all over the world (there were 10,000 participants in 2009) and there are full and half marathons as well as a 5km run. Contact the park for more information.

Sleeping

With your own transport, you have many options for sleeping.

Tienhsiang

Silks Palace Hotel HOTEL $$$
(太魯閣晶英酒店; Tàilǔgé Jīngyīng Jiǔdiàn; ☎869 1155; www.grandformosa-taroko.com.tw; r incl breakfast from NT$7000; @ 🏊) Most likely the first building you'll see upon entering Tienhsiang, the former Grand Formosa now sports a new name and an updated style: think clean lines, liberal use of wood and stone, and red tile floors. In addition to multiple eating and drinking venues, the hotel now boasts a rooftop pool and tennis courts with big views of the gorge. Shuttle buses can pick up guests from Hualien airport or train station. There are discounts of 40% to 50% during the week.

Tienhsiang Youth Activity Centre HOTEL/HOSTEL $$
(天祥青年活動中心; Tiānxiáng Qīngnián Huódòng Zhōngxīn; ☎869 1111; http://cyctsyac.myweb.hinet.net; dm NT$650, d/tw incl breakfast NT$1800/3600) Up the hill from the

Catholic Hostel, the airy, expansive Youth Activity Centre offers far superior private and dorm rooms to the Catholic Hostel. Expect two-star comfort but a lot of space to hang out, including a cafe-bar with outdoor seating. Rooms are discounted by 15% midweek.

Catholic Hostel HOSTEL $
(天祥天主堂; Tiānxiáng Tiānzhǔ Táng; ☎869 1122; dm NT$250, s/d without shower NT$350/600, with shower d/tw 1000/1200) The Catholic Hostel has been the principal budget hotel in Tienhsiang for 50 years. The place is getting a bit long in the tooth but it still offers clean, decent rooms and dorms at no-nonsense prices. However, the dorm rooms are a bit stark, with old metal-frame bunk beds and zero decorative touches.

Bulowan

Meaning 'echo' in Atayal, Bulowan (布洛灣; Bùluòwān) is a former Taroko mountain village. In the lower village a few aboriginal families sell and display good-quality arts and crafts (from 8.30am to 4.30pm, closed first and third Monday of each month).

TOP CHOICE **Leader Village Taroko** CABINS $$$
(立德布洛灣山月村; Lìdé Bùluòwān Shānyuè Cūn; ☎861 0111; www.leaderhotel.com; 2-person cabins incl breakfast from NT$4700) In the upper village, on a high meadow surrounded by postcard-perfect scenery, the Leader Village Taroko offers 36 quality wood cabins with old-time porches to let you relax and take in the views. This is by far the best place to stay in the park. Book online for weekday/low-season discounts.

Thankfully, there is no karaoke TV (KTV) or loud entertainment permitted (although there are nightly aboriginal musical performances). Management encourages guests to be quiet and enjoy what nature has to offer, which includes a small trail behind the cabins where endemic butterfly and bird species flit about year-round, and where monkeys, civets and deer are often spotted.

Taroko

An increasingly popular option for travellers is to stay in the little village (太魯閣) at the base, just metres from the park entrance, and 5km from Hsincheng train station. A number of inexpensive restaurants and hotels line the main road, including **Liwu Inn Youth Hostel** (立霧客棧; Lìwù Kèzhàn; ☎861 0769; liwu.hotel@msa.hinet.net; dm/d/tw incl breakfast NT$650/2200/3100; @) on the right near the end of the strip. The owner speaks some English and can help with bike and scooter rental.

Guanyun (Kuanyun)

Youth Activity Centre HOSTEL $
(觀雲山莊; Guānyún Shānzhuāng; ☎04-2599 1173; http://kwan.cyh.org.tw/eng; dm/d/tw NT$300/2000/3000) At an altitude of 2374m, the revamped activity centre in tiny Guanyun (觀雲), 57km up from Tienhsiang, offers solid food (breakfast/lunch/dinner NT$80/150/150) and accommodation literally in the clouds (most days). It's usually the first night's stop for cyclists on the way to Lishan or Hehuanshan from Taroko. However, for most travellers the centre is a bit too far away from the main sights to be of much use.

The centre is 400m off Hwy 7. Look for the sign in Chinese around the KM117 mark.

Camping

Arrive early if you wish to stake out a spot at the campgrounds at **Holiu** (合流; cleaning fee NT$200) and **Lushui** (綠水; free). Both campgrounds sit in superb locations on flats above the river, and bathrooms with showers are available.

Eating

Leader Village Taroko RESTAURANT $$
(Bulowan; lunch & dinner set meals from NT$280) The Leader Village resort in Bulowan serves excellent aboriginal food prepared by aboriginal chefs. Portions are large, and every last bite is a delight. A typical set meal might include both barbecued wild pig and mountain chicken; soup; rice steamed in bamboo tubes; and exotic mountain vegetables. English menus.

Silks Palace Hotel RESTAURANT $
(Tienhsiang; lunch/dinner buffet for nonguests NT$650/800) Excellent buffet spreads available in either the Western or Chinese restaurants.

Tienhsiang Youth Activity Centre RESTAURANT $
(Tienhsiang; lunch & dinner NT$160) Meals are available to guests and nonguests. Buy tickets in advance. For breakfast (NT$100), buy a ticket before 9pm the night before.

The cafeterias around the bus station in Tienhsiang deserve a sign above them reading 'Serving barely edible food since 1986'.

Information

There are no ATMs in the park that take international cards.

National Park Headquarters (國家公園管理處; Guójiā Gōngyuán Guǎnlǐ Chù; www.taroko.gov.tw; ⌚8.30am-4.45pm) Found at the entrance to gorge. It has useful information on the status of trails and road conditions, and free maps and brochures of hiking trails. There's also a bulletin board with bus schedules and notices, a cafe, and a souvenir shop with books for sale. Other visitor centres can be found throughout the park.

Getting There & Away

Bus

We don't recommend taking a public bus through the gorge, not least because, when you are trying to return or move on, it's difficult to spot them among the hundreds of other buses. Check the visitor centre at the Hualien train station for the latest schedule.

Buses run hourly from Hualien to the park entrance (NT$82, one hour) starting at 5.30am. There are four buses a day from Hualien to Tienhsiang (NT$162, 1½ hours); the first bus leaves at 6.30am and the last bus leaves Tienhsiang at 6.30pm.

Taxi

A day trip from Hualien to Taroko Gorge costs up to NT$3000, and a one-way trip from Hualien to Tienhsiang costs NT$1500.

Train

Hsincheng Station (新城站), also known as Taroko Station, lies closest to the park entrance (about 5km away). It's used by travellers staying in Taroko village or in the gorge. All buses to Taroko Gorge stop here. A fast/slow train from Taipei to Hsincheng costs NT$441/284 and takes 2½/3½ hours.

HIGHWAY 11

Two main routes run north–south along the east coast – whichever road you choose to travel will make all the difference to your journey. Highway 9 cuts through the verdant East Rift Valley (Huādōng Zòng Gǔ), while Hwy 11 winds down the narrow strip between the sea and the Coastal Mountains, a series of steep volcanic arcs. There are few large settlements but plenty of small aboriginal villages, fishing harbours, beaches and ocean terraces. There are several places to camp along the way, and more and more guesthouses seem to spring up every year.

Much of Hwy 11 falls under the auspices of the East Coast National Scenic Area. Its **visitor centre** (☎089-841 520; www.eastcoast-nsa.gov.tw; Cheng Gong; ⌚9am-5pm) is between Duli and Cheng Gong.

Getting Around

Personal transport (scooter, car, bicycle) is best for travelling Hwy 11.

Bus

See the visitor centre at Hualien train station for the latest schedule.

Dingdong Bus Company (鼎東客運; http://diingdong.myweb.hinet.net; 138-6 Guo Lian 1st Rd) Hualien to Taitung (NT$475, 3½ hours, three times daily).

Hualien Bus Company (花蓮客運; www.hl.gov.tw/bus) Buses from Hualien to Taitung (NT$492, 3½ hours, twice daily) and hourly buses from Hualien to Chengkung.

Bicycle

The 180km from Hualien to Taitung (and perhaps on to Chihpen hot springs) comprises the most popular long-distance cycling route in Taiwan. An average cyclist will take three days, with overnight stops in Shihtiping and Dulan. The road winds, but the only major climb, to the Baci Observation Tower, lies behind you after the first morning. From Hualien to Chihpen, the highway has a smooth, wide, double-lined shoulder marked for cyclists and scooters only.

Hualien Ocean Park

花蓮海洋公園

(Hualien Far Glory Ocean Park; Huālián Hǎiyáng Gōngyuán; www.hualienoceanpark.com.tw; adult/child NT$890/790; ⌚9am-5pm) A large aquarium/amusement park south of Hualien off Hwy 11. The facilities here are first class and attractions include dolphin shows, sea-lion exhibits and a water fun-park. Kids love this place.

If you don't have your own transportation, the easiest way to get here is to take a **Taiwan Tour Bus** (☎0800 011 765) from outside the visitor centre in front of the Hualien train station. The price is around NT$1000 person and includes transportation and tickets. Enquire at the visitor centre for details.

Baci Observation Tower 芭崎眺望台

A mandatory highway stop, this **rest area** (Bāqí Tiàowàngtái) affords a mesmerising cliff-side view over the blue waters off Jici Beach and down 40km of rugged mountainous coastline. For cyclists this is the summit of the longest climb on Hwy 11.

Jici (Chichi) Beach 磯崎海濱遊憩區

This **beach** (Jīqí Hǎibīn Yóuqì Qū; admission NT$100) is one of only two that you can swim at between Hualien and Taitung, so if you're looking for a dip, a paddle, or a bit of surfing, don't pass by – at least from May to September between 9am and 6pm.

The beach is developed, to a degree, meaning you'll find showers, changing rooms and rental equipment, as well as a **campground** (☎03-871 1251; per site NT$500). All Hualien and Dingdong buses (NT$116) pass by the beach, so you should never have to wait more than an hour for a ride.

Highway 11 甲

The first of three routes connecting Highways 11 and 9, 11甲 runs along the **Dingzilou River** (丁子漏溪; Dīngzǐlòu Xī), over a narrow ridge, and then past pretty fields before ending in Guangfu, 19km to the west. A good day trip from Hualien entails riding Hwy 11 to the turn-off at Fongbin, the 11甲 to County Rd 193, and then following that superb road back to Hualien.

Shihtiping 石梯坪

The rich Kuroshio current runs closest to Taiwan at Shihtiping (Shítīpíng), and more species of whale and dolphin can be spotted here than anywhere else in Taiwan. Misty conditions along the coast also make the vegetation greener and denser than elsewhere and, as a final touch, the volcanic coastline has eroded to form beautiful natural stone steps. Shihtiping in fact means 'stone steps', and if you love exploring rocky, rugged coastlines you'll be in your element here. Whale- and dolphin-watching tours leave from the harbour from May to October but the quality is said to be poor.

Shihtiping is divided into a rough-hewn village nestled on a terrace below towering headlands; a fishing harbour below this; and a nicely landscaped park south of the harbour. Further up the road are a number of tiny Ami settlements where traditional life goes on. Hunters hunt in the hills, fishermen cast nets at the mouths of rivers, and woodcraftsmen can be seen transforming driftwood into furniture and sculptures.

At 80km from Hualien, Shihtiping is usually the first night's resting area for cyclists.

Sleeping & Eating

Sea Fan Guesthouse BOUTIQUE HOTEL $$
(石梯緣景觀咖啡 民宿; Shítī Yuán Jǐngguān Kāfēi Mínsù; ☎03-878 1828; www.seafan.idv.tw/; d NT$2200, ocean-facing d NT$3200; wi-fi) This cosy boutique hotel at the start of the park has small well-furnished rooms and, more importantly, views that are hard to top. From the balconies of the doubles with lofts, for example, you look north at 40km of an undeveloped coastline that's all dark-green hills and blue ocean. Other rooms feature mountain views but, really, it's so worth spending a little more to face the sea.

Meals are available and locally sourced by your humble, genial host, Mr Wang. There are 20% discounts midweek.

Pakelang HOTEL $
(巴歌浪船屋民宿; Bāgēlàng Chuánwū Mínsù; ☎089-881 400; http://pakelang.e089.com.tw; d/tw NT$1500/2500, camping per site NT$250) A few kilometres past Shihtiping, and just before the Tropic of Cancer monument at the KM72.5 mark, look for a wood sign marked 'Pakelang'. Head down the narrow path to this quirky beachside guesthouse (some rooms are set in a cement boat; others are in a house made of betel-nut palms) run by a local Ami family. You've got about 2 acres of land in which to stretch out here, as well as a long undeveloped beach (swimmable in summer only). Rooms are discounted 20% on weekdays.

Xin Yang Live Seafood Restaurant HOTEL & RESTAURANT $
(昕陽活海鮮餐廳; Xīnyáng Huóhǎixiān Cāntīng; ☎0911-277 442; 96 Shihtiping; r NT$1000) Basic guesthouse accommodation is available above the restaurant, which, as the name suggests, serves some fresh (and cheap) seafood. Xin Yang is to the right off Hwy 11 as it runs through the village.

In the park area of Shihtiping, the national scenic administration runs a well-laid-out **campground** (☎03-878 1452; per site Sat & Sun NT$500, Mon-Fri NT$300) with raised platforms that face the sea. Check in at the visitor centre at the end of the road.

Ruigang Hwy (Township Road 64) 瑞港公路

More winding country road than highway, the 22km cross-mountain Ruigang Hwy follows the contours of the Hsiukuluan River from a high-enough perch to let you take in all the surrounding natural beauty. If you're cycling, plan on it taking two hours to get to Rueisui – and bring water: there is only one small farming settlement along the way.

Caves of the Eight Immortals 八仙洞

This mandatory stop (Bā Xiān Dòng) for all tour buses going up and down the east coast is the site of the earliest human inhabitation of Taiwan. While a good place to spot wild monkeys, most people will want to give the place a miss. The insides of most caves have been turned into tacky Buddhist shrines. Archaeology is an afterthought.

Platform of the Three Immortals 三仙台

Also known as Sansiantai (Sānxiāntái), this is a series of **arched bridges** leading to a small coral island that was once a promontory joined to the mainland. The island's three large stone formations have been likened to the three immortals of Chinese mythology – hence the name.

Sansiantai is a very pleasant spot to wander around for a couple of hours, although on holidays and weekends it's a bit of a madhouse with all the tour-bus crowds.

Highway 23

The last route connecting Hwys 11 and 9, the 23 is windy, steep and sparsely populated – unless you count the numerous monkey troops that hang out on the sides of the road.

Jinzun Recreation Area 金樽遊憩區

Just south of Hwy 23 on Hwy 11 is this recreation area (Jīnzūn Yóuqì Qū), centred on a beautiful 3km-long sand beach hemmed in by high cliffs. There's not much to do here other than head down the stairs to the beach, stroll around and admire the view (and maybe have a picnic, get your feet wet in the surf, take some photos, paint a seascape, read a book, write a book...).

Dulan 都蘭

POP 500

Years ago, the tiny town of Dulan (Dūlán) hardly merited a nod as you passed by on the way south. But in recent years this has changed, as a thriving local arts scene has taken off with both local and foreign artists beating a path here. One long-term expat likened the current buzz around Dulan to what he felt in Goa in the 1970s. Perhaps no surer sign that he may be on to something is the interest big hotel chains in Taipei have suddenly taken in this former backwater.

The Dulan area has been inhabited for thousands of years, as evidenced by the stone coffins and other archaeological ruins of the Beinan culture in the hills west of town. These days it has one of the largest Ami settlements along the east coast, and the aboriginal presence in the arts scene (music and woodcarving) is strong.

Dulan is small, in essence a couple of blocks on either side of Hwy 11, and a few backstreets (which teem with bird and butterfly life) winding into the hills.

Sights & Activities

Dulan Sugar Factory ART CENTRE

(都蘭糖廠; Dūlán Tángchǎng; 61 Dulan Village; ☎089-530 060; admission free; ⏲24hr) Once a busy processing plant and a source of local employment, the factory closed its doors in the 1990s. Local artisans and craftspeople soon began to reopen the abandoned warehouse space as makeshift studios: a genuine local art scene developed and continues to gain in reputation. Weekdays it's often pretty quiet but weekends you can usually watch carvers at work and also make purchases of some unique articles.

As you ride into Dulan from the north it's easy to spot the factory on the right, near

ABORIGINAL FESTIVALS ON THE EAST COAST

Dates for festivals are only roughly the same each year, so it's important to find out the exact schedule before you go. Call the 24-hour **tourist hotline** (☎0800 011 765), or contact the **East Coast National Scenic Administration** (www.eastcoast-nsa.gov.tw) or the **National Youth Commission** (www.youthtravel.net.tw).

» **Yami Flying Fish Festival** – the Yami on Lanyu Island hold this festival every March to May (different villages hold it at different times) during the beginning of the flying-fish season. Like the Puyuma festival, this celebrates a young man's passage into adulthood.

» **Bunun Ear Shooting Festival** – the Ear Shooting Festival is held in towns throughout the East Rift Valley around the end of April. It's meant to honour the legendary hunting heroes of the tribe and to teach young boys how to use bows and arrows.

» **Millet Harvest Festival** – this festival is held after the April millet harvest, and takes place in towns throughout the East Rift Valley.

» **Ami Harvest Festival** – this festival is the largest in Taiwan and takes place every July or August in various towns around Hualien and Taitung Counties. In June tribal chiefs choose the exact date.

» **Rukai Harvest Festival** – one highlight of this harvest festival is watching tribal youth play on giant swings. The swings are built to allow guys to show their affection for the gals by sending them higher and higher into the air. The festival takes place every July or August.

» **Paiwan Bamboo Pole Festival** – the Paiwan tribe holds this festival every five years in October to honour its ancestors and to pray for a good harvest. The festival takes place in Daren Township, Taitung. The next festival will take place in 2012.

» **Puyuma Tribe Annual Festival** – this festival combines the old monkey and hunting rituals with the larger coming-of-age ceremony for young men. The festival is celebrated by tribal members in Beinan Township, near Taitung, at the end of December.

» **Festival of Austronesian Cultures** – held annually in December at various locations around Hualien and Taitung Counties, this festival includes aboriginal groups from several South Pacific nations that are believed to share a common ancestry with Taiwan's indigenous people.

» **Dulan Sugar Factory** – while the sugar factory grounds are the site of many aboriginal festivals such as the Harvest Festival, it's worth mentioning that there are also weekly live music concerts by aboriginal players.

the edge of town: it looks like a factory, with high walls and smokestacks, except for an incongruous driftwood stage and a small cafe.

Moonlight Inn ART CENTRE/CAFE
(月光小棧; Yuèguāng Xiǎo Zhàn; admission free; ⌚24hr) In the hills above Dulan sits a quaint old forestry building from Japanese times. Nicknamed the 'Moonlight Inn', it hosts frequent local arts exhibitions. Handcrafted items are for sale inside a cafe area.

To get to the inn, follow the English signs off Hwy 11. Along the way there's a stone coffin site that's worth checking out.

Water Running Up NATURAL ODDITY
Just south of Dulan is the geological oddity known as Water Running Up (水往上流; Shuǐ Wǎng Shàng Liú). See if you can figure out why it's doing this.

Sleeping & Eating

Enquire at Dulan Café about guesthouse rooms (d NT$1000). If you have a tent, the local police station allows camping on its grounds for free.

Taitung Sea Art Hostel HOMESTAY $
(Motherland; 台東海之藝民宿-大地之母; Táidōng Hǎizzhīyì Mínsù – Dàdì Zhīmǔ; ☎in English 0988-243 108, in Chinese 0935-061 578; s/tw/q

NT$600/1000/2000) Up in the wooded hills above Dulan. One of the nicest couples you'll ever meet in Taiwan have set up a dreamy little rustic homestay, complete with funky rooms (designed by your host, Roman), curious pets, and as much wildlife as you're likely to see anywhere outside a national park. Motherland is a bit off the road, so call first to make reservations (and a pick-up, if needed). Home-cooked meals (breakfast and dinner) are available for an extra NT$350 a day. To see photos, check out the hostel's Facebook site.

Marino's Kitchen ITALIAN $$
(馬利諾廚房; Mălìnuò Cúfáng; ☎089-531 0955; 436-6 Dulan Village; 都蘭村436-6號; dishes from NT$120; ⊙noon-6.30pm Sat & Sun) By the time you read this, Marino's might still be making the best Italian pastas and pizzas on the east coast, or the owner may have gone full time into baking his hand-milled breads (which you can buy from Wednesday to Sunday). We hope it's the former. Or both.

Marino's is on the northern edge of Dulan, around the KM146.2 mark.

☆ Entertainment

Dulan Café CAFE/MUSIC VENUE
(都蘭糖廠咖啡屋; Dūlán Tángchǎng Kāfēiwū; ☎089-530 060; Dulan Sugar Factory; admission free, coffee NT$50; ⊙8am-whenever) It all began with the cafe, people say. Run by an Ami family who are heavily involved in the music and arts scene, the cafe sponsors the weekly live-music performances that have put Dulan on the map. If there is a heart to modern Dulan, this is certainly it.

The performances start every Saturday evening and go into the night. Most musicians are local Amis, but guest performers come from elsewhere. The audience is a wild mix of Dulan locals and Taiwanese from all over the island, with a few Japanese, Koreans, Hong Kongers and Westerners.

Shanyuan Beach 杉原海水浴場

Beautiful Shanyuan Beach (Shānyuán Hǎishuǐ Yùchǎng) is the closest beach to Taitung and the longest swimmable one between Hualien and Taitung. With its soft yellow sands, tropical blue waters and stunning mountain backdrop, it's a fantastic place to enjoy the natural life.

Unfortunately, the beach has been officially closed for some time to make way for the construction of a monstrously unattractive and environmentally inappropriate 'five-star' hotel. In 2008, local protests over zoning irregularities brought construction to a halt, where it is very likely to remain. It's uncertain what this means for the future of the beach.

Currently you can still enjoy parts of the beach by entering from the northern end, beside a temple.

Hsiao Yeliu 小野柳

Just a few kilometres north of Taitung is Hsiao Yeliu (Xiǎo Yěliǔ), a coastal park known for its bizarre rock and coral formations, formed over thousands of years by wind and water erosion. The landscape is truly unearthly here, with rocks curving and twisting into all manner of fantastic shapes.

A large park has been developed around the most interesting stretch of coastline, and most nature lovers would have a happy time here exploring the rocks and tidal pools. It's also a fun spot for families with young children, as the area is compact but full of surprises. It's simple to get around and there are English signs.

There's a good **campground** (per site NT$350) at the back of the park, with wooden tent platforms facing the sea. Bring your own food. A **visitor centre** (☎089-280 093; ⊙9am-5pm) has English maps and information about the various rock formations.

HIGHWAY 9 & THE EAST RIFT VALLEY

Highway 9 is the main transport artery through the East Rift Valley, a long alluvial plain that just happens to sit right on the seam of the collision point between the Philippine and Eurasian plates. The valley has some of Taiwan's best farming country, to say nothing of rural scenery: bordered by the Central Mountains on one side and the Coastal Mountain Ranges on the other, stunning views are in every direction.

The valley offers plenty of hiking and biking routes and even a white-water-rafting venue to keep the outdoor enthusiast happy, while numerous hot springs (just one result of the tectonic activity in the area) are there for those who want to indulge themselves. A few quirky highlights include the fields of orange day lilies that bloom in late summer, the wetlands in Mataian, and the Liji Badlands. Those interested in organic farming should check out the scene at Loshan.

The East Rift Valley falls under the watchful eye of the **East Rift Valley National Scenic Area Administration** (www.erv-nsa.gov.tw).

Getting Around

There are good train services all down the Rift Valley, and most small towns have bike rentals.

Bicycle

Hwy 9 is flatter and straighter than Hwy 11, but it has more traffic, especially trucks. Many cyclists take back-country routes such as County Rds 193 and 197, popping back onto Hwy 9 for meals and accommodation. However, if you do that you miss some of the best sights.

Liyu Lake 鯉魚潭

Though the entire Rift Valley was most likely once a giant lake, it drained long ago, leaving 2km-long Liyu Lake (Lǐyú Tán) as the largest natural body of fresh water on the east coast. Shaped somewhat like a carp (Liyu means 'carp' in Chinese), Liyu is tucked into the green foothills of the Central Mountain Range about 19km southwest of Hualien.

Families with small children who enjoy camping or picnicking will like it here. There are safe bike trails around the lake, and there are short hikes in the nearby hills. In April fireflies are out in force.

Backpackers, and others looking for a bit of adventure, should come midweek and rent a bike to ride out to nearby Hwy 14, which runs up a canyon that's like another Taroko Gorge.

In recent years a number of stylish B&Bs have opened and the lake can now compete with Hualien as a base for exploring the county.

Sights & Activities

Cycling

For the casual biker, several easy routes start out near the lake: a 4km **bike path** winds round the lake itself; another route just north connects the lake with Hualien; and a very scenic **10km path** along the Baibao River begins off the side road leading up to the Chihnan National Forest Recreation Area. At the time of writing, the last route connected with Hwy 9 for a short distance and then veered off to join another series of signposted bike routes on farm roads.

Mugua River Gorge SCENIC GORGE/BIKE ROUTE

For a real cycling adventure, head out to narrow, snaking Hwy 14, cut into the marble walls of the **Mugua River Gorge** (6.30am-4pm), which is a chasm as dramatic in appearance as Taroko Gorge but far more raw.

To get to Hwy 14 head north along Hwy 9 from Liyu Lake. Cross the bridge heading back to Hualien and then turn left to follow the river upstream. Cross the next bridge and continue upstream (now on the left bank). Register at the police station and pay NT$10 to receive your permit (bring your passport). A short distance later, hand a copy of your permit to the officer on duty at a gated booth. Note that there's a 300-person daily limit into the corridor, and on summer weekends this fills fast. Try to arrive before 8.30am.

The road now goes on for 10km or so, ending at a hydroelectric power plant. After that a very narrow (but also ride-able) farm road continues up a side canyon until washouts render it impassable.

Several popular **swimming holes** can be found in the gorge down a side road. After passing the police station, continue a few kilometres until you reach a large red bridge. Don't cross, but instead take the lower road to the left going upstream along the Chingshui River. After the first tunnel, look down to the right. See the massive, marble-lined natural swimming hole with deep, bluish green, crystal-clear water? To get down into the water look for a trail about 30m up on the other side of the cement barrier.

Decent-quality bikes can be rented at the **Giant** (捷安特; Jié Ān Tè; 03-864 1892; rental per day NT$150-450; 9am-6pm) bicycle shop on the west side of Liyu Lake. Headlights are essential if you plan on entering the gorge. The series of winding cathedral tunnels can be nerve-racking enough without attempting them in the dark.

Hiking

You can walk around the lake in about an hour, or do the **Liyu Mountain** (鯉魚山; 600m) circuit in three to four hours.

Chihnan National Forest Recreation Area SCENIC PARK
(池南國家森林遊樂區; Chínán Guójiā Sēnlín Yóulè qū; www.forest.gov.tw; admission NT$50; ⌚8am-5pm) This small forest reserve preserves the history of Taiwan's logging industry. The old steam locomotive engines steal the show, though the museum of old logging equipment and the cable system are pretty interesting, too. The visitor centre has an informative English brochure that includes a simple map. Sometimes there are English-speaking tour guides available.

The reserve is just west of the lake. There are clear signs to it in English.

Sleeping

Monet Garden HOTEL $$
(莫內花園民宿; Mònèi Huāyuán Mínsù; ☎0988-796 279; www.monetgarden.com.tw; d/tw incl breakfast from NT$2200/2800) Part of a row of stylish B&Bs tucked into a grove south of the lake, Monet is the lovechild of a retired journalist-turned-coffee trader. As your host specialises in Guatemalan beans, expect the spacious rooms to be decorated with solid wood furniture and knickknacks imported from Latin America.

Monet is about half a kilometre south of the lake on Hwy 9. Look for the sign for Balanjoyo Café, which shelters the rooms from the main road.

Liyu Lake Campground CAMPGROUND $
(鯉魚潭露營區; Lǐyú Tán Lùyíng qū; ☎03-865 5678; per site NT$800) The campground is 1km south of the lake off Hwy 9 and features showers, barbecue areas and covered sites.

Eating

A row of simple restaurants and noodle shops sits across the road from the lake. Balanjoyo Café at Monet Garden has decent set meals for NT$180 and, of course, has good Guatemalan coffee.

Getting There & Away

From Hualien, buses (NT$52, 20 minutes) leave every two hours – catch a bus heading to Shoufong (壽豐).

Lintianshan

林田山林業文化園區

Once a Japanese logging village, Lintianshan (Lin Tien Shan; Líntiánshān) housed a population of over 2000. It's an odd piece of Taiwan: a quaint ghost town (with a few remaining residents) highlighting a colonial heritage that involved stripping this fair island of much of its ancient forests. But it's worth a visit if you are in the area. The surrounding mountains are beautiful and there is a genuine historical atmosphere to the village, which is made entirely out of cypress.

When you visit, do check out the nearby Wanli River, its waters such a striking blue-green colour that you might think it's terribly polluted. In fact, the colour is the natural result of minerals washing into the water from the eastern mountains. You see some of this same colouration in Taroko Gorge, but never so vivid.

The turn-off for Lintianshan is marked in English on Hwy 9. From Hualien, there are two trains in the early morning (fast/slow NT$67/56, 55 minutes, 5.50am and 6.30am) and one at 1.19pm. Get off at Wanrong Station (萬榮) and turn left down a short lane. Turn left again at the end and follow the road (Hwy 16) about 2.5km to Lintianshan. There are English signs along the way.

Hualien Sugar Factory

光復糖廠

Despite the history here, there's no confusing this old **factory** (Guāngfù Tángchǎng; Guangfu) with the Dulan Sugar Factory, a genuine venue for local culture. This is a tourist trap, with gift shops galore, tacky music and a freak-show museum out back. However, if you're driving down the highway it's still worth a pit stop for the **ice cream** (NT$35; ⌚8am-8pm). While you eat your cone or dish, wander around the factory grounds and check out the row of old Japanese-built wooden buildings. Here's a bit of trivia for you: the large carp pools beside the ice-cream shop are craters from the US bombing of Taiwan during WWII.

The sugar factory is just south of the town of Guangfu (光復) on Hwy 9. There are signs in English on the highway directing you there.

Mataian 馬太鞍

☎03 / POP 500

On the west side of Hwy 9, close to the Hualien Sugar Factory turn-off, is the wetland area known as Mataian (Mǎtàiān). An ideal place for farming and fishing, Mataian has supported generations of Ami. Recent efforts by the Taiwanese government to protect wetlands have seen the area turned into a bit of an ecological classroom.

To arrange an English speaking ecotour, contact **Shin-liu Farm** (欣綠農園; Xīnlǜ Nóngyuán; ☎870 1861; www.shin-liu.com). The farm – really more of a resort – is crisscrossed with a network of wooden bridges and narrow walking paths (with English-Chinese interpretative signs) over a large section of wetland. Food and lodgings are also available.

Bicycles can be rented at Shin-liu by nonguests for touring the maze of farm roads. In June look for lotus flowers in bloom, and in autumn and winter glow-in-the-dark mushrooms sprout in the nearby hills.

For an intimate homestay with a local family enquire at **Cifadahan Cafe** (紅瓦屋文化美食餐廳; Kwangfu Hong Wa Wu; Hóngwǎwū Wénhuà Měishí Cāntīng; www.cifadahan.net; 9-course set meal NT$300; ⏲10am-10pm). Also, don't miss the food (English menu available) at this Mataian institution. Run by a talented Ami artist whose aboriginal-themed carvings and furniture adorn the restaurant, dishes include a 19-vegetable salad, and a hot pot (石頭火鍋; NT$500) brought to the boil with fire-heated stones. The huge set meals offer a range of dishes to sample.

ℹ Getting There & Around

Car & Scooter

Coming from the north, look for signs in Chinese at the KM251.5 mark on Hwy 9. Turn right. Head straight until the road ends. Turn left and follow signs (now in English) to farm or cafe.

Train

From Hualien (fast/slow NT$98/76, 45 minutes/one hour, hourly). Exit at Guangfu Station and walk to Hwy 9. Turn right and walk 1km south. Turn right at sign for Mataian.

Fuyuan Forest Recreational Area 富源國家森林遊樂區

In the late 19th and early 20th century Taiwan dominated the world market of camphor production. Extracted from the stately camphor tree, which grew in abundance at midlevel elevations, the substance was used in everything from embalming fluid to medicine to insect repellent.

A few kilometres off Hwy 9, the 235-hectare **Fuyuan Forest Recreational Area** (Fùyuán Guójiā Sēnlín Yóulè Qū; www.forest.gov.tw; admission NT$100; ⏲6am-5pm) protects the largest pure camphor forest left in Taiwan. Quiet trails runs through the reserve to waterfalls and special bird and butterfly corridors. About 100 species of birds can be found in Fuyuan, and you have a good chance of spotting the gorgeous Maroon Oriole. As for butterflies, this is one of the richest areas in the east: swallowtails are in abundance, including the exquisite Golden Birdwing.

A series of open-air stone and wood **hot-spring pools** (admission NT$300; ⏲6am-10pm) nestle under the camphor trees not far from the ticketing booth and are open late. At the time of writing, bike paths were being marked around the surrounding countryside and bike rentals should be available at Fuyuan train station, the closest to the reserve.

Rueisui 瑞穗

☎03 / POP 5000

Bland Rueisui (Ruìsuì) opens up into some very scenic countryside within a few minutes from the train station. In particular, look for a deep gorge cutting through the Coastal Mountains, formed by the longest river in the east. In the summer months, Taiwanese flock here to raft and then later soak in Rueisui's carbonated hot springs.

At 70km from Hualien (depending on your route), and at the junction of three excellent cycling roads (Hwy 9, County Rd 193 and the Ruigang Hwy), Rueisui is often used as an overnight stop for cyclists.

Activities

Rueisui Hot Springs HOT SPRINGS

The carbonated Rueisui hot springs (瑞穗溫泉; Ruìsuì Wēnquán) were first opened by the Japanese in 1919. The water boasts a temperature of 48°C and is rich in iron, giving it a pale-brown colour and a slightly salty, rusty flavour (so we've heard). Many Taiwanese still believe that frequent bathing in the spring water increases a woman's chance of bearing a male child.

The hot-spring area is a few kilometres directly west of Rueisui town (on the other side of Hwy 9). As you drive down the highway there are English signs pointing to the area.

Rafting

Rafting trips (泛舟; Fànzhōu) can be arranged from May to September at the **Rueisui Rafting Service Centre** (瑞穗泛舟服務中心; Ruìsuì Fànzhōu Fúwù Zhōngxīn; ☎887 5400; 215 Jhongshan Rd, Sec 3; 中山路3段215號) at the start of the rafting route. The standard fee is NT$750, which includes transportation from and to Hualien, lunch, equipment and insurance.

Boats usually run between 7am and noon and take 3½ hours to complete the 24km-long route down the Hsiukuluan River (Xiùgūluán Xī) from Rueisui to Takangkou. For the most part, this is leisurely rafting, unless there has been a typhoon recently.

To get to the centre, head out from Rueisui train station and continue straight along Jhongshan Rd for about 4km to 5km. A taxi will cost around NT$100.

There's a good campground (per site NT$250) with toilets and showers at the centre.

Sleeping

Rueisui Hot Springs Hotel GUESTHOUSE **$$**
(瑞穗溫泉山莊; Ruìsuì Wēnquán ShānZhuāng; ☎887 2170; 23 Hongye Village; d/tw NT$2500/4000, dm per bed NT$500) At over 90 years old, this place lays claim to being the first and longest-running hot spring and guesthouse in the area. Managed by a local family and offering tatami-style dorm rooms and bike storage, it's a popular place for cyclists to spend the night. Others might prefer the more modern and stylish hotels nearby. The Rueisui Hot Springs Hotel is up a small road off the main road through the hot-spring area (there are signs in English).

Eating

Most hot-spring hotels have restaurants in them. Around the train station there are numerous small noodle stands and restaurants, as well as convenience stores for snacks, sandwiches and drinks.

Getting There & Away

There are hourly trains from Hualien to Rueisui (fast/slow train NT$146/112, one/1½ hours).

Yuli 玉里

☎03 / POP 3000

In the mid-19th century, Hakka immigrants from Guangzhou established Yuli (Yùlǐ) as one of the earliest nonaboriginal settlements on the east coast. Today, with the Central Mountains looking over its shoulder, and the Rift Valley under its nose, Yuli is well based for day trips to hot springs, mountains covered with day lilies, the organic rice-growing valley at Loshan, and the eastern section of Yushan National Park.

Activities

Cycling

While the circuit around the town wasn't complete at the time of writing, a marked path to the right of the train station (as you exit) led to the Walami Trail (12km away), with a branching route to Antung Hot Springs: the latter runs on a section of abandoned rail line adjacent to fields of rice and swaying betel-nut palms. By the time you read this, a cycling route along the bucolic back roads from Yuli (starting off the road to the Walami Trail) to Fuli and possibly Haituan on the South Cross-Island Hwy should be marked.

Shops around the train station rent out cheap bikes. However, the **Giant** (捷安特; Jié Ān Tè; ☎888 5669; 981和平路47號; ⌚8am-10pm) bicycle shop on Heping Rd has a better selection (per three hours NT$150, per three days NT$1200) for short or extended trips. To find the shop head straight from the train station and turn left at the second intersection. The shop is on the left a block up the street.

Sleeping & Eating

TOP CHOICE **Wisdom Garden** HOMESTAY **$$**
(智嵐雅居民宿; Zhìlán YǎJū Mínsù; ☎0921-986 461; www.wisdom-garden.com; 玉里鎮大禹里5鄰酸甘98-1號; r from NT$2400; @) This guesthouse, just north of the train station off Hwy 9, is *the* place to stay in the Yuli area. Without doubt it's our favourite B&B in Taiwan. The house sits in an orchard

high above the Rift Valley, looking across to Chikha Mountain. Make sure to take your meals out on the front lawn.

The owner, a Buddhist and former hotel manager, has made a true retreat here. It's both soothing and nurturing. Each room has its own character, and is flooded with light and green views. Furnishings are country quaint, bathrooms are large and modern, and the owner's original paintings and tie-dye work add a special decorative touch.

If you're driving, the turn-off for Wisdom Garden is at the Km289.4 mark on Hwy 9. Just follow the English signs from here. If you make prior arrangements the owners will pick you up from Yuli train station.

Shalom RESTAURANT/TEAHOUSE
(五餅二魚複合式茶舖; Wǔbǐng Èryú Fùhéshì Chápù; ☎888 0087; 174 Zhongshan Rd; 中山路二段174號; set meals NT$190, drinks NT$140; ⏲11am-10pm) At this teahouse, set in a 100-year-old former police station, baseball, woodworking and teaching form the trifecta of interests of the genial owner. If you have an interest in any of these, or just desire a meal, a drink or a chinwag with an agreeable host, you're always welcome. To reach the shop head straight out from the train station and turn left on Zhongshan Rd.

Yuli's eponymous noodles (玉裡麵; Yùlǐmiàn) won't strike you as much different from Rueisui noodles, or Taitung noodles, or Taipei noodles, but they are cheap (per bowl NT$40), filling and ubiquitous.

Two cheap hotels sit across the road from the train station. We like **Walami Inn** (瓦拉米客棧; Wālāmǐ Kèzhàn; ☎888 6681; 214 Datong Rd, 大同路214號; d/tw NT$1200/1800) best because of the name, the friendly front desk staff, and the slightly more-updated rooms.

 Getting There & Away

Frequent trains run from Hualien to Yuli (fast/slow train NT$191/123, one hour and 20 minutes/two hours).

Antung (Antong) Hot Springs 安通溫泉

About 8km south of the town of Yuli on the new Hwy 26, Antung hot springs (Āntōng Wēnquán) have been soothing tired bodies since Japanese times. The clear alkaline waters (slightly odorous) have a temperature of 66°C. The water is drinkable, and hotels here use it to make coffee (the only place we know of in Taiwan that does so).

Modern hotels with a range of rooms and pools for soaking have popped up in the upper and lower village: the former are most enjoyably reached by bicycle from Yuli along the old train tracks. A good option for spending the night is in the upper village at **New Life Hot Springs Resort** (紐澳華溫泉山莊; Niǔàohuá Wēnquán Shānzhuāng; ☎03-888 7333; www.twspring.com.tw; dm with IYH card NT$800, d from NT$2100, unlimited use of public pools per person NT$250). Rooms are airy and wood panelled and open to views across the Coastal Mountains. To get to the hotel look for the English sign as you ride into the hot-springs area.

Walami Trail 瓦拉米古道

A must-do hike, the Walami Trail (Wǎlāmǐ Gǔdào) begins high above the Nanan River, about 12km southeast of Yuli in the Nanan section of Yushan National Park. Along the path there are high waterfalls, suspension bridges, lookouts, sections cut straight into the cliff walls, and the constant sound (and occasionally sight) of monkeys crashing through the trees. It's a jungle out there – one of the best preserved in Taiwan. The views down the valley and across the mountains are chillingly beautiful.

The trail hails from the Japanese era and was built to facilitate the opening of the east as well as maintain a careful eye on aboriginal tribes. As such, this is as much a walk through history as it is through nature. The trail has been fortified (meaning barriers have been placed on the sides of the trail, where you can drop hundreds of metres to your death) and improved in recent years. This makes it safe for most people to travel on, especially for the first couple of kilometres, which you can do without any permits.

The Walami Trail forms part of the much-longer Japanese Occupation Era Batongguan Traversing Route (see p195), which goes all the way to Dongpu. The 14km up to the attractive Walami cabin takes about six to seven hours and is not a particularly difficult route for anyone who's in decent shape. The A-frame cabin looks like a visitor centre in a Canadian national park and has room for 24 hikers.

Hiking all the way to the cabin and spending the night is highly recommended. There's rough bedding (bring your own sleeping bag), water and solar-powered lights. You do need to apply at least a week ahead of time for a permit (see boxed text, p28). On the day of your hike check in at the **Nanan Visitor Centre** (南安遊客中心; ☎03-888 7560; ⏲9am-4.30pm) and then pick up a mountain permit at the police station. If you plan to return the same day you can pick up a one-day pass on that day at the visitor centre.

If you don't have your own transportation, take a taxi from Yuli to the visitor centre (NT$300), then walk the last 6km to the trailhead (after arranging permits). Along the way you'll pass **Nanan Waterfall** (南安瀑布; Nánān Pùbù).

You can also rent a bike in Yuli. It's a great route, first passing old Hakka villages dating back to the 1850s, then along open fields, and finally up the deep wooded Nanan River gorge, which just gets more lush and wild with every kilometre.

Sixty Stone Mountain 六十石山

Once a typical rice-growing area, Sixty Stone Mountain (Liùshí Dàn Shān; 952m) became a centre for growing day (tiger) lilies (金針; *jīnzhēn*) a few decades ago. The orange-coloured lilies are popular with Taiwanese consumers who eat them fresh or dried in tea drinks and a host of other products. The harvest time from August to early September is popular with Taiwanese tourists who come to enjoy the mesmerising sight of entire green mountainsides carpeted with pretty orange blossoms.

You need your own transport to get here. There are English signs on Hwy 9 as you head south of Yuli.

Loshan (Luoshan) Scenic Area 羅山風景區

Just north of Fuli (富里), in an area called the rice barn of Taiwan, lies this valley (Lóshān) that Hakka farmers have transformed into the centre of the organic rice industry in Hualien. Some highlights include bucolic splendour in every direction, the 120m-long **Luoshan Waterfall** (羅山瀑布; Lóshān Pùbù) and a number of small bubbling mud volcanoes.

The **visitor centre** (☎03-882 1725; ⏲8.30am-5.30pm) runs a free campground that features the Coastal Mountains as its backdrop. Call ahead to reserve a tent platform (a formality that ensures the bathrooms will be open).

The centre can also help with homestays (an average single/double costs NT$1000/2000 per night) and with joining a group to make the area's speciality cuisine: 'volcanic tofu'.

SOUTH CROSS-ISLAND HIGHWAY

In August 2009 Typhoon Morakot wiped out large sections of this old mountain highway (南部橫貫公路), one of Taiwan's grandest. At the time of writing there was no access on the west side from Meishan to Yakou and little left of interest from Baolai to Meishan either. We've been told the Meishan to Yakou stretch will never reopen so we've included what's left of the eastern half in this chapter. Please ask about road conditions before you head out.

ℹ Getting There & Around

At the time of writing, twice-daily buses (NT$351, 4½ hours, 6.20am and 1.05pm) ran as far as Litao from Taitung.

Wulu 霧鹿

POP 100

The first real stop on the way up the highway, about 20km from Haituan, the tiny Bunun village of Wulu (Wùlù) sits on a ledge over the wild S-shaped **Wulu Canyon** (Wùlù XiáGǔ). As you ride through the area watch for steamy fumaroles and hot-spring water spitting out from cracks in the canyon walls, and long cliff faces stained with colourful mineral deposits.

Wulu's water has a pH of about 7.5 and is odourless and silky to the touch. It is, in fact, almost identical to the water at Taian, our favourite hot spring in Taiwan. The **Chief Spa Hotel** (天龍飯店; Tiānlóng Fàndiàn; www.chiefspa.com.tw; d/tw NT$4200/3600; ☎089-935 075) looks out onto the canyon, which you can cross on the highest suspension bridge in the east. If the hotel is not busy, nonguests can use the outdoor pools

STOPPING TO SMELL THE FLOWERS

Taiwan is not hurting for beautiful flowers to appreciate. The blooming period is long and you can usually see something all year round. Here are a few scented petals to watch out for, besides the sublime day lilies.

» **Flamegold tree** – appropriately named native tree with large yellow and red blooms in autumn. It grows in lowland forests, and it's widely planted on city streets as it does well in polluted air.

» **Youtong** – the large white flowers of the Youtong tree bloom all over the north in April. Around the Sanxia Interchange on Fwy 3, entire mountainsides go near-white in good years.

» **Rhododendron & azalea** – native species bloom from low to high altitudes from April to June.

» **Formosa lily** – one of the tallest of lilies, with long trumpetlike flowers. Blooms wild all over Taiwan twice a year in spring and autumn.

» **Orchid** – there are many wild species but large farms around Tainan and Pingtung also grow these delightful flowers. Taiwan is, in fact, the world's largest orchid exporter.

» **Lotus** – Baihe in Tainan County has a two-month-long summer festival devoted to this flower.

» **Cherry blossom** – cherry trees bloom in great numbers in February and March in Yangmingshan, Wulai and Alishan Forest Recreation Area.

» **Calla lily** – these beautiful long-stemmed white lilies bloom in large fields in Yangmingshan in spring. There's even a festival for them.

» **Plum blossom** – the national flower (at least for the Kuomintang) blooms in February in orchards all over the island at midaltitudes. Intoxicating scent.

» **Butterfly ginger** – a hopeless romantic, the white flower of the native butterfly ginger gives off its strongest scent at night. Blooms from spring to autumn all over the island.

» **Awn grass (silvergrass)** – a tall swaying grass, with light, airy blooms. Its blooming signals the end of autumn in the north. The Caoling Historic Trail is one of the best places to see entire hillsides covered in it.

» **Alpine flowers** – Taiwan has dozens of petite flowers that splash a bit of colour above the treeline all summer long.

(NT$300). Comfortable rooms with piped-in-hot spring water are also available and there's a 30% discount from Sunday to Friday. Audrey, the hotel's manager, speaks fluent English and is a great source of local information.

Wulu is well known for birdwatchers, and organised tours frequently stop there. Endemic species to watch include the Taiwan partridge, mikado pheasant and rusty laughing thrush.

Litao 利稻

POP 300

Another 8km up the highway from Wulu, Litao (Lidao, Lìdào), with an elevation of approx 1000m, functions as a rest stop, or as an overnight stay that's cheaper than at Wulu – at one of the many **homestays** (民宿) run by the Bunun.

Lisong Hot Spring 栗松溫泉

Arguably the most beautiful natural hot springs in Taiwan, Lisong (Lìsōng Wēnquán) is a must-visit for any lover of the sublime in nature. For here, at the base of a deep river valley, aeons of mineral deposits have painted a small limestone grotto shades of deep green, white, red and black. Steam rises from the rocks, and hot-spring water bubbles and spits and streams from fissures and cracks in the canyon walls.

Stand in the right place and you're in a hot-spring shower. It's as good as it sounds.

If Lisong wasn't already well known among Taiwanese hot-spring fans we'd probably keep it a secret. Fortunately, the remoteness of the spring and the very steep trail down keep it from being wrecked by crowds. In fact, on a weekday you most likely won't see another soul.

The trail to Lisong exits the highway about 8km to 9km up from Lidao, near the village of **Motian** (摩天). Take the farm road to the right about 1.5km to the end. Turn right across a farmer's field and look for the trailhead on the other side. It's pretty much straight down from here, and there are many sections where you must use ropes (already in place) to assist you. When you reach the river, cross and head up the bank about 30m. Cross back using the rope that's in place. Scramble up the bank to the now-obvious springs. People have contrived a small pool out of rocks and you can dip into the deep pools of the Lidao River when you get too hot.

Siangyang Forest Recreation Area & Jiaming Lake National Trail

向陽森林遊樂區、嘉明湖

Another 12km along from Lisong Hot Spring, this new forest recreation area (Xiàngyáng Sēnlíng Yóulè Qū), with an elevation of 2300m, was at the end of the drivable road at the time of writing. Not a bad end, all things considered, as Siangyang offers prime birdwatching in the old cypress and pine forests, and a three-day national trail to Jiaming Lake (嘉明湖; Jiāmíng Hú). The elliptical alpine lake (elevation 3310m), gemlike on a sunny day, resulted from a meteor strike 4000 to 10,000 years ago, making it possibly the youngest meteor lake on earth. On the edge of the wilds of Yushan National Park, the lake attracts a great deal of wildlife and your chances of spotting endemic yellow-throated martens and sambar deer are good.

The trail was officially closed at the time of writing but was slated to reopen by the time you read this. Only a mountain permit is required and it can be picked up at the police station below the **visitor centre** (☎089-345 493; http://taitung.forest.gov.tw). However, because of the popularity of the trail, hikers must prebook beds at one of the two mountain cabins with the **Forestry Bureau** (www.forest.gov.tw). See the boxed text p28) for more on permits.

The 10.9km trail to the lake from Siangyang is clear and well marked, though fog at higher altitudes can make navigating difficult. The route begins in a pine and hemlock forest, but once you ascend the ridgeline it's all rolling hills of dwarf bamboo dotted with rhododendron bushes and wind-twisted alpine juniper.

A typical itinerary is as follows:

Depending on the time you arrive at Siangyang and arrange your permits, you can hike two to three hours up a very steep trail to the spacious wood **Siangyang Cabin** (向陽工寮), which has water and basic toilet facilities, or five to seven hours to the well-worn **Jiaming Lake Cabin** (嘉明湖避難山屋), where the elevation is 3350m (note that the water supply is unreliable here). If they have spent the night at Siangyang Cabin, many hikers make a two-hour side trip up **Mt Shangyang** (向陽山), with an elevation of 3602m, on the way to the second cabin.

From Jiaming Lake Cabin the trail runs along the lower edge of the ridge skirting a chain of rugged peaks. Climbing **Mt Sancha** (三叉山), with an elevation of 3496m, is another popular side trip.

The lake itself is down from Mt Sancha in a wide hollow that's carpeted in soft dwarf bamboo. Camping is permitted but be sure to make your toilet on the other side of the watershed to avoid contaminating the lake water (which can be drunk after purifying). In the evening be on the lookout for sambar deer coming down to drink.

From Jiaming Lake Cabin to the lake and back is six to eight hours. It's another four to five hours from here back to the visitor centre.

Kuanshan (Guanshan) 關山

POP 2000

Back on Hwy 9, the former logging community of Kuanshan (Guān Shān) features a **riverside park** (admission NT$50; ⏲7am-5.30pm) that draws in the weekend crowds with bike paths through yellow rice paddies and fields of colza and sugar cane. Flat and relatively short at 10km, the main path won't appeal to serious cyclists, though side routes up or down County Rd 197, a lovely quiet back road, can be tackled for a longer ride. There's also an excellent **birdwatching path** (with pavilions and lookouts) nearby for the twitching-cycling enthusiast.

To get to the park turn left as you exit the train station at Kuanshan, then take the first left and walk up the road about 1km. You can rent bicycles (per day NT$150 to NT$500) at any number of shops on your way. There are trains to Kuanshan from Hualien (fast/slow train NT$287/221, two/three hours) about every two hours.

Luye 鹿野

The township that ugliness forgot, Luye (Lùyě) stands out for its fine climate, even finer teas and pineapples, its stunning plateau, and a community spirit that has helped its villages win awards.

The Luye region was first settled by Ami and Puyuma aboriginals who hunted the abundant herds of deer. After the Japanese occupied the area in the 1920s, they reportedly claimed that Luye was the best place to live in Taiwan. Today the township is a prosperous tea-growing region, a popular retirement destination and, rather incongruously, a centre for paragliding.

Township Rd 33 is the main route through Luye. Note that the grubby sprawl around the Luye train station off Hwy 9 is not at all representative of the region.

Sights & Activities

Luye Gaotai SCENIC AREA

Luye's pastoral charms don't grow on you; they embrace you fast, like a person you want to marry after a first date. And do!

There's no better place to fall for the township than the area known as the Gaotai (鹿野高台; Lùyě Gāotái), a fecund plateau rising sharply above the alluvial plains. In addition to the orderly fields of tea and pineapples, and panoramic views, the lower villages of Longtian (龍田村) and Yongan (永安村) have maintained much of their historical character as Japanese immigrant villages, and are worth a visit.

Parasailing PARASAILING

The Gaotai drops sharply at the southern end for expansive views over the plains. Nicely, this is also the site of one of the best paragliding venues in Taiwan. The launch site sits across from a teahouse and **campground** (per site NT$500), so expect plenty of spectators. Solo pilots can use the site, although the local tandem flyers have right of way here, especially if they are taking tourists up with them (per sail NT$1500).

Flying is best from March to October, when the winds blow from the south. Every summer there is an international competition attracting pilots from all over the world. Check out the **Wings Taiwan** (http://wingstaiwan.com) website for a good overview of paragliding here and elsewhere in Taiwan by an expat flyer.

Sleeping & Eating

In addition to the campground at the parasailing venue, the plateau has a half dozen or so cosy little B&Bs and an equal number of cafes and restaurants. Agricultural products are on sale at various shops around the plateau. Fulu Tea, a type of oolong, is the region's most popular product, and in many ways is the source of its modern prosperity.

Zixi Garden Lodge LODGE $$

(紫熹花園山莊; Zǐxī Huāyuán Shānzhuāng; ☎089-550 617; fax 089 550 621; d/tw NT$2420/3469) This enormous lodge sports wood-panelled rooms, Chinese- and Japanese-style wings, and a mezzanine reading floor. It might be a bit tricky to find, as it's off the southern end of Township Rd 33. If coming from the north, drive past the northern entrance to the 33, keep going past the train station, and a few kilometres later look for the southern entrance to the 33 on the right. Zixi Garden Lodge is on the left about a kilometre up from Hwy 9. Look for the massive wooden arch fronting the grounds. Weekday discounts of 20% are available.

Getting There & Around

You need your own transport.

Taitung

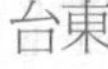

☎089 / POP 110,192

The sprawl and traffic of Taitung (Táidōng) often comes as a rude shock after days in the idyllic countryside to the north. Still, if you have your own vehicle the small city makes for a decent base. The weather is sunny most of the year, the people are relaxed, and while food isn't usually brilliant there is more selection than ever. If you like fruit, you will never go hungry here.

Taitung became frustratingly divided into two after the railway station moved across town. While the new station area is seeing more development, and is by far the greener part of town, with wide streets and calmer traffic, there aren't many places to eat here so you'll need to head into the centre of town often.

History

The earliest people living in the Taitung region were the Puyuma and Amis, who maintained a traditional life of hunting and fishing. Until the late 19th century, when the Qing government reversed its no-immigration policies, there were few non-aboriginal settlements.

Under the Japanese, Taitung was built up as an air and naval base for the empire's expansion into the Pacific. The region's continuing strategic military importance is reinforced nearly daily with F-16s roaring across the sky from Chih-hang Air Base.

In the 1950s and '60s Taitung received an influx of new immigrants, first retired servicemen (mostly Chinese mainlanders) and later Hakka, who came to work on the highways and rail lines. Today the Hakka make up the largest ethnic group in Taitung, though other groups, such as Amis and Bunun aboriginals, are by no means invisible.

Sights & Activities

Taitung's tourist sites are mostly of the small-park and local-exhibition-hall type, such as the Railway Art Village area on the grounds of the old railway station, and Liyushan (鯉魚山; Lǐyúshān), a hill with good views from the top. If you're interested in **surfing** around the Taitung area, talk to Dave at KASA (p187).

National Museum of Prehistory MUSEUM
(國立臺灣史前文化博物館; Guólì Táiwān Shǐqián Wénhuà Bówùguǎn; www.nmp.gov.tw; admission NT$80;) The two most-touted sites of Taitung, this museum and the associated **Peinan Culture Park** (卑南文化公園; Bēinán Wénhuà Gōngyuán; admission free) are a bit disappointing. Though highly informative, the museum features too many exhibits that are nothing more than pictures and dioramas with write-ups. It is in the western part of town near Kangle railway station.

The culture park (west of the new railway station), meanwhile, is the site of the largest prehistoric settlement found in Taiwan, and the largest stone coffin culture site in all of Southeast Asia. Over 1500 stone coffins and more than 20,000 stone and pottery artefacts were excavated but, unbelievably, most have been shipped to Taipei for storage, while the site itself has been reburied (except for one tiny area). As the park's website states, 'There are bountiful prehistoric cultural relics beneath its ground.'

OK, but can we see some of them, please?

Cycling

Taitung's new **22km circle path** (自行車道; Zìxíngchē dào) runs north to the Beinan River and the **Liji Badlands** (利吉惡地), a fantastical muddy, barren moon-world of sheer slopes, ravines and pointy ridges. On the opposite bank of the river, the more durable cliffs have been eroded into kilometres of craggy ridges and steep-sided outcrops. The area goes by the name **Little Huangshan** (小黃山), after the famous Chinese landscape. Both Liji and Little Huangshan are worth a few hours' exploring.

The easiest entrance points for the cycle path are at the Railway Art Village and behind the monstrous Environmental Protection Agency building (a former stadium), which is up the street and right from the new train station.

You can rent good-quality bikes at the **Giant** (捷安特; Jié Ān Tè; 934 7416; giant.d21078@msa.hinet.net; 377 Chunghua Rd; per hr NT$150; 8am-10pm) bicycle shop. This shop also rents bikes for multiday trips.

Festivals & Events

Bombing Master Handan LANTERN FESTIVAL
This is an old festival (well, from the '50s) that is getting a new lease on life as activities get bigger and bigger each year. During the festival, volunteers dress as Handanyeh (the money god) and are carried through the streets. Since the god reportedly hates the cold, people shell him with exploding firecrackers to warm him up and thus win his favour. The festival takes place on the 15th and 16th day of the Lunar New Year. Every year volunteers appear on TV a few days earlier to remind the public that the god doesn't like firecrackers thrown directly at his face.

Sleeping

Taitung Travel Hostel HOSTEL $
(台東旅遊民宿; Táidōng Lǚyóu Mínsù; 235 043; www.gotaitung.tw; 21 Shin-Sheng Rd; 興盛路21號; s/d NT$600/800) Just a couple

Taitung

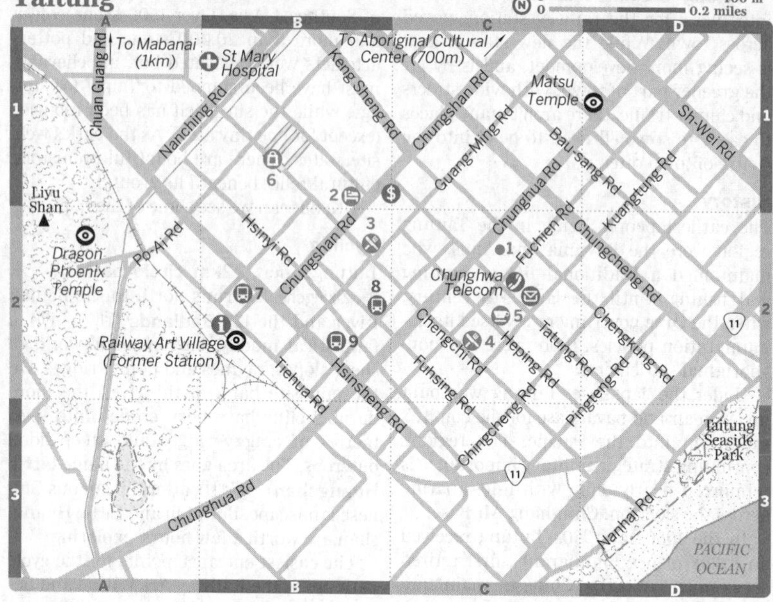

of minutes' walk from the new train station, this hostel is more cosy B&B than backpacker hangout (not that backpackers aren't most welcome). The friendly husband-and-wife team who run this place out of their three-storey home are both heavily involved in Taitung tourism (as advisors and realtors) and started the hostel to meet travellers to the east, and to learn about their impressions. There are 10% discounts for travellers with an IYH card, and 15% discounts for any cyclist. Book via email and ask for an airport or train station pick-up as it's a little tricky getting here.

Longxing Holiday Cabins HOTEL $
(龍星花園渡假木屋; Lóngxīng Huāyuán Dùjià Mùwū; ☎228 193; www.long-xing.com.tw; 625 Xinxing Rd; 新興路625號; d/tw NT$1100/1900) The cabins, actually connected rooms around a central garden, are in a perfect location if you're arriving late or heading out early from the train station: just two blocks straight ahead on the right from the station exit. Rooms are small but comfortable and clean and there are a few restaurants nearby. There are 15% discounts midweek.

Fuh Tuan (Fu Yuan) Hotel HOTEL $
(富源大飯店; Fùyuán Dàfàndiàn; ☎331 1369; 72 Wenhua St; 文化街72號; d/tr NT$800/1000) This basic budget hotel is centrally located in a busy market area in the middle of everything. Wenhua St is off Chungshan just up from Chengchi Rd.

Aboriginal Cultural Centre HOTEL $
(原住民文化會館; Yuánzùmín Wénhuà Huìguǎn; ☎340 605; www.tac-hotel.com.tw; 10 Chungshan Rd; 中山路10號; d/tr NT$1150/1650) The cultural centre has clean, spacious rooms with just a couple of chips and smudges here and there. There are 15% discounts on weekdays.

Eating & Drinking

The lanes between Chungshan Rd and Chingcheng Rd are chock-a-block full of cheap eateries and cafes. Some local delicacies to try are sticky rice (筒仔米糕; *tǒngzǐ mǐgāo*) and pork blood soup (豬血湯; *zhū xiě tāng*), a Puyuma dish.

Mabanai ABORIGINAL $$
(米巴奈; Mǐbānài; 470 Chuan Guang Rd; dishes from NT$200; ⏲lunch & dinner) Like Cifadahan Cafe in Mataian, Mabanai is taking traditional aboriginal food to a whole other level. Though the restaurant has all the style of a wedding banquet hall, the food

Taitung

Activities, Courses & Tours
1 Giant Bicycle Shop C2

Sleeping
2 Fuhyuan Hotel B1

Eating
3 Beikang Xiao Chi Pu B2
4 Old Taitung Noodle Shop....................C2

Drinking
5 KASA C2

Shopping
6 Fruit Street B1

Transport
7 Dingdong Coastal Bus Station............B2
8 Dingdong Inland Bus Station B2
Hualien Bus Station......................(see 7)
9 Kuo Kuang Hao Bus Company............B2

more than compensates. Make sure you try the signature dish of wild-boar-bacon-wrapped baby corn (yes, corn!). Some other fine dishes include betel-nut flower salads and sticky rice and corn.

Old Taitung Noodle Shop NOODLES **$**
(老台東米苔目; Lǎo Táidōng Mǐtáimù; 134 Chengchi Rd; noodles NT$43; ⏲10am-10pm) This is where Taiwanese head when they want their version of a '50s dinner. In business for decades, the noodle shop sells bowls of slightly sour rice noodles with a boiled egg thrown in for good measure. It tastes about like it sounds.

Nearby are a number of stalls and small shops selling street food and fruit drinks.

Beikang Xiao Chi Pu TRADITIONAL RESTAURANT **$**
(北港小吃部; Běigǎng Xiǎochībù; 212 GuangMing Rd; sticky rice NT$25-40; ⏲8am-7pm) The Beikang is an unassuming little place that has been around for over 25 years. The sticky rice here is one of the best in town. Try it with some thick meat soup (roù gēng).

KASA CAFE **$$**
(www.wretch.cc/blog/kasataitung; 102 Heping St; ⏲6pm-midnight) KASA has been around Taitung for many years, in various manifestations. The latest, off Heping Rd, is a rustic little cafe made out of driftwood and recycled yellow cedar. It's got a great laid-back atmosphere and a friendly crowd of regulars, both Taiwanese and foreign, who come for coffee, Tex-Mex snacks, or a drink or two.

☆ Entertainment

Every Saturday night there is live music at the Dulan Sugar Factory, a short drive up Hwy 11.

Shopping

Taitung has some of the freshest and most delicious fruit in Taiwan. In central Taitung, between Po'ai and Chungshan Rds, there's a lively fruit street (水果街; *Shuǐguǒ jiē*) selling a colourful assortment of fruit, including pineapples, coconuts, bananas, mangoes, dragon fruit and papayas. There's also Taitung's most famous fruit, the delicious custard apple, nicknamed 'Buddha head fruit' (釋迦; *shìjiā*) because its shape resembles the head of the curly-haired Sakyamuni Buddha.

Aboriginal arts and crafts are on sale at the gift shops of the National Museum of Prehistory and the Peinan Culture Park.

ℹ Information

Railway Art Village Visitor Information Centre (遊客服務中心; ☎359 085; ⏲9am-5pm) There are also smaller visitor centres at the new train station and airport. Except for the volunteers, the staff's English ability tends to be weak. Has written-English information on buses and trains, as well as some useful brochures.

Money

Many 7-Elevens have ATM service.

Bank of Taiwan (台灣銀行; Chungshan Rd) Will exchange foreign currency and has an ATM that takes international debit cards.

Websites

Department of Culture & Tourism (http://tour.taitung.gov.tw)

Taitung County Government (www.taitung.gov.tw)

ℹ Getting There & Away

Air

There are flights from Taitung's **Fong Nian Airport** (www.tta.gov.tw) to Taipei, Taichung and Lanyu and Green Islands. The airport has a nice tropical feel to it, and is a pleasant way to enter the south. There's a **visitor centre** (⏲9am-5pm) to help you out. The following airlines have booking counters at the airport:

Daily Air Corporation (www.dailyair.com.tw)

Mandarin Airlines (www.mandarin-airlines.com)

Uni Air (www.uniair.com.tw)

Bus

Taitung has multiple bus stations, and finding which bus goes to where, from where, can be confusing. Ask at the visitor centre for the latest.

Dingdong Coastal Bus Station (鼎東客運海線總站; ☎333 433) Across from the visitor centre. Has buses to Hualien via Hwy 11 (NT$475, three hours, four per day).

Dingdong Inland Bus Station (鼎東客運山線總站; ☎333 433; cnr Fuhsing & Ancing Rds) Has buses to: Chihpen Hot Springs (NT$58, 40 minutes, hourly); new Taitung train station (NT$22, hourly); and Litao on the South Cross-Island Hwy (confirm schedule at the visitor centre). Note: there are no direct buses to Kenting.

Kuo Kuang Hao Bus Company (國光客運公司; www.kingbus.com.tw, 92 Hsincheng Rd) Has buses to Kaohsiung (NT$443, 4½ hours, six daily).

Train

If taking a taxi to the train station, be clear with your driver that you mean the new station. From central Taitung it will cost around NT$250. Buses (NT$22) to the station leave from the Dingdong Inland Bus station. There are trains to Hualien (fast/slow train NT$346/222, 2½/3½ hours, hourly) and Kaohsiung (fast/slow train NT$364/234, 2½/3½ hours, hourly).

Getting Around

To/From the Airport

A taxi will cost you NT$250, but a bus from the Dingdong Coastal Bus Station will cost NT$22 (20 minutes, hourly).

Scooter

Rentals are available from shops across from new train station (per day NT$400 to NT$500). You need a Taiwanese licence to be able to rent (they are very strict about this).

SOUTH OF TAITUNG

South of Taitung there are a few interesting little stops where you can enjoy hot springs, beachcombing and a fascinating banyan forest.

Cyclists can continue riding south (Hwy 11 is a nicer ride out of Taitung than the 9) to connect with the 199 to Kenting, but be aware that the cycling shoulder lane ends past Chihpen. Many find sharing the twisting and rising narrow lanes with speeding trucks more of a challenge than they care for. Consider taking the train down to Dawu or getting a very early morning start.

Chihpen (Zhiben) 知本

☎089 / POP 3000

The **Chihpen Hot Springs** (Zhīběn Wēnquán) lie about 15km southwest of Taitung in a canyon at the foot of the Dawu Mountains. The quality of the sodium bicarbonate spring water (colourless, tasteless, and 90°C) was first recognised by the Japanese, who built a resort here in the early 20th century. They dubbed the area 'Chihpen', meaning 'source of wisdom'.

Nowadays, Chihpen is a locally top-rated tourist draw, with rows of five-star hotels, garish KTVs and traffic clogging the road into the canyon. Luckily, getting away from all the noise and bustle isn't difficult. Some of the better resorts sit on high shelves, and at the far end of the canyon in a thick jungle park you'll find quiet walking paths where the likelihood of spotting deer and monkeys is high.

Sights & Activities

Chihpen (Zhiben) Forest Recreation Area FOREST PARK
(知本森林遊樂區; Zhīběn Sēnlín Yóulè Qū; www.forest.gov.tw; admission NT$100; ⏲7am-5pm) It's worth coming to Chihpen just to wander this jungly landscape's trails, especially the upper slopes to see the giant white-bark fig trees. Unlike the vines of willows, with these 'weeping figs' it's the aerial roots that make the trees seem soulful.

On almost every visit to the forest park, you will see Formosan macaques crashing about overhead and may even catch a glimpse of the tiny Reeves' muntjac deer (barking deer), which makes a strange barking sound like a dog.

To get to the forest recreation area, either catch a bus from Taitung (all buses to the hot-spring area should stop here) or simply follow the signs to Chihpen Hot Springs and drive through the hotel wonderland to the end of the road. The visitor centre has English maps.

Hot Springs

Most hotels have hot-spring facilities that are open to nonguests.

Toyugi Hot Spring Resort & Spa HOT SPRINGS
(東遊季溫泉渡假村; Dōngyóujì Wēnquán Dùjiàcūn; www.toyugi.com.tw; admission NT$300; ⏲8am-9pm) This resort sits a few kilometres down County Road 58東 on a large shelf

above the river valley, giving it a private feel in the madhouse that is Chihpen. Facilities include a multipool complex, restaurant and cabins, should you wish to stay the night (from NT$3500). To get to the hotel look for the sign in English saying 'Journey to the East'.

Hotel Royal Chihpen HOT SPRINGS
(老爺大酒店; Lǎoyé Dàjiǔdiàn; www.hotel-royal-chihpen.com.tw; hot-spring admission NT$350; r from NT$7800) A few kilometres past Toyugi, up a side road to the left, sits what many consider to be the finest hotel in Chihpen, with the swankiest pools.

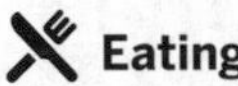

Eating

The main road through Chihpen (Longchuan Rd) has plenty of small restaurants and noodle stands selling decent local food at standard prices.

Getting There & Away

There's a bus from Taitung to Chihben (NT$58, 40 minutes, every hour); the first bus to Chihben leaves at 6am, while the last bus to Taitung leaves at 7.05pm.

Taimali 太麻里

It sounds like a Mexican dish, but Taimali (Tàimálǐ) is a little nothing-town south of Chihpen. Ah, but there is something here, a beach, a long, beautiful palm-studded beach that stretches on and on. There's no swimming (far too rough) but the crashing surf, the wide soft-sand beach, the green mountains rising to the west, and the long coastline sweeping out to the north make this an absolutely fabulous place for a couple hours' strolling. There's also plenty of driftwood, should you want to build a fire, and of course no one would object if you set up a tent and camped out.

Interestingly, the BBC chose this beach as one of the 60 best places in the world to watch the sunrise of the new millennium on 31 December 1999.

It's best to have your own transport to get here.

Yushan National Park & Western Taiwan

Includes »

Best Places to Eat

» Cantonese Restaurant (p204)

» Matsu Temple Market (see p217)

» Full House Resort (p221)

Best Places to Stay

» Alishan House (p208)

» Roulan Lodge (p210)

» Laurel Villa (p220)

» Dasyueshan Forest Recreation Area (p199)

» Aowanda National Forest Recreation Area (p226)

» Mountain Fish Water Boutique Hotel (p225)

Why Go?

The west puts on a good show for travellers with some of Taiwan's biggest celebrations of gods and nature alike. If the fireworks blow-out at Yenshui is the season opener, the Matsu Pilgrimage is most definitely the year's highlight. This nine-day parade across half of Taiwan is far more entertaining than Chinese New Year. Expect endless fireworks, feasting, prostrating, praying, great acts of generosity and (since this is Taiwan) a little bit of gangster intrigue.

Not to be outdone, the natural world presents some of the most wild and untrammelled landscapes in Taiwan, as well as yearly migrations of both butterflies and raptors. For DIY entertainment, head to Yushan National Park to climb the highest peak in Northeast Asia. It takes two days to reach the top, and if you continue down the backside trails, you won't see anyone else for days at a time. We're sure you can keep yourself amused.

When to Go

Taichung

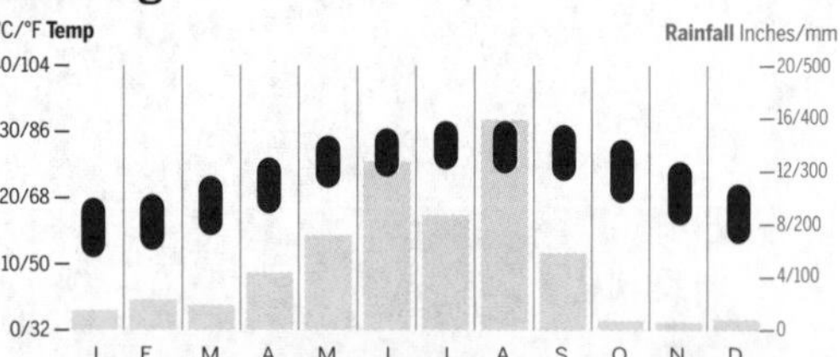

April Matsu Pilgrimage.

March–April Purple Crow butterfly migration.

September–December Best time for hiking in Yushan National Park.

National Parks & Forest Recreation Areas

Western Taiwan has its share of parks including pristine Yushan National Park, home of 3952m Yushan (Jade Mountain), the highest peak in Taiwan. Tame Alishan Forest Recreation Area is the polar opposite, with an old alpine train and cherry-blossom trees being the draw. Dasyueshan Forest Recreation Area and Aowanda National Forest Recreation Area offer the best birdwatching venues in the country, while rugged Hehuanshan Forest Recreation Area offers scenic hikes above the treeline. Huisun, Sitou and Shanlinhsi Forest Recreation Area are cool mountain retreats with short hikes and plenty of good scenery.

The Linnei area has a reserve for the globally threatened Fairy Pitta, and is also a mass gathering point on the Purple Crow butterfly's yearly migration. Changhua's

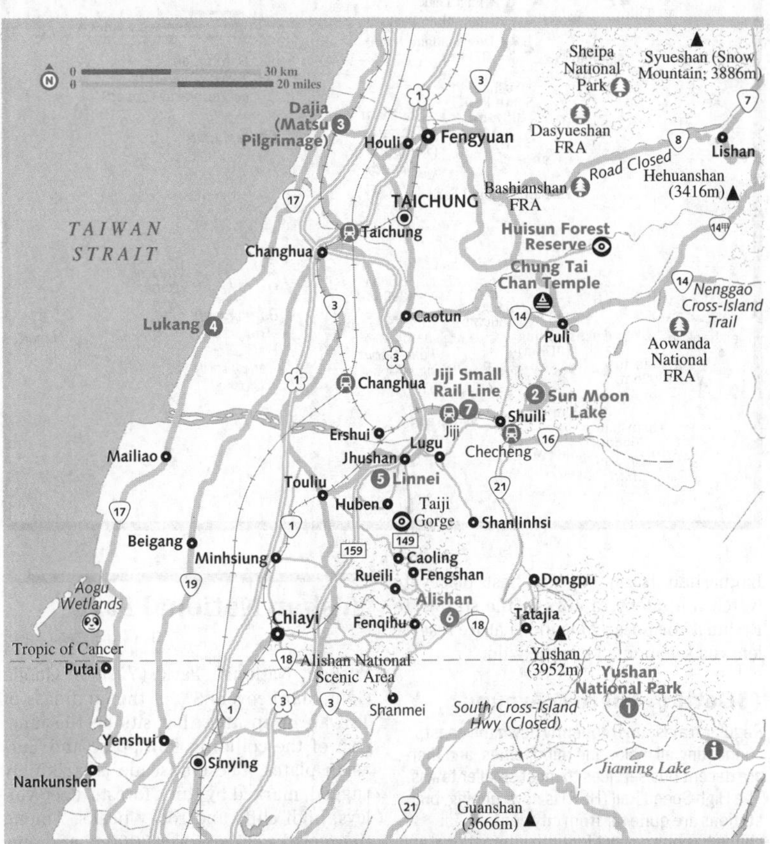

Highlights

1. Climb Yushan, Northeast Asia's highest mountain, in **Yushan National Park** (p192)
2. Cycle, boat and stroll along **Sun Moon Lake** (p218)
3. Become a pilgrim for Matsu in **Dajia** (see boxed text, p201)
4. Wander the old merchant streets of **Lukang** (p214)
5. **Bird-** and **butterfly-watch** around the west (see boxed text, p212)
6. Ride an old train and explore ancient forests at **Alishan** (p205)
7. Explore the quaint countryside and rugged mountains around the **Jiji Small Rail Line** (p224)

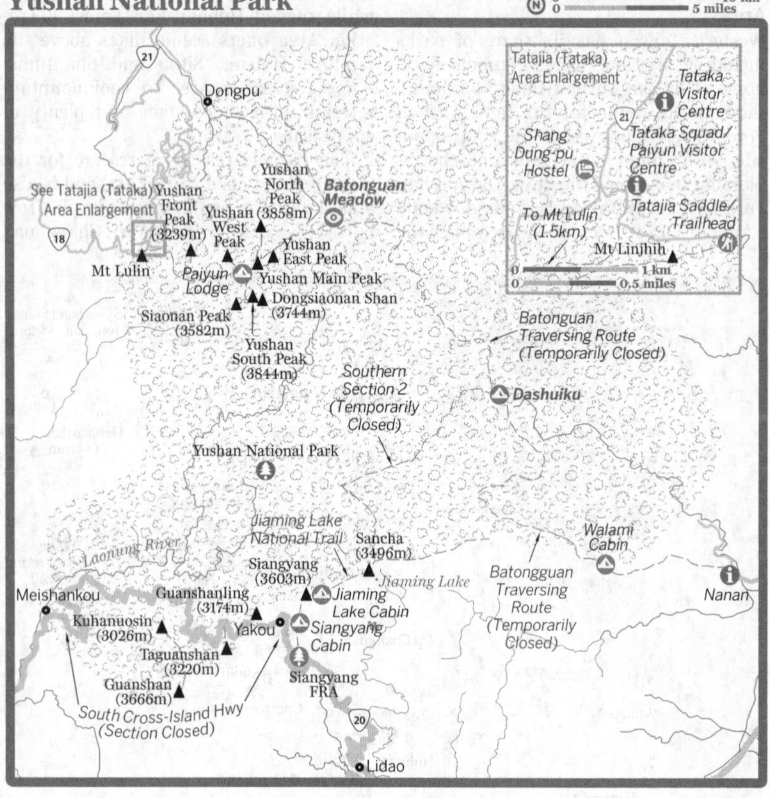

Baguashan is one of the best places to watch migratory raptors in the spring. In Ershui a Formosan Macaque nature reserve lets you see monkeys in the wild.

Getting There & Around

Regular trains run frequently down the coast, connecting all major and minor cities, and there are decent bus services to most smaller towns. The High Speed Rail (HSR) is now running, but stations are quite far from city centres. Taichung has one airport for both international and domestic services. A narrow-gauge alpine train (temporarily out of commission at the time of writing) does the route from Chiayi to Alishan. In most cities you'll find scooter and car-rental outlets.

The only areas where public transport is inconvenient are Yushan National Park, the more remote parts of the Alishan National Scenic Area and Hwy 14 past Puli.

Yushan National Park

玉山國家公園

Yushan National Park (Yùshān Guójiā Gōngyuán) covers 3% of the landmass of Taiwan in an area that sits on the junction of the colliding Philippine and Eurasian plates. The landscape is strikingly rugged, marked by thick forests, deep valleys, high cliffs and rocky peaks. Among these peaks, 30 are over 3000m, and one, the eponymous Yushan (Jade Mountain), is the highest mountain in Northeast Asia at 3952m and attracts hikers from all over the world.

The park's six vegetative zones harbour 151 species of birds, 34 mammals, 17 reptiles, 228 types of butterflies and over 4000 species of vascular plants. Given that recent studies have shown that little Taiwan harbours about 2.5% of the world's species of plants and animals, this national park is rightly considered a natural treasure trove.

Yushan National Park covers areas of Chiayi, Nantou, Kaohsiung and Hualien Counties. A 20km drive west will take you to the Alishan Forest Recreation Area. From Yuli in the east, you can reach the Nanan section of the park, with its fantastic Walami Trail. The South Cross-Island Hwy, which skirts the southern borders of the park, is no longer passable.

You can visit the park year-round for hiking or sightseeing. In general, the area is wet in summer and dry in winter.

History

In 1697 Chinese travel writer Yu Yung-ho wrote, 'Yushan stands amidst ten thousand mountains. It is white like silver, and appears at a distance covered in snow. It can be seen, but not reached. The mountain is like jade.'

It was the first recorded account of the mountain and its Chinese name. Around the same time Bunun aboriginals were starting to emigrate to the central mountains and they gave the highest peak their own name: Tongku Saveq (The Sanctuary). More renamings were to come.

In 1896 a Japanese officer made the first recorded ascent of Yushan. By the 1920s two hiking routes had opened: one from Alishan and another from Dongpu. High-school kids started to climb the mountain as a graduation trip, much as they still do today.

During the Japanese colonial era, Yushan was the highest mountain in the empire: 176m higher than Mt Fuji. In 1897 it was renamed Niitakayama (New High Mountain; which incidentally was the code name for the attack on Pearl Harbor: 'Climb Niitakayama').

The Japanese recognised the Yushan area as one of Taiwan's most biodiverse. In the late 1930s they drew up plans for an 1800-sq-km national park. WWII scuttled the plans, but by the late 1970s the Kuomintang (KMT) had revived the idea.

The 105,000-hectare Yushan National Park came into official existence on 10 April 1985. In 2009 the main peak was shortlisted by the New7Wonders foundation in a contest to choose seven modern wonders of nature.

Activities

Hiking

Park trails are well maintained and usually clear to follow. Signs are in English and Chinese, and there are frequent distance posts. Before beginning a hike to the main peaks make sure you drop into the Tataka Squad and Paiyuan Visitor Centre to get your permits in order. The park's staff will ask you to watch a movie afterwards that introduces Yushan and encourages green behaviour.

The best time to hike in the park is during autumn and early spring (October to December and March to April). May has seasonal monsoon rains, and typhoons are a problem from June to September, though if there is no typhoon, you can certainly hike. In winter the main peaks are usually closed for almost two months to give the environment a rest, though the day hikes around Tatajia are open year-round.

DAY HIKES

For the superb Walami Trail in the southeast corner of the park, see p180.

Most day hikes are concentrated at Tatajia (塔塔加; Tǎtǎjiā) around the Km108 mark on Hwy 18. As these can get over 2800m, bring adequate warm, all-weather clothing, some food and water before you head out. Pick up a copy of the excellent *Tatajia: Guide to the Tataka Recreation Area* at any visitor centre for an overview of the system.

A pleasant 1.7km walk through grassland and pine forest runs from the Tataka Visitor Centre (塔塔加遊客中心) to the Tataka Squad (塔塔加小隊; Tǎtǎjiā Xiǎoduì) and adjacent Paiyun Visitor Centre.

From the Tataka Squad you can follow the (traffic controlled) road an easy 3.5km to the **NCU Lulin Observatory** (鹿林天文台; NCU Lùlín Tiānwéntái). Another paved route runs south 2km to **Tatajia Anbu** (塔塔加鞍部; Tǎtǎjiā Ānbù; Tatajia Saddle), the start of the trail to Yushan. From Tatajia it's 1km of steep trail up to **Mt Linjhih** (麟芷山; Línzhǐ Shān; elevation 2854m) or you can take an easier 1.8km route that skirts the peak from the south.

Mt Lulin (鹿林山; Lùlín Shān; elevation 2881m) can be tackled from the road to the observatory or on a trail connecting with Mt Linjhih. The area is largely open grassland, with superb views. Give yourself all day if you plan to hike the whole circuit.

IF YOU CAN'T CLIMB YUSHAN, TRY...

With over a thousand people applying for the 90 permits to climb Yushan each day, you need some options if you want to climb a 3000m plus mountain in Taiwan. Here are a few worthy options that are easier to secure permits for:

» **Snow Mountain** (p144) Taiwan's second-highest peak. Amazing geology and vistas.

» **Wuling-Quadruple** (p144) Climb four peaks in two days, with superb views over the Holy Ridge.

» **Beidawushan** (p265) Most southerly 3000m-plus peak. Long, sweeping ridgeline walk to the summit. Only a police permit needed.

» **Hehuanshan Peaks** (p229) Series of short hikes starting above the treeline. No permits needed.

» **Dabajianshan** (p149) The holy peak of the Atayal with a magical landscape.

» **Jiaming Lake** (see p183) Sublime high-alpine scenery at a young meteor lake. Only a police permit needed.

» **Nenggaoshan North Peak & Chilai South Peak** (p228) In the heart of the central mountains. Big views. Only a police permit needed.

» **Holy Ridge** (p144) Five-day adventure on a thin ridgeline that never dips below 3300m.

» **Nenggao–Andongjun Trail** (p228) Six days through alpine lake country. Unlikely to see another person after the first day. Only a police permit needed.

OVERNIGHT HIKES

The Yushan Peaks HIKES

The trail to the main peak is straightforward and can be done by anyone in decent shape (though plenty of horribly unfit Taiwanese do it, too). From the Tatajia Squad and Paiyun Visitor Centre (a short walk up a sideroad from Hwy 18) where permits are processed, a shuttle bus transports hikers to Tatajia Saddle, the official start of the trail to the **main peak** (玉山主峰; Yùshān Zhǔfēng; elevation 3952m).

The trail runs relatively wide and flat most of the way, skirting the northern slopes of the deep V-shaped Cishan River (旗山溪) valley. Elevation is gained in a couple of short steep sections. While Yushan National Park harbours six forest zones, you're squarely in a cool-temperate zone. The pure forests of hemlock are sublime. The yellowish grass trying to reclaim the trail is actually dwarf bamboo (Yushan cane).

At **Paiyun Lodge** (排雲山莊; Páiyún Shānzhuāng; elevation 3402m) hikers rest for the night in preparation for the ascent on the main peak. Be on the lookout for yellow-throated martin at the cabin, and even serow on the slopes.

If you arrive early at Paiyun Lodge and still have energy to spare, **Yushan West Peak** (玉山東峰; Yùshān Dōngfēng; elevation 3518m) can be tackled. The trail starts to the left of the cabin.

The next day most hikers get a 3am start in order to reach the summit by daylight. It's switchback after switchback until a loose gravel slope. At the top of the slope hikers enter a steel cage, exit onto a tiny rocky pass, and then make a final scramble up the roughest and most exposed section of the trail to the ingot-shaped peak.

On the way up, watch for the hemlock and spruce forest giving way to fields of rhododendron and stands of juniper, at first tall and straight and then twisted and dwarfed. At the highest elevations lichens and tenacious alpine flowers clinging to the windswept rocks are about all the life you'll find. This is also when the views start to chill you to the bone.

After resting on the summit, and taking in the views, hikers return to Paiyun Lodge to gather their stuff and hike back to Tatajia.

If the weather is clear, consider hiking across to **Yushan North Peak** (玉山北峰; Yùshān Běifēng; elevation 3858m). The way is obvious and the view from the weather station on the peak shows the classic sweeping ridgeline of Yushan portrayed on the NT$1000 note.

If tackling the southern set of peaks that include **Yushan South Peak** (玉山南峰; Yùshān Nánfēng; elevation 3844m) and **Dongsiaonan Shan** (玉山東小南山; Yùshān Dōngxiǎonán Shān; elevation 3744m), hikers stay at the lofty **Yuanfong Cabin** (圓峰營地; Yuánfēng Yíngdì; 3752m) about 2.5km (1.5 hours) south off the main trail. You'll need a couple more days to bag these extras.

OTHER HIKES

The following trails may have been repaired by the time you read this, so we are including them as they are among the best in Taiwan.

Japanese Occupation Era Batongguan Traversing Route HIKE

This 90km, seven-day-long trail (八通關日據越道線; Bātōngguān Rìjù Yuèdào Xiàn) was hacked across the mountains in 1921 during the Japanese era, following in part an earlier Batongguan route built by the Qing in 1875.

The alternative name of the Japanese trail, 'The Pacifying the Natives Old Rd', gives an idea what purpose it served besides facilitating travel, trade and communication between east and west Taiwan. A small number of old police stations (or forts really) can be seen abandoned along the trail, and at least half a dozen stelae that commemorate battles between Japanese and aboriginal forces.

The trail climbs for three days to reach Dashuiku, a meadow of Yushan cane high above the treeline. It then begins to descend and by the fifth day, most hikers will be back in mixed temperate forest around Dafen, site of a former trading post. This area is now a Formosan black-bear reserve and if you were going to see one of these elusive creatures anywhere, this would be it.

The Batongguan trail starts in Dongpu and ends in Nanan, near Yuli on the east coast. If restored (and we expect it will be), expect good cabins, campgrounds and mostly reliable water sources along the way.

Southern Section 2 Trail HIKE

This is an eight-day trail (南二段線; Nán Èrduàn Xiàn) running from the South Cross-Island Hwy to Dongpu, or Tatajia via the back route to Yushan. It's one of Taiwan's toughest high-mountain hauls, with almost daily climbs of 1000m, followed by descents of 1000m just to even things out. Knees beware.

The challenges keep the crowds away (you're likely to be alone on the trail for days at a stretch), but also lets the relationship between altitude and forest cover unfold before your very eyes. By the end of the trip you'll be able to make rough guesses of your altitude just by the surrounding vegetation: 'If this is juniper, we must be above 3500m!'

When the trail is reopened, you can expect good cabins, campgrounds and water sources along the length. The first two days follow the trail up to **Jiaming Lake** (嘉明湖; Jiāmíng Hú). For more details, see p183.

Bird- & Butterfly-Watching

About 150 bird species can be sighted in the park. Rusting Laughing Thrush and Yushan Yuhina are commonly seen on the trails. At Tatajia Saddle the endemic Mikado Pheasant can be spotted as often as not.

Butterflies can be found all over the park, but Tatajia is the funnel point of a remarkable and little-understood butterfly corridor. In late spring winds from Puli sweep the immense valley below Tatajia, carrying every little winged creature upwards. Hundreds of butterflies can pass the saddle per minute, and even in late June we have watched awestruck as dozens were blown up overhead every minute, spun around in the turbulence and then carried away.

A STANDARD YUSHAN HIKING ITINERARY

» Tatajia trailhead to Paiyun Lodge: 8.4km, four to six hours

» Paiyun Lodge to Yushan West Peak: 2.5km each way, three hours return

» Paiyun Lodge to Yushan Main Peak: 2.4km, three hours

» Yushan Main Peak to Yushan North Peak (detour): 3km each way, 2½ hours return

» Yushan Main Peak to Paiyun Lodge: 2.4km, 1½ hours

» Paiyun Lodge to Tatajia trailhead: 8.4km, four hours

About 100 species can be spotted, including a good number of migratory Purple Crows, who have either got caught in the wrong winds (they should be following the currents north) or have taken a detour to look for food. Mid-May mornings are the best time to see this phenomenon, though it continues until late June.

Sleeping & Eating

On the trail, cabin quality varies. Paiyun Lodge below the summit of Yushan has bunk bedding, flush toilets, running water, solar lighting and a rough kitchen. There is space outside for three tents, but tenting is only allowed on weekends. By the time you read this, restoration work should have been completed to bring the lodge up to international standards.

Other cabins around the park are usually sturdy A-frames, with open floors for crashing out on (some have a nice thick black underpadding), a loft for extra bedding, solar lights, a water source and ecotoilets. Some cabins also have clear space around them for camping and a deck for cooking and lounging.

You can book meals at Paiyun Lodge for NT$500 per person. This gives you access to a multicourse buffet prepared by Bunun porters. In the morning you get rice porridge and hot water.

Other cabins are unmanned, so you must bring your own supplies.

Shang Dung-pu Hostel HOTEL $
(東埔山莊; Dōngpǔ Shānzhuāng; ☎049-270 2213; dm NT$300) The only place to stay in the park if you are not on a trail is this hostel at Tatajia. The rustic old wood building has simple bunk dorm beds, showers and toilets. Simple meals can be arranged if you give advance notice, and you can buy instant noodles and snacks at the front desk. Book ahead if you want to stay here.

Tours

The park organises hikes to Yushan Main Peak twice monthly from October to December. Call for reservations. For other organisations, see the Taiwan Outdoors chapter.

Information

There are no banks in the park. Wi-fi is available on the summit of Yushan (no kidding!). All of the following visitor centres provide maps in English, brochures and information on current trail conditions. For permits and maps, see p25.

Nanan Visitor Centre (南安遊客中心; ☎03-888 7560; 83-3, Choching; ⌚9am-4.30pm)

Tatajia (Tataka) Visitor Centre (塔塔加遊客中心; ⌚9am-4.30pm)

Yushan National Park (www.ysnp.gov.tw)

Yushan National Park Headquarters (玉山國家公園管理處; www.ysnp.gov.tw; 515 Jungshan Rd, Sec 1, Shuili, Nantou County; 水里鄉中山路一段515號; ⌚8.30am-5pm)

Getting There & Away

Public transport is nonexistent in the park. If you don't have your own vehicle or driver, you might be able to hire a taxi in Alishan, or catch the sunrise tour buses.

Dongpu (Tungpu) 東埔

POP 500 / ELEV 1200M

Just over the northern tip of Yushan National Park, or directly south of Sun Moon Lake, sits the hot-spring village of Dongpu (Dōngpǔ). The carbon-acid hot spring delivers high-quality, clear, odour-free water with an average temperature of 50°C.

Dongpu's status as a gateway to Yushan National Park is threatened by severe washouts on the trail up to the Batongguan meadows (a junction of trails, which includes a back route to Yushan Main Peak). Even before Typhoon Morakot this section was in such rough shape that Bunun porters were reluctant to take it. Although it's currently completely impassable, it's expected to be repaired.

There are plenty of hot-spring hotels in Dongpu. For an inexpensive option, try the **Youth Activity Centre** (青年活動中心; Qīngnián Huódòng Zhōngxīn; ☎049-270 1515; r from NT$700) at the high end of town.

Yuanlin Bus Company (員林客運; ☎049-277 0041) runs buses between Dongpu and Shuili (NT$115, 80 minutes) approximately hourly between 6am and 5pm.

TAICHUNG COUNTY

Taichung 台中市

☎04 / POP 1,021,290

Under Japanese, and later KMT, economic planning, Kaohsiung became the centre of heavy industry; Taipei the centre of colonial administration; and Taichung? The centre of light industry. If your image of Made in

Taiwan still conjures up visions of cheap toys, shoes and electrical goods, then you've got old Taichung in mind.

Today the name Taichung tends, among locals anyway, to conjure up visions of great weather. Taipei and Taichung may have very similar average temperatures but Taichung is much drier, receiving around 1700mm of rain a year compared with Taipei's 2170mm. In many ways the city is a decent place to live but there is very little here for the traveller. New transport routes created by the HSR also mean you can largely bypass the city when travelling to Sun Moon Lake or Lukang.

But if you're stuck for a few hours in the 'Chungle', the following might help to pass the time.

Sights & Activities

For information on cycling in the Taichung area, see http://poweredbyusana.blogspot.com/2010/01/exploring-taichung-by-bike.html.

FREE National Taiwan Museum of Fine Arts MUSEUM

(台灣美術館; Táiwān Měishù Guǎn; 2 Wuquan W Rd) The open modern design is visually sophisticated and there are high-quality exhibits of both Taiwanese and foreign artists. Exhibits change often.

For children there is a good hands-on play area and storybook centre on the lower floors.

Taichung Folk Park FOLK PARK

(台中民俗公園; Táizhōng Mínsú Gōngyuán; 73 Lu Shun Rd, Sec 2; admission NT$50; ⌚9am-5pm, closed Mon) The park is divided into several sections but most of the interesting material is to the far right as you enter (to the left are cheap souvenir stalls). Don't miss the collections of folk artefacts (everything from ceramic pillows to farming implements).

Dakeng SCENIC AREA

To the east of the city is a hilly area known as Dakeng (大坑; Dàkēng). If you are going to spend any time in the city, Dakeng is worth exploring, as there are pleasant hiking trails and even a few hot springs.

Paochueh Temple BUDDHIST TEMPLE

(寶覺寺; Bǎojué Sì; 140 Jianxing St; ⌚8am-5pm) This Buddhist temple features one of the largest and fattest Milefo (laughing) Buddhas in Taiwan.

Sleeping

The Taichung train-station area has been cleaned up a bit in recent years and makes for a decent base, having all your life-support systems nearby.

Plaza Hotel HOTEL $

(☎2229 3191; www.plazahotel.com.tw; 180 Jianguo Rd; 建國路180號; d/tw incl breakfast NT$1380/2400; @) Just a stone's throw from Taichung train station, this rather smart-looking business hotel is a great bargain for those who need a bit more comfort than what the other budget hotels provide.

Fuh Chun Hotel HOTEL $

(富春大飯店; Fùchūn Dàfàdiàn; ☎2228 3181; fax 2228 3187; 1 Zhongshan Rd; 中山路1號; s/d/tw NT$600/780/1000; @) This place, just across from Taichung train station, has been around forever and is popular with foreign travellers and Taiwanese students. Rooms are small without appearing too cramped and...is that an slight recent upgrade we noticed?

Chance Hotel HOTEL $

(巧合大飯店; Qiǎohé Dàfàdiàn; ☎2229 7161; 163 Jianguo Rd; 建國路163號; d/tw NT$950/1200; @) Rooms are clean and in need of a style change (the '70s are dead, long live the '70s) but will do fine for a night or two.

Eating

Taichung has a pretty decent assortment of restaurants serving a wide range of Asian and Western cuisines. A few popular areas for restaurant dining are the streets south of the National Taiwan Museum of Art (for lunch and dinner only) and the area marked on our Taichung map.

There are dozens of cheap noodle, Japanese fast-food and pizza places clustered around the train-station area.

Shantung Dumplings & Beef Noodles RESTAURANT $

(山東餃子牛肉麵館; Shāndōng Jiǎozi Niúròumiàn Guǎn; 96 Gongyi Rd, Sec 1; dishes NT$60-190; ⌚11am-9pm) Year after year this place serves consistently tasty traditional home-cooked dumplings, beef noodles and other staples with a Shantung province flavour. English menu.

Finga's Base Camp RESTAURANT/DELI $$

(風格餐廳; Fēnggé Cāntīng; 61 Zhongming S Rd; ⌚10am-10pm) A deli, restaurant, butchery and bakery all in one.

Taichung

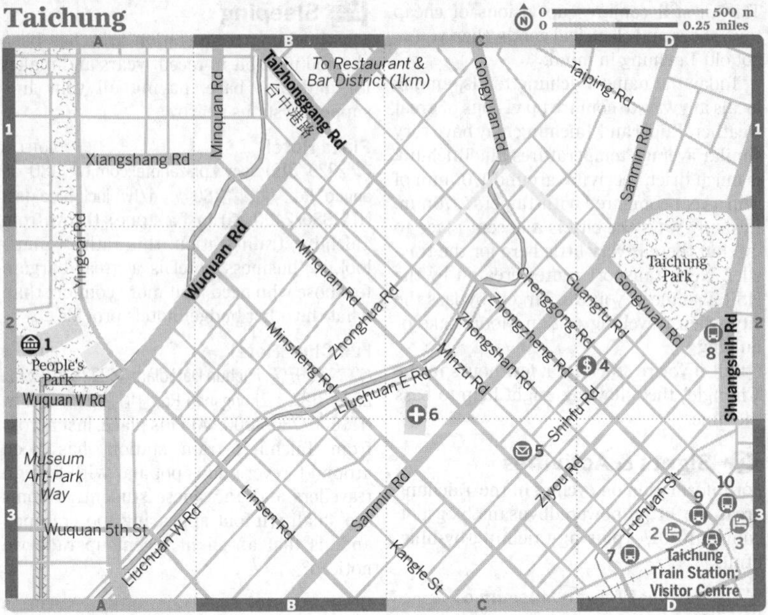

0 500 m
0 0.25 miles
To Restaurant & Bar District (1km)
Taizhonggang Rd 台中港路
Minquan Rd
Xiangshang Rd
Gongyuan Rd
Taiping Rd
Sanmin Rd
Yingcai Rd
Wuquan Rd
Minquan Rd
Zhonghua Rd
Taichung Park
Chenggong Rd
Guangfu Rd
Gongyuan Rd
Zhongzheng Rd
Zhongshan Rd
Minzu Rd
Minsheng Rd
Liuchuan E Rd
Shuangshih Rd
People's Park
Wuquan W Rd
Shifu Rd
Museum Art-Park Way
Linsen Rd
Sanmin Rd
Ziyou Rd
Luchuan St
Liuchuan W Rd
Wuquan 5th St
Kangle St
Taichung Train Station; Visitor Centre

Drinking

Chun Shui Tang Teahouse TEAHOUSE
(春水堂; Chūn Shuǐ Táng; Chingming St; ⊙8.30am-10.30pm) Taiwan bubble tea is famous worldwide tand this is supposedly the company that began it all. The modern teahouse is at the start of Chingming St, known as one of Taichung's famous tea streets, though today it's almost all clothing shops. Still, the pedestrian-only street has outdoor seating and is pleasant on cool evenings.

Smooth Bar & Grill BAR
(☎2329 3468; 5-7 Lane 50, Jingcheng Rd; drinks from NT$150; ⊙3pm-1am) If you need something a little stronger than bubble tea, try this long, long-running bar and grill just a block north of Chun Shui Tang Teahouse. The bar is well stocked and has a big-screen TV for watching sports. There's also an international menu offering curries, steaks, pastas, goulash and more.

Information

There are plenty of banks and 7-Elevens with ATMs around Taichung train station, and further up along Zhongzheng and Taizhonggang Rds.

Internet places come and go frequently; ask at the Visitor Information Centre. Wi-fi is common in cafes and hotels.

Bank of Taiwan (台灣銀行; 144 Zhongzheng Rd) Offers moneychanging facilities in addition to an ATM.

Taichung County Government (www.taichung.gov.tw) The county's official website.

Visitor Information Centre (☎2221 2126; ⊙9am-6pm) Located in Taichung train station. Staff speak English and have an abundance of useful information, including bus schedules (and prices), hotel rates and travel brochures.

Welcome to Taichung (http://english.tccg.gov.tw) The city government's website.

Getting There & Away

Taichung has an **airport** (www.tca.gov.tw), but it's unlikely you'll ever use it.

Bus

Near Taichung train station, **Fengyuan Bus Company** (豐原客運; ☎2222 3454) runs buses once a day (NT$464, six hours, 8am) to Hehuanshan and Lishan. There is also a bus connection at Lishan to Wuling Farm (NT$70, departs at 2pm). The Hualien Bus Company has a connection to Hualien via Taroko Gorge.

Nantou Bus Company (南投客運; www.ntbus.com.tw; 35-8 Shuangshi Rd) has frequent buses to Puli (NT$52, one hour) and Sun Moon Lake (NT$175, 1½ hours), though you can also catch the bus at the HSR station. Buses to Aowanda travel in winter and spring. Call for a

Taichung

Sights
1 National Taiwan Museum of Art A2

Sleeping
Chance Hotel .... (see 10)
2 Fuh Chun Hotel D3
3 Plaza Hotel D3

Information
4 Bank of Taiwan D2
5 Post Office C3
6 Taichung Hospital C2

Transport
7 Fengyuan Bus Company D3
8 Nantou Bus Company D2
9 Taichung Bus Company Station D3
10 UBus D3

schedule or enquire at the Visitor Information Centre.

UBus (統聯客運; www.ubus.com.tw) has frequent buses to Taipei (NT$150, 2½ hours) and Kaohsiung (NT$200, 4½ hours).

High Speed Rail

A commuter train connects the HSR station with central Taichung and Taichung train station (NT$15, 10 minutes, every 20 minutes). Shuttle buses also travel to central Taichung from the HSR station (average price NT$30, 20 to 40 minutes, every 15 minutes).

An HSR train travels to/from Taipei (NT$700, 60 minutes, three trains hourly). There are also buses from the HSR station to Sun Moon Lake, Puli and Lukang.

Train

There is train service from Taipei (fast/slow train NT$375/241, two/three hours) and Kaohsiung (fast/slow train NT$470/303, 2½/three hours).

Getting Around

Taichung lacks a useful public-transport system (see the Visitor Information Centre for information on the services and schedules available).

At the time of writing two Mass Rapid Transit (MRT lines) had begun construction.

A taxi from Taichung train station to the National Taiwan Museum of Art costs around NT$150; a taxi from the Museum of Art to the HSR station costs NT$250.

Dasyueshan Forest Recreation Area

大雪山國家森林遊樂區

At the western edge of the Snow Mountain Range, the **Big Snow Mountain Forest Recreation Area** (Dàxuě shān Guójiā Sēnlín Yóulè Qū; admission NT$200; ⊙8am-5pm), also known as Anmanshan, rises from 1000m to just under the gold standard of 3000m. This is big country, with densely forested ranges offering panoramic views to rival the Rockies.

There are some fantastic hiking opportunities here and great wildlife viewing, in particular birdwatching. The climate is humid and cool with an average temperature of 12°C, making it a popular retreat during summer. Fogs and mists are common but only add to the supernatural beauty.

Sights & Activities

Hiking

Forestry Road 200 SCENIC AREA

Here's another of those incredible routes in Taiwan that take you from one forest zone to the next in record time. But the 49km-long 200 from Dongshi to, well, the end of the line, may offer the fastest change of all, going from a subtropical landscape of fruit orchards and broadleaf forest, through a magical mixed zone where cypress and cedar stand beside giant tree palms and ferns, to a pure high-mountain coniferous forest in just 1½ hours. The Alishan Forest Train, by contrast, does the same in 3½ hours.

If you want to know what it would be like to bike this road, check out this blog: http://peaceandride.eklablog.net/by-train-to-dasyueshan-forest-road-a748780.

Yuanzui–Shaolai–Xiaoshue National Trail HIKING TRAIL

This popular trail (鳶嘴稍來小雪山國家步道; Yuānzuǐ Shāolái Xiǎoxuěshān Guójiā Bùdào) runs northwest of the road, and though its total length is only 15.5km, it takes two days to complete. Most hikers just do a small portion (five to six hours) starting at the Km27 mark. It's about one to 1½ hours uphill on a great path to **Yuanzui Shan** (鳶嘴山; elevation 2130m), where a steel observation tower gives you views of Yushan on a clear day.

THE MATSU PILGRIMAGE

In the pantheon of gods that are regularly worshipped in Taiwan, only Guanyin has a status that rivals Matsu. Although often referred to as the goddess of the sea, Matsu in fact is officially Tianhou (Empress of Heaven) and her divine efficacy extends from protecting fishermen, to helping women in childbirth, to restoring social order. The unquestioned patron deity of Taiwan, and a powerful symbol of Taiwanese identity, Matsu's common name is an affectionate term meaning something like granny.

Of course, she was once simply Lin Mo-niang (林默娘; born 960 AD) from Meizhou, Fujian. Or maybe not so simply. Even as a young girl Mo-niang was noted for her exceptional intelligence, and quickness to master Taoist and Buddhist texts. A girl after Hermione Granger's heart, she learned magical arts as a teen and soon began to be regarded as a female shaman. Her particular forte was helping fishermen survive at sea and one of her most famous exploits was rescuing her own father.

Mo-liang died young (aged 28), but almost immediately people in Meizhou began to worship her. As word of her divine efficaciousness spread (ie her ability to grant wishes and offer protection), so did her cult. Over the centuries Matsu received imperial recognition after recognition for her good works. Her highest title, Empress of Heaven, was conferred after she reportedly assisted in overthrowing Dutch rule in Taiwan (by stemming the tides it is said).

Matsu worship came to Taiwan with the earliest settlers and her oldest temples date back to the 16th century. Today there are at least 1500 Matsu temples around the island. Statues of the goddess usually depict her with black skin, a beaded veil and a red cape (which she wore to guide ships to harbour). Standing next to her are her loyal attendants, Eyes that See a Thousand Miles and Ears that Hear upon the Wind, two demons that she subjugated and rescued from hell.

Chenlan Temple 鎮瀾宮

Pilgrimages from daughter temples to mother (see boxed text, p343) have long been a part of the Matsu cult in Taiwan. The most famous is associated with the Chenlan Temple in Dajia, Taichung. But it wasn't also so.

Worshippers from Chenlan began a pilgrimage to Beigang's Chaotien Gong some time in the 19th century, but they were one of many and clearly in a subordinate position. The change in status came in the late 1980s when an ambitious temple chairman (and convicted criminal) named Yen Ching-piao made two controversial decisions: first to travel to Meizhou (Matsu's birthplace) and bring back the first statue from China since the lifting of martial law. Second, to declare that this new statue gave Chenlan Temple such a boost in divine powers that it was now the equal of Chaotien Gong.

The move rocked the Matsu community and Chaotien Gong's board of directors outright refused to accept the equal relationship. Not one to be deterred, Yen simply changed the traditional route of the pilgrimage from Chaotien Gong to the more accommodating Fengtian Gong, Chaotien's longstanding rival (see boxed text, p207).

Throughout the 1990s the Chenlan pilgrimage grew in size and importance under Yen's leadership, which involved, among other things, very clever manipulation of the media. Today it is likely to be one of the largest mass religious pilgrimages left on earth.

Matsu & National Politics

Matsu has been called the kingmaker for the way top politicians vie for her support (or that of her most famous temples). And not just politicians in Taiwan. In 2010 Beijing had

From here another two to three hours along steep rocky ledges (like a high-altitude Wuliao Jian) takes you to **Shaolai Shan** (稍來山; elevation 2307m). Another hour takes you back to the main road at the Km37 mark. You can also just hike up to Shaolai Shan and back. It's possible to continue walking to **Anmashan** (鞍馬山; Ānmǎshān) and down to the village at the Km43 mark but that would take another day.

Matsu culture inscribed on Unesco's intangible heritage list, an obvious long-term political move to both subsume Taiwanese culture under China's and possibly win hearts here with the recognition of Matsu's importance.

Yen Ching-piao, a hard-core unificationist, has vowed he will use Matsu to deliver Taiwan to China. Given that most Matsu believers have a strong sense of a distinct Taiwanese identity (and that Matsu belief is a focal point of that identity), it's going to be interesting to watch how this plays out.

The Pilgimage

The pilgrimage is the largest and most celebrated religious and folk activity in the country. Hundreds of thousands of pilgrims and spectators from all over the island and abroad escort a palanquin graced by a statue of Matsu from Dajia to Hsinkang, southern Taiwan, and then back again, covering a distance of over 350km. The goddess is carried through 50 towns, and over a million people will see her pass their homes. Some reports say five million people will be involved with the pilgrimage in some way.

Many devotees will follow Matsu for the full nine days (it was extended a day in 2010). They'll jostle each other to touch the sedan chair, while the most devout will jump to the front and actually kneel down on the road to allow the goddess to be carried over them. According to legend, touching the palanquin will make one lucky for a whole year.

The dates for the pilgrimage are announced every year in March. *Bwah bwey* (casting moon blocks) are used to determine the starting dates, though the goddess is only given weekends as a choice. The first, fourth (when the palanquin reaches Fengtian Gong) and last days are the most spectacular, but now many subordinate temples are starting to let their statues and palanquins arrive early to avoid overcrowding and the frequent gang fights that erupt on the last day.

If you decide to join the pilgrimage, note that temples and volunteers along the way provide basic water, meals and accommodation (not that a 7-Eleven is ever far from sight). In 2010 the schedule was as follows:

» Day 1: Pilgrims left Dajia around midnight and ended their walk at **Nanyao Temple** (南瑤宮), Changhua city.

» Day 2: **Fuhsing Temple** (福興宮) in Siluo Township, Yunlin County.

» Day 3: **Fengtien Temple** (奉天宮) in Hsingang Township, Chiayi County.

» Day 4: Main blessing ceremony and a second night at Fengtien Temple.

» Day 5: **Fuhsing Temple** (福興宮) in Siluo Township, Yunlin County.

» Day 6: **Chengan Temple** (奠安宮) in Beidou Township, Changhua County.

» Day 7: **Tienhou Temple** (天后宮) in Changhua city.

» Day 8: **Chaohsing Temple** (朝興宮) in Qingshuei Township, Taichung County.

» Day 9: Pilgrims returned to Chenlan Temple.

For information on the dates and events of each year's pilgrimage, check the website www.dajiamazu.org.tw.

To reach Dajia take a train from Taipei. Chenlan Temple is a few blocks straight ahead as you exit the front of the train station.

No matter which route you take, be prepared. In 2010 a group of foreign hikers wandered off the (clear) trail and spent a bitterly cold night in the mountains before being rescued in the morning.

Wildlife-Watching

Despite being a former logging area, much of the forest cover was not cut, which is one reason it is still so stocked with wildlife. Commonly seen are martins, weasels, white-faced flying squirrels, barking deer and Formosan Macaques.

Even the casual visitor will be rewarded with a little time spent twitching here, Long regarded as Taiwan's top birding location. At least 12 of the 17 endemic species can be spotted here, including the majestic Swinhoe's Pheasant and Mikado Pheasant. We've heard that locals wait at the Km23 mark on Forestry Road 200 for Swinhoe's Pheasant to appear, and the Km47 mark for the Mikado Pheasant.

Sleeping & Eating

There are very pleasant wood **cabins** (04-2587 7901; d Mon-Fri NT$1800, Sat & Sun NT$3600) at the village at the Km43 mark. Set meals (NT$150) are also available and it's best to book both ahead of time. You can book online (http://tsfs.forest.gov.tw; in Chinese) but do call afterwards to confirm.

Information

The **visitor information centre** (遊客中心; 9am-5pm) in the village at the Km43 mark has simple maps of the recreation area.

Getting There & Away

You need your own transport.

ALISHAN NATIONAL SCENIC AREA

05

If you want to see Taiwan's natural environment raw in tooth and nail, visit a national park. If you want to see how humans have tried to make a go at settling on landslide-prone mountains and battered escarpments (as spectacular as they are to merely gaze upon), come to the Alishan National Scenic Area.

From a starting altitude of 300m in the west at Chukou, the 327-sq-km scenic area quickly rises to heights of more than 2600m. The great diversity of climate, soils and landscapes allows for the growing of everything from wasabi and plums to high-mountain oolong tea, the latter some of the best in the world. From the Zhou aboriginals, the original settlers, come foods you've never heard of, such as bird-nest fern, tree tomatoes, *ai yu* jelly and millet wine.

Tourists have been finding their way to this region since the early days of the Japanese period. They come for the local specialities, the natural and manmade landscapes (who doesn't like terraced tea fields?), and more recently the legacy of the colonial period, which includes a very rare narrow-gauge forest train.

Tourism took a massive hit in 2009 after Typhoon Morakot wiped out roads, villages and large sections of the railway tracks. At the time of writing, Hwy 18 was once again passable, but the railway was expected to take years to fully repair. Check on conditions before going up and avoid the days after a typhoon or earthquake or when heavy rains are predicted.

Chiayi 嘉義

05 / POP 270,340

While Chiayi (Jiāyì) is not part of the Alishan National Scenic Area, almost every traveller will have to pass through here on the way there. The narrow-gauge train to the Alishan Forest Recreation Area leaves from Chiayi train station, as do buses and taxis. There are a few better-than-OK sights to recommend in Chiayi, so plan to spend a half day or so before moving on.

Central Chiayi is small enough to walk across in 30 minutes, though air pollution often makes it unpleasant to do so. Most road signs appear with pinyin also. Taxis are plentiful, except in the area west of the train tracks.

History

Chiayi is the capital of Chiayi County and one of the oldest cities in Taiwan. The area was once the home of plains aborigines, but during the Dutch occupation of Taiwan Fujian farmers began to settle in numbers. The name Chiayi was given by the Emperor Chien-lung, intended as a reward for Chiayi citizens taking the 'right' side in an 18th-century islandwide rebellion. The city prospered under Qing and later Japanese rule (when it was the capital of the sugar industry and one of the most modern cities in Taiwan), but today sadly there is too little of this prosperity and heritage remaining.

Sights

FREE **Cochin Ceramic Museum** MUSEUM

(交趾陶館; Jiāozhǐtáo Guǎn; 275 Jungshiao Rd; 9am-noon & 1.30-5pm Wed-Sun) An excellent

Chiayi

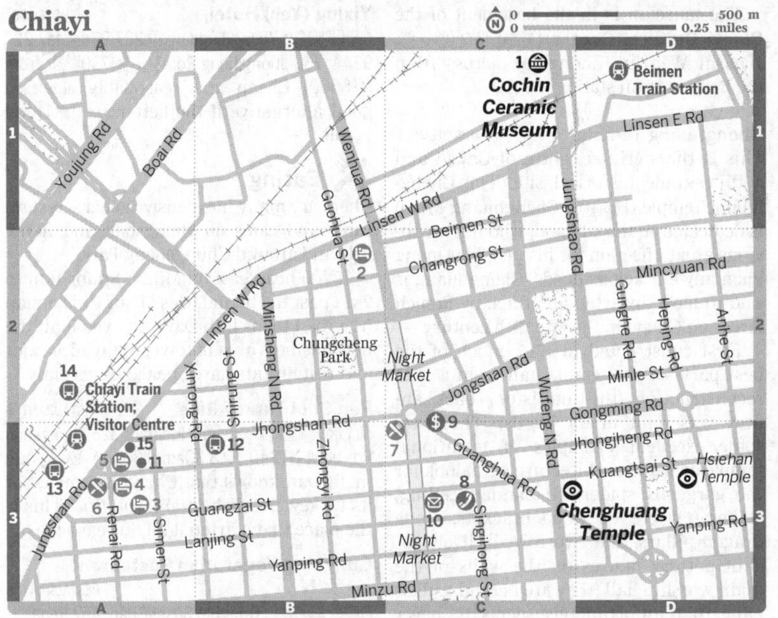

Chiayi

Top Sights
- Chenghuang Temple C3
- Cochin Ceramic Museum C1

Sights
- 1 Chiayi Cultural Centre C1

Sleeping
- 2 Maison de Chine B2
- 3 Country Hotel A3
- 4 Jiaxin Hotel A3
- 5 Yixing (Yes) Hotel A3

Eating
- Cantonese Restaurant .... (see 2)
- 6 Gongbing Vegetarian Restaurant A3
- 7 Pen Shui Turkey Rice C3

Information
- 8 Chunghwa Telecom C3
- 9 First Commercial Bank C3
- 10 GPO C3
- 11 Laundromat A3

Transport
- 12 Chiayi Bus Company B3
- 13 Chiayi County Bus Company A3
- 14 Kuo Kuang Hao Bus Company A2
- 15 Scooter Rentals A3

little museum dedicated to cochin *(jiāo zhǐ táo)* a low-fired, brightly coloured glaze style of ceramic traditionally used for temple decoration. You've probably seen cheap work in this style in tourist shops around the island but much of the work here is outstanding. Look for the set of figurines performing what look like different opera gestures: you'd swear they had muscles and bone under their robes, so realistic is the motion captured by the artist.

Cochin artists have been working in the Chiayi area since the Qing dynasty and have won praise from as far afield as Japan and France. **Yeh Wang** (1826–91) is widely regarded as a founder of the cochin tradition in Taiwan and one of its top practitioners. Pictures of his work are featured on a large poster (look for the fat and skinny guys), but to see the real thing you need to visit the Yeh Wang Museum in Tainan County (see boxed text, p245).

The museum is in the basement of the **Chiayi Cultural Centre** (嘉義市文化中心; Jiāyìshì WénHuà Zhōngxīn), across from the Beimen train station.

Chenghuang Temple TAOIST TEMPLE
This is the spiritual centre of Chiayi and a third-grade historical site. The Chenghuang Temple (城隍廟; Chénghuáng Miào) is dedicated to the city god, who has an obvious great affection for his people. Among his many efficacious deeds, Chenghuang is said to have thwarted an attack by French forces on Chiayi in the late 19th century.

First constructed in 1715, much of the best parts of the temple hail from a 1941 reconstruction (the multistory back annexe was built in the 1980s). There are some excellent examples of traditional temple arts and architecture here: look for the gorgeous spiderweb plafond ceiling, elaborately carved wood brackets, stone dragon pillars, and two rows of lively cochin pottery figures on the walls of the main worship hall (they are behind a glass pane that unfortunately seems to never be washed). The traditional double-eave roof sports elegant swallowtail ridges and colourful figures in *jiǎnniàn* (mosaiclike temple decoration. You can check it out from the upper floors of the back annexe.

Sleeping

Jiaxin Hotel HOTEL $
(嘉新大飯店; Jiāxīn Dàfàndiàn; ☎222 2280; 685 Jhongjheng Rd; 中正路685號; d/tw from NT$600/1200; @) Rooms are clean, not too small and overall good value for money. Some have ADSL (for an extra NT$200).

Maison de Chine HOTEL $$
(兆品酒店; Zhàopǐn Jiǔdiàn; ☎229 2233; 257 Wenhua Rd; 文化路257號; d/tw NT$3600/4000; @) One of the top hotels in town, offering a 30% discount on weekdays. Facilities include a business centre, small fitness room and VIP lounge, restaurant and cafe. English service is available.

Country Hotel HOTEL $
(國園大飯店; Guóyuán Dàfàndiàn; ☎223 6336; fax 223 6345; 678 Guangzai St; 光彩街678號; d/tw NT$1260/2300;@) A little more expensive and with a better atmosphere than other hotels offering similar rooms, but offers a car park next door and free snacks in the evening. Usual weekday rates for a double are NT$950.

Yixing (Yes) Hotel HOTEL $$
(義興旅館; Yìxīng Lǚguǎn; ☎227 9344; fax 227 9344; 730 Jhongjheng Rd; 中正路730號; r from NT$600) Cheap and reasonably clean, a good alternative if the better Jiaxin Hotel is full.

Eating

There are many inexpensive generic restaurants and cafes on Jhongshan and Renai Rds and around Chungcheng Park.

If you head east on Minzu Rd for 1km to 2km past the boundaries of our Chiayi map (the road turns into Daya Rd), you'll hit the new business area of town. Many nice cafes and restaurants have opened up recently.

Pen Shui Turkey Rice RESTAURANT $
(噴水火雞飯; Pēnshuǐ Huǒjīfàn; 325 Jhongshan Rd; bowl NT$40; ☎8.30am-9.30pm) Everyone in Taiwan knows that Chiayi is famous for its turkey rice dish *(huǒ jī ròu fàn)*. This is the place that started it all 60 years ago.

Gongbing Vegetarian Restaurant RESTAURANT $
(宮賓素食館; Gōngbīn Sùshí Guǎn; 457 Renai Rd; average meal NT$100; ⏲6.15am-7.30pm) Long-running buffet-style vegetarian restaurant.

Cantonese Restaurant RESTAURANT $
(Maison de Chine, 3rd fl, 257 Wenhua Rd; dishes from NT$120) One of the best high-end restaurants in Chiayi, serving a great dim sum.

Night Market MARKET $
(Wenhua Rd) Good for cheap food. Located between Mincyuan and Chuei Yang Rds.

Information

Internet cafes are located around the train station; ask at the Visitor Information Centre for the latest details. Most hotels offer free ADSL.

There are numerous banks and ATMs on Renai Rd near Chiayi train station.

Chiayi City Government (www.chiayi.gov.tw) Good for general information about the city, including sights and activities for tourists.

First Commercial Bank (第一商業銀行; 307 Jhongshan Rd) ATMs and currency exchange.

Laundromat (投幣式洗衣店; 701 Jhongjheng Rd; ⏲24hr) This DIY place is just up the road from the Jiaxin Hotel.

St Martin De Porres Hospital (天主教聖馬爾定醫院; ☎275 6000; 565 Daya Rd, Sec 2).

Visitor Information Centre (遊客服務中心; ☎225 6649; ⏲8.30-5pm) The centre is located inside Chiayi train station, it provides English brochures and travel information about Chiayi, Alishan and pretty much anywhere else you want to go. Staff speak English.

Getting There & Away

Chiayi is the gateway to the Alishan National Scenic Area.

Bus

Chiayi Bus Company (嘉義客運; ☎275 0895; 503 Jhongshan Rd) has buses to Guanziling (NT$78, one hour, every 30 minutes).

Chiayi County Bus Company (嘉義縣公車; ☎224 3140) runs buses from early morning to late afternoon to Alishan (NT$212, 2½ hours, hourly). Check the full English schedule at the Visitor Information Centre. There is also frequent service to Beigang (NT$62, 45 minutes) and Budai Port (NT$109, 1½ hours, hourly), and less-frequent service to Ruili and Fenqihu (see the Visitor Information Centre for the schedule).

Kuo Kuang Hao Bus Company (國光客運公司; www.kingbus.com.tw) offers buses to Taipei (NT$330, three hours, every 30 minutes) and other cities on the west coast. Buses leave from its new bus station at back of the train station. Other intercity bus companies also leave from here.

Boat

All Star (www.aaaaa.com.tw) runs in the summer months between Putai Port (near Chiayi) and Makung on Penghu (NT$1000, 1½ hours).

High Speed Rail

A free shuttle bus connects the HSR station with Chiayi train station (40 minutes, every 20 minutes). At the time of writing the shuttle bus stop was being moved to the back of the train station along with the intercity bus companies.

Trains travel frequently to Taipei (NT$1080, 90 minutes, four trains hourly).

Train

At the time of writing the famous narrow-gauge train to Alishan was out of commission until 2013 at the earliest (though parts were repaired further up the line).

Trains travel to/from Taipei (fast/slow train NT$600/386, three/4½ hours) and Kaohsiung (fast/slow train NT$246/158, one/two hours).

Getting Around

Scooter rentals (機車出租; per day NT$200 to NT$400) are available from shops across from Chiayi train station. An International Driving Permit (IDP) and ID is required to rent.

Alishan Forest Recreation Area 阿里山

☎05

The high-mountain resort of **Alishan** (Ālǐshān; admission NT$200) has been one of Taiwan's top tourist draws since the 1920s. While other spots around the island offer equally good or better mountain scenery, Alishan has a peerless draw in a charming old narrow-gauge railway, and a reputation for glorious sunrises, sunsets and the 'sea of clouds' phenomenon. It's a good thing, too, as the village is looking very tired these days and would not otherwise be high on the list of travelling destinations.

You can visit Alishan at any time of year but weekdays are best when the crowds are thinner. In spring the cherry trees are in bloom, while in autumn and winter the sunrises and sunsets are said to be the best. Summer is busy with city folk looking for a cool retreat.

Late-afternoon thunderstorms are common in spring and summer, and during winter the mountaintops may get a light dusting of snow. Summer temperatures average from 13°C to 24°C, while those in winter are 5°C to 16°C. You should bring a sweater and a raincoat no matter what time of year you visit.

Despite its size, it's simple to get your bearings in Alishan and the visitor centre across from the car park has an excellent English map. Most people stay in what is technically Zhongzheng Village, though most just refer to it as Alishan Village. The village comprises a car park, post office, bus station, visitor centre, and most of the hotels and restaurants.

Paths around the park are broad and attractions are usually marked with English signs. Traffic is not permitted (except work vehicles) in the park, so you can walk on roads as well as trails without concern.

History

In former times the recreation area was likely Zhou hunting grounds rather than the site of permanent settlements. Modern development began with the Japanese, who became aware of the abundant stands of cypress *(hinoki)* growing in the misty mountains. In 1906 the first railway into the mountain was established and by 1913 the tracks had reached Alishan at Chaoping station. This is the famous Alishan Forest Train still in operation today.

Logging was the mainstay of activity in Alishan, but the area attracted hikers and sightseers early on. The Japanese, in fact, encouraged tourism as a way to open up the region and excuse their pacification of aboriginal tribes. In 1926 they opened a 43km trail from Chaoping to the summit of Yushan, later shortening it by extending the train to Tatajia.

Logging continued into the 1970s when the first steps towards creating a forest park were taken. In the 1980s Hwy 18 opened, and the fast connection between Alishan and Chiayi caused an explosion in tourism. In 2001 the Alishan National Scenic Area (which covers far more than just this recreation area) opened with the mandate to regulate and limit development. These days the administration's hands are filled repairing typhoon damage and getting things back to how they were.

Sights & Activities

Alishan Forest Train OLD TRAIN

Running on narrow-gauge track (762mm) and ascending to 2216m from a starting altitude of 30m in just 3½ hours, the forest train offers a ride that can be found today in only two other locations: the Chilean Andes and the Indian Himalayas. It's rightly seen by Taiwanese as a national treasure and a potential candidate for Unesco Heritage status.

The total length of track is 86km and, remarkably, within this short distance three climatic zones are traversed. From a usual muggy start at Chiayi train station (30m above sea level), the train rolls slowly though a tropical zone comprised of banana and longan plantations and then forests of figs, longans, acacia and bamboo. From 800m to 1800m the train runs through a subtropical zone with camphor, Machilus and Japanese cedar, in addition to tea fields. Finally, in the last section, with the temperatures cooling, a temperate forest of cypress, Taiwania, hemlock and pine predominates.

This 'rolling botanical museum', as it has been called, is one of the most enjoyable ways to take in a sampling of Taiwan's astonishing biodiversity.

As you ride up it may feel like the train is going backwards. It is! The track system employs a unique system of switchbacks (much like hiking trails on a steep mountainside) that allow it to traverse slopes ordinarily too steep for trains.

At the time of writing the line was operating only from Alishan village to the Chushan sunrise area. The forestry bureau was promising to have the 72km stretch from Chiayi to the village restored by 2013. We wish them good luck.

Sunrise

We're not big fans of sunrise viewings but it's *de rigueur* here. When you check into a hotel you will inevitably hear the question *'Yàobúyào kàn rìchū?'*, which means 'Do you want to see the sunrise?' Say no, and you'll get a funny look as if you just admitted to wearing diapers.

Assuming you do go, there are two main viewing venues: the summit of **Chushan** (祝山; Zhùshān; 2489m) and **Tatajia** (塔塔加; Tǎtǎjiā), a mountain pass 2610m above sea level in nearby Yushan National Park.

To reach Chushan you can either take the train from Chaoping station (departure time varies according to the season), or hike up along the **Chushan Sunrise Viewing Trail** (祝山觀日出步道; Zhùshān Guānrìchū Bùdào). The train takes about 25 minutes, while hiking can take up to 1½ hours if you start in the village.

If you wish to see the sunrise at Tatajia, pay for a seat on one of the sunrise-tour minibuses (NT$300, three hours). Every hotel can arrange it for you. Buses come directly to your hotel.

The minibus has several advantages over the train, one being that it stops at numerous scenic locations, such as the monkey-viewing area and the site of a few ancient trees, on the way back from the sunrise viewing.

Hiking

There are many trails in the park, ranging from strolls around flower gardens to hikes up mountaintops requiring several hours or more to complete. On the **Giant Tree Trail** (巨木群棧道; Jùmùqún Zhàndào) you'll find majestic old cypresses up to 2000 years old. This trail is best done towards dark when the crowds have left.

For a bit of peace and quiet and a few hours' workout on a natural path, the **Duei-Kao-Yueh Trail** (對高岳步道; Dùigāoyuè Bùdào) is just the ticket. The Chushan Sunrise Trail, and the viewing platform, is so

A TALE OF TWO TEMPLES

Rivalry among temples is all too common in Taiwan where the rewards for the victor are not only prestige, but access to pilgrims (and hence fundraising powers). Two of the oldest and most impressive Matsu temples in Taiwan have been at it for six decades, only patching things up in 2009.

What was the dispute all about? The leaders of both were unhappy with the other's claim that it represented the area's orthodox Matsu lineage.

Fengtian Temple (Fengtian Gong) 奉天宮

The committee that runs this temple (Fèngtiān Gōng), founded in 1622, claims it was the first Matsu temple on mainland Taiwan. The story goes that one day a man named Lin brought a statue of Matsu from her original temple on Meizhou and established a small shrine at the goddess' request. Over time the shrine (and later small temple) became an important centre of worship in the area.

But it was not without its troubles. With a history worthy of a Monty Python sketch, the original temple is said to have collapsed, been rebuilt, collapsed again and then been destroyed by flood. Relocated, the new temple was ruined by successive earthquakes until finally, finally, the present structure – built in 1922 – has survived to this day.

Chaotian Temple (Chaotian Gong) 朝天宮

Just a few kilometres away from Fengtian Gong, this temple (Cháotiān Gōng) was founded in 1694 when a monk brought a Matsu statue to the area and, like Mr Lin, was instructed by the goddess to leave her image there. Also like Fengtian, the Chaotian Temple was at one time or another razed by fire, flood and earthquake. It was even occupied by Japanese troops in 1895. In 1908 a major restoration was undertaken and it is this structure (minus a few neon tigers) that is largely the one you can see today.

The Rivalry

The rivalry between the Fengtian and Chaotian is conditional on the complex web of relations between what are called mother and daughter temples (see boxed text, p343). Fengtian stresses that it is the oldest link to the Meizhou mother temple, while Chaotian stresses that its temple is, in fact, the older (since it was not relocated) and that the power of Matsu is more obviously shown by its history and development.

The rivalry took a turn for the worse in 1989 when the famous Dajia Matsu pilgrimage was rerouted from Fengtian to Chaotian temple (thus increasing the latter's claim to greater status). Reconciliation finally took place in 2009 when the respective temple committees agreed that worshipers at Fengtian Temple would take their Matsu statue on an 'ice breaking' visit to Chaotien Temple and burn incense together.

It's well worth taking a day out of your travels in Taiwan to visit these temples. Both are beautiful structures filled with elaborate relief in wood and stone, and many historical relics. Chaotian Temple in particular has a grand open stone structure quite unlike any other temple in Taiwan. Of course, both are riots of parading, prostrating, praying and merry-making pilgrims around the time of Matsu's birthday.

Getting There & Away

Buses to Beigang leave frequently from the **Chiayi County Bus Company station** (嘉義縣公車站; fare NT$62) located by the Chiayi train station. The trip takes 45 minutes and Chaotian is just a couple of minutes' walk from the station. It's also possible to take the High Speed Rail (HSR) to Chiayi train station and then a taxi (NT$400).

To get to Fengtian Temple, catch a taxi from Beigang.

busy at dawn but empty of people by the late morning.

For more information, including times and distances for trails, pick up the brochure at the visitor centre.

Festivals & Events

The **Cherry Blossom Festival** runs in March or April for two weeks while the trees are in bloom. This is an extremely busy time for the park. To our eyes though, Taiwanese cherry trees look spindly.

Sleeping

Alishan has more than a dozen hotels, the majority of which are in the village below the car park. Most hotels offer weekday and low-season discounts, which can be up to 50%, though prices have been rising in recent years, and quality is dropping.

The high season is considered Chinese New Year and during the Cherry Blossom Festival. Saturday nights have increased rates, too.

Alishan House HOTEL $$$

(阿里山賓館; Ālǐshān Bīnguǎn; ☎267 9811; r from NT$7620) The management has been strangling the old-world charm from this Japanese-era hotel for years, but for now it's still Alishan's top hotel. The food in the restaurant is not much better than what's available around the carpark, but the outdoor cafe has a lovely setting among the cherry trees. Make sure to get the hotel to pick you up as it's a bit of walk from the village car park or train station.

Shermuh HOTEL $

(神木賓館; Shénmù Bīnguǎn; ☎267 9511; fax 267 9667; s/d/tw NT$800/2800/3700) Newish hotel with clean, simply furnished rooms. For single travellers there are a limited number of the tiny single-bed rooms, so book ahead. The hotel is located off a lower road, which you can reach by taking a set of stairs beside the visitor centre.

Catholic Hostel HOTEL $

(天主堂; Tiānzhǔtáng; ☎267 9602; dm/d/tw NT$400/1200/2400) Nothing fancy, and there is a slight institutional feel about the place, but this is it for rock-bottom budget accommodation in Alishan. The hostel, down a side road to the left of the park entrance gate, is not always open (especially on weekdays) so call before you go.

Kao Feng (KF) Hotel HOTEL $$

(高峰大飯店; Gāofēng Dàfàndiàn; ☎267 9411; www.alishan.net.tw/kaofeng; d/tw NT$3500/4800) Close to Shermuh in both location and comfort, though rooms are slightly more spacious.

Eating

Most of the restaurants in Alishan are clustered around the car park and serve similar decent fare at similar prices: hotpots, stir-fries and local vegetable and meat dishes for around NT$100 to NT$200. Most are open for breakfast, lunch and dinner, though occasionally places close for one shift. English menus are usually available. There is a 7-Eleven in the car-park area selling the usual sandwiches, noodles and drinks.

Shopping

Alishan High Mountain Tea (阿里山高山茶; Ālǐshān Gāoshān Chá), dried plums, cherries, fruit liqueurs, *moji* (sticky rice) in almost every conceivable flavour, and aboriginal crafts are sold in the shops just back from the car park.

Information

There's free internet at the Chunghua Telecom (中華電信) office beside the visitor centre. Both the village post office (郵局) and the 7-Eleven have ATMs but you'd be advised to bring cash with you.

Alishan National Scenic Area (www.ali-nsa.net) The English version has not been updated to reflect the typhoon damage.

Public health clinic (衛生所; Wèishēngsuǒ; ☎267 9806) The clinic has irregular hours, but is always open in the mornings and usually the afternoons. It's just down the road from the Catholic Hostel, near the entrance gate to the park.

Visitor centre (旅客服務中心; ☎267 9917; ⌚8.30am-5.30pm) Offers maps and brochures in English.

Getting There & Away

Bus

Buses to Chiayi (NT$214, 2½ hours, hourly) run from 9am to 5pm and leave from in front of the 7-Eleven. An English schedule is posted.

Train

There are three train stations in Alishan; however, there were no trains running at the time of writing.

Alishan station In Zhongzheng Village (main train station).

Chaoping station A few minutes by train up the track.

Chushan station Twenty-five minutes by train up the track. It's where passengers watch the sunrise.

Fenqihu 奮起湖

A former repair and maintenance station for the Alishan Railway, Fenqihu (Fènqǐhú) sits about halfway up the line at an altitude of 1405m. Once a popular stop for both tour-bus and rail passengers, the future of this old Hakka village is uncertain. At the time of writing, the road in was barely passable and the village's water supply sporadic.

Sights & Activities

The **train station** platform is an obvious place to begin your exploration of Fenqihu, especially the garage accommodating two old engines. Across the tracks and up a small set of stairs to the left is a fenced-in strand of the curious **square bamboo** (四方竹; *sìfāng zhú*).

If the 7km **Fenqihu–Rueili Historic Trail** (奮瑞古道; Fèn-Ruì Gǔdào) is repaired, you can hike it from, you guessed it, Fenqihu all the way to Rueili in about three to four hours. Much of the trail runs through bamboo forests that look like something out of a *wushu* (martial arts) film. In Rueili the trail ends (or begins) on the main road into town, close to hotels and restaurants, and the visitor centre. The trail should be mapped and signed in English.

Sleeping

Catholic Hostel HOTEL $
(天主堂; Tiānzhǔtáng; ☎256 1134; http://aj-centersvd.myweb.hinet.net/; dm/d with shared bathroom NT$250/500) Run by a sweet Swiss sister (who speaks good English), the hostel (on the grounds of the Arnold Janseen Activity Centre) is as clean as a whistle and a cozy, quiet place to stay. The hostel is a few minutes' walk downhill from the train station.

Eating

Restaurant hours in Fenqihu are not fixed but expect places to close early (or not open at all) on weekdays. A meal for two of mountain vegetables and game costs NT$600.

> **UNSTABLE ALISHAN**
>
> Typhoon damage to roads and basic infrastructure made travel into much of the Alishan National Scenic Area difficult, if not impossible, during the time of writing. The following areas may be open by the time you read this, but check before going, especially after heavy rains or earthquakes. We expect temporary and possibly permanent impassable conditions in much of this region for years to come.

Some local specialities to look for include fresh Alishan wasabi and 'tree tomatoes' (樹番茄; *shù fānqié; Cyphomandra betacea*), which tastes like a combination of tomato and passionfruit.

Fancylake Hotel LUNCHBOX OUTLET $
(奮起湖大飯店; Fènqǐhú Dàfàndiàn; lunchbox NT$100) Just behind the train station at the start of the 'old street', Fancylake is famous for its lunchboxes (鐵路便當; *Tǐelù Biàndāng*; rice, vegies and meat) served in special wooden souvenir containers.

Getting There & Away

Check at the visitor centre in Chiayi for the latest bus schedule. Everything is up in the air these days due to the typhoon damage. If all goes well, the forest train will run at least from Chiayi to Fenqihu by 2012.

Rueili (Juili) 瑞里

POP 970 / ELEV 1000M

Rueili (Ruìlǐ) was one of the first places that 18th-century Fujian pioneers into the Alishan region established as a permanent settlement. Today the small, quiet, temperate mountain community thrives on tourism and tea growing. In addition to panoramic mountain scenes, bamboo forests, waterfalls and historic walking trails, pesticide-free Rueili offers one of the best venues in Taiwan for watching fireflies.

Sights & Activities

Rueili has several beautiful waterfalls, including **Cloud Pool Waterfall** (雲潭瀑布; Yúntán Pùbù), just past the Km22 mark on County Rd 122.

The **Ruitai Old Trail** (瑞太古道; Ruìtài Gǔdào) was once used for transporting goods between Rueili and Taihe. It's now part of the overall hiking system that connects Fenqihu to Rueili.

Fireflies (螢火蟲; *yínghuǒchóng*) show off their bioluminescent skills from March to June. The mountainsides literally sparkle throughout the night.

Sleeping & Eating

The Rueitai Tourist Centre can help with homestays and hotel bookings.

Most hotels and homestays have their own restaurant (set meals NT$100 to NT$200) and there are scattered places to eat around town as well. A small grocery sells instant noodles, canned goods, eggs, fruit and vegies, and drinks.

Roulan Lodge HOTEL **$$**
(若蘭山莊; Ruòlán Shānzhuāng; ☎250 1210; fax 250 1555; 10 Rueili Village; d/tw NT$1800/2400, cabins from NT$3200) One of the most popular places to stay in Rueili, especially during the firefly season when nightly tours are on offer. The owners of the lodge have been recognised nationwide for their efforts at preserving the natural heritage of Rueili. There is a weekday discount of 30%.

Information

Rueitai Tourist Centre (瑞太遊客中心; ☎250 1070; 1-1 Rueili Village; ⏲8.30am-5pm) Offers brochures, internet and a very knowledgeable, friendly staff of locals.

Getting There & Around

If you aren't hiking from Fenqihu, there are buses to/from Chiayi. See the Chiayi visitor centre for the latest schedule.

You need your own transport to get around Rueili.

Fengshan 豐山

POP 365 / ELEV 750M

When Chinese immigrants began to settle in the mountainous regions of Alishan, life was a challenge. In remote Fengshan (Fēngshān) it hasn't gotten much better. The village and its pesticide-free fields of tea, sugar cane and mountain vegetables appear to remain intact only by the grace of God. And in many ways they do. Typhoons and landslides (and the occasional earthquake) ravage Fengshan almost yearly. After the extensive destruction brought by Typhoon Morakot, we don't expect this area to be open to travellers for many years.

Keep an eye open for any news, though, as there's an appealing ruggedness to Fengshan that makes it one of the best off-the-beaten-track destinations in Taiwan. This land of stratified canyons and dark-green mountains that fill up half the sky is a treasure trove for DIY exploration.

Shanmei 山美

From 1989 to 1999 the Zhou people of Shanmei (Shānměi) closed off the dying Danayigu Creek to all outsiders. The plan was to clean up the river and protect and restock the dwindling fish population. The success of the project, soon called the **Danayigu Ecological Park** (達娜伊谷自然生態保育公園; Dánàyī Gǔ Zìrán Shēngtài Bǎoyù Gōngyuán), amazed everyone. The river teemed with life and the surrounding parkland became a model of ecological diversity.

At the time of writing, however, the park was in tatters. It would be worth checking out the status in Chiayi if you are planning to head into the area. To reach Shanmei, take Hwy 18 east of Chiayi towards Alishan. At Lungmei (龍美; Lóngměi) turn south on County Rd 129, from where it's an hour from Chiayi by car. There is no public transport.

CHANGHUA & YUNLIN COUNTIES

Changhua

☎04 / POP 234,310

Changhua City (Zhānghuà), the capital and political heart of Changhua County, has usually been thought of as a gateway to the old town of Lukang, but there are some treats in the town itself, including stately old temples, a giant Buddha on a hilltop, some good biking and a rare fan-shaped train garage that nestles a half-dozen old steam engines.

Birders should note that Changhua is on the migratory route of the grey-faced buzzard and that the hilltop with the Great Buddha Statue affords a 360-degree panoramic view.

Changhua is not a compact city, but you needn't wander too far from the train station during your stay. Even the Great Buddha Statue is only a couple of kilometres to

Changhua (Zhanghua)

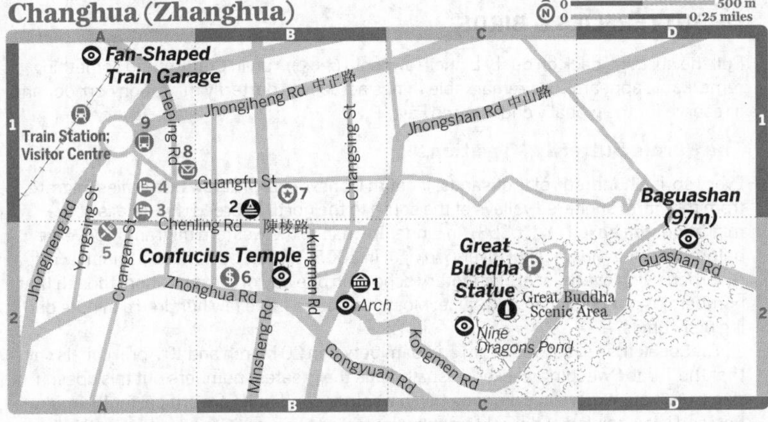

Changhua (Zhanghua)

Top Sights
Baguashan (97m) ... D2
Confucius Temple ... B2
Fan-Shaped Train Garage ... A1
Great Buddha Statue ... C2

Sights
1 Changhua Arts Museum & Hongmao Well ... B2
2 Yuanching Temple ... B1

Sleeping
3 Ing Shan Hotel ... A1
4 Rich Royal Hotel ... A1

Eating
5 Cat Mouse Noodle ... A2

Information
6 Bank Of Taiwan ... B2
7 National Immigration Agency ... B1
8 Post Office ... A1

Transport
9 Changhua Bus Company ... A1

the east. Road signs around the town are large, bright and green, displaying easily read pinyin.

Sights & Activities

Confucius Temple CONFUCIUS TEMPLE
(孔廟; Kŏng Miào; 30 Kungmen Rd; 8am-5pm, closed national holidays) This 1726 beauty both ranks as one of the oldest Confucian temples in Taiwan and as a first-class historical relic. There's an inscribed plaque in the ancestral hall donated by the Qing dynasty emperor Chien Long. Don't miss this temple if you are in Changhua.

Every year on Confucius' birthday (28 September) there is a colourful dawn ceremony.

Baguashan SCENIC AREA
Changhua is best known for the 22m-high **Great Buddha Statue** (八卦山大佛像; Bāguàshān Dàfóxiàng) that sits atop **Baguashan** (八卦山; Bāguàshān) looking down over the city. The statue and its surrounding parkland are noted for a harmonious and tranquil atmosphere. But it wasn't always so.

Baguashan slopes towards Changhua, affording views not only over the whole of the city, but far out to sea. Not surprisingly, it was for centuries an important military observation zone. After the Sino-Japanese War ceded Taiwan to Japan, a great battle was fought on these grounds between Taiwanese resistance fighters and imperial troops. The militarisation of Baguashan seems to have ended after this.

In 1962 the Great Buddha was completed after 10 years of work and in recent years the entire mountain has been turned into a park, with wooden walkways, pavilions and playground areas for children. It makes for pleasant strolling, especially in the spring when the snow-white flowers of the Youtong trees are in bloom.

OF BUTTERFLIES & BIRDS

Pull the curtains back on dusty Linnei Township (林內), Yunlin County, and something remarkable appears. Two remarkable things actually: a butterfly migration corridor and a reserve for the globally endangered Fairy Pitta.

The Purple Butterfly Migration

Every spring hundreds of thousands, if not millions, of purple crow butterflies migrate from the warm sheltered valleys of the south to the north to breed (for details of the migration, see boxed text, p358). In Linnei Township, the western migrants converge before crossing the Choshui River (濁水溪). In 2005, 10,000 butterflies a minute were recorded flying over a local elementary school on one day of the migration, though that number has not been matched since. Most years it's a *mere* few hundred a minute during peak times.

That peak time is between 7am and 9am between 20 March and 10 April. Locals say that the Tomb Sweeping weekend usually sees the greatest numbers but this doesn't ring true in our experience. For one thing, weather conditions are critical for the migration and if it is raining or if a cold front has come in blowing winds from the north, the butterflies won't be moving. Suffice to say, there are no guarantees.

The best place to see the butterflies on the move is **Linbei Village Chukou** (林北村觸口; Línběicūn Chùkǒu), where Provincial Hwy 3 and National Fwy 3 almost touch. It's a couple of kilometres east of Linnei (the town) on Provincial Hwy 3 and is literally just a shrine, a water-management office and a couple of rice fields under the freeway overpass.

You can't miss this place during migration time as there will be posters everywhere (and on weekends other spectators). Just to confirm your location, look up at the freeway overpass. If you don't see 600m of netting, designed to help the butterflies pass over the highway safely, you are in the wrong spot.

The nets have become part of the migration lore. First set up in 2004, they have helped reduce the road kill from 3% of migrating purples to a negligible 0.3%. During the peak morning hours, traffic is also brought to a crawl and the outside lanes of the freeway closed.

In addition to Linbei Village Chukou, the ridgetop tea-growing village of **Pingding** (坪頂; Píngdǐng) is a good place to spot the butterflies. The abundance of nectar plants on the forested slopes are one reason the purple butterflies make a stop in the region on their way north.

The turn-off for Pingding (marked in English) is just past the main strip in Linnei and before Linbei Village Chukou. Follow the main road 5km up to the ridgetop village. There are trails along the ridges and open fields for viewing butterflies.

Baguashan is a prime **birdwatching** area. During late March and early April migratory Grey-Faced Buzzards and Chinese Sparrow Hawks appear in great numbers. Contact the **Changhua County Wild Bird Society** (☎728 3006) for information.

FREE **Fan-Shaped Train Garage** TRAIN GARAGE

(扇形車庫; Shànxíng Chēkù; ☎724 4537; 1 Changmei Rd; ⏲8am-5pm) A pilgrim's site for train buffs and photographers, the Changhua fan-shaped train garage is the last of its kind in Taiwan. How do we describe this odd bit of engineering? Well, in essence, a single line of track connects with a short section of rotatable track from which 12 radial tracks branch out. A train engine rides up onto the short track, rotates in the direction of its garage, and then proceeds into this garage for maintenance and repairs. The 12-garage depo in Changhua is shaped like a fan and so hence the name; and hence the attraction to aficionados.

The garage accommodates the oldest steamed train engine in Taiwan (CK101, built in 1907) and several others of lesser vintage but still great lustrous mechanical beauty. Visitors need to show ID to enter the garage

The Fairy Pitta

From Pingding village the road continues another 10km winding through subtropical forests until the village of **Huben** (湖本; Húběn). Keep on for another 2.5km and you'll pop out again on Provincial Hwy 3, completely, in essence, a big loop.

A 17.4-sq-km area between the two villages has been designated a major wildlife habitat by Taiwan's Forestry Bureau, and an **Important Bird Area** (IBA) by BirdLife International. The habitat is the world's largest breeding ground for the globally threatened Fairy Pitta (八色鳥; *bā sè niǎo*). This enchanting migratory bird (aptly called the eight-coloured bird in Chinese), arrives in Taiwan in April for the breeding season (which lasts till May). By August the adults and their young have started migrating south, some travelling as far as Borneo.

The whole area has a soft, almost magical, atmosphere. In addition to rare plants, 100-plus bird species (including the Taiwan Partridge, Swinhoe's Pheasant, the Blue Magpie and the rare Malayan Night Heron), almost two dozen amphibians, dozens of butterfly species, Formosan macaques and a whole lot more can be found here. There are various trails and interpretation signs in the areas, mostly with English translations.

And yet 200 hectares of this ecoparadise is under threat from the Hushan Reservoir project, scheduled to be completed in five years. The Taiwanese government claims the dam will have negligible impact on the fairy pitta population, but environmental groups worry that the reservoir will fragment the area, with a resulting great loss of biodiversity. Get here while there's still something to 'get'.

Sleeping & Eating

Nearby Linnei has plenty of noodle shops and other basic eateries.

Eight Color Bird Cafe HOSTEL $

(八色鳥咖啡館; Bā Sè Niǎo Kāfēiguǎn; 0975-209 605; Huben; 湖本; dm Mon-Fri NT$450, Sat & Sun NT$500) Set in an old brick courtyard, this cafe offers meals and drinks and very basic dorm lodging on tatami mats. It's popular with Taiwanese birders on weekends, so try to reserve a spot. The cafe is 2.5km up Township Rd 67 (the road that connects with Pingding) off Provincial Hwy 3 in Huben.

Getting There & Around

During the butterfly migration period a free shuttle bus (8am to 4.30pm) runs from Linnei train station on weekends to Chukou. Alternatively, a bike would be a great way to get around. The entire loop from the train station out to Linbei Village Chukou, up to Pingding, down to Huben and back to the train station is only around 20km. If driving, take National Fwy 3 south and exit at the Linnei Interchange. Head east on Provincial Hwy 3 and look for signs for Huben Eco Village, Pingding or Linbei Village Chukou.

area, but you are allowed to walk right up to the engines and across the radial tracks.

Changhua Arts Museum & Hongmao Well MUSEUM

(彰化藝術館; Zhuānghuà Yìshù Guǎn; 542 Jhongshan Rd, Sec 2; 1.30-9pm Wed-Fri, 9am-9pm Sat & Sun, closed Mon) The museum sits in Jungshan Hall, a lovely heritage building that once again serves as a performance theatre, lecture hall and art gallery.

On the grounds of the museum is the 300-year-old **Hongmao Well** (紅毛井; Hóngmáo Jǐng), the last of the original Dutch-built wells (hence the name Hongmao, meaning 'red hair') in central Taiwan.

Yuanching Temple BUDDHIST TEMPLE

This splendid southern-style temple (元清觀; Yuánqīng Guàn; founded in 1763), just a *bwah bwey* throw away from the Confucian temple, was under repair at the time of writing. When it reopens check out the elegant rooftop swallowtail eaves and the wealth of fine interior woodcarvings.

Cycling

The rolling hills between Baguashan and Ershui offers some fine road cycling. There are a number of marked routes, but you can just follow roads such as the **County Rd 139**, which is a sweet rural route down to Jiji. OK-quality **bikes** (per day NT$100) can be rented across from the train station.

Sleeping

Rich Royal Hotel HOTEL $
(富皇大飯店; Fùhuáng Dàfàndiàn; ☎723 7117; 97 Changan St; 長安街97號; d from NT$800-1200, tw NT$1800) This place feels like a love hotel when you walk down the long garage (where you can park if you are driving) to the check-in counter but it is, in fact, popular with families. Rooms are slightly frilly in design, and ageing a bit, but it's probably your best value for money in town.

Ing Shan Hotel HOTEL $
(櫻山大飯店; Yīngshān Dàfàndiàn; ☎722 9211; 129 Changan St; 長安街129號; d/tw NT$900/1500) A decent budget hotel, with friendly owners.

Eating & Drinking

Changhua is famous for its *ròu yuán* (肉圓; meatballs) and you'll find many places to try them out on Chenling Rd. For more local foods, check out the city's website. For cheap eats and cafes, there are plenty of places around the train station and on Guangfu St. For a beer, head up Chengling Rd past Heping. There are a few bars in the area, some more respectable looking than others.

Cat Mouse Noodle RESTAURANT $
(貓鼠麵; Māoshǔmiàn; 223 Chenglin Rd; noodles from NT$35; ⏲9am-8.30pm) The Changhua tourist website claims this shop's special noodle dish is one of the three culinary treasures of the city. It's a stretch, but the tangy-flavoured noodles are pretty tasty. The shop's odd name arose because the owner's nickname sounds like 'cat mouse' in Taiwanese and not because of anything you'll find in the food.

Information

Bank of Taiwan (台灣銀行; 90 Zhonghua Rd) You can change money here.

Changua County website (http://tourism.chcg.gov.tw) A valuable source of travel information.

Changua city website (www.changhua.gov.tw) Also very helpful.

Visitor centre (☎728 5750; ⏲9am-5pm) Located in the train station, with some of the most helpful English- and Japanese-speaking staff anywhere.

Getting There & Away

Buses to Lukang (NT$47, 30 minutes, every 15 to 30 minutes) depart from the **Changhua Bus Company** (彰化客運; ☎722 4603; 563 Jhongijeng Rd) station, located near the train station.

Trains travel from Taipei (fast/slow train NT$416/268, 2½/three hours) and Kaohsiung (fast/slow train NT$430/276, two/three hours) to Changhua.

Lukang (Lugang) 鹿港

☎04 / POP 84,770

Ninety percent of Lukang (Lùgǎng) is as nondescript as most small towns in Taiwan. But then there is that other 10%. Comprising some of the oldest and most gorgeous temples in the country, and featuring curiously curved streets, art museums in heritage buildings, and dusty old shops where equally dusty old masters create colourful fans, lanterns and tin pieces, it is this small part of Lukang that justifiably brings in the crowds.

People call Lukang a 'living museum' and this is true as much for the food as it is for the buildings and streets. Traditional dishes are cheap and readily available near all of the major sights. Look for the enticingly named phoenix eye cake, dragon whiskers and shrimp monkeys, among many other dishes.

On the central coast and just half an hour from Changhua by bus, Lukang is easily reached from anywhere on the west coast.

You can cover the sights on foot in one long day and there are many more worthy ones than we can list here. English signs point to the major attractions, and most roads sport a pinyin road sign or two (sometimes with different spellings one block to the next).

History

Lukang translates as 'deer harbour', and once large herds of deer gathered here in the lush meadows adjacent to one of the best natural harbours on the west coast. In the 17th century the Dutch came to hunt and trade pelts (which they sold to the Japanese to make samurai armour) and venison. Trade grew and diversified in the 18th century (centred on rice, cloth, sugar, timber and pottery) and Lukang became one of the most thriving commercial cities and ports in Taiwan. Over the years settlers from different provinces and ethnic groups in China made their home here and, almost as a gift to the future, left a legacy of temples and buildings in varying regional styles.

In the 19th century silt deposits began to block the harbour and in 1895 the Japanese closed it to all large ships. The city began to decline. To make matters worse, conservative elements in Lukang refused in the early 20th century to allow trains and modern highways to be built near their city. Lukang became a backwater, only to be reborn decades later when modern Taiwanese began to search for a living connection with the past.

Sights

Longshan Temple BUDDHIST TEMPLE

Built in the late 18th century at a time when Lukang was enjoying its heyday as a vital trade link between Taiwan and China, Longshan Temple (龍山寺; Lóngshān Sì) remains a showcase of southern temple design. The temple is expansive, covering over 10,000 sq metres within its gated walls, so give yourself a few hours to take in the grandeur and admire the minutiae.

Some highlights include the front **mountain gate**, with its elegant *dǒugǒng* (special bracketing system for Chinese architecture) and sweeping eaves. Before the front of the Hall of Five Gates you'll find the most famous **carved dragons** in Taiwan: note that the head of one runs up the column while its twins runs down.

Also check out the hall's window lattice for two fish that curl around each other in the shape of the **yin yang symbol**. Inside the hall you'll find one of the most stunning **plafond ceilings** in Taiwan, as well as brackets and beams carved into a veritable smorgasbord of traditional symbols: there are clouds, dragons, bats, lions, flowers, melons, elephants, phoenixes, fish and more.

The resident deity at Longshan Temple is the Bodhisattva Guanyin and you'll find her shrine at the back worship hall, along with an old cast bronze bell.

Matsu Temple TAOIST TEMPLE

Another large, splendid and holy structure, this Matsu Temple (天后宮; Tiānhòu Gōng) was renovated in 1936, a high period in Taiwan's temple arts. The wood carvings are particularly fine in the front hall, and do look up as you enter: that's one gorgeous deep plafond ceiling above your head.

It is said that the Matsu statue in this temple was brought to Taiwan by a Qing-dynasty general. The statue is now called 'The Black-Faced Matsu', as centuries of incense smoke have discoloured her original complexion.

The area around the Matsu Temple is pedestrian only and great crowds gather here on weekends, though the atmosphere feels festive and not touristy. Vendors and the surrounding stores sell a variety of traditional snacks, sweets and drinks.

Folk Arts Museum MUSEUM

(民俗文物館; Mínsú Wénwùguǎn; 152 Jhongshan Rd; admission NT$130; 9am-5pm, no entry after 4.30pm, closed Mon) The Folk Arts Museum has always been one of our favourite heritage sites in Lukang. Built in the Japanese era and originally the residence of a wealthy local family, the museum houses a large collection of daily-life artefacts from a bygone age.

The museum can now be accessed via the **Din Family Old House** (丁家進士古厝; Dīngjiā Jìnshī Gǔcuò; 132 Zhongshan Rd; admission free; 9am-5pm), the last remaining imperial scholar's house in Lukang.

Old Market Street OLD STREET

The merchant streets of old Lukang are well represented by the shops lining both sides of the curved, red-tiled lanes of what is now called the Old Market St (古市街; Gǔshì Jiē). Almost all the shop fronts have been restored and interiors decorated with antiques. You can shop for traditional items, try some local delicacies or just enjoy a stroll through history.

Nine-Turns Lane (Chinseng Lane) OLD STREET

Don't bother counting the turns as you wend your way past some of the oldest and most charming residences in Lukang on Nine-Turns Lane (九曲巷; Jiǔqū Xiàng). The number nine refers to September, the ninth month. Cold winds blow down from Mongolia at this time of year and the turns functioned as a natural windbreak, giving new meaning to the phrase 'clever by turns'.

Breast Touching Lane (Mo-Lu Lane) 摸乳巷 OLD STREET

The narrowest alley in Lukang, also called Gentleman's Lane (Mōlǔshàng), gets it comical label from the fact that a man could

Lukang (Lugang)

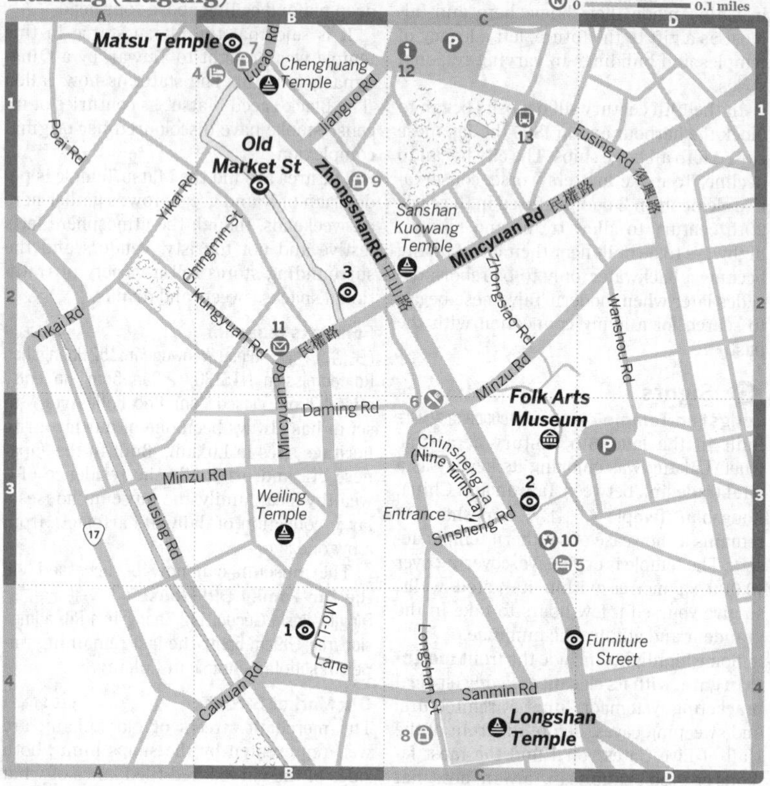

not pass a woman down the narrow inner passageway without her breasts brushing against him. The true gentleman would always wait for a lady to pass through first. Take a stroll through the lane with someone you love – or hope to.

Tours

Taiwan Tour Bus (☎0800 011 765; http://taiwan.net.tw) Has day tours of Lukang (NT$1500) leaving from the train station, HSR stations, and major hotels in Taichung and Taipei.

Festivals & Events

Every year Lukang hosts a four-day **folk-arts festival** that begins three days before the Dragon Boat Festival (see p370). This is a crowded but rewarding time to visit Lukang. Matsu's birthday, the 23rd day of the third lunar month (usually in April; see boxed text, p201), is also cause for intense celebration at the Matsu Temple.

Sleeping

Matsu Temple Believer's Hotel HOTEL $
(鹿港天后宮香客大樓; Lùgǎng Tiānhòugōng Xiāngkè Dàlóu; ☎775 2508; 475 Zhongshan Rd; 中山路475號; d/tw NT$950/1680) You don't have to be a believer to stay here, though it might help you to ignore how bland the rooms are (hospital-room bareness comes to mind). Note that the entire hotel may be booked out months in advance of Matsu's birthday and other important festivals.

Quanzhong Hotel HOTEL $
(全忠旅社; Quánzhōng Lûshè; ☎777 2640; 104 Zhongshan Rd; 中山路104號; d/tw NT$700/1050) This hotel is getting old but at least the location is good. Rooms are small, cheaply furnished and a little musty, but clean enough for a night's stay.

Lukang (Lugang)

Top Sights
Folk Arts Museum ... C3
Longshan Temple ... C4
Matsu Temple ... B1
Old Market St ... B1

Sights
1 Breast Touching Lane (Mo-Lu Lane) ... B4
2 Din Family Old House ... C3
3 Half-Sided Well ... B2

Sleeping
4 Matsu Temple Believer's Hotel ... B1
5 Quanzhong Hotel ... C3

Eating
6 Yu Chen Chai ... C3

Shopping
7 Mr Chen's Fan Shop ... B1
8 Wan Neng Tinware ... C4
9 Wu Tu-Hou Lantern Shop ... B1

Information
10 Police Station ... C3
11 Post Office ... B2
12 Visitor Centre ... C1

Transport
13 Changhua Bus Company Station ... C1

Eating

There's hardly a street in Lukang that doesn't offer wall-to-wall eating, and the pedestrian-only zone around Matsu Temple is a lively market of food stalls and small restaurants. Some famous local dishes to try are steamed buns, shrimp monkeys (溪蝦; *xī xiā*), oyster omelettes (蚵仔煎; *é ā jiān*), meatballs (肉圓; *ròu yuán*) and sweet treats, such as cow-tongue crackers (牛舌餅; *níushé bǐng*) and dragon whiskers (龍鬚糖; *lóngxū táng*).

Yu Chen Chai TRADITIONAL SNACKS $
(玉珍齋食品有限公司; Yùzhēnzhāi Shípǐn Yǒuxiàn Gōngsī; 168 Minzu Rd; ⏲8am-11pm) This fifth-generation shop sells pastries based on original Qing-dynasty recipes. Try the phoenix eye cake (鳳眼糕; *fèngyǎn gāo*) or the green bean cake (綠豆糕; *lùdoù gāo*).

Shopping

Lukang offers great shopping (or just browsing) if you're in the market for original crafts. Several shop owners have received 'Living Heritage' awards for their skill and dedication in preserving old crafts.

Down near the end of Zhongshan Rd is a row of old furniture makers, still plying their trade in such items as sedan chairs for carrying touring gods. It's unlikely you will want to make a purchase here, but browsing is welcome.

Wan Neng Tinware TINWARE
(萬能錫舖; Wànnéng Xípù; ☎777 7847; 81 Longshan St) The master here is in fact a fourth-generation tinsmith. His elaborate dragon boats and expressive masks cost thousands but are worth the price for their beauty and craftsmanship.

Mr Chen's Fan Shop TRADITIONAL FANS
(陳朝宗手工扇; Chéncháozōng Shǒugōngshàn; ☎777 5629; 400 Zhongshan Rd) The shop is just on the right before you enter the pedestrian-only area near Matsu Temple. Fans range from a few hundred dollars to many thousands for the larger creations. Mr Chen has been making fans since he was 16.

Wu Tun-Hou Lantern Shop TRADITIONAL LANTERNS
(吳敦厚燈籠舖; Wúdūnhòu Dēnglóngpù; ☎777 6680; 312 Zhongshan Rd) Mr Wu has been making lanterns for about 70 years and has collectors from all over the world come to make purchases. These days, however, you're more likely to see his sons (highly skilled themselves) and grandsons at work outside. Lanterns start at a few hundred dollars but the really creative works cost thousands.

Information

Lukang website (www.lukang.gov.tw) An informative introduction to the town's history and sights.

Visitor centre (遊客中心; ☎784 1263; Fusing Rd; ⏲9am-5.30 Mon-Fri, to 6pm Sat & Sun) This new visitor centre is easy to spot, located in a large field/car park across from the Changhua Bus Company station. Pick up a brochure in English for more sights than we can cover here.

Getting There & Away

There are direct buses from Taipei's main bus station to Lukang (NT$300, three hours) with **U-bus** (統聯汽車客運; www.ubus.com.tw). Buses to Changhua (NT$47, 30 minutes, frequent) leave from the **Changhua Bus Company station** (彰化客運站; ☎722 4603; Fusing Rd). The last bus returns at 9pm.

SUN MOON LAKE NATIONAL SCENIC AREA

Sun Moon Lake 日月潭

☎049

Sun Moon Lake (Rìyuè Tán) is the largest body of fresh water in Taiwan and has one of the island's most lovely natural landscapes. In his blue period, Picasso would have had no end of inspiration. At an altitude of 762m, the lake is backed by high-forested mountains and boasts good weather year-round. Boating is popular, as is hiking and biking.

Sun Moon Lake is part of the 90-sq-km Sun Moon Lake National Scenic Area under the control of the central government. The scenic area stretches north to include the Formosan Aboriginal Cultural Village, south to the Snake Kiln in Shuili and the old train station at Checheng, west to Great Jiji Mountain and east to Mt Shueishe. It's also close to Puli (30 minutes) and makes for a nice base to explore that town (as accommodation in Puli is poor). Note that you can get to all these places from the lake by public transport.

Accommodation is more than plentiful, with the majority of hotels centred in Shueishe Village and Itashao. Itashao is not the quiet backwater it once was, though the strong presence of the Thao aborigine (the area's original inhabitants) contrasts it very obviously with the predominately Taiwanese atmosphere at Shueishe.

Sights

Shuieshe Village SCENIC AREA

People often refer to Shueishe Village (水社村; Shǔishè Cūn) as Sun Moon Lake Village. The cobbled main road, Minsheng Rd, is supposed to be pedestrian only but this rule is not being enforced very strictly. The area by the **Shueishe Pier** (水社碼頭; Shǔishè Mǎtóu) is particularly attractive and a great place to hang out day and night. Most of the hotels along the waterfront have added new facades and constructed leafy decks offering food and beverage service.

Lakeside walking paths extend from the village in either direction. Going east you can walk all the way to Wenwu Temple. **Meihe Garden** (梅荷園; Méihé Yuán), on a ledge above the village, is a heavenly spot to hang out on a sunny day (and the night view is pretty charming, too).

Sun Moon Lake Ropeway GONDOLA

(日月潭纜車; Riyuètán Lǎnchē; return NT$300; ⊙9am-5pm, closed 2nd Wed every month) The law of diminishing returns sadly comes into play here if the queues you face getting on this new gondola are anything like ours. The seven-minute, 1.9km ride may give you an unparalleled bird's-eye view of the lake as you rise into the nearby hills, but, well, you may have had other plans that day.

The gondola terminates at the **Formosan Aboriginal Cultural Village** (九族文化村; Jiǔzú Wénhuà Cūn), an amusement park-cum-culture-venue.

Wenwu Temple TAOIST TEMPLE

This temple (文武廟; Wénwǔ Miào) has superb natural lookouts. Faux northern-style temple architecture.

Syuanzang Temple BUDDHIST TEMPLE

Szuanzang Temple (玄奘寺; Xuánzàng Sì) stores a fragment of skull from the monk Tripitaka (600–664 AD), immortalised in the novel *Journey to the West*.

Tsen Pagoda PAGODA

This temple (慈恩塔; Cīēn Tǎ) was built by Chiang Kai-shek in honour of his mother.

Activities

Boating

Boat tours (NT$100 each way) are a popular way to take in the scenery and sights, and leave every 30 minutes between 9am and 6pm. You can get on or off at any of the three piers, wander round and catch the next boat out. You can take bikes on the boats.

Most hotels will sell you a ticket without commission. Otherwise, pick one up at any pier. Private boats can be rented at Shueishe Pier and **Itashao Pier**.

Cycling

The cycling craze that hit Taiwan in 2007 certainly didn't exclude Sun Moon Lake. While circling the 29km-round-the-lake road is the most popular option, many cyclists are now riding down to towns along

Sun Moon Lake

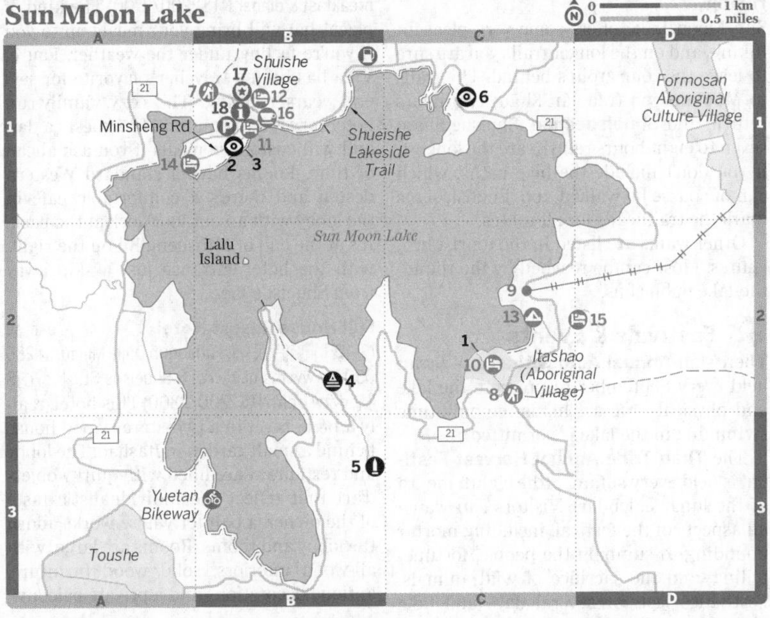

Sun Moon Lake

Sights

1 Itashao Pier C2
2 Meihe Garden B1
3 Shueishe Pier B1
4 Syuanzang Temple B2
5 Tsen Pagoda B3
6 Wenwu Temple C1

Activities, Courses & Tours

Giant Bicycle Shop .... (see 18)
7 Maolanshan Trailhead B1
8 Shuisheshan Trailhead C2
9 Sun Moon Lake Ropeway C2

Sleeping

10 Full House Resort Hotel C2
11 Harbor Resort Hotel B1
12 Lake House B1
Laurel Villa .... (see 11)
13 Sun Moon Bay Campsite C2
14 Teachers Hostel A1
15 Youth Activity Centre D2

Eating

Full House Resort Hotel .... (see 10)

Drinking

16 Del Lago Hotel Tea Shop B1

Information

17 Police Station B1
18 Visitor Information Centre B1

the Jiji Small Rail Line via County Rd 131. The 18km or so from the lake to Checheng (the end of the Jiji line) passes quiet villages, thickly forested hills and a final stretch following the downstream flow of the Shuili River, dammed in several places to store water released from Sun Moon Lake for the generation of hydroelectric power.

At the time of writing the scenic administration had begun construction on a path that would join Shueishe Village with the 8km **Yuetan Bikeway** (月潭自行車道; Yuètán Zìxíngchē Dào) and a circular route through **Toushe** (頭社; Tóushè), a scenic peat soil basin south of the lake.

You can rent a variety of bikes at the **Giant** (捷安特; Jié Ān Tè; per hr NT$200-1000; ⌚7am-6pm) bicycle shop, located beneath the Visitor Information Centre.

Hiking

Sun Moon Lake offers some very pleasant hiking, and on the longer trails you are sure to leave the tour groups behind. The trails to **Maolanshan** (Māolán Shān; two hours return) and **Shueisheshan** (Shǔishè Shān; seven to eight hours return) are the longest, if you don't include the bike paths, which can of course be walked, too. English signs mark the trailheads for all routes.

Other walks are listed in the tourist brochures. Most can be reached by the round-the-lake public bus.

Festivals & Events

There's an **Annual Across the Lake Swim** held every September to promote the lake and physical fitness. This is the only time swimming in the lake is permitted.

The **Thao Tribe Annual Harvest Festival** is held every summer (the eighth month of the lunar calendar). Visitors can watch all aspects of the festival, including mortar pounding to summon the people, fortune-telling, and the sacrifice of wild animals. Festivities last for several days and take place in Itashao.

Sleeping

All hotels at the lake offer discounts of up to 50% during the week and often on weekends, too. Rooms that face the lake are always the most expensive and are usually booked out.

Homestays on the main road are one of the best options at the lake. For comfort some can rival rooms at bigger hotels that go for two or three times the price. As you wander down from the Visitor Information Centre towards the village (around the 7-Eleven), a dozen or so small homestays will announce themselves in obvious ways: usually with a picture board so you can see what you're getting.

Lake House HOTEL $

(日月潭-潭之戀民宿; Rìyuètán-Tánzhīliàn Mínsù; 122 Jhongshan Rd; 中山路122號; ☎285 5207; r from NT$1500) One very friendly place where a little English is spoken is Lake House. It's like staying with a friend who's clean, sees to it you have a proper bed and shower, but doesn't feel the need for spoiling you with frills.

Laurel Villa HOMESTAY $$

(桂月村; Guìyuè Cūn; ☎285 5551; www.laurelvilla.com.tw; 28 Minsheng Rd; 名勝街28號; s/d incl breakfast & dinner NT$2200/2700) The kind of place that will bring your meals up to you if you're feeling under the weather, Laurel Villa has been a traveller's favorite for several years running. The cozy, family-run hotel serves a maximum of 15 guests a day, and will customise meals if you ask ahead of time. Rooms have a standard Western design and there's a comfortable cafe in the lobby with an outdoor deck at the back. It's at the end of Minsheng Rd on the right, with the hotel entrance just a skip away from Shueishe Pier.

Full House Resort Hotel B&B $$

(富豪群渡假民宿; Fùháoqún Dùjià Mínsù; ☎285 0307; www.fhsml.idv.tw; 8 Shueishe St; 水秀街8號; d/tw from NT$2200/2800) This hotel, really a B&B, is set in a two-storey wood house behind a small garden in Itashao. The lobby and restaurant are filled with quirky objets d'art that reflect the individualistic taste of the owner, a painter whose works adorn the lobby and rooms. Rooms are large, with all-wood interiors, solid wood furniture, antique decorations and a private balcony.

Teachers Hostel HOTEL $

(教師會館; Jiàoshī Huìguǎn; ☎285 5991; www.t-welfare.com.tw/edumoon; 136 Zhongxing Rd; 中興路136號; with Youth Travel Card dm NT$500) A proper hotel, not hostel, travellers with a Youth Travel Card (p367) can nonetheless stay here in surroundings far above their budget. The hotel is a 10-minute walk up the hill from the village. Single female travellers without transport should be aware that parts of the walk are isolated and dark at night.

Youth Activity Centre HOSTEL $

(日月潭青年活動中心; Rìyuètán Qīngnián Huódòng Zhōngxīn; ☎285 0071; www.cyh.org.tw; 101 Jhongjheng Rd, 中正路101號; dm with IYH card NT$550, d/tw 1800/2300) This centre is a 20-minute ride or so from Shueishe Village (the round-the-lake bus stops here), but it has its own restaurant (meals NT$150), store, bikes for rent and large grounds for simply hanging out.

Harbour Resort Hotel HOTEL $$

(碼頭休閒大飯店; Mǎtóu Xiūxián Dàfàndiàn; ☎285 5143; 11 Minsheng Rd; 名勝街11號; d/tw NT$3000/4500) The last hotel on Minsheng before the dock. Lakeside rooms are bright and airy and have a modern decor that includes flat-screen TVs. Although the room windows are small, there are excellent lake views from the balconies. There is a simple spa in the basement for guests.

Sun Moon Bay Campsite CAMPGROUND $
(日月灣露營農場; Rìyuèwān Lùyíng Nóngchǎng; ☎285 0559; www.rock-camp.com.tw; per site NT$500) Set beside the lake, with clean grounds, shady trees and on-site bathrooms (with showers), this campground was a solid budget choice before the gondola opened nearby. No, it's not the crowds, but the noise, though if you are out all day you may not be bothered. To reach the campground, take a round-the-lake bus to the Youth Activity Centre. Continue on foot just a little further and turn right onto a small road heading down to the lake.

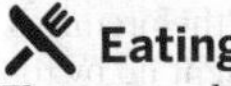

Eating

The general breakdown for eating is Shueishe for Chinese food (and a few attempts at Western cuisine) and Itashao for aboriginal. If you are on a budget there's a 7-Eleven in Shueishe for noodles and sandwiches, and cheap stir-fries and filling set meals are available from the nearby restaurants (dishes from NT$80, set meals NT$200). Most of the expensive hotel restaurants don't seem to serve anything better than the shops on the main street.

Restaurants in Itashao are largely set up for groups, but solo travellers can head to the snack street across from the pier for all manner of aboriginal-style foods, including mountain pig and chicken, sticky rice and wild vegetables.

Full House Resort RESTAURANT $$
(set meals from NT$220; ⏲24hr) Tasty and filling set meals with a vegie option. The outside garden gets a bit too much noise from the streets these days, but it hasn't completely lost its charm.

Drinking

Along the waterfront, both in Shueishe and Itashao, many hotels runs cafes where you can take in the lake views from your table. The Starbucks beside the Del Lago Hotel in Shueishe actually has one of the nicest views, so don't knock it off your list.

Del Lago Hotel Tea Shop TEASHOP
(大淶閣大飯店; Dàláigé Dàfàndiàn, 101 Jhongshan Rd) The 2nd-floor lobby, accessed off the main street beside Starbucks, sports a room for sampling tea with stunning views over the lake. Make sure you don't pass over the high-mountain oolong and locally grown Assam black tea. During Japanese times the black tea enjoyed a worldwide reputation, and it's slowly gaining that back. Grown in the misty mountains above the lake, the leaves produce a richly flavoured tea that can be enjoyed without milk and sugar.

Information

There are no banks but the 7-Eleven on the main road up from the village has an ATM.

Sun Moon Lake National Scenic Area (www.sunmoon lake.gov.tw) Excellent resource, now with full bus information for both getting there and around.

Visitor Information Centre (遊客服務中心; ☎285 5668; 163 Jhongshan Rd, Shueishe Village; ⏲9am-5pm) Now in a large modern building off the main road just before the turn-off for the village. English-speaking staff are usually on hand to help with all your needs. If you see a kind elderly gentleman called Hsu Ting-fa (Tim), thank him for all the great work he has done to make Sun Moon Lake easy for English-speaking tourists to get around. Generous retirees like him are truly a national treasure.

Getting There & Away

Purchase bus tickets at the kiosk outside the Visitor Information Centre. On the kiosk side of the road, **Nantou Bus Company** (南投客運; www.ntbus.com.tw) has hourly buses to Puli (NT$52, 30 minutes), Taichung HSR (NT$175, 1½ hours) and Taichung city (NT$175, two hours).

Across the street from the kiosk, **Green Transit Bus** (Fengrong Bus Company; 豐榮客運; ☎285 5219) has buses to Shuili Snake Kiln (NT$49, 20 minutes, every one or two hours) and Shuili train station (NT$50, 30 minutes, every one or two hours).

Getting Around

The round-the-lake bus (all day pass NT$80, every 30 minutes from 9.30am to 6.30pm) leaves from in front of the Visitor Information Centre and turns back at Xuanguang Temple. An English schedule is available at the Visitor Information Centre.

Chung Tai Chan Temple
中台禪寺

Opened in 2001, this 43-storey **temple** (Zhōng Tái Chán Sì; www.chungtai.org) is more than just one of the quirkiest buildings in Taiwan (think tiled mosque meets rocket ship) – it's an international centre of Buddhist academic research, culture and the arts.

The temple was designed by Taipei 101 architect CY Lee, and took 10 years and the donations of countless members of the Chung Tai Chan Buddhist community to complete. Chung Tai Chan is an international branch of Buddhism founded by the Venerable Master Wei Chueh – the master who is said to have revived the Chan (Zen) tradition in Taiwan.

From the start, Master Wei Chueh was determined to build something grand, something that would appeal to the modern eye as much as the soul. Technology was embraced rather than shunned and the temple has deservedly won numerous awards for its lighting and design.

From the entrance doors with their giant wooden guardians to the seven-storey teak pagoda, only top-quality materials and artists, both Taiwanese and foreign, were used during construction. One master craftsman is said to have spent 10 years collecting coloured jade for the delightful 18 Lohan reliefs. Another struggled (successfully) to adapt Taiwanese folk-art colours and techniques to traditional ceiling design. Marble from 15 different countries was imported and pure teak used for the seven-storey indoor pagoda, which was built without metal nails or screws.

Beyond the skilled artwork and engineering, however, the temple exists for those who have an interest, curiosity or passion for Buddhism. Several resident nuns speak good English, and it is their responsibility to give guided tours to any and all visitors.

Unlike temples where the emphasis of the tour is on teaching you purely about the religious and ritual aspects of Buddhism, at Chung Tai Chan the nuns will help you to understand the statues, motifs and iconography as well as the art and engineering feats of the temple, as if you were in a museum. They will explain the 22 physical markings of the Buddha, why one holds a medicine ball in his hand while another holds a lotus, and why one sits on a white elephant with six tusks and another is so fat.

There is no accommodation at the temple, but there are weekly meditation classes in English, and weeklong retreats during Chinese New Year and summer. Other retreats, lasting three days, are held irregularly. During retreats, guests stay at the temple.

To get to the temple, first take a bus to Puli and then a taxi (NT$300). If you are driving, head north on Jungjeng Rd out of Puli and then follow the signs. The temple is about 6km away.

Shuili Snake Kiln 水里蛇窯

Snake kilns were first developed in China during the late Ming dynasty, and named sensibly after the long, narrow, snakelike appearance of the kilns. This 30m-long **Shuili snake kiln** (Shǔilǐ Shéyáo; admission NT$150; ⏲8am-5.30pm), constructed in 1927 and one of the last to still operate in Taiwan, is housed in a small artisan village founded by the third-generation owner of the kiln. Potters still work on the premises, and much of their work is bought up by top hotels in Taiwan.

Informative displays (in English) explain how the abundance of good clay and cheap wood from the mills at nearby Checheng made Shuili a centre for pottery production in Japanese times. Don't miss the display of WWII-era man-sized vats that were designed to hide soldiers on the beach.

Buses connecting Shuili train station with Sun Moon Lake stop outside the kiln (NT$49, 20 to 30 minutes, every hour or two).

Puli 埔里

Thirty minutes north of Sun Moon Lake, the hectic town of Puli (Pǔlǐ) lies in a basin surrounded by low mountains. Known in modern times as the epicentre of the 921 earthquake in 1999 and the home of Shaohsing wine, Puli was once a centre for butterfly exports. The area still flitters with winged life year-round and is the source of the mysterious butterfly dispersal over Tatajia every May and June.

Accommodation in Puli is as expensive as Sun Moon Lake, but dreary, and the town is irredeemably committed to putting as many scooters and cars on the road as possible.

Sights & Activities

FREE **Puli Wine Museum & Factory**

WINE MUSEUM

(埔里酒廠; Pǔlǐ Jiǔchǎng; 219 Zhongshan Rd; ⏲8am-4pm Mon-Fri, 8.30-5pm Sat & Sun) The history of the Puli winery is tied with the monopoly system established by the Japanese (and continued by the KMT) on core

WORTH A TRIP

HUISUN FOREST RESERVE 惠蓀林場

This combination **forest research station** (Hùisūn Línchǎng; http://huisun.nchu.edu.tw/home.php; admission NT$150; ⏲7am-10pm) and recreation park offers a range of trails for light hiking through protected forests that are also prime spots for spotting endemic bird and butterfly species.

Huisun is also simply a quiet mountain retreat with mild weather and some knockout scenery. Many visitors are student researchers and there is a pleasantly quiet atmosphere and tone of respect often absent in other forest recreation areas. There are simple rooms and cabins for rent (from NT$1400; check its website for details) and meals (breakfast NT$60, lunch or dinner NT$190) served in the centre at the end of the reserve (about 5km from the entrance gate on the only road through). Vegie options are available if you book ahead.

Huisun is 25km from Puli by road. It's a great route through sparsely developed hill country on Provincial Hwy 21, with the last few kilometres following a side road up the wild Beigang River canyon.

Buses to Huisun (NT$114, one hour) leave Puli at 8.50am and 2.20pm with **Nantou Bus Company** (南投客運; www.ntbus.com.tw; ☎049-299 6147) on Zhongzheng Rd.

Huisun to Donghsih

Continuing along Provincial Hwy 21 past the turn-off for Huisun there's a small area of hot-spring resorts and campgrounds on a shelf beside the Beigang River. Past these there is little but lovely countryside, the occasional hamlet and distant views of craggy mountaintops until Dongshih, a typical sprawling, traffic-infested midsized Taiwan town that seems particularly offensive after travelling through so much natural beauty.

About halfway to Dongshih the old Central Cross-Island Hwy 8 breaks off and you can travel east as far as the overdeveloped hot-spring town of Guguan and the nearby (and polar opposite to Guguan) **Bashianshan Forest Recreation Area** (八仙山國家森林遊樂區; Bāxiānshān Guójiā Sēnlín Yóulè Qū; www.forest.gov.tw; admission NT$150; ⏲8am-5pm), a former logging area now a popular day-hike venue. At Dongshih itself look for the narrow road up to **Dasyueshan Forest Recreation Area** (p199) covering one of the most stunning mountain regions in Taiwan.

If you're biking, there is one long climb starting about 10km past the turn-off for Huisun but otherwise the route is flat to gentling rolling.

industries such as alcohol, tobacco and logging. In 1917 the factory began producing sake, and some five decades later switched to Shaohsing wine, traditional Chinese firewater made from glutinous rice and wheat. The amber-coloured liquid has a kick and a bite, and while rarely appreciated by the Western palate, the jugs and jars it comes in are attractive and make for nice gifts or knick-knacks.

On the 1st floor of the factory a display and sample area now lets you try the spirits and a number of flavoured Shaohsing items, such as popsicles, cakes and sausages. Upstairs the entire history (in English) of the factory (and other monopoly industries), and even Chinese spirits in general, is laid out in mesmerising detail.

A taxi from the bus station to the factory will cost less than NT$100.

Hot Springs

On the outskirts of Puli at **Carp Lake** (鯉魚潭; Lǐyú Tán), a pretty willow-lined pond with a lush green mountain backdrop, you'll find hot springs *(wēnquán)* at **Solas Resort** (天泉溫泉會館; Tiānquán Wēnquán Huìguǎn; www.solasresort.com; unlimited time NT$250; ⏲5-10pm Mon-Fri, 2-10pm Sat & Sun). It's a nice modern set-up spilling over from a covered area to the edge of the lake. Facilities include outdoor and indoor pools, a wrap-around jet contraption, and a long trench with picnic tables and swings built inside. Bring your own towels.

Getting There & Away

Hourly buses are available with **Nantou Bus Company** (南投客運; www.ntbus.com.tw) between Puli and Sun Moon Lake (NT$52, 30 minutes).

You'll need a taxi to get around Puli.

JIJI SMALL RAIL LINE

049

Branching off the west-coast trunk line in flat rural Changhua, this 29km former narrow-gauge line (集集小火車線; Jíjí Xiǎohuǒchē Xiàn) chugs past some lovely stretches of rural Taiwan before coming to a halt in Checheng, a vehicle yard and former logging village in the foothills of Nantou County.

While the ride is short (45 minutes), the list of things to see and do at the seven stops is long: you can cycle, hike and monkey-watch, as well as visit temples, museums, kilns, dams and historical buildings. The line is open year-round, though the popular stops are a madhouse on summer weekends. Consider a winter day, when the weather is dry and mild, and the hordes are at home.

There are seven stations along the way, the most visited of which are Ershui, Jiji, Shuili and Checheng. You can sometimes get a map at the train stations, but in Chinese only.

Most of the towns have 7-Elevens with ATMs. There's a **visitor centre** (9am-5pm) at the Ershui station.

History

Like the Pingxi, Alishan and Neiwan lines, the Jiji line once served in the industrial development of Taiwan. Completed in 1922 under Japanese rule, the line supported the construction of the Daguan Power Station downstream from Sun Moon Lake. This was the first hydroelectric plant in Taiwan and power from it was used as far away as Taipei. Tourism began in earnest just 10 years ago, and now, along with farming, forms the core of the local economy.

Getting There & Around

Bus

Buses from Sun Moon Lake stop at Shuili station.

Train

A Jiji line all-day train pass costs NT$80, with 12 daily trains in either direction, from 6am to 10pm. The schedule is available at any station along the small rail line.

Ershui, the first station of the Jiji Small Rail Line, is connected to the main West Coast Line, but not every train stops here. A train from Changhua (fast/slow NT$73/47, 30 minutes, frequent) takes 30 minutes.

When you arrive at Ershui station, alight and transfer to the Jiji Small Rail Line (follow platform signs in English).

Road Biking Around the Line

Ershui and Jiji have short cycling paths but the rural roads all over this area are great for longer rides:

» Ershui to Jiji on County Rd 152: 20km

» Jiji to Shuili on Township Rd 27: 7km (can also take 139 north to Changhua: 50km)

» Shuili to Sun Moon Lake on County Rd 132: 22km

Ershui 二水站

POP 300

Ershui is the first station on the Jiji Line and where you'll transfer if coming by train from Changhua. It's worth a few hours' stop to cycle the dedicated bike paths through the farm fields.

Sights & Activities

Cycling

The cycling-only **bike path** *(jiǎotàchē zhuānyòng dào)* begins to the right of the train station, and intersects with quiet country roads that are also good for cycling. The countryside is picturesque, with lush fields and temples, shrines, traditional brick villas and pagodas popping up in unexpected places. Just to the north stands Songbo Ridge, a holy spot for Taiwan's Taoists. With its thick forests and crumbling cliff faces, the ridge helps to break up the flat landscape along the bike path.

You can rent bikes outside the train station (per day NT$100 to NT$200).

FREE **Ershui Formosan Macaque Nature Preserve** MONKEY RESERVE
(二水台灣獼猴自然保護區; Èrshuǐ Táiwān Míhóu Zìrán Bǎohùqū; 04-879 7640; 9am-5pm, closed Mon) The 94-hectare park covers the slopes of Songbo Ridge and contains well-preserved mid-elevation forests favoured by the Formosan Macaque, the island's sole monkey species. Today hundreds of monkeys live in the reserve and are easiest to spot in the morning.

The reserve and exhibition halls are 6km east of Ershui off County Rd 152 (look for the English sign 'Ershuei Formosan Macaque Education Hall'), which is a pleasant rural route to take should you wish to ride the 20km to Jiji.

Jiji (Chi Chi) 集集

POP 12,035

Lying at the feet of Great Jiji Mountain, Jiji (Jíjí), the fifth stop down the Jiji Small Rail Line, has a real country charm with fields of banana and betel-nut trees, grape vines and cosmos flowers lining the roads. The old cypress train station is a reproduction of the original Japanese-era station that was levelled in the 921 earthquake.

Sights & Activities

Endemic Species Research Institute RESEARCH INSTITUTE

(特有生物研究保育中心; Tèyǒu Shēngwù Yánjiù Bǎoyù Zhōngxīn; www.tesri.gov.tw; 1 Minsheng East Rd; admission NT$50; ⏲8.30am-4.30pm) The institute functions as a research centre and natural-history museum for plant and animal species endemic to Taiwan. Displays are highly informative and now feature full English text (proper English, too). The institute is about 1km east of the train station on the bike path.

Wuchang Temple TAOIST TEMPLE

One of the oddest sites billed as an attraction you're likely to come across in Taiwan, Wuchang Temple (武昌宮; Wǔchāng Gōng) made its name after the 921 earthquake collapsed its lower floors leaving the roof to lie in ruins on the ground. Very photogenic in its state of disrepair, the temple is now one of the first things people rush to see when they come to town.

To get to the temple turn right as you leave the train station and walk about 10 minutes to Ba Zhang St (八張街). Turn left and walk another 10 minutes. You can also reach the temple on the bike path.

Cycling

Jiji's **bike path** is for the most part scenic and easy to follow, with distance markers and clear turning signs. Note that when you get down near the weir the bike path takes you back to town, but it's fun to explore this area as well. Riding up County Rd 152 takes you through the **Green Tunnel** (綠色隧道; Lûsè Suìdào), a section of road with a high canopy formed by interlocking camphor-tree branches, while County Rd 27 rises to take you past the trailhead to **Great Jiji Mountain** (集集大山; Jíjí Dà Shān; elevation 1390m) before a fast descent into Shuili and the backdoor to Sun Moon Lake.

You can rent bikes (per hour NT$100) at numerous locations around the train station.

Sleeping & Eating

Jiji is not hurting for places to eat, both around the train station and at various stops along the bike routes. Cafes and convenience stores abound, and there's a night market on weekends.

Mountain Fish Water Boutique Hotel HOTEL $$

(集集山魚水渡假飯店; Jíjí Shān Yú Shuǐ Dùjià Fàndiàn; ☎276 1000; www.mfwhotel.com.tw; 205 Chenggong Rd; 成功路205號; d/tw NT$2240/4060; @) With its great location off a quiet leafy road, big mountain views and cozy rooms that offer comfort and style beyond their costs, this is one of the best options for the traveller who wants to relax for a couple days in the countryside. A buffet breakfast and use of the swimming pool (fed with mountain spring water), steam room and spa are included (summer only). To reach the hotel, go north from the train station to Cheng Gong Rd and turn right. Discounts of 30% are usual on weekdays.

Shuili 水里

POP 1000

The penultimate stop on the Jiji Small Rail Line, bland Shuili (Shuǐlǐ) serves mostly as a base for travelling somewhere else.

Yushan National Park Headquarters NATIONAL PARK OFFICE

(玉山國家公園管理處; Yùshān Guójiā Gōngyuán Guǎnlǐchù; ☎277 3121; www.ysnp.gov.tw; 515 Jungshan Rd, Sec 1; 水里鄉中山路一段515號; ⏲8.30am-5pm) For English brochures and films about the park, as well as the latest road and trail information. Usually someone working can speak English.

Getting Away

Buses to Sun Moon Lake (NT$50, 30 minutes, hourly) are available with **Green Transit Bus Company** (Fengrong Bus Company; 豐榮客運; ☎277 4609). **Yuanlin Bus Company** (員林客運; ☎277 0041) has buses to Dongpu (NT$115, one hour 20 minutes, eight buses daily). Note that buses to these places run during daylight hours only (6am to 5pm or so). To reach the

Yuanlin Bus Company, exit the train station and turn left on Minquan Rd. The bus station is on the opposite side of the road from the 7-Eleven. The Fengrong Bus Company is further down the road on the same side.

Checheng 車埕

At the end of the Jiji Small Rail Line, and conceived initially as little more than a car yard due to its large shelf of flat land, Checheng's (Chēchéng) fortunes were closely tied to the railway's functions as both supply mule for hydroelectric development and logging.

Sights & Activities

A few decades ago more than 2000 residents lived in Checheng, most working for the Chen Chang Corporation that had won the rights to log the region in 1959. A moratorium on logging in 1985 left Checheng nearly a ghost town. The remains of the logging industry and the old wood and brick houses now form the backbone of this charming little stop. The upper village exists more or less as it was, while the lower village has been gentrified, with a nice mix of wood walkways, grassy parks, open decks, new cedar wood buildings, cafes and restaurants.

Checheng Wood Museum (Logging Exhibition Hall) MUSEUM
(車埕木業展示館; Chēchéng Mùyè Zhǎnshìguǎn; admission NT$40; ⏲9am-5pm) This stylish museum, under an enormous wood A-frame, highlights the area's logging.

Mingtan Reservoir SCENIC AREA
This reservoir (明潭水庫; Míngtán Shuǐkù) sits just above the village and feeds a power station billed as the largest pumped-storage generating plant in Asia. Is that impressive? Who knows, but the system uses surplus electricity at night from the 2nd and 3rd nuclear power plant to pump water back up to the original source of the reservoir's water (Sun Moon Lake). During the day, in peak hours, the water is released to generate extra power. And that's kinda cool.

Sleeping & Eating

In the lower village there are a number of cafes, teahouses and restaurants.

Mommy Chang Hostel HOSTEL $
(陳銀花民宿; Chén Yín Huā Mínsù; ☎0920-389 808; dm NT$300) At the end of a row of squat yellow and green brick houses that couldn't say 'old Taiwan' more if they had a water buffalo lowing outside, the genial Mrs Chang offers a couple of simple rooms each night to crash out in. To find her place just head up from the Checheng Wood Museum and turn left at the signpost, which conveniently reads 'Mommy Chang Hostel'. Mrs Chang's house is the last on the right about 150m down.

Checheng Wood Museum LUNCHBOX OUTLET $
(Chēchéng Mùyè Zhǎnshìguǎn; railway lunchbox NT$80-270; ⏲9am-5pm) At the Wood Museum you can pick up a railway lunchbox (*tiělù biàndēng*), from simple paper lunchbox meals to more expensive options in cedar boxes that you can take away as souvenirs.

HIGHWAY 14

Although it begins just south of Taichung in the bland town of Caotun, Hwy 14 makes up for a poor start in no time. After Puli, which is worth stopping into to visit the marvellous Chung Tai Chan Temple, the elevation rises and one turn after another brings stunning mountain views. Along the way you can break for sightseeing and some of the best hiking in Taiwan.

Hwy 14 ends at Tayuling, just north of the forest recreation area of Hehuanshan (which sits at over 3300m), and from here you can go east to Taroko Gorge or north to Wuling Farm and Ilan. Public transport is not great, or even good, along the highway. Only Puli has anything like regular bus service from Taichung. By driving, and not stopping much, you can cover the route in four to five hours but give yourself at least two days.

Aowanda National Forest Recreation Area 奧萬大國家森林遊樂區

As you drive along Hwy 14 east of Puli, you reach the mountain community of **Wushe** (霧社; elevation 1150m) in less than an hour. It's very scenic up here and if you are interested in Taiwanese history there is a monument (just up the main road on the left) to the Wushe Incident, the last large-scale revolt against the Japanese, which led to a massacre of Atayal aborigines.

WORTH A TRIP

JOURNEYS FROM JIJI

Not far south of the Jiji Small Rail Line, the western plains give way to the foothills of the Alishan Range. There are few permanent settlements but lots of narrow roads through some of the best scenery in Taiwan: think endless river valleys, dense green forest canopies and blue-tinged ranges. In short, think superb country for scootering, or cycling if you're very fit.

Here are a few gems to keep in mind when you want to ramble and roll.

Taichi Gorge 太極峽谷

It's not hard to see why the 921 earthquake of 1999 closed **Taichi Gorge** (Tàijí Xiágǔ; admission NT$50; ⏲9am-5pm) off to the public for over a decade. The precipitously high, narrow and rocky terrain just doesn't allow for easy trail development. Kudos to the forestry bureau for the wall-hugging wood steps and the thrilling 136m **Ladder to Heaven** (天梯; Tiāntī), one of Taiwan's longest and certainly its only suspension bridge with built-in steps (to help you descend faster).

Taichi Gorge is 15km south of the town of Jhushan (itself about 20km southwest of Jiji) on Township Rd 49投. You'll need a few hours here if you want to explore some of the narrower chasms, and waterfall pools at the bottom of the gorge.

Caoling 草嶺

Also south of Jhushan (about 32km), though much deeper into the Alishan Range, is the village of Caoling (Tsaoling), which also witnessed heavy damage during the 921 earthquake. In fact, much of the land here simply slid away: 120 million cubic metres of rock and debris that clogged the river valley below, forming a lake upstream that lasted for a year.

These days County Rd 149 to Caoling is in good shape, the village is back on its feet, and by the time you read this it may even be possible to continue riding over the hills to Fengshan and Ruili. (Check at the Caoling police station before you try.)

Sitou (Hsitou or Chitou) & Shanlinhsi 溪頭、杉林溪

Taking County Rd 151 south of Jhushan leads first to the emerald tea terraces of **Lugu** (鹿谷; Lùgǔ), Taiwan's largest tea-growing area, and then the old forest reserves of Sitou (Xītóu; elevation 1150m) and Shanlishi (Shānlínxī). Both the latter are noted for beautiful stands of bamboo, China Fir and cedar, but can be shockingly overrun on weekends.

For sleeping check out the **Youth Activity Centre** (青年活動中心; Qīngnián Huódòng Zhōngxīn; ☎049-261 2160; http://chitou.cyh.org.tw; dm with IYH Card NT$500) in Sitou.

Note that this whole area is often shrouded in mist. The oolong tea growers love it, but it can make for challenging driving conditions.

Huashan Coffee Area 華山咖啡園區

Locals claim coffee has been grown in the foothills of Gukeng Township (古坑鄉; Gǔkēng Xiāng) since the Dutch occupation of Taiwan. If true, it was only after – you guessed it – the 921 earthquake destroyed everything that locals turned to coffee as their savior. The timing was fortuitous to say the least. Coinciding with Taiwan's recent coffee craze, Gukeng has since become one of the most prosperous rural townships.

The Huashan Coffee Area (Huáshān Kāfēi Yuánqū) is built on the steep hillsides east of National Fwy 3. It's all narrow roads lined with orchards, betel palms and coffee fields, with the occasional house offering a deck or a garden for sipping a pot of Gukeng coffee (古坑咖啡; Gǔkēng Kāfēi). A number of B&Bs in the area rent out rooms should you want to spend the night.

To get to Gukeng take County Rd 149 towards Caoling and then follow the signs.

The **Wushe Youth Activity Centre** (霧社山莊; Wùshè Shānzhuāng; ☎049-285 0070; www.cyh.org.tw.tw; d NT$1600) is a popular place for cyclists to spend the night when coming from Taroko Gorge.

Half an hour south, down a long and winding road, is the national forest recreation area of **Aowanda** (Àowàndà; http://trail.forest.gov.tw/index.aspx; admission NT$200). It's well worth a stop here, or even an overnight stay in the quaint **wooden cabins** (cabins NT$1500) surrounded by plum and maple trees. Aowanda has a **visitor centre** (☎049-297 4511; ⏲8.30am-5pm), with maps and brochures in English.

The park ranges in altitude from 1100m to 2600m, making it a cool retreat from the heat in summer. On the developed trails you can walk from one end of the reserve to the other in about two hours. All signs are bilingual and trails are simple to follow.

Aowanda is famous around Taiwan for its **maple trees** *(fēngshù)*. November to late January, when the leaves change colours, is a busy time for the park. **Birdwatching** is popular here and a visit to Aowanda is usually on the itinerary for tours from Western countries. In all, 120 species of bird live in the park, and of the 15 endemic bird species in Taiwan, 10 can be found here, including Swinhoe's pheasant and the Taiwan partridge. The park has set up a **birdwatching platform** *(shǎngniǎotái)* and benches, one of which bears an amusing dedication to Jo Ann McKenzie, a Canadian twitcher who has been to Aowanda many times.

From Taichung, the **Nantou Bus Company** (☎04-2225 6418; 35-8 Shuangshi Rd) usually has buses from autumn to spring. Call for the schedule.

Nenggao (Neng-Gao/ Nengkao) Cross-Island Trail 能高越嶺國家步道

This 200-year-old high-mountain trail (Nénggāo Yuèlǐng Guójiā Bùdào) was first used by the Taiya to help them ply trade between Puli and Hualien. During the Japanese occupation it was expanded and used, ironically, to police aboriginal tribes. During the later half of the 20th century, the path was expanded further by Taipower, which used it when laying high-voltage powerlines. (Hence you will sometimes also hear the trail called the 'Nenggao Powerline Trail'.)

It was possible until a few years ago to hike the entire trail to Liyu Lake in Hualien County, but landslides and washouts have made that route impassable. There are no plans to restore it, so we've included those sections that can still be hiked.

Activities

Nenggaoshan North Peak & Chilai South Peak MOUNTAIN HIKE

Also called the Nenggao West section, this trail starts at **Tunyuan** (屯原; elevation 2041m) at the end of Hwy 14 and ends the first day at **Tienchi** (天池; elevation 2860m), with the average hiker taking about five or six hours to walk in. Tienchi has a cabin where you'll find beds, a kitchen and water. You can also camp.

The next day **Nenggaoshan North Peak** (能高北峰; elevation 3184m) and **Chilai South Peak** (奇萊主山南峰; elevation 3358m) can be climbed in one long day with a return to Tienchi cabin.

The return to Tunyuan takes three hours.

Nenggao–Andongjun MOUNTAIN HIKE

An epic six-day hike across the spine of Taiwan, the Nenggao–Andongjun (能高-安東軍; Nénggāo–Āndōngjūn) hike is for the very fit and experienced only. The first day's hike follows the same route as the others to Tienchi but after that veers south to cross a rugged high-mountain landscape of deep-set lakes, rolling meadows of dwarf bamboo, deep-cut valleys and endless dark ranges. There is great beauty here and deeper solitude. The last day's hike down the Aowanda River ends in the Aowanda National Forest Recreation Area.

Be prepared to carry your own supplies, including a tent, for the whole trip. A guide who knows the route is an absolute necessity.

Information

The Nenggao Cross-Island Trail is part of the National Trail System (p27). Only a mountain permit is needed to hike and one can be picked up at the **police station** (☎049-280 2520) in Wushe.

Getting There & Away

You need your own vehicle or arrangements for someone to drop you off and pick you up. Note that past Wushe, Hwy 14 splits into Hwy 14甲, which heads north, and Hwy 14, which heads east to the trailhead at Tunyuan.

Hehuanshan (Hohuanshan) Forest Recreation Area

合歡山森林遊樂區

The last interesting stop on Hwy 14甲 before the descent into Taroko Gorge is **Hehuanshan** (Héhuān Shān Sēnlín Yóulè Qū; www.forest.gov.tw). At over 3000m, the recreation area sits mostly above the treeline, and the bright, grassy green hills of the Mt Hehuan Range roll on and on, often disappearing into the fog or a spectacular sea of clouds.

If you've driven up from the western plains of Taiwan, in a few hours the change from urban sprawl to emerald hills seems miraculous. It is, so stop and admire some of the highest and most loved peaks of the central mountains: the Hehuan peaks, Cilai Ridge, Nanhudashan and Chungyanjian.

Hwy 14甲 passes right through the park and at Wuling Pass (not to be confused with the forest recreation area called Wuling) it reaches the highest elevation of any road in Taiwan at 3275m. It snows up here in winter and when it does the road becomes a skating rink, parking lot and playground for the Taiwanese. Best to avoid the area at this time.

Summer is delightfully cool, and highly scenic as different alpine flowers bloom from May to September. Autumn and spring are excellent times for hiking. In the autumn the 'sea of clouds' formations are at their best.

Despite its chilly temperatures (12°C average), Hehuanshan has a remarkable amount of plant and animal life to admire. It's even considered a good spot for birding. Check out the website for details.

Activities

There are a number of short hikes starting close to the former Hehuan Cabin, now an information centre without information. Most trails have English signs at the trailhead but you are advised to still get a proper map of the area (see Outdoor Taiwan). Be aware that fog or rain can come in suddenly in the mountains, so always be prepared with warm clothing and some kind of rain protection. Be aware also that if you have driven up straight from lower altitudes, your body may take time to get used to exercising at 3000m plus. You don't need permits to tackle the following hikes.

The trail to **Hehuanshan East Peak** (合歡山東峰; Héhuān Shān Dōngfēng; elevation 3421m) starts next to the Ski Villa. It's a two- to three-hour return hike to the top.

The marked trailhead to **Hehuanshan North Peak** (合歡山北峰; Héhuān Shān Běifēng; elevation 3422m) starts a few kilometres north of the info centre off the highway. It's a three- to four-hour return hike.

The trailhead for **Shimenshan** (石門山; Shímén Shān; elevation 3237m) is just north of the information centre on the east/left side of the road. It's a short walk to the top and people often go here to watch the sunrise.

The paved path up to **Hehuanshan Main Peak** (合歡山主峰; Héhuān Shān Zhǔfēng; elevation 3417m) starts just before Wuling and is about a two-hour return hike.

The trail up to **Hehuan Jian Shan** (合歡尖山; Héhuānjiān Shān; elevation 3217m) starts just behind the information centre. It takes about 15 minutes to reach the top.

For overnight hikes, check the website.

Sleeping & Eating

Camping is possible in the parking lot at the information centre. The Youth Activity Centre in Kuanyun (see p170), about 15km from Hehuanshan, is also an option.

Simple dishes can also be picked up from vendors at Wuling.

Ski Villa HOTEL $
(滑雪山莊; Huáxuě Shānzhuāng; ☎04-2522 9797; dm incl dinner NT$700) You can stay overnight in the Ski Villa down the lower lane from a toilet block across from the information centre. The upper lane leads to the overpriced Song Syue Lodge (松雪樓). If you stay in the villa, you need to book ahead and bring a sleeping bag, towel, your own toiletries and some food. Note that the villa doors close at 8pm and there will be no one around to let you in or out after this.

Getting There & Away

The **Fengyuan Bus Company** (☎2222 3454) runs buses once daily to Hehuanshan from Taichung (NT$464, four hours, 8am). If you want to continue north from Hehuanshan, catch the next day's Fengyuan bus as it passes Hehuanshan heading to Lishan. The bus arrives in Lishan at around 2pm, where you can connect to a bus at 4pm to Wuling Recreation Area, and the next day continue by bus down to Ilan or Taroko Gorge.

You could also rent a scooter in Jiaoshi (p134) to get to Hehuanshan, but it's a long ride. Consider renting a car.

For information on biking to Hehuanshan from Taroko Gorge, see p169.

Southern Taiwan

Includes »

Best Places to Eat

» 5 Cent Driftwood House (p240)
» Jade Room Restaurant (p239)
» Escape 41 (p253)
» By the Sea (p262)

Best Places to Stay

» Teacher's Hostel (p237)
» The King's Garden Villa (p244)
» International Friendship House (p252)
» Sunset Beach Resort & Spa (p252)
» De En Gorge Guesthouse (p259)
» Chateau Beach Resort (p269)

Why Go?

They burn boats down here. Not as political protest (although this is the hotbed of Taiwan independence), but as a reminder of the hardships their ancestors faced in adapting to a new world. In the south, ties to tradition and folk culture are strong and the yearly calendar is chock-full of some of Taiwan's most unforgettable festivals.

Outside of Taipei, the cities most worth visiting are in the south. Tainan, the island's former capital, is a treasure trove of temples, relics and original night-market snacks. Kaohsiung has turned its industrial heritage on its head, converting warehouse districts into art studios and harbour fronts into biking routes.

Southern summers are scorching, but no one cares when the beaches of Kenting National Park are so close. Winters are balmy and some 15 million purple butterflies return each year to overwinter in the pristine mountain valleys around Maolin. They've chosen well.

When to Go

Tainan

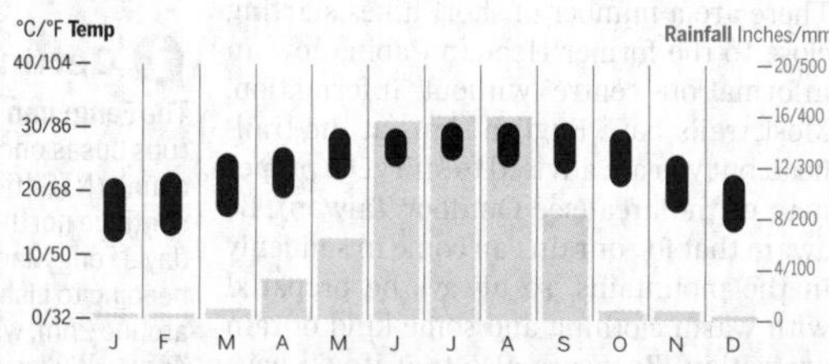

February Yenshui fireworks festival.

April 'Spring Scream' music festival in Kenting National Park.

September–October Raptor migration over Kenting National Park.

National Parks & Forest Recreation Areas

There are three national parks in the south: Kenting, a beach playground with some well-protected areas into which few people venture; Taijiang, Taiwan's newest national park and a storehouse for ecological and cultural heritage along the southwestcoast; and Yushan, unfortunately now inaccessible from the south because of typhoon damage.

Beautiful, remote Maolin Forest Recreation Area is a stronghold for aboriginal culture but also holds an important overwintering valley for the purple butterfly. Shuangliou Forest Recreation Area has a

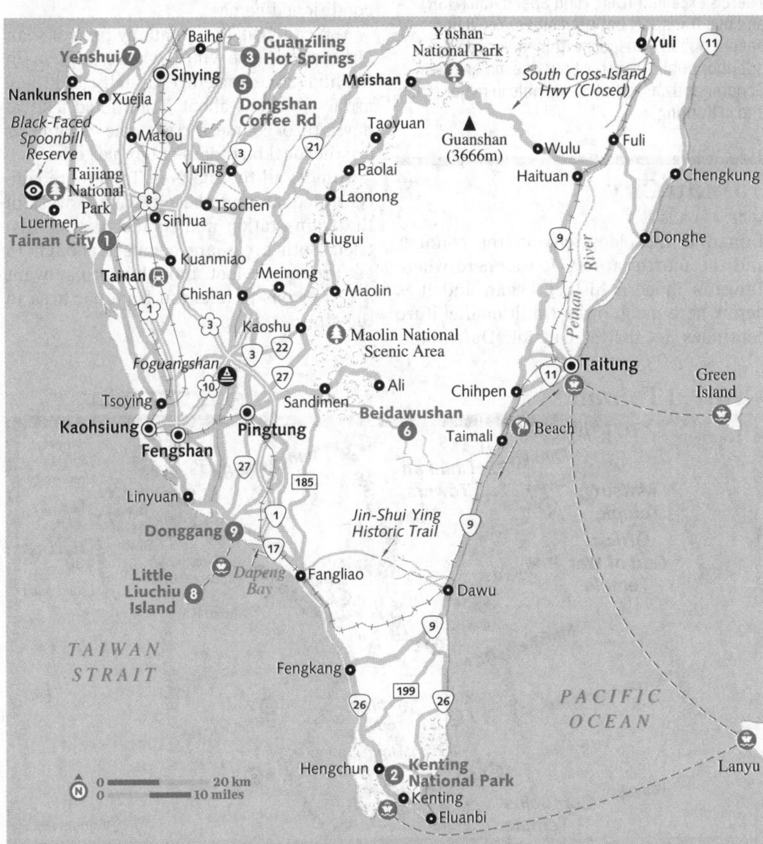

Highlights

1 Explore Taiwan's temple heritage in and around the old capital of **Tainan** (p232)

2 Swim, surf and cycle year-round in **Kenting National Park** (p266)

3 Soak in rare mud springs among the maple trees at **Guanziling hot springs** (p244)

4 **Bird-** and **butterfly-watch** year-round at some of Taiwan's top protected areas

5 Cycle charming back-country routes like the **Dongshan Coffee Road** (p247)

6 Climb **Beidawushan** (p265), the most southerly of the 3000m-plus peaks in Taiwan, and admire the view from the clouds

7 Get rained on with fireworks at **Yenshui** (p243)

8 Scooter and snorkel around Taiwan's only coral island, **Little Liuchiu Island** (p262)

9 Watch a ceremonial boat burn to the ground in **Donggang** (p260)

gorgeous waterfall, while much of Tengchih Forest Recreation Area boasts intact virgin forest. Shanping Forest Recreation Area offers peaceful trails, abundant plant life and excellent birdwatching. There's something for everyone in this part of Taiwan.

Getting There & Around

There's excellent train, High Speed Rail (HSR) and bus transport between cities. You'll find decent public transport within major cities, but poor public transport outside major cities. Scooter and car rental is available in major cities and in Kenting.

Tainan City 台南市

☎06 / POP 754,917

Tainan is the oldest city in the country, and the fourth largest. It was here where Taiwan's modern history began and it is here where much of its traditional culture continues to thrive. Outside Dutch-built forts, lively night markets sell dishes that are exclusive to the region. Inside temples that are hundreds of years old, people *bwah bwey* (cast moon blocks) to determine the best course of actions, just as their ancestors did when the temple first opened. The only difference is that, today, people then jump into their cars and head to their air-conditioned homes.

You can visit Tainan at any time of year, although we love winter when it's warm (in the high 20s, on average) and dry and there are few tourists about. Traditional festival days are, of course, a great time to come, as are the local birthdays of temple gods.

Almost all the sights in Tainan are concentrated around the city centre west of the train station and in the Anping District. Both areas are compact enough to get around on foot, though you may want a taxi or bus to take you from one area to the other.

Central Tainan

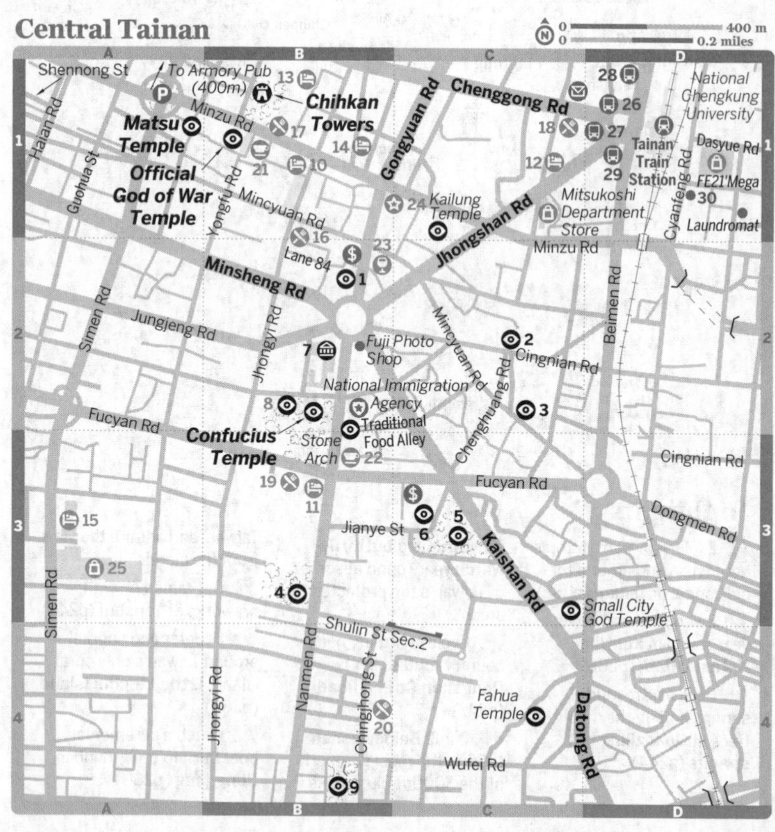

History

Fujianese first settled in the Tainan area in the late 1600s, but it was the Dutch East India Company (VOC) that encouraged immigration. After being booted off Penghu by the Qing dynasty, the Dutch established Tainan as an operational base for their trade with Japan and China. However, unable to persuade Taiwanese aborigines to grow rice and sugar for export, and unable to persuade Dutch rulers to allow immigration, the VOC looked to China for cheap labour.

When the Ming loyalist Koxinga defeated the Dutch, he established a central government in Tainan and started building up the city (a project later continued by his sons). Koxinga's son constructed Taiwan's first Confucian temple, helping to establish Tainan as a cultural and educational centre.

In 1683, when the Qing dynasty gained control of Taiwan, Tainan was chosen as the capital. The city remained the political, cultural and economic centre under the Qing, but lost this status in 1919 when the Japanese moved their colonial capital to Taipei. If you have a discerning eye, Tainan's pedigree is apparent by the stately quality of the city's temples and historical sites.

Modern Tainan has industries producing metals, textiles and machinery, and a few old masters working on traditional crafts, as well as a new science park that promises to bring the city into the avant-garde of Taiwan's hi-tech revolution. In 2009 Tainan city and county were approved for merger into one giant metropolitan area.

Sights

CENTRAL TAINAN

Confucius Temple CONFUCIAN TEMPLE

(孔廟; Kǒng Miào; http://confucius.cca.gov.tw/; 2 Nanmen Rd; admission NT$25; 8.30am-5pm)

You expect a Confucian temple to exude the calm, grace and dignified beauty of traditional Chinese culture, and this, the first such temple in Taiwan, doesn't disappoint. Nor do the grounds, which contain one of the largest and most beautiful banyan trees in all of Taiwan.

The temple grounds are free, and are nice to sit in at night, but you must pay to enter the palace area. The receipt comes with an excellent short brochure and map

Central Tainan

Top Sights

	Chihkan Towers	B1
	Confucius Temple	B2
	Matsu Temple	A1
	Official God of War Temple	B1

Sights

1	Altar of Heaven	B2
2	City God Temple	C2
3	Dongyue Temple	C2
4	Great South Gate	B3
5	Koxinga's Shrine	C3
6	Lady Linshui's Temple	C3
7	National Museum of Taiwanese Literature	B2
8	Old Tainan Martial Arts Academy	B2
9	Wufei Temple	B4

Sleeping

10	Cambridge Hotel	B1
11	Teacher's Hostel	B3
12	Hann Gong Hotel	C1
13	Ing Wang Hotel	B1
14	Ta Lee Hotel	B1
15	Tayih Landis	A3

Eating

16	A Xia Restaurant	B1
17	Chi Kin Dandanman	B1
18	Jade Room Restaurant	C1
19	Lily Fruit Shop	B3
20	Yu Shen Restaurant	B4

Drinking

21	A Chuan Melon Drink	B1
22	Narrow Door Café	B3
23	Hud La Voos	B2

Entertainment

24	Vie Show Cinemas	C1

Shopping

25	Shin Kong Mitsukoshi Department Store	A3
	Tainan Kuang Tsai Embroidery Shop	(see 21)

Transport

26	City Bus North Station	D1
27	City Bus South Station	D1
28	Ho-Hsin Bus Company	D1
29	Hsingnan Bus Company	D1
30	Scooter Rentals	D1

of the temple. Make sure you look out for the stone tablet on the right as you enter the Edification Hall (the tablet is not shown on the brochure). The words on the tablet explain the school rules (the site was once a centre for Confucian studies), such as prohibitions against gambling, drinking and cheating.

The temple is part of a larger cultural zone that includes the **Old Tainan Martial Arts Academy** (台南武德殿; Táinán Wǔdé Diàn), a renovated Japanese dojo built in 1926 and once used to train the colonial police force (not open to the public).

Across the street from the temple entrance is a **stone arch** that was built in 1777. It's now the gateway to a pedestrianised street filled with cafes and small eateries.

Chihkan Towers HISTORIC SITE
(赤崁樓; Fort Proventia; Chìkǎn Lóu; 212 Minzu Rd; admission NT$50; ⌚8.30am-9pm) This old fort is one of the best preserved, or perhaps we should say reconstructed, historical sights in Tainan. It's a splendid place in which to roam around, or even to enjoy an outdoor concert on the weekends.

Chihkan has gone through many masters – Ming, Qing and Japanese, and the Kuomintang (KMT; China's Nationalist Party) – since the foundations were first laid by the Dutch in 1653. At that time the seashore reached the fort's outer walls. Our favourite features are the nine stone turtles with tablets on their backs. These stelae hail from the Qing dynasty and if you check the backs you can see where the carver made a mistake on one and, rather than starting over with a fresh slab, simply turned the stone over and redid everything on the other side.

There are English explanations around the site, as well as a brochure you can pick up when you enter. At night the whole area around the fort is filled with shops and vendors selling traditional foods.

Matsu Temple TAOIST TEMPLE
(大天后宮; Dà Tiānhòu Gōng; 18 Lane 227, Yongfu Rd, Sec 2) This lively temple once served as the palace of Ning Jin, the last king of the Ming dynasty. If you wish to confirm visually that a king's status is lower than an emperor's, count the steps to the shrine. There are only seven; an emperor would get nine.

Matsu is the most popular folk deity in Taiwan (see boxed text, p201), with over 500 temples dedicated to her around the island. Some features to note at this particular temple (besides the nicely detailed wood carvings and paintings) include the 300-year-old Matsu statue, and, in the back, the shrine to Matsu's parents, in an area that used to be King Ning Jin's bedroom. Look up and you'll see the roof beam where the king's concubines hanged themselves so many years ago (see Wufei Temple, opposite).

For fun, check out the eyes and feet of the door guards in the annexe to the left. Notice something odd?

Official God of War Temple TAOIST TEMPLE
(祀典武廟; Sacrificial Rites Temple; Sì Diǎn Wǔ Miào; 229 Yongfu Rd, Sec 2) This is the oldest and most impressive temple in Taiwan dedicated to Guan Di (Guan Gong), a Han-dynasty general deified as a patron of warriors and those who live by a code of honour.

The temple's overall size and structure were established in 1690, although much splendid artwork and many historically valuable objects have been added over the years. For us, the long, deep-rose-coloured walls of this temple have always been one of its highlights. Other interesting features to note are the beggar seats built into the doorframe (so that the poor could beg alms from every visitor), the high threshold at the entrance (originally designed to keep women out!), and the bamboo-shaped poem on a scroll at the back, which contains words said to have been written by Guan Di himself.

Dongyue Temple TAOIST TEMPLE
(東嶽殿; Dōngyuè Diàn; 110 Mincyuan Rd) People often come to this temple to communicate with the dead through spirit mediums. It's a fascinating place to catch a glimpse of Taiwanese folk culture.

The first chamber of the temple holds the city god, Chenghuang; the second, Zizang Wang, the Buddhist king of the underworld; the last, a number of demon gods who rule the underworld.

The disturbing yet fascinatingly grim murals on the walls of the second chamber are as graphic as the depictions of hell by Hieronymus Bosch: there are disembowelments, eye gougings, stabbings, boilings and so much more.

City God Temple TAOIST TEMPLE
(城隍廟; Chénghuáng Miào; 133 Cingnian Rd) The city god (Chenghuang), officially the Lord of Walls and Moats, and protector of towns, also tallies this life's good and bad

deeds after we die. Hence it is not unusual that his image appears in the Dongyue Temple, dedicated to the underworld, nor that these two temples sit in close proximity to each other.

When you enter the City God Temple, look up for the two large abacuses used to calculate whether you have done more good than bad in life. And check out the gold scripted plaque: it translates roughly as 'You've come at last', meaning death escapes no one.

In the worship hall look for pink slips of paper on the altar. They're from students asking for help to pass an exam. Yep, school is hell everywhere.

Though a relatively small structure, the City God Temple has some outstanding wood and stone work in the entrance portico and worship hall.

FREE Koxinga's Shrine HISTORIC SITE

(延平郡王祠; Yánpíng Jùnwáng Cí; 152 Kaishan Rd; ⏲8am-6pm) When the Ming dynasty was overthrown by the Manchus in 1661, Koxinga (Cheng Cheng-kung) led his army to Taiwan with plans to restock supplies and then retake the mainland. He found the Dutch already here, but after nine months' battle they surrendered and departed Taiwan.

Koxinga did much to improve conditions on the island. But, like the KMT of modern times, he did not live to see the mainland retaken. He died after only a year in Taiwan, and his grandson surrendered to the Manchus in 1683.

There's a certain atmosphere of dignity surrounding Koxinga's Shrine, even though most of it is of rather recent origin: the original southern-style temple was rebuilt in a northern style by the KMT government in the '60s. Many of the artefacts are historical, however, including the boxes in the shrine that hold the original imperial edict from 1874, permitting the shrine to be built.

The free **museum** to the left of the shrine features rotating exhibits of varying degrees of interest.

Lady Linshui's Temple TAOIST TEMPLE

(臨水夫人媽廟; Chen Ching Gu Temple; Línshǔi Fūrén Mā Miào; 1 Jianye St) For generations, women have come to this temple to ask Lady Linshui to protect their children. This is demanding work and the goddess employs 36 assistants (three for each month), whose statuettes can be seen in little glass vaults around the inside walls of the temple.

In addition to offerings of incense, you'll often see flowers, face powder and make-up left at the temple. If you are extremely lucky you might see the unique southern-temple spectacle associated with Lady Linshui called the **Twelve Grannies Parade**.

Wufei Temple TAOIST TEMPLE

(五妃廟; Wǔfēi Miào; ⏲8am-6pm) When Koxinga's grandson surrendered to the Manchus in 1683, all hope of restoring the Ming dynasty ended. King Ning Jin, the last contender for the Ming throne, knew his time was up. However, before he committed suicide, he urged his concubines to 'get thee to a nunnery'. The concubines refused, claiming their honour was as important as the king's, and hanged themselves on a roof beam in the bedroom of his palace. The palace is now the shrine to Matsu's parents at the Matsu Temple and the beam is still in place.

The dainty Wufei Temple was constructed in the concubines' honour and now sits in a 2000-sq-metre garden park off Wufei Rd. Note that the real tombs of the concubines are behind Koxinga's Shrine and are covered with cement.

FREE Great South Gate HISTORIC SITE

(大南門城; Dà Nánmén Chéng; Lane 34, Nanmen Rd; ⏲8.30am-5pm) The garrison commander in you will love the martial feel of this old city gate, the only one in Tainan that still has much of its defensive wall intact. The inner grounds feature several cannons and a section of the old wall that is marvellously overgrown with thick roots. As with the Confucius Temple, the trees here are an attraction in themselves.

At the far end of the park look for a collection of handsome **stelae** that commemorate centuries of battles, bridge buildings, official promotions and anything else thought worthy of a large slab of engraved rock.

FREE National Museum of Taiwanese Literature MUSEUM

(國家台灣文學館; Guójiā Táiwān Wénxué Guǎn; www.nmtl.gov.tw; 1 Jungjeng Rd; ⏲9am-9pm) The building that houses the museum was once the Tainan District Hall. Built in 1916 by the Japanese, it's a gorgeous example of colonial architecture. Even if literature isn't your greatest interest, it's worth coming here just to wander the halls and relax in the foyer.

The museum highlights the development of Taiwanese literature from pre-Han aborigines, through the colonial periods, up to the modern era. All exhibits and displays have English signage.

Altar of Heaven TAOIST TEMPLE

(天壇; Tiāntán; 16 Lane 84, Jhongyi Rd, Sec 2) Have you had a run of bad luck lately? Then visit this temple and pray to the supreme Taoist entity, the Jade Emperor (Lord of Heaven), to help you out. Tainan families have been doing this for generations on the 1st and 15th of every month.

The temple is noteworthy for two things. First, it has no statue of the god as the original temple was established as a temporary measure – 300 years ago! Second, there's a famous *Yī* (One) inscription over the altar that signifies there is only one true way for heaven and earth: humanity and righteousness.

ANPING

Besides central Tainan, the western district of Anping (安平區; Ānpíng) has the most interesting concentration of relics and temples. For several years the area has been undergoing a dramatic facelift as part of a multi-billion-dollar plan to revive the old historical district. It's coming along nicely, with work not only restoring old buildings, but establishing parks, bike lanes, waterfowl reserves and a modern harbour-front area.

The centre of Anping is the intersection of Anping Rd and Gubao St. Buses from central Tainan (Bus 2 or 88) stop just west of here across from the square in front of the Anping Matsu Temple. This is a good place to start your explorations from.

As in central Tainan, there are English interpretation signs and map boards everywhere. Also note that our list of sights and activities is not exhaustive.

History

When the Dutch established their colony on Taiwan, they built their first fort and commercial centre here in Anping. Anping was a very different harbour back then, being part of a giant inland sea called Taijiang (now the name of the eighth national park). But silting has always been a major problem with western seaports and in 1822 most of Taijiang was filled in – almost overnight, it was reported! Researchers now speculate the cause was landslides sparked by rainfall even heavier than the deluge Typhoon Morakot brought in 2009.

In 1858 the Tianjin Treaty opened Anping to western powers and their business interests, something readily apparent in the number of old merchant houses about town. By the early 20th century, however, continued silting had made Anping lose almost all function as a workable harbour.

Anping Matsu Temple TAOIST TEMPLE

This temple (安平天后宮; Ānpíng Tiānhòu Gōng) is one of many claiming status as the oldest in Taiwan. But it does genuinely display what many believe is the oldest Matsu statue. Our sources say it's not the one the temple brochure claims (the biggest one in the back shrine), but is, in fact, the middle one on the second row of smaller Matsu statues.

The temple interior is far more elaborately decorated than most in central Tainan, and features a splendidly ornate and deep plafond (decorative ceiling) above the main shrine. Near the altar, little packets of 'safe rice' are available for you to take home to help keep you and your family safe. If you do take one, make a donation to the temple.

Anping Fort HISTORIC SITE

(安平古堡; Fort Zeelandia; Ānpíng Gǔbǎo; admission NT$50; ⌚8.30am-5.30pm) The fort was a stronghold of Dutch power until captured by Koxinga in 1661 after a nine-month battle. Though most of the structure has been reconstructed, it's still an impressive site. A small **museum** on the grounds highlights the history of the Dutch occupation of Taiwan.

The fort sits behind the Matsu temple.

Anping Old Streets OLD STREET

Anping has some of the oldest streets in Taiwan, including **Siaojhong Street** (效忠街; Xiàozhōngjiē), and **Yenping Street** (延平街; Yánpíngjiē), both of which are to the right of Anping Fort as you face the entrance. Siaojhong St is the more interesting and leads to a number of back alleys with restored brick buildings. Yenping St, site of the first market in Taiwan, has been turned into a dull tourist lane, although it's worth a visit to sample traditional Tainan foods.

As you wander about, look for **stone lion masks** (劍獅; *jiànshī*) with swords across the mouth. These were once used to both protect a house against evil and to identify it. There are a few dozen left in Anping and no two are alike.

Former Tait & Co Merchant House and Anping Tree House OLD HOUSE
(德記洋行暨安平樹屋; Déjì Yángháng Jì Ānpíng Shùwū; Gubao St; admission NT$50; ⏲8.30am-6pm) The merchant house was built in 1867 and holds a permanent exhibit of household artefacts from the 17th century, donated by the Dutch government. Through a series of decorated rooms, the exhibit highlights the lifestyle of Dutch, Chinese and aboriginal families.

But nobody comes for that. Instead, it's the Anping Tree House (Ānpíng Shùwū) that draws in the curious with its massive banyan strangling the gutted roofless walls of the back quarters.

Both houses are up Gubao St and behind the primary-school grounds.

Medicine God Temple TAOIST TEMPLE
Just south of Anping Rd on Gubao St, this small temple (妙壽宮; Miào Shòu Gōng) boasts a lovely example of a swallowtail eave roof, and two small lion statues with an interesting tale (not tail) behind them.

Long ago in the days of the Qing dynasty, a young scholar prayed to the Medicine God to help him pass an imperial exam. Since Chinese religion is largely based on quid pro quo, he promised that if successful he would reward the god by paying for two stone temple lions to be carved and placed out front. Well, the scholar did pass the exam but, poor man that he was, could only afford the two diminutive felines you see today.

Eternal Golden Castle HISTORIC SITE
(億載金城; Yìzài Jīn Chéng; admission NT$50; ⏲8.30am-5.30pm) Like many famous sights around Tainan, this fort goes by different names: Erkunshen Cannon Fort, Anping Big Cannon Fort and Eternal Golden Castle. The fortress was built in 1876 to shore up Taiwan's defences against the Japanese threat.

Not much remains of the original fortress; oddly, though, the intact arched front gate was built with bricks pilfered from Anping Fort. The reconstructed fort and the cannons make for good photo ops. It's possible now, and recommended, to walk to the castle from the other sights in Anping.

City buses 2 and 14 stop at the castle, as does tour bus 88. You can walk from Anping St along the harbour in about 30 minutes.

Walking & Cycling

Anping is dead flat and has lots of open areas and pavements, so walking or cycling are both good ways to get around. In addition to the sites around the centre, head north a few blocks to the restored wetlands along the Yanshui River banks. A **riverside bike path** runs west a couple of kilometres to the coast, where you can continue north through Taijiang National Park or south along the Taiwan Strait and into the harbour area.

Cheap bikes (per day NT$100) can be rented on Gubao St across from Anping Fort or from the Tainan City program at Anping Fort, Eternal Golden Castle and Anping Tree House.

Tours

Barking Deer Adventures NATURE TOURS
(www.barking-deer.com) Offers hiking trips outside the city, birdwatching tours, and kayaking in the mangrove swamps.

Taoyuan Culture Tourism Association CULTURAL TOURS
(☎0927-927 791; w741224@ms51.hinet.net) A historical society that offers half- or full-day tours in English around Tainan, with Yvon Hsu.

Festivals & Events

Traditional Chinese holidays such as the **Dragon Boat Festival**, **Lunar New Year** and **Lantern Festival** are celebrated in a big way in Tainan. In addition, the birthdays of the various temple deities – **Matsu** (the 23rd day of the third lunar month), **Confucius** (28 September) – usually feature colourful and lively events at the respective temples.

Sleeping

Teacher's Hostel HOTEL $$
(劍橋南商教師會館; Jiànqiáo Nánshāng Jiàoshī Huìguǎn; ☎214 5588; www.tainan-teachers-hostel.com.tw; 4 Nanmen Rd; 南門路4號; d/tw incl breakfast from NT$2000/3200; @) Formerly the Confucius Inn, this professionally run hotel, directly south of the Confucius Temple, could easily charge much more. Rooms have spiffy modern decor, with large comfy beds. Extras like ADSL and laundry service are available, and while the free breakfast used to be a lot better it can still offer a hearty start to the day. There are 30% discounts midweek.

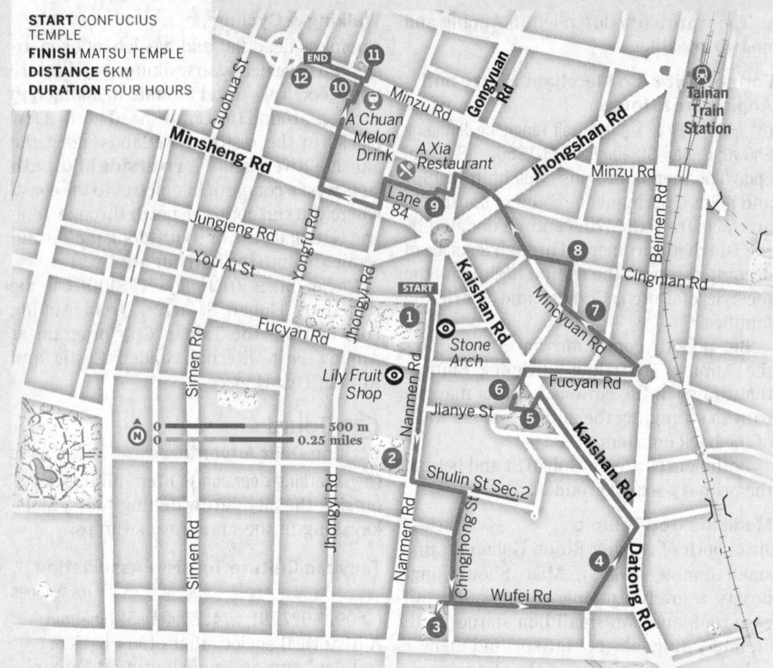

Walking Tour

Tainan Temples

After admiring the classical layout of peaceful ❶ **Confucius Temple**, head a few blocks south. After passing martial ❷ **Great South Gate** turn left on Shulin St and then take the first right. When you reach Wufei St, check out dainty ❸ **Wufei Temple**, shrine to the concubines to the last contender for the Ming Empire.

Head east down Wufei Rd and turn left just past building No 76. Quickly you'll see the grounds of 300-year-old ❹ **Fahua Temple**.

Continue up the alley until you reach a large intersection. Head north up Kaishan Rd until you see stately ❺ **Koxinga's Shrine** on the left. When you leave the compound, take the back right gate to visit ❻ **Lady Linshui's Temple**. You'll mostly see women here, asking for their children's protection.

Now get back on Kaishan Rd and turn right at the intersection. Head east down Fucyan Rd and turn left at the big intersection onto Mincyuan Rd. At ❼ **Dongyue Temple** check out the terrifying paintings of hell.

Continue up Mincyuan to Chenghuang Rd and turn right. At the end of this short street you'll see ❽ **City God Temple**. The god has been waiting for you!

Now head west down Cingnian and turn right up Mincyuan. Cross Gongyuan and turn left. You'll see a bank and then a small alley. Turn right into the alley to get to ❾ **Altar of Heaven**. Say a prayer to relieve any bad luck.

When you leave the alley, it's a quick left and then a right onto Minsheng Rd. A block later, turn right up Yongfu Rd. Two blocks ahead you'll see the beautiful deep-rose-coloured walls of ❿ **Official God of War Temple**.

Now continue to the end of Yongfu Rd to ⓫ **Chihkan Towers**. On the opposite side of the street, a tiny alley leads to ⓬ **Matsu Temple**. Don't forget to check out the door gods and roof beams.

Ing Wang Hotel HOTEL $

(英王賓館; Yīngwáng Bīnguǎn; ☎2263 3151-4; 26 Lane 233, Jhongyi Rd, Sec 2; 忠義路2段233巷26號; r from NT$590; @) A popular budget hotel just a stone's throw from Chihkan Towers (down the back alleys). Rooms are small but bright, and a small breakfast (and very friendly owners) is thrown into the deal. The location is a bit tricky to find the first time, so from the corner of Chenggong and Jhongyi Rds, head south. Look for the turn for Lane 233 about 50m up on the right. Follow this lane for 150m as it winds along walled compounds to the hotel.

Tayih Landis HOTEL $$$

(大億麗緻酒店; Dàyì Lìzhì Jiǔdiàn; ☎213 5555; www.tayihlandis.com.tw; 660 Simen Rd, Sec 1; 西門路1段660號; d/tw/ste incl buffet breakfast NT$6200/6800/8800; @) This established five-star hotel is noted for its good service, management and top-notch food and beverage outlets. Rooms have a pretty standard luxury design, but are spacious and feature very cosy large beds. The hotel is close to the upmarket Shin Kong Mitsukoshi Department Store, as well as a number of cultural attractions. Package deals for two people usually run for around NT$4000 a night.

Ta Lee Hotel HOTEL $

(大立大飯店; Dàlì Dàfàndiàn; ☎222 0171; http://talee.hotel.com.tw; 6 Jhongcheng Rd; 中成路6號; r from NT$1220; @) Rooms are surprisingly fresh looking and well appointed, for the price. There are a variety of styles from which to choose, and they could be described as airport-lounge cosy, sauna interior (ie wood-panelled), very junior executive, and Plain Jane.

Hann Gong Hotel HOTEL $

(漢宮大飯店; Hànggōng Dàfàndiàn; ☎226 9115; 199 Jhongshan Rd; 中山路199號; s/d/tw from NT$700/800/1350) Rooms are nondescript but clean, and the location, near the train station, is good. Singles and doubles are NT$100 cheaper on weekdays.

Cambridge Hotel HOTEL $$

(劍橋大飯店; Jiànqiáo Dàfàndiàn; ☎221 9966; www.cambridge-hotel.com.tw; 269 Minzu Rd, Sec 2; 民族路2段269號; d/tw NT$2800/3400; @) Run by the same company as the Teacher's Hostel, but ageing a little less gracefully, the Cambridge is well positioned in the business district, a stone's throw from the Chihkan Towers. Facilities include underground parking, business centre, ADSL in every room and direct service to the Tainan Science Park. Midweek discounts are 20% to 30%.

Tainan City Labour Recreation Centre HOSTEL $

(台南市勞工育樂中心; Táinánshì Láogōng Yùlè Zhōngxīn; ☎215 0174; fax 215 0177; 261 Nanmen Rd, 南門路261號; s NT$550) Part of the Youth Guesthouse Network, but anyone can stay here. Rooms are very basic, in an institutional kind of way. It's just south of Jiankang Rd on the left inside a large complex. To get to the centre take a bus 2 from the City Bus North or South Stations.

Eating

For simple inexpensive noodle, dumpling, rice and Japanese fast-food outlets, check out the area around Vie Show Cinemas, or behind the train station (the student area) – or really anywhere in the city. You'd be hard-pressed to find any city street not chock-a-block with eateries.

For traditional food you can't beat the areas around Chihkan Towers and Anping Fort. Look for *dan zai mian* (擔仔麵; *dànzǎi miàn*), coffin cake (棺材板; *guāncáibǎn*), and seafood congee (海鮮粥; *hǎixiānzhōu*).

Some of the best areas for casual eating in Tainan are down narrow back alleys. Yenping St in the Anping area dates back to a Dutch-era market and is lined with shops selling snacks, drinks and simple traditional dishes.

In central Tainan, the leafy old street directly east of the Confucius Temple (through the gate) is another pleasant pedestrian-only area with cafes and small restaurants.

Chihkan East Rd, just up from the Chihkan Towers, has a row of eateries across from a crumbling block of old buildings that give a cool old-world feel to the street.

The newcomer on the block (though really another charming old character-filled lane) is Shennong St, a narrow alley off Hai'an Rd just north of Mincyuan St. The mouth of the alley opens up onto a number of outdoor eateries serving beer and fried dishes, while down the lane itself a few studios, cafes, bars and restaurants are starting to get established.

CENTRAL TAINAN

Jade Room Restaurant CHINESE/WESTERN $$$

(翡翠廳; Fěicuì Tīng; 1 Chenggong Rd; buffet lunch/dinner NT$720) This long-running restaurant inside the Tainan Hotel has one of the best buffets in town.

Lily Fruit Shop FRUIT $
(莉莉水果店; 199 Fucyan Rd, Sec 1; ⌚11am-11pm, closed 2 Mon per month) Across from the Confucius Temple is this well-known shop, serving delicious *bào bīng* (刨冰; shaved iced and fruit; NT$50) and fruit drinks (NT$50).

Chi Kin Dandanman TRADITIONAL SNACKS $
(赤崁擔仔麵; Chì Kǎn Dànzǎimiàn; 180 Minzu Rd, Sec 2; dànzǎi miàn bowl NT$50; ⌚24hr) This is a fun place to try traditional *dànzǎi miàn,* because the restaurant is set in a Japanese-era merchant's house. *Dànzǎi miàn* means 'two baskets and a stick' and refers to the baskets used to carry the noodles around for sale. The dish is a simple, refreshing mix of noodles with a tangy meat sauce. This shop uses no MSG.

Yu Shen Restaurant VEGETARIAN $
(優鮮素食西餐; Yōuxiān Sùshí Xīcān; 180 Chingjhong St; dishes from NT$60; ⌚10am-10pm) A popular vegetarian restaurant serving à la carte dishes including noodles, dumplings and salads.

A Xia Restaurant SEAFOOD $$$
(阿霞飯店; Āxiá Fàndiàn; ☎221 9873; 7; Lane 84, Jhongyi Rd, Sec 2; dishes NT$500-700, 4-person set meals NT$6000; ⌚11am-2.30pm & 4.30-9pm, closed Mon) A popular venue for weddings and other celebrations, now sporting a modern look. Not really suitable for single diners.

ANPING

The area close to Fort Anping is also well known for its local foods. Some snacks to look out for include shrimp rolls (蝦捲; *xiājuǎn*) and fish ball soup (魚丸湯; *yúwántāng*).

An-Ping Gui Ji Local Cuisine Cultural Restaurant TRADITIONAL FOOD $
(安平貴記美食文化館; Ānpíng Guìjì Měishí Wénhuàguǎn; 93 Anping Jie; set meals NT$129; ⌚11am-8pm) Set in the Yang family's ancestral home on Yenping St, this restaurant offers a host of traditional Tainan snacks at low prices. The shop features a big photo display of traditional foods and a multilanguage brochure to help visitors. The restaurant also sells Chou family shrimp rolls (周氏蝦捲; Zhōushì Xiājuǎn; NT$50), an Anping staple.

5 Cent Driftwood House CHINESE/WESTERN $$
(伍角船板; WǔJiǎo Chuánbǎn; 88 Guangjhou Rd; set meals from NT$480; ⌚11.30am-9pm, closed Mon) This is one place that you should at least have a gander at. It's across from the Eternal Golden Castle. Designed by an artist from Tainan County, who had no previous background in architecture, the house will either strike you as daring, original and awesome, or proof that people should stick to their field of expertise. The outside is indescribable, though if we had to describe it we'd say it looks like a castle battling cancer. If this sounds harsh it isn't meant to be – the restaurant is a quirky, idiosyncratic work of love and we quite like it just the way it is.

 Drinking

There are cafes and teahouses all around Tainan. Check out the back alleys mentioned on p231 if you're looking for something with old Tainan character.

Former Julius Mannich Merchant House PUB
(德商東興洋行; Déshāng Dōngxīng Yángháng; beer from NT$100; ⌚10am-10pm Sun-Thur, to midnight Fri & Sat) The first Opium War between the British Empire and China led to the opening of ports in Taiwan to European trade. This fine old wood and brick structure is mildly interesting to tour as a site but is also highly enjoyable as a place to hang out. The garden restaurant serves good German beer and sausage plates under the shade of spreading banyan trees.

The merchant house is just a few minutes' walk from the Tree House, and just behind a row of houses across from Anping Fort.

Narrow Door Café CAFE
(窄門咖啡; Zhǎimén Kāfēi; 67 Nanmen Rd; drinks from NT$120; ⌚11am-11pm; 📶) The Narrow Door has been around for over a decade serving drinks and simple meals in a white stucco tearoom overlooking the Confucius Temple. It's easy to miss the entrance to the 2nd-floor cafe but if you look for a tight alley entrance just south of the arch across from the temple, the cafe's choice of name will become apparent.

Hud La Voos BAR
(6 Lane 82, Jhongshan Rd; drinks from NT$100; ⌚8pm-3am) A family-run bar sounds a bit quirky, but the Bunun clan that runs Hud La Voos embraces that difference. The bar is decorated with aboriginal carvings, paintings and embroidery and has a funky

world-music feel to it. Hud La Voos offers standard drinks but also millet wine and a range of exotic aboriginal fare (fried bees, for example). There's an English menu to help you out.

Other recommendations:

A Chuan Melon Drink FRUIT STAND

(義豐阿川冬瓜茶; Yìfēng Āchuān Dōngguāchá; 216 Yongfu Rd, Sec 2; drinks from NT$20; ⌚9am-10pm) Well-known melon (or winter squash, technically) drink stand across from the Official God of War Temple. Look for the line-up.

Willy's Second Base PUB

(葳苙二壘酒吧餐廳; Wēilì Èrlěi Jiǔbā Cāntīng; 321 Jiankang Rd, Sec 2; drinks from NT$100; ⌚6pm-2am) Loud and fun, with good British pub fare on offer (meals NT$200 to NT$300).

Armory Pub PUB

(http://armorypub.com.tw/; 82 Gongyuan S Rd; drinks from NT$100; ⌚8pm-late) A staple of the bar scene. Serves meals with a decent range of vegetarian options.

☆ Entertainment

Vie Show Cinemas MOVIE THEATRE

(華納威秀影城; Huánà Wēixiù Yǐngchéng; www.warnervillage.com.tw; 8F 60 Gongyuan Rd) You can book tickets online in English.

Shopping

Tainan Kuang Tsai Embroidery Shop TRADITIONAL EMBROIDERY

(府城光彩繡莊; Fǔchéng Guāngcǎi Shòu Zhuāng; ☎227 1253; 186-3 Yongfu Rd, Sec 2; ⌚8am-10pm) Across from one treasure of Tainan (the Official God of War Temple) is this other treasure, Mr Lin, one of the last remaining embroidery masters in Tainan. Mr Lin has been working at his craft since he was 16 (he's in his late 60s now) and in recent years he and his daughter have taken the craft to a new, modern level. All his pieces have the light touch and expressiveness of a craftsman truly at the peak of his skills.

The most famous and expensive samples of his work are the long Eight Immortals panels, which used to be popular at weddings and other special occasions. Such panels cost tens of thousands of Taiwanese dollars but this doesn't stop buyers from all over the world coming to the shop. Smaller pieces can be purchased for a few thousand, and even browsers are more than welcome (as the sign outside the shop says).

Shin Kong Mitsukoshi Department Store DEPARTMENT STORE

(台南新天地新光三越; Táinán Xīntiāndì Xīng uāng Sānyuè; 658 Simen Rd, Sec 1) Most older locals remember when this housed a prison and an execution room, not an upscale mall.

ℹ Information

After Taipei, Tainan is probably the most English-friendly city in Taiwan. Nearly every sight worth seeing has English interpretation signs around it. Large map boards guide you along a walking-tour route that's similar to ours, though not identical (ours was first).

Internet Access

ADSL is widely available in hotels. There's free wireless available at many sites including Chihkan Towers, Anping Fort, Anping Tree House, Eternal Golden Castle and Koxinga's Shrine.

National Museum of Taiwanese Literature (www.nmtl.gov.tw; 1 Jhongjheng Rd; ⌚8am-5pm, closed Mon) Internet access is free in the museum library.

Laundry

Laundromat (洗衣店; 111-1 Yu Le St; ⌚8am-midnight) Down the street behind the FE21'Mega department store is a DIY Laundromat.

Medical Services

National Cheng Kung University Hospital (成大醫院; www.hosp.ncku.edu.tw; 138 Sheng Li Rd) Reputable local hospital across from the north side of the National Cheng Kung University campus.

Money

There are ATMs in most 7-Elevens (which are everywhere) in Tainan. You can use the ATMs or change money at **Bank of Taiwan** (台灣銀行; 155 Fucyan Rd, Sec 1).

Photography

Fuji photo shop (照相館; 5 Nanmen Rd)

Tourist Information

Visitor Information Centre (遊客服務中心; ☎229 0082; ⌚9am-6pm) There are two centres in Tainan but the most convenient one for travellers is right in the train station. Staff speak English and have all the information you could need.

Websites

Tainan City Government (www.tncg.gov.tw) Wealth of information (and pictures) on everything to see, do and consume in the city.

Getting There & Away

Bus

Ho-Hsin Bus Company (和欣客運; www.ebus.com.tw; 23 Beimen Rd) This company takes you to Taipei (small/large seat NT$350/600, five to six hours, every 30 minutes), as do other bus companies nearby.

High Speed Train

The HSR station is a 30- to 40-minute drive or bus ride south of the city centre. Trains to Taipei (NT$1350, two hours) leave every half-hour.

Train

Tainan is a major stop on Western Line. Fast/slow train to Taipei – NT$738/475, four/5½ hours; to Kaohsiung – NT$107/69, half-hour/one hour.

Getting Around

To/From the Airport & HSR

Bus 5 connects the airport with City Bus North Station (NT$18, 20 minutes). HSR shuttle buses connect HSR station with City Bus North station (NT$40, 40 minutes, every 20 minutes).

Bus

CITY BUS

This bus covers most of the city (http://ebus.tncg.gov.tw). Basic fares are NT$18, and buses run every 15 to 30 minutes. The hub across from the train station is divided into City Bus North Station and City Bus South Station. Most city buses stop at both stations, as do the tourist buses.

TOURIST BUS

Free tour bus 88 runs daily (every 30 minutes from 9am to 6pm) to all major historical sites. Free tour bus 99 runs to Sihcao Dazhong Temple, in Taijiang National Park, only on weekends (every 30 minutes from 9am to 6pm). The visitor information centre has a map of all routes and stops.

Cycling

The city has a decent government bicycle-rental program (per four hours NT$50, from 9am to 5pm). Note: it's not always obvious where to find bikes. Rental sites include Chihkan Towers, Koxinga's Shrine, Eternal Golden Castle, Anping Fort and Anping Tree House. You can return bikes to any station.

Scooter

Rentals (機車出租) cost NT$250 to NT$400 per day and are available at shops behind the train station. You only need an International Driver's Permit and ID.

SOUTHWEST COAST

Taijiang National Park

台江國家公園

The 8th and newest national park in Taiwan, **Taijiang** (Táijiāng Guójiā Gōngyuán; www.tjnp.gov.tw) covers a patchwork of coastal lands north of Anping Harbour (see the website for a map of the areas included). The almost 50 sq km of land and 340 sq km of sea include tidal flats, lagoons, mangrove swamps and wetlands that are critical habitats for rare fish, crustaceans, mammal, and bird species, including the endangered black-faced spoonbill.

That a national park would seek to preserve a diverse natural environment is not surprising. What is surprising is that the traditional economic activities in the area are also protected. But then Taijiang covers an area dear to the hearts of Taiwanese, as it was here that their ancestors first landed after the dangerous crossing of the Black Ditch (the Taiwan Strait). Once a giant inland sea, Taijiang silted up during the 18th century, facilitating the development of local salt and farm-fishing industries. These days only the fish farms remain active, and they will face greater environmental regulations under national-park law.

The potential for Taijiang to become a prime biking destination is great. The land is completely flat and the climate is sunny year-round. One day you'll be able to idle away the day riding from mangrove swamps, to historical saltpans, to bird-watching areas, to beautiful old temples, concluding with a view of a glowing sunset over a lagoon. Taijiang is not quite there but work turning back the clock on decades of environmental abuse is progressing fast, and even at the time of writing this was still a rich little area to explore.

Sights & Activities

Boating

You can boat through the mangrove swamps and further out to the estuary of the Yenshui River from a pier close to the **Sihcao Dazhong Temple** (四草大眾廟; Sìcǎo Dàzhòng Miào). A 30-minute ride through the **Mangrove Green Tunnel** (紅樹林綠色隧道; Hóng Shùlín Lùsè Sùidào) is NT$150 while the 70-minute ride that goes out to larger channels and into the mouth

YENSHUI FIREWORKS FESTIVAL 鹽水蜂炮

There may be nothing stranger in this land than the annual Yenshui Fireworks Festival (Yénshǔi Fēngpào) – or battle, or blow-out – in which thousands of people place themselves willingly in a melee of exploding fireworks. Officially, the festival re-enacts when the people of Yenshui turned to Kuan Kong (the god of war and righteousness) to save them from a terrible epidemic.

It was 1875, and cholera was killing off the town; nothing known to man was helping. In desperation, people began to parade their gods through the town and set off noisy and smoky firecrackers to scare away evil disease-spreading spirits.

For the older generation, the current Yenshui festival still honours the old event, but for the younger crowd it's an opportunity to live life on the edge. Crowds of 100,000 or more can gather. It's hot, smoky, and tense, very tense. When a nearby 'beehive' is set off thousands of bottle rockets fly at you and over you (though hopefully not through you). The noise deafens, the smoke blinds and the rockets sting.

Some people travel from overseas every year to be part of the excitement. Tens of thousands more come in from all parts of Taiwan. Accidents, burns and lost eyes are all common, though most try to mitigate damage by wearing protective clothing. A motorcycle helmet is considered mandatory, as is thick, nonflammable clothing and earplugs. Many people also wrap a towel around their neck to prevent fireworks from flying up under their helmet.

If you're injured you should be able to find medical help nearby, but don't expect any sympathy. And certainly don't expect any compensation. You participate at your own risk.

Yenshui is in the north of Tainan County. You can reach the town by taking an express train to nearby Sinying and then a taxi. Be prepared to be out all night, and take care of your valuables. The festival takes place every year during the Lantern Festival, two weeks after Chinese New Year.

of the Yenshui River is NT$200. Boats (☎06-284 1610) leave when full so most weekdays you will be waiting a long time.

Bus 10 (NT$36, every hour) from Tainan runs out to the temple daily while the free tourist bus 99 (every 30 minutes) runs from 9am to 6pm on weekends. You can take bikes on the buses, which is useful if you want to explore the national park.

Barking Deer Adventures (www.barking-deer.com) offers kayaking through the mangroves.

Black-Faced Spoonbill Reserve 野生動物保護區

The **reserve** (Yěshēng Dòngwù Bǎohùqū; ☎06-786 1000; Cigu Township) is a small section of wetlands on the west coast of Tainan County that's dedicated to protecting the extremely rare black-faced spoonbill. The bird, which gets its name from its comically long black bill, spends summers (May to September) in Korea and northern China and migrates to Tainan County for the winter. Once down to just a few hundred members, the species now has closer to 2000, though this is still tiny and the bird's future is by no means assured.

If you visit the reserve you won't be able to see the birds up close, but there are high-powered binoculars you can use for free. To get to the reserve head north up Hwy 17 from Tainan and look for the English signs around the Km162 mark after crossing the Zengwen River, or contact **Barking Deer Adventures** (www.barking-deer.com) for private tours.

Taiwan Salt Museum 台灣鹽博物館

Although not a must-see, this **museum** (Taíwān Yén Bówùguǎn; Cigu Township; admission NT$130; ⌚9am-5pm, closed 3rd Wed of month) makes for a nice diversion on a long day exploring Taijiang National Park (although, technically, it's just outside the park's boundaries). The 1st floor has English interpretation signs, and there are several movies to watch, including one on the black-faced spoonbill. The 2nd-floor display of salt crystals from around the world is fascinating in its variety.

Next to the museum are several **salt mountains** (admission NT$50; ⌚9am-6pm) that kids can climb, and, where the salt has not hardened, even slide down.

The museum and salt mountains are off Hwy 17 north of Tainan. Look for the turn-off's English signs at around the Km156 mark.

Aogu Wetlands 鰲鼓濕地

Just when you think you've got Taiwan pegged as a mountainous island covered in dense forest, you discover yet another aspect to its rich ecological diversity: in this case, its coastal wetlands, considered some of the best in the world.

The sprawling 13-sq-km wetland preserve known as Aogu (Áogǔ Shīdì) includes sandbars, mud beaches, marshes, lagoons, fish farms and forests of beefwood, as well as tracts of thick shrub. Dozens of bird species can be spotted here by the inexperienced amateur with nothing more than his or her naked eyes: these include varieties of drongos, egrets, cranes, ducks, cormorants from south China, hawks and eagles. Occasionally a rare black-faced spoonbill can also be spotted. In total, 221 species have been recorded in the wetlands, with the majority being migratory. If all goes well, in the coming years about half the total area will be turned into a wildlife conservation zone.

Aogu is easily reached off Hwy 17 if you have your own vehicle, but be aware that the reserve is a maze of dirt roads.

Guanziling (Kuanziling) 關子嶺

☎06 / POP 2000

Aficionado alert! Only three places in the world can lay claim to having mud hot springs, and this little northern Tainan mountain village (Guānzǐlǐng) is one of them.

The Guanziling area is essentially one long dip off County Rd 172 on leafy Township Rd 96. The village, on the eastern end of the dip, is divided into lower (the older part of town) and upper sections joined by a series of stone steps for walking, or a regular road for cars. There's an ATM in the 7-Eleven in the lower village.

Sights

Red Leaf Park PARK

The Japanese built this park (紅葉公園; Hóngyè Gōngyuán) and, as usual, they knew what they were doing. The feng shui is fantastic but, more importantly, so are the clear, unspoiled views of Dadongshan and the sight of maple leaves changing colours in autumn. To reach the park, head up from the 7-Eleven in the lower village and look for a wooden arch to the left about 200m along. The stairs lead directly to the park.

Water & Fire Mix NATURAL ODDITY

(水火同源; Shǔihuǒ Tóng Yuán) Guanziling is famous for two geological oddities. The first concerns the mud hot-spring water, which isn't really muddy but is rather a light grey colour, owing to the heavy concentration of minerals it picks up on the way to the surface.

The second oddity, only slightly less remarkable, is a small grotto where fire and water really do mix – natural gas from far underground bubbles up through a pool of water and ignites spontaneously on the surface. The result is a surreal dance of flames atop pure water.

Sadly, the site seems to be slowly losing life. Years ago it was like standing before a bonfire, but at the time of writing it's, well, more like a yuletide log. The grotto is in a small park across from a car park about 5km west of the hot-spring area.

Temples

On the ride up to Guanziling the road passes two popular Buddhist temples, the expansive **Dasian Temple** (大仙寺; Dàxiān Sì) and the Ming-dynasty era **Biyun Temple** (碧雲寺; Bìyún Sì) dedicated to Guanyin, the goddess of mercy. The latter is a small affair, but commands excellent views over the plains.

Activities

Hot Springs

The Japanese built the first hot-spring resort in Guanziling and considered the muddy waters (found elsewhere only in Japan and Sicily) particularly therapeutic. If you are staying overnight, look for bargains in the lower village hotels.

King's Garden Villa HOT SPRING

(景大渡假莊園; Jǐngdà Dùjià Zhuāngyuán; ☎682 2500; www.myspa.com.tw; admission NT$450; ⌚9am-10pm) The leafy garden complex of this resort gets the hot-spring

WORTH A TRIP

TEMPLE TOURING ON THE SOUTHWEST COAST

The southwest coast, as one of the oldest settled parts of Taiwan, naturally contains some of the most ancient temples. In most cases these centre on the stars of southern folk faith: Matsu and the Wang Yeh.

At Luermen, look for the massive **Luermen Matsu Temple** (鹿耳門天后宮; Lùěrmén Tiānhòugōng), which is near the location where Koxinga is said to have landed during his campaign against the Dutch. Close by is the **Orthodox Luermen Matsu Temple** (聖母廟; Shèngmǔ Miào), which reached its outlandish size after a battle for spiritual (and funding) supremacy with the Luermen Matsu in the '80s (bigger meaning better in the eyes of many donating believers). Both temples are near the Sihcao Dazhong Temple and can be reached easily by bike.

Two temples off Provincial Hwy 19 are well worth the effort to find if you have any interest in traditional temple arts. The **Zhenxing Temple** (振興宮; Zhènxīng Gōng) in Jiali (佳里), just past the Km119 mark, contains some fantastic tableaux of figures in *jiǎnniàn* (mosaiclike temple decoration). However, these figures are not on the roof, as is usual, but on the sides of the entrance portico, so you can really examine them in detail.

At the front of the temple, above the main supports, check out the unique cochin (brightly coloured, glazed ceramic) figures of an old man and woman crouching as if to support crossbeams. They were created by Master Yeh Wang (see Cochin Ceramic Museum, p202) and are called *The Fool Crouching to Raise the House*. Also look for the two squirrels just under the roof ridgeline. They are probably the only temple squirrels you will see in Taiwan.

About 5km north of Jiali, in the town of Xuejia (學甲), the **Ciji Temple** (慈濟宮; Cíjì Gōng; 170 Jisheng Rd; 濟生路170號) protects more of the remaining works of Master Yeh Wang. The works are collected in a four-storey **museum** (admission free; ⏲8.30am-noon & 2-5pm) beside the temple. These little treasures show the full range of Yeh Wang's interests: gods, imperial officials, animals, mythological creatures and tableaux of classical historical events, as well as his obvious joy in creating riding and moving figures.

A few pieces of Yeh Wang's pottery remain in the temple but you'll have to ask where they are. On the whole, Ciji is a lovely southern-style temple, with a graceful swallowtail roof and stone work and wood carvings from the 19th century. The figurines in *jiǎnniàn* to the left and right of the front steps are over 100 years old and are superb examples of this folk art.

Heading to the coast from Xuejia, and connecting with Provincial Hwy 17, takes you quickly to **Nankunshen Temple** (南鯤鯓代天府; Nánkūnshēn Dàitiān Fǔ). Established in 1662, this temple is the centre of Wang Yeh worhsip (don't confuse these gods with Master Yeh Wang) in Taiwan. Like the Luermen Matsu temples, the size of Nankunshen is the direct result of rivalry with a local upstart over who had paramount status in the world of Wang Yeh. Nankunshen won (as it should).

On most Sundays the temple explodes with exuberant displays of ritual devotion: there are fireworks, parades, chanting and, occasionally, self-mutilation. If possible, try to visit during the Welcoming Festival for Wang Yeh (20 April, lunar calendar) or the Birthday of Wu-tzu-yeh (10 September, lunar calendar).

If you don't need a temple time-out by now, and would like to end your tour on a high note, head west to Beigang and Xigang for two beautiful Matsu temples (rivals, of course; see boxed text, p207) that have preserved much of their traditional style and adornments.

experience right, in our opinion. With 15 stone and wood pools to test, in addition to a swimming pool, mud-bath room, and lounging area, the hours spent here melt away. Rooms and cabins are also available for private soaking or overnight stays.

To get to the resort, which is 500m up a side road, look for the signs in English as you drive up the main road in the upper village.

Sleeping

You'll find a few remaining hotels from the Japanese era in the lower village. The posher resorts are in the upper village.

Guanziling Hotel HOTEL
(關子嶺大旅社; Guānzǐlǐng Dàlǚshè; No 20; ☎682 2321; s/d/tw NT$1200/1600/2600) This wooden hotel dates back to 1905, making it one of a handful of places left over from Japanese times. It has guest-only springs, and while a typical Westerner will have trouble cramming into the tubs from a bygone era, this is one of the cheapest places to stay in town, and certainly the most character filled. Discounts of 20% are available midweek.

To get to the hotel, walk uphill about 50m from the 7-Eleven in the lower village and then cross a bridge to the right. You can enter the hotel from a wooden-framed portico up the side lane but you must check in on the far side up a flight of stairs.

Eating & Drinking

There are plenty of cafes and restaurants around Guanziling. Across from the bus stop sits a row of barbecue stalls, although these usually serve group-sized portions. Most of the hotels have restaurants, and decent *tǎocān* (set meals) can be had for around NT$200.

Getting There & Around

It's best to take your own transport. Consider scooter rental in Chiayi (per day NT$200 to NT$400). Buses from Chiayi (NT$78, one hour, every hour) stop at the two temples and 7-Eleven in the lower village. The last return bus to Chiayi leaves at 8pm.

Kaohsiung City 高雄市

☎07 / POP 1,512,677

If you were ever asked to define 'bustling harbour city', you could always point to the southern city of Kaohsiung (Gāoxióng). This is Taiwan's largest port, second-largest city and centre of the heavy and petrochemical industries.

If that last reference conjures up Dickensian nightmare images, you'd be right – about a decade ago. Today's Kaohsiung has largely been transformed from grim industrial warrens into a modern urban landscape of shiny cafes, wide streets, river- and harbour-side parks, mass public transit, bicycle lanes, and cultural venues that have embraced, rather than shunned, the manufacturing past. There are also two swimming beaches within the city area, and 1000 hectares of almost-pristine forest right on its doorstep. If there's a vibe to Kaohsiung, it's 'on-the-move, but still chillin' out'.

Kaohsiung is divided into 11 districts, but most of what you want to see is clustered in a few areas that are within walking distance or a short bus ride (or cycle) from a Kaohsiung Mass Rapid Transit (KMRT) station: the harbour and lower Love River area (in the Yancheng and Gushan and Sizihwan Districts); the Lotus Pond area in Tsoying District in the north; and Cijin Island.

History

The Chinese settled on Cijin Island in the late Ming dynasty, and throughout the Qing period Kaohsiung was an administrative centre for the Taiwan territory. As usual, the Japanese were responsible for its modern character. 'Rice in the north and sugar in the south' was the colonialist policy, and under it Kaohsiung became a major port for the export of raw materials. During this time the grid pattern of streets was laid out, the harbour was expanded and rail lines were built.

The Japanese called the harbour area Hamasen, a name still used by older residents and the tourism bureau. The area lay in ruins after Allied bombing at the end of WWII but was slowly rebuilt under the KMT. Once again, with central planning, Kaohsiung became the heavy industry centre.

Under mayor Frank Hsieh (1998–2005), the city started to clean up (literally getting potable water for the first time), and to shift its industrial base towards tourism, high technology, automation and other capital-intensive industries. These days a massive land-reclamation project called South Star is creating space for a pop-music centre, and for the expansion of Kaohsiung's yacht-building industry, already the largest in Asia.

Sights

Ciaotou Sugar Factory OLD FACTORY
In 1902 the flat, fertile strip of land in Ciaotou Township (to the north of Kaoh-

WORTH A TRIP

GUANZILING TO TAINAN

Guanziling's mountain roads see little traffic during the week, and offer some fine road cycling. A particularly scenic route of about 70km follows County Rd 174 and Provincial Hwys 3 and 20 down to Tainan city.

DONGSHAN COFFEE ROAD

Some signs refer to County Rd 174 as the Dongshan Coffee Rd. You won't see much sign of coffee growing from roadside, but you will get expansive views over the alluvial plains of Tainan County and the choppy foothills of the Central Mountains.

It's 25km of rolling pitch from the start of the 174 to Nansi. If you want to continue riding through more undeveloped natural landscape, head up the east side of Tsengwen Reservoir.

PROVINCIAL HIGHWAY 3

After riding about 30 kilometres through sparsely developed hills from Guanziling, you descend into the fruit-growing plains south of Tsengwen Reservoir and connect with Provincial Hwy 3. Keep your eyes peeled for the **Jiang Family Heritage Village** (鹿陶洋江家古厝; Lùtáoyáng Jiāngjiā Gǔcuò), probably the largest collection of traditional southern Fujian-style homes left on the main island of Taiwan. All the families in the 3-hectare village are surnamed Jiang and all trace their lineage back to one Jiang Ru-nan, who migrated from Fujian in 1721.

Houses are neatly arranged in six rows, safeguarding a central shrine to the ancestors. While most houses are red brick with roof tiles, some have a mud and bamboo construction, while others display the washed pebble style popular during Japanese times. A large cement courtyard, the scene of much play and tea drinking during the day, fronts the houses. Villagers are very friendly and quite happy to have visitors wander around.

The village sits back a short distance from Hwy 3, and it would be easy to pass by without noticing that it was there. Look for a large English sign at the 370km mark.

PROVINCIAL HIGHWAY 20

In the town of Yujing our route connects with Provincial Highway 20, which you can continue on to reach Tainan city. However, when you pass through **Tsochen** (左鎮; Zuǒzhèn), it's worth heading out to **Mt Tsao Moon World** (草山月世界; Cǎoshān Yuè Shìjiè), a grimly picturesque landscape of barren eroded cliffs and pointy crags. There are places in Taiwan that feel as remote, but few that feel as bewitchingly desolate.

To reach the Moon World, turn left around the 27km mark toward Nanhua on Hwy 20甲. Proceed about 1km and then turn right at the sign for the moon world. Five kilometres further, turn left at the next set of signs. From here it's 9km to **Hill 308**, which has panoramic views over the badlands.

A few kilometres in look for the Chinese sign to the **Grand Canyon** (大峽谷; Dàxiágǔ), a unique section of jagged white hills that needs no comparison to greater things.

siung) saw the start of industrial development in Taiwan with the opening of a modern sugar factory. Now the opening of the KMRT has been instrumental in breathing life back into this charming bit of old Taiwan.

Ciaotou (橋頭糖廠; Qiáotóu Tángchǎng) consists of a defunct yellow factory (which you can walk into, and explore the old mechanisms and vats) and an old village that retains most of its early-20th-century flavour. In addition to clumps of common red-brick residences, there are a number of handsome old offices in what is called the Japanese Dutch Colonial style.

The sugar factory and village grounds begin as soon as you exit Ciaotou Sugar Factory KMRT station. There are good English interpretation signs around.

Lotus Pond

SCENIC AREA

The **pond** (蓮池潭; Liánchí Tán; Map p252) in the north of the city has been a popular

Central Kaohsiung

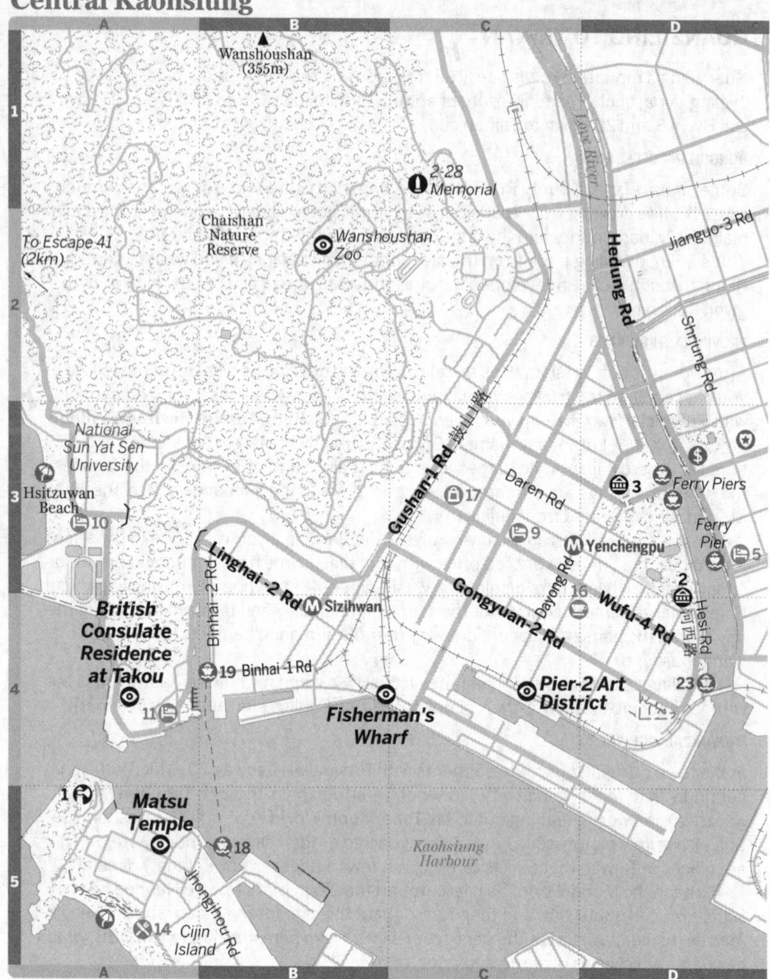

destination since the Qing dynasty and is well known for the 20 or so temples dotting the shoreline and nearby alleys. In recent years much money and effort has gone into returning the lake and its cultural and natural heritage to something of their former glory. There's now a path right around the lake, and efforts are underway to restore the wetlands on the west side. At night coloured lights give the lake a very festive appearance.

Starting from the southern end and heading clockwise around the lake, you'll first encounter sections of the **Old Wall of Fengshan** (Fèngshān Jiùcháng), built in 1826. The intact north-gate wall runs along Shengli Rd.

Next, extending out onto the pond itself are the **Dragon and Tiger Pagodas** (Lónghǔ Tǎ), built in the '60s as an extension of the Ciji Temple opposite. Enter the dragon and exit the tiger for good luck.

Next along are the **Spring and Autumn Pavilions** (Chūnqiū Gé), dedicated to Kuan Kung, the God of War, and featuring Kuanyin riding a dragon. The pavilions extend onto the lake and make for good photos.

Across the road is the **Temple of Enlightenment** (Tiānfǔ Gōng), the largest temple

in the area and worth a visit to see the two giant temple lions draped over equally giant stone balls.

As you will have noticed so far, most structures around the lake are modern and fairly garish. Look for older temples in the back streets such as the delightful **City God Temple** (城隍廟; Chénghuáng Miào). To get here, take the side road to the left past the pavilions, and then take the first left again down a small alley. In the entrance hall look up to admire the detailed plafond; the traditional woodcarvings are filled with symbolism such as the fish representing Yin and Yang, and the crabs representing official promotion. The roof, which you can reach via a set of stairs, has some fine examples of dragons and phoenixes in *jiǎnniàn* (mosaiclike temple decoration).

Back at the pond, follow the pier to the walkway out to the imposing 24m statue of **Xuantian Shang-di** (Xúantiān Shàngdì), the Supreme Emperor of the Dark Heaven, and guardian of the north.

The final temple of note is the **Confucius Temple** (Kǒng Miào) on the lake's northern end. Completed in 1976, it's the largest Confucius temple in Taiwan.

To get to the lake, take bus R35 from KMRT Ecological District station.

Kaohsiung Harbour HARBOUR

The opening of the **harbour** (Gǎngkǒu; Map p248; MRT Yanchengpu or Sizihwan) to the public is still a work in progress, but down by Pier 12 (the Love Pier), Gushan Ferry Pier (渡船站) and **Fisherman's Wharf** (高雄港漁人碼頭; Gāoxióng Gǎng Yúrén Mǎtóu) you'll find walkways, bike paths, cafes and beer gardens. Check at the train station visitor centre about harbour cruises.

The **Pier-2 Art District** (駁二藝術特區; Bóèr Yìshù Tèqū) is an old warehouse area that was renovated into art studios (following European and North American examples of similar urban-regeneration projects). Exhibitions and concerts are frequently held indoors and out. Check at the visitor centre for a schedule of events.

Cijin Island SCENIC AREA

This thin **island** (旗津; Qíjīn; Map p248), almost a sandbar really, acts as a buffer to the harbour and extends down the city coastline. It's a popular day trip from the mainland, with its frenetic **seafood street** (Hǎichǎn Jiē), beach, **lighthouse** (Qíjīn Dēngtǎ; admission free; 9am-4.30pm) and biking routes being the main attractions. The oldest temple in the Kaohsiung area is Cijin's **Matsu Temple** (天后宮; Tiānhoù Gōng), the origins of which go back to the late 17th century when the area was the first commercial centre in Kaohsiung. Much of the excellent stone relief and pillar carvings go back to the 18th century.

As on the mainland, you can rent bikes on Cijin or take your bike over on the ferry (NT$15, 10 minutes), which runs from 5am to 2am between the Gushan Ferry Terminal (鼓山碼頭; Gǔshān Mǎtóu) and the Cijin Ferry Terminal (旗津碼頭).

Central Kaohsiung

Top Sights
British Consulate Residence at Takou ... A4
Fisherman's Wharf ... B4
Matsu Temple ... A5
Pier-2 Art District ... C4

Sights
1 Lighthouse ... A5
2 Municipal Film Archives ... D4
3 Museum of History ... D3
4 Tuntex Sky Tower ... E5

Sleeping
5 Ambassador Hotel ... D3
6 Happy Hotel ... F1
7 Hotel Skoal ... F2
8 Hwa Hung Hotel ... F1
9 Kingship Hotel ... C3
10 Sunset Beach Resort & Spa ... A3
11 Uni Resort ... A4

Eating
12 Lai Lai Seafood Barbecue Restaurant ... E3
13 Liuhe Night Market ... F2
14 Seafood Street ... A5
15 Vegetary Restaurant ... E4

Drinking
16 Dog Pig Art Cafe ... C4

Shopping
17 Bamboo Street ... C3

Transport
18 Cijin Ferry Terminal ... B5
19 Gushan Ferry Pier ... B4
20 City Bus Hub ... F1
21 Kaohsiung Ke Yuan ... F1
22 Kuo Kuang Bus Company Station ... F1
23 Pier 12 ... D4

FREE British Consulate Residence at Takou (Dagou) HISTORIC SITE

(打狗英國領事館; Dǎgǒu Yīnguó Lǐngshì Guǎn; Map p248; 20 Linhai Rd; 9am-midnight) The handsome red-brick consulate residence was built in 1865 by a British trading company. Sitting about 70m above the mouth of Kaohsiung harbour, the location is perfect for watching giant container ships sail through the tiny mouth of the harbour. There's also an interesting clash of cultures to observe on the steps as mainland Chinese tourists react in bewilderment to the open presence of Falun Gong posters and protesters decrying the Beijing government.

While in the area, check out a tiny **temple** to the left of the larger temple beside the consulate. It's the only shrine in Taiwan to deify 17th-century Dutch naval commanders, much in the way old Chinese generals have been deified over the centuries.

The consulate is a five-minute walk from Sizihwan Beach. There's an open-air cafe on the grounds servings drinks and light meals.

Love River SCENIC AREA

Some have compared Kaohsiung's **Love River** (愛河; Ài Hé; Map p248; MRT Yanchengpu) to Shanghai's Bund – only a whole lot cleaner! It's a bit of a stretch (except the clean part) but this once open sewer certainly has seen a remarkable transformation in recent years. The waters flow clean, and the bankside promenades with their benches, shady trees and outdoor cafes are popular hangouts for both locals and visitors.

You can cruise along the river day and night (20-minute boat rides are NT$80, and run from 4pm to 11pm). Boats leave often and are usually full on weekends.

Just back from the river is the wonderful **Municipal Film Archives** (電影圖書館; Diànyǐng Túshūguǎn; 10 Hesi Rd; admission free; 1.30-9.30pm, closed Mon), where you can enjoy on-site private and public viewings of the archives' films. It's just a shame they won't sell those movie posters in the lobby.

A few blocks north of the archives is the classy-looking **Museum of History** (歷史博物館; Lìshǐ Bówùguǎn; http://w4.kcg.gov.tw/~khchsmus/english/index.htm; 272 Jhongjheng-4th Rd; 9am-5pm, closed Mon; admission free), which was the city government building during Japanese times. Tucked into neat rooms down the blond-wood and marble hallways are photographic displays, a permanent 2-28 Memorial, and special seasonal exhibits.

Beaches

Kaohsiung is lucky to have two decent beaches right within the city borders, open for swimming from May to October. At both you'll find showers and changing rooms.

The beach on **Cijin Island** (Map p248; admission free) is just a 10-minute ferry ride from Gushan Ferry Pier (NT$20) and another five-minute walk. When going in the water, be aware that there are serious rip tides along the more-open parts of the beach.

Hsitzuwan Beach (Sizi Bay; Xīzǐwān; Map p248; admission NT$70; ⏲8am-6pm; Ⓜ MRT Sizihwan) is smaller than Cijin, but it's a calmer swimming beach and is also an excellent place for hanging out and watching the sunset. The beach has a cool tropical feel to it and a lovely mountain backdrop.

Museums

FREE Kaohsiung Museum of Fine Arts MUSEUM

(高雄美術館; Gāoxióng Měishùguǎn; Map p252; http://english.kmfa.gov.tw; 80 Meishuguan Rd) Has a stylish interior with exhibits highlighting Taiwanese artists and local themes. Exhibits change frequently. Take Bus 35 from KMRT Aozihdi station.

National Science & Technology Museum MUSEUM

(科學工藝博物館; Kēxué Gōngyì Bówùguǎn; www.nstm.gov.tw; 720 Jiou Ru Rd; foreigners with passport NT$50) Features an hourly IMAX show and high-quality, hands-on science exhibits designed for children. The exhibit on the Industrial History of Taiwan, one of the few in English, is so informative that it alone is worth the price of admission. Take the Bus 60 to the museum from the main train station.

Other Recommended Sights

Formosa Boulevard KMRT Station STAINED-GLASS DOME

Stop to see the resplendent **Dome of Light** (光之穹頂; Guāng Zhī Qióng Dǐng), by Italian glass artist Narcissus Quagliata. Formosa Blvd is south of the main train station.

Tuntex Sky Tower LOOKOUT

This was the tallest **building** (Map p248; Gāoxióng 85 Dàlóu; 高雄85大樓) in Taiwan before Taipei 101, with a look inspired by the character 高 (gāo), meaning 'tall'. Take the elevator (NT$100) to 75th floor for sunset views.

World Games Main Stadium MODERN ARCHITECTURE

The ultramodern design of this **stadium** (世運主場館; Shìyùn Zhǔchǎngguǎn; Map p252) by Toyo Ito looks like a metallic spine. Take KMRT World Games station exit 2, turn right on Jhonghai Rd and then walk for 10 minutes.

Activities

Hiking

Within Kaohsiung City there is good hiking in the 1000-hectare **Chaishan Nature Reserve** (Cháishān Zìrán Gōngyuán), preserved since Japanese times. The Chaishan reserve is famous for its macaque population, which has been getting increasingly aggressive with visitors and locals alike in recent years. Don't carry food into the area and watch out that the monkeys don't steal your camera!

To reach the start of the trails into the reserve take Red Bus 35 from Aozihdi KMRT station (outside exit 1) to Longcyuan Temple (龍泉寺), where the trails begin. The reserve is northwest of the city centre.

Just walking around the university and getting lost in the hills is pleasant, too. Some trails will take you up to the zoo, and also up to the nature reserve.

Cycling

Kaohsiung is leading the country in urban biking, with 100km (and growing) of dedicated paths around the city. The cheap and effective **C-bike** (www.c-bike.com.tw; per hour NT$30) program has 50 stations around the city – you can rent a bike with a credit card at one location, and drop off at any other location when you are finished. There are obvious-looking stands of the green bikes outside every KMRT and also at major tourist sights such as the Love River. The website has a list of all the stations but they aren't hard to find and bikes are usually available.

You can pick up a map of the bike routes at the visitor centre. The most interesting route so far runs along the Love River and through the old warehouse district at the harbour.

Volunteering

Started by husband and wife team Christian Leroux and Natasha Hodel in 2005, **BARK** (www.atkaohsiung.org) is now leading the pack in animal welfare in the south. The organisation is particularly active in re-homing, CNR (catch-neuter-release) programs, and rescues, in addition to raising awareness of the huge problem of stray animals in Taiwan.

Lotus Pond

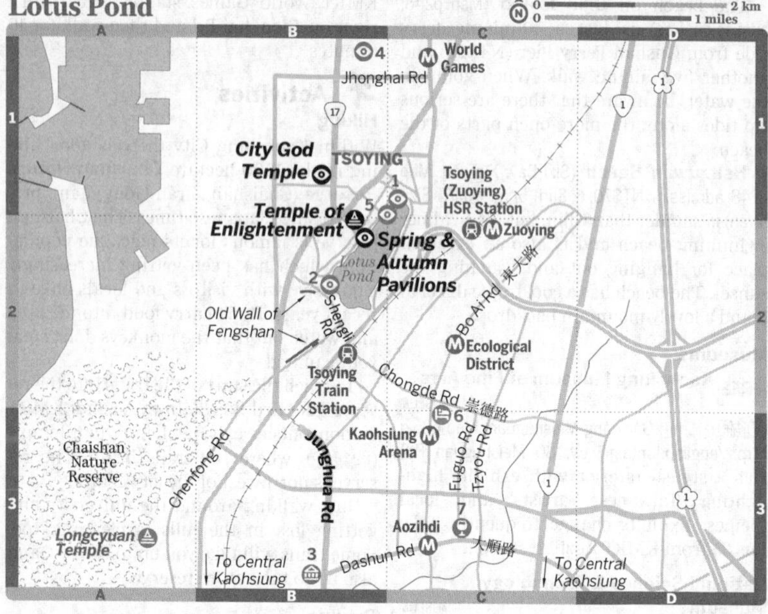

Festivals & Events

As befitting a port city, a quirky **International Container Arts Festival** (Guójì Huògùi Yìshù Jié) is held in December. Containers are used as art material.

There are also praiseworthy shows during Chinese New Year at the Kaohsiung Cultural Centre, and the colourful (and often hi-tech) lantern displays along the Love River during the Lantern Festival.

Sleeping

International Friendship House HOSTEL $
(☎0971-119 930; Map p252; internationalfriendshiphouse@gmail.com; 83 Lane 129, Wun Tze Rd, Tsoying; 左營文自路129巷83號; dm/d NT$300/750; @) The house is a modern five-storey apartment 2km southeast of Lotus Pond. Run by a long-term Canadian expat, it features a homey atmosphere with all the fixings: full shared kitchen, TV, stereo etc. There are two rooms (each for two to four people) per floor and each floor has its own bathroom. Should you need them, towels and toiletries are provided, and there is a laundry and a ton of travel information.

The house is down a quiet lane not far from Ecological District KMRT station. Long- and short-term stays are accepted but call or email Melissa first to reserve a room.

Hwa Hung Hotel HOTEL $
(華宏大飯店; Huáhóng Dàfàndiàn; Map p248; ☎237 5523; www.hhhotel.com.tw; 243 Jianguo-2nd Rd; 建國2路243號; d/tw NT$950/1600; @) The fresh, funky interior of this hotel looks like it was taken out of a comic book. Rooms are large, casually furnished, and overall great value for the money. The only downside is the neighbourhood. The train station is nearby if you need it, but otherwise this is a depressing part of town.

Sunset Beach Resort & Spa HOTEL $$
(西子灣沙灘會館; Xīzǐwān Shātān Huìguǎn; Map p248; ☎525 0005; www.seasbay.com.tw; 51 Lianhai Rd; 蓮海路51號; s/d/tw NT$2112/3300/4200; @) The rooms are a good size and feature soft beds, good bedding and other midrange comforts. But it's the location that really sells the place. It is literally on the beach, and the hotel has its own private entrance. It's also right within the university grounds, giving you access to tennis courts, jogging tracks, hiking trails and lots of greenery. The hotel has a restaurant and cafe on the premises with a deck overlooking the beach. There are seasonal and midweek discounts.

Lotus Pond

Happy Hotel HOTEL **$**
(華賓旅館; Huábīn Lǚguǎn; Map p248; ☎235 8800; www.happyhotel.com.tw; 221 Nanhua Rd; 南華路221號; d/tw NT$850/1500, @) A solid new budget hotel with pleasant decor that will hopefully shame others nearby (those that are a bit cheaper, but nasty) to similar upgrades. Rooms are small but bright and there's efficient use of space so they don't feel cramped. The staff are pleasant and there is internet and free breakfast. There are 10% discounts midweek, making this about the cheapest price for any train station hotel you'd really want to stay at.

Uni Resort HOTEL **$$$**
(統一渡假村; Tǒngyī Dùjiàcūn; Map p248; ☎533 6676; 14 Shaochuan St; 哨船街14號; d/tw NT$4000/5500; @) An excellent place to stay if you want both a comfy environment and lots of room to move around. The hotel is right on the waterfront, with walking paths to the ferry and the university right on your doorstep. There's a small spa in the basement. Expect discounts of 20% to 40%, depending on the season.

Ambassador Hotel HOTEL **$$$**
(國賓大飯店; Guóbīn Dàfàndiàn; Map p248; ☎211 5211; www.ambassadorhotel.com.tw; 202 Minsheng-2nd Rd; 民生2路202號; d/tw/ste NT$5500/6500/12,000; @) Part of a group of luxury hotels in Taiwan, the Ambassador is rated one of Kaohsiung's best. Facilities include business centre, outdoor pool, health club and a host of food and beverage options. The Ambassador attracts as many families and leisure travellers as business types so you won't feel out of place in a plaid shirt. Prices are considerably lower if you have Taiwanese ID. Expect discounts of 20% to 25% off the rack rates.

Kingship Hotel HOTEL **$$$**
(漢王洲際飯店; Hànwáng Zhōujì Fàndiàn; Map p248; ☎531 3131; fax 531 3140; 98 Cisian-3rd Rd, 七賢3路98號; r from NT$4800; @) The Kingship updates its look every few years, which helps it remain perennially fresh and modern in a local hotel market that's not particularly known for either of those traits. With its proximity to the Love River and the shopping and restaurants along Wufu-4th Rd, the Kingship makes for a solid midrange option. Discounts of 50% off the rack rates are usual.

Hotel Skoal HOTEL **$**
(世國商旅; Shìguó Shānglǚ; Map p248; ☎287 6151; fax 288 6020; 66 Min Jhu Heng Rd; 民主橫路66號; d/tw NT$1380/2280; @) This place is not as cheap as it used to be, but rooms have been updated and are a little brighter and bigger than before. It's a decent option if the cheaper places by the train station are full. Min Jhu Heng Rd runs north–south off Bade Rd.

Eating

There's food everywhere in Kaohsiung, at all times of day or night. Fuguo Rd east of Bo'ai (near Aozihdi MRT station) is filled with midrange restaurants and has a good range of Thai, Italian, barbecue and seafood. Kaohsiung arena, north of the city centre, is another good area.

Escape 41 WESTERN **$$**
(海洋天堂歐風餐館; Hǎiyáng Tiāntáng Ōufēng Cānguǎn; ☎525 0058; 41-2 Caishan, Gushan District; 鼓山區柴山路41之2號; dishes NT$90-380; ⏲noon-11pm) Did you catch that address? This place is on the mountain, or, rather, just down the slopes of it, a few metres above the blue sea. With good attention to food, Escape is worth the effort to get here. Pizza is the best dish but there are good vegie options, and a broad cocktail and wine selection if you want to hang out in the evenings on a hot summer night after sunset.

Taxis from Sizihwan station will cost about NT$150 to NT$200. Escape is the last house down a winding road through the little fishing village.

Lai Lai Seafood Barbecue Restaurant SEAFOOD $$

(來來碳烤海鮮餐廳; Láilái Tànkǎo Hǎixiān Cāntīng; Map p248; 53 Minsheng-2nd Rd; ⏲5pm-3am) For fresh seafood head over to Cijin Island's **seafood street**, or try the locally recommend Lai Lai. It's the kind of place you go to eat good seafood, drink cheap beer (NT$70 a pint), and be loud like the locals. You can barbecue right at your table or just tell the staff how much you want to spend and they will arrange dishes for you. Be sure to tell them of anything you don't eat (like fish head, perhaps?).

Vegetary Restaurant VEGETARIAN $$

(李記素食工坊; Lǐjì Sùshí Gōngfǎng; Map p248; 145 Wufu-3rd St; set meals from NT$290; ⏲6.30-9.30am, 11am-9pm) A comfortable vegie place with set meals and à la carte dishes. The speciality here is hot pot.

Bagel-Bagel 3 WESTERN $$

(貝果貝果3; Bèiguǒ Bèiguǒ 3; 158 Minsheng-1 Rd; sandwiches from NT$89, set meals from NT$199; ⏲10am-10pm) One branch of a long-running Kaohsiung restaurant chain serving a fix of Western staples such as bagel sandwiches, pasta, pizza and soups. There's a useful information board on the premises.

Night Markets

Locals recommend the food at **Ruifong Night Market** (瑞豐夜市; Ruìfēng Yèshì; ⏲closed Mon & Wed; Ⓜ MRT Kaohsiung Arena), though there is little space to even move here. **Liuhe Night Market** (Liùhé Yèshì; Map p248; Ⓜ MRT Formosa Boulevard) is famous islandwide for its 100-plus food stalls. The latter is the far more open and clean of the two markets, if that's important to you.

Other places to try traditional foods include the Lotus Pond area, especially on Shengli Rd, and around the Gushan Ferry Pier.

Drinking

Cafes, tea shops, fruit stalls and the like are everywhere. The outdoor cafe within Central Park may have reopened by the time you read this. Along the Love River, outdoor cafes offer shade in the daytime and stay open into the late evening. Some serve beer at night. The British Consulate Residence, a popular university student hangout, has an outdoor patio cafe commanding fine views over the harbour and city. Fisherman's Wharf has a row of outdoor bars, though the atmosphere was decidedly downscale at the time of writing. Wufu-4th Rd, a traditional pub street, is looking very tired these days.

Dog Pig Art Cafe ALTERNATIVE ART CAFE

(豆皮文藝咖啡館; Dòupí Wényì Kāfēiguǎn; ☎521 2422; 2F 131 Wufu-4 St; coffee NT$70-130; ⏲5-11pm Tue-Fri, 2-11pm Sat & Sun) This is a long-running cafe and alternative art space at the heart of the scene in Kaohsiung. Documentary movies and alternative theatre are shown on the 3rd floor on weekends. As owner Leo Liu says, 'We show things that are interesting to us, not necessarily what is commercially successful'.

The cafe serves good curries and has a decent foreign-beer selection.

Lighthouse Bar & Grill BAR & GRILL

(燈塔美式酒館; Dēngtǎ Měishì Jiǔguǎn; Map p252; 239 Fuguo-1st Rd; ⏲6pm-late) A popular hangout in the Tsoying District, with good service, live sports broadcasts, and a wide selection of bar favourites like pizza and sandwiches.

Entertainment

Free movies are shown night at the Municipal Film Archives.

Dog Pig Art has alternative theatre and documentary showings on the weekend. Pier-2 Art District is often the site of concerts and outdoor performances. Pick up a seasonal events calendar at the visitor information centre.

Shopping

Bamboo Street TRADITIONAL WARES

(玉竹街; Yùzhú Jiē; Map p248) At the end of Wufu-4 Rd you'll find wares from the past, including traditional hats, raincoats and household articles made from bamboo.

Information

Cultural Centres

Kaohsiung Cultural Centre (高雄文化中心; Gāoxióng Wénhuà Zhōngxīn; ☎222 5136; 67 Wufu 1 Rd; ⏲9am-5pm, closed Mon; Ⓜ KMRT Cultural Center) The centre has lecture and concert halls, galleries and a library.

Dangers & Annoyances

If you want to head out to a club, or even a bar, you're advised to get a recommendation first. Kaohsiung can be a rough town, and foreign men (and sometimes women) in clubs are an easy target for nasty beatings. Many expats simply avoid the club scene entirely now.

Internet Access

ADSL is widely available in hotels. There's free wi-fi at the Kaohsiung Cultural Centre, as well as outside the MRT station at Central Park. Internet cafes come and go, so ask at the visitor centre for locations.

Medical Services

Chung-Ho Memorial Hospital, Kaohsiung Medical University (高雄醫學大學附設中和紀念醫院; www.kmuh.org.tw; 100 Zihyou 1st Rd) Just east of Houyi KMRT Station.

Money

There are banks and ATMs everywhere, including most 7-Elevens. You can change money at the **Bank of Taiwan** (台灣銀行; 264 Jhongjheng-4th Rd).

Tourist Information

Train Station Visitor Centre (火車站遊客服務中心; ⏰9am-7pm) In the main train station. Staff speak English and are a good source of information.

Websites

Kaohsiung City (http://khh.travel) Excellent city tourism website.

Getting There & Away

Air

The airport, south of the city, connects seamlessly to downtown by KMRT. Domestic and international terminals are joined and you can quickly walk from one to the other. Facilities include money changing, a post office, and bilingual signage.

There's a **visitor information centre** (遊客服務中心; ⏰9am-10pm) in each terminal. Staff speak passable English and can help with hotels, tours, MRT travel, car rentals etc.

Siaogang Domestic Airport Terminal (www.kia.gov.tw) has flights to Kinmen and Penghu. **Uni Air** (www.uniair.com.tw) and **Daily Air Corporation** (www.dailyair.com.tw) fly from here.

Siaogang International Airport Terminal has flights to most Southeast Asian countries, Japan, Korea and China. **EVA** (www.evaair.com) and **China Airlines** (www.china-airlines.com) fly from here.

Boat

Taiwan Hangye Company (www.taiwanline.com.tw/taiwu01.htm) There are year-round boats from Kaohsiung to Makung, Penghu (NT$860, 4½ hours). The schedule changes every three months and is unreliable in winter.

Bus

Kaohsiung Ke Yuan (高雄客運; Map p248; ☎746 2141; 245 Nanhua St) has buses to: Donggang (NT$91, 50 to 70 minutes, every 15 to 30 minutes); Foguangshan (NT$80, 30 minutes, eight per day); Kenting (every 30 minutes, 24 hours a day – by Kenting Express, NT$355, 2½ hours; by regular bus, NT$309, 3½ hours); and Meinong (NT$124, 1½ hours, every one or two hours).

Kuo Kuang Bus Company (國光客運東站; Map p248; ☎236 0962; www.kingbus.com.tw; 306 Jianguo Rd) has buses to Taipei (weekday/weekend NT$400/520, five hours, every half-hour 24 hours a day) and Taitung (NT$443, four hours).

High Speed Rail

The HSR travels from Tsoying Station to Taipei every half-hour (NT$1490, two hours).

Train

Kaohsiung is the terminus for most west-coast trains. Trains run frequently from early morning until midnight. To Taipei, fast/slow NT$845/544, 4½/seven hours; to Taichung, fast/slow NT$470/303, 2½/three hours, every two hours.

Getting Around

To/From the Airport & High Speed Rail

Taking the KMRT Red Line to the airport and HSR costs NT$35. Taxis to the airport or HSR cost NT$300 from the city centre.

Bus

The city has a decent bus system that ties in with the KMRT. The bus hub is directly in front of the train station, and buses have English signage at the front and electronic English displays inside indicating the next stop.

Routes are clearly mapped in English at every KMRT station, and a one-zone fare is NT$12.

Car

Both of the following have English-speaking staff and do pick-ups:

Car Plus (☎0800-222 568; www.car-plus.com.tw)

Central Auto (☎802 0800; www.rentalcar.com.tw)

Kuohsing Mass Rapid Transit

Rivalling the Taipei MRT for cost, cleanliness and efficiency, the Kaohsiung **system** (www.krtco.com.tw; ⏰5.55am-11.40pm) surpasses its northern cousin for convenience. Locals complain that the system doesn't go where they live, but it does go where travellers want to visit. Abundant English signs and maps make the system easy to use.

Individual fares start at NT$20 and can be purchased at every station. A day pass costs NT$130 (plus NT$70 deposit) – buy directly from any staffed station booth. A bus/MRT/ferry combo pass is NT$200 (no deposit).

AROUND KAOHSIUNG

Foguangshan 佛光山

☎07

The **Foguangshan** (Light of Buddha Mountain; Fóguāngshān; www.fgs.org.tw) is a 52-acre temple complex about a 30-minute drive from Kaohsiung. The complex serves as a monastery, university and meditation centre. It's considered *the* centre of Buddhism in southern Taiwan.

The most famous feature here is the **Great Buddha Land** (大佛城; Dàfóchéng), where a towering 36m Amitabha Buddha stands over a garden of 480 smaller Buddha statues. For many, the Disneyland-like **Pure Land Cave** (淨土洞窟; Jìngtǔ Dòngkū), with its animated figures and light show, is the more interesting sight.

Tours in English of up to a half-day can be arranged with the nuns at **reception** (信徒中心; Xìntú Zhōngxīn; ☎656 1921, ext 6203-05). Temple tours stress the ceremonial aspects of Buddhism and you will be requested to bow, kowtow and otherwise observe all forms of respect and devotion. Wear appropriate clothing and do not carry any food or drinks. In return, you will be instructed in Buddhist thought, history and iconography and may receive advice and blessed trinkets.

The **Pilgrim's Lodge** (Cháoshān Huìguǎn; dm/d free/NT$2000) invites devotees and tourists to spend the night. The accommodation is surprisingly good. The meditation centres host frequent retreats for beginners and experienced practitioners. Check the website for details, and for more on the history and mission of the temple. Arrangements for meditation classes or an overnight temple stay can be made in advance.

There are eight buses a day between the temple and Kaohsiung (NT$80, 30 minutes).

Meinong 美濃

☎07 / POP 45,187

In 1736 the intrepid Lin brothers led the first Hakka immigrants to settle the plains of Meinong (Měinóng). While the Hakka make up about 10% to 15% of the population of Taiwan, in Meinong the percentage today goes up to 95%. A hardworking people, who value higher education, the Hakka of Meinong can count a disproportionate number of PhDs (and in the past, imperial scholars) among its population.

Thoroughly rural in character, and once the centre of a thriving and well-protected tobacco industry, Meinong was hit hard by Taiwan's entry into the World Trade Organization (WTO) in 2002. With the monopoly system – which had been in place since the 1930s – abolished, the town began to refashion itself into a country retreat. Hakka culture, historical sites, tobacco history and (a little more incongruously) butterfly-watching became the cornerstones of the new economy.

Winters are a great time to visit, as the weather is perfect – warm and dry – and the tourists are few. Summer is the season of the yellow butterflies and in the valleys to the northeast they swarm in the hundreds of thousands.

Sights & Activities

Yellow Butterfly Valley BUTTERFLY VALLEY

If you want to see for yourself just why Taiwan was and is known as the kingdom of the butterfly, then head to this remarkable reproductive **valley** (黃蝶翠谷; Huángdié Cuìgǔ) in the late spring and summer. Over 100 species can be found here, and the chances of having a dozen (species, that is) of them flittering about you at any moment are high. In late July you may see half a million individuals within a couple of hectares of open riverbed and the surrounding forest. Yes, half a million. No one is entirely sure how many exist in the entire region.

The flighty, midsized yellow emigrant butterfly *(Catopsilia pomona)* lends its name to the valley and is the most commonly seen species. It breeds in the spring, and with the explosion of its numbers in summer, devours most of the available food sources. Around July it is common to see swarms of yellows crossing Hwy 10 as they disperse to richer pastures.

To reach the valley, head north on the 106 and follow the signs to the valley. At a wide intersection with a temple on one side, take the road to the right. When you see the temple with butterfly cut-outs on its frame you are close. A few hundred metres up, the river makes a bend and widens. This is your spot.

Meinong

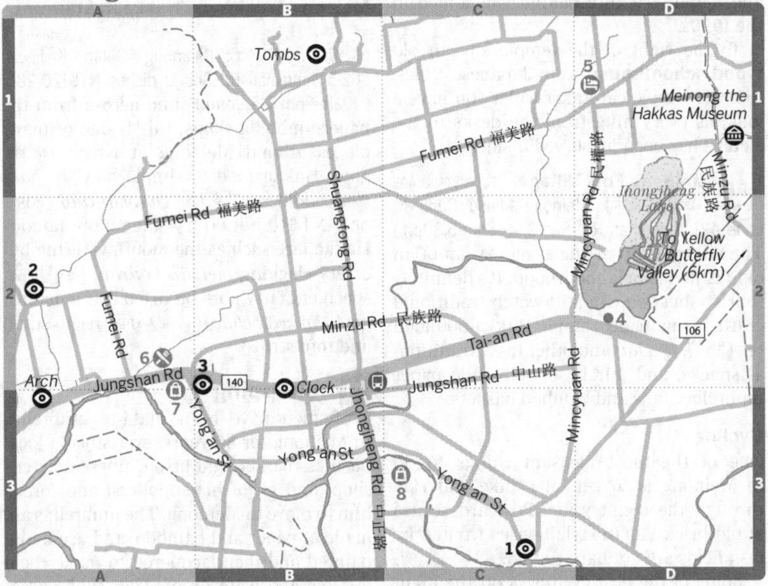

0 — 500 m
0 — 0.25 miles

Yong'an Street
OLD STREET

This was the first street (永安路; Yǒngān Lù) in Meinong, and some of the oldest family residences can still be found in the narrow back alleys. It's a good place for photographs but don't expect a solid row of traditional buildings.

Just behind the **East Gate** (東門; Dōngmén) at the end of the street is a famous **Bogong shrine** (伯公神壇; Bógōng Shéntán), Bogong being the distinctly Hakka designation for the earth god. In old Hakka style no statue is used, just a stone tablet and incense. There are over 400 Bogong shrines around Meinong although this is the most valued. Bow three times to this or any other shrine to bring peace to your life.

Meinong residents have long placed a high premium on learning, which, in traditional society, meant book learning. Oblation furnaces such as the **Minongjhuang Oblation Furnace** (瀰濃庄敬字亭; Mínnóngzhuāng Jìngzìtíng), 300 hundred years old, at the start of Yong'an St were designed to dispose of paper that contained written text, thus signifying such paper's exalted status.

Guangshan Temple
TAOIST TEMPLE

'If you don't stop fighting we're going to build a temple.' It doesn't sound like much of a threat, but in 1915 Gu A-Jhen and 12 other local worthies were true to their word and miraculously, after they constructed this charming little temple (廣善堂; Guǎngshàn Táng) in 1918, peace was restored to Meinong. The overall structure today is a great example of a southern temple complete with a nicely intact and highly

Meinong

Sights
- Bogong Shrine.............(see 1)
- 1 East Gate.............C3
- 2 Guangshan Temple.............A2
- 3 Minongjhuang Oblation Furnace.............B2

Activities, Courses & Tours
- 4 Meinong Bicycle Travel.............D2

Sleeping
- 5 Jhong Jheng Hu B&B.............D1

Eating
- 6 Meinong Traditional Hakka Restaurant.............A2

Shopping
- 7 Guan De Xin Paper Umbrella Shop.............A3
- 8 Jing Shing Blue Shirts Shop.............C3

decorated swallowtail roof. The bulkier and bland structure behind was added in the 1990s.

To the right of the temple sits an old **wood schoolhouse** from Japanese times. Ask the temple caretaker to let you have a look, as everything from the desks to the lectern has been preserved inside.

FREE **Meinong Folk Village** TOURIST VILLAGE
(美濃民俗村; Měinóng Mínsú Cūn; 80 Lane 421, Jungshan Rd, Sec 2; ⏲8am-5.30pm) The village is an artificial recreation of an old-fashioned neighbourhood. It's definitely touristy but you can still watch traditional crafts being made, sample Hakka pounded tea (擂茶; *léi chá*) and other tasty traditional snacks, and purchase well-made paper umbrellas, fans and bamboo baskets.

Cycling

One of the most pleasant things to do in Meinong is to get on a bike and ride through the countryside. Postcard scenes of old brick Fujian-style houses fronted by lush fields are not hard to find.

Some of the best cycling is off the main road towards the mountains and out to the Yellow Butterfly Valley. On the weekend you can hire rickety bikes at shops around the bus station, although another shop, **Meinong Bicycle Travel** (美濃自行車行; Měinóng Zìxíngchēháng; ☎681 2433; 789 Taian Rd), a few minutes' walk from the bus station, has a bigger and better selection.

Sleeping

Jhong Jheng Hu B&B HOMESTAY $$
(中正湖民宿渡假山莊; Zhōngzhènghú Mínsù Dùjià Shānzhuāng; ☎681 2736; www.minsu.com.tw/cc-fu; 30 Fumei Rd; r from NT$1800) The owner of this pleasant B&B is a local tour guide. She doesn't speak English but her son does. Stay in the newer building for the larger windows overlooking the fields and a lovely sunset over palm trees and low mountains. Bikes are free for guests.

Guangshan Temple TEMPLE HOSTEL $
(☎681 2124) The temple has a small pilgrim's house in which you can stay, if you reserve in advance. A four-bed room is NT$600 for the first person, and NT$100 per person for each additional person (if you are in a group).

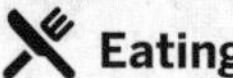

Eating

Meinong Traditional Hakka Restaurant HAKKA $
(美濃古老客家菜; Měinóng Gǔlǎo KèJiācai; 362-5 Jungshan Rd Sec 1; dishes NT$120-280; ⏲9am-2pm & 5-9pm) Found across from the paper-umbrella shops, this is one of many places around Meinong at which to try good Hakka food. A simple bowl of *bantiao* noodles (炒粄條; *chǎobǎntiáo*) costs only NT$40 but do try some more famous Hakka fare such as the mouthwatering but artery-clogging *méigān kòuròu* (梅干扣肉; succulent fatty pork on dried leaf mustard) or *kèjiā xiǎochǎo* (客家小炒; fried squid and tofu strips).

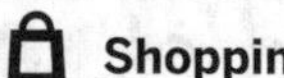

Shopping

Craftsmen have been making umbrellas in Meinong for 80 years, ever since a local businessman bought up a Chinese master's shop (and all of his suppliers) and forced him to move to Meinong. The umbrellas are made of paper and bamboo, and are hand-painted and then lacquered to make them durable and waterproof. They make great decorations and gifts.

Guan De Xin Paper Umbrella Shop TRADITIONAL UMBRELLAS
(廣德興紙傘; Guǎngdéxīng Zhǐsǎn; 361 Jungshan Rd, Sec 1) If you're looking to buy, this is one of the best places. An umbrella here costs between NT$250 and NT$1200.

Jing Shing Blue Shirts Shop TRADITIONAL CLOTHING
(錦興行藍衫店; Jǐnxīngháng Lánshāndiàn; 177 Yong'an St; ⏲7.30am-9pm) This little family-run shop opened in the 1930s making traditional Hakka-style blue clothing. The man who started it, Mr Hsieh, is still around, though he had to retire a few years ago, as he just doesn't have the stamina of when he was merely in his 90s. Mr Hsieh's children and grandchildren now run the operation. A loose-fitting shirt costs NT$3000.

Getting There & Around

Buses between Meinong and Kaohsiung (NT$124, 1½ hours) run every one or two hours.

Meinong is small but the surrounding countryside is expansive and you'll need a vehicle or bicycle to get around. B&B owners may be able to help you hire a scooter.

Meinong to Maolin

This is a scenic ride, but at the time of writing the road betweeen these towns was chewed up from the twin effects of Typhoon Morakot in 2009, and a 6.5-magnitude quake in March 2010. Assuming it is back in shape by the time you read this, you can look forward to the craggy karstlike **18 Lohan Mountains** (十八羅漢山; Shíbā Lóhàn Shān) along the Laonong River, the bell fruit capital of **Liugui** (六龜; Liùguī), and two forest reserves: **Tengchih** (藤枝森林遊樂區; Téngzhī Sēnlín Yóulèqū; www.forest.gov.tw) and **Shanping** (扇平森林生態科學園區; Shànpíng Sēnlín Shēngtài Kēxué Yuánqū).

Tengchih is said to have one of the best-preserved natural forests in Taiwan, while little-visited Shanping offers peaceful trails and excellent bird- and wildlife-watching. Bring a high-powered torch (flashlight) to catch flying squirrels in action after dark.

Maolin Recreation Area 茂林遊憩區

07

Though a small corner of the much larger Maolin National Scenic Area, the **recreation area** (Màolín Yǒuqì Qū; www.maolin-nsa.gov.tw) covers a protected region rich in pristine mountain landscapes, vertiginously high suspension bridges, waterfalls, natural swimming pools and wild hot springs. Maolin's greatest hit, however, is its Purple Butterfly Valley, one of 15 overwintering sites that stretch across southern Taiwan from Maolin to Dawu in Taitung.

There's only one main road through the recreation area, County Rd 132 connecting Maolin village at the start with Dona at the end. Rukai aboriginal culture remains strong in both villages, and in Dona you can still find traditional stone slab houses.

At the time of writing the road to and into the recreation area was in horrendous shape, so do check on conditions before you go. There should be a new visitor centre in Maolin village by the time you read this; the old centre literally washed away during Typhoon Morakot.

Sights & Activities

Because of the typhoon damage it's difficult to predict what will be reopened when you arrive. Keep an eye out for signs to waterfalls, suspension bridges and hiking trails.

Purple Butterfly Valley BUTTERFLY VALLEY

The **valley** (紫蝶幽谷) is not one geographical location, but a number of sites around the recreation area. Some will be signed as you drive along the main road, but enquire at the visitor information centre for good locations.

The best time to watch the butterflies is between 9am and 11am, when the sun first comes over the mountains and rouses the insects from sleep. On cooler or rainy days the butterflies remain motionless, hanging from the trees like garlands (though it's not easy to spot them). It's possible to arrange a tour with De En Gorge Guesthouse.

See boxed text, p358, for more on the mass overwintering and migration of the purple butterfly.

Sleeping

There are guesthouses in Dona charging around NT$1500 a night for a double. Just walk around and you will see them.

De En Gorge Guesthouse HOMESTAY $

(Dé Ēn Gǔ Mínsù; 0955-055 132; dm/2-person cabins NT$500/1500) Set high above the river on a grassy meadow, and run by a friendly local family that offers good ecotours, this is the default accommodation in Maolin. Camping is permitted on the grass bluff (per person NT$200; bring your own equipment), while the cabins, made of grey stone, offer a more stylish option.

To get to the guesthouse head up County Rd 132 until you see the signs for Maolin Valley (茂林谷; Màolíngǔ, also Maolin Gorge). Turn right down a side road and cross the bridge. When the road ends at a fork, head left and up about a kilometre or so. The first building you see is the guesthouse.

Eating

Options for eating are very limited in Maolin. Little stalls are set up on the main road in both villages but be aware that these places close early (by 6pm or 7pm) on weekdays.

Getting There & Away

You need your own vehicle. Consider renting a scooter in Tainan (per day NT$200).

PINGTUNG COUNTY

Oddly, Taiwan's poorest county has some of the country's best beaches, most fertile farmland, richest fish stocks, balmiest weather and liveliest festivals. But if Pingtung County (屏東) seems a little rough around the infrastructure edges lately, at least it won't kill you. In the old days, if the 'Black Ditch' didn't sink your ship coming over, and the coastal pirates didn't rob you in the harbour, and the aborigines didn't take your head on land, well, there were still those pesky microbes flourishing in the hot, humid southern air.

Disease, or the prevention of it, is at the heart of one of the most exuberant festivals in Pingtung, if not all of Taiwan: the Burning of the Wang Yeh Boats. Other top draws that might also help keep the doctor away include swimming, snorkelling and birding at Kenting National Park, and cycling along the quiet county roads that roll slowly past calming fields and foothills.

Dapeng Bay 大鵬灣

Taiwan's answer to Chicago's Big Dig, the bay (Dàpéngwān) features the world's most expensive bicycle path: half a billion dollars for every kilometre, and counting, although after eight years the 16km loop is (incredibly) still not quite ready for prime time.

In 1997 the Dapeng Bay National Scenic Area was initiated to transform the bay, actually a lagoon, into an international resort. It seemed a good idea at the time: the sun shines 300 days a year, on average, here and the sheltered waters offer excellent conditions for sea kayaking, windsurfing, swimming and sailing.

Ironically, Dapeng Bay was first considered for development in the 1970s and many of the king palms around the bay were first planted at that time. Locals were rightly sceptical the second time around and we suspect they are stretching out this project for as long as possible, unwilling to let another 30 years go by for the central government to notice them.

When completed, the bicycle path, and whatever else may be planned (which we are told includes a golf course, marina and luxury hotels), could be brilliant. Most of the wetlands around the lagoon are being restored, and the sections of the path that take cyclists round the coast look back over the glassy bay to a ring of green mangroves with blue-tinged mountains in the far distance.

Donggang 東港

POP 50,000

Sadly, the port of Donggang (Tungkang) that featured importantly in Taiwan's history is not at all apparent in the grubby face it presents to most travellers. During the Qing dynasty, Donggang was one of three main commercial ports in Taiwan, the landing site for the ancestors of millions of modern Taiwanese (in particular the Hakka), and, according to records, a rather prosperous little town.

Pictures from Japanese times show a bustling main street with smart colonial facades. The harbour hosted the Imperial Navy, and nearby Dapeng Bay was a kamikaze training base. It all was reduced to rubble by Allied bombers at the end of WWII. Today the town of 50,000 remains an important centre for fishing, especially the prized blue-fin tuna and mullet, but its best days are long behind it.

Except for one week every three years.

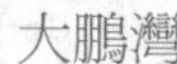 Festivals & Events

Burning of the Wang Yeh Boats

This is, without doubt, one of Taiwan's top folk festivals, both for its paramount exhibition of traditional faith, and for the wild rituals. In short, a boat burning involves inviting gods to earth, feasting them, and then asking them to carry trouble-causing demons and plague away with them on a boat. In the spectacular conclusion to the festival, the boat is torched to the ground on the beach.

In Donggang, hundreds of millions of dollars are spent on getting the details right, but much of what makes the festival so highly enjoyable is that everyone around you, the faithful and the spectators, are so taken in by it. Sublime, dignified, bizarre, entertaining and stirring: the boat burning is all that, and for most people, usually all at once.

The festival is sponsored every three years by the resplendent **Donglong Temple** (東隆宮; Dōnglóng Gōng), established in 1706 and long one of the centres of folk faith in southern Taiwan. The exact dates vary, but the festival always starts on a Saturday and ends on a Friday night (into Saturday

THE WANG YEH BOATS

The boats used in the boat-burning festival are typical southern Chinese wooden junks. Dimensions are approximately 4m x 4m x 14m, but vary each time and must be determined by *bwah-bwey* (tossing divination discs).

Carpenters can refer to a general blueprint but before each portion can be built, it must be approved by Donglong Temple's resident god, and preceded by Taoist rituals.

The 100 volunteer carpenters at Donglong Temple are all former boat builders. The current master builder is 61, and no one on his team is younger than 50. What will happen when these men are too old to work is anyone's guess, because the younger generation does not have the skill set to continue their work.

After boat construction is done, the outside is painted with traditional colours and classical motifs. Hand-carved figurines, representing the crew, are attached to the gunwales. If you happen to see the boat while it's still in its shed, look for the 'captain' sitting on a small altar at the bow. A real cigarette will be burning in his hands at all times.

morning). The next boat burning will take place in autumn 2012.

History

In essence, boat-burning festivals are large-scale plague-expelling rituals. Their origins go back over 1000 years to the Song dynasty and are connected with the Wang Yeh, deities once worshipped for their ability to prevent disease.

In Fujian, the festivals reached their heyday in the 18th and 19th centuries, which coincided with the time of peak immigration from that province to Taiwan. Naturally, the practice spread here (early settlers were constantly beset by plague), but surprisingly it also expanded under the early Japanese colonial period (when it was dying out in China) and has continued into modern times. Many southern temples still hold their own small boat burnings, but a greater number have simply merged their traditions with Donglong Temple, giving it both spiritual and funding primacy.

In these days of modern medicine, the meaning of boat burnings has changed considerably, and they are now held as prayers for peace and stability. But the dark and solemn plague-expulsion rituals remain central to the festival.

Known officially as the **Sacrifice of Peace and Tranquillity for Welcoming the Lords** (東港迎王平安祭典; Dōnggǎng Yíngwáng Píngān Jìdiǎn), the festival runs for eight consecutive days. Most visitors (and you can expect tens of thousands of them) attend the first and last.

The Ceremony

DAY ONE (SATURDAY): INVITING THE GODS

Around noon a procession leaves Donglong Temple for the beach, where they will meet with five Wang Yeh returning to earth for this year's festival. At the beach, **spirit mediums** *(jītóng)* write the names of Wang Yeh in the sand when they sense their arrival. When the leader of the five Wang Yeh arrives his surname is written on a large yellow banner and the procession then slowly returns to the temple.

Local Donggang leaders carry the Wang Yeh (on sedan chairs) over live coals before they enter Donglong Temple.

Things to watch for on this day include people with **paper yokes** around their necks. Square yokes represent that a wish has been asked. A fish or round yoke means a wish has been fulfilled.

Down at the beach there will be hundreds of other temple representatives with their gods and sedan chairs. Many will take the chairs into the ocean for a rough watery blessing. Painted troupes representing the **Soong Jiang Battle Array** will also be around, though they usually perform earlier.

DAYS TWO TO SIX

The Wang Yeh are carried around town on an inspection and are then feasted. The boat is also blessed.

DAY SEVEN (FRIDAY NIGHT TO SATURDAY MORNING)

Volunteers **parade the boat** through town to allow it to collect every bit of misfortune and evil that it can. The boat returns to Donglong Temple around 7pm and is loaded with all manner of goods, as if truly going on a voyage.

In the courtyard, watch for **Taoist priests** burning pieces of paper and chanting. This ritual relieves hundreds of gods and their thousands of foot soldiers from the duties they have performed this past week. Watch also (and have your camera ready) for a priest with a wok, *bagua* symbols, broom, rice shifter and sword. He is directing stray demons onto the boat.

Around midnight the leaders of the temple offer the Wang Yeh one last special **feast** of 108 dishes, which includes famous traditional palace foods, local snacks, fruit and wine. This is one of the most solemn and beautiful rites of the festival.

Around 2am the boat is dragged on wheels out of the temple grounds through a famous **gold foil arch** (it's a sight you'll never forget) and down to the beach. Expect a lot of exploding fireworks.

At the beach hundreds of tons of ghost paper is packed around the ship to help it burn, and the anchors, mast, sails (made of real cloth), windsock and lanterns are hoisted into place.

Finally the five Wang Yeh are invited onto the boat and firecrackers are used to start a fire, which slowly engulfs the entire ship. The **burning** takes place between 5am and 7am and it's proper to flee as soon as the boat is lit to avoid having your soul taken away. But these days only older locals follow this custom.

Eating

Bluefin tuna (黑鮪魚; hēi wěiyú) is Donggang's second claim to local fame. One recommended place to try it (or perhaps not, as many environmental groups are calling for an outright ban on bluefin-tuna fishing) and other delicacies such as mullet roe (信魚; *xìnyú*) and sea grapes (海葡萄; hǎi pútáo) is **By the Sea** (海這裡餐廳; Hǎi Zhèlǐ Cāntīng; www.bythesea.com.tw; 53 Xinsheng 1st St; 新生一路53號; dishes from NT$200; ⏲10.30am-9pm, closed Mon), which is actually more *by the port*.

Getting There & Away

Buses from Kaohsiung (NT$91, 50 to 70 minutes, every 15 to 30 minutes) and Pingtung (NT$63, 40 minutes, every hour) drop you off near the McDonald's in central Donggang. Facing the McDonald's, turn left and take a left at the first intersection. The temple is about 500m down the road on the left.

After the festival consider taking a bus or taxi down to Kenting. You'll need some rest.

Little Liuchiu Island 小琉球

☎08 / POP 13,000

This pretty coral island (Hsiao Liuchiu Island; Xiǎo Liúqiú) offers more than enough sea vistas, convoluted caves, sandy beaches, odd rock formations and temples (over 100) to keep you happy for a long, long day. Best of all, it's simple to get to and around.

There's a new spirit and look to Liuchiu as zoning regulations allowing for homestays have seen the locals becoming involved in improving the look of their villages. Narrow backstreets have been cleared of clutter, facades are going up, and every old structure is getting a little well-deserved TLC.

You can visit Liuchiu all year round, but winters, like most of the south, are lovely: warm and dry, with temps averaging in the mid-20°C range.

History

The original inhabitants of Little Liuchiu, Siraya aborigines, called it Samaji. During the Dutch occupation, the island was under VOC control and when the crew of the shipwrecked *Golden Lion* were killed by the Siraya, the Dutch forcibly removed the entire population. This act included a notorious slaughter of several hundred Siraya holed up in a cave. The massacre is now remembered, in a completely bowdlerized fashion, in the legend on the plaque in front of the Black Dwarf Cave.

In the 18th century, Taiwanese fishermen started to settle Hsiao Liuchiu in small numbers. Until recently about 80% of the island's residents made their living from fishing.

The inclusion of Hsiao Liuchiu into the Dapeng Bay National Scenic Area has been a boon for the environment. Access to larger resources has meant funds for replanting vegetation, protecting coral, and proper garbage disposal. However, one thing that hasn't really been solved is what to do with the dead.

As you ride around the island, try to keep count of the graveyards: they are outnumbered probably only by temples. Taiwan law states that tombs can't be closer than 500m to a residence but on an island 4000m long this just has to be ignored. For most Western travellers, the site of so many

Little Liuchiu Island

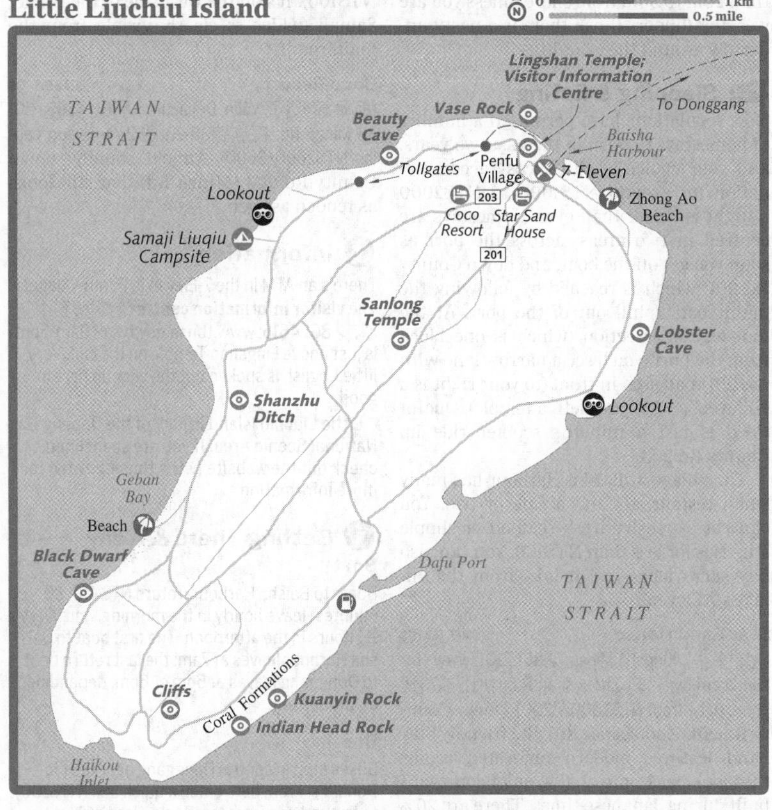

exotic tombstones just adds to the charm of this little island. Asian visitors tend to think a little differently.

Sights & Activities

You can ride around the island on a scooter in about 30 minutes but give yourself at least half a day. This island was made for exploring.

Some attractions to look out for are **Vase Rock** (花瓶岩; Huāpíng Yán), a giant eroded coral with a thin base and large head, **Black Dwarf Cave** (烏鬼洞; Wūgǔi Dòng; 8am-5pm) and **Beauty Cave** (美人洞; Měirén Dòng; 8am-5pm). Note that some sites require an entrance ticket; one ticket for NT$120 is good for all of them.

Other must-sees include the narrow, twisting, root-strangled coral passageways at **Shanzhu Ditch** (山豬溝; Mountain Pig Ditch; Shānzhū Gōu) and **Lingshan Temple** (靈山寺; Língshān Sì), just up from the pier. The temple offers, like dozens of others around the island, fine clear views across the Taiwan Strait.

The temple that ate half of Little Liuchiu, aka ginormous **Sanlong Temple** (三隆宮; Sānlónggōng), sponsors a boat-burning festival every three years. The festival takes place in the autumn a couple of weeks after Donggang's Donglong Temple holds its festival.

The best place for a swim is at **Zhong Ao Beach** (中澳沙灘; Zhōng Ào Shātān). The beach at **Vase Rock** is nice for wading or snorkelling as you search for sea life, while the tiny but picturesque stretch of shell-sand beach at **Geban Bay** (蛤板灣; Gébǎnwān) makes for a sweet picnic spot. You can go for a dip here as well, but only up to your knees.

Be sure to wear something on your feet if you go into the water as the coral rocks can really cut you up. Also, don't go more than 20m to 30m from shore unless you are wearing flippers (fins); there is a nasty undertow around the island.

Sleeping & Eating

New regulations have permitted a number of homestays to open in the past two years, and your choice of clean, cosy accommodation for around NT$1000 to NT$2000 a night is better than ever. Homestays are centred in two areas: across the port as soon you get off the boat; and down County Rd 201, which is reached by following the main road uphill out of the port. At the four-way intersection (which is one block from the port) you'll see a narrow lane with the 201 road sign in front (to your right is a 7-Eleven, and to your left, a temple). Quaint Coco is just a minute's scooter ride up County Rd 203.

The village at Baisha Harbour has many small restaurants and a cafe or two. You can eat expensive fresh seafood or simple stir-fries for less than NT$100. You can also buy sandwiches and drinks from the village's 7-Eleven.

Star Sand House HOMESTAY $$
(星沙民宿; Xīngshā Mínsù; ☎861 2101; www.starsand.com.tw; 173-1 Zhongshan Rd; 中山路173號之一; d/tw from NT$2000/3200) Down County Rd 201 (Zhongshan Rd), the friendly Star Sand features modern renovated rooms that look back onto a wide quiet courtyard built during Japanese times. There are 20% discounts midweek.

Samaji Liuqiu Campsite CAMPGROUND $
(沙瑪基島露營渡假區; Shāmǎjīdǎo Lùyíng Dùjiàqū; ☎861 4880; www.samaji.com.tw; per site NT$400, cabins from NT$1600) Samaji offers the cheapest accommodation on Liuchiu (if you bring your own tent), but also some of the most scenic from its expansive cliffside perch. There's a restaurant on the grounds and bike rental (per hour NT$100). It's on the west side of the island, Samaji (which is clearly visible from the main road).

Coco Resort CABINS $$
(椰林渡假村; Yélín Dùjiàcūn; ☎861 4368; 20-38 Minzu Rd; 民族路38-20號; 2-/4-person cabins NT$2600/3600) An old standby down County Rd 203 (Minzu Rd) that still looks as tended as ever.

Information

There's an ATM in the 7-Eleven in Penfu Village. The **visitor information centre** (遊客服務中心; ☎861 4615; www.tbnsa.gov.tw; ⏰9am-5pm) is just above Lingshan Temple on the cliff. Very little English is spoken but the view up here is good.

Little Liuchiu Island is part of the Dapeng Bay National Scenic Area. If you are so inclined, check out the website (www.tbnsa.gov.tw) for more information.

Getting There & Away

Boat

Boats to Baisha Harbour (return NT$410, 30 minutes) leave hourly in the morning, and every 1½ hours in the afternoon. The first boat to Baisha Harbour leaves at 7am; the last return boat to Donggang leaves at 5pm or 6pm, depending on the season.

Bus

Buses stop in central Donggang near the McDonald's. From here catch a quick taxi (NT$100) to the harbour ferry terminals. Use the first terminal on the right before the fish market. Buses leave from Pingtung every 20 minutes (NT$63, 40 minutes), and from Kaohsiung (NT$91, 50 to 70 minutes) every 15 to 30 minutes.

Getting Around

The island is only 9km around so you could easily walk it in a day. Scooters rentals (per half-/full day NT$150/300) are available from

PINGTUNG CITY TO KENTING NATIONAL PARK

The top attraction in the south is Kenting National Park, and getting there is half the fun if you take the right route. Going directly south from Kaohsiung runs through such a blighted industrial zone that you'll wonder if you've been given the wrong directions.

The most delightful way to reach Kenting, and the only way to go by bike, is to start in Pingtung city and ride 30km to Sandimen on Provincial Hwy 27 and then head south on County Rd 185. This absolutely idyllic road runs flat for 60km to Fangliao where it joins Provincial 1. From here it's another 50km to the edge of Kenting. There's a little bit of blight on this stretch, but you can minimise it by taking the coastal roads into Kenting once you pass Checheng.

A STANDARD BEIDAWUSHAN ITINERARY

Trailhead to Summit (9.5km, eight to 10 hours)

» Trailhead to campground: 4km, four to five hours

» Campground to summit: 5.5km, four to five hours

Summit to Trailhead (10km, six hours)

» Summit to campground: 5.5km, three hours

» Campground to trailhead: 4.5km, three hours

touts at the harbour – you don't need ID or a licence.

Pingtung 屏東

☎08 / POP 216,777

Though Pingtung (Píngdōng) is actually not a bad-looking little town, there is nothing for the traveller here except to begin a journey to somewhere else. If you need to spend the night, there are obvious places around the train station where you can get a room for under NT$1000 a night.

Trains from Kaohsiung to Pingtung (fast/slow NT$31/48, 25 minutes) run about every 15 minutes. **Pingtung Bus Company station** (☎723 7131) is a block left of the train station as you exit.

There are buses to Donggang (NT$63, 40 minutes, every hour) and also to the Indigenous People's Culture Park.

Sandimen 三地門

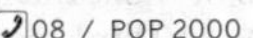

☎08 / POP 2000

This small aboriginal community (Sāndìmén), 30km east of Pingtung, is known for the **Indigenous People's Cultural Park** (台灣山地文化園區; Táiwān Shāndì Wénhuà Yuánqū; www.tacp.gov.tw; Majia Village; admission NT$150; ⏲8.30am-5pm, closed Mon). The park, set in forested mountains, displays true-to-life examples of traditional aboriginal houses and communal structures. A museum near the entrance has exhibitions of daily, ceremonial and martial items, though there is less emphasis these days on showing artefacts, and more on videos.

From Sandimen it's possible to get further into the mountains to very remote aboriginal villages such as Wutai, but check on road conditions: this area is often inaccessible. Driving or riding north on County Rd 185 takes you to Maolin Recreation Area. It's best to have your own vehicle to get here.

Beidawushan 北大武山

A side route off the 185 south of Sandimen takes you to the trailhead to Beidawushan (Běidàwǔshān), the most southerly mountain in Taiwan over 3000m. A holy peak, home to spirits of the Rukai and Paiwan, it has one of the best-loved short overnight hikes. On a clear day from the summit you can observe both the Pacific Ocean and the Taiwan Strait, and look down upon a reserve that might be the last refuge of the clouded leopard (if not completely extinct).

At the time of writing the trail was not open because of damage caused by Typhoon Morakot. However, we were assured by the Forestry Bureau that work was well underway. When reopened, the well-made trail to the summit should still be exactly 10km in length. Signposts will be in English and Chinese.

Activities

Hiking

The hike begins at an elevation of 1520m. The trail is normally wide and clear but there is a lot of scrambling near the end. After a final thrilling crossing over a thin and high stone causeway you reach a campground that features running water and flush toilets.

The next day you need to be on the trail by 6am. Expect a lot of switchbacks, with some tricky rope sections before the ridge. Some highlights include a **1000-year-old red cedar** (with a 25m circumference), a Japanese-era shrine, and forests of rare hemlock spruce. Keep your eyes open for **raptors**: grey-throat eagles, crown eagles and black kites are all fairly common.

The last couple of hours to the summit run along a wooded ridgeline, at times only a few metres wide. It is not particularly challenging to navigate this section, except that you want to keep stopping to gasp at the sublime sight of clouds hanging in the air at eye level.

The summit is the end of the line and you simply retrace your steps to reach the trailhead.

Getting There & Away

You need your own vehicle to get to the trailhead and we aren't going to promise that you won't get lost at least a few times getting here. As you ride along County Rd 185 heading south, turn left just past the 40km mark, heading towards the hills and Jiaping Village (佳平村; Jiāpíng Cūn), also known as Taiwu Village.

One kilometre up the hill, stop at the police station to apply for mountain permits (see boxed text, p28). From then on, consult a good map.

Jin-Shui Ying Old Trail

Part of the National Trail System (see p27), this Qing-dynasty road (Jìnshuǐ Yín Gǔ Dào) once started at Fangliao and crossed the entire southern part of the island. Today it still covers about half and takes a full six hours of downhill walking to reach the end of the trail near Dawu on the east coast. Along the way you pass the remains of a Qing-dynasty army camp, a nature preserve, and a rich butterfly valley near the suspension bridge at the end of the trail.

The trail begins in the mountains east of Fangliao and runs along the point where the summer and winter monsoon airstreams meet. It's a jungle here (the area receives the second-highest rainfall in Taiwan) and the relative remoteness of the trail and its long history mean you have a good chance of spotting local wildlife, including the Formosan macaque, the Reeves' muntjac, wild boar and over 80 species of birds. For what it's worth, this is the only trail on which we've ever seen a wild pangolin.

The last section of trail after the suspension bridge is washed out and it's a bit tricky to navigate the new paths over the ridge and onto the back roads to Dawu. During the winter months (and *only* the winter months) you can simply walk the last 5km stretch along the dry bed of the Dawu River, almost 1km across at this point.

To hike the trail you need a police permit (see boxed text, p28) and your own transportation.

Kenting National Park

墾丁國家公園

☎08

It's the end of the road down here, but there's nothing remote or isolated about at all about Kenting National Park (Kěndīng Guójiā Gōngyuán). Over five million visitors a year flock here to swim, surf, snorkel and dive, visit museums, hike, hot spring, eat good food and enjoy a little nightlife – all year round. The average January temperature is 21°C (many days are much warmer). Unless a cold front has hit the island, you can usually swim even in January. In July it can get to a scorching 38°C.

The park occupies the entire southern tip of Taiwan, an area known as the Hengchun Peninsula. Low mountains and hilly terraces prevail over much of the land, along with, in a few places, rugged high cliffs and sandy deserts. The swimming beaches won't stun you with their beauty like those in Thailand, but they are lovely nonetheless, with yellow sands and turquoise waters. All in all, the topography is wonderfully suited for recreation, in particular cruising around sightseeing on a scooter or bicycle.

The park is a sanctuary for wildlife, including the reintroduced Sika deer, which is now commonly seen in Sheding Nature Park. In autumn, migratory raptors can be spotted overhead in the tens of thousands, and these are just a few of the 340 bird species recorded in the park. Kenting is without doubt one of Taiwan's top birdwatching destinations.

In many ways, the park gets better every year, but also worse. You can no longer just pitch a tent anywhere, but then fireworks are banned on the beaches. There's a greater emphasis on cleanliness but with more and more travellers visiting, some places are trashed during the busy season (summer and Chinese New Year). And there's still no plan for a pavement in Kenting village!

The national park covers 180 sq km but as there are few major roads you can get around easily with our map in hand.

Sights

Kenting Forest Recreation Area NATURE PARK

(Kěndīng Sēnlín Yóulèqū; admission NT$100; ⏲8am-5pm) Once an undersea coral reef, the forest area is now a quirky landscape of limestone caves, narrow canyons, and cliff walls straggled with the roots of banyan trees. It's one of the most visited places in the park, so try to arrive early.

FREE **Sheding Nature Park** NATURE PARK

(社頂自然公園; Shèdǐng Zìrán Gōngyuán; ⏲8am-5pm) This well-protected expanse of scrubby hills and open grasslands is a favourite with picnickers and ecotourists. The reintroduced Sika deer is often spotted in the brush, as are endemic bird species (we saw two in one tree just in the car park), dozens of butterfly species (in particular colourful swallowtails) and even wild boar.

National Museum of Marine Biology MUSEUM

(國立海洋生物博物館; Guólì Hǎiyáng Shēngwù Bówùguǎn; www.nmmba.gov.tw/; 2 Houwan Rd, Checheng; admission NT$450; ⏲9am-6pm) The museum is rated highly by visitors for the live displays of colourful and exotic sea life that are professionally and imaginatively designed.

Jialeshui SCENIC AREA

(Jiālèshuǐ; admission NT$100; ⏲8am-5pm) A 2.5km-long stretch of coral coastline with rocks eroded into the shapes of animals.

Reserve Areas

The park maintains strict access controls over ecologically sensitive regions, such as the area around **Lake Nanren** (Nánrén Hú) and the fine shell beach at **Shadao** (Shādǎo). You can apply on the park's website ahead of time for permits to enter these areas.

Activities

Swimming

Taiwan was formed by the intense upward thrust of tectonic plates colliding. The land rises steeply from the sea and as a result the waters have treacherous currents and undertows not far offshore. Some sound advice from a long-term expat is to go no deeper than where your feet can still touch the sand.

Kenting Beach, the longest swimming beach in the area, is now once again free to the public. At the time of writing a park was being constructed across from the beach after a long-overdue move to tear down a field of grubby outdoor barbecue stalls.

The beach across from the Caesar Hotel is smaller but set in picture-perfect **Little Bay** (小灣; Xiǎowān). There's a beach bar and showers (free for Caesar Hotel guests, a nominal fee for others). This beach is very family oriented.

The vibe at **Nanwan** (南灣; Nánwān; South Bay) is young, brash and entirely eco-oblivious. Expect trash and tractors on the beach, and jet-ski heroes making runs at the sand with complete disregard for whomever might be in their way.

The sweet little crescent beach at **Baisha Bay** (白砂灣; Báishā Wān) is a little further afield but worth taking the extra time to visit. It is not as unvisited as years ago, but it is still the least crowded. However, national-park plans to take control of the area around the beach seem to have gone nowhere.

Jumping off the chin (and other protuberances) of **Sail Rock** (船帆石; Chuánfán Shí), aka Nixon Rock, and swimming round the landmark is also a popular swimming option.

Surfing, Snorkelling & Diving

The waters around **Jialeshui** and the nuclear power plant at **Nanwan** have the best surfing waves. Jialeshui is by far the more laid back and less crowded of the two. It also has a small row of B&Bs up near the toll booth, catering to those looking to escape the regular madness in Kenting. You can hire surfboards (per day NT$500) almost everywhere these days. See Sleeping (p269) for places that offer lessons.

For snorkelling, check out the coral formations near **Sail Rock**. You can hire gear across the road.

For snorkelling and scuba tours, as well as lessons, contact **John Boo** (www.udive.com.tw).

Birdwatching

With its grasslands, forests, lakes and coastline, Kenting is a prime birdwatching area, and the visitor centre has several good books and brochures on the species that you may encounter (now totalling over 340). **Eluanbi** (鵝鑾鼻; Éluánbí), **Sheding Nature Park**, **Manjhou** and **Longluan Lake** (龍鑾潭; Lóngluántán) are considered prime spots. A **visitor centre** and observation area at Longluan Lake was about to reopen at the time of writing.

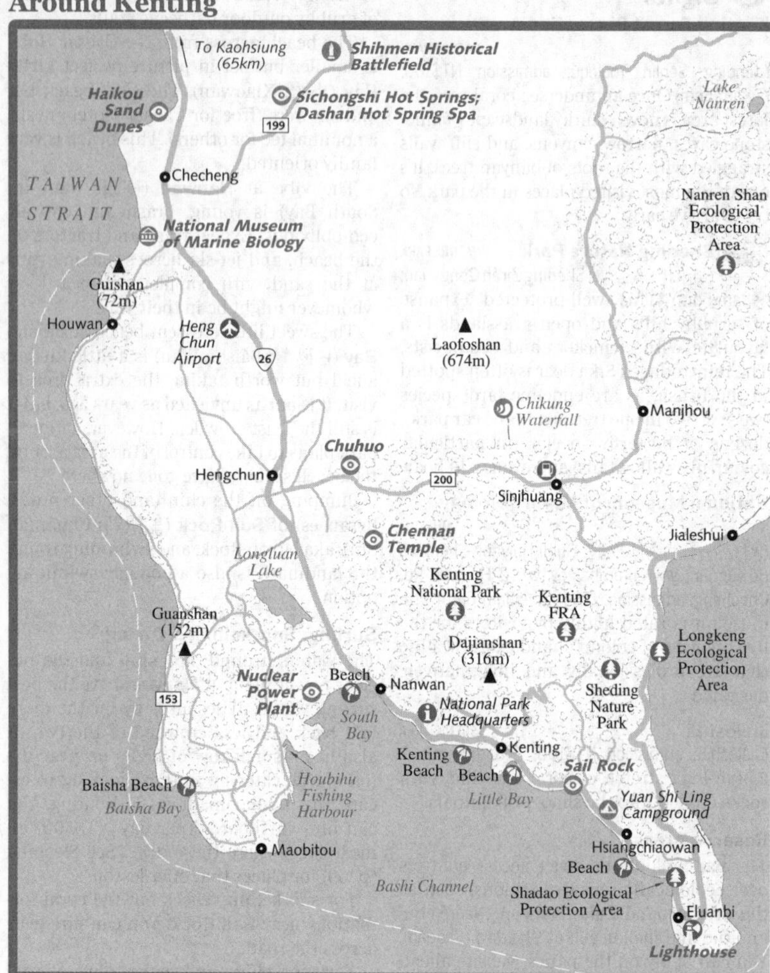

The Hengchun Peninsula is listed as one of the most important sites for raptor migration in east Asia and is one of the top 20 raptor-migration sites worldwide. In a single autumn day, over 50,000 raptors have been recorded flying overhead. Among the more famous to sail the Kenting skies are the Chinese goshawks and grey-faced buzzards.

Goshawks start arriving early to mid-September on their journey south to Indochina. The best time and place to see them is morning in Sheding Nature Park.

Around 10 October, grey-faced buzzards pass through the park, also on their way to Indochina. The best times and places to see these 'National Day Birds' are Sheding in the mornings, and Manjhou between 3pm and 6pm.

The revival of raptor numbers in the past decade is one of the great environmental success stories of Taiwan. See the **Birding in Taiwan** (www.birdingintaiwan.com/gray-facedbuzzard.htm) website for the story.

Cycling

The sunny, scenic Hengchun Peninsula is one of Taiwan's best riding destinations.

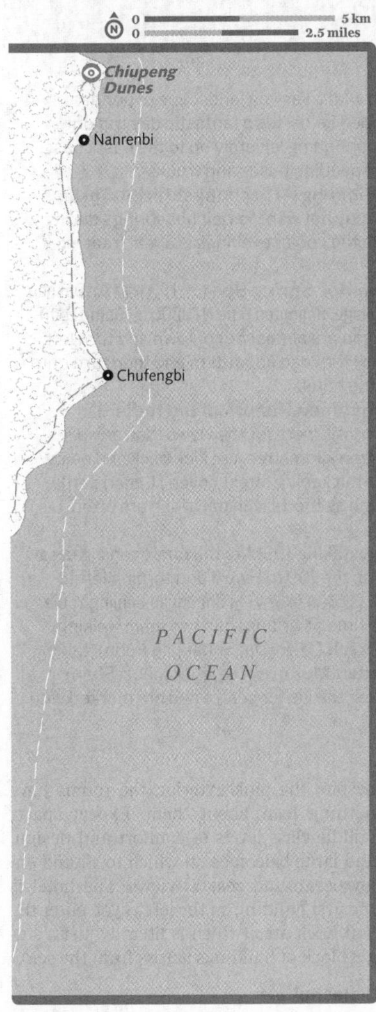

As with elsewhere, it's important to choose the right route to avoid blight. Hwy 26 from Kenting to Checheng is congested and runs through a lot of ugly small towns, so after Nanwan head west and take the quiet coastal roads as far north as possible. At Checheng head east on the County Rd 199, one of the sweetest rural roads in the south (see boxed text, p270).

South of Kenting and up the coast to Jialeshui the roads are not usually busy and run through a beautiful landscape of beaches, scrubby hills and coastal bluffs. The 200 is also another great road for riding.

For getting to Kenting by bike, see boxed text, p264.

Festivals & Events

Indie-music fans should definitely try to time their Taiwan visit for April when **Spring Scream** (www.springscream.com) takes over Kenting. The country's longest-running music festival, this multistaged event brings together names big and small in Taiwan's indie-music scene, along with some imported bands. It's currently held in Eluanbi, but that may change, so check the website.

Sleeping

Bookings are advisable if there's a particular hotel you wish to stay at. Otherwise, it's possible, even during Chinese New Year, to just show up and find accommodation.

Summer (approximately May to September), Chinese New Year and other public holidays are considered the high season. Discounts of 40% or more for midrange and top-end hotels are standard on weekdays and during the low season.

Kenting Village

Kenting Village has the lion's share of hotels along the main strip (charging under NT$1000 on low-season weekdays) but this particular street is a noisy, charmless place to stay.

Chateau Beach Resort BEACH RESORT **$$$**
(夏都沙灘酒店; Xiàdū Shātān Jiǔdiàn; ☎886 2345; www.ktchateau.com.tw; 451 Kenting Rd; 墾丁路451號; r from NT$6600; @) There's a light, breezy, whimsical and secluded feel to the pastel-coloured Chateau, the only resort in Kenting to sit right on the beach. Room interiors could have come from anywhere, but the dazzling views of the sea and mountains are pure Kenting. The Chateau has facilities for both business travellers and families with kids.

Tz Shin Resort Hotel HOTEL **$$**
(澤信旅店; Zéxìn Lǚdiàn; ☎276 006; http://uukt.idv.tw/inn/gc/htm; 260 Dawan St; 大灣路260號; d from NT$2400) Dawan St has a row of stylish three-storey B&Bs all facing onto the new park (or car park) and beach. To reach this street, turn right just past the McDonald's as you enter Kenting village. At Tz Shin, rooms are spiffy and feature large beds and big windows. Low-season midweek prices for a single traveller can go down to NT$800 – an absolute steal for the location and quality.

WORTH A TRIP

COUNTY ROAD 199

This quiet country road rewards at every turn with a varying landscape of ponds, farms, aboriginal villages, wooded hills and open fields. It's a fantastic day trip out of Kenting and the preferred route for those continuing leisurely on to the east coast (Hwy 9 is straighter and faster but thick with speeding buses and trucks).

The first sight of note along the 199 is the **Sichongsi (Szchongshi) Hot Springs** (四重溪溫泉; Sìchóngxī Wēnquán). While you may not want to visit hot springs during the summer days, a soak in an outdoor pool in the cooler evenings is a real treat, so maybe save this one for the trip back.

Recommended by Kenting locals is **Dashan Hot Spring Spa** (大山溫泉農場; Dàshān Wēnquán Nóngchǎng; 60-1 Tamei Rd, Wenquan Village; unlimited time NT$200; ⌚6am-11pm) at the far end of Wenquan Village. Drive until you are almost out of town and turn left 30m or so before the castlelike building. Follow the road about 1km and then turn onto a dirt road marked with a sign in Chinese for the hotel.

East of Sichongsi, on a high meadow, the **Shihmen Historical Battlefield** (石門古戰場; Shímén Gǔzhànchǎng) is worth a visit more for the views than any historical remains. After this, for the next few dozen kilometres just kick back and enjoy as the road winds and curves through an ever-thickening forest cover. Human settlements are few, but flocks of endemic birds such as the Taiwan partridge are often seen roadside.

Just before the coast, you have the choice of taking 199甲 to the photogenic **grasslands** around Shiuhai (Xùhǎi), or continuing up the 199 to Hwy 9 and turning left to reach **Shuangliou Forest Recreation Area** (雙流森林遊樂區; Shuāngliù Sēnlíng Yóulè Qū; www.forest.gov.tw). The park (closed at the time of writing) has two main walking trails, one to the gorgeous **Shuangliou Waterfall** (雙流瀑布; Shuāngliú Pùbù), taking two hours return, and the other to 630m **Mautzu Mountain** (帽子山; Màuzi Shān), taking three hours return. Both trails begin near the visitor centre and are marked with English signs.

Kenting Youth Activity Centre HOTEL $$ (青年活動中心, Qīngnián Huódòng Zhōngxīn; ☎886 1221; www.cyh.org.tw; 17 Kenting Rd; 墾丁路17號; d/tw from NT$2500/3000) The centre occupies 25 hectares of land and features a reproduction traditional Fujian-style courtyard dwelling for guests to sleep in. The centre will appeal to families, not only for the rather fun design (kids just love playing around the old-style buildings) but also for the fact that it's on its own secluded road.

The activity centre is at the far edge of Kenting village. Look for a road on the right with a toll booth (no toll is charged) at the start (it's just across from a Starbucks and mini-mall on the left). The centre is at the end of this road.

Sail Rock

Seafood Hotel HOTEL $$ (品喬海鮮旅店; Pǐnqiáo Hǎixiān Lǚdiàn; ☎885 1496; fax 885 1263; 720 Sail St; 船帆路720號; d from NT$2200) The hotel sits above a busy seafood restaurant (hence the name) and, despite the pink exterior, the rooms have nothing fishy about them. Expect space, middle-class levels of comfort and design, and large balconies on which to sit and enjoy ocean and coastal views. The hotel is the first building on the left as you enter the Sail Rock area (which is literally just a single block of buildings across from the sea).

Jialeshui

Winson House HOSTEL $ (☎880 1053; www.tbay.com.tw; 244 Chashan Rd; 茶山路244號; dm/s/d NT$400/800/1200) Just 100m before the toll booth into Jialeshui is this bare-bones guesthouse run by Winson, a well-known local surfer. Lessons are available (per day NT$2000), as are surf tours and equipment rental (board per day NT$800). The surfing beach, which is considered the best in the Kenting area if not one of the best in Taiwan, is just down the hill from the house. On the same strip as Winson you'll find several higher-end B&Bs.

Eluanbi

The Eluanbi campground did not seemed staffed at the time of writing, but we were assured by the park that it was getting on its feet. To get here, drive past the lighthouse and take the first right 100m past the Km41 mark. The campground is at the very end of the road and has bathroom facilities.

Hengchun

Surf Shack HOSTEL $
(☎0958-856 645; www.taiwansurfshack.com; 224 Hengnan Rd, Hengchun, 恆春鎮, 恆南路224號; s/d with shared bathroom NT$400/700; breakfast NT$200; 📶) Run by an expat (but long-term Kenting resident) and his local wife, the Surf Shack pulls in a largely young and fun crowd from all over the world. The owners, both avid surfers and divers, know Kenting's aquatic secrets as well as anyone. Rooms are basic, but clean, and there is laundry and free wi-fi. The 1st-floor restaurant has a good reputation for Western hostel standards like burgers and sandwiches (dishes from NT$180), and functions as a bar at night. Surf Shack is across from the bus station in Hengchun, and is near scooter and bike rentals.

Eating & Drinking

Kenting Village is a tourist town and there is no shortage of food, including Thai, Chinese, Italian and even South African. Prices are reasonable and most places are open late. There are a couple of breakfast shops along Kenting St, and numerous fruit-drink stands.

The strip in Nanwan is also loaded with restaurants, while Sail Rock has big seafood joints where you can point at what you want. Hengchun is a small town, so if you're staying here you'll have no problem finding food.

Warung Didi CURRY $$
(迪迪小吃; Dídí Xiǎochī; ☎886 1835; 26 Wenhua Lane, Kenting Rd, Kenting Village; dishes NT$180; ⏲5.30pm-1am) This long-running restaurant draws in the crowds every night with the promise of excellent Thai and Malay curries, good music, beer and lively beach atmosphere. Reservations are recommended on weekends.

Amy's Cucina ITALIAN $$
(Nánxīng Dàfàndiàn; 131-1 Kenting Rd, Kenting Village; dishes NT$200; ⏲10am-late) This was the first place in Kenting to serve pizza and it still has some of the best Italian food in the park. The casual red-brick and wooden design makes it suitable for hanging out and enjoying a nice meal.

Bossa Nova Beach Cafe CAFE/RESTAURANT $$
(巴沙諾瓦; Bāshānuòwǎ; 100 Nanwan Rd, Nanwan; dishes NT$180; ⏲11am-late; 📶) This cafe sits on the main drag in Nanwan, across from the beach. Sandwiches are filling and there's free wi-fi. The cafe also runs a B&B, should you want to stay in the Nanwan area.

Many restaurants, such as Warung Didi's and Amy's, also serve as bars (beer from NT$120), with music played loudly in the evenings. The **Caesar Hotel** (Kǎisà Dà Fàndiàn; beer from NT$140; ⏲11am-10pm) runs an outdoor bar-cafe on Little Bay beach.

Information

There's free wireless internet at the National Park Headquarters, and you'll find ATMs in the 7-Elevens in Kenting Village, on the main road.

Kenting National Park (www.ktnp.gov.tw) The official website is more than thorough in its introduction to the park.

National Park Headquarters (國家公園管理處; ☎886 1321; 596 Kenting Rd; ⏲8am-5pm) You'll find English-speaking staff and several useful English brochures and maps. The centre is a few kilometres north of Kenting so you'll probably need to check into your hotel and rent a scooter before visiting.

Getting There & Away

Bus

From Kaohsiung, the Kenting Express (2½/3½ hours NT$355/$309) leaves every 30 minutes. Buses from the HSR station are less frequent (NT$383, three hours, every 1½ to two hours).

Taxi

Taxis take groups of passengers from the main train station in Kaohsiung for NT$400 per person (1½ hours). Single travellers can wait until the taxi fills, which usually doesn't take long. However, it's difficult for a single traveller to take a shared taxi from the HSR (per person NT$500) unless your hotel has arranged this.

Getting Around

You need your own transport. There are no buses, except those coming in from Kaohsiung and Hengchun. Hotels can arrange car, 4WD or scooter rental. Scooter-rental shops (per day NT$400 to NT$500) are to the right as you enter Kenting village from the north. Some shops now refuse to rent to travellers unless they have a Taiwanese driver's licence.

Taiwan's Islands

Includes »

Best Places to Eat

» Hung Lou (p278)
» Leemo's Shop (p288)
» Good Friend Vegetarian House (p296)

Best Places to Stay

» Penghu Sunrise B&B (p300)
» Enhui Mingsu Zijia (p304)
» Shuitiaogetou (p283)
» Coast Hotel (p288)

Why Go?

To get off the beaten path, that's why. And be rewarded for it. Taiwan's outer islands are as chock-full of culture, history, and scenic eye candy as you're going to find in East Asia. Volcanic Lanyu is Taiwan's furthest outpost, both geographically and culturally, and combines a fantastical landscape with the deep charms of an indigenous people living off the sea. Kinmen and Matsu, lying in the Taiwan Strait, are a twitcher's dreamland, and boast some of the country's oldest traditional villages and festivals. They also offer a superb window into the Cold War struggles that saw the island groups turned into frontline battlefields.

Green Island and Penghu appeal to the young set looking for perfect sand beaches, coral reefs and a bit of nightlife. Each has a top draw you won't find anywhere else: for Green Island, one of the world's rarest seawater hot springs; for Penghu, Asia's top windsurfing destination.

When to Go

Makung (Penghu Island)

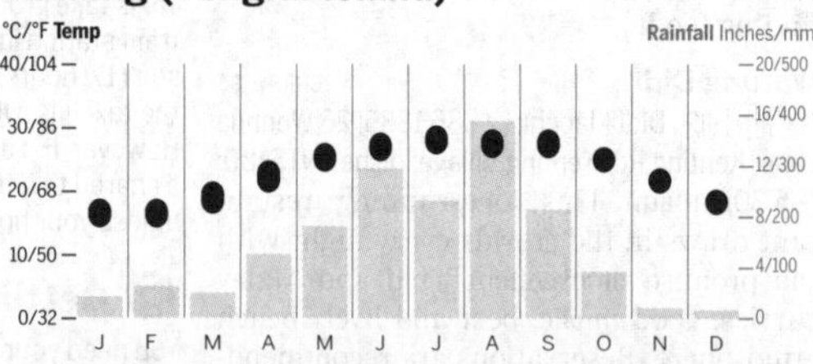

March–May Flying Fish Festival on Lanyu, the most important yearly event for Yami people.

April Welcoming the City God parade on Kinmen, a vibrant pilgrimage with unique rites and festivities.

September–March World-class windsurfing around Penghu. September/October are best for beginners.

Taiwan's Islands Highlights

1 Sleep in a traditional, and lovingly restored, Fujian-style village in **Matsu** (p284) or **Kinmen** (p274)

2 Soak in **Chaojih Hot Springs** (p308), a rare seawater spring just off the beach on Green Island

3 Spend a few days living in a Yami family home on **Lanyu** (p301) for a glimpse at a traditional seafaring way of life

4 Bird-, butterfly- and deer-watch in the parks and on the ponds and beaches of Taiwan's islands

5 Temple-hop and windsurf on **Penghu** (p291), a windswept archipelago of almost 100 islands

6 Snorkel the pristine reefs off **Green Island** (p306), home to more than 200 species of coral

7 Witness the historical remains of the Cold War between the Chinese communists and nationalists, on **Kinmen** (p274)

ISLAND OVERVIEW

ISLAND(S)	IN 10 WORDS OR LESS	WHO SHOULD GO	BEST TIME TO VISIT	PAGE
Kinmen	ancient towns & front-line military outpost transformed into national park	military enthusiasts, cyclists, birdwatchers, traditional-architecture buffs	summer, autumn	below
Matsu	military stronghold on beautiful archipelago, with tunnels & beaches aplenty	traditional-architecture buffs, war historians, butterfly lovers, people who want to get seriously off the beaten path	summer, autumn	p284
Penghu	spectacular beaches & more temples than you'd think possible	windsurfers, beachcombers, spiritual travellers	spring, summer, autumn, (winter if you like high winds)	p291
Lanyu	tribal island with other-worldly feel	hikers, butterfly lovers, birdwatchers, those interested in authentic aboriginal culture	spring, summer, autumn	p301
Green Island	yesterday's prison, today's playground	political-history enthusiasts, snorkellers, divers, hot-spring lovers	year-round (but crowded in summer)	p306

National Parks & Forest Recreation Areas

Though you'll find higher mountains and larger stretches of green in Taiwan proper, the outer islands have things well covered when it comes to parkland. Reforested Kinmen itself is a national park (quite fitting, we think, as the whole area was once totally deforested by Ming-dynasty general Koxinga to build a sailing fleet), and there's talk of eventually turning Green Island into one too. Except for a few small towns, mountainous Lanyu is almost entirely covered by forests, and its indigenous Yami inhabitants are quite militant about fighting any improper development. Most of the Penghu Archipelago consists of volcanic islands covered with low-lying cacti and other succulents. Trees in Penghu's Lintou and Chitou parks tend to all grow at a pronounced angle thanks to the persistent wind.

KINMEN

☎082 / POP 45,000

Kinmen (金門; Jīnmén) oozes old-world (Chinese) charm and if you want to explore traditional villages, ancient pagodas, arches, stelae and temples, there is no better place in Taiwan. On the other hand, the pollution-free islands also boast open fields, sandy beaches, thick forests, landscaped parks and artificial lakes that attract hundreds of species of migratory birds. For cyclists and twitchers alike, it's a small paradise.

And then there is a third side to the islands. Along with Matsu, Kinmen is a small chunk of Fujian province (yes, officially Kinmen is part of Fujian) occupied by Republic of China (ROC) forces and administered from Taiwan. Lying only 2km off the coast of mainland China, the island is an odd remnant from the bitter civil war between communist and Nationalist forces. This struggle is not only a major part of Kinmen's history but of great appeal to travellers.

As a result of its strategic position, Kinmen is a fairly well-developed place. Soldiers have been put to good use planting trees, maintaining roads and restoring the island's old villages, many built during the Ming and Qing dynasties. Roads are wide and well cared for (so they can double as runways, just in case), parks are everywhere, and in general the environment is relaxed. But don't lose sight of the fact that Kinmen remains a military outpost. Restricted areas still exist and more than one beachfront property bears serious landmine warnings.

Kinmen

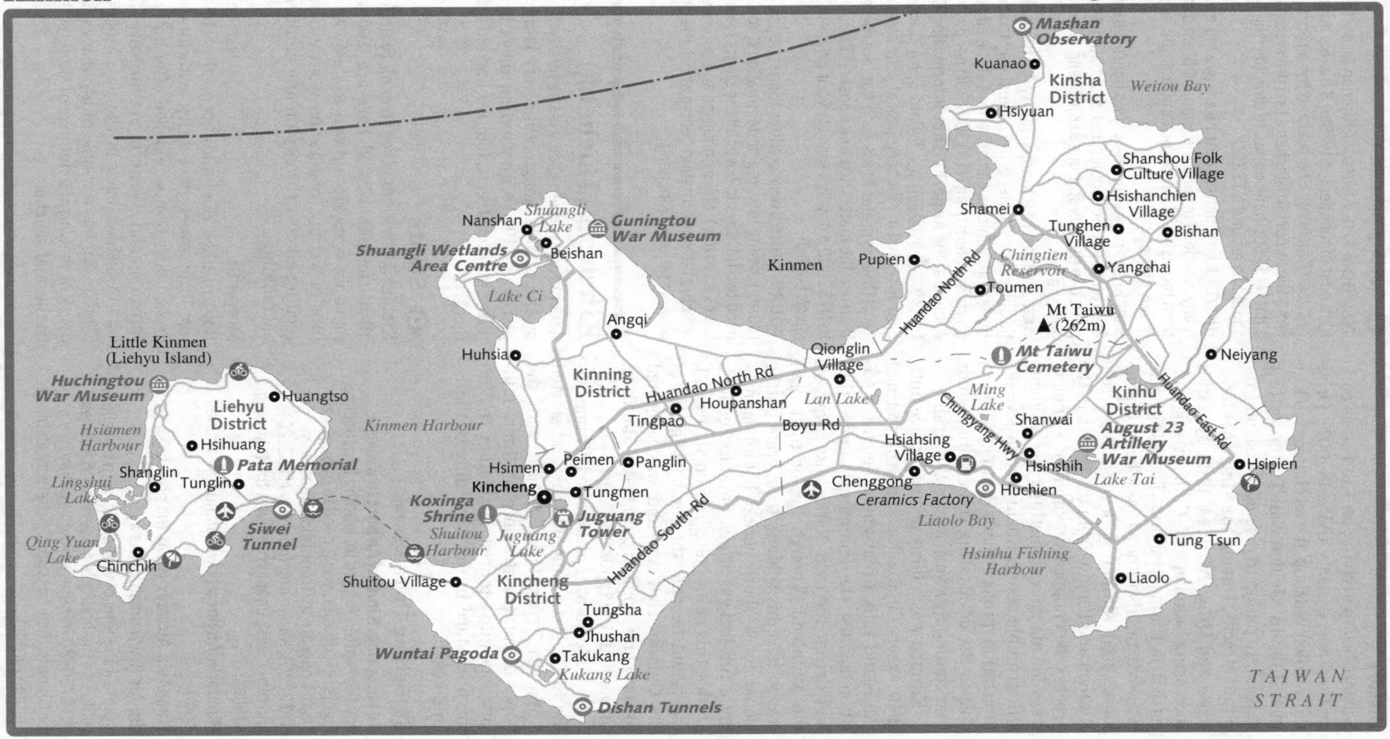

0 5 km
0 2.5 miles
Mashan Observatory
Kuanao
Kinsha District
Weitou Bay
Hsiyuan
Shanshou Folk Culture Village
Hsishanchien Village
Shamei
Tunghen Village
Bishan
Chingtien Reservoir
Yangchai
Pupien
Kinmen
Huandao North Rd
Toumen
Mt Taiwu (262m)
Neiyang
Mt Taiwu Cemetery
Qionglin Village
Kinhu District
Huandao East Rd
Ming Lake
Lan Lake
Boyu Rd
Chungyang Hwy
Shanwai
August 23 Artillery War Museum
Hsiahsing Village
Hsinshih
Hsipien
Lake Tai
Chenggong
Ceramics Factory
Huchien
Liaolo Bay
Hsinhu Fishing Harbour
Tung Tsun
Liaolo
Taiwan Strait
Nanshan
Shuangli Lake
Guningtou War Museum
Beishan
Shuangli Wetlands Area Centre
Lake Ci
Angqi
Huhsia
Kinning District
Houpanshan
Tingpao
Hsimen
Peimen
Panglin
Kincheng
Tungmen
Koxinga Shrine
Juguang Tower
Shuitou Harbour
Juguang Lake
Huandao South Rd
Shuitou Village
Kincheng District
Tungsha
Jhushan
Wuntai Pagoda
Takukang
Kukang Lake
Dishan Tunnels
Kinmen Harbour
Little Kinmen (Liehyu Island)
Huchingtou War Museum
Huangtso
Liehyu District
Hsiamen Harbour
Hsihuang
Pata Memorial
Shanglin
Tunglin
Lingshui Lake
Siwei Tunnel
Qing Yuan Lake
Chinchih

History

Settlers began arriving on Kinmen as early as the Tang dynasty (AD 618–907). Originally called Wuzhou, it was changed to Kinmen (literally 'Golden Gate') after fortified gates were put up to defend the island from pirate attacks. During the Ming (AD 1368–1644) and Qing (AD 1644–1912) dynasties, increasing numbers of Chinese migrants settled on Kinmen's shores. The Ming loyalist Koxinga, also known as Cheng Chengkung, used Kinmen as a base to liberate Kinmen and Penghu from the Dutch. In the process, he chopped down all of Kinmen's trees for his navy, something the residents still grumble about. Koxinga's massive deforestation project made Kinmen vulnerable to the devastating soil-eroding winds that commonly sweep across the strait.

Kinmen was a fairly peaceful place until 1949, when Chiang Kai-shek transformed the island into a rear-guard defensive position against the communist forces that had driven his own Nationalist army off the Mainland. Though his original plan was to have his soldiers recuperate on the island for a short period before launching a full-fledged attack on Mao Zedong's armies, this never quite happened. Instead, the island became the final flashpoint of the Chinese civil war and was subjected to incessant bombing from the Mainland throughout the 1950s and '60s.

In 1995, Taiwan established Kinmen as the ROC's sixth national park and started a massive reforestation project with the hopes of turning the once off-limits military zone into a tourist destination. In 2010 the final stage in the de-mining of the island began.

Getting There & Away

AIR In spring, **Kinmen Airport** (www.kma.gov.tw) is often fogged in, leading to cancelled flights; in summer, you'll need to book ahead. Flights operate to/from Taipei (one-way NT$2220), Kaohsiung (one-way NT$2120) and other west-coast cities with the following airlines:

Mandarin Airlines (www.mandarin-airlines.com)

TransAsia Airways (www.tna.com.tw)

Uni Air (www.uniair.com.tw)

BOAT At the time of writing, foreign travellers could use the hourly ferry service to Xiamen (NT$750, 80 minutes) providing they had a visa for China in their passport; tickets available at Kinmen Airport.

Getting Around

TO/FROM THE AIRPORT Kinmen Airport is 8km east of Kincheng city. Bus 3 travels hourly between Kincheng, Shanwai and the airport. From the airport to Kincheng taxi drivers charge a flat NT$250; in the opposite direction the fare should be around NT$200.

BICYCLE Free bicycle rentals are available in many locations around the island. Obtain a map from the visitor information centre at the airport or bus station.

BUS Buses run every one or two hours between 6am and 5pm. Schedules and destinations are posted in the bus stations in Kincheng, Shanwai and Shamei.

CAR & SCOOTER Kinmen has very little traffic and car or scooter is the easiest way to see the island. Vehicles can be rented at the airport (cars/scooters from NT$1300/300 per day); enquire at the **Airport Visitor Information Centre** (機場遊客服務中心; ⏲8am-6pm). Cars can also be rented in Kincheng (ask at your hotel).

TAXI Drivers prefer to ask for a flat fare rather than use the meter. Taxi tours cost NT$2000 to NT$2500 a day; it's unlikely your driver will speak English.

TOURIST BUS There are four tourist buses with routes running to all major destinations. You'll need two full days to cover all the sights (two buses each day). Make enquiries and purchase tickets at the information centre above the public bus station in Kincheng.

Kincheng (Jincheng) 金城

Kincheng (Jīnchéng) city is the busiest town on the island (though still a very laid-back place) and filled with winding alleys, brick-paved market streets, temples and old architecture.

Sights

Kincheng is a great place to explore on foot; all of the sights listed here are free, and most are open from dawn to dusk. At the time of writing, restoration work was proceeding all over the city on any number of old buildings.

Mofan St HISTORIC SITE

Built in 1924, the buildings on this charming little street have brick exteriors and arched door fronts modelled after both the Japanese and Western architecture that was in fashion back in the day. Mofan St (Mófàn Jiē) has a couple of hip places for a drink or meal and a number of shops selling traditional snacks.

Memorial Arch to Qiu Liang-Kung's Mother HISTORIC SITE

What a shining example of filial devotion was Qiu Liang-Kung, a native of Kinmen who became governor of China's Zhejiang province. When his mother refused to remarry after his father died, living her remaining 28 years as a widow, he had this Kincheng landmark erected in 1812 in her honour. The Memorial Arch to Qiu Liang-Kung's Mother (Qiū Liánggōng Mǔ Jiéxiào Fǎng) now dominates narrow Juguang Rd in the old market area.

Kuei Pavilion HISTORIC SITE

(奎閣; Kuí Gé; ⏲8.30am-5pm) The very elegant-looking two-storey Kuei Pavilion was built in 1836 to worship the god of literature, and it's here that aspiring scholars would come to pray for success in the civil-service examinations. Surrounding the pavilion are a number of stately (if decaying) Western-style buildings, and fanning back an entire neighbourhood of old dwellings connected by narrow lanes. We implore you to explore this tradition-rich area, especially in the evening.

The pavilion is down a side alley to the left just past the Memorial Arch to Qiu Liang-Kung's Mother. It's a bit of a maze but there are signs and the pavilion is no more than 100m from the arch.

Kinmen Qing Dynasty Military Headquarters HISTORIC SITE

(清金門鎮總兵署; Qīng Jīnménzhèn Zǒngbīngshǔ; ⏲10am-8pm) This is the oldest surviving Qing government building in Taiwan; a 10-year restoration project has seen the spacious compound restored to its original design. It's lit at night with lanterns.

Wú Jiāng Shū Yuàn (Wu River Academy) HISTORIC SITE

This walled complex was built in 1780 to house one of Kinmen's ancient schools. Inside, the **Chutzu Shrine** (朱子祠; Zhūzǐ Cí) honours neo-Confucian scholar Chu Hsi, who sought a revival of Confucian values during the Sung dynasty (AD 960–1279).

Festivals & Events

Welcoming the City God TRADITIONAL FESTIVAL

On the 12th day of the fourth lunar month the **City God Temple** (城隍廟; Chénghuáng Miào) in Kincheng hosts this mass multiday festival. A parading route covers most of the western side of the island and everywhere you'll find traditional opera and dancing, fireworks and costumed troupes. One unique part of the festival involves children dressed as characters from history and mythology. Depending on the village they come from the kids will be riding on tricycles or rickshaws. The Juguang Tower (p279) has a super-informative introduction (with tons of pictures) to this festival.

Sleeping

In recent years a number of homestays have opened up in restored dwellings in the traditional villages around Kinmen. If you can speak a little Chinese, these are infinitely preferable to the mostly mediocre accommodation on offer in Kincheng, though you will still be likely return to town for meals.

Ru Yi Jia HOMESTAY $

(如一家; Rúyìjiā; ☎322 167; ru.jia@msa.honet.net; 35-1 Zhupu North Rd, 珠浦北路35-1號; d/tw NT$1280/1980) A quaint and friendly homestay right in the heart of Kincheng. Rooms feature modern decor and furnishings and there's a relaxing cafe at the front. The homestay is almost directly across from the old Wu River Academy.

King Ring Hotel HOTEL $$

(金瑞 大飯店; Jīnruì Dàfàndiàn; ☎323 777; kr@quicknet.com.tw; 166 Minquan Rd, 金城 民權路166號; d/ste NT$1600/2000; @) The King Ring enjoys a good reputation among travellers and tour groups, meaning it's often fully booked. Rooms are cosy and modern, though a little dark.

Ta Chen Hotel HOTEL $

(大成大飯店; Dà Chéng Dàfàndiàn; ☎324 851; 16 Minsheng Rd, 金城 民生路16號; d/tw incl breakfast NT$1000/1200; 📶) This hotel is right in the thick of things, just down the road from the Kincheng bus station. Rooms are basic but clean and include wi-fi.

Six Brothers Hotel HOTEL $

(六桂飯店; Liù Guì Fàndiàn; ☎372 888; 166 Juguang Rd, 金城 莒光路166號; s/d NT$1000/1200) Decent rooms and friendly management.

Hong Fu Hotel HOTEL $

(宏福大飯店; Hóngfú Dà Fàndiàn; ☎326 768; 169-175 Minzu Rd, 民族路169-175號; r NT$1000-1200; 📶) Rooms could use an update but they are perfectly clean and have excellent wi-fi reception.

Kincheng

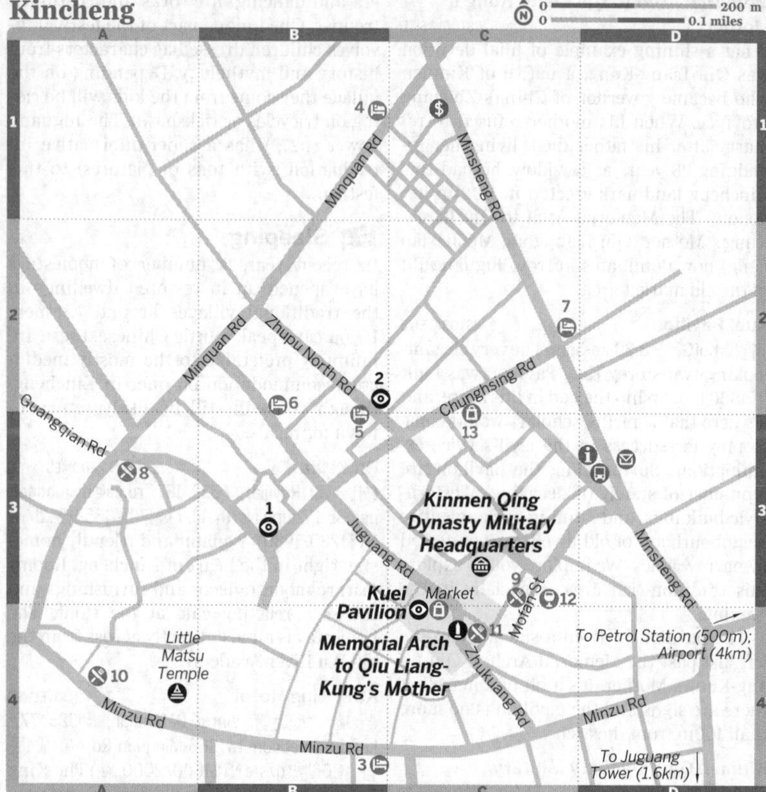

Eating

The area around Mofan St is chock-a-block with small stands and restaurants selling a variety of Kincheng snacks and sweets. Some of Kinmen's specialities include *gòng táng* (hard candy), *miàn xiàn* (sticky rice noodles) and *chǎo shāchóng* (fried sandworms). Go to the market in the early morning or evening to get the best of what's on offer.

For small restaurants check out Juguang Rd and Minzu Rd. Minzu Rd is also loaded with fruit shops.

Hung Lou SET MEALS $$
(戀戀紅樓; Liànliàn Hóng Lóu; 24 Mofan St; set meals NT$160-200, ⏲10am-10pm) This place is extremely funky, with walls covered in political art representing both sides of the cross-Strait conflict. Set meals are great value and rather tasty as well.

Niu Jiazhuang BEEF NOODLES $
(牛家莊; Niújiāzhuāng; 5 Lane 318, Minzu Rd; beef noodles NT$70; ⏲5-10pm) This popular *níu'rìu miàn* (beef noodles) restaurant uses ox beef in the traditional Kinmen way. It's just off Minzu Rd down an alley across from the county stadium.

Shou Ji Kuangtung Zhou CONGEE $
(壽記廣東粥; Shòujì Guǎngdōng Zhōu; 50-1 Zhukuang Rd, Sec 1; congee NT$60; ⏲6.30am-noon) This restaurant, more than 80 years old, serves up steaming bowls of Cantonese-style congee. Locals favour the *zhū dù (*pig-stomach) congee but there are other varieties available.

Damiaokou SEAFOOD $$
(新大廟口; Xīn Dàmiàokǒu; cnr Minquan & Guangqian Rds; dishes NT$60-180; ⏲lunch & dinner) Right next to a small temple on the west side of Kincheng, this restaurant serves up some mighty fine seafood.

Kincheng

Top Sights

Kinmen Qing Dynasty Military Headquarters C3
Kuei Pavilion C4
Memorial Arch to Qiu Liang-Kung's Mother C4

Sights

1 City God Temple B3
2 Wu River Academy B2

Sleeping

3 Hong Fu Hotel B4
4 King Ring Hotel B1
5 Ru Yi Jia B3
6 Six Brothers Hotel B2
7 Ta Chen Hotel C2

Eating

8 Damiaokou A3
9 Hung Lou C3
10 Niu Jiazhuang A4
11 Shou Ji Kuangtung Zhou C4

Drinking

12 Bar Sa C3

Shopping

13 Kinmen Minsu Wenwu Chih Jia C3

Weather permitting, management sets up tables so guests can sit outside and feast next to the temple.

Drinking

Bar Sa BAR
(Bāsà Shāokǎo Diàn; 13 Mofan St) Bar Sa is a chic bar-cafe selling a range of rice and noodle dishes as well as fruity drinks and coffees.

Shopping

Visitors to Kinmen generally leave with two of the island's most famous products: a potent liquor made from sorghum, and extremely sharp knives constructed from spent shell casings lobbed over from the Mainland. Booze and weaponry: always a good combination.

First the liquor. At 58 proof, Kaoliang liquor is sold all over the island; try a few shots at a local bar before purchasing any serious quantities to take home. 'Blinding' is an adjective often used to describe the liquor's effects. As for the knives, these unusual souvenir items are made from melted-down artillery shells left over from the Mainland bombardments. They are some of the best cutting knives you'll find and your chef friends will be drooling with envy when they see them.

The knives are available all over Kinmen and come in a variety of shapes and sizes. The most fun place to shop for them is at the Chin Ho Li Steel Knife Factory just outside the city, where you can watch Maestro Wu as he crafts high-quality knives (see the boxed text, p280). And of course, don't forget to pack your knives (or meat cleavers, swords or axes) in your checked baggage before boarding the plane.

Kinmen Minsu Wenwu Chih Jia SOUVENIRS
(金門民俗文物之家; Jīnmén Mínsú Wénwù Zhī Jiā; Lane 1, 124 Chunghsing Rd) A wonderful little curio shop in central Kincheng, where you can find all sorts of ceramic knick-knacks, dishes and one-of-a-kind items to take home.

Information

Bank of Taiwan ATM (台灣銀行; Minsheng Rd) On the west side of Minsheng Rd, just before Minquan Rd.

Kinmen County Tourism (www.kinmen.gov.tw) Excellent resource for background on sights and general cultural information.

Visitor Information Centre (遊客服務中心; 9am-9.30pm) Above the bus station; has brochures and information on free bike rentals and bus tours.

Around Kincheng

Twenty kilometres long and roughly bow-tie shaped, Kinmen is easy to get around by bike or scooter. The island is full of ancient towns, battlefield monuments, lakes, forests and well-laid-out little parks (technically speaking, the whole island is a national park). We recommend you spend at least two days on the island if you want to begin to see what it has to offer.

Note that all the sights following are free.

Sights

Juguang Tower HISTORIC SITE
(莒光樓; Jǔguāng Lóu; 8am-10pm) This three-storey tower just southeast of Kincheng should be your first stop for an overview of the rich history and culture of Kinmen. The 1st floor covers food, architecture, alcohol, industry, wind lions and even local proverbs ('better to marry a man from the west than east'). The 2nd floor is

WATCHING THE MAESTRO AT WORK

Living under bombardment has taught the people of Kinmen to make the best of things, and the island has done a good job transforming war history into tourist trade. One place where you can see this done with unique aplomb is at the **Chin Ho Li Steel Knife Factory** (金合利鋼刀; Jīnhélì Gāngdāo; 236 Bóyù Rd, Sec 1; ⏲8.30am-6.30pm), otherwise known as the factory of Maestro Wu. It's here where spent shell casings are transformed into one-of-a-kind knives. What makes a Maestro Wu knife so unique is what they're made from: old propaganda-laden shells lobbed by the communist Chinese in the 1950s. These are shaped into beautiful steel blades of various sizes, intended for both kitchen and ornamental use. Prices start at around NT$800, and if you want to watch yours being made, don't come between noon and 2pm – that's when Maestro Wu rests.

The current Maestro Wu is a wiry middle-aged fellow named Wu Tsong-shan, who studied smithing and weapon crafting under the tutelage of his father (another Maestro Wu, as the title is passed down). Wu says that the countless tons of shells that were lobbed over are ideal for making knives. Unlike regular shells, which are designed to shatter into killing fragments, propaganda shells are made of high-grade steel, designed to split neatly open and demoralise the opponent.

dedicated to a unique festival called Welcoming the City God (see p277), while the 3rd explains the origin of the tower itself.

Juguang Tower was built in 1952 as a memorial to the fallen soldiers of Kinmen. A striking-looking building, it was constructed in the 'National style', a key feature of which is a traditional sweeping roof on a modern base.

ANCIENT VILLAGES

Kinmen has the best collection of old dwellings in one small area in all Taiwan. Seven villages retain most if not all of their original feng-shui-beholden layout and clan structure, while many more have sections to admire among the newer constructions. Almost everywhere you go on Kinmen you'll spot old houses, and nicely, restoration work has not destroyed the original character.

Note the following as you walk around. Most traditional dwellings in Taiwan sport a simple gabled roof with overhanging eaves. But on Kinmen many feature the long, elegant swallowtail roof that you usually find only on temples elsewhere. The reason for this is that Kinmen was once a very wealthy place and swallowtail roofs symbolise high social position.

Many of Kinmen's old houses also feature some fabulous looking high gable fronts, either shaped like a saddle or a thick fan jutting straight up. Traditional symbols are usually painted on the gable face and mentally collecting the various symbols and gable types is a fun way to enjoy looking at old buildings. Just be careful: gable-gazing can make you walk into things!

Some other dwelling features to admire include stone courtyards and stone wall bases (made with high-quality Quanzhou stone); woodcarvings on the front gates; stone or wood lattice windows (often in a hexagonal shape); long panels of cochin pottery where the walls and eaves meet; lion statues; and painted or carved traditional symbols such as bats symbolising luck and vases symbolising peace.

Beishan & Nanshan — ANCIENT VILLAGES

The two villages of Beishan (北山; Běishān) and Nanshan (南山; Nánshān) around Lake Ci and Shuangli Lake are part of the area known as Guningtou, famous for a bloody battle between communist and Nationalist forces in 1949. These days the villages retain much of their old character, adding a charming backdrop to the lakes.

The most visited of the old dwellings is called the **Beishan Old Western-style House** (北山古洋樓; Běishān Gǔ Yánglóu). Get up close and you'll see why: it's still riddled with bullet holes from the Guningtou battle. To find the house, head straight when you see the sign for the turn-off to the 'Nature Centre' (the Shuangli Wetlands Area Centre). The house is about 100m further up the road.

Shuitou Village — ANCIENT VILLAGE

There's an old saying, 'You can be as rich as Shuitou, but you can't build houses like Shuitou.' And they have a point. The 700-year-old community of Shuitou Village (水頭村; Shuǐtóu Cūn) boasts one of the best collections of old houses, both Chinese and Western-style, in all of Taiwan.

First the Western buildings. There are over 100 of them around Kinmen, all built by Kinmen emigrants who made it big in business across Southeast Asia during the late 19th and early 20th centuries. The **Deyue Mansion** (得月樓; Déyuè Lóu) is probably the most famous. Built in 1931 by Huang Hui-huang, it features an unmistakable four-storey **gun tower** that was for years Kinmen's tallest structure.

Huang Hui-huang was part of the Huang clan, the earliest settlers in Shuitou and also builders of the rows of traditional Fujian houses just a stone's throw from the Deyue Mansion. Follow the signs to **Youtang Villa** (酉堂; Yǒu Táng), a 200-year-old former school that is a showcase of traditional design.

Oddly, for such a famous place the village is not properly signed, so as you head towards Shuitou harbour look for a large white statue of an alcohol bottle at a major intersection. The village is just off the road down a slope.

Jhushan Village

ANCIENT VILLAGE

There's another old saying on Kinmen: 'Even if you have the houses of Shuitou, you don't have the wealth of Jhushan.' Again, they have a point. During the late 19th century emigrants from Jhushan Village (珠山村; Zhūshān Cūn) made huge profits in the Philippines and sent much of it back to build the gorgeous houses you see today.

In the centre of the village is a large brick-lined pond; at the back a small mountain (well, hillock really). In the world of feng shui it doesn't get much better than this potent wealth-retaining arrangement.

Shanshou Folk Culture Village

ANCIENT VILLAGE

This grouping of 18 Fujian-style buildings, all interconnected by narrow alleys and bricked walls, was built over a 25-year period in the late Qing dynasty. Again, money made overseas was used for funding, and all materials – even the master craftsmen – were brought in from China.

The Kinmen government restored Shanshou in 1979 after most of the original residents had moved out. Today Shanshou Folk Culture Village (山后民俗文化村; Shānhòu Mínsú Wénhuà Cūn) sits as a near-perfect example of a traditional village.

Go in the morning if you want to take pictures – the back of the village faces west and the late-afternoon sun makes it difficult to shoot.

Qionglin Village (Cyonglin or Chiunglin)

ANCIENT VILLAGE

Qionglin Village (瓊林村; Qiónglín Cūn) in Kinhu is famous for having more shrines than any other village on Kinmen. Head off the main road for the best atmosphere and buildings.

BATTLE HISTORY & WAR MUSEUMS

FREE Guningtou War Museum

MUSEUM

(古寧頭戰史館; Gǔníngtóu Zhànshǐ Guǎn; ⌚8.30am-5pm) Guningtou was the site of a ferocious battle between the communist Chinese and Taiwan in 1949. The war museum, on the actual battlefield site, provides an interesting look into a gruesome conflict that saw 5000 soldiers from both sides lose their lives over a 56-hour period. Nearby are the traditional villages of Beishan and Nanshan, still bearing the scars of the Guningtou battle on some old buildings.

The turn-off for the museum is only marked in Chinese but it's to the right just before the turn-off for the Shuangli

WIND LIONS

Travelling around Kinmen, you'll notice an abundance of stone lions. These are Kinmen's Wind Lions (風獅爺; Fēngshīyé), traditional totems said to have the power to control the winds and keep the land fertile. According to locals, these totems began appearing after Kinmen was deforested to build Koxinga's navy. The locals, forced to turn to supernatural aid as the denuded soil of their island ceased bearing crops, began placing the lions around the island. While the island has since been reforested, the Wind Lions can still be found in almost every village around the island. Many stand upright and are draped in flowing capes, giving them the appearance of a dapper Pokemon.

Check out www.kinmen.gov.tw for a complete list with locations.

THE AUGUST 23RD ARTILLERY WAR

In August 1955, Sino–US talks about the status of Taiwan had left China feeling bitter and angry. The United States insisted that Beijing renounce the use of force against Taiwan. China returned that Taiwan was Chinese territory and it had the right to liberate it from Chiang Kai-shek. Dead centre in the dispute, Taiwan declared a state of emergency and prepared for the full force of a Chinese attack.

That came on the morning of 23 August 1958, as Beijing launched a ferocious bombardment on Kinmen. In just two hours the island was hit with over 42,000 shells. Alarmed, the US acted quickly to help defend Kinmen, realising that if the island fell, Taiwan was likely to be next. A shipment of jet fighters and anti-aircraft missiles were sent to Taiwan, along with six supporting aircraft carriers.

China created a tight blockade around Kinmen's beaches and airstrip in an effort to prevent any military supplies from reaching the Nationalist military. In response the US sent several warships into the Taiwan Strait to escort a convoy of Taiwan military-supply ships. The convoy got within 5km of the blockade and was surprised that the communists refused to fire.

Instead, Beijing offered Taiwan a very odd ceasefire – it would fire on Kinmen only on odd-numbered days. On even-numbered days the island would be left alone. Taiwan agreed to this reluctantly. The Chinese held to the ceasefire and continued to bomb Kinmen throughout September and October on odd-numbered days. By November, tensions had decreased and the bombing stopped. Tragically, almost 500,000 shells had struck Kinmen, killing over 3000 civilians. More than 1000 soldiers were also killed or wounded.

Wetlands Area Centre (marked 'Nature Centre' on the road sign).

FREE **Dishan Tunnels** HISTORIC SITE
(翟山坑道; Díshān Kēngdào; ⌚8.30am-5pm) Blasted out of solid granite by soldiers in the early 1960s, these tunnels stretch 357m to the ocean and were designed to protect boats from bombs during wars. Tourists are allowed to walk through the spooky interior or follow a bridge over the entrance that leads to the piers.

FREE **August 23 Artillery War Museum** MUSEUM
(八二三戰史館; Bā Èr Sān Zhànshǐ Guǎn; ⌚8.30am-5pm) This museum documents the horrific battle that occurred on 23 August 1958, when the communists launched an artillery attack against Kinmen that lasted for 44 days and pummelled the island with almost 500,000 shells. Outside are fighter planes, tanks and cannons used during the siege. The museum is on the grounds of Banyan Park.

PARKS & NATURE PRESERVES

With its beautiful lakes, forests and bird sanctuaries, Kinmen truly is, as locals say, 'a garden built upon a fortress'. So much so that the island attracts visitors with no interest in military history.

Lake Ci SCENIC AREA
Though one of the most scenic and popular spots to visit on Kinmen, saltwater Lake Ci (Cí Hú) did not even exist until the 1970s. Once an open harbour, the lake was formed after the Nationalists constructed a causeway along the western seashore following the battle of Guningtou. Today the causeway is the perfect spot to take in the lake (and its great variety of birds; see p284) and also the pretty stretch of beach and parkland on the other side looking west to Xiamen.

Lake Tai SCENIC AREA
Just south of Shanwai is Lake Tai (Tài Hú), a 5m-deep body of water that was dug entirely by hand in the 1960s. The views from the south side take in Mt Taiwu, which from this angle looks far more imposing than it's 262m height would suggest.

Mt Taiwu SCENIC MOUNTAIN
The highest mountain on Kinmen, Mt Taiwu (Tàiwǔ Shān) rises a colossal 262m above sea level. A road takes you about halfway up to a shrine and **soldiers' cemetery** *(gōng mù)* built in 1952 to honour the ROC soldiers who died in battle. From here a walking path takes you to the top (one hour). Be on the lookout for a famous inscription on a stone of one of Chiang Kai-

shek's favourite one-liners: 'Wú Wàng Zài Jǔ Lèshí' or 'Don't forget the days in Chu' (a reference to a doomed battle that was saved at the last moment).

TEMPLES & SHRINES

Koxinga Shrine SHRINE

To the southwest of Kincheng sits the Koxinga Shrine (延平郡王祠; Yánpíng Jùnwáng Cí), built in memory of the Ming general Koxinga who fought against the Dutch occupation. The shrine seems to be most popular with Taiwanese tourists – locals haven't quite forgiven Koxinga for cutting down all their trees.

As you leave the temple, head right and 150m down the road look for a lane heading left down to the sea. This leads to a walkway over to a tiny island you can reach when the tide is out.

Wuntai Pagoda HISTORIC SITE

Considered one of the oldest constructions in Taiwan, the five-level hexagonal Wuntai Pagoda (文臺寶塔; Wéntái Bǎotǎ) was originally built for the Ming emperor Hungwu as a place to honour the stars and celestial deities. Within the stone pagoda is the **Hsuchianghsiao Ancient Inscription** (虛江嘯臥碣群; Xūjiāng Xiāo Wò Jié Qún), carved by the Ming general Hsuchiang. The general, they say, used to come here to look at the sea and the inscription reads 'Hsuchiang is shouting and lying here'.

Sleeping

There are 49 homestays scattered around Kinmen, most offering rooms in traditional buildings over a century old. See http://guesthouse.kmnp.gov.tw for a complete list (in Chinese only).

Lexis Inn HOMESTAY $$

(來喜樓; Láixǐlóu; ☎325 493; http://guesthouse.kmnp.gov.tw/hotel/hotel_view2.asp?Tkey=12; 82 Jhushan Village, 珠山82號民宿; s/d NT$1400/1600; wi-fi) This newly renovated house in Jhushan was built in a Western style by emigrants who made their fortune in the Philippines in the 19th century. Rooms are simple but everything else is full of character and history and beauty. There's 20% discount outside summer months.

Shuitiaogetou HOMESTAY $$

(水調歌頭; Shuǐdiào Gētóu; ☎0932-517 669, 322 389; http://guesthouse.kmnp.gov.tw/hotel/hotel_view2.asp?Tkey=17; 40 Shuitou Village; 水頭40號民宿; s/d incl breakfast NT$1000/1600) The rooms in this traditional Fujian-style house in Shuitou Village feature wood and red-brick interiors and lots of lovely old touches. Rates include airport pick-up/drop-off.

Eating & Drinking

Some of the smaller towns have a noodle shop or restaurant (though they aren't always easy to spot) and there are a few 7-Elevens on strategic corners. It's probably best to carry a lunch if you're going out all day.

Tranquil Tea House TEAHOUSE

(文學茶坊; Wénxué Cháfǎng; ⏰10am-5pm Sat & Sun) In the village of Chenggong overlooking a pretty bit of coastline is this former military dorm turned teahouse. To get here just head up the road into Chenggong and at the very top of the road look for the big arch to the left. Head through and about 100m down you'll spot the teahouse to the right.

Little Kinmen 小金門

Little Kinmen (Xiǎo Jīnmén) is the common name for Liehyu Island (Lièyǔ Xiāng), a small, 15-sq-km patch of land west of the main island. If Kinmen is an outpost, then Little Kinmen is an outpost of an outpost, a chunk of ROC territory so close to the People's Republic of China (PRC) that mobile phones automatically switch to Fujian-based networks (mind those roaming charges!). Pretty and windswept, Little Kinmen is basically an island park that just happens to sit atop the 1958 war's last front lines.

Sights & Activities

Cycling is the best way to see Little Kinmen and the price can't be beat – the Kinmen tourism department loans visitors bikes for free! Just head left towards the Siwei Tunnel when you get off the boat from Kinmen and head up the stairs to the main visitor centre (not the one at the harbour).

Little Kinmen's perimeter is ringed by an 18.5km bike path passing through lovely forests and coastal scenery, much of which is currently being de-mined by teams from Mozambique. There are a couple of small stores that sell local specialities such as deep-fried oyster cake, in addition to groceries, but you'd be wise to carry a lunch with you.

BIRDING ON KINMEN

Lying along the migratory routes of hundreds of bird species and boasting a variety of habitats in a small area (seashore, lakes, marshes, mudflats, open fields and forests), Kinmen is rightly seen as a paradise for birdwatchers. Over 300 species of birds have been recorded, with about 40 resident species and the rest migratory. Lake Ci is considered one of the top twitching spots, especially in winter when thousands of great cormorants come to nest.

To the east, Lake Tai is a feeding ground for cormorants and ospreys, species best seen in the early morning. Later in the day look for the comical resident woodpecker-like hoopoe feeding in the grass of nearby Banyan Park.

On Little Kinmen, Lingshui Lake is a popular twitching venue. It's also a good place to spot fiddler crabs in the mudflats.

For more information on the birds of Kinmen visit the **Shuangli Wetlands Area Centre** (雙鯉溼地自然中心; Shuānglǐ Shīdì Zìrán Zhōngxīn; ⌚8.30am-5pm), a research facility devoted to wetlands preservation. Also pick up a copy of *Birdwatching at Kinmen*, published by the Kinmen County Government. It's available at most visitor centres.

FREE **Siwei Tunnel** HISTORIC SITE
(四維坑道; Sìwéi Kēngdào; ⌚8.30am-5pm) The underground Siwei Tunnel, blasted through a granite reef, is 790m in length (twice as large as the Dishan Tunnels on Kinmen) and the top tourist attraction on the island. It's also home to Little Kinmen's only coffee shop. The Liehyu visitor centre is right next to the tunnel entrance.

Lingshui Lake SCENIC AREA
The pretty, artificial, saltwater Lingshui Lake (陵水湖; Língshǔi Hú) is home to a number of species of waterbirds native to Fujian province.

FREE **Huchingtou War Museum** MUSEUM
(湖井頭戰史館; Hújǐngtóu Zhànshǐ Guǎn; ⌚9am-5pm Tue-Sun) The Huchingtou War Museum contains war memorabilia and an observation room with pay binoculars from which you can see Xiamen on a clear day.

Getting There

There are frequent ferries from Shuitou harbour on the main island (NT$60, 20 minutes).

MATSU

☎0836 / POP 9000

If you're looking for an off-the-beaten-path experience, look no further than this green archipelago directly off the coast of mainland China's Fujian province. Like Kinmen, Matsu (馬祖) retains much of its feel as a place perpetually on the military defensive. However, while both are still considered military posts, the Matsu vibe is a bit more martial; for one thing, half the people you run into in Matsu are in uniform. For another, while Kinmen's military sites tend to be more memorials, in Matsu you can expect to scurry down narrow tunnels and, emerging to the clear light of day, enjoy a superb ocean lookout with a real 80mm anti-aircraft cannon at your side.

The people of Matsu – though nominally schooled in Mandarin – speak a dialect mostly unintelligible to speakers of Taiwanese. Politically, most folk identify with their kin across the narrow strait separating them. For over a generation they could only watch these others through binoculars, but now they form a substantial part of the visitor population.

Eighteen islands make up the area collectively known as Matsu and are grouped

into townships: the main townships are Nangan, Beigan, Dongyin and Jyuguang, which are connected by ferry boats.

History

The development of Matsu began in the 1400s with the arrival of Fujianese mainlanders escaping political turmoil in their homeland. Later, the migrant waves of the 1600s from mainland China to Taiwan saw an increase in Matsu's population as boatloads of Fujianese fishermen arrived on the island. They brought with them the language, food, architecture and religious beliefs of their ancestors, much of which is still around today.

Throughout the 1700s and 1800s piracy plagued the islands, causing residents at various times to temporarily abandon their homes to seek shelter elsewhere. Matsu was largely politically insignificant until the Nationalists fled to Taiwan in 1949 and established Matsu, along with Kinmen, as a front-line defence against the communists. Matsu residents saw their quiet islands transformed into battlefields and had to adjust to the constant threat of war. The Mainland bombed Matsu intermittently until the deployment of the US 7th Fleet in 1958 prevented any further escalation.

Martial law was lifted from Matsu in 1992, a number of years after it was lifted over in 'mainland' Taiwan. In 2001, Matsu (along with Kinmen) became an early stepping stone in cross-Strait travel when the 'Three Small Links' policy was instituted, permitting limited trade and limited travel between ROC- and PRC-controlled territory. Cross-Strait direct flights, inaugurated in 2008, have stolen much of the business traffic that was flowing through Matsu and the government is now set on transforming this military zone into a major tourist destination.

Dangers & Annoyances

Travellers in Matsu, especially Nangan, should be mindful of the fact that live-firing exercises are conducted regularly. Warning signs should be obeyed and straying too far off marked roads is a bad idea.

Nangan 南竿

Shaped like a poorly baked croissant, Nangan (Nángān, Nankan) is Matsu's largest island. Compared with the rest of Matsu, it's a veritable hotbed of activity. The largest settlement is **Jieshou Village** (介壽村; also spelled Chiehshou), which is where you'll find places to rent scooters, and the island's only bank. The walk to Jieshou from the airport takes about 20 minutes, and is quite pretty. Ferries to outlying islands leave from Fu'ao harbour (Fúaò Gǎng), just a few kilometres northwest of Jieshou. The central bus station is in Jieshou Village, at the end of the main road just before the start of the seaside park.

Sights & Activities

Unlike on Taiwan's other outer island groups, the main roads of Matsu do not skirt the flat bits, but roll with the hilly terrain. For the visitor on a scooter this means endless pretty scenes unfolding before your eyes, in particular of the deep-blue sea dotted with green islets. It also means that exploring beyond the sights is well worth the petrol. The northwestern corner of Nangan is a particularly lovely area.

Note that all sights and activities on the islands are free.

Military History

Matsu is replete with forts, tunnels and other sights connected with the islands' important position in the struggles between communist and Chinese Nationalist forces. Authorities claim that the islands actually have the highest concentration of tunnels and warrens in the world. Some of these sites have already been opened for tourism, but you can expect dozens more in the coming years.

Iron Fort MILITARY SITE

One of the most impressive military sites is the abandoned Iron Fort (鐵堡; Tiě Bǎo), really a rocky strip of coral jutting out over the sea and hollowed out to house Matsu's amphibious forces. Visitors are allowed to enter and have a look at the spartan living quarters of the soldiers who once lived there. Be sure to look out over the ocean through sniper slots. Gruesome stories are told by Matsu residents of how Mainland frogmen would sneak inside the fort at night, slit the throats of the Taiwanese guards on duty and carry back an ear to show their comrades.

Beihai Tunnel & Dahan Stronghold MILITARY SITES

(北海坑道; Běihǎi Kēngdào; ⏲8am-5pm Mon-Fri) The 700m Beihai Tunnel was carved out of a sheer rock face by soldiers using only simple hand tools. Begun in 1968, the

Nangan

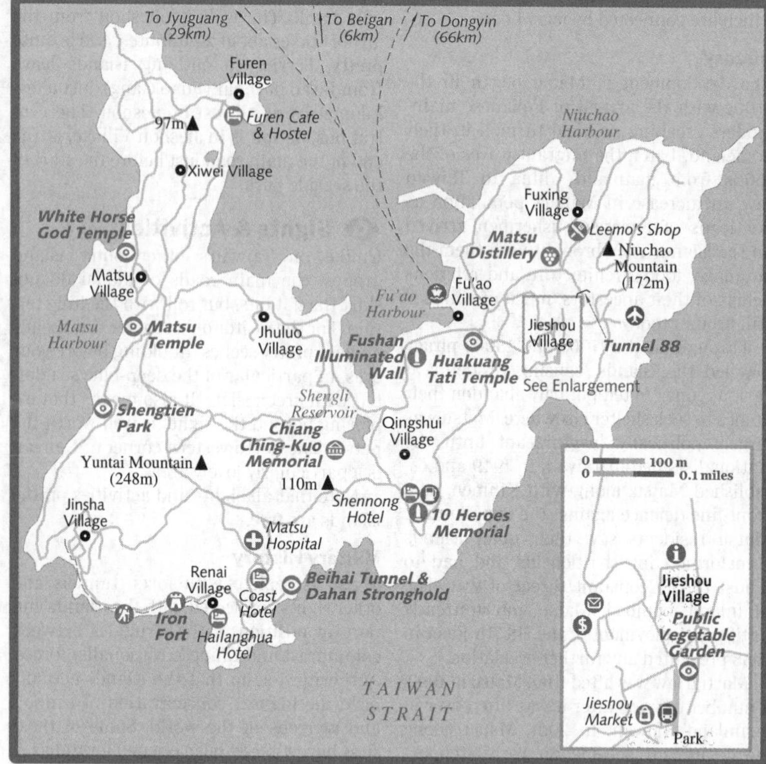

project took more than three years and many young men lost their lives in the process. The tunnel was used as a hiding place for military boats and is supposedly large enough to hide 120 small vessels inside its cavernous interior in case of attack.

Just across a rocky beach from the Beihai Tunnel is the recently opened Dahan Stronghold (大漢據點; Dàhàn Jùdiǎn), a fortification built directly into a granite peninsula. A warren of narrow and low tunnels leads visitors to emplacements where real 80mm anti-aircraft cannons and machine guns peak out from caves overlooking the sea.

Fushan Illuminated Wall MILITARY SITE

Overlooking Fu'ao harbour is the Fushan Illuminated Wall (枕戈待旦; Zhěngē Dàidàn), in essence a concrete billboard that faces mainland China and warns communist forces to 'sleep on spears'. Translation: Chiang Kai-shek is coming to get you (one day). The wall is easy to pass on the road without seeing it, so head to the harbour and look back at the hills.

Temples

Temples in Matsu are largely uninspiring modern restorations, interesting more for their histories than anything else. Some, however, do sport striking-looking high gable ends that jut up like waves on the ocean, or, licking flames. In fact the roofs are called fire walls, and you'll not find them anywhere else in Taiwan.

Not surprisingly, numerous Matsu temples can be found on Matsu's islands. Many feature statues of the goddess as a sweet-faced young woman, again something only found in this part of Taiwan.

Matsu Temple TAOIST TEMPLE

Adjacent to Matsu harbour (Mǎzǔ Gǎng) in Matsu Village (Mǎzǔ Cūn), Matsu Temple (馬祖天后宮; Mǎzǔ Tiānhoù Gōng) has the oldest history on the Matsu islands. Legend has it that during an attempt to save her father from shipwreck, Matsu herself drowned and was washed to shore here. The temple is considered one of the most sacred spots in Taiwan. Show up on Matsu's birthday (the 23rd day of the third lunar month) to check out a serious festival.

Huakuang Tati Temple TAOIST TEMPLE

In the Ming dynasty, a villager dreamt that the god of fire told him an incense burner was buried in Fu'ao. The man later discovered it and Huakuang Tati Temple (華光大帝廟; Huáguāng Dàdì Miào) was built in the god's honour.

White Horse God Temple TAOIST TEMPLE

The small White Horse God Temple (白馬文武大王廟; Báimǎ Wénwǔ Dàwáng Miào) is devoted to a deified general who once defended Fujian. During storms a mysterious light appears to guide ships.

Bird- & Butterfly-Watching

Matsu's offshore islets attract thousands of breeding terns in the spring and summer months. In 2000, the area around Snake Island, a tiny bit of land off the northwestern shore of Xiju, was declared a **tern reserve** and serious twitchers can hire boats to take them around this and other locations. See www.birdingintaiwan.org for more.

While seldom mentioned, Matsu is one of the best places in summer to see a variety of Taiwan's large and exquisite **swallowtail butterflies**. You don't need to search for these; there are colonies literally everywhere. Most of what you'll see are common species such as **Great Mormons** but the sheer numbers floating about roadside will astound anyone with the slightest naturalist impulses.

Some places to see them swarm in the hundreds are the coastal road past Jinsha Village, the road up from the Chiang Ching-Kuo Memorial, and the road to Yuntai Mountain (Yúntái Shān; 248m), Nangan's highest peak. Butterflies are for the most part quite used to people and you can get up pretty close for photos.

Jinsha Village ANCIENT VILLAGE

This collection of old stone houses lies just back from the sea in a sheltered cove. Restoration work on the village was under way at the time of writing. If you visit, check out the toilets down by the entrance to the beach. They are reportedly (and we have no reason for doubt) the only loos in Taiwan ever constructed from an old military fort. Beside them a bunker filled with paintings bears the great old propagandist slogan to 'Fight against the communists, resist the Russians, kill Je De, and remove Mao Zedong'.

FREE **Matsu Distillery** DISTILLERY

(馬祖酒廠; Mǎzǔ Jiǔchǎng; 208 Fuxing Village; 8.30-11.30am & 1.40-5pm Mon-Fri, 1.40-4.40pm holidays, last tour 40min before closing) Like booze but don't like paying for it? Well, friend, a tour of Matsu Distillery may well be for you. The factory produces two of Matsu's best-loved products: *Gāoliáng jiǔ* (Kaoliang liquor), made from sorghum, and *làojiǔ* (medicinal rice wine). There's honestly not much to see, but if you can tag along with a Chinese-language tour, you can partake of the samples that are given out liberally at the end of each session.

Sleeping

At the time of writing, there was much work being done restoring Nangan's old villages and in general trying to make the towns a better match to their lovely surroundings. In the future the villages of Fuxing, Jinsha and Qingshui might be worth checking out for homestays.

Furen Cafe & Hostel HOMESTAY $

(夫人咖啡館; Fūrén Kāfēiguǎn; 25138; www.furen.com.tw; Furen Village; dm NT$700) The hostel is literally just some floor space in a cool old wood loft of a traditional stone building, but you've plenty of room out on the terraced patio overlooking a pretty cove. If there's a more charming spot on Nangan we haven't found it, and to top it off there's a small swimming beach about 100m down the road. Call to make a reservation.

Hailanghua Hotel HOTEL $

(海浪花客棧; Hǎilànghuā Kèzhàn; 22569; Renai Village, 仁愛村; s/d NT$1000/1200) Clean, modern rooms, friendly management and ocean views from the coffee-shop patio make the Hailanghua Hotel a great budget choice.

Shennong Resort HOTEL $$

(神農山莊; Shénnóng Shānzhuāng; 26333; www.shennong.com.tw; Qingshui Village, 清水村; d/tw NT$1600/1800; @) With Yuntai Mountain on one side and the ocean on the other, this five-storey hotel offers some beautiful views. The cosy modern rooms with broadband could easily go for twice this price anywhere else.

Coast Hotel BOUTIQUE HOTEL $$
(日光海岸海景旅館; Rìguāng Hǎiàn Hǎijǐng Lǚguǎn; ☎26666; www.coasthotel.com.tw; Renai Village, 仁愛村; s/d/ste incl breakfast NT$2680/2880/3240) This small boutique hotel boasts a Japanese minimalist design, fabulous ocean views, and an excellent restaurant and coffee shop serving both Western and Asian dishes. In the low season, the basic doubles go for around NT$2000.

Eating

There are a number of Taiwan-style restaurants along the main streets in the villages of Jieshou, Matsu and Fu'ao. The morning market in Jieshou (Jièshòu Shìzǐ Shìchǎng) is a good place for a traditional breakfast including fish noodles, oyster pancakes and a variety of cakes.

Leemo's Shop SEAFOOD $$
(依嬤的店; Yīmā de Diàn; http://hogoema.pixnet.net/blog; 72-1 Fuxing Village; set meals NT$290; ⌚lunch & dinner; 📶) Unless you come with a group your only option is the one set meal (*tǎocān*): all nine dishes of it, which includes in-season seafood, soup, vegetables and fruit.

The restaurant is a little tricky to get to. First head down the side road to the right of the distillery (towards Fuxing Village, aka Niujiao Village). Take the first right (following the English signs to Leemo's) and then another right in 50m. Look for the stone house with big glass windows in a quaint old neighbourhood of other stone houses.

Furen Cafe CAFE $
(夫人咖啡館; Fūrén Kāfēiguǎn; www.furen.com.tw; Furen Village; dishes NT$150) Even if you don't stay here, come for the excellent coffee and simple dishes served on the stone patio overlooking the sea.

Information

Taiwan's tourism department has information booths at the airport, the ferry terminal and any number of attractions (seems a bit of a make-work project to be honest) but none had much English material at the time of writing. If you can find it, pick up the super-informative brochure *Let's Backpack in Matsu*.

There's not much internet access on the island but a few places have wi-fi, including the airport.

Bank of Taiwan (台灣銀行; Táiwān Yínháng; Jieshou Village) The only place in Matsu to change money; also has a 24-hour ATM on the Cirrus network. You'd be smart to take what you expect to spend in Matsu.

Getting There & Away

AIR Uni Air (www.uniair.com.tw), and only Uni Air, flies to Matsu. There are six flights daily from Taipei (NT$1962, 55 minutes) to Nangan Airport (Nángān Jīchǎng).

BOAT Shinwa Boat Company (☎in Keelung 02-2424 6868, in Nangan 22395; http://order.shinhwa.com.tw/Web.Order.aspx) runs an overnight boat from Keelung (9.50pm, eight hours). Boat schedules alternate, going directly to Nangan one night and to Nangan via Dongyin the next. The service is very unreliable, however; expect cancellations without notice. Even tourism offices recommend you call *every day* to confirm sailings.

Getting Around

TO/FROM THE AIRPORT It's a 20-minute walk to Jieshou or Fuxing Villages; most hotels offer airport pick-up.

BUS There are two bus lines on the island: mountain and shore. Services run hourly around the island (NT$15 per trip, NT$50 per daily pass, from 6.10am to 6pm); schedules are posted on bus stops except, oddly, at the central bus station.

SCOOTER Rental costs NT$500 per day, including petrol. The information counter at the airport can help with bookings but you might have a hard time finding your hotel the first time, so it's probably best to get your hotel to help with scooter rental after you've checked in.

TAXI Drivers are supposed to use the meter (NT$100 for the first 1.25km, NT$5 for every additional kilometre).

Beigan 北竿

Nangan too boisterous for you? A quick ferry brings you to Beigan (Běigān, Peikan), which boasts spectacular coastal scenery, fine beaches and wonderfully preserved Fujian villages you can stay in overnight.

Ferries to Beigan dock in Baisha harbour. The island's largest settlement is **Tangci Village** (塘岐村; Tángqí Cūn, Tangchi). Beigan is a relatively small island, so you could see the whole place in a long day on foot, though it would be a slog with all the steep hills. A scooter is best.

Sights & Activities

Military History

TOP CHOICE **Peace Memorial Park** MILITARY SITE
The western edge of Beigan, with its thin, high, rocky peninsula, was once

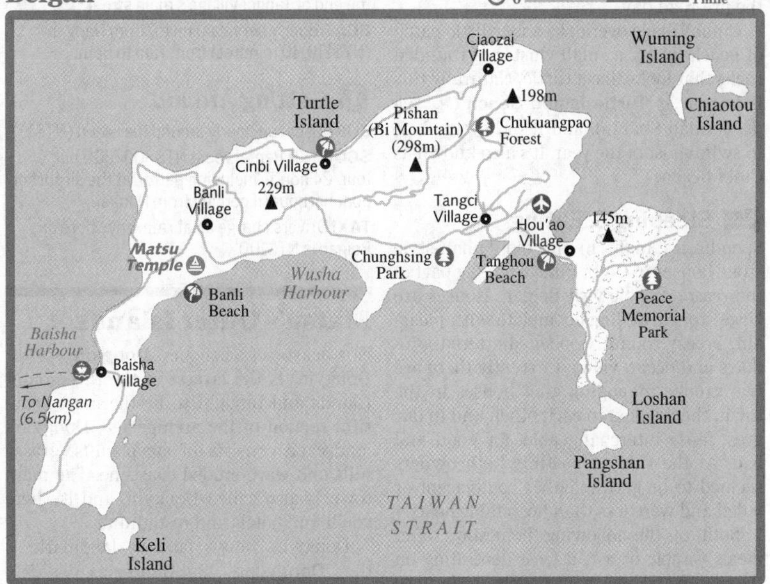

an important part of the ROC's military defence of Matsu. In recent years the entire zone has been turned into one of the island's most intriguing, to say nothing of scenic, military parks, the Peace Memorial Park (戰爭和平紀念公園; Zhànzhēng Hépíng Jìniàn Gōngyuán). After riding a very steep road to the top of the peninsula, follow the paths to a number of 'strongholds' where you'll find tunnels, bunkers, foxholes, forts and lookouts as well as outdoor displays of real tanks and anti-aircraft cannons pointing out to sea.

Ancient Villages

Chief among the preserved villages of Beigan is **Cinbi Village** (芹壁村; Qínbì Cūn), comprising low-lying interconnected one- and two-storey homes built into the side of Pishan (Bi Mountain), overlooking Turtle Island. The houses are built from slabs of granite and feature high, narrow windows to protect the inhabitants from wind and pirates. Roofs have bright-red or black tiles. About half of the homes in the small village have been transformed into guesthouses, and spending the night in one of these should be one of the highlights of your trip to Matsu.

A walk of a kilometre or so up the coastal road takes you to the foot of Leishan (Thunder Mountain), where you'll find **Ciaozai Village** (橋仔村; Qiáozǎi Cūn). The village, nestled in a cove that protects it from the northeast monsoons, has several temples devoted to the thunder god sporting very high and stylish 'fire wall' gables. Nowadays the village is mostly empty save for a few elderly residents who maintain the temples and are outnumbered by the gods inside (or so the not-so-inaccurate joke goes).

At the very eastern edge of the island is **Hou'ao Village** (后澳; Hòuào, Houwo), a small village that used to be cut off from the main island during high tide. There's a small section of old houses off the main street worth navigating the twisting alleys to check out. The Peace Memorial Park is just up the road.

Swimming

Beigan's longest and prettiest beach, **Banli Beach** (坂里沙灘; Bǎnlǐ Shātān) is just up the road from where boats dock. There are changing rooms and showers and supposedly you are allowed to camp here.

Tanghou Beach (塘后道沙灘; Tánghòu Shātān) is a thin strip of sand, divided by a road, which connects the villages of Tangci and Hou'ao. Before the road was built locals had to wade through water during high tide to travel between the two villages.

Some locals that we've spoken to pine for the pre-road days.

Cinbi Village overlooks a nice little patch of beach facing a small cluster of rounded rocks that looks like a turtle. Naturally this is known as **Turtle Island Beach** (龜島沙灘; Guīdǎo Shātān), and it's a lovely place to swim most of the year. It's also known as Cinbi Beach.

Sleeping & Eating

Spending a night in the old Fujian-style stone houses in Cinbi Village is a big part of the reason people visit Beigan. Houses are large stone dwellings complete with pleasant, breezy rooms, wooden-shuttered windows and ocean views. Currently there are two groups managing guesthouses in the town; they're next to each other, and in our eyes, fairly interchangeable, for good and bad. At the time of writing, both owners seemed to be getting either complacent or jaded and were less than hospitable hosts.

Both of the following homestays offer meals (simple or a real feast depending on the season and how many people are around) and drinks either indoors or on a terraced patio overlooking the sea that is simply one of the most serene spots to linger in all Taiwan.

If staying in a stone building that's more than 100 years old doesn't do it for you, there are a number of hotels in Tangci Village, though you'd be better off staying on Nangan and just coming over for the day. Tangci Village has a number of restaurants but opening hours and days are subject to random change so just look for whatever's open that day. Many places have picture menus.

Chin-Be Village Homestay HOMESTAY **$**
(芹壁民宿村; Qínbì Mínsù Cūn; ☎55456; http://hotel.matsu.idv.tw/chinbe; 49 Cinbi Village; d NT$800-1200) This homestay is run out of Cafe Cinbi and has stylish loft rooms with cosy bedding.

Di Zhonghai Homestay HOMESTAY **$**
(地中海民宿; Dìzhōnghǎi Mínsù; ☎56611; www.chinbe-village.com.tw/index.php; 54 Cinbi Village; dm/d NT$800/1200) Run out of the Di Zhonghai Restaurant, Di Zhonghai offers breakfast and free pick-up from the airport or ferry pier. Rooms are more basic than at Chin-Be Village Homestay.

Getting There & Away

AIR Uni Air (www.uniair.com.tw) has three flights daily from Taipei (NT$1862, 55 minutes) to Beigan Airport (Běigān Jīchǎng), which is at the end of Tangci Village's main street.

BOAT Hourly services run to/from Nangan (NT$110, 10 minutes) from 7am to 5pm.

Getting Around

BUS Buses run hourly around the island (NT$15).

SCOOTER Rentals cost NT$300/500 per four/24 hours, including petrol, at the airport or boat harbour (if coming from Nangan).

TAXI Drivers charge a flat rate: anywhere on Beigan is NT$100.

Matsu's Outer Islands

Northeast of Beigan, **Dongyin** (東引; Dōngyǐn) is the largest of the three outer islands and thought to be the most beautiful section of the archipelago. Dongyin's landscape consists of steep cliffs, grassy hills and wave-eroded coastline. The main town is also called Dongyin, and it's here you'll find hotels and restaurants.

Dongyin's most famous landmark is the **Dongyung Lighthouse** (東湧燈塔; Dōngyǒng Dēngtǎ), a simple white structure on a grassy hill overlooking the ocean. The lighthouse was built by the British in 1904 and remains an important part of Taiwan's coastal defence system.

The islands of Jyuguang Township, **Dongju** (東莒; Dōngjǔ, Tongchu) and **Xiju** (西莒; Xījǔ, Hsichu), are the most southerly of Matsu's islands. Both are remote and sparsely inhabited, but with some pretty scenery. The commercial centre of Dongju is **Daping Village** (大坪村; Dàpíng Cūn). Sights include the **Dongquan Lighthouse** (東犬燈塔; Dōngquǎn Dēngtǎ), which sits high on a hill at the northeast tip of the island. Built by the British in 1872, the white-granite building aided the navigation of merchant ships during the Opium Wars.

The other main attraction of Dongju is the **Dapu Inscription** (大埔石刻; Dàpǔ Shíkē), on the south side of the island. The memorial is dedicated to a general from the Ming dynasty who successfully drove pirates off the island without losing a single one of his soldiers.

Xijju is rowdier than its sister island, but not by much. This small island was once a busy seaport, though there's little evidence of that now. During the Korean War, American companies set themselves up in **Chingfan Village** (青帆村; Qīngfán Cūn) and nicknamed it 'Little Hong Kong'.

Getting There & Away

From Nangan there's one boat daily to Dongyin (NT$350, two hours) and three boats daily to Jyuguang's two islands (NT$200, 50 minutes). Check at Fu'ao harbour for current schedules.

PENGHU

06 / POP 90,000

Penghu (澎湖; Pénghú), also known as the Pescadores, is famous for its beautiful beaches, glorious temples and a plethora of traditional Chinese-style homes surrounded by walls made from coral. Penghu is famous for another thing as well: though the weather in the summer is hot and beautiful, in winter and spring the archipelago is quite possibly the windiest place in the northern hemisphere. Wind not a tourist draw, you say? Tell that to the droves of windsurfers who consider Penghu a sporting mecca and the Canary Islands of the Orient.

A flat, dry place covered mostly with low bush and grasslands, Penghu is quite a change from the mountainous subtropical environment on Taiwan proper. Geologically it is also significantly different, being formed from the solidified lava of volcanic eruptions some 17 million years ago. If you need evidence of this, just check out the stunning rock formations everywhere, including towering basalt columns and stacks.

Penghu County includes almost 100 islands (only a quarter of which are inhabited) but there's plenty to see and do on the main archipelago, four interconnected islands that collectively form a horseshoe containing the townships of Makung, Huhsi, Paisha and Hsiyu. Ferries run daily during high season between Makung and the two largest outer islands, Chimei and Wang'an, and tours are available to bring you to some of the smaller islands as well. Makung (on Penghu Island) is the only city, and though you can find whatever you need here, by Taiwanese standards Makung is more like a large town.

For more information see http://tour.penghu.gov.tw.

History

Windswept Penghu has served for centuries as a strategic connection point between Taiwan, China, Japan and Southeast Asia. But its strategic position has proved both a blessing and a curse, and over the centuries Penghu was grabbed by various colonisers from Asia and Europe looking to get a toehold in the Taiwan Strait.

The Dutch were the first to take the islands, in 1622, but they moved to the Taiwanese mainland when they learned that the Ming imperial court had plans to remove them from Penghu by force (a stele in the Matsu Temple in Makung inscribes this threat). In 1662 the Ming loyalist Koxinga was sent to oust the Dutch from Taiwan for good. Penghu was a convenient place to station his troops as he drew up his battle plans. Some troops stayed in Penghu after the Dutch were gone and set up their own regime, which was short-lived, however, because the Qing court threw them out in 1683. The French were the next to arrive, in 1884, followed in 1895 by the Japanese, who settled down and stayed for the next 50 years, only to be replaced by the Nationalists in 1945.

Penghu is rich with historical relics, evidence of its long colonial history. To capitalise on this history and boost a drooping economy, the islands were transformed into a beach mecca for local and foreign visitors. The Penghu Archipelago has been designated a national scenic area and the main islands at least have been given a makeover that nicely blends tradition with modern comforts.

Getting There & Away

AIR There are over 50 daily flights between **Makung Airport** (www.mkport.gov.tw) and Taipei (NT$2050, 40 minutes), Kaohsiung (NT$1718, 40 minutes) and other west-coast cities with the following airlines:

Mandarin Airlines (www.mandarin-airlines.com)

TransAsia Airways (www.tna.com.tw)

Uni Air (www.uniair.com.tw)

BOAT Information in English on boat travel is nonexistent but it is a viable option, although schedules change often. Hotels and guesthouses in Penghu can arrange tickets for trips between the Makung Harbour Terminal Building (馬公港務大樓; Mǎgōn Gǎngwù dàlóu) and Kaohsiung Pier 1 and Putai Port (near Chiayi).

Tai Hua Shipping (www.taiwanline.com.tw/taiwu01.htm) has boats from Kaohsiung to Makung (NT$860, 4½ hours); **All Star** (www.aaaaa.com.tw) from Putai Port to Makung (NT$1000, 1½ hours).

Penghu

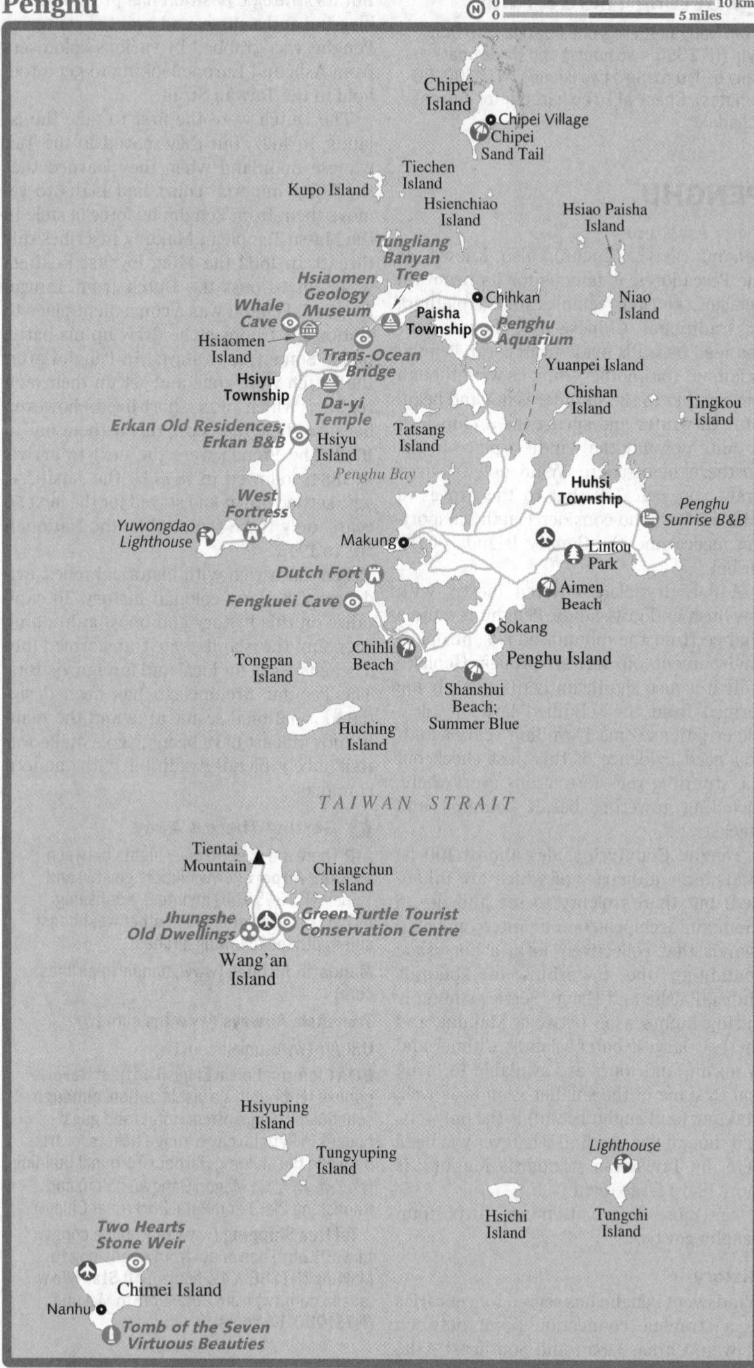

0 10 km
0 5 miles
Chipei Island
Chipei Village
Chipei Sand Tail
Tiechen Island
Kupo Island
Hsienchiao Island
Hsiao Paisha Island
Tungliang Banyan Tree
Hsiaomen Geology Museum
Whale Cave
Hsiaomen Island
Chihkan
Niao Island
Paisha Township
Penghu Aquarium
Trans-Ocean Bridge
Hsiyu Township
Yuanpei Island
Chishan Island
Tingkou Island
Da-yi Temple
Erkan Old Residences; Erkan B&B
Hsiyu Island
Tatsang Island
Penghu Bay
Huhsi Township
Penghu Sunrise B&B
West Fortress
Yuwongdao Lighthouse
Makung
Lintou Park
Dutch Fort
Aimen Beach
Fengkuei Cave
Sokang
Chihli Beach
Penghu Island
Tongpan Island
Shanshui Beach; Summer Blue
Huching Island
TAIWAN STRAIT
Tientai Mountain
Chiangchun Island
Jhungshe Old Dwellings
Green Turtle Tourist Conservation Centre
Wang'an Island
Hsiyuping Island
Tungyuping Island
Lighthouse
Hsichi Island
Tungchi Island
Two Hearts Stone Weir
Chimei Island
Nanhu
Tomb of the Seven Virtuous Beauties

Getting Around

TO/FROM THE AIRPORT There's an hourly airport shuttle bus to Makung. The taxi fare to/from Makung Airport is NT$300; most hotels and B&Bs offer airport pick-up.

BUS Bus travel is inconvenient but possible. There are two lines with hourly buses from the main bus station (車站; *chēzhàn*) in Makung.

CAR & SCOOTER Hotels and B&Bs can handle rentals (car/scooter per day NT$1300/350); an international or Taiwan licence is needed to rent cars.

TAXI Drivers prefer flat rates to using the meter; most trips cost NT$200 to NT$300. Taxi tours are available for NT$2500 to NT$3000 per day, but it's unlikely your driver will speak English.

Makung (Magong) 馬公

Makung (Mǎgōng, Magong, Makong) is a pretty seaside town with a history stretching back to the 14th century. Though it's thoroughly modern (there's even a McDonald's, something which Makung people seem unusually proud of), you won't have to look far to find remnants of bygone dynasties. The Japanese have also left their mark in Makung with a number of Japanese-style administrative buildings around town. It's definitely worth spending a day exploring Makung before heading out to see the rest of the archipelago or any of the outer Penghu Islands.

Summer is prime time in Makung, with streets full of tourists and hotel prices rising like the temperature. In winter, when the howling of the wind sometimes becomes deafening, the town is markedly more subdued. Autumn and spring, however, can be perfectly lovely, with the weather warm enough to swim, cheaper accommodation and low-to-no crowds.

Sights

Makung is great to explore by foot or bicycle. Its old buildings, narrow cobblestone alleys, temples and remnants of the old city wall are waiting to be checked out. Jhongjheng Rd is basically the main drag and it's here where you'll find more coffee shops than you'd think a small Taiwanese city could ever support.

TOP CHOICE **Matsu Temple** TAOIST TEMPLE

(馬祖天后宮; Mǎzǔ Tiānhòu Gōng; Huian Rd; ⌚4.30am-8.30pm) One of Penghu's most celebrated spots, the Penghu Matsu Temple was first established as a small shrine in the late 16th century. Locals say it's the oldest Matsu temple in Taiwan and the discovery of a **stele** in 1919 inscribing an order by General Yu Tzu-kau (made in 1604) to the Dutch to get out of Taiwan gives a lot of credence to this claim.

The current structure hails from a wonderful 1922 restoration by a famous architect. The first thing you'll notice are the steep stone steps to the main floor, a necessity as the temple is built on a slope. Some highlights of the temple include an unusually high and sweeping **swallowtail eave roof**, and a wealth of gorgeous woodcarvings, such as the hanging **flower pots** under the front eaves. In the main hall, look for a **swastika design** in the wood door panels: it represents endless good fortune.

The temple is dedicated to Matsu (see p201), and sailors have been coming here for centuries to pray to the goddess for a safe voyage. Take a few minutes to soak in the palpable feeling of antiquity and spirituality that pervades this first-grade historical site.

Makung Central Street OLD STREET

Behind Matsu Temple is Central St (中央街; Zhōngyāng Jiē), the oldest street in Makung. This series of winding, brick-paved pedestrian lanes is home to a number of interesting sights such as the **Shihkung Ancestral Shrine** (施公祠; Shīgōng Cí) and **Well of a Thousand Soldiers** (萬軍井; Wàn Jūn Jǐng). In 1682 the goddess Matsu is said to have bequeathed a magical well to Ming soldiers massing for an invasion of Taiwan.

Also in this warren of backstreets is an eclectic mix of early 20th-century homes mixing Western and Fujian elements. The **Chienyi Tang Chinese Traditional Medicine Store** (乾益堂中藥行; Qiányì Táng Zhōngyào Háng; 42 Chungyang St; ⌚7am-9.30pm) is one of the more handsome. The proprietor speaks no English but it's a fun place to browse for traditional Chinese remedies.

Living Museum MUSEUM

(澎湖生活博物館; Pénghú Shēnghuó Bówùguǎn; www.phlm.nat.gov.tw; 327 Sinsheng Rd, 馬公市新生路327號; admission NT$80; ⌚10am-5pm Fri-Wed) The newest museum in the city offers a fantastic introduction to every aspect of Penghu life: from child-rearing techniques to religious customs. Displays are filled with real artefacts (there's even a full-size traditional junk on the 2nd floor) and

Makung (Magong)

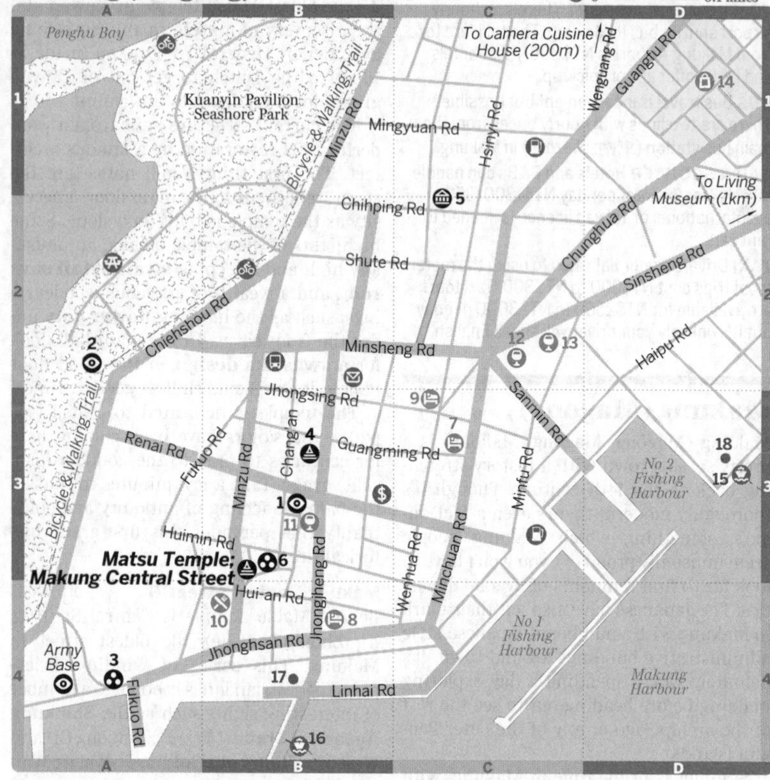

Makung (Magong)

Top Sights
- Makung Central Street B3
- Matsu Temple B3

Sights
1. Chienyi Tang Chinese Traditional Medicine Store B3
2. Kuanyin Pavilion A2
3. Makung Old Wall A4
4. Peichen Temple B3
5. Penghu Reclamation Hall C2
- Shihkung Ancestral Shrine .... (see 6)
- Shuncheng Gate .... (see 3)
6. Well of a Thousand Soldiers B3

Sleeping
7. Blue Sky Hotel C3
8. Bowa Hotel B4
9. Chunghsin Hotel C3
- Makung Traditional Homestay .... (see 6)

Eating
10. Jang Jin Restaurant B4
- Ma Lu E .... (see 4)

Drinking
11. Colony Bar B3
12. Freud Pub C2
13. Sha Ai Chuang C2

Shopping
14. Peichen Market D1

Transport
15. Boats to Chimei, Wang'an & Tongpan D3
16. Boats to Kaohsiung & Putai Port B4
17. Makung Harbour Terminal Building B4
18. South Seas Tourist Service Centre D3

while explanations were only in Chinese at the time of writing, we were promised they would also have them in English by the end of 2010.

Next to the museum is the very grand **Confucius Temple** (孔廟; Kǒng Miào). The temple was formerly the Wenshi College, built in 1766 and an important centre of learning during the Qing dynasty. The name of the college was changed to the Confucius Temple during the Japanese occupation to take advantage of the Japanese respect for Confucius, in the hope that the college wouldn't be torn down.

Makung Old Wall HISTORIC SITE

A quick walk west along Jhonghsan Rd takes you to **Shuncheng Gate** (順承門; Shùnchéng Mén) and a section of the Makung Old Wall (馬公古城; Mǎgōng Gǔ Chéng). City walls were constructed around Makung as a defensive measure. After the occupying French left the city in 1885, the walls were mostly knocked down by the Japanese. Parts of the wall are in the process of being overrun by cacti and aloe plants the size of ponies. The old neighbourhood around the wall is worth exploring. At the time of writing, further up the hill there was restoration work happening on a small neighbourhood of old buildings and an adjacent army base.

Kuanyin Pavilion TAOIST TEMPLE

(觀音亭; Guānyīn Tíng; ⏲5am-8pm) At Makung's western shoreline you'll find the city's fabulous waterfront park, which has an enclosed bay that's great for swimming. The park is named for the 300-year-old Kuanyin Pavilion, dedicated to Kuanyin (Guanyin), goddess of mercy. This is one of the most important places for Buddhist worship, which says a lot, as there are a great many places for Buddhist worship in Penghu. The most important artefact in the temple is the old bell, which dates back to 1696.

Penghu Reclamation Hall MUSEUM

(澎湖開拓館; Pénghú Kāituò Guǎn; 30 Chihping Rd; admission NT$30; ⏲10am-5pm Wed-Sun, closed national holidays) Stylish Japanese-era building with displays of Penghu culture and history.

Peichen Temple TAOIST TEMPLE

Just off Jhongjheng Rd is the large, ornate Peichen Temple (北辰宮; Běichén Gōng).

Festivals & Events

Lantern Festival LUNAR FESTIVAL

Though the Lantern Festival (Yuánxiāojié) is a sight to behold anywhere in Taiwan, Penghu's festival is truly a unique celebration. It takes place on the 15th day of the first lunar month (about 15 days after the first day of Chinese New Year, which begins anywhere from mid-January to mid-February, depending on the year). Penghu's celebrations include a bacchanalian parade with dancers and fireworks through the streets and past the many temples of Makung. One twist particular to Penghu is the parading of gigantic golden turtle effigies through the streets. In the days before the festival, most bakeries in town devote half their oven space to the production of turtle cakes, which are given away and eaten during the course of the festival.

Peichi Temple (北極殿; Běijí Diàn) in Sokang near Shanshui Beach is a hub of activity at this time of year.

Sleeping

During summer, hotel prices in Makung rise dramatically, and rooms are hard to come by on weekends and holidays. But with more than 400 B&Bs around the archipelago, there's likely to be something available at any time. Following we list places that are in Makung itself.

Autumn through spring is considered low season, and though it's windier than in summer, the weather is usually still hot in autumn and spring; sizeable discounts can generally be had at even the most expensive of hotels.

Makung Traditional Homestay HOMESTAY **$$**

(馬公老街民宿; Mǎgōng Lǎojiē Mínsù; ☎926 6161; www.069266161.com; 8 Alley 1, Jhongyang St, 中央街1巷8號; d NT$2400) The most affordable of the homestays on the old Makung Central St, the Makung offers simple modern comforts and friendly hosts. And the location, of course. If you don't mind a bit of noise, get a room with a balcony over the old street. To get to the homestay head down the narrow alley beside the Matsu Temple. The even narrower alley entrance to the B&B is just past the Shihkung Ancestral Shrine.

Blue Sky Hotel HOTEL **$**

(藍天大飯店; Lántiān Dàfàndiàn; ☎926 5231; 2-1 Guangming Rd, 光明路2-1號; d/tw NT$1000/1500) On a road with other

TURTLES OF PENGHU

Fifteen days after the start of the lunar year, the evening of the Lantern Festival, Penghu residents crowd into temples around the islands and offer sacrificial images of turtles to the deities. They pray for prosperity and give thanks for the good things that happened to them the previous year. The sea turtles that migrate through the coastal waters off Penghu have a special meaning to the islanders, who believe that they represent longevity and fortune. Rice cakes and dough are formed into the shape of turtles and offered to temple deities. Sacrificial turtles are also made from gold coins, noodles, sponge cakes and sometimes offered live. Turtles can be offered to any of the gods or goddesses, though Matsu seems to be the local favourite. During the festivities, parades are held, with men carrying giant palanquins down the streets bearing local gods and goddesses, accompanied by singing, dancing and plenty of fireworks.

Some of the beliefs about turtles come from ancient Chinese myths about the reptiles being special conduits between heaven and earth and capable of divining the future through marks on their shells. To the Chinese, the turtle is considered one of the four spiritual beasts of the world, along with the dragon, chimera and phoenix. In ancient times they were thought to have magical powers.

Unfortunately, there are more rice-cake turtles in Penghu now than the real things. Once dispersed throughout Taiwan's coastal regions, including Kinmen, Lanyu and Penghu, sea-turtle nesting sites are now found only on Penghu and Lanyu. In the summer of 2010, however, a new nesting site along the Taitung coastline was discovered, much to the surprise and joy of conservationists.

Is this the beginning of a turnaround for the species? For more on the plight of the green sea turtle and efforts to revive its numbers visit the Green Turtle Tourist Conservation Centre (p300) on Wang'an Island.

inexpensive hotels, the Blue Sky stands out for its friendly front-desk staff and a generally clean atmosphere. Rooms are fairly spacious for the money and are a good deal in the high season. In the low season prices are comparable with much nicer B&Bs.

Bowa Hotel HOTEL $$

(寶華大飯店; Bǎohuá Dàfàndiàn; ☎927 4881; 2 Jhongjheng Rd, 中正路2號; s/d/tw incl breakfast NT$2600/2800/3800;) Adjacent to Makung harbour, the Bowa offers spotless rooms, some with ocean views. B&Bs are generally cheaper, especially in the low season, but it's a good choice if you prefer hotels. Discounts of 30% are available midweek and in the low season.

Chunghsin Hotel HOTEL $

(中信大旅社; Zhōngxìn Dàlǔshè; ☎927 2151; 22 Chunghsing Rd, 中興路22號; r from NT$700) The lobby and stairs are dreary and the rooms a little smoky but they're clean, and for this price you won't get anything better, especially in the high season.

Eating

First and foremost, Makung is a seafood-lover's paradise, though locally caught seafood is expensive (much of what you'll find at restaurants is flown in from other parts of Taiwan). Raw *lóng xiā* (lobster) and fried *wǔ xiāng cìhétún* ('five-flavour' balloonfish) are favourites. In addition, look for the following local specialities: *jīnguā mǐfěn* (pumpkin rice noodles); *xián bǐng* (salty biscuits); *shāo ròu fàn* (grilled meat with rice); and *hēi táng gāo* (brown-sugar sponge cakes). Penghu is famous for the latter.

There are restaurants all over town and you'll find street food cooking in front of just about any temple, especially during high season. Jhongjheng and Guangfu Rds are particularly rich in places to eat or just nibble.

Camera Cuisine House WESTERN $$

(卡麥拉; Kǎmàilā; 104-2 Wenguang Rd; set meals from NT$180; ⊙11am-9.30pm;) Camera is a stylish corner restaurant serving very tasty and filling multicourse set meals for a bargain price. Dishes have an Italian theme but are heavy on seafood and feature Penghu side dishes (such as pumpkin soup).

Good Friend Vegetarian House VEGETARIAN $

(好朋友; Hǎo Péngyǒu; 320 Sanduo Rd; dishes from NT$100; ⊙lunch & dinner;) Though it's on Makung's northern edge, we had to tell you about this primarily vegetarian restaurant, which makes some of the best Taiwanese *niúròu tāngmiàn* (beef noodle soup) we've ever eaten. Quite the paradox, eh? To get to the restaurant head up Guangfu Rd and then turn left on Sanduo Rd.

Jang Jin Restaurant SEAFOOD **$$**
(長進餐廳; Chángjìn Cāntīng; www.jangjin.idv.tw/; 9 Minzu Rd; dishes NT$180-350; ⏲lunch & dinner) A loud and popular locally recommended seafood place with a wide range of fresh dishes. Not really suitable for one person as dishes are designed for sharing.

Ma Lu E TRADITIONAL FAST FOOD **$**
(馬路益; Mălùyì; 7 Jhongjheng Rd; dishes NT$40-80; ⏲3.30-11.30pm) Across from Peichen Temple is this simple warehouse of a restaurant serving quick Taiwanese-style fast food such as oyster omelettes (蚵仔煎; *kēzaǐjiān,* pronounced locally 'uh-ah-jian') and stinky tofu (臭豆腐; *chòu dòufǔ*). There's a picture menu out front or just ask one of the student groups at a table nearby to help you order.

Drinking

For cafes and fruit or tea shops head to the little alleys around the Matsu Temple and off Jhongjheng Rd.

Sha Ai Chuang TEAHOUSE, BAR
(傻愛莊; Shǎ Ài Zhuāng; 14 Sinsheng Rd; ⏲10am-midnight) Loosely translated as 'foolish love pub', this place was once the home of Penghu's first county chief. It has since been transformed into a colourful cafe-bar with great ambience. The fruit-juice cocktails are especially good on a warm night.

Colony Bar BAR
(陽光殖民地; Yángguāng Zhímíndì; 6 Lane 3 Jhongjheng Rd) This bar is a trendy place to spend the evening. Speciality drinks include Penghu *xiánrénzhǎng zhī* (cactus juice) mixed with alcohol.

Freud Pub BAR
(弗洛伊得; Fúluòyīdé; 2-1 Sinsheng Rd) The house special in this slightly cramped but laid-back sports bar is the potent cocktail 'Absolutely Drunk', made with six kinds of alcohol.

Shopping

Makung is full of shops selling all kinds of Penghu speciality items such as pink and black coral, shells and veined stones. We recommend against buying coral items as it only hastens the destruction of coral reefs and the decline of the marine creatures that live within them. If you need to bring home a nonedible souvenir, why not go for some nautically themed jewellery or perhaps a wind-chime set?

Edible items are especially popular with Taiwanese tourists, and stores selling squid jerky, smoked fish and dried seafood in general (but thankfully not shark's fin) can be found all over Makung. And of course, you can buy just about anything edible, from freshly caught fish and oysters to local vegetables and cooked snacks, at the bustling **Peichen Market** (北辰市場; Běichén Shìchăng) in central Makung.

Information

Penghu's not the most wired of places, but more and more hotels and guesthouses offer wi-fi connections.

Bank of Taiwan (台灣銀行; 24 Renai Rd) Foreign-currency exchange and ATMs.

Tourist Information Centre (Pénghú Yóukè Fúwù Zhōngxīn; http://tour.penghu.gov.tw; 171 Kuanghua Lane; ⏲8am-5pm) Inconvenient location, so pick up travel brochures at the airport or ferry terminal travel kiosks. Your best source for boat and plane schedules, and other information, will be your hotel or guesthouse.

Around Penghu Archipelago

Though it's actually four islands, this horseshoe-shaped archipelago is referred to by most locals as the main island, or simply Penghu. The U-shaped route 203 shoots north from Makung on the west side of the main island, passing through the Paisha Township before heading on to Hsiyu Island via the Trans-Ocean Bridge. Hsiyu is a long, narrow island, and route 203 continues to the West Fortress and Yuwongdao Lighthouse on its southern tip. The total distance of the one-way trip is just under 37km, so you can spend a full day exploring the sights along that road on a scooter and still make it back to Makung before dark.

Sticking to the main roads is not advisable unless you are in a hurry to get from major sight to sight. Much of the magic of Penghu is found in its endless seaside hamlets with their stocky grey houses and narrow winding roads bordered by low coral walls.

Sights

Erkan Old Residences TRADITIONAL VILLAGE

Set on emerald slopes above the blue sea, Erkan Village (二崁古厝; Èrkǎn Gǔ Cuò) oozes charm from every coral wall, stone walkway and brick facade. The 50 or so houses are built in a melange of southern Fujian, Western and Japanese styles, and mostly hail from the early 20th century. Residents on the main street keep their front gates open and invite visitors to check out their unique homes and possibly sample a few local treats.

Just down the road towards the coast is the **Guoyeh Prismatic Basalt** (大菓葉柱狀玄武岩; Dàguǒyè Zhùzhuàng Xuánwǔyán), a beautiful example of the basalt cliffs formed from the cooling lava that created Penghu.

Whale Cave SCENIC AREA

The western coast of Hsiyu is visually dramatic, full of steep cliffs, basalt formations, shallow coves and headlands. Whale Cave (鯨魚洞; Jīngyú Dòng) is a hole in a rock that kinda-sorta looks like a whale; locals say the hole was created by a gigantic whale crashing into the rock, but we kinda-sorta doubt that. Checking it out gives you a fine excuse to ride over the Trans-Ocean Bridge, of which Penghu folks are quite proud.

Nearby is the **Hsiaomen Geology Museum** (小門地質博物館; Xiǎomén Dìzhì Bówùguǎn; 11-12 Xiaomen Village), undergoing a facelift at the time of writing.

FREE **Dutch Fort** SCENIC AREA

The ruins of the Dutch Fort (風櫃尾紅毛城遺址; Fēngguìwěi Hóngmáochéng Yízhǐ), abandoned when the Dutch were driven out of Penghu by the Ming army in 1624, are at the end of the peninsula. There's nothing of the fort to see, but the grassy terraces offer some fine walks and even finer views. To get to the fort follow the signs to Snakehead Hill (蛇頭山; Shétóu Shān).

Sokang Pagodas TAOIST RELICS

On the way to Shanshui Beach on County Rd 25 are the Sokang Pagodas (鎖港子午寶塔; Suǒgǎng Zǐwǔ Bǎotǎ), two north- and south-facing stone towers. Blessed by a Taoist priest, they are reputed to contain supernatural powers that ward off evil and protect residents from natural disasters. So far they're working.

Note that the towers are about two blocks from each other. From the north tower just keep heading down the main road and look for the south tower to the left down a side road.

Penghu Aquarium AQUARIUM

(澎湖水族館; Pénghú Shǔizú Guǎn; 58 Chitou Village; admission NT$200; ⌚8am-5pm) The two-storey marine exhibition centre provides information on all the aquatic creatures swimming around Penghu. Kids and adults alike will have a great time communing with the sea turtles. The highlight of the aquarium is the 14m glass tunnel allowing visitors and fish to meet eye-to-eye.

West Fortress FORT

(西台古堡; Xī Tái Gǔ Bǎo; admission NT$30; ⌚8am-5.30pm) Built in 1887 following the Sino-French War; 5000 soldiers were once stationed here. It's possible to go inside and wander around.

FREE **Yuwongdao Lighthouse** LIGHTHOUSE

(漁翁島燈塔; Yúwēngdǎo Dēngtǎ)

In the 19th century, British lighthouse keepers stayed on for 10-year shifts. Look for the stone cross marking the grave of Nellie O'Driscol, daughter of one of the keepers.

Temples

Some call Penghu the Hawaii of Asia, but how many temples does Hawaii have? We lost count of how many we saw in Penghu, but we think the person-to-temple ratio is 10 to one. Travelling around Penghu you'll undoubtedly stumble across some. On the wide, flat plains the huge, colourful complexes are a bit hard to miss. Inside, listen for the often cacophonous chattering of birds (mostly buntings and swallows) – something rarely heard in temples on Taiwan proper.

Tungliang Banyan Tree OLD TREE, TAOIST TEMPLE

The astonishing 300-year-old Tungliang Banyan Tree (通梁古榕; Tōngliáng Gǔróng) wraps and creeps and twists round a cement frame that stabilises the tree like the lattice arch of a bower. The spread of branches and aerial roots cover 600 sq metres, enough to give shade to you and the endless roll of tour-bus-driven visitors who rightly see this as a must-visit.

It's said that during the Qing dynasty a ship sunk off the coast of Penghu and a small seedling floated to shore and was planted by locals. A temple complex was built later, and the tree and hall of worship are now inseparable.

There's a little snack shop next to this temple that sells cactus-fruit sorbet, something you'll only find in Penghu. Well worth trying.

Da-yi Temple TAOIST TEMPLE

On Hsiyu Island, the 200-year-old Da-yi Temple (大義宮; Dàyì Gōng) is dedicated to Guan Di, the god of war, or more accurately, patron of knights. Some say that when the French tried to attack Penghu, mysterious forces kept them away from the temple.

The temple is a massive structure with 4m bronze guardians of Guan Di, **Guānpíng** (關平) and **Zhōucāng** (周倉), flanking the stairs. The interior features several large and detailed plafond ceilings, some good dragons in *jiǎnniàn* (mosaic-like decoration), and, brace yourself, an **underground coral cavern** with a collection of giant (living) sea turtles. The legality of this is a grey area, but we'd be remiss not letting you know about it.

The temple is off route 203, down a side road towards the sea. There is an English sign for it after you cross the Trans-Ocean Bridge.

Beaches

The archipelago has several hundred kilometres of shoreline with more than 100 beaches. The following are among the best found on Penghu, and indeed anywhere in Taiwan.

Shanshui Beach BEACH

Southeast of Makung the excellent Shanshui Beach (山水沙灘; Shānshǔi Shātān) has smooth white sand and breaking waves, and is a great place to relax. On weekends the beach is fairly crowded with sun worshippers from Taiwan, but during the week you may well wind up sharing the beach with just a handful of other bathers. The beach is popular with Penghu's surf set when the waves are up.

Chihli Beach BEACH

Up the coast from Shanshui to the northwest, Chihli Beach (蒔裡沙灘; Zhílǐ Shātān) is a great little spot with a real community feel. The shell-sand beach stretches for over 1km and is popular with beach-sport enthusiasts and sunbathers.

This stretch of coast is also known for its bizarre rock formations, created thousands of years ago by cooling basalt magma. Sea erosion has created many unusual gullies and crevices that have taken the imagination of Penghu residents and tourists. Not far is **Fengkuei Cave** (風櫃洞; Fēngguì Dòng), on Penghu's southwest shore, a sea-eroded gully that reportedly makes a peculiar sound when the wind rushes through it during high tide.

Aimen Beach BEACH

Aimen Beach (隘門沙灘; Àimén Shātān) is a favourite among locals for all kinds of water sports and beach activities. The nearby expanse of pines in **Lintou Park** (林投公園; Líntóu Gōngyuán) borders a white-sand beach that's a superb spot for a picnic but not so suitable for swimming as the coral is very sharp.

Activities

Windsurfing

With wave and wind conditions similar to Gran Canaria's Pozo Izquierdo, or the Columbia River Gorge in USA, Penghu is fast becoming Asia's premier spot for windsurfing – in winter! From September to May the same Arctic-Mongolian cold fronts that send temperatures in Taipei down into the single digits also blast strong winds down the Taiwan Strait. Wind speeds around Penghu can reach 40 and even 50 knots.

In 2010, Asian RSX championships were held in October for the first time. Organisers are hoping that the archipelago can become a serious training ground for Asia's Olympic windsurfing athletes.

Windsurfing lessons and equipment rental are available at both the Penghu Sunrise B&B (p300) in Guoyeh, and in Makung at **Liquid Sport** (www.liquidsport.com.tw). The first lesson is NT$1500, including equipment, and Liquid Sport owner Alex Mowday says he can teach most beginners to windsurf in 'about two hours'. Recommended are the months of September and October for good weather and wind conditions that haven't become too extreme yet.

Diving & Snorkelling

Though it was possible to get in some great snorkelling and diving even off the main beaches just a few years ago, a freak cold snap killed off most of the shallow-water coral in 2008. Although the coral is growing back, it will be years before the reefs return to their former glory.

There are still great sites on the smaller islands and in less accessible locations on the main archipelago. **Liquid Sport** (www.liquidsport.com.tw) does diving lessons and easy day trips in summer and now has clear-bottomed sea kayaks for rent – a marvellous way to see the underwater world. Another reputable local dive instructor and guide is **Mr Liu** (☎0928-370 035; padi470704@yahoo.com.tw); by appointment only.

Sleeping

Literally hundreds of B&Bs have popped up in the past few years and you can find a place to stay almost anywhere. While nearby food options will probably be limited, Makung is not more than a 30-minute ride from any of the following.

TOP CHOICE **Penghu Sunrise B&B** B&B $$
(澎湖民宿-菓葉觀日樓; Pénghú Mínsù-Guǒyè Guānrìlóu; ☎992 0818; www.sunrisebb.idv.tw; 129-3 Guoyeh Village, 菓葉村129-3號; s/d incl breakfast NT$1500/2000; 📶) Run by Jan and Sylvia, a Taiwanese couple who decided to swap the rat race for windsurfing and sunshine, the Sunrise is a bona fide B&B with ocean views, fresh morning coffee and English-speaking hosts. Rooms are bright, airy and comfortably furnished, and there's a great communal lounge area with a panoramic view of the ocean. The B&B is in Guoyeh, 12km east of Makung, close to some great beaches. Scooter, bicycle, windsurfing and sea-kayaking equipment are available for rent. There is a 25% discount weekdays and during the low season, or any day after the first night's stay.

Erkan B&B HOMESTAY $$
(二崁民宿; Èrkǎn Mínsù; ☎998 4406; www.phnet.com.tw/erkan; d NT$2400; 📶) If you want accommodation with modern comforts that opens up onto a traditional village, this block of old residences at the end of charming Erkan Village is your top choice. According to the owners, the rooms were originally remodelled to encourage extended family to relocate. When that didn't happen, well, a B&B was born. The rooms, part of a larger family complex, are on the far side of Erkan Village. Head towards the temple, turn left and then make a quick right, making your way in essence around a knoll.

Summer Blue HOMESTAY $$
(藍海風晴; Lánhǎi Fēngqíng; ☎995 2115; www.summer-blue.com; 17-21 Shanshui Village, 山水里17之21號; d/tw from NT$1980/3180) Just back from Shanshui Beach is this cosy and friendly homestay with big (if somewhat bland) rooms. A few have balconies but all have access to a large patio garden for hanging out. The homestay offers free scooter rental and airport pick-up with rooms and has a 10% discount on weekdays. Summer Blue is at the end of a short row of hotels and B&Bs off the beach. Look for a mustard-coloured block called C'est La Vie and then turn your head slightly to the right.

Outer Islands

The two largest of Penghu's outer islands are Wang'an and Chimei. Both are south of the main island and have boat and air service to Makung. Third largest is Chipei, north of Paisha, which has some great beaches. Tongpan is a small island ringed with some fantastic basalt column cliffs. Several of the smaller islands ringing the archipelago are reserves for migratory waterfowl but can be visited or at least sailed by.

WANG'AN 望安鄉

About 30 minutes by boat from Makung harbour, Wang'an (Wàng'ān) is home to the **Green Turtle Tourist Conservation Centre** (綠蠵龜觀光保育中心; Lùxīguī Guānguāng Bǎoyù Zhōngxīn; admission free; ⏲8.30am-5pm). Inside are bilingual exhibits about the state of sea turtles in Taiwan and around the world. There's also information on wildlife preservation efforts in the Strait Islands and Taiwan proper.

The protected areas for the turtles are on the southwest side of the island. However, green turtles are extremely rare and even during the breeding and hatching season (May to October) you are very unlikely to see one. The beaches here are golden, however, and can be swum during the day (after 8pm all activity is prohibited).

The **Jhungshe Old Dwellings** (中社古厝; Zhōngshè Gǔ Cuò) are a group of abandoned but well-preserved houses in Jhungshe Village (Zhōngshè Cūn). Nearby is the highest point on the island, **Tientai Mountain** (Tiāntái Shān), actually a grassy hill with some cows. The mountain is the oldest bit of basalt on Penghu but is most famous for the footprint of Lu Tungbin, one of China's Eight Immortals, impressed on a rock here. Lu's other footprint can be found on one of the smaller of Penghu's Islands and the story goes that he made these marks as he squatted down to urinate.

CHIMEI 七美鄉

Chimei (Qīměi) means 'Seven Beauties' and refers to a legend (a somewhat common one in Chinese culture) involving seven women who, in the Ming dynasty, threw themselves into a well rather than lose their chastity to Japanese pirates. The island's coastline is one of the finest on Penghu and it's well worth your time to stop on your scooter ride and head down to the sea to explore cliff and cove.

The **Two Hearts Stone Weir** (雙心石滬; Shuāng Xīn Shí Hù), a ring of stones literally shaped like two hearts, is a Penghu icon and probably the most photographed sight on the islands. The original purpose of the weir was to catch fish during low tide.

There are several excellent **snorkelling** spots in the shallow coves around Chimei, and one-day tours (NT$1100 to NT$1300, including transport and food) can be arranged beforehand by your hotel or homestay.

There are several seafood restaurants at Nanhu harbour, as well as a couple of small inns and homestays.

Alumi Home (阿魯米家; Ālǔmǐjiā; ☎0911-659 639; set meals from NT$80), at the end of the row of shops to the left as you get off the boat, has excellent meals made largely with local ingredients (the pickled cactus is excellent). The restaurant also has rooms, should you want to spend the night on Chimei.

CHIPEI 吉貝

With its lovely sand-shell beaches, Chipei (Jíbèi) buzzes with tourists in summer but shuts down almost completely in winter. **Chipei Sand Tail** (吉貝沙尾; Jíbèi Shāwěi) is the most popular beach on the island and the only one that isn't trashed with garbage. This long strip of golden sand juts out into the water, its size changing with the coming and going of the tides. During summer, windsurfing, boating and even parasailing and karaoke singing are popular activities here. Equipment is available for rent at the beach resort or in the small shops around the beach. During winter, you'll have the whole place to yourself.

Chipei Village has an assortment of homestays and small hotels but most people just come over for the day.

TONGPAN 桶盤嶼

The shoreline of this small island is barricaded by walls of natural basalt columns, giving it an imposing appearance. Boats to Chimei will slow down to let you observe the columns, and some will even stop for an hour, just enough time to walk around the island and observe the walls up close.

ℹ Getting There & Away

AIR TransAir Asia (www.tna.com.tw) has flights between Kaohsiung and Chimei (35 minutes), and Chimei and Makung (15 minutes).

BOAT South Seas Tourist Service Centre (南海遊客服務中心; Nánhǎi Yóukè Fúwù Zhōngxīn; ☎926 4738; No 3 Fishing Harbour, Makung Harbour; ⏲6.30am-9.30pm) has boats to Chimei, Wang'an and Tongpan, as well as many options for day trips in the high season. A full-day tour (NT$550) hits three or four islands with one- or two-hour stops depending on how many islands you are visiting. Schedules and prices are jealously guarded at the centre – get your hotel to book tickets for you.

North Sea Tourist Service Centre (北海遊客服務中心; Běihǎi Yóukè Fúwù Zhōngxīn; ☎993 3082; Chihkan, Paisha Island; ⏲6.30am-9.30pm) operates boats to Chipei (round-trip NT$300, 15 minutes, every 30 minutes) and some smaller islands north of Paisha.

ℹ Getting Around

Rental scooters are available on Chimei, Wang'an and Chipei for NT$400 to NT$500 a day or for NT$150 if you are just stopping as part of a one-day island tour. Tongpan is small enough to walk around in the hour that most tours give you.

LANYU

☎089 / POP 3000

The Yami people call their island home 'Pongso No Tao' (Island of the People) in their native tongue. The Taiwanese call it Lanyu (蘭嶼; Lányǔ, Orchid Island), naming it after the flowers that have almost been picked to near extinction. A volcanic, mountainous island covered with a carpet of tropical rainforest, Lanyu lies about 65km southeast of the city of Taitung, making it the southernmost outpost of Taiwan.

Lanyu's status as a far-flung outpost isn't merely geographical, but cultural as well, as the island is by far the least Chinese part of Taiwan. The Yami people are of Australasian descent, speak their own distinct language, and have a culture well

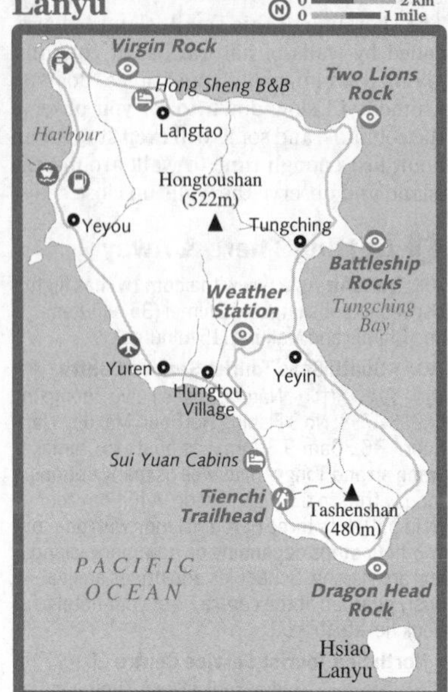

removed from that of the people 'on the mainland' (as they sometimes refer to the Taiwanese).

Coral reefs, perhaps the least spoiled in Taiwan, surround the rocky coastline, and at first glance the island appears a tropical paradise. In many ways it is. But to its inhabitants, the island is a sacred land, one mistreated for decades by a larger colonising neighbour, and there are certain frictions between natives and outsiders. The opening of the island to tourism in the 1960s, coupled with controversial government policies, have forced the Yami to struggle particularly to retain their culture in the face of increasing outside influence. The Yami are well aware that most Taiwanese visitors view them as an oddity, so Western visitors to Lanyu should tread especially lightly (see p305).

Summer is high season on Lanyu, and plane tickets are hard to get and accommodations scarce and more expensive. After mid-September, however, and in the spring, Taiwanese visitors are few and far between (especially during the week), despite the fact that the weather leans towards the idyllic end of the scale.

Lanyu is made up of two steep, jungle-covered mountains surrounded by a thin strip of coastal land. The 37km road circling both mountains can be driven in about 1½ hours; a shorter, twisting road winds between both mountains from just south of the village of Hungtou on the west coast to the village of Yeyin on the east. This road also branches off to reach the weather observation centre at the top of Hongtoushan (Red Head Mountain). There are six villages located on the narrow flat strip of land wedged between the mountains and the sea.

History

For centuries the Yami were the only tribal group on their island and it wasn't until the 20th century that their way of life began to be seriously disturbed by outsiders.

During the Japanese occupation, the Japanese were fascinated by the local customs of the Yami and did little to interfere with their way of life. Things changed drastically after the Kuomintang (KMT) came to power and attempted to introduce Chinese language and culture to the Yami.

It began with a name change: from Dawu (the people) to Yami, reportedly because the latter sounded better. Boatloads of mainland Chinese were also shipped to the island in the hope that interracial marriages would Sinicise the Yami population. The Yami resisted this encroachment and years of fighting with the mainlanders ensued. In the late 1960s Soong Mei Ling (wife of Chiang Kai-shek) declared that the traditional underground homes of the Yami were not fit for humans and ordered they be torn down and new cement structures built in their place. The houses were poorly made and couldn't hold up to the typhoons that whip through the island every year. At about the same time the housing law was passed, the island was opened to tourism and Taiwanese tourists began to arrive in droves. Christian missionaries also arrived, converting a large percentage of the population who are, to this day, primarily Christian.

Hardly based on mutual respect, the relationship between the Taiwanese government and the Yami took a turn for the worse when the government decided that the island would be a good place to dump nuclear waste. Long Men (Dragon Gate), at the southern tip of the island, was selected as a temporary storage facility for mid- and low-level nuclear waste. The site, which government representatives told locals was 'a fish cannery', became a depository for up to 100,000 barrels of nuclear waste in 1982. When islanders discovered the truth from Taiwanese news reports they raised a furious outcry, protesting both on Lanyu and in front of the various government buildings in Taipei. Despite government promises that the dump would be removed, the barrels remain and there is evidence that approximately 20% of the original barrels are beginning to leak and the concrete trenches they are buried in are cracking. Soil samples from the south end of the island show higher than normal levels of radioactivity and the possibility of health problems resulting from long-term contamination is of great concern to Yami people.

The Yami are doing their best to preserve their culture in the face of various social issues not uncommon in aboriginal communities. Alcoholism is a problem on the island, as is the overall brain drain caused by so many young people leaving to find greater economic prosperity in Taiwan. Even so, Yami traditions on Lanyu remain alive and one of the benefits that tourism has brought to the island has been to encourage the younger generation to learn more about their heritage before heading off to Taiwan to seek their fortunes.

Sights & Activities

Swimming, Diving & Snorkelling

Because of heavy currents and an overall dearth of sandy beaches, most of Lanyu's shores are best suited for strong swimmers, or left alone entirely. Locals recommend three small bays for swimming near Langtao but they are not marked so you'll need to ask where they are.

For snorkelling, Lanyu offers some of Taiwan's most unspoiled coral reefs. Two popular areas are Langtao and Dragon Head Rock. Most homestays can arrange for snorkelling, or contact **Badaiwan Diving** (八代灣潛水; Bādàiwān Qiánshuǐ; ☎0937-608 854; 126 Hungtou village), run by a Lanyu native called A-Xiong. Snorkelling costs NT$400 for a half-day (including equipment and guide); it's NT$1000 for diving but you must have at least eight in your group. A-Xiong's wife, Teresa, is a local guide, speaks excellent English, and will translate for him.

Wildlife-Watching

Despite its relatively small size, Lanyu is home to a few endemic butterfly and bird species. The diminutive **Lanyu scops owl** is relatively common in the more remote forests and most homestays can arrange for a night visit where the odds of spotting a few are high.

The gorgeous **Magellan's iridescent birdwing butterfly** has one of the widest wingspans in the world: up to 20cm across for males. Just riding around the main roads in April and May or October and November you may spot one or two, but for a tour of prime areas contact Mr Si, a well-known local carver, at his **Si Kang Chai Art Studio** (希岡菜木雕工作室; Xī Gāng Cài Mùdiao Gōngzùoshi; ☎0989-729 966; 38 Tungching village).

Rock Formations

Visiting Lanyu is an otherworldly experience indeed and one of the features that gives Lanyu a vaguely Lovecraftian vibe is the twisted, jagged volcanic rocks jutting dramatically out of the ground and out to sea off the coast. Naturally, some of these strange geological formations have been named. Taiwanese tourists like to pose before formations with imaginative monikers such as **Dragon Head Rock** and **Two Lions Rock**. On the north coast of the island one rock has been dubbed **Virgin Rock**; this is likely because the elliptical rock is hollow, save for a stalactite-like formation in the middle that gives the whole affair an appearance reminiscent of...well, you get the picture. Come see for yourself. In any event, the rocks' monikers have been assigned by the Taiwanese and not the Yami themselves (who generally find the names somewhat silly).

Hiking

The narrow island road winding past craggy cliffs, waterfalls, deep caves and the occasional village is really the only part of Lanyu level enough to be settled. This leaves the interior open for some magnificent hiking. One of the best hikes on Lanyu leads up to **Tienchi** (Tiānchí; Heaven Lake), an often-dry pond formed inside a volcanic crater on top of Tashenshan (Tashen Mountain). The hike to the lake and back is moderately difficult, with one section requiring hikers to navigate their way through a large, rocky ravine. As you climb higher into the jungly elevations the views open up and there are good opportunities for both bird- and butterfly-watching. Allow three to four hours to do the round-trip hike.

Tours

Most homestays can arrange snorkelling and wildlife tours. If you have an interest in a special part of Yami culture or Lanyu, contact **Canaanland Workshop** (迦南園工藝坊; Jiānányuán Gōngyìfǎng; ☎0912-103 639; 224 Langtao; ⏲8am-6pm), about 500m from the main strip in Langtao. Look for the really big canoe on the left. The workshop also has a restaurant serving locally grown food and a gift shop area with handmade carvings and beadwork on sale.

Teresa (☎0937-608 814; tbunnyteresa@yahoo.com.tw) is one of the few people on Lanyu fully fluent in English. Though employed as a nurse at the island's health clinic, Teresa also acts as a guide for those interested in Yami culture, as well as an interpreter for Westerners looking for hotels, homestays or activities on Lanyu. Rates for her guide service are quite reasonable, but she asks that visitors contact her in advance. Teresa is keen on promoting both responsible travel and the culture of her people and will generally know the dates of various villages' Flying Fish Festivals.

Festivals & Events

Flying Fish Festival ABORIGINAL FESTIVAL

The Flying Fish Festival (飛魚季; Fēiyú Jì) is a traditional coming-of-age ceremony for young men whose societal standing was based on how many fish they could catch. The spring festival is a very localised affair and each of the villages holds theirs on a different day chosen by the elders of the village. During the festival the men of the village wear traditional Yami loincloths, bark helmets and breastplates, and smear the blood of a freshly killed chicken on the rocks by the sea, all the while chanting 'return flying fish' in unison before heading out to sea in their canoes. According to custom, women are not allowed to view the festival, but most villages will make exceptions for visitors.

The festival usually takes place between March and May. Contact Teresa (above) to find out about exact times.

If you have at least eight companions, you can arrange for fishermen to take you out fishing during the flying fish season.

Sleeping

Most villages now offer homestays or small B&Bs. Rooms vary from a basic bed in a square room to some reasonably fancy digs. Though the families running these places have limited to zero English, they're generally pleased to have Western guests. Most homestays provide at least breakfast and some offer dinner as well if given a few hours' notice.

TOP CHOICE **Enhui Mingsu Zijia** HOMESTAY $

(恩惠民宿之家; Ēnhuì Mínsù Zhījiā; ☎732 979; Yeyin village, 野銀部落; per person NT$300) Staying in the home of husband-and-wife team Li Ge and Li Sao is a great way to get to know both Lanyu and the Yami. Their home, located on a hill in Yeyin on the east side of the island, is spotless and has four doubles and a large dorm on the upper floor. Li Ge is an excellent guide, highly knowledgeable about both culture and botany, and offers night-time owl and sea-life tours, and visits to his parents' underground house in the mornings. Li Sao is a fine cook and for an extra NT$100 per person she'll cook up a suppertime feast.

Hong Sheng B&B HOMESTAY $

(鴻昇民宿; Hóngshēng Mínsù; ☎732 462; 186 Langtao village, 朗島村186號; dm/d NT$500/800; @) The whitewashed exterior of this Langtao homestay features Greek columns, while the interior looks like a modern downtown Taipei apartment, complete with a bar-style kitchen, plasma TV, internet and a few flowery frills. And yet Hong Sheng is nestled in a small hamlet at the base of the green hills just west of the main strip in Langtao, one of the most traditional villages on Lanyu. From the front steps of the B&B you can look down a range of forested slopes to Tashenshan, 20km in the distance. Some of the best swimming and snorkelling areas on Lanyu are just down the road.

Sui Yuan Cabins CABINS $$

(隨緣小棧; Suíyuán Xiǎozhàn; ☎0955-562 842; 30-1 Hungtou village, 紅頭村30-1號; d NT$1900) Set on a low bluff overlooking the sea is this row of five cabins run by a Yami who calls himself Goodbye. The cabins look like yellow square boxes from the outside but are pretty cosy where it counts and each unit has its own porch overlooking the sea. A bacon-and-egg breakfast is included and Hungtou village is just a few hundred metres down the road for more eating options.

Mermaid & the Cat B&B HOMESTAY $

(人魚和貓民宿; Rényú Hé Māo Mínsù; ☎732 943; 23-3 Tungching village, 東清村23-3 號;

LOCAL KNOWLEDGE

QUAN YUMAN: RESPECTING LOCAL TRADITIONS

The majority of Yami on Lanyu were raised in the old traditions and it's important for visitors to travel carefully. Local craftswoman Quan Yuman (全玉滿) is part of Canaanland Workshop, an association in Langtao working to educate both visitors and locals on the culture, history and ecology of Lanyu. Here are her suggestions for minimising cross-cultural misunderstandings:

» In general, Yami do not like being watched when performing their common daily activities, and bristle at being looked upon as exotic or different.

» Following the above point, don't take photos without asking for permission. This applies not just to people, but to their houses and their possessions, including livestock.

» Don't touch or sit or pose by traditional canoes without asking for permission. The canoes are private property and not placed on the beach for tourists.

» During the flying-fish season, don't stand or walk under or take pictures of racks of drying fish. This is considered extremely impolite.

» If you see someone hauling in a large catch of fish don't comment on how many fish there are. As with many traditional cultures, the Yami feel this not only jinxes the fisherman (meaning his next catch will be small) but also puts an obligation on him to give you some of his catch.

» The traditional platforms you see everywhere are for resting during the day and cooling off. Yami dislike having their picture taken when they are sitting or sleeping in these. Visitors are free to use the platforms but ask first and be aware that the owner always has right of way.

» Yami men fish at night and so often sleep or hang about in the daytime. Suggestions that they have an easy or lazy life because they never seem very busy are not appreciated.

» Yami graves are often not marked, so don't go wandering off the trails in the forest as you might inadvertently step on one. In general keep to the roads and paths. This applies to bird- and butterfly-watchers, too. If you want to explore, get a guide.

» If you are curious about Yami culture it's best to ask your homestay or the association to find someone who is willing to answer your questions. Local people don't always appreciate a lot of direct questions from strangers and may just make up their answers.

d NT$1200; wi-fi) Next door to the restaurant with the same name in Tungching village, this brick annexe has a few private doubles. The exposed-cement walls and floor have an almost urban bohemian appeal, though this was probably not intentional. The B&B sits across from a rocky beach and just down from a trail to a sunrise lookout.

Eating & Drinking

The Yami diet consists primarily of fish and locally grown vegetables, with a bit of pork and goat (there are goats wandering freely all over the island) on special occasions. In addition to enjoying homestay meals you can eat and drink at a growing number of restaurants and cafes on both sides of the island. Non-local dishes tend to be prepackaged stews and the like, so stick to fish if possible. Most villages also have one breakfast shop that opens around 6am.

Mermaid & the Cat RESTAURANT **$**

(人魚和貓; Rényú Hé Māo; 23-3 Tungching village; dishes from NT$60; 11am-8.30pm; wi-fi) Run by a couple of young women from the 'mainland' (one is married to a local Yami), the clapboard and driftwood Mermaid has a bright, airy beachtown feel. The food is nothing special but there's free wi-fi and some pleasant chatty company to pass the time.

Epicurean Cafe RESTAURANT **$$**

(無餓不坐; Wúè Búzuò; 77 Yuren village; drinks from NT$60, meals NT$160-300; 11am-8.30pm; wi-fi) Like the Mermaid's, the food here won't turn your head, but the hillside perch of this cafe-restaurant-bar is a great location for sipping a coffee or beer while you enjoy the views of Lanyu's coral coastline. If there are customers the cafe will stay open late, in effect turning into a late-evening bar.

Shopping

One of the most important Yami cultural traditions is the building of elaborately carved wooden canoes, made from 27 individual pieces of wood, ingeniously held together without nails. Buying such a canoe is unfeasible unless you intend to row it home (not advisable). **Canaanland Workshop** (迦南園工藝坊; Jiānányuán Gōngyìfǎng; ☎0912-103 639; 224 Langtao; ⊙8am-6pm) does sell some good replicas, however, and other crafts at their shop in Langtao. **Three Sisters** (三姐妹; Sān Jiě Mèi; 23 Tungching village) sells woven bracelets, woodcarvings and paintings.

Information

The cancellation of flights is common, so prepare extra cash for unplanned days. There are no international ATMs on Lanyu; the post office at Hungtou accepts Taiwanese cards.

Wi-fi is available at a growing number of cafes, restaurants and homestays. There's an internet cafe (網咖; *wǎngbā*) in Yeyin village.

Getting There & Away

AIR Daily Air Corporation (☎362 489; www.dailyair.com.tw) has six flights a day (NT$1380, 20 minutes) between Taitung and Lanyu. The 19-seat planes fill up quickly all year round, so book both ways as far ahead as possible. In the winter months scheduling is unreliable because of the weather.

BOAT Boats run on an erratic schedule from May to October between Fugang harbour (Taitung) or Houbitou (Kenting) and Lanyu (just north of Yeyou village). Schedules are dependent both on weather and the number of passengers. Booking further than a day in advance can be unreliable; verify on day of travel with the travel agency in Taitung or at the harbour. The three-hour trip can be extremely rough.

Getting Around

TO/FROM THE AIRPORT Hotels and homestays provide transport to and from the airport if notified in advance.

BUS A public bus circles the island four times a day; it can be flagged down anywhere.

CAR & SCOOTER There's a rental shop next to the Lanyu Hotel in Hungtou but any hotel or homestay can arrange rental (car/scooter NT$1800/400 per day). In winter, renting a car is safer and more comfortable than a scooter because of slippery road conditions.

TAXI There are few taxis on the island; anywhere by taxi costs around NT$250.

GREEN ISLAND

☎089 / POP 3000

Beautiful and lush, boasting good beaches and one of only three seawater hot springs in the world, Green Island (Lǜdǎo; 綠島) is a popular resort destination for Taiwanese looking for rest and recreation. But in the not too distant past, the phrase 'off to Green Island' didn't conjure up visions of leisure pursuits in the Taiwanese psyche; quite the opposite, in fact, for once upon a time the very name of this tiny volcanic island, 30km east of Taitung, was synonymous with repression. It was where, under martial law, political opponents of the regime were sent to languish at the island's notorious prison camp, sardonically referred to as 'Oasis Villa'.

Today, the prison's metal doors have been flung open and this once potent place of repression has been transformed into a museum and human-rights memorial. To a new generation of Taiwanese the island is thought of not primarily for its infamous past, but as a place to see pristine coral reefs and gorgeous tropical fish through glass-bottomed boats and hang out on the beach and soak in the hot spring under the night sky.

Smaller than Lanyu, Green Island is ringed by a 19km road that you can get around on a scooter in 30 minutes. With one main road hugging the shore and another leading up to Huoshao Mountain (great for hiking), getting lost is pretty difficult.

Sights

FREE **Green Island Human Rights Cultural Park** MEMORIAL PARK

(綠島人權文化園區; Lǜdǎo Rénquán Wénhuà Yuánqū; ⊙8am-5pm) Standing forlorn on a windswept coast, its back to a sheer cliff, this park complex documents Taiwan's White Terror and Martial Law periods (1949–1987). The park is the site of a former prison where dissidents, activists and others considered 'hooligans' by the KMT were sent to languish. At the time of writ-

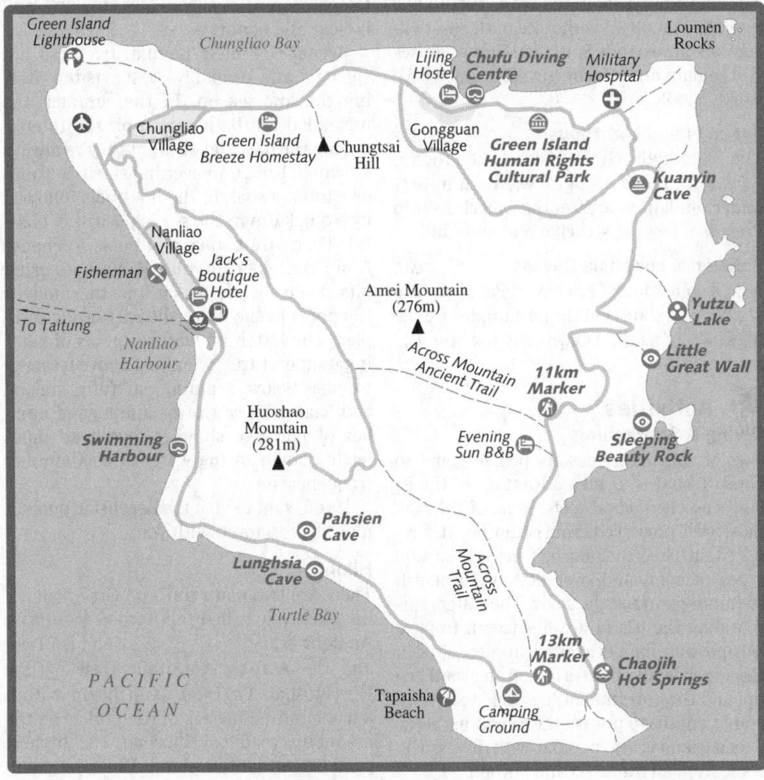

ing, the entire complex was undergoing repairs to make it accessible to the public. For the time being visitors are welcome to walk around the prison area popularly called **Oasis Villa** (綠島山莊; Lùdǎo Shānzhuāng) and inspect the cells where former prisoners such as former vice-president Annette Lu and Taiwanese writer Bo Yang (author of *The Ugly Chinaman*) once spent years. It's a sombre place, of course, so visit here first and devote the rest of the trip to more cheerful pursuits.

Little Great Wall — VOLCANIC CRATER

Green Island has some intriguing volcanic-rock formations scattered around the coast, leading some Taiwanese to give the rocks curious names. The promontory called Little Great Wall (小長城; Xiǎo Chángchéng) is probably the most inaptly named, as it is in fact the rugged northern wall of the crater of the volcano that formed Green Island. The path to the promontory edge is only 300m long but ends at a pavilion where you can look down to **Haishenping** (海參坪; Hǎishēnpíng), the crater bay. Across the bay is **Sleeping Beauty Rock** (睡美人; Shuì Měi Rén), one of the formations that actually does resemble its name (once you figure out the neck the rest of the figure will fall into place).

Kuanyin Cave — TAOIST SHRINE

The underground Kuanyin Cave (觀音洞; Guānyīn Dòng) is dedicated to Kuanyin and features a stalagmite wrapped with a red cape. Legend has it that during the Qing dynasty a fisherman became lost at sea and a fiery red light came down from the sky and led him to safety in the cave. The fisherman believed the light to be the goddess Kuanyin and the stalagmite in the cape to resemble the form of the goddess. The cavern was designated a sacred spot on the island and people come here from all over Taiwan to pay their respects.

Yutzu Lake SCENIC AREA

Not a lake but a sheltered cove, Yutzu Lake (柚子湖; Yòuzǐ Hú) is the site of the first village on the island. Some old stone houses still remain and nearby is a sea-eroded cave worth a look.

Green Island Lighthouse LIGHTHOUSE

The 33m-high Green Island Lighthouse (綠島燈塔; Lùdǎo Dēngtǎ) was built in 1937 under the Japanese after the American ship *President Hoover* struck a reef and sank.

Pahsien & Lunghsia Caves CAVES

A cool collection of sea caves, Pahsien Cave (八仙洞; Bāxiān Dòng) and Lunghsia Cave (龍蝦洞; Lóngxiā Dòng) are just off the main road.

Activities

Diving & Snorkelling

One of the main reasons people come to Green Island is to take advantage of the island's excellent coral reefs, some of Taiwan's most well preserved. Tourist authorities report that Green Island has more than 200 types of coral and over 602 types of fish swimming around the coast. The waters surrounding the island are filled with tropical fish, possibly thanks to nutrients deposited in the water by the hot spring on the southern tip, and the government has gone to considerable lengths to protect the remaining reefs. Green Island is also popular with divers, who come from all over Asia and beyond.

Most hotels and guesthouses can arrange snorkelling and diving trips. Equipment can be rented at shops in Nanliao village and around the harbour. Rates depend on how many people you have in your group and the type of equipment you need to rent.

Tapaisha Beach (大白沙; Dàbáishā) has fine white coral sand and is known for its stunning coral reefs, making it a good spot for snorkelling, as is the small stretch of beach east of the Green Island Lighthouse.

One reputable dive shop is the **Chufu Diving Centre** (居福潛水; Jūfú Qiánshuǐ; ☎672 238; 78-3 Kungkuan village), run by diving enthusiast Mr Tsai.

Hot Springs

History and strange rock formations aside, what brings people to Green Island is the sea; not just in the form of beaches, but also hot springs.

TOP CHOICE **Chaojih Hot Springs** (朝日溫泉; Zhāorì Wēnquán; admission NT$200; ⏲5am-2am) is one of the planet's three known seawater hot springs. The water temperature varies from 53°C to 83°C, and is clear and odourless.

Because of their popularity, these hot springs are probably best visited during the low season. In the summer, the unshaded hot baths are a bit too intense during the day, and at night they're always crowded. Under an evening sky in autumn or winter, a soak in the hot pools followed by a quick dip in the sea is positively blissful. There are two sets of pools to choose from: the older circular stone hot-spring pits down by the beach and the modern tile pools in the better-lit part of the complex. The latter set features pools of varying temperatures, from just above freezing to just below scalding, artfully shaped artificial privacy grottos and a good number of massage showers (overhead pipes jetting down spring water at jackhammer frequencies).

If you want to visit the beachside pools at night, take a torch with you.

Hiking

There are two main trails on Green Island, imaginatively called the **Across Mountain Ancient Trail** (過山古道; Guòshān Gǔ Dào) and the **Across Mountain Trail** (過山步道; Guòshān Bù Dào). Both begin within a few hundred metres of each other on the mountain road to Huoshao, the highest peak (281m) on the island. You can't climb Huoshao because of the military base at the summit, but these two trails heading down to the seashore more than make up for that.

The trails are about 1.8km long each and run through thick, natural tropical forest. Paths are wide and clear, and have informative interpretation signs that nicely explain the common English names of plants. Best of all, the chances of spotting sika deer or the tiny barking deer are high. On a casual stroll on a Monday morning we spotted half a dozen deer, and heard many more crashing in the bushes.

Tours

Green Island Adventures (www.greenislandadventures.com) arranges year-round transport to the island, accommodation, and tailor-built tour packages including snorkelling, diving, hiking and, of course, hot springing. It also arranges the use of a glass-bottomed boat for tours around the island's fabulous coral reefs.

Sleeping

There are accommodation options all over Green Island. The greatest concentration is on the main street in Nanliao Village close to the harbour, but these tend to be older hotels. Some newer and more modern (dare we say even stylish) B&Bs have recently opened up around the island and have quite reasonable prices.

Green Island is a popular place in summer for Taiwanese tourists, which means that most hotels will be booked solid on weekends. During the low season (or even weekdays in summer), you'll probably be met by people at the boat offering to bring you to their hotels and guesthouses; most hotels offer discounted prices.

Jack's Boutique Hotel HOTEL $$
(傑克飯店; Jiékè Fàndiàn; ☎0963-221 279; www.jack.e089.com.tw; 20 Yugang Rd, Nanliao Village, 南寮村漁港路20號; d/tw NT$2200/3600; @ 📶) With its bright colours and dudish beach decor, this place feels more like an upmarket hostel than boutique hotel. If you're coming to Green Island for the works (snorkelling, hot springs, scooter riding) consider its packages (from NT$2300 per person in summer).

Green Island Breeze Homestay HOMESTAY $$
(綠島微風民宿; Lùdǎo Wéifēng Mínsù; ☎671 617; 58-1 Chaokou, Chungliao Village, 公館村柴口58之1號; d/tw incl breakfast NT$2200/3200) Rooms are new and massive in this modern house with a washed-pebble exterior. The location is a bit out of town but across from one of the best swimming and diving beaches on the island. Airport pick-up is included and the homestay can help with scooter rentals. Good weekday discounts and discounts for single travellers.

Evening Sun B&B HOMESTAY $
(幸福月光民宿; Xìngfú Yuèguāng Mínsù; ☎672 126; http://eveningsun.okgo.tw; 41 Gongguan Village Wenquan, 公館村溫泉41號; r from NT$1200) If you want to stay on the other side of the island this is a pretty good choice. Rooms are small but brightly painted and airy, and the homestay is just a couple of minutes from the hot springs and hiking trails. To find Evening Sun head north from the hot springs and take the second left into Gongguan Village, a tiny settlement across from the sea. The homestay is a few houses in.

CHECKING IN & OUT

Green Island hotels have a strict 2pm check-in, so book ahead if you are catching an early ferry or flight. You'll wait in the lobby for a long time if you just show up. Also, take advantage of pick-ups, especially from the airport, which has no scooter rental nearby.

Be aware that most hotels also have a 10am checkout. You can usually store your bags if you have a later flight but be sure to take them out of your room on time or you will be charged extra.

Lijing Hostel HOTEL $
(麗景山莊; Lìjǐng Shānzhuāng; ☎672 000; 47 Kungkuan Village, 公館村47號; dm/s/d NT$500/800/1000) A friendly place run by local Mrs Tien, the Lijing offers very basic dorm accommodation and rooms that are ageing but clean and about as cheap as you're going to get in summer. Good location in a village with lots of dive shops.

Camping Ground CAMPGROUND $
(露營區; Lùyíng Qū; ☎672 027, 671 133) Under reconstruction at the time of writing, but should be reopened by the time you read this. The visitor information centre takes all reservations and may rent out equipment as it did in the past. Prices should be around NT$300 per grass site. The area can be a bit buggy, though, so bring repellent.

Eating

Nanliao Village has quite a few seafood restaurants and a few awful attempts at Western food. Most shops are only open for lunch and dinner, so don't wait to eat. There are a couple of breakfast-only places on the main street and two convenience stores selling the usual drinks (the only places for fresh coffee), sandwiches and noodle concoctions.

Local dishes include sea mushrooms (海香菇; *hǎi xiānggū*) and garlic octopus (蒜香章魚; *suàn xiāng zhāngyú*).

Restaurants go in and out of business often. At the time of writing, **Fisherman** (釣漁人; Dìaoyúrén; dishes NT$50-100; ⏰lunch & dinner; 📋), on the main street of Nanliao Village with a deck facing the Pacific, was popular with the crowds for cheap seafood and a laid-back atmosphere.

THE GREEN ISLAND VOMIT BARGE *JOSHUA SAMUEL BROWN*

Green Island is among Taiwan's loveliest offerings, and as a traveller and writer I recommend a visit highly. However, a word on the boat. I am an islander, of sorts (Staten Island, New York, where the ferry to and from Manhattan, though hardly a strenuous voyage, was a daily routine for a decade). I've travelled extensively by ship and ferry around Taiwan, by riverboat through China's Pearl River Delta and Southeast Asia, and by a host of seagoing vessels large and small around Maritime Canada and in the Pacific Northwest.

Only twice in my extensive travels have I found myself, face pressed against a rolling floor, stinking of my own vomit, begging for the sweet, sweet release of death.

The first time was on the boat to Green Island. The second was on the boat back.

Information

There's good wi-fi at the airport. The one ATM in Nanliao Village is not reliable, so bring the cash you need.

Visitor Information Centre (遊客中心; Yóukè Zhōngxīn; ☎672 027; 298 Nanliao Village; ⌚8am-5pm) A minute's walk from the airport, the centre has maps and information about the island's history, culture and ecology. Staff can make reservations for the campground in the south of the island but have poor English-speaking skills.

Getting There & Away

AIR Daily Air Corporation (☎362 489; www.dailyair.com.tw) has three daily flights between Taitung and Green Island (NT$1028, 15 minutes) on small 19-seat propeller planes. During winter flights are often cancelled due to bad weather. In summer you must book several weeks ahead. Note that the tiny airport on Green Island is literally at the edge of Nanliao Village, about 500m from the main drag. Just walk out the front door and you are on the road.

BOAT From June to September boats run hourly between Taitung's Fukang harbour and Green Island (NT$460, 50 minutes). The first boat leaves Fukang at 7.30am, Green Island at 8.30am. The schedule outside summer changes daily and is unreliable because of weather conditions. At all times it's a very uncomfortable ride that makes most people seasick.

Getting Around

BICYCLE There's free rental at the airport if you've flown to Green Island; you'll need to show a passport or Alien Resident Certificate (ARC) and boarding pass.

BUS Buses circle the island eight times a day, stopping at various tourist points, and can be flagged down anywhere. Schedules are posted at each stop.

SCOOTER Scooter rentals (NT$300 to NT$400 per day) are available at the harbour or from your hotel; none available at airport.

TAXI There are very few taxis on Green Island; arrange one through your hotel or at the visitor information centre.

Understand Taiwan

population per sq km

TAIWAN

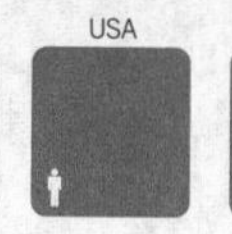

USA

CHINA

≈ 30 people

Taiwan Today

An Island in Flux Clings to Its Identity

Sovereign nation or renegade Chinese province? Taiwan or Republic of China? At the start of the second decade of the 21st century, Taiwan retains its political autonomy even as political and economic realities seem to draw it closer into China's orbit. Today's Taiwanese are increasingly aware of their own strength as a society, one that's managed to transform from authoritarian rule to democracy, weather economic recessions better than other countries in the region and maintain a unique cultural identity in the face of a much larger neighbour seeking to absorb it. While Taiwan's future as a fully autonomous political entity is uncertain, you'll find little self-pity in the island's collective spirit. Instead, you'll discover collective pride at Taiwan's long list of historical, technological and economic accomplishments, along with a sense that, even if most of the world's nations don't 'officially' recognise Taiwan, Taiwan certainly recognises itself.

Government

A multiparty democracy, Taiwan's government is dominated by its two largest political parties, the Kuomintang (KMT) and the Democratic Progressive Party (DPP). The current head of state is Ma Ying-jeou (KMT), whose party holds 74 of the seats in Taiwan's legislative branch, the Legislative Yuan. The DPP is a distinct minority, controlling 33 seats, with smaller parties and independents holding the remaining four. Though Ma's 2008 election was seen as a turning point in modern Taiwanese history, his approval ratings around the island have been lacklustre at best. Elected on a promise to stimulate the economy by moving closer to China, something his predecessor had sharply rejected, the administration's opening years have been strongly affected by the global economic crisis, which have sent the island's exports into a tailspin.

Must-See Films

» **Cape No. 7** Director Wei Te-Sheng's 2008 romantic comedy became the second-highest grossing film in Taiwanese history.

» **Au Revoir Taipei** Director Arvin Chen's 2010 drama won the Best Asian Film (NETPAC) prize at the Berlin International Film Festival.

» **Eat Drink Man Woman** Ang Lee's 1994 drama is still a must-see for anyone interested in Taiwanese culture and cuisine.

» **Super Citizen Ko** Wan Jen's 1995 film was one of the first films to examine Taiwan's White Terror period.

» **Formosa Betrayed** Though not perfect, Adam Kane's 2009 film is a good primer on the last days of martial law in Taiwan, as seen through Western eyes.

belief systems
(% of population)

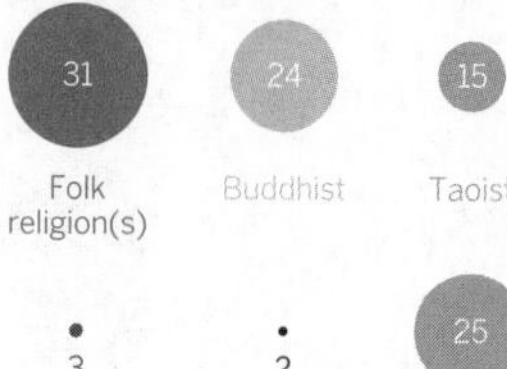

if Taiwan were 100 people

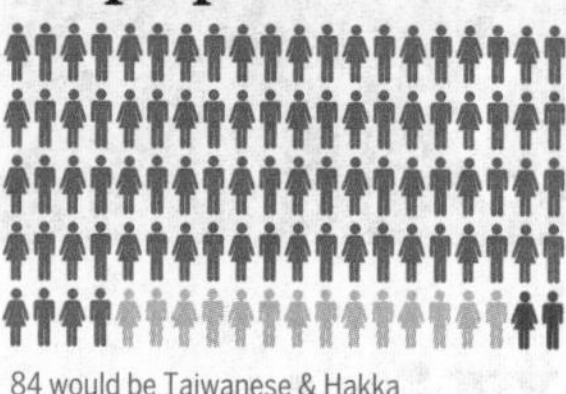

84 would be Taiwanese & Hakka
14 would be mainland Chinese
2 would be indigenous

The administration's handling of other issues, from its slow response to Typhoon Morakot to continuing corruption and vote-buying scandals involving both parties have likewise served to keep Ma's overall approval rating around the island below 50%. Also an issue is the fear that the KMT, a political party whose name is inexorably intertwined with the darkest days of Taiwan's martial-law period, may be in the process of reigning in hard-won democratic reforms in order to retain its grip on power. Although most basic freedoms are intact, international human-rights groups Freedom House and Reporters Without Borders have issued statements expressing concern over issues such as judicial impartiality and press independence.

Economy

Even folks who couldn't find the island on a map have seen the phrase 'Made In Taiwan' on hundreds of items, ranging from clothing and bicycles to electronics and computer parts. Manufacturing is the backbone of Taiwan's economy, with major trading partners including China, the US and Japan. Since the mid-1980s, Taiwan has become one of the world's leaders in high-tech production, especially in computer technology.

Taiwan's economy has proved fairly resilient to the economic storms that have battered most of its neighbours, and despite a decrease in exports due to the global economic downturn, Taiwan's standard of living remains fairly high. Issues such as inflation, overpriced housing and stagnating wages are regular topics of discussion.

Due to Taiwan's unique diplomatic situation, trade relations between Taiwan and countries around the world have taken on an added element of importance: trade delegations often double as diplomatic entourages and trade offices around the world stand in as permanent quasi-embassies.

Taiwan has one of Asia's highest literacy rates, with 96.1% of the island's population able to read and write. No mean feat, considering that the Chinese language contains 80,000 characters (though to be fair, only a fraction of these are in regular use!).

Dos & Don'ts

» Do bring business cards. You never know who you might meet. Business cards should be handed and received with both hands.

» Don't be afraid to talk politics. Taiwanese people of all political stripes cherish their democracy and value the free exchange of ideas.

» Do offer to pay the bill when dining out with Taiwanese friends. They won't let you, of course, but your offer will make their face-gain even greater.

» Don't forget to take your shoes off when entering someone's home!

» Don't give four of anything as a gift. The word 'four' in Mandarin sounds like the word 'death' and is considered inauspicious.

History

Writing a historical overview of any place in just a few pages necessitates being both sweepingly general and highly selective. But writing about Taiwan's history is especially tricky, because it's a history of two different entities: Taiwan, the island, and Taiwan, the political entity known as the Republic of China (ROC). Though unified currently, the history of the former is far older, and the origin of the latter is found many miles elsewhere. Since history is a big part of Taiwan's appeal to travellers, and because Taiwan's history is so mired in politics, we endeavour to tread delicately, but boldly, stopping along the way to suggest places where the reader might find living reminders of days gone by.

Information about Taiwanese history (from the point of view of the Taiwanese) can be found on www.taiwandc.org/history.htm. The site has a lot of interesting photographs and an excellent recommended reading list.

Early History

Taiwan has been settled for a long time, this much is certain. There is evidence of human settlement in Taiwan dating as far back as 30,000 to 40,000 years ago, and one theory holds that Taiwan is the linguist homeland of various Austronesian languages currently spoken throughout the Pacific. Whether the earliest inhabitants of Taiwan are related to the descendents of the aboriginal tribes currently living on Taiwan (or were in fact overrun by them and forced to migrate elsewhere) is still being debated.

Prehistoric Taiwan was likely a wetter place than it is today (a fact that will seem impossible to anyone who has hiked up Yaming Mountain – or just dared to step outside of an air-conditioned mall or Mass Rapid Transit (MRT) station, for that matter – on a typical humid August day). The mountains surrounding present-day Taipei were still majestic, but the land between them, on which now sits a great metropolis, was mostly under water. At some point, over 6000 years ago, the now (mostly) dry basin between the mountains began to be settled by people who, according to some theories, migrated to Taiwan from

TIMELINE

50,000–10,000 BC

Human skeletons found in eastern Taiwan and in the Taipei Basin point to prehistoric human habitation of the island during the late Palaeolithic era.

c 10,000 BC

Ancestors of Taiwan's present-day aboriginals first come to the island by sea and begin settling around the island.

AD 1544

Passing Portuguese sailors become the first Europeans to lay eyes on Taiwan; they are so enchanted they name the island Ilha Formosa (Beautiful Island).

LIVING HISTORY: PREHISTORIC TAIWAN

Di-re Valley, Beitou Scalding steam rising from craters filled with sulphurous water gives a taste of the less-than-hospitable place prehistoric Taiwan must have once been.

Dulan Ancient stone coffins still out in the fields are said to be the final resting place of some of Taiwan's earliest inhabitants. Tread lightly.

Shihsanheng Museum of Archaeology, Bali Offers exhibits on the archaeological history of Taiwan's earliest residents, tracking the movements of the various tribes from prehistory to the present day.

Shitoushan This mountain on the border of Hsinchu and Miaoli Counties is home to a river-crab species that scientists think is as old as Taiwan itself.

Taroko Gorge Formed by the same tectonic plate action that gave birth to the island itself, it doesn't get any more prehistorical than Taiwan's most gorgeous (pardon the pun) area of natural splendour.

other islands in the Pacific. Anthropologists would later collectively describe the first settlers as 'Pingpu' or 'plains aboriginal people'. Their descendants still live in Taiwan.

Fast forward to the last millennium. Having been 'discovered' by Han Chinese, Taiwan was subject to a slow but inexorable influx of settlers from China's east coast. For most of its long history, China seemed fairly indifferent to Taiwan. Early Chinese texts from as far back as AD 206 contain references to the island, but for the most part it was seen as a savage island, best left alone. Contact between China and Taiwan was erratic until the early 1400s, when boatloads of immigrants from China's Fujian province, disillusioned with the political instability in their homeland, began arriving on Taiwan's shores. When the new immigrants arrived, they encountered two groups of aboriginal people: one who made their homes on the fertile plains of central and southwestern Taiwan and the other, seminomadic, who lived along the Central Mountain Range.

Over the next century, immigration from Fujian increased, these settlers being joined by the Hakka, another ethnic group leaving the mainland in great numbers. By the early 1500s there were three categories of people on the island: Hakka, Fujianese and the aboriginal tribes. The current population of Taiwan is descended from these early Chinese immigrants, as well as from later Chinese settlers arriving throughout the time of the Ming and Qing dynasties. Centuries of intermarriage between Han Chinese and members of aboriginal tribes means that a fair number of Taiwanese have some aboriginal blood as well.

1622–1662

The Dutch establish colonies on both Taiwan Island and Penghu to facilitate trade with China and Japan during this 'Dutch Formosa' period. They also encourage migration of Han Chinese to Taiwan.

1662

After a campaign lasting two years, Dutch forces are driven off Taiwan by Ming loyalist Admiral Koxinga; they surrender to him in Tainan.

1662–1683

Following Koxinga's death in 1662, son Zheng Jing sets up the first Han Chinese government on Taiwan, as a base to try to regain China from the Qing dynasty.

1683

Following Zheng Jing's death in 1682, son Zheng Keshuang rules briefly before being defeated at Battle of Penghu, resulting in a surrender to Qing forces.

Taiwan in the Ming Dynasty

Taiwan was once a haven for pirates in the 15th and 16th centuries.

PIRATE HAVEN

In 1544 a Portuguese fleet 'discovered' the island. Enamoured by the lush plains, rugged mountains and rocky coasts, they declared Taiwan Ilha Formosa, meaning 'beautiful island'. Less romantically minded Europeans soon took notice, and before long the Dutch (national proprietors of the recently formed Dutch East India Company) set up a trading base on the Penghu Islands (p291) in the Taiwan Strait.

This did not sit well in China's Ming court, who sat up suddenly and took notice of Taiwan. The Ming government sent its navy to Penghu, and before long had thrown the Dutch off the island. But being particularly tenacious, the Dutch soon returned and established a colony in Penghu in 1622, remnants of which can still be seen in the Dutch Fort ruins (p298) a few kilometres out of present-day Makung City.

The first thing the Dutch did on their return was to establish a trading route between Batavia (now Jakarta), Makung, China and Japan. For a short period of time, Dutch trade dominated the Taiwan Strait, much to the chagrin of the Ming court, who issued a decree in 1623 banning all entry of ships into the Taiwan Strait from southeast Asia. Realising the ineffectiveness of the decree, Ming troops were sent to attack the Dutch, who gave in and agreed to remove themselves from Penghu. Oddly, the Ming allowed the Dutch to establish trading ports in Taiwan proper.

Spain, ever envious of the Dutch hold on Taiwan and their growing wealth, decided they wanted in on the action themselves. In 1626 the Spanish invaded what is now Keelung and established their territory all the way down the west coast to Danshui and eventually all over northern Taiwan. Unfortunately, Taiwan's climate took revenge and a series of catastrophes took its toll on the Spanish traders. Typhoons and malaria devastated the Spanish, and attacks by local aboriginal people caused them to relinquish their territory. In 1638 the Spanish withdrew from Danshui and the Dutch (ever tenacious) moved in to snatch up the remains, taking control of Keelung in 1642.

LIVING HISTORY: MING TAIWAN

Kinmen Island Though normally associated with a period much later in Taiwan's history, it was this island that Koxinga completely deforested to construct his final fleet.

Koxinga Shrine, Tainan Originally constructed in 1663 (it's been rebuilt since), this shrine is dedicated to the pirate/admiral who expelled the Dutch from Taiwan during the final days of Ming rule.

West Fortress, Penghu One of the earliest examples of Dutch influence in Taiwan can be found at this fort on the western edge of the archipelago.

1683–1895
Taiwan governed by the Qing dynasty as part of Fujian province. Early years of Qing rule are marked by frequent rebellion, riots and civil strife.

1871
Japanese sailors stranded on the southern tip of Taiwan are killed in a conflict with local Paiwan tribespeople. The Japanese government demands compensation from the Qing court.

1874
A Japanese assault on Taiwan is repelled by a combination of locals and Qing troops. Japan withdraws its troops after suffering casualties caused by both battle and disease.

1895 (April)
After being defeated by Japan in the first Sino-Japanese War, a Qing delegation signs the Treaty of Shimonoseki, granting Japan control over Taiwan and the Penghu Islands in perpetuity.

LIVING HISTORY: QING-DYNASTY TAIWAN

Guandu Temple, Taipei First built in 1661, this fabulous temple dedicated to the Goddess of the Sea is among the oldest temples in Northern Taiwan.
Lukang A town featuring temples and streets that date back to the Qing.
Sansia (Sanxia) Though there's a bit of Japanese influence here, this town's Qing street is nearly perfectly restored to its initial splendour.
Taijiang National Park A national park preserving not only the environment but also the traditional Qing industries such as salt making.
Taipei City Gates Though the wall that once encircled Taipei – the last walled city of the Qing dynasty – is long gone, four of her five gates are still standing. Of these, Beimen (the one closest to the train station) is the most authentic, the other three having been 'restored' from southern- to northern-Chinese style.

Though continued western encroachment into Taiwan undoubtedly displeased the Ming court, over in Beijing the emperor had bigger problems; the dynasty itself was in collapse. One staunch Ming loyalist in exile would have a lasting impact on Taiwanese history; Admiral Cheng Cheng-kung, also known as Koxinga, sought refuge with his troops on the small island of Kinmen (p274) off China's Fujian province. On Kinmen, Cheng met a disgruntled former interpreter for the Dutch East India Company who convinced him to invade Taiwan and overthrow the Dutch.

Intrigued, Cheng somehow managed to amass an army on Kinmen and build a fleet of ships (in the process deforesting the island, from which it's now only just recovering). Cheng set sail for the Penghu Islands, where he swiftly deposed the Dutch before moving on to Taiwan proper. Arriving in Taiwan, he was greeted by local supporters anxious to be free of the Dutch once and for all. Realising their days in Taiwan were numbered, the Dutch surrendered to Cheng in 1662 and left for good.

With Cheng came 30,000 mainland Chinese, who established Taiwan island as their home. Others soon followed, and would do so for the next 200 years. Taiwan's growing population accelerated development on the island, especially in the north and along the fertile plains of the west coast. To manage Taiwan's fast growth, Cheng set up an efficient system of counties, some of which remain today. However, his dreams of overthrowing the Manchu remained unfulfilled; he died a year after landing on Taiwan. Many Taiwanese today regard Cheng as a hero for driving the Dutch out of Taiwan.

1895 (May)

Unhappy with being incorporated into Japan, local Taiwanese (assisted by disenchanted Manchu officials) establish the Taiwan Republic, the first independent republic in Asia.

1895 (October)

After a five-month campaign during which Japanese forces capture towns in a southward march, Republican forces surrender the capital of Tainan, bringing to an end the short-lived Taiwan Republic.

1912

Following the collapse of the Qing dynasty, Sun Yat-sen declares the birth of the Republic of China (ROC). Taiwan is still under Japanese rule.

RICHARD CUMMINS

» Statue of Dr Sun Yat-sen

Taiwan in the Qing Dynasty

After Cheng's death his son and grandson ruled the island but their ineptness caused wide-scale poverty and despair. In 1683 the Qing government overthrew Cheng's descendents and took over the island, placing it under the jurisdiction of Fujian province. Having 'retaken' Taiwan, the Qing court's attitude towards Taiwan was about as lax as the Ming's before them, and Taiwan was again mostly ignored by China, save the boatloads of Chinese immigrants yearning for space to spread out.

In the West, however, Europeans were not blind to Taiwan's advantageous position, and the 'beautiful island' was quite well known among traders both for its strategic location and hazardous coastline. (The latter would eventually play a part in the Qing court's surrender of Taiwan to Japan.) After the second Opium War ended, Taiwan was opened to trade with the West in Keelung and Suao. The southern ports of Kaohsiung and Tainan were also opened. Foreign trade increased rapidly, with Taiwan's main exports being camphor, rice, tea and opium.

Despite Taiwan's importance as a trading centre, the island remained a wild and unruly place, and the Qing government did little to control the frequent unrest between settlers, foreign sailors and the aboriginal population. In 1872 the crew of a shipwrecked Japanese junk was killed by an aboriginal tribe; after being told by the Qing emperor that the aboriginal people on the island were beyond his court's control, Japanese troops invaded Taiwan. Before the annexation was complete, the Qing government offered compensation to the families of the dead sailors, as well as pledging to exert more control over Taiwan. Placated for the time being, the Japanese withdrew from Taiwan.

The withdrawal, however, was to prove temporary.

LIVING HISTORY: TAIWAN UNDER JAPANESE OCCUPATION

Ciaotou Sugar Factory, Kaohsiung City Only recently opened to the public, this was the first modern factory in Taiwan and the start of industrialisation under the Japanese. The entire grounds are open, including the factory and a lot of cool old colonial offices and houses.

Jinguashi's Ecological Gold Park Displays what Japanese-era Taiwan looked like better than almost anywhere else.

Presidential Building, Taipei Both this building and several others in the area are excellent examples of Japanese colonial architecture.

Taiwan Literature Museum, Tainan One of the largest colonial buildings and nearby is a restored dojo where the police used to practice.

1919

Den Kenjiro appointed first civilian governor-general of Taiwan and begins policy of Doka (assimilation), in which Taiwanese are viewed as Japanese rather than colonial subjects.

1930

More than 130 Japanese and 700 Taiwanese aboriginals are killed in the 'Wushe Incident', after an altercation between Japanese authorities and members of the Sediq tribe in Nantou County.

1945

After Japan's defeat in WWII, Taiwan is placed under administrative control of Chiang Kai-shek's Republic of China. Taiwan's social order is thrown into chaos.

1947

In an already tense environment, the arrest of a cigarette vendor by police leads to clashes between soldiers and citizens. Thousands are killed or imprisoned in the ensuing violence, known as the 2-28 Incident.

Japanese Occupation & 'Retrocession'

In 1894 war broke out between Japan and China over the Japanese invasion of Korea. China's poorly equipped navy was no match for Japan's modern fleet, and in 1895 China was forced to sign the humiliating Treaty of Shimonoseki which ceded the Ryukyu Islands (Okinawa), Taiwan and the Penghu Archipelago to Japan.

Taiwan responded to the treaty with alarm and a group of intellectuals formed the Taiwan Democratic Republic, writing a Declaration of Independence and claiming the island as a sovereign nation. Japan was not deterred, and after subduing the areas of Keelung and Danshui, the Japanese took over the ex-Qing governor's office in Taipei. Control over the rest of the island was not as easy as in the north and the Japanese met strong resistance as they moved further south. Employing over a third of its army in Taiwan, the Japanese eventually overcame the Taiwanese, who had confronted the modern weapons of the invaders with bamboo spears and outdated weapons.

Taiwan was declared a Chinese province only in 1887, just a few years before being ceded to Japan.

The hopes of the nascent Taiwan Democratic Republic were crushed, and Japan was to stay on the island for 50 years. It's believed that in the first several months after the Japanese arrived, over 10,000 soldiers and civilians lost their lives.

Once the Japanese felt they had things under control, they set out to modernise the island, building highways and railways to improve trade and to open up formerly isolated areas, especially along the east coast. They also constructed hospitals, schools and government buildings in an effort to improve the infrastructure of the island. Despite these improvements, the Japanese rule on the island was harsh, with brutal crackdowns on political dissent.

Over 80,000 Taiwanese served in the Japanese military during WWII.

The loss of Taiwan to Japan was merely one in a string of humiliations heaped by foreign hands upon the tottering Qing dynasty, and by 1900 it was obvious that a strong breeze would bring about its collapse. That wind came in the form of a revolutionary doctor named Sun Yatsen, founder of China's Nationalist party, Kuomintang (KMT). In 1912 China's last dynasty finally collapsed; Sun's KMT stepped in to fill the void, and Imperial China became the Republic of China (ROC). By this time Taiwan had been under Japanese control for nearly two decades, and the nascent ROC had far bigger things to worry about than reclaiming Imperial China's former and furthest-flung possession. From the creation of the ROC in 1912 until the defeat of Japan in 1945, Taiwan remained firmly in Japanese hands, while the ROC battled for its very existence on the Chinese mainland.

All this would change on 25 October 1945 (known as Retrocession Day in Taiwan). Japan, defeated in WWII, was forced to cede all

1949
The nationalist army is driven from mainland China by the communists. Chiang Kai-shek moves the ROC government to Taiwan with the intention of using the island as base to retake the mainland.

1951
Japan signs the Treaty of San Francisco, formally relinquishing all claims to Taiwan and its surrounding islands. However, the treaty does not clearly indicate to whom Taiwan belongs.

1954
The First Taiwan Strait Crisis begins when the People's Liberation Army (PLA) shells ROC-occupied Kinmen and Matsu. The conflict leads to the Sino-American Mutual Defense Treaty.

1958
The Second Taiwan Strait Crisis erupts when the PLA again attempts to seize Kinmen and Matsu from the ROC. Despite intense shelling the ROC maintains control of the islands.

2-28 INCIDENT

On 27 February 1947 a trivial incident led to a massacre that still reverberates to this day. Having declared a government monopoly on the sale of all tobacco, the Kuomintang (KMT) went after merchants selling black-market cigarettes. In Keelung, police from the Alcohol and Tobacco Bureau seized cigarettes and money from a middle-aged widow and pistol-whipped her into unconsciousness. Angry crowds formed and attacked the officers, who responded by shooting into the crowd, killing an innocent bystander.

The next morning crowds protested outside the Taipei branch of the Monopoly Bureau, attacking employees and setting the offices on fire. This was followed by a protest outside the governor's office. But the KMT was in no mood for negotiations. On the order of Governor Chen Yi – orders handed down, many maintain, by Chiang Kai-shek himself – troops fired on the crowds, killing dozens. A state of emergency was declared, and all public buildings were shut down as civilians took to the streets. Soon news of the event spread and riots erupted islandwide. Government offices and police stations were attacked and mainland immigrants were targeted for beatings.

The government's crackdown was brutal, and in the weeks following the incident intellectuals, political activists, and innocents were arrested, tortured and executed. Some estimate that up to 30,000 Taiwanese were murdered.

The 28 February incident evokes powerful memories even today for those who lived through the event. To commemorate those who died during the tragedy, 28 February was declared a national holiday 50 years later and Taipei New Park was renamed the 2-28 Peace Park (p45).

overseas possessions. Taiwan, now a spoil of war, was handed over to the ROC.

Though some say the Taiwanese were relieved to be rid of the Japanese, others maintain that most had already grown accustomed to the stability offered by the Japanese. In any event, any goodwill towards their Chinese 'liberators' would be short-lived. Almost immediately following the defeat of Japan, civil war broke out on the mainland between the KMT (led by Chiang Kai-shek) and Chairman Mao's communist forces. Embroiled in civil war, Chiang sent an inept general named Chen Yi to govern Taiwan; Chen Yi and his thugs plundered Taiwanese homes and shops, sending anything of value back to the mainland to help support the Nationalist fight against the communists. Riots against the KMT broke out, leading to the deaths of tens of thousands of civilians.

Taiwan under Chiang Kai-shek

At the beginning of 1946 things looked good for the KMT in China. The defeated Japanese were gone, and the KMT, with material back-

1971

UN General Assembly Resolution 2758 transfers the UN seat from the Republic of China to the People's Republic of China. From here on in, the UN no longer recognises the Taiwan as sovereign nation.

1975

Nationalist leader and ROC president Chiang Kai-shek dies aged 87; the government declares a month of mourning and Chiang's body is entombed in his former residence in Taoyuan County.

CRAIG FERGUSON

» Chiang Kai-shek Memorial Hall, Taipei

ing from America, seemed in a good position to defeat their rivals and re-assert full dominance over the Chinese mainland. How different the history of Taiwan might have been had this come to pass.

Alas, Chiang's army, demoralised and crippled by corruption from above and lack of support from the Chinese people at large, proved unable to defeat Mao Zedong's more disciplined red army, battle hardened from the years of conflict with Japan. By 1948 the communists were well on the way to driving the KMT from the mainland. Fully defeated by 1949, Chiang Kai-shek fled to Taiwan, followed by a steady stream of soldiers, monks, artists, peasants and intellectuals. One of the first things Chiang did when he arrived in Taiwan was to send Chen Yi back to the mainland (he was later executed). When Chairman Mao declared the birth of the People's Republic of China (PRC) on the Chinese mainland on 1 October 1949, the ROC found itself, as a geographical entity, consisting only of Taiwan, Penghu, and a number of islands off the Chinese coast including Matsu and Kinmen. These straits islands were quickly set up as military zones, both to rebuff any mainland attack and to set up a base of operations from which Chiang vowed he would use to retake the Chinese mainland.

On Taiwan, Chiang proved the able state governor that he never had been in China, instituting a series of land-reform policies that successfully laid the foundation for Taiwan's future economic success. While advertising his government in exile as 'Free China', based on the democratic ideals of Sun Yat-sen, Chiang's Taiwan was anything but free. While economic development was swift, Chiang's rule was quick to crush any political dissent. The White Terror (p322) era of the 1950s was a frightening time in Taiwanese history, when people literally disappeared if they spoke against the government. Political dissidents were either shipped to Green Island (p306) to serve long sentences or executed outright.

LIVING HISTORY: TAIWAN UNDER CHIANG KAI-SHEK

2-28 Memorial Museum This beautiful museum follows the events of 28 February 1947, and the decades of political repression that followed.
Cihu Statue Park This park gives visitors a good idea of the cult of personality formed around Chiang Kai-shek.
Green Island Though the island's political prison is now closed, many visitors claim to still be able to sense the spirits of former inhabitants who didn't live to see the end of Taiwan's White Terror (p322).
Kinmen & Matsu For decades these now-peaceful islands were at the frontline of the conflict between the Republic of China (ROC) and the People's Republic of China (PRC).

1976

Taiwanese Stan Shih starts a small company called Multitech in Hsinchu with his wife and an investment of US$25,000. Later renamed Acer, the company goes on to become a global computer producer.

1978

Chiang Ching-kuo becomes ROC president. While continuing many of his father's autocratic policies, the younger Chiang generally rules with a softer touch.

1979

The Taiwan Relations Act is passed by US Congress following the breaking of official relations between the US and Taiwan. The Act establishes quasi-diplomatic relations between the two countries.

1979

Known as the Kaohsiung Incident, a major gathering for Human Rights Day in Kaohsiung sees demonstrators clash with military police, and well-known opposition leaders arrested.

During the Korean War the Americans were protective of Taiwan, assuring the Taiwanese that they would repel any communist attacks. Military outbreaks between China and Taiwan were common in the 1950s and 1960s, with Kinmen subjected to regular shelling. Events such as the August 23rd Artillery War kept Chiang's 'Free China' firmly entrenched in the hearts and minds of anticommunist America.

At the time of the KMT arrival, the Taiwanese had been heavily influenced by decades of Japanese rule, spoke little Mandarin, and by and large felt little kinship with the newly arrived mainland Chinese. They were also accustomed to a higher standard of living than the mainland Chinese and felt an ingrained superiority towards the poorer and less well-educated immigrants, especially soldiers who often came from humble backgrounds. The KMT issued laws requiring all Taiwanese to speak Mandarin, in an attempt to 're-Sinisise' the population. The Taiwanese resented the heavy-handedness of the KMT, and there were various outbreaks of rebellion and clashes with military police.

Though Taiwan prospered during the 1950s and 1960s, her economy becoming one of the richest in Asia, and her population growing to 16 million, big changes were on the horizon as the 1970s began. In 1971 Chiang Kai-shek withdrew the ROC from the UN Security Council after the council's admission of the PRC. In 1979, America, the ROC's staunchest international ally, switched official recognition from the ROC to the PRC. US policy towards Taiwan would now be dictated by the Taiwan Relations Act, which, while promising to protect Taiwan militarily in the case of attack by mainland China, recognised Beijing as the sole capital of a China which included Taiwan.

Chiang Kai-shek died in 1975, his presidential duties taken over by his son, Chiang Ching-kuo. While this administration was marred by a

TAIWAN'S WHITE TERROR

One of the bleakest times in Taiwan's history was the White Terror, when the government started a large-scale campaign to purge the island of political activists during the 1950s. Many who had spoken out against government policies were arrested, charged with attempting to overthrow the government and sentenced to death or life imprisonment. Some who were arrested were indeed political spies but most, it's believed, were unjustly accused. Over 90,000 people were arrested and at least half that number were executed. Taiwanese were not the only targets; a large number of mainland Chinese were arrested or killed. Today Taiwan's White Terror period, though an unpleasant memory, is not forgotten. Green Island's once-notorious political prison, now empty of prisoners, has been transformed into a human-rights museum, serving both as a focal point for mourning and a reminder of the human cost of tyranny.

1987

After 38 years, martial law is lifted in Taiwan, setting the stage for the island's eventual shift from authoritarian rule to democracy.

1988

ROC President Chiang Ching-kuo dies of heart failure at age 78. He is succeeded by Lee Teng-hui, the first native-born president of Taiwan.

1996

Lee Teng-hui re-elected in Taiwan's first fully democratic ROC presidential election, winning 54% of the vote in a three-way race.

1996

The first line of Taipei's Mass Rapid Transit system – which will eventually expand to encompass the entire city and suburbs – begins operating to much fanfare.

THE AUGUST 23RD ARTILLERY WAR

On the morning of 23 August 1958, Beijing, determined to take Kinmen from Chiang Kai-shek's Nationalist army, launched a ferocious bombardment against the island. In just two hours the island was hit with over 42,000 shells. Alarmed, the US acted to defend Kinmen, realising that if it fell, the security of America's 'unsinkable battleship' (as Harry Truman called Taiwan) would be in severe jeopardy. The US sent a shipment of jet fighters and antiaircraft missiles to Taiwan, along with six aircraft carriers.

Communist forces created a tight blockade around Kinmen's beaches and airstrip, preventing any military supplies from getting in. On 7 September the US sent several warships into the Taiwan Strait to escort a convoy of Republic of China (ROC) military-supply ships; the convoy got within 5km of the blockade and was surprised that the communists refused to fire.

Realising that its navy was outclassed (and no doubt wary of factions in America threatening China with nuclear bombs), Beijing offered the nationalists a very odd ceasefire – it would only fire on Kinmen on odd-numbered days. The deal was agreed to, and the Chinese side continued to shell Kinmen throughout September and October only on odd-numbered days. By November tensions had decreased and the bombing stopped, but not before nearly half a million shells had struck Kinmen, killing and wounding thousands of civilians and soldiers.

scandal involving the assassination of an overseas Taiwanese professor on US soil (an event which became the basis for the book and film *Formosa Betrayed*), the younger Chiang was a pragmatist, and his rule over Taiwan was softer than that of his father; in an effort to improve relations with native Taiwanese, Chiang allowed more Taiwanese to take up political positions. The late 1970s saw increasing political dissent in Taiwan. One of the most noteworthy uprisings of the late martial-law period occurred in December 1979.

Considered a turning point in Taiwan's shift from authoritarian rule to democracy, the Kaohsiung Incident occurred when editors of *Meilidao,* a publication often critical of the government, organised a rally to celebrate International Human Rights Day. The day before the rally, two organisers were arrested and beaten by police when they were caught handing out promotional flyers. On the day of the rally, scuffles broke out between police and protestors and the situation turned violent, changing from a peaceful event into a full-scale riot. Eight of the organisers were arrested, including Taiwan's future vice-president Annette Lu. Among the lawyers who represented the organisers was future Taiwanese president Chen Shui-bian. Though it was a short-term

1999

Taiwan is hit by a massive earthquake measuring 7.3 on the Richter scale. Centred in Nantou County, the quake causes massive damage, loss of life and injury throughout the island.

2000

Former Taipei Mayor Chen Shui-bian is elected ROC president, winning 39.3% of the popular vote in a three-way race, ending over 50 years of Kuomintang (KMT) rule in Taiwan.

2000

In an early sign of thawing relations between Taiwan and China, the 'Three Small Links' commence, opening limited trade between China and the Taiwanese-held islands of Kinmen and Matsu.

2003

Efforts at containing the SARS epidemic are hampered by the refusal of the People's Republic of China (PRC) to allow Taiwan to participate in the World Health Organization's anti-SARS effort.

defeat for the democracy advocates, the violence brought increasing support for democratic reforms. Public sentiment eventually forced the KMT to make political concessions. In 1986, with martial law still in effect, Taiwan's first opposition party, the Democratic Progressive Party (DPP), was formed. Chiang Ching-kuo, surprisingly, did not shut the party down, resulting in a large number of DPP candidates being elected to office, and culminating in the official formation of Taiwan's first opposition party.

In 1987 Chiang Ching-kuo announced the end of martial law. The following year Chiang passed away and his vice-president, Lee Teng-hui, became the first Taiwanese-born ROC president. For Taiwan, a new era had begun.

MARTIAL LAW

2009's *Formosa Betrayed* is a Hollywood film dealing with politics, intrigue and murder during the waning days of Taiwan's martial-law era.

The Post-Martial-Law Period Begins

With Taiwan all but excluded from the international community and China growing economically and militarily, Lee Teng-hui had his work cut out for him. Early in his presidency, Lee paid lip service to the 'One China policy', but as the years progressed he developed a more pro-independence stance. Mistrustful of Lee, China launched a series of missiles only 25km away from the Taiwanese coast in 1995. But the scare tactics backfired, and Taiwan re-elected Lee Teng-hui in open elections the following year.

Sensing that the 'stick' approach had failed, China switched to carrots, and in 1998 offered to lift the ban on shipping and direct flights. The offer was rebuffed by Lee, who incensed China even further the next year by declaring openly his belief that China and Taiwan, as two separate countries, should enjoy 'state to state' relations.

In 2000, with Taiwan's presidential elections looming on the horizon, there was much cross-strait sabre rattling. Despite this, DPP candidate Chen Shui-bian won in a three-party race, ending 54 years of KMT rule in Taiwan. Though the election signalled pro-independence, Chen was widely seen as a disaster by Beijing. The newly elected Chen soon softened his stance somewhat, declaring in his inauguration speech that the status quo would be maintained as long as China did not attempt to take Taiwan by force. But Beijing was hardly won over by Chen's words, demanding a firm commitment to the 'One China policy'.

Chen found himself between a rock and a hard place, unable to please either his supporters or his detractors. As a result, cross-strait relations stalled during Chen's first term, with the only glimmer of improvement being the opening of limited trade and travel between China and Taiwan's offshore islands. Though often overshadowed by the more high-profile presidential election, Taiwan's legislative election of 2001 was equally revolutionary, reducing the KMT (albeit temporarily) to

2004

Chen Shui-bian is re-elected by the slimmest of margins; the day before the election both president and vice-president are mildly wounded by the same bullet in a botched assassination attempt.

2004

Taipei 101 opens in Taipei's Xinyi district. Designed to resemble a graceful bamboo stalk, the building is also wind- and earthquake-resistant. It holds the 'world's tallest building' title for five years.

CRAIG FERGUSON

» Taipei 101 towers over Taiwan's capital

LIVING HISTORY: A NEW TAIWAN IS BORN

Democracy Plaza/Chiang Kai-shek Memorial, Taipei Originally constructed as a solemn continuation of Chiang's cult of personality postmortem, the park has instead become a place where Taipeiers come to play.

Ximending Shopping District, Taipei Brightly lit plazas filled with the young and trendy, alleyways offering tattoo and piercing parlours, and cafes popular with Taiwan's gay and lesbian communities show how far the country has progressed from authoritarian dictatorship to liberal democracy.

minority party status in a legislature they'd once controlled with an iron grip.

Chen's re-election in 2004, by the slimmest of margins, was surrounded by strange circumstances to say the least; an assassination attempt on the day before the election resulted in both president and vice-president being mildly wounded, both by the same bullet. Some felt the event was staged for sympathy. China, fearing that Chen's re-election would embolden pro-independence factions, caused cross-strait tensions to be ratcheted to their highest level in years with the issuing of an 'anti-secession law'. The law, in brief, codified China's long-standing threat to attack Taiwan should the island's leaders declare independence. Though Beijing's move was protested by massive rallies throughout Taiwan, cross-strait tension seems to have abated somewhat since, and there's been little outside of the usual sabre rattling for the past few years.

Richard C Bush's *Untying the Knot: Making Peace in the Taiwan Strait* provides a number of interesting insights into the difficulties inherent in the Taiwan–China conflict.

In 2006 a number of interesting political developments occurred, as two major figures from Taiwan's 'old guard' made much-touted visits to mainland China. Other major political stories of 2006 and 2007 were the changing of names of various state-run departments and buildings to incorporate the word 'Taiwan' instead of 'China', and the large-scale removal of thousands of statues of former dictator Chiang Kai-shek from many public spaces in Taiwan. Talk of removing Chiang's statue from one of Taipei's most famous landmarks, Chiang Kai-shek Memorial Hall (p47), came to naught, but the name of the park itself was changed to Democracy Plaza (though the MRT stations still say 'Chiang Kai-shek Memorial Hall'. All in all, 2007 was for Taiwan a year of near-total political gridlock thanks to a number of high-profile corruption scandals involving major figures from both the KMT and the DPP.

These scandals would prove to be a foreshadowing of things to come in the post-Chen era.

2005

China enacts an 'anti-secession law', formalising its commitment to use military force if Taiwan declares independence. Protests against the law draw huge crowds around the island.

2006

After winning 19 games with a 3.63 earned run average (ERA) for the New York Yankees in US major league baseball, Taiwanese phenomenon Wang Chien-ming wins the Starting Pitcher of the Year award.

2006

In the largest move towards Taiwan localisation and 'de-Chiangification' to date, Chiang Kai-shek International Airport is renamed Taoyuan International Airport.

2007

Chiang Kai-shek Memorial Hall is controversially renamed the National Taiwan Democracy Memorial Hall. A compromise sees the hall name restored, with the plaza renamed Liberty.

2008 & Beyond – The Return of the KMT

2008 did not open well for the ruling DPP as the opposition KMT won a decisive victory in legislative elections held in January. These elections – held just two months before the presidential election, an election in which embattled president Chen Shui-bian was barred by term limits from running – would auger a total return to power by the party whose political death many Taiwan-watchers had pronounced just a few years before. The causes of the DPP's legislative defeat are complex. Many Taiwanese blamed the DPP for poor stewardship of Taiwan's economy, anaemic throughout much of the Chen years in the face of an uncertain global economy. Others worried that Chen, by coming closer to officially acknowledging Taiwan's status as a de-facto independent state than any other president before him, had gone too far in provoking confrontation in the Taiwan Strait. The world was a vastly different place than it had been in 1995, when China's military posturing towards Taiwan resulted in the US sending warships to the area to make clear US commitment to maintaining the status quo. But in 2008, with the US economically weakened and weary from long years of involvement in two wars, the idea that Taiwan's most powerful ally would play knight in shining armour in a cross-straits conflict with a China that was steadily rising in power (both militarily and economically) was far from certain.

HISTORY IN COMICS

A History of Taiwan in Comics – http://edu.ocac.gov.tw/local/history_of_taiwan/index.htm

Although members of both parties were implicated in ongoing and complicated scandals involving corruption and money laundering, the fact that President Chen – easily the highest-profile DPP member – was himself under investigation certainly did nothing to help the DPP's legislative chances. Following the KMT legislative victory, President Chen Shui-bian resigned as chairman of the DPP.

Two months later Ma Ying-jeou won a decisive victory, winning 58% of the vote against DPP candidate Frank Hsieh. Ma's platform promised a radical departure from the Chen years, especially concerning cross-strait relations. Among the proposals of his candidacy were that Taiwan and China should form a common market, that direct air-links

LIVING HISTORY: POST-CHEN TAIWAN

Taipei 101, National Palace Museum, Sun Moon Lake A visit to any of these famous Taiwanese tourist spots, now nearly almost always crowded with visitors from mainland China, will give you an idea of just how much cross-straits relations are warming up.

Taipei Zoo Is reunification between Taiwan and China already in progress? Some say that the Taipei Zoo's newest residents, a pair of pandas called 'Tuan Tuan' and 'Yuan Yuan' (which together mean 'Reunion') are a sign that such a reunion is already underway.

2007

Taiwan's High Speed Rail (HSR) begins operation to much fanfare and publicity. With speeds of up to 350 km/h, the HSR cuts rail travel from Taipei to Kaohsiung to 90 minutes.

CRAIG FERGUSON

» Taiwan's High Speed Rail

2006

Following a series of scandals involving the Chen Shui-bian administration, one-time Chen ally Shih Ming-teh leads a massive rally calling for the president's resignation.

2008

Former Taipei mayor and long-time KMT favourite Ma Ying-jeou is elected president of Taiwan, regaining control of the executive branch after eight years of Democratic Progressive Party (DPP) rule.

across the straits should be normalised, and that the maintenance of the status quo between Taiwan and China – neither independence nor reunification – was the wisest path to follow.

After stepping down as president, Chen Shui-bian immediately lost presidential immunity; within six months of losing this immunity, the former president was arrested on charges of money laundering, bribery and embezzlement of government funds, charges which Chen has steadfastly denied. Chen was sentenced to life imprisonment in September 2009, charges which were reduced to 20 years in June 2010. Many supporters of Chen maintain that the charges against him were fabricated, and that the former president's imprisonment is a deliberate attempt to frighten supporters of Taiwan independence into political silence. Current president Ma Ying-jeou has remained largely silent on the issue of his predecessor (and one-time political rival's) incarceration.

Denny Roy's *Taiwan: A Political History* is a very readable and balanced account of Taiwan's progress towards democracy.

Since 2008 tensions between Taiwan and mainland China have eased markedly as the KMT government led by President Ma – an avowed opponent of Taiwan independence and widely viewed as being conciliatory towards Beijing – has taken steps to bring the two sides closer together. Regularly scheduled flights from Taiwan to cities throughout mainland China began in 2008, and are now so common as to no longer be noteworthy. Tourism from mainland China is now equally common (though still regulated), and on any given day a large percentage of visitors to Taiwan's famous spots such as Sun Moon Lake, the National Palace Museum and Taipei 101 are likely to be mainlanders on group travel packages.

Not long into Ma's first term, however, many in the now-minority DPP are claiming that the KMT is solidifying its rule through the use of political repression, citing a spate of arrests of a number of DPP officials on charges of corruption. Only time will tell whether this heralds a return to Taiwan's predemocracy days.

2008
In a further indication of warming cross-Strait ties, regularly scheduled direct flights between Taiwan and mainland China begin.

2009
Bringing high winds and record rainfall, Typhoon Morakot causes severe damage to the island, particularly in the southern counties. The storm kills hundreds and causes billions of dollars in damage.

2009
Former president Chen Shui-bian is sentenced to life imprisonment (later reduced to 20 years) on corruption charges; supporters of the former president claim the charges are politically motivated.

2010
President Ma Ying-jeou signs the Economic Cooperation Framework Agreement, a controversial trade agreement between the PRC and ROC governments, lowering economic barriers between the two sides.

The People of Taiwan

Hardly Homogeneous Han

The casual academic might be forgiven for assuming that Taiwan has only slightly more ethnic diversity than a Korean soap opera. Technically speaking, it's true that 98% of Taiwan's population is made up of Han Chinese with the other 2% being of Taiwanese aboriginal descent. But does this statistic define Taiwan's cultural diversity (or lack thereof)? Consider the number of dialects spoken over the public address system of the Taipei Metro:

'Xia yi jian shi...' is the first thing you'll hear as the train leaves the platform, followed by a few syllables ending in the word *jian* (station). And then you'll hear it again, in a dialect that to even the untrained ear sounds different. And then you'll hear it a third time in yet another dialect. Finally, the announcement will be repeated in English.

Just why does the capital city of a statistically homogeneous country need three dialects? And what are these dialects anyway?

The answer to the first question is that Taiwan is a place whose ethnic diversity is belied by the numbers found on a demographic pie chart or table (even our own; see p220). And the answer to the second question will give you an idea as to who these ethnic groups are.

The dialect of the first announcement is standard Mandarin (Guóyǔ), the same language spoken by a billion-plus people across the strait in the People's Republic of China. It was the language of Chiang Kai-shek, and the primary tongue of the two million or so Chinese citizens – nationalist soldiers, their dependents and assorted others – fleeing mainland China after the defeat of the Nationalists by the communists in 1949. Collectively, this group might be referred to as Wàishěngrén (People from Outside the Province). Though far from a majority, these Wàishěngrén held the reins of power for much of Taiwan's postwar history.

Just why does the capital city of a statistically homogeneous country need three dialects? And what are these dialects anyway?

The second dialect is Taiwanese (Táiyǔ). This dialect is a kissing cousin to what you'll hear spoken directly across the strait in China's Fujian province. This is no accident, as it's from this part of the Chinese mainland that many of the earliest Han Chinese settlers came. The descendants of these early pioneers, primarily Fujianese fleeing their home province during the Ming and Qing dynasties, form the largest percentage of Taiwan's current population. This group, if asked to provide a phrase that might differentiate them from fellow Taiwanese of more recent mainland descent, might call themselves Běnshěngrén.

The third announcement is spoken in the Hakka dialect (Hak-kā ngin). Between 14% to 20% of Taiwanese are Hakka, though over the years much intermarrying has made it difficult to determine exact numbers. Though genetically a subgroup of the Han Chinese, the Hakka have fiercely maintained their own customs, language and culture despite a diaspora that's seen the group migrate throughout China and Asia. Some of the earliest nonaboriginal settlers in Taiwan were Hakka, and major centres of Hakka population in Taiwan can be found in Hsinchu, Miaoli and Pingtung.

The last announcement, naturally, is provided for your benefit, and that of anyone else on the train who might not understand Guó-yǔ, Táiyǔ or Hak-kā ngin.

'Next Stop...Taipei Main Station!'

Taiwan's Indigenous Tribes

They only represent 2% of Taiwan's overall population, and you won't hear any of their many languages coming over the Taipei Metro's public-address system. Nonetheless, Taiwan's aboriginal groups continue to play a crucial role in the shaping of Taiwan's distinct identity. It's not at all unusual, for example, to run into a taxi driver of apparent Han lineage in Taipei wearing a traditional aboriginal hat. If you ask him, he'll tell you proudly that his great-grandmother is a member of the Atayal tribe, making him one-eighth Atayal himself. The fact is that many of Taiwan's Běnshěngrěn have some aboriginal ancestry.

With a few exceptions, most of Taiwan's indigenous communities are found in the mountains or along the eastern coast. Nearly all aboriginal people speak Mandarin in addition to their own tribal languages. Some villages offer Disneyesque re-creations of 'traditional' tribal life and others are hardly distinguishable from any other small Taiwanese town.

While the lines are blurred, in recent years more attention has been paid to providing more precise numbers for Taiwan's aboriginal groups. One of the results of this has been an increase in the number of 'recognised' tribal groups (that is, recognised by the Taiwan government), who as of this writing count 14 official tribes. Readers should keep in mind that the identification, naming and population counts of the indigenous tribes of Taiwan enjoys spirited ongoing debate, and that the numbers and classifications in the boxed text on p330 reflect only one census conducted in 2010.

TAIWAN'S ABORIGINES

One of the most comprehensive websites on Taiwan's aboriginal peoples is www.atayal.org. In addition to providing detailed information on the history and customs of Taiwan's indigenous peoples, the website also offers links to volunteer opportunities in aboriginal villages around Taiwan.

Taiwan's Women: Holding Up Half the Sky

Taiwanese society is about as sexually equitable as any in Asia. The Republic of China (ROC) constitution forbids discrimination on the base of gender, and women are found in the upper echelons of many companies and businesses. In education there are a few interesting gender gaps: while graduating classes of both high schools and universities tend to be evenly split, graduate programs skew heavily on the male side, with roughly three of five masters students being men, and only one in three doctorate students being women.

An interesting byproduct of the strong role that women play in Taiwanese society is an increasing reluctance by many women in Taiwan to conform to what's been for centuries considered the traditional role for them set up by society, namely that of mother, caretaker and homemaker. A significant percentage of Taiwanese women, unwilling to give up their independence and careers in order to raise a family, have simply opted out, choosing to remain unwed, or to marry much later in life than their sisters on the Chinese mainland or in other Asian societies. This has caused Taiwan to have the lowest birthrate in Asia, the lowest in the world by many statistics. This low birthrate makes itself felt in various ways, from concerns over a future labour shortage to a decline in the number of teaching jobs available on the island (where just 10 years ago being a Westerner whose mother tongue was English was a near-sure ticket to a teaching job).

The National Psyche

One of the first things that people usually mention after visiting the island is the friendliness of the Taiwanese people themselves. A Western visitor standing on a train station trying to decipher the train schedule can pretty much take it for granted that someone will approach them within minutes asking, 'Can I help you?'

'Friendly' is often used to describe the Taiwanese, often followed by 'relaxed'. The latter is especially true when compared with Taiwan's close neighbours (physically and to some extent culturally), Japan and South Korea, where people are often described as 'industrious', 'polite' and 'reserved' – but rarely 'relaxed'.

Why is this? It's interesting to compare the national psyche of the three countries. Economically the three have followed roughly similar trajectories (low-tech agrarian to high-tech industrial) to roughly similar demographics featuring largely middle-class populations. Though dissimilar in many ways, the 20th century was filled with periods of trauma for all three nations. South Korea, like Taiwan, bears the scars of foreign colonialism, oppressive dictatorship, military occupation and the always-looming spectre of catastrophic war. The Japanese psyche is scarred by military defeat and occupation.

But Taiwan, which endured the shackles of colonialism, decades of brutal martial law and dictatorship, continual low-level threat of invasion and the added ignominy of existing in the strange political limbo of being an officially politically unrecognised entity has managed to

TAIWAN'S TRIBES

TRIBE	REGION	POPULATION
Amis	throughout Taiwan, and predominantly Ami towns and villages on the east coast, from Taitung to Hualien	184,820
Paiwan	Kaosiung, south of Pingtung	88,805
Atayal	in the hills and mountains of northern Taiwan, Wulai	80,460
Bunun	originally from the central and southern mountains of the island	51,770
Truku	around Hualien, on Taiwan's central east coast	26,065
Rukai	Taiwan's southeast coast	11,950
Puyuma	Taiwan's southeast coast	11,975
Tsou	Kaohsiung, north of Chiayi	6760
Sediq	mostly in Nantou County	6740
Saisiyat	in the hills around Hsinchu and Miaoli	5965
Yami (also known as Dao)	Lanyu island	3780
Kavalan	Ilan	230
Thao	around Sun Moon Lake	700
Sakizaya	around Hualien	5000

A 'TYPICAL HAKKA FAMILY HOME'

In the mid-1990s I lived with the Yeh family, Hakkas living in a medium-sized village just a stone's throw away from Hsinchu Science Park, one of Taiwan's major computer and high-tech manufacturing centres. The Yehs lived in a four-storey house, part of a chain of row houses that stretched fairly far in either direction along the town's main street. Half of the 1st floor was taken up by an indoor garage, which had a prominently displayed aquarium filled with goldfish. According to feng shui principles, goldfish bring luck. The garage was also home to the family dog Lai-fu, whose name meant 'Come Fortune'. The garage also had two nice cars, three or four motorcycles and some bicycles for the kids. Lai-fu and the fish, it seemed, were bringing fortune, thus earning their keep.

Behind the garage was the living room where at any given time friends, family and extended family might be found drinking tea, eating sunflower seeds or otherwise just hanging out. The centrepiece of the living room was an expensive, beautifully ornate wooden table carved from a single piece of wood. Next to the living room was a kitchen in which meals were cooked but almost never eaten. Instead, Yeh Tai-tai ('Mr Yeh's Wife', which was how I always addressed the family matriarch) and Mr Yeh's mother (who I called Ayi, or Auntie) brought the meals they cooked into the kitchen of the house next door through a side door that was never closed. This was the home of Mr Yeh's brother and his wife. Their kitchen was equipped with a large round table with a lazy Susan. There was always a pot of soup on sister-in-law's stove, as well as a rice cooker filled with rice.

Grandfather and Grandmother lived in an apartment somewhere behind the two kitchens. They were only home around half the year; the rest of the time they were off travelling around the world, a popular pursuit for Taiwanese retirees of decent physical and economic health.

The 2nd floor was where the parents and children lived. The Yehs had the idea that renting a room to a foreigner would be a good way for their youngest son to practise his English, though the boy, called Jem, wound up being my principal Chinese-language tutor instead.

The 3rd floor contained the bedroom of the Yeh's oldest sons, who only came home for the holidays, and a parlour with a folded-up ping-pong table and disused snooker table that Mr Yeh had bought some years ago when snooker had been a passing craze in Taiwan.

The 4th floor was divided into two sections. In the back was the little apartment I lived in, a simple affair. But the front was the most beautiful room in the house, containing an outdoor garden, complete with a tiled fish pond and dozens of plants, and a large, open room with an ornately tiled ceiling, an incense brazier and a large mahogany table pressed against the northern wall.

This was the shrine of Yeh Ken-fu, the grandfather of Mr Yeh. It was here that the family came on holidays to pay their respects. Most of the time it was only me, the foreign boarder, who spent any time on the 4th floor, except on weekends when Mrs Yeh would come upstairs to clean and dust, and very early in the predawn hours, when Mr Yeh's father would come up to tend to his own father's shrine.

Joshua Samuel Brown, Lonely Planet author

produce a population of 21-odd-million citizens whose disposition could be summed up with the word 'sunny'.

Consider the possibility that the same factors that have brought about Taiwan's unique geopolitical position may also have had a hand in shaping the disposition of its people. Taiwanese people are painfully aware of their island's diplomatic isolation, and this lack of 'official' international recognition is a big part of the Taiwanese psyche.

This may be part of why Taiwanese people are so genial. By the very act of applying for a visa, or of passing through customs at Taoyuan

International Airport, a foreign visitor is recognising (in some sense at least) Taiwan's legitimacy to control its own borders.

There's another possible way in which Taiwan's curious diplomatic situation may have helped to shape the disposition of its people. Although the USA does not technically recognise Taiwan as a sovereign nation, it has pledged to come to Taiwan's aid in the event of military conflict. Like Japan and Korea, Taiwan enjoys the 'protection' of the world's most powerful military force. However, unlike either of these nations, Taiwan has long been free from the obligation of having to quarter American soldiers. Cultural misunderstanding (and occasionally worse) involving foreign soldiers has long been a source of irritation, fear and hostility from Seoul to Okinawa. In Taiwan, however, the curse of political isolation may have spit up a gift. No Western visitor to Taipei need learn how to say 'I'm a tourist, not a soldier' in Mandarin.

Perhaps both of these theories are mostly hogwash. Maybe Taiwanese people are friendly because of a combination of good weather and a mixture of Buddhist philosophy. Or maybe there is something in the theory of collective national hunger for recognition from the world community, a sentiment that filters down only partly through the lips of people on the street. Perhaps when a Taiwanese person is especially nice to a Western visitor (as often happens), following some random act of kindness with the commonly spoken words, 'Welcome to Taiwan', they're only telling part of the story.

Maybe what they're really saying is simply *'Thank you for realising that we're here'.*

Taiwan's Musicians – Voices of Formosa

We began this chapter using language to illustrate Taiwan's cultural diversity and make-up. It feels fitting, therefore, to end it on a musical note. After all, what is music if not a language in and of itself, and what better way to project an image of a people than by offering a brief introduction to a few of the musicians that represent Taiwan at home and abroad?

Perhaps the most internationally well-known Taiwanese musician is A-mei (阿妹; Ā Mèi), a singer-songwriter from Taiwan's Puyuma tribe. With 18 albums to her name, A-mei is among Taiwan's most prolific pop singers. In the mid-2000s A-mei's career was flavoured with cross-Strait controversy after the singer performed the ROC national anthem at the first inauguration of newly elected president Chen Shui-bian, resulting in a short-lived ban on her performing (or her music being played at all) in China. A-mei's face has graced the cover of magazines such as *Time* and *Newsweek,* making her among the most recognised Taiwanese entertainers in the world.

Web presence of Taiwan's most beloved death-metal band, www.chthonic.tw, complete with photos, music videos and tour info.

Equally as well known – certainly in the Chinese-speaking world – is Wu Bai (伍佰; Wǔ Bǎi), Taiwan's 'King of Live Music'. An excellent guitarist and lyricist, Wu Bai regularly plays to sold-out arenas both in Taiwan and internationally with his band China Blue. Those who understand Mandarin or Taiwanese (the artist records equally in both languages) may detect a certain amount of pathos in Wu Bai's lyrics, unusual for Asian pop in general. Wu Bai is also the face of a number of Taiwanese products, including Hey Song Soda and Taiwan Beer – you're as likely to see his face on advertisements on buses around Taipei as you are to hear his music being played in a taxi.

One Taiwanese group unlikely to become a household name anytime soon (or be asked to sell soft drinks, for that matter) has nonetheless managed to carve an interesting niche for themselves as a spokesband for Taiwanese interests. Death-metal band ChthoniC (閃靈樂團/Shǎnlíng Yuètuán) has made headlines over the past few years, touring

WHAT IS TAIWAN HIP HOP?

You don't need to understand Chinese to realise that Kou Chou Ching doesn't fit the mould of the stereotypical Western hip-hop-aping Asian rap act. The Taipei-based hip-hop band has been playing clubs, festivals and events around Taiwan since 2003, mixing politically charged lyrics in Mandarin, Hoklo (Taiwanese) and Hakka with sampled flavours drawn from the far corners of Taiwanese musical history. Kou Chou Ching's MC Fan Jiang spoke a bit about Taiwanese hip hop, music and identity:

'Like everywhere else in the world, hip hop is getting more popular in Taiwan. A lot of Taiwanese hip-hop artists start by mixing music on computers, then mixing in various Western influences, including of course old- and new-school rap from African-American hip-hop artists.

Kou Chou Ching has tried to take it in a different direction, aiming for a more clearly Taiwanese-flavoured hip-hop music, drawing influences not primarily from the West but from the music of our home, from traditional Taiwanese music; Kou Chou Ching songs sample Beiguan and Nanguan, Taiwan opera, Hakka Ba-yin and mountain songs, south Chinese Huamei Diao, with some Beijing opera and classical Chinese music thrown into the mix.

Our language and lyrics reflect the new generation of Taiwan, people who have transcended so-called 'ethnic differences'. Our songs attempt to realise this desire for harmony among Taiwan's diverse ethnic groups. One of our songs is called 'Your name is Taiwanese'. The word 'Taiwan' is sung many times throughout this song. This repetition, the beat and lyrics combined remind listeners to use their hearts when considering their roots.

These days many people forget their roots. Parents send their children to study English, but where do the children learn to speak their mother tongue? Kou Chou Ching songs are about reminding people that it doesn't matter what language you speak at home; if you grew up eating Taiwanese rice, drinking Taiwanese water, then you are a Taiwanese person.'

Check out Kou Chou Ching's music and performance schedule online at www.kou.com.tw.

the globe with their own unique brand of heavy metal, which incorporates both metal and traditional Taiwanese instruments and influences. Lyrically, the band incorporates elements of classical Mandarin, Taiwanese and aboriginal languages, and some Japanese. The band's political views have caused them to be banned from playing on the Chinese mainland.

Taiwan has a number of home-grown drama and dance troupes. The best-known internationally is the Cloud Gate Dance Company, founded in the early 1970s by Lin Hwai-min. Combining modern dance techniques with Chinese opera, Cloud Gate's early works were based on stories and legends from Chinese classical literature, while their more recent works have tended to explore Taiwanese identity. The company tours most of the year, both domestically and internationally. Check its website, www.cloudgate.org.tw, for performance schedules.

Another group pushing the boundaries of world music while remaining true to its Taiwanese roots is A Moving Sound. Mixing elements of modern dance, taichi and deep-breath work, the four-piece group combines Eastern and Western instruments, vocals and dance styles to create a sound that is both ancient and modern, at once universal and distinctly Taiwanese. Like Cloud Gate, A Moving Sound tours internationally for part of the year. Check its website, www.amovingsound.com, for performance schedules and updates.

Religion in Taiwan

Introduction

A funny thing happened to Taiwan on the way to its future. Instead of losing its religion as economic growth, mobility and education brought it into the First World, the very opposite happened. There are more Buddhists today, for example, than ever before: in fact, you'd be hard-pressed to find a larger (per capita) monastic population in all of Asia.

But the old Taoist gods, and the old acts of worship, have hung on, too. When a modern Mr Wang is troubled he is as likely to burn incense and joss paper, toss moon blocks *(bwah bwey)* and pray at the altar of a favourite deity as his ancestor was. Of course, before asking Baosheng Dadi to help cure his glaucoma, Wang will take the medicine his doctor prescribed knowing full well which one is more efficacious. But if he is cured, it's still the temple that will get the fat donation.

At the Dizang Temple in Xinzhuang, Taipei County, thousands of people come yearly to file indictments with Bodhisattva Dizang against people who they believe have wronged them in some way. A bit of an indictment against the legal system, too, we would say.

Perhaps the biggest change has been the way the media, feeding the public demand for religious content, has made nationwide stars of regional temple cults and festivals. Religious associations understand this very well, and several Buddhist and Taoist groups now control their own image by running independent TV stations. Probably only in the USA, with its tradition of fiery evangelists spreading the word of God on TV, can you find such a potent fusion of technology with tradition.

All of which is to say that the more things change in Taiwan, the more they stay the same. No matter what form it's received in or propagated, religion in Taiwan continues to foster a sense of shared culture and identity, and to provide the individual with satisfying rites of passage and intimations of the divine.

A Brief History

The early immigrants to Taiwan faced conditions not unlike the settlers in the New World did: a harsh environment, hostile natives, a lack of wives and a host of devastating diseases. Faith in the local cults of their home village in China was vital in forming new and strong community bonds in Taiwan.

During the late Qing dynasty into Japanese times, a period of increasing wealth and mobility, many temples began to expand their influence beyond the village level. Famous pilgrim sites arose, and Matsu started her rise to pan-Taiwan deity status.

The Kuomintang (KMT) at first tolerated local religion but then attempted to both suppress and coopt it, fearing that it was at best superstitious nonsense and at worst a rallying point for Taiwanese independence. They were largely unsuccessful and even before the lifting of martial law had abandoned trying to direct local culture.

Three Faiths (Plus One)

The Taiwanese approach to spirituality is eclectic and not particularly dogmatic; many Taiwanese will combine elements from various religions to suit their needs rather than rigidly adhering to one particular spiritual path. Religion in Taiwan is largely about an individual relationship to a deity, dead spirit or even spiritual leader. Many of the gods, customs and festivals have little to do with any of the three official religions and are sometimes described as part of an amorphous folk faith. But don't expect anyone to ever tell you they are a believer in this faith: instead, they will say they are Taoist or Buddhist.

Confucianism

Confucian values and beliefs (Rújiā Sīxiǎng) form the foundation of Chinese culture. The central theme of Confucian doctrine is the conduct of human relationships for the attainment of harmony and overall good for society. Society, Confucius taught, comprises five relationships: ruler and subject, husband and wife, father and son, elder and younger, and friends. Deference to authority and devotion to family are paramount.

The close bonds between family and friends are one of the most admirable attributes of Chinese culture, a lasting legacy of Confucian teachings. But Confucianism's continuing influence on modern Taiwan society is often overstated. The effects of modernisation, which include greater mobility, mass education (for both males and females) and democratic elections (which allow ordinary citizens to make demands of their rulers) are all centrifugal forces acting to push society away from a simple adherence to Confucian values.

Wonder why temples offer worshippers so many statues of the same god? Well, different statues can play different roles. In the Tainan Matsu Temple, the Great Matsu statue oversees the local neighbourhood; a second watches over the internal affairs of the temple; yet another is a helper of the Great Matsu. Each is said to have a different personality and be receptive to different requests.

Taoism

Taoism (Dàojiào) is easily the most confusing facet of Chinese culture, consisting of a vast assembly of philosophical texts, popular folk legends, various organised sects, a panoply of gods and goddesses numbering in the thousands, alchemists, healers, hermits, martial artists, spirit-mediums, alcoholic immortals, quantum physicists, New Age gurus…and the list goes on. Controversial, paradoxical and – like the Tao itself – impossible to pin down, it is a natural complement to rigid Confucian order and responsibility.

Taoism began with Lao-Tzu's *Tao Te Ching*. Its central theme is that of the Tao – the unknowable, indescribable cosmic force of the universe. Organised Taoism came into being in the 2nd century at which time there was an emphasis on mystical practices to cultivate immortality. Taoism reached a high point during the Tang dynasty when there was a fierce (but productive) battle with Buddhism and when many branches became increasingly tied to popular religion.

In modern Taiwan, Taoist priests still play a vital role in the worship of deities, the opening of temples, the exorcising of bad luck (and sometimes illness) and the presiding over funeral services.

For a more thorough look at Taoism, including the myriad deities, see the Daoist Encyclopedia at http://en.daoinfo.org/wiki/Main_Page.

Buddhism

Buddhism (Fójiào) came to Taiwan in the 17th century with the Ming loyalist Cheng Cheng-kung but there were few orthodox associations until Japanese times. Many Japanese were devout Buddhists and supported the growth of the religion during their occupation.

In 1949 thousands of monks, fearing religious persecution in China, fled to Taiwan with the Nationalists. Under martial law, all Buddhist groups were officially organised under the Buddhist Association of the Republic of China (BAROC). By the 1960s, however, independent associations were emerging, and it is these maverick groups that have had the most influence in modern times.

Buddhism in Taiwan is largely Chan or Pure Land, though few groups are strictly orthodox. The main Buddhist associations are Foguangshan (the Light of Buddha), Dharma Drum, Tzu Chi and Chung Tai Chan.

A god's ability to grant requests is critical to popularity. In the past he or she might be asked for protection against plague. Today it could be advice on which job to take; help passing an important test; or even, as we saw once on a prayer card at Donglong Temple, that the young believer grow to over 160cm tall.

The Bodhisattva Guanyin, the embodiment of mercy, is the most popular Buddhist deity in Taiwan.

Folk Religion

Beliefs about ancestor worship permeate almost every aspect of Chinese philosophy. Most homes in Taiwan have their own altar, where family members pay their respects to deceased relatives by burning incense and providing offerings.

Closely tied to ancestor worship is popular or folk religion, which consists of an immense celestial bureaucracy of gods and spirits, from the lowly but important kitchen god *(zào jūn)* to the celestial emperor himself *(tiāndì* or *shàngdì)*. Like the imperial bureaucrats on earth, each god has a particular role to fulfil and can be either promoted or demoted depending on his or her job performance. Offerings to the gods consist not only of food and incense, but also opera performances, birthday parties (to which other local gods are invited) and even processions around town.

Other Faiths

Presbyterian are few in number but are politically influential. Aboriginals tend to be overwhelmingly Catholic or of other Christian faiths; church steeples are a common fixture in villages as are ageing nuns and priests from Europe.

In addition Taiwan has a small number of Tibetan Buddhists, Muslims, and a number of followers of cults such as Falun Gong, Yiguan Dao and those that occasionally arise around a single person.

RÉNJIĀN FÓJIÀO: THIS-WORLDLY BUDDHISM

You won't get far understanding the Buddhist influence on modern Taiwanese society if you simply try to grasp doctrine and schools. In the past 40 years a special form of socially active Buddhism (Rénjiān Fójiào; this-worldly Buddhism) has emerged to redefine what that religion means to its practitioners. Rénjiān Fójiào draws inspiration from the thoughts of the early-20th-century reformist monk Taixu in China, but has been completely localised by masters such as Chengyan of Tzu Chi (see boxed text, p165).

A central tenet of Rénjiān Fójiào is that one finds salvation not by escaping in a monastery but by bringing Buddhist compassion into ordinary life and adapting the dharma to the conditions of modern life. Taiwanese Buddhist groups stress humanitarian work, and teach that traditional beliefs, such as filial piety, should be expanded to encompass respect and consideration for society at large. With a combined de-emphasis on ritual and a central role for lay followers to take in the organisations, Taiwanese Buddhist groups have made themselves the religion of choice for middle-class urbanites and professionals. The older folk gods, on the other hand, remain more typically attractive to the working class.

The Main Folk & Taoist Deities

Those outlined here are just a few of the dozens, even hundreds, of folk and Taoist gods you will come across in temples. Among the most important deities in the south, the Wang Yeh (the Royal Lords), who number in the hundreds, were either once real historical figures (such as Koxinga) or plague demons. Today they are regarded as general protectors.

Matsu (Empress of Heaven) is the closest thing to a pan-deity in Taiwan (see boxed text, p201). She is worshipped as a general protector.

GuanGong, or Guandi, is the so-called God of War, but better thought of as a patron of knights and those who live by a righteous code. More generally he is worshipped as a god of wealth and literature. He is easy to recognise by his red face, beard and halberd.

Baosheng Dadi (the Great Emperor Who Preserves Life) is the god of medicine. He played an important role for early immigrants faced with a host of diseases and plagues.

The top god in the Taoist pantheon, the Jade Emperor fulfils the role of emperor of heaven. In Taiwan he is usually represented by a plaque rather than a statue.

The City God (protector of cities), also officially the Lord of Walls and Moats, is also the moral accountant of the world, recording people's good and bad deeds for their final reckoning. People pray to him for protection and wealth.

Tudi Gong, the Earth god (and minor god of wealth) has the lowest ranking in the Taoist pantheon. As governor of local areas, he was very important in pre-industrial Taiwan and his shrines can be found everywhere. Look for statues of an old bearded man with a bit of a Santa-like visage.

Pilgrimage

As an integral part of the religious life in Taiwan, it's not surprising that pilgrimage fulfils many roles besides worship: it gives people an excuse to travel; it helps reinforce the relations between daughter and mother temples (see boxed text, p343); and it's a major source of funding.

Jìnxiāng, the Chinese term for pilgrimage, means to visit a temple and burn incense to the god. But not any temple will do. Famous pilgrim sites have a reputation for divine efficacy (靈, *líng*); that is the magical power to answer a worshipper's prayers. Pilgrims visiting such sites expect to have a direct experience of the god's powers, and to return home with both good-luck trinkets and good results (ie prayers granted). In return they usually make a donation to the temple.

The most famous pilgrimage in Taiwan is in honor of Matsu (see boxed text, p201). But there are many others, such as those to Beigang's Chaotian Gong, Maokong's Zhinan Temple, Tainan's Nankunshen and Donggang's Donglong Gong.

Religious Festivals

In all phases of Taiwan's history, the wealthier society got, the bigger the religious festivals. Well, there's never been a wealthier Taiwan, which means bigger, flashier, more extravagant festivals than ever. Good places to catch random celebrations are Lukang and Tainan.

Top Festivals

Matsu Pilgrimage (see boxed text, p201)
The Burning of the Wang Yeh Boats (p260)
Ghost Festival (p127)
Welcoming the City God (p277)

SPIRIT MEDIUMS

A common sight at religious festivals are the spirit mediums (*jītóng* in Mandarin, *tangki* in Taiwanese). Not sure who these are? Look for wild bare-chested guys lacerating themselves with swords and sticking blades through their cheeks to prove the god is within them.

Acts of Worship & Prayer

Worship is known as *baibai* and doesn't have to take place in a temple, as most families have a household shrine devoted to their ancestors. In addition to the following, typical acts of worship include offerings of food, candles and thanks, as well as fasting or refraining from eating meat.

It's been said that the most important part of a temple is not its statues but its incense censer. In every temple in Taiwan you will see worshippers holding burning incense in their hands as they do the rounds, bowing first before the main deity and then the host of subdeities. Afterwards the incense is placed in the censer.

Want to learn more about religious life in Taiwan? Pick up a copy of Mark Caltonhill's *Private Prayers and Public Parades – Exploring the Religious Life of Taipei.*

Burning joss paper is another common act of worship and there are four different types, each used for a variety of purposes, such as supplicating the gods, worshipping ancestors and literally providing spirits with money to use in the afterlife.

Going to a temple to ask gods or ancestors for answers to questions is common. The most typical form of divination is *bwah bwey,* which involves tossing two wooden half-moon divining blocks after a yes-or-no type question has been asked.

If the curved ends of the *bwey* both land upwards, the request has been denied. If one is up and one down, the request has been granted. If they both land curved-side down, it means the god is laughing at your request or suggesting you try again.

There is no limit to how many times you can perform *bwah bwey* but if you get the same answer three times in a row, you should accept it.

Temple Arts & Architecture

In Taiwan anyone can have a temple built; and almost anyone does it seems. Government statistics from 2009 show 14,993 registered temples, or approximately one for every 1500 residents (just a little higher than the average for convenience stores). This figure does not include unregistered temples, family shrines and the ubiquitous Earth God shrines.

What's more astonishing is that the majority of these temples are relatively new. In 1930 there were 3336 registered temples; in 1981 there were 5331.

Taiwanese clearly love their temples. And why not? In addition to being houses of worship, temples fill the role of art museum, community centre, business hall, marketplace, recreation centre, orphanage, pilgrim site, and even recruitment centre for organised-crime gangs and front for money laundering. Temples have launched political careers, and been used to bolster the positions of both those who seek Taiwan's formal independence and those who desire unification with China.

For more information on the Taiwanese and temple worship, see p338.

Temple Etiquette

- » In general, temples welcome visitors
- » You can take pictures but be courteous
- » Don't go past gated altar areas
- » Remove your hat when entering and don't smoke
- » Some Buddhist temples might ask you to remove your shoes

History

Historians generally divide temple development in Taiwan into three periods.

In the early immigrant stage (16th to 17th centuries), settlers, mostly from Fujian, established branch temples in Taiwan based upon the gods worshipped in their home villages. These temples were simple affairs, sometimes little more than a thatched shrine. For information on two of the oldest Matsu temples in Taiwan, see boxed text, p207.

In the age of prosperity (18th to 19th centuries), as Taiwan grew wealthier (and it was always more prosperous than the mainland), the small shrines were replaced with wood and stone temples. Wages for craftsmen were high and top artisans from China were eager to work here. Most materials were imported.

During this period temple ceremonies also started to become more elaborate and certain temples became regionally famous as pilgrim sites.

The modern period began with the colonisation of Taiwan by the Japanese in 1895. Restricted trade with China forced a reliance on local materials and craftsmen. Several highly talented schools developed and much of the fine and most daring work you'll find in temples hails from this period.

Architectural Features

The basic characteristics of any temple building are a raised platform that forms the base for a wood post-and-beam frame. This frame is held together by interlocking pieces (ie no nails or glue are used) and supports a curved roof with overhanging eaves. Think of any pagoda you have seen as a ready example.

Temple Roofs

Stand outside a traditional Taiwanese temple and look up at the gabled roof. It will be single or multitiered (ie have one or two levels). The ridgeline, slung low like a saddle, will curve upwards at the end, tapering and splitting prettily like the tail of a swallow. Not surprisingly this is known as a swallowtail roof, or swallowtail ridgeline.

The slopes of the roof will be covered with glazed tile and often highly, even gaudily, decorated with colourful cochin pottery and figures in *jiǎnniàn*. Fish and some dragon figures symbolise protection against fire (always a threat with wood structures).

Bracketing

Wooden brackets help to secure posts and beams but they are also decorative features. In fact, one of the pleasures of visiting temples is to record different bracket carvings. They vary from dragons and flying phoenixes to flowers and birds, or tableaux of historical scenes.

Examples are Longshan Temple (p215) and Fengtian Temple (see boxed text, p207).

TEMPLE STYLES

South vs North

The first thing you should recognise about traditional Taiwanese temples is that their style is southern (sometimes called Minnan). What does this mean? Well, during the Ming and Qing dynasties architecture in the north of China moved away from the aesthetics principles of the Song dynasty (a high period in Chinese culture) towards a stiff, formal and grandiose expressiveness best exemplified by Beijing's Forbidden City.

In the more remote regions of the empire, however, Song principles of beauty, playfulness and experimentation persisted. As all early Taiwanese emigrated from the south, when it came time to building temples they naturally had them constructed in the style they knew. And this is just one reason why Taiwan's traditional temples are worth investigating. They are heirs to a thousand-year-old high tradition that has died out pretty much everywhere else.

Buddhist vs Taoist vs Confucius

The second thing you should recognise is how to distinguish between Buddhist, Taoist and Confucian temples. One of the easiest ways is to look at the actual name. A Buddhist temple name will end with the character 寺 *(sì)*, while a Taoist temple will end with the character 宮 *(gōng)* or 廟 *(miào)*. A Confucian temple is always called a Kǒng Miào (孔廟).

The general architectural features (such as a raised structure with a post-and-beam frame) will be the same for all three types of temple, though modern temples can incorporate foreign influences such as the mosque-meets-rocket-ship design of the Chung Tai Chan Monastery in Puli. But Buddhist temples will generally have fewer images and less elaborate decorations. The atmosphere inside will be solemn, hushed and profound.

Confucian temples, which are always large walled complexes, will be even more sedate, not simply because few people bother to worship at them anymore. About the only time you'll find a serious ruckus at a Confucian temple is on the Sage's birthday.

Taoist and folk temples on the other hand will generally be loud, both in noise levels and decoration. They tend to be a lot of fun to explore because of this.

Dǒugǒng

Stand under the eaves of a temple roof and look up. Notice the complex system of two- or four-arm brackets? These brackets, a little hard to describe but so apparent when you see them, are called *dǒugǒng* and are unique to Chinese architecture. In fact, they are considered the very heart of the system.

Dǒugǒng gives a builder complete freedom to make a roof as large or as small as he likes and is one reason why Chinese architecture can be found across a wide region so varying in climate.

Spiderweb Plafond Ceilings

This type of inverted ceiling (like in a cathedral) is constructed with exposed *dǒugǒng* arms that extend up and around in a spiderweb pattern. Again, when you see it you will recognise it instantly. Plafond ceilings are the most striking and spiritually uplifting of all temple architectural features.

Examples are Anping Matsu Temple (p236), Tzushr Temple (the ceiling design here swirls upwards creating a vortex effect; p122) and Hsinchu's City God Temple (p145).

When the USA stopped pegging gold at US$35 an ounce in the 1970s, the price of the precious metal skyrocketed. Many temples in Taiwan, traditionally big recipients of gold donations, suddenly found their worth doubling and even tripling. Many restoration projects from this era got their funding from this unexpected windfall.

Temple Decorative Arts

Jiǎnniàn

One of the most delightful of temple arts when done well, *jiǎnniàn* is a method of decorating figurines with coloured shards. Imagine a three-dimensional mosaic.

The best examples of *jiǎnniàn* use sheared ceramic bowls for raw material. The irregular pieces are then embedded by hand into a clay figurine (a laborious and costly process). The second-best examples use premade glass pieces but still embed them by hand. The worst examples are simply prefab whole figurines.

Jiǎnniàn figures are usually found on the rooftops of temples. The figures include dragons (check out the teeth and the long irregular whiskers), phoenix, qilin (mythical creatures), flowers, the eight immortals and stories of filial piety.

Examples are Bao-an Temple (p53), Kaohsiung's City God Temple (p249) and Zhenxing Temple (see boxed text, p245).

Cochin Pottery

A type of colourful low-fired lead-glazed ceramic, cochin (also spelled *koji*) is one of Taiwan's unique temple decorative arts. The style is related to Chinese tri-colour pottery and came to Taiwan in the 18th century with immigrants. Common themes include human figures, landscapes, flowers and plants, as well as tableaux depicting stories from mythology and history.

In a temple, cochin pottery is found either on the uppermost panel of a wall or on the rooftop.

Examples are Chenghuang Temple (p204), Zhenxing and Ciji Temples (see boxed text, p245), and Cochin Ceramic Museum (p202).

Jiǎnniàn figures are found on the roof of a temple. Stairs on the sides of the main hall often lead to an upper balcony where you can view the work up close.

Woodcarving

Wood carving is usually found on cross beams, brackets, hanging pillars (often carved in the shape of flower pots), doors, window lattice and screen walls. Its basic function is decorative, though many parts that are carved are integral to the temple structure.

Examples are Makung's Matsu Temple (p293), Longshan Temple (p215) and Fengtian Temple (see boxed text, p207).

Painting

Painting is mainly applied to beams and walls. Though decorative, painting also helps to preserve wood, and is said to drive away evil, bless and inspire good deeds. Common motifs include stories from literature and history.

Probably the most distinctive paintings at any temple are the vibrant depictions of guardian gods on the doors to the front hall. Guardians vary according to the temple (Buddhist temples, for example, always display the guardians of the four directions) and the main deity worshipped inside. The eyes and feet of some door gods point at you no matter where you stand in relation to them.

Examples are Tainan's Matsu Temple (p234) and Hsinchu's City God Temple (p145).

Most larger temples are incorporated, and run by a manager appointed by a board of directors. His office will usually be to one side of the main hall, and nearby will be desks where you'll find the accountants, PR reps, website designers and volunteers who help run the show.

Stone Carving

Before the 20th century most stone came from China, and was often used as ballast in the rough ship ride over. Later locally sourced Guanyin stone became the preferred choice, though today cheaper Chinese imports are often used.

Stone is most commonly used for courtyard surfaces, stairs and doorposts (the design is often a stylised drum), dragon columns, lion statues and wall panels, where high relief shows scenes from history and literature.

TOURING THROUGH A TYPICAL TEMPLE

Temple layout can seem intimidating, what with talk of axis and feng shui, but most temples follow a similar and comprehensible pattern.

» Most temples are surrounded by a neighbourhood of shops, usually selling all manner of items the faithful will need for worship. The temple was likely to have owned the land these sit on, and either sold it (often to pay for reconstruction or a pilgrims' house) or rents it out.

» A main gate fronts the actual temple followed by a large open courtyard with a stone surface. Some temples in cities no longer feature a gate because of space constraints.

» After the courtyard comes a front hall (basically a colonnaded entrance portico) with two stone lions (a male and female) at the front and two dragon pillars before the main door. These both protect the temple and welcome guests. At this hall, stop to look for cochin pottery figures, *dǒugǒng,* carved brackets and posts, painted beams and possibly a plafond ceiling inside. A plafond here is known as an *algal well* and is designed to fool fire-causing demons into believing the temple is underwater (and hence impervious to fire). Note it is respectful to enter via the right door and exit via the left. The main door is reserved for the temple's god.

» Following the front hall there is another courtyard, often covered. Sometimes there is a large incense burner here and cochin panels or stone relief panels on the walls. There may also be tables piled high with offerings.

» The main roofed hall appears next, with more tables piled high with ghost paper, flowers, food, candles and statues. This prayer area is sometimes called the worship hall. At the back of the main hall is a black lacquered altar and shrine with the statue of the main deity inside. The shrine is almost always elaborately carved and often Buddhist light towers will stand on either side.

» Most temples will also feature a rear hall with shrines to various deities, and side rooms with more shrines, administrative offices, bathrooms and sometimes a library of religious materials.

» Observing the variations on this basic outline is part of the pleasure of visiting temples.

BRANCH TEMPLES & THE DIVINE POWER OF THE MOTHER

As we wrote at the beginning of this chapter, anyone can have a temple built in Taiwan, and when they do, it's usually as a branch (or daughter) temple of a larger and more famous mother temple. This involves a rather fascinating process called *fēnxiāng* (分香; spirit division).

In this practice, representatives from the newly built temple go to the elder one to obtain incense ash or statues. By doing so they bring back a little of the *líng* (靈; divine efficacy) of the original temple deity to their own humble house of worship.

Periodically representatives from the daughter temple must return to the mother to renew or add power to the *líng* of their statue. At the mother temple they once again scoop out incense ash to place in the incense burner of their own temple and also pass their statue through the smoke of the mother temple's incense burner.

Examples are Tzushi Temple (p122) and Chaotian Temple (see boxed text, p207).

Temples Today

Temples are fragile structures and prone to weathering, and subject to outright destruction by fire, flooding, earthquakes, typhoons, landslides, wars, occupations, indifference and so on. Nearly every temple in Taiwan has been rebuilt at least once since 1945, in many cases radically re-altering the original style.

In fact, most temples you see in Taiwan today will not have a traditional southern style at all. Since the 1960s the trend has been to build in the northern palace style. Such temples are squat and broad, with a flat roof ridgeline and a flat interior ceiling. Decorations tend to be repetitive and gaudy and are often prefabricated in China. The reason for the change? Such temples are easier to build and decorate, meaning money can be spent simply on giving them an impressive size.

In every temple you visit look for animals in the paintings, carvings and ceramic figures. The dragon, phoenix, tortoise and Chinese unicorn are known as the 'four Spiritual beasts'. The tiger, leopard, lion and elephant are also important symbols in both Buddhism and Taoism.

The Dying Masters

Taiwan has a serious problem ahead with the lack of fresh blood moving into the traditional decorative-arts field. The last survey of *jiǎnniàn* masters in 2004, for example, showed that only 37 remained. A combination of low prestige, long hours and low pay because of competition from cheaper Chinese imports has made traditional craftwork unattractive to younger Taiwanese. One master woodcarver we met from Pingdong even said he refused to pass his skills on to his children, not wanting them to get stuck in a dead-end career.

Taiwan's Cuisine

What's That Dangling from My Chopsticks?

No doubt about it, there's a lot to love about Taiwanese food, and a lot of it to love. And crikey, do the Taiwanese love food. Taiwanese people tend to eat out often, and are hardly known as sombre diners. Looking for a good restaurant? Just follow the noise. That said, some of the best food is not found in restaurants but on the street, and gourmands know that some of Asia's best street eats are found in night markets in and around Taiwan's cities.

If you're an academic, the sort who enjoys pontificating over the ethnic and geographical roots of stuff like food, you'll have your brainpan full sorting through the various foods you'll find around Taiwan. But keep in mind that while Taiwanese cuisine can be divided into several general styles of cooking, these boundaries are often blurred. While you'd be hard pressed to find some of Taiwan's more emblematic dishes (stinky tofu, for example) anywhere in mainland China (outside of restaurants specialising in Taiwanese cuisine, of course) you may find stuff that's pretty close in Fujian province. Straddling both sides of the Taiwan Strait, Hakka food is distinct enough to warrant its own category, though Hakka cuisine you'll find on Taiwan will be more seafood heavy than what you'd find in the inland regions of China. And of course, anything you'd find on the Mainland – Cantonese, Sichuan, Beijing, Shanghai and so forth – you'll find in Taiwan.

RECIPE FOR AN OVERVIEW OF TAIWANESE CUISINE

Assemble the following ingredients:

» one medium-sized subtropical island well suited for growing rice, vegetables, tubers and fruit

» one surrounding ocean teeming with fish (seafood-rich outer islands optional)

» several thousand years of indigenous Pacific Islander culinary tradition

» several hundred years of southeastern Chinese culinary tradition

» equal parts of Buddhist, Taoist and indigenous culinary roots.

Mix well, adding a long dash of Japanese culinary influence. Continue to cook under subtropical heat until 1949, then rapidly infuse long- and slow-cooking mixture with traditions of chefs from all corners of China fleeing political turmoil. Continue cooking under high pressure for around 35 years.

Begin liberalising in 1987. Continue to infuse and then mix regularly with random dashes of international influence and increasing aboriginal seasonings to taste.

Serve hot, cold or in between and until all diners are fit to burst. Serves around 23 million locals plus three million visitors per year.

KNOW YOUR STINKY TOFU

The staple of any night market, *chòu dòufǔ* (臭豆腐; stinky tofu) is the Taiwanese dish that – figuratively speaking – separates the men from the boys. An acquired taste most outsiders prefer to leave unacquired, the dish is actually tofu that's been fermented to an aromatic pungency and cut into rectangular cubes.

The most common variety of the dish – usually served at night markets – is deep-fried and served with pickled vegetables (usually cabbage, daikon and carrot), as well as soy sauce, garlic, and chilli sauce. Restaurants specialising in nonfried, or wet, stinky tofu can be found all over Taiwan. This version – often even more odiferous than the first – is served in a spicy soup base. A third variety, usually sold on the street, is served glazed and grilled on two bamboo sticks.

Cultivating a taste for *chòu dòufǔ* is a good way to set yourself apart as a Westerner with an appreciation for the finer aspects of Taiwanese culture.

Taiwanese

Taiwanese cooking has a long, storied and complex history, with influences ranging from all over China mixed with a rather unique aboriginal/Polynesian base. In general, food that you see people enjoying at roadside markets and restaurants tends to emphasise local recipes and ingredients (though often curious about things foreign, most Taiwanese tend to buy local when it comes to their food). Seafood, sweet potatoes, taro root and green vegetables cooked very simply are at the heart of most Taiwanese meals. Chicken rates second in popularity to seafood, followed by pork and beef. *Xiǎoyú huāshēng* (fish stir-fried with peanuts and pickled vegetables) is an example of a Taiwanese favourite. *Kézǎi* (oysters) are popular, and *kézǎi tāng* (clear oyster soup with ginger) is an excellent hangover cure and overall stomach soother. Though the Taiwanese like to cook with chilli, Taiwanese dishes are rarely as mouth-searing as those in Sichuan cuisine.

Need a quick, cheap protein fix? Grab a *cháyè dàn* (tea egg). They're those dark-brown things floating in a cauldron in nearly any convenience store. The darker they are, the longer they've been cooking.

Hakka

Hakka dishes are very rich and hearty, which makes sense for people who historically made their living as farmers and needed plenty of energy to work the fields. Dishes are often salty and vinegary, with strong flavours. Pork, a favourite of the Hakka, is often cut up into large pieces, fried and then stewed in a marinade. Our favourite Hakka dish is *kèjiā xiǎo chǎo* (stir-fried cuttlefish, leeks, tofu and pork).

Hakka cuisine is also known for its tasty snacks, including *zhà shūcài bǐng* (fried, salty balls made from local mushrooms and flour), *kèjiāguǒ* (shrimp and pork turnip cakes) and *kèjiā máshǔ* (sticky rice dipped in sugar or peanut powder).

Aboriginal

Travellers who visit Taiwan without sampling the dishes of the tribal peoples who called the island home millennia before the first Han sailor ever laid eyes on Ilha Formosa are definitely missing out. The product of hunters, gatherers and fishing people, aboriginal dishes tend to be heavy in wild game and mountain vegetables, as well as a variety of seafood. One must-try dish is *tiěbǎn shānzhūròu* (鐵板山豬肉; fatty wild mountain pork grilled, sliced, and grilled again with onions and wild greens). A staple that's easy to carry and an excellent source of calories to bring along hiking is *zhútǒng fàn* (竹筒飯; steamed rice – with and without meat – stuffed into a bamboo stalk).

Even if your travels don't take you past Taipei, you should still make a trip to Wulai (40 minutes by bus from the Taipei MRT's southernmost station, Xindian), both to enjoy the views and to sample some traditional aboriginal cuisine (p114). Should your journey take you down the southeast coast, there are two restaurants specialising in aboriginal cuisine that you'll definitely want to visit – Mabanai (p186) in Taitung, and Cifadahan Cafe (p178) in Mataian.

Fujianese

Much of Taiwanese cuisine has Fujianese roots, as the earliest wave of Han Chinese immigration to the island comprised primarily Fujian mainlanders who immigrated in the 18th and 20th centuries. Fujianese cuisine particularly abounds on the Taiwan Strait islands of Matsu and Kinmen (both of which are a stone's throw away from Fujian province), but you'll find Fujianese cuisine all over Taiwan. One of the most popular dishes is *fó tiào qiáng* ('Buddha Jumps Over the Wall'; a stew of seafood, chicken, duck and pork simmered in a jar of rice wine). Apparently the dish is so good that even the Buddha – a vegetarian, of course – would hop over a wall to get a taste.

Chiayi's must-try dish seems deceptively simple, but folks come for miles around to get themselves a bowl of *huǒ jī ròu fàn* (火鶏肉飯; Turkey rice). Shredded turkey strips served with a delicate yet savoury sauce ladled over rice, it's a local speciality and available pretty much everywhere in Chiayi, from the cheapest street eatery on up.

Cantonese

This is what non-Chinese consider 'Chinese' food, largely because most émigré restaurateurs originate from Guangdong (Canton) or Hong Kong. Cantonese flavours are generally more subtle than other Chinese styles – almost sweet, with very few spicy dishes. Sweet-and-sour and oyster sauces are common. The Cantonese are almost religious about the importance of fresh ingredients, which is why so many restaurants are lined with tanks full of finned and shell-clad creatures.

Cantonese *diǎnxīn* (dim sum) snacks are famous and can be found in restaurants around Taiwan's bigger cities. As well as *chāshāobāo* (叉燒包; barbecued pork dumplings), you'll find *chūn juǎn* (spring rolls), *héfěn* (flat rice noodles), *zhōu* (rice porridge) and, of course, *jī jiǎo* (chickens' feet) – an acquired taste.

Sichuan

Sichuan food is known as the hottest of all Chinese cuisines, so take care when ordering. Lethal red chillies (introduced by Spanish traders in the early Qing dynasty), aniseed, peppercorns and pungent 'flower pepper' are used, and dishes are simmered to give the chilli peppers time to work into the food. Meats are often marinated, pickled or otherwise processed before cooking, which is generally by stir-frying.

Famous dishes include *zhāngchá yāzi* (camphor-and-tea-smoked duck), *mápó dòufǔ* (Granny Ma's tofu; spiced mincemeat sauce and tofu) and *gōngbǎo jīdīng* (spicy chicken with peanuts). Sichuan is an inland province, so pork, chicken and beef – not seafood – are the staples.

EAT YOUR WAY THROUGH THE NIGHT

One experience you shouldn't miss out on is eating at a night market. Though Taipei's night markets are arguably the most famous, all cities in Taiwan have at least a few of their own, and even a medium-sized town will have a street set up with food stalls selling traditional Taiwanese eats late into the night. Whether it's a major popular-with-tourists spot (like Keelung Miaokou, or Shilin and Shida in Taipei city) or a neighbourhood set-up catering mostly to locals, night markets are an excellent place to tap into the heart, soul and stomach of Taiwan. Find the nearest market in our On the Road section.

DOS & DON'TS FOR DINING OUT

» In restaurants, every customer gets an individual bowl of rice or a small soup bowl. It is quite acceptable to hold the bowl close to your lips and shovel the contents into your mouth with your chopsticks. If the food contains bones, just put them out on the tablecloth, or into a separate bowl if one is provided. Restaurants are prepared for this – the staff change the tablecloth after each customer leaves.

» Remember to fill your neighbours' teacups when they are empty, as yours will be filled by them. You can thank the pourer by tapping your middle finger on the table gently. On no account serve yourself tea without serving others first. When your teapot needs a refill, signal this to the waiter by taking the lid off the pot.

» Taiwanese toothpick etiquette is similar to that of neighbouring Asian countries. One hand wields the toothpick while the other shields the mouth from prying eyes.

» Probably the most important piece of etiquette comes with the bill: although you are expected to try to pay, you shouldn't argue too hard, as the one who extended the invitation will inevitably foot the bill. While going Dutch is fashionable among the younger generation, as a guest you'll probably be treated most of the time.

Vegetarian

Vegetarian visitors to Taiwan may well consider applying for citizenship once they've experienced the joys of Taiwanese vegetarian cuisine. Taiwan's Buddhist roots run deep, and while only a small (but still sizeable) percentage of Taiwanese are vegetarian, a fair chunk of the population abstains from meat for spiritual or health reasons every now and again, even if only for a day or a week.

Buddhist vegetarian restaurants are easy to find. Just look for the gigantic *savastika* (an ancient Buddhist symbol that looks like a reverse swastika) hung in front of the restaurant. If the restaurant has a cassette or CD playing a soothing loop of *ami tofo* (Buddhist chant) and a few robed monks and nuns mixed among the lay patrons, you're in business. Every neighbourhood and town will generally have at least one vegetarian buffet; some are a bit on the plain side, others are places of unparalleled food artistry.

The Taiwanese are masters at adding variety to vegetarian cooking and creating 'mock meat' dishes made of tofu or gluten on which veritable miracles have been performed. Some vegetarians might find these items 'too meatlike for comfort'.

If you're in Tainan and someone asks you if you'd like a *guāncái bǎn* ('coffin cake'), don't worry – this isn't some inscrutable Taiwanese threat. A Tainan speciality, the coffin cake is a fat toast plank hollowed out and filled with a thick chowder of seafood and vegetables.

Drinks

Tea & Coffee

Tea is a fundamental part of Chinese life. In fact, an old Chinese saying identifies tea as one of the seven basic necessities of life, along with fuel, oil, rice, salt, soy sauce and vinegar. Taiwan's long growing season and hilly terrain are perfectly suited for producing excellent quality tea, especially high-mountain oolong, which is prized among tea connoisseurs the world over (and makes a great gift for the folks back home).

There are two types of teashop in Taiwan. The first are traditional teashops (more commonly called teahouses) where customers brew their own tea in a traditional clay pot, sit for hours playing cards or Chinese chess, and choose from several types of high-quality leaves. These places can be found tucked away in alleys in almost every urban area, but are best visited up in the mountains. Taipei's Maokong is an excellent place to experience a traditional Taiwanese teahouse (see p103). The second type of teashop are the stands found on every street corner. These specialise in bubble tea, a mixture of tea, milk, flavouring, sugar and giant black tapioca balls. Also called pearl tea, the sweet drink is popular with students who gather at tea stands after school to socialise and relax, much in the way that the older generation gathers at traditional teahouses.

Coffee, once hard to come by, is now widely consumed all over Taiwan, at prices ranging from cheap (NT$35 per cup) to expensive (NT$100 and up). Not only is Taiwan big on coffee consumption, the island is experimenting with growing coffee as well; in the past few years a number of coffee plantations in southern Taiwan have begun producing coffee for domestic consumption and export. See boxed text, p227, for more on Taiwan's coffee-growing culture.

TEA

The Chinese were the first to cultivate tea, and the art of brewing and drinking tea has been popular since the Tang dynasty (AD 618–907).

Juices

Fresh-fruit stands selling juices and smoothies are all over Taiwan, and these drinks make wonderful thirst quenchers on a hot summer day. All you have to do is point at the fruits you want (some shops have the cut fruit already mixed in the cup) and the person standing behind the counter will whiz them up in a blender for you after adding water or milk. Especially good are iced-papaya milkshakes.

Popular juices include *hāmìguā* (哈密瓜; honeydew melon), *xīguā* (西瓜; watermelon), *píngguǒ* (蘋; apple) and *gānzhè* (甘蔗; sugar cane). Sugar-cane juice is usually sold at speciality stands selling raw sugar cane rather than run-of-the-mill fruit stands.

Harder Stuff

The Taiwanese tend to be fairly moderate drinkers (with some exceptions, banquets being a time when much drinking abounds), but Taiwan does have a number of locally produced inebriants well worth trying. The most famous of these is *gāoliáng jiǔ* (Kaoliang liquor). Made from fermented sorghum, Kaoliang is produced on Kinmen and Matsu, the islands closest to mainland China. Another local favourite is *wéishìbǐ* (Whisbih), an energy drink with a fine mixture of dong quai, ginseng, taurine, various B vitamins, caffeine, and some ethyl alcohol to give it a kick.

The Landscape of Taiwan

Taiwan's Topography

Lying 165km off the southeast coast of mainland China (from which it's separated by the Taiwan Strait), the island of Taiwan straddles the Tropic of Cancer and is shaped kind of like a yam. (Perhaps this is why *'wo shi zhen di guo'* – 'I am a real Yam' – is sometimes said with pride by Taiwanese natives wishing to distinguish themselves from their genetic cousins across the strait.) Criss-crossed with many small rivers that empty into the sea, the plains and basins of western Taiwan essentially provide the only land suitable for either agriculture or industry. The east coast, with its towering seaside cliffs and rocky volcanic coastline, is utterly spectacular; outside the three cities of Ilan, Hualien and Taitung, the area is among the most sparsely populated on the island.

Territories controlled by the Republic of China (ie Taiwan) include a number of small islands, including the Penghu Archipelago and the islands of Matsu and Kinmen in the Taiwan Strait, and Green Island and Lanyu off the east coast. Visitors to Taiwan and the surrounding islands can experience a stunningly broad variety of landscapes, from rugged mountains in the centre of the main island (there's even snow in winter at higher altitudes) to low-lying wetlands teeming with wildlife on the western coast, rice paddies and farmland in the south, and lonely windswept beaches punctuated with basalt rock formations on the outer islands.

At 36,000 sq km Taiwan is roughly the size of the Netherlands and only about 20% more populous. Yet the two countries could hardly feel

ENVIRONMENTALLY RESPONSIBLE TRAVEL

In an age of dwindling forests, melting icebergs and politicians in deep denial, Taiwan is a nation that seems to have pulled itself back from the precipice of environmental disaster. Here are some ways tourists can encourage the island to keep moving boldly forward towards its goal of becoming the 'Switzerland of Asia'.

» When buying snacks, avoid taking a plastic bag if you don't really need one. Try saying *'wǒ bù xūyào dàizi'* ('I don't need a bag').

» Recycling is the rule in most places, so place your rubbish in the appropriate bins.

» Use rechargeable batteries; digital cameras will run longer on them anyway.

» Taiwan offers myriad temptations for those turned on by technology; just keep in mind that improperly disposed-of mobile phones, laptop computers and MP3 players wind up contributing to the growing and ever-toxic high-tech trash heaps of southern China, India or Africa. Choose your purchases wisely and dispose of them even more so.

more different. The reason: landscape. Flat and at sea level (and in places, below it), the Netherlands stands in stark contrast to the island of Taiwan, which is mostly mountainous. It's this extreme landscape that forces the majority of Taiwan's 23 million people to live on the small expanses of plains to the west of the Central Mountains range, a series of jagged mountain peaks that stretches for over 170km from north to south. It's this topography that makes Taiwan's capital, Taipei, feel considerably more crowded than, say, Amsterdam.

Natural Disasters

Sitting atop the ever-colliding (albeit slowly colliding) Eurasian and Philippine plates has given Taiwan the beautiful mountains, scenic gorges and amazing hot springs that keep people coming back. Alas, these same geological forces also put the island smack dab in earthquake central, meaning that nary a week goes by without some form of noticeable seismic activity. Most of these quakes are small tremors, only noticed by folks living in the upper storeys of buildings as a gentle, peculiar rocking sensation. Others can be far more nerve-wracking to locals and visitors alike.

One quake on the southern coast in late 2006 caused only a few casualties, but severed several underground cables, disrupting telephone and internet service across Asia. On 4 March 2010 an earthquake measuring 6.4 on the Richter scale with an epicentre 362km south of Taiwan's southernmost city caused buildings to tremble as far north as Taipei, knocking out power and rail service for a short time and causing several injuries. The most devastating earthquake to hit Taiwan is remembered locally simply as '9-21' after the date it occurred, 21 September 1999. Measuring 7.3 on the Richter scale, the earthquake collapsed buildings and killed thousands. Damage caused by the 9-21 earthquake – especially the dramatic collapse of buildings in commercial and residential neighbourhoods – led to the passage of laws requiring that new buildings be designed to withstand future earthquakes of high magnitude.

VOLUNTEER

For years, Animals Taiwan (www.animalstaiwan.org) has been saving Taiwan's stray dogs and cats from life on the streets by connecting abandoned animals with prospective adoptive homes. The organisation provides volunteer opportunities for visiting animal lovers and advice for expats looking to take their pets in or out of Taiwan.

Typhoons are another frequent, unwelcome visitor to Taiwan. The island experiences yearly tropical storms, some of which reach typhoon level. Having better infrastructure than many of its neighbours, Taiwan tends to weather most typhoons fairly well, with the majority resulting in flooding, property damage, delays and headaches – but little loss of life. In August 2009, however, Taiwan found itself in the direct path of Typhoon Morakot. The island was unable to cope with the massive rainfall brought by the typhoon (up to 254cm, or 100in, in some parts of the country), which, combined with winds of up to 150km/h, triggered heavy flooding and landslides, especially in the southern counties of Pingtung, Chiayi, Tainan and Kaohsiung. One such mudslide buried an entire village and its inhabitants, erasing the town of Xiaolin in rural Kaohsiung county (a town inhabited mostly by indigenous peoples) from the map entirely.

Although there has been no official consensus on precisely why Morakot was so devastating, many who study local climate and land-use issues in Taiwan factor in poor land management, excessive draining of aquifers and wetlands, and climate change in general as being partially responsible.

A fact of life for people living in Taiwan, natural disasters are also something that travellers need to take into account when planning their trip. Earthquakes, of course, can't be predicted. Typhoons, however, usually come between July and October, so travellers planning to visit for more than a few days during these months might wish to factor in the possibility of witnessing a storm firsthand. Typhoons tend to hit the east coast particularly hard, so if you're planning a trip down the coast or to Lanyu or Green Islands, plan accordingly. (There are reports of diehard surfers actually heading to the beaches along the east coast specifically to catch the waves in the hours preceding a big storm.)

Aside from the obvious dangers that may arise from being in the vicinity while one is occurring, typhoons and earthquakes have the potential to actually alter the landscape, rendering once-scenic areas unreachable and roads impassable. Some roads, though still appearing on outdated maps, remain closed indefinitely. Outdated guidebooks may also lead readers astray (this writer's one-time favourite outdoor hot spring, the Wenshan spring in Taroko Gorge, is still closed several years after bathers were killed by a rockslide). Sections of the Central Cross-Island Hwy that once stretched across the middle of the island from Taichung to Hualien will probably never be rebuilt, and large sections of the Southern Cross Hwy are still impassable after being altered beyond recognition by Typhoon Morakot in 2009.

Taiwan's Green Party (www.greenparty.org.tw) is active in issues of ecological sustainability and social justice, coordinating with other environmental organisations throughout the island.

National Parks & Reserves

The Republic of China (on Taiwan) National Park Act was passed in 1972, and since then six national parks have been established. This puts the percentage of Taiwan's acreage designated as national parkland at around 9%, which is pretty substantial for a country of Taiwan's relatively diminutive size.

Environmental Issues

When Chiang Kai-shek's nationalist troops were driven off the mainland, they brought more than just millions of Chinese people fleeing communism with them: they also brought capital, much of which was

TAIWAN'S NATIONAL PARKS

NATIONAL PARK	FEATURES	ACTIVITIES	BEST TIME TO VISIT	PAGE
Kenting	popular beach resort with 'Cancún of Taiwan' vibe	swimming with tropical fish, diving in pristine coral reefs, migratory birdwatching, surfing, camping, 3-day rock concerts	year-round	p266
Kinmen	once off-limits military outpost replete with history, ancient villages and temples, transformed into a beautiful island park	hiking, bike riding, birdwatching	summer, autumn	p274
Sheipa	second-highest mountain in Taiwan, diverse terrain, Formosan landlocked salmon	hiking, birdwatching	summer, autumn, spring	p143
Taroko	spectacular gorge, Formosan macaque, pheasants	hiking	summer, autumn, spring	p164
Yangming-shan	beautiful mountain park with varied climate, hot springs, butterflies	hiking, birdwatching	summer, autumn, spring	p94
Yushan	tallest mountain in Taiwan, rare Formosan salamander, Formosan black bear	hiking alpine, tundra & cedar forests	summer, autumn, spring	p192

ORGANIC FARMING IN TAIWAN

In recent years, increasing numbers of farmers have switched to organic farming methods, resulting in a dramatic upswing in the number of organic farms springing up around the island (both in rural communities and the suburbs of major cities).

One such urban collection of organic farms sits just south of Tucheng station, the second-last stop on the western end of Taipei Metro's blue line. While close enough to the city that Taipei 101 can be seen to the east on all but the worst air-quality days, the land on which this series of farms is set (former military property that's reverted to its original owners since martial law) exudes a bucolic splendour not easily found so close to a Metro line. Like organic farmers in the west, the Tucheng farmers rely on strict nonuse of pesticides and chemical fertilisers to maintain their organic ratings. Produce – including fruits and vegetables of all kinds – grown in Tucheng is sold in markets and speciality stores throughout Taiwan, usually commanding higher prices than their nonorganic counterparts. Some Taipei-based expats come to Tucheng on the weekends and work for a few hours, returning home with sacks full of farm-fresh groceries.

Visitors interested in more-formal volunteer opportunities should check out an organisation called **WWOOF Taiwan** (☎02-2571-1677; www.wwooftaiwan.com), which connects interested travellers with host farms throughout the island. Farms vary in size and production, but what they all have in common is a total commitment to sustainable organic agriculture. While there are some farms on the outskirts of cities, many of them are located in rural areas, bringing volunteers into some of the island's most pristine and beautiful spots. Membership provides access to a list of host farms (in English and Chinese) as well as a description of what jobs need to be filled, where the farms are located and what the linguistic abilities of the farmers are. Many of the farms are owned by members of Taiwanese aboriginal tribes, providing an excellent opportunity to study the languages and cultures of Taiwan's aboriginal groups in addition to sustainable farming techniques.

Tip: the word for 'organic' is *yǒujī* (有機). To ask if something is organic, you can say *'Shì bù shì yǒu jī de?'* (是不是有機的?).

used to transform a primarily agrarian society into a major industrial powerhouse. Taiwan became wealthy, quickly, but it also became toxic, with urban air quality ranking among the world's worst, and serious pollution in most of its waterways. Indeed, Taiwan's 'economic miracle' came at a serious price, and pollution, urban sprawl and industrial waste have all taken a heavy toll on the island.

When the Excavators Came to the Rice Fields (www.dfun.com.tw/?p=28023) is a heartbreaking account of farmers in Miaoli county being removed from their land in the name of economic progress.

Things have improved markedly over the last decade. Environmental laws, once largely ignored by industry and individuals alike, are now enforced far more rigorously across the board, and the results have been tangible (the Danshui and Keelung Rivers in Taipei, for example, once horribly befouled, are significantly cleaner in sections). Urban air quality is noticeably better, thanks to a combination of improved public transport, more stringent clean-air laws, and a switch to unleaded petrol. Taipei's air quality, once almost as bad as Mexico City's, now hovers somewhere around London's. The Taiwanese collective unconscious has changed as well: so much of the emerging 'Taiwanese identity' is tied in with having a clean and green homeland that people are tending to take environmental protection far more seriously.

Lest we paint too rosy a picture, it's possible to counter any perceived step forward with another step back towards the bad old days.

One of the bigger issues belying the image that the Taiwan government hopes to project as an environmentally conscious democracy is that of land expropriation – that is, the legal removal of farmers from privately owned lands. In March 2010, otherwise unaffiliated farmers from Hsinchu, Miaoli, Taichung, Changhua and Hualien Counties travelled to Taipei to hold a joint protest against the compulsory 'purchasing' of their lands in order to build factories and resorts. Government and industrial proponents of expropriation point to the issue of common good, saying that transforming farmland into industrial areas creates jobs, reducing the country's climbing unemployment rate. However, opponents say that the main beneficiaries are a conglomerate of large corporations and real-estate developers. Although Taiwan's High Speed Rail (HSR) has been touted for making travel around the island even more convenient, many feel that placement of the stations – in the far outskirts of Taiwan's westernmost cities as opposed to in the city centres themselves – has actually promoted both increased traffic and urban sprawl. And of course, the ongoing issue of decaying barrels of nuclear waste buried on the aboriginal island of Lanyu has also yet to be resolved to anybody's satisfaction.

Interested in taking a course in permaculture design in Taiwan? Check out the Taiwan Permaculture Institute (www.permaculture.org.tw).

Taiwan's environmental issues are a global concern as well. Despite its diminutive size, Taiwan is a major CO_2 producer. One study contends that the 4130-megawatt coal-burning Taichung power station is the biggest CO_2 emitter on the globe, with yearly CO_2 emissions from the one plant alone roughly equal to the emissions of Switzerland.

So while it's fair to say that Taiwan has made great strides on the environmental front, it's clear that yet more remains to be done.

Taiwan Wildlife Guide

To most of the world Taiwan is best known as one of the Asian Tigers, an economic powerhouse critical to the world's IT supply chains. Decades earlier it had a reputation (now overtaken by China) as a manufacturer of cheap toys and electronics. But going back even earlier, Taiwan was not just the 'beautiful island' but also the kingdom of the butterfly and an endemic species wonderland where one could find the most astonishing variety of native plants and animals.

Is there anything left of this old world? Plenty. Taiwan is still 50% forested, with about 20% (and growing) of the land officially protected as national park or forest reserve. One of the absolute highlights of any trip to Ilha Formosa involves getting to know the flora and fauna, much of which you can't find anywhere else on earth.

The Endemic Species Research Institute in Jiji (see p225) is a great place to learn more about Taiwan's remarkable natural heritage.

Taiwan lies across the Tropic of Cancer and most fact books record its climate as subtropical. But with an extremely mountainous terrain (it's almost 4000m high in the centre), Taiwan's climate can range from subtropical to subarctic, and its vegetation zones can range from coastal to montane to alpine. It's been said that a journey 4km up to the 'roof' of Taiwan reproduces a trip of many thousands of kilometres north from Taiwan to the Russian steppes.

In this chapter we'll cover some of what you can reasonably expect to see in the wilds of Taiwan.

Plants

Taiwan has 4000 to 5000 plant species, with an estimated 26% found nowhere else. Travellers will be most interested in the forest zones, which is a good thing because Taiwan has plenty of forest cover.

Foothills (Tropical Zone): 0–500m

Most of Taiwan's original tropical forests have long been cleared to make room for tea fields, orchards, and plantations of Japanese cedar, camphor and various bamboos. Intact lowland forests still exist along the east and in parts of Kenting National Park. In other areas you will find dense second-growth forests.

TAIWAN'S WILDLIFE HIGHLIGHTS

- » Super-high rate of species endemism
- » Huge variety of flora and fauna within a small area
- » Easy access to wild areas
- » Fascinating yearly migrations of birds and butterflies

THE NATIONAL BIODIVERSITY RESEARCH PROMOTION PROJECT

In 2009, a seven-year study by the Biodiversity Research Centre of Academia Sinica reported that Taiwan had 50,164 native species in eight kingdoms, 55 phyla, 126 classes, 610 orders and 2900 families. To cut to the chase, this means that Taiwan, with only 0.25% of the world's land mass, holds 2.5% of the world's species. It's a rate of endemism 100 times the world average.

The study, the first since British diplomat and naturalist Robert Swinhoe completed his own in the late 19th century, was a revelation – to put it mildly. Altogether, it was found that 70% of Taiwan's mammals, 17% of its birds, 26% of its plants and 60% of its insects are endemic species.

What accounts for such a high rate of bio-density? It's Taiwan's long isolation from the mainland, as well as a geographic environment that harbours a variety of ecosystems in a small area. About the only ecosystem that Taiwan is missing, scholars have noted, is a desert.

Submontane (Subtropical Zone): 300–1500m

It's in these broadleaf forests that most people get their first taste of just how unspoiled and luxuriant Taiwan's forests can be. It's a jungle-like environment teeming with birds, insects, snakes and so many ferns that you often can't count the number of species in one patch. Though ferns can grow as high as trees (giving forests a distinct 'Lost World' feel), common larger plant species include camphor, *Machilus,* crepe myrtle, maple tree, gums and cedar.

Where to see submontane plants:

» Nanao (p135)

» Pingxi Branch Rail Line (p115)

» Walami Trail (p180)

» Wulai (p111).

Montane (Temperate Zone): 1600–3100m

The montane forests vary greatly because the elevation changes mean there are warm temperate and cool temperate zones. You might start your journey in a mixed broadleaf forest that soon turns to evergreen oaks. At higher elevations conifers such as Taiwan red cypress, Taiwania, alder, hemlock and pine start to predominate. In areas that have been disturbed by landslide or fire you often get large tracts of Taiwan red pine. When their needles fall, the forest floor becomes almost ruby in colour.

Between 2500m and 3100m in elevation a natural pine-hemlock zone runs down the centre of Taiwan. This is one of the most pristine parts of the country (logging never went this high) and many trees are hundreds and even thousands of years old. A good part of any hike to the high mountains will be spent in this zone.

Where to see montane plants:

» Alishan Forest Train (p206)

» Forestry Rd 200 (p199)

» hiking trails in Yushan National Park (p193) and Snow Mountain (p144).

There are no comprehensive English books on Taiwan's wildlife, but the visitor centres at the country's national parks sell a wide range of individual books and DVDs that cover butterflies, birds, mammals, reptiles and more. Many books can be bought at www.booksfromtaiwan.com.

Subalpine (Cold Temperate Zone): 2800–3700m

You might think that this high-altitude zone is inaccessible unless you hike in, but you can actually reach sections of it by road. Taiwan's highest pass sits at 3275m on Hwy 14, just before Hehuanshan (Hohuanshan) Forest Recreation Area. The rolling meadows of Yushan cane (a type of dwarf bamboo) that you can see from the roadside stand as one of the most beautiful natural sights on the island.

Less accessible are forests of tall straight Taiwan fir and juniper (a tree-line species). To see these you will need to put on your boots and strap on a knapsack.

Where to see subalpine plants:

» Hehuanshan (Hohuanshan) Forest Recreation Area (p229)

» Snow Mountain (p144)

» Tatajia (p193)

» Wuling Pass (p229).

Alpine (Subarctic Zone): 3500m+

If you manage to climb your way to this elevation you'll be above the tree line. The zone is divided into a lower scrub zone and an upper herb zone where tiny patches of vegetation cling to the exposed rocks. It's a chilly place even in summer but the views are worth every effort to get here.

Where to see alpine plants:

» Snow Mountain peaks (p144)

» Yushan National Park peaks (p192).

Animals

Mammals

There are about 70 species of mammals in Taiwan, and about 70% of those are endemic. Once over-hunted and threatened by development, species like the Formosan macaque, wild boar, martin, civet, sambar deer, and the delightful and diminutive barking deer (Reeves' muntjac) have made great comebacks and are relatively easy to spot in national parks and forest reserves. Sika deer, which once roamed the grasslands of the west from Kenting to Yangmingshan, have been reintroduced to Kenting National Park and are doing well. Head out at night in submontane forests with a high-powered torch (flashlight) if you want to catch Taiwan's flying squirrels in action.

Though tropical at lower elevations, Taiwan lacks large species of mammals such as elephants, rhinos and tigers. Taiwan's biggest cat, the spotted cloud leopard, is almost certainly extinct, while the Formosan black bear is numbered at fewer than 1000. Your chances of seeing one of these creatures are pretty slim. In 15 years of hiking the wilds of Taiwan we have seen only one.

Where to see mammals:

» Chihpen (Zhiben) Forest Recreation Area (p188)

» Jiaming Lake National Trail (p183)

» Kenting National Park (p266)

» Nanao (p135)

» Sheipa National Park (p143)

» Yushan National Park (p192).

Taiwan's Birds

» Birding in Taiwan (www.birdingintaiwan.org)

» Birdlife International (www.birdlife.org/regional/asia)

» Wild Bird Society of Taipei (www.wbst.org.tw)

» *Birds of East Asia* by Mark Brazil

Birds

With its great range of habitats, Taiwan is an ideal place for birds, and birdwatchers. Over 500 species have been recorded here: 150 are considered resident species, 69 are endemic subspecies, and 15 are endemic species (though some authorities say there are 24, or more). It's an impressive list and compares very well with larger countries in the region such as Japan.

Bird conservation has been a great success over the past two decades, and it's therefore easy to spot endemics like the comical blue magpie, or multicoloured Muller's Barbet even in the hills surrounding Taipei. For one of the world's truly great shows, however, check out the raptor migration over Kenting National Park. Once threatened by over-hunting, bird numbers have tripled in the past decade. Several years back, over 50,000 raptors passed over the park in a single day.

Where to see birds:

» Aowanda Forest Recreation Area (p226)

» Dasyueshan Forest Recreation Area (p199)

» Kenting National Park (p266)

» Kinmen (p274)

» Tatajia (p193)

» Wulai (p111)

» Yangmingshan National Park (p94).

Taiwan has many relic species that survived the last ice age. One of the more intriguing is the Formosan landlocked salmon, which never leaves the mountain streams in which it was born. See p141.

Butterflies

In the 1950s and '60s Taiwan's butterflies were netted and bagged for export in the tens of millions (per year!). Remarkably, only three species became extinct, though numbers plummeted for decades. These days top butterfly areas are well protected, and these delightful creatures can be seen everywhere year-round.

Taiwan has over 400 species of butterflies, of which about 60 are endemic. Some standouts include the Blue Admirals, Red-base Jezebels and Magellan's Iridescent Birdwing, which has one of the largest wingspans in the world. Prominent sites include Yangmingshan National Park's Datunshan, where chestnut tigers swarm in late spring; the overwintering purple butterfly valleys in the south (see boxed text, p358); Fuyuan Forest Recreational Area; and the Yellow Butterfly Valley outside Meinong.

Where to see butterflies:

» Fuyuan Forest Recreational Area (p178)

» Linnei (see boxed text, p212)

» Maolin (p259)

» Tatajia (p193)

» Yangmingshan National Park (p94)

» Yellow Butterfly Valley (p256).

Other Wildlife

Taiwan has a host of reptiles including a wide variety of beautiful but deadly snakes. Lizards, frogs and a long list of insects including stag beetles, cicadas and stick insects can be found anywhere where there's a bit of undisturbed land.

Marine life (whales and dolphins, as well as corals and tropical fish) is abundant on the offshore islands and the east coast where the rich Kuroshio Current passes. Many species of river fish are also making a good comeback, though sports fishermen are sadly too quick to catch (and not release) fry.

Where to see other wildlife:

» Green Island (p306)

» Lanyu (p301)

» Shihtiping (p172)

» Wulai (p111)

» Yangmingshan National Park (p94).

Conservation

Today, conservation projects all over Taiwan are restoring mangroves and wetlands, replanting forests and protecting the most vulnerable

ON WINGS OF GOSSAMER

Butterfly migration is fairly common the world over, but Taiwan's purple crow migration can hold its own. Each year in the autumn, as the weather cools, bands of shimmering purples (four species of Euploea, also known as milkweed butterflies) leave their mountain homes in north and central Taiwan and begin to gather in larger and larger bands as they fly south. By November they have travelled several hundred kilometres, and in a series of 12 to 15 warm, sheltered valleys in the Dawu Mountain Range, 10 to 15 million of them settle in for the winter.

This mass overwintering is not common. In fact, Taiwan is one of only two places in the world where it happens: the other is in the Monarch Butterfly Valleys of Mexico. The most famous overwintering site in Taiwan is in Maolin Recreation Area but according to experts this is actually the least populated valley. It simply had the advantage of being the first to be discovered and written about.

The discovery happened in 1971 when an amateur entomologist was invited into Maolin by local Rukai aboriginals. Though not aware of just how significant the find was, the entomologist (and others) continued to study the valley. By the mid-'80s it was obvious that a north–south migration route existed, though it wasn't until 2005 that the 400km route along the west could be roughly mapped out. Since then a second migration path along the east coast and a connecting path joining the two have also been discovered.

The northern migration usually begins around March, and, astonishingly, it involves many of the same individuals who flew down in the autumn (purples have been found to live up to nine months). Some good places to spot the spring migration are Linnei, Dawu (in Taitung County), Pingtung County Rd 199, Taichung's Metropolitan Park, Baguashan, and coastal areas of Jhunan (Miaoli County) where the purples stop to breed. In May and June large numbers of purples appear to take a mysterious detour and are blown back south over the high mountain pass at Tatajia.

If you're curious as to just how the migration occurs in the first place, the answer is relatively simple: seasonal winds. In the autumn they come strong out of Mongolia and China, while in the spring they blow up from the Philippines. Without them the purples would be unlikely to move such great distances and this would mean their death when the temperatures drop during northern winters.

From spring until autumn, purple butterflies are easily spotted all over Taiwan. So give a nod to these brave wayfarers when you encounter them in a park or mountain trail. They may have come a long way.

For a mostly accurate look at the discovery of the western migratory route check out *The Butterfly Code*, a Discovery Channel DVD.

species. A 10-year moratorium on river fishing has succeeded in restocking streams, while hundreds of small community projects are bringing back balance to urban neighbourhoods; even in Taipei the sound of song birds and the flittering of butterfly wings is common stuff. There are also vast areas now inaccessible to the public because of the closing of old forestry roads (a deliberate policy).

For a closer look at the variety of snakes in Taiwan, check out Snakes of Taiwan (www.snakesoftaiwan.com).

However, it's not all good news. The oceans and rivers are still treated as dumping grounds by industry; overdevelopment is rampant (constrained in many cases only by the extreme terrain); and official attitudes towards wildlife can be shockingly indifferent. In 2010, during a debate on the expansion of a science park, Taiwan's premier, Wu Den-yih, casually explained that the critically endangered pink dolphin should be smart enough to swim around a proposed jetty that would extend far out to sea.

It was a clear sign of how much still needs to change here. On the other hand, the lambasting of the premier (by the public and the media) in the days following was an equally clear sign of how far things have come.

The Future of Taiwan

May you live in interesting times.

If writing an abbreviated history of a place requires being highly selective, then predicting its future makes one tread even more lightly. This can be no more true than in Taiwan, where the last few years have seen a near 180-degree shift in the political winds.

In 2007, Taiwan's pro-independence government seemed to be inching ever closer to declaring the island's status as a separate nation. Chiang Kai-shek's name had been removed from the international airport, and the name of the park surrounding his ostentatious memorial had been changed to 'Democracy Plaza'.

Three years later, and much has changed. The election of 2008 saw a return to power of the anti-independence Kuomintang (KMT). It also saw the ascension of Ma Ying-jeou as president, who promised a return to the status quo that had once dominated Taiwan's political landscape.

Since then, many of the changes brought about by the previous administration have been rolled back, and relations between the governments of the Republic of China (ROC) and the People's Republic of China (PRC; which, for better or worse, is always the elephant in the room in any discussion about Taiwan's future) have gone from openly hostile to something that could be perceived as 'nearly fraternal'. Indeed, by many objective measures, some form of détente has occurred. The two sides seem to be inching ever closer to something approaching harmonious relations.

Perhaps the most politically and economically significant expression of the closening ties between Taiwan and China is the Economic

THE DEBATE OVER ECFA

On paper, the Economic Cooperation Framework Agreement (ECFA) seems fairly simple. Signed in Chongqing in the summer of 2010 between the governments of the People's Republic of China and the Republic of China, this trade agreement promises a reduction of tariffs and commercial barriers across the Taiwan Strait, strengthening economic ties between the two sides. Proponents claim the agreement will cause investment to flow from China into Taiwan, creating jobs, markets and opportunities while also enabling Taiwan to engage in similar agreements with other nations. Opponents see the pact as a cover for a quasi-unification between Taiwan and China. They also say that it threatens to reduce manufacturing jobs inside Taiwan, as well as opening up the island to an influx of white- and blue-collar workers (thus lowering salaries) and inferior-quality and potentially hazardous goods from China.

Cooperation Framework Agreement (ECFA), a recently inked (and somewhat controversial) trade agreement.

It's still too early to tell what level of integration the agreement will bring the two economies, but the very fact of its existence – unthinkable four years ago – speaks volumes as to how much has changed. What is certain is that warming ties between the two sides are bringing – and will continue to bring – change.

From a tourism perspective, these changes can already be seen and felt at some of Taiwan's top tourist spots. A Western traveller to Sun Moon Lake, the National Palace Museum or Taipei 101 will find themselves elbowing for space with tour groups of middle-class visitors from Beijing, Shanghai and other points in China, something definitely not seen just a few years back.

It's worth noting that other regular features at these spots are members of groups such as Falun Gong, whose rights to gather freely, practise and protest are still protected by the ROC constitution. It's possible that many Chinese travellers are bringing home not only photos and memories of their Taiwan sojourns, but questions about the far more restrictive regime under which they live. If so, perhaps democratic Taiwan will serve to hasten China's transformation into a more politically open society, in precisely the way that ultracapitalist Hong Kong hastened China's change from tight state control of the economy to an almost anything-goes free market. Only time will tell.

Tourism from China is clearly on the rise, and while most visitors still come with tour groups (a legal requirement), it's likely that the coming years will bring further relaxation, opening the floodgates for younger, more independent travellers. This should serve to strengthen social and cultural ties across the Taiwan Strait.

The *View from Taiwan* is an excellent, regularly updated blog about where Taiwan is heading culturally, politically and otherwise. http://michaelturton.blogspot.com.

Another by-product of warming ties (with future ramifications for the globetrotter) is that air travel between Taiwan and cities in China is now both possible and practical. In the past, travellers wishing to visit both Taiwan and China were forced, by law, to make a stopover in a 'neutral' port (usually Hong Kong). Time- and money-consuming, this was often a deciding factor that did not work in Taiwan's favour, causing travellers to skip Taiwan entirely in favour of China (whose power to draw tourists in 1997 dwarfed Taiwan's by a factor of around 15 to 1).

No longer forced to choose between the two, it's possible that more and more casual travellers will decide to include Taipei and Taroko Gorge in their trip-of-a-lifetime itinerary, which includes Shanghai, the Forbidden City and the Great Wall. Rising prices in China (which has gone, in relation to Taiwan, from being *far cheaper* to merely *slightly cheaper*) might even convince people to budget a few more days to see Taiwan.

The speculations we've made about Taiwan's future are based purely on observations of current trends. From within, Taiwan's electorate has

TAIWAN'S ECONOMIC FUTURE

Economically, Taiwan has proven itself to be flexible. In a few short decades this one-time producer of textiles and cheap consumer goods transformed itself into the world's leading high-tech producer. It fuelled the digital boom of the late 20th century, in the process becoming one of Asia's most durable and dynamic economic powerhouses, weathering financial storms that capsized other economies in the region. As Taiwan proceeds into the second decade of the 21st century, an influx of Chinese money in Taiwan is bound to give Chinese business increasing leverage over Taiwan's economy. Look for tourism, biotech and green technology to play increasingly important roles in Taiwan.

TAIWAN'S DIPLOMATIC ALLIES

One by-product of Taiwan's ambiguous national status is that only a handful of states recognise Taiwan (as the Republic of China) as a sovereign state. At the time of writing, the following nations maintained diplomatic relations with Taiwan: Belize, Burkina Faso, Dominican Republic, El Salvador, Gambia, Guatemala, Haiti, Honduras, Kiribati, Malawi, Marshall Islands, Nauru, Nicaragua, Palau, Panama, Paraguay, Saint Kitts and Nevis, Saint Lucia, Saint Vincent and the Grenadines, São Tomé and Príncipe, Swaziland, Solomon Islands, Tuvalu and the Vatican.

proven somewhat fickle, and the same forces that brought the KMT to power in 2008 could easily take them out again in 2012. Beijing has never renounced the use of force as a possible means of attempting to control Taiwan's destiny. Trade pacts, tour groups and pandas aside, there are still missiles pointed eastward across the Taiwan Strait. This makes the likelihood of peace, prosperity and harmony in the region anything but certain.

It's worth noting that the changes Taiwan is currently experiencing would have seemed highly unlikely (at best) when this book last went to print a mere three years ago. Therefore, forgive us for being reluctant to peer too deeply into our crystal ball to offer any rock-solid predictions into the future.

There's an old Chinese blessing (almost a cliché, but appropriate here) that says, 'May you live in interesting times'. What the future holds for Taiwan is unclear, save for one certainty – it will be interesting.

However, lest anyone forget, this blessing can also be considered a curse...

Survival Guide

Accommodation

Taiwan provides the full range of lodgings, from basic hostels to world-class resorts. Air-con is standard and no key deposit is required but you'll need your passport or ID to check in. Note that the quality can vary, even at the same price range. Foreigner visitors are not overcharged. Outside of popular areas in summer there is usually no need to prebook rooms.

Accommodation is generally priced per room (or number of beds per room) and not per guest. What is called a 'single' room in other countries (one single bed) is rare; a 'single' in Taiwanese hotel lingo usually means a room with one queen-sized bed, suitable for a couple. 'Double' generally means a double bed but could also mean a twin, ie two beds per room. A suite is generally called a *taofang* (ie a room with a separate living area). In the countryside many hotels and homestays have rooms called *tongpu* (東埔). These have no beds but offer thick quilts and floor mats. Usually you must book the whole room but if it's not busy you can often have the room to yourself and just pay for a single person.

Summer, Chinese New Year and Saturday nights are high season. Discounts off the rack rate are the norm even in high season except for a very few hotels (mostly strictly budget) that always charge the same price. Sometimes you must ask, but mostly discounts are given automatically (often they are written on the hotel's price list). Discounts range from 10% to 50%. For resort discounts try midweek and for business hotel discounts try the weekends.

Making Reservations

Reserving by phone is better, though some high-end hotels take online reservations. Visitor information booths at airports, train stations and High Speed Rail (HSR) stations can make hotel reservations for you. If you're phoning someone at a hotel and do not speak Chinese, you may run into trouble at all but the high-end hotels. Hint: speak clearly and if the last name does not work, try the first name. Asking for a room number is best.

Symbols Used in this Guide

The following accommodation price ranges are indicated by $ within the guide:
$ = budget <NT$1600
$$ = midrange NT$1600 to NT$4000
$$$ = top end >NT$4000

Camping

Camping is generally safe, clean and cheap. It is best to bring a free-standing tent, as many sites have raised wooden platforms. You can pick up a cheap tent in Taiwan for NT$1000. Public campgrounds tend to have the best facilities. Along the east coast you can set up a tent on pretty much any beach. Be warned that camping in summer on the beach sounds good, but at sunrise the inside of your tent will become as hot as a pizza oven – look for campgrounds with covered sites.

Homestays/B&Bs

Mínsù (民宿; homestays) offer travellers a way to meet local people. There has been an explosion of new homestays in the past few years – most are well run and offer good accommodation at a fair price.

Tourism Bureau website (www.tai wan.net.tw) lists the 40 best homestays. Most charge in the NT$2000 to NT$3000 range, with off-season and midweek rates dropping considerably. If you have a Youth Guesthouse Network card (see p366), you get a discount rate on most of the Top 40 homestays. Signs for homestays are everywhere, concetrated on the east coast, Alishan National Scenic Area, and offshore islands.

Hostels

Each year more and more hostels are opened, often by young, well-travelled Taiwanese. A basic dorm bed starts at NT$250, though the better places charge NT$400 to NT$500 per

PRACTICALITIES

English Newspapers

» *Taipei Times* (www.taipeitimes.com)

» *China Post* (www.chinapost.com.tw)

» *Taiwan Today* (http://taiwantoday.tw)

Magazines

» *Taiwan Panorama* (formerly *Sinorama;* www.sinorama.com.tw) An intelligent look at Taiwanese language and culture, sports, finance, history, travel and more.

» *Commonwealth Magazine* (www.cw.com.tw) The Taiwanese *Economist*.

» *Travel in Taiwan* (www.tit.com.tw) An excellent resource for all things cultural and touristy, with calendars of events and colourful coverage.

Radio & TV

» International Community Radio Taipei (ICRT) broadcasts nationwide in English 24 hours a day at 100MHz (FM) with a mix of music, news and information.

» Taiwan has three broadcast networks: CTS, CTV and TTV, with shows in Chinese, including dubbed foreign shows.

» Cable TV is available throughout Taiwan, with some English movie channels (HBO, AXN), news channels (CNN, CNBC) and the like.

Electricity

» Taiwan has the same electrical standard as the USA and Canada: 110V, 60Hz AC. Electrical sockets have two vertical slots. If you bring appliances from Europe, Australia or Southeast Asia, you'll need an adaptor or transformer.

Weights & Measures

» Taiwan uses the metric system alongside ancient Chinese weights and measures. For example, apartment floor space is measured by *píng* (approximately 4 sq metres), fruit and vegetables are likely to be sold by the catty (*jīn*, 600g) and teas and herbal medicines are sold by the tael (*liǎng*, 37.5g).

Smoking

» Smoking is common but not allowed in public facilities, public transport, restaurants and many hotels.

night. Private rooms, when available, are usually tiny and start at NT$500. You can often arrange weekly or monthly rates. Taiwanese hostels affiliated with **Hostelling International** (http://taiwan.yh.org.tw) usually offer discounts for cardholders. Some hostels are technically illegal, though there is nothing dodgy about them. Hostels generally have laundry, simple cooking facilities, a TV, computer hook-up with ADSL (or wi-fi) and a room for socialising. Some Taipei hostels are dingy and old, having catered to a different era. Choose carefully in the capital. Also see the Youth Guesthouse Network, p366.

Hotels

Taiwan offers a great range of options among hotels. Budget options from NT$550 to NT$800 give you threadbare accommodation, private bathroom (no shower curtain), TV and phone. No English will be spoken. Quality varies greatly from NT$800 to NT$1600. Above NT$1200 rooms are usually good enough that you wouldn't feel embarrassed putting family up there.

For a midrange price range of NT$1600 to NT$4000, you're likely to find a fancy lobby, one or more restaurants on site, ADSL and possibly plasma TVs. Private bathrooms include shower (or bathtub with shower) and a shower curtain. Decor can range from a little dated to very slick. Unless you're looking for a luxury experience, most travellers will feel comfortable here. In the big cities usually at least one or two staff members speak some English.

The big cities abound with international-standard top-end hotels. Typical amenities include business centres, English-speaking staff, concierge services, spa and/or fitness centre, massage services and a sense of style.

Rental Accommodation

English-language newspapers carry rental listings, usually luxury accommodation catering to expats on expense accounts. For upscale or even good midrange apartments it's useful to hire an agent, whose number you can find by looking in newspapers. The usual agent fee is about half a month's rent. For mid- to low-range accommodation by area and price in Taipei check out **Tsui Mama** (www.tmm.org.tw) and the websites catering to the foreign community (see p15). You can also look around the area in which you want to live and ask building guards. They usually know when their building has apartments for rent.

Basic studio apartments (with no kitchen) in Taipei cost from around NT$5000 to NT$10,000 per month. Small three-bedroom apartments start at NT$15,000 to NT$20,000 – in good downtown neighbourhoods rents are at least double this. You'll find the best value in suburbs such as Muzha, Xindian, Neihu and Guandu. Outside of Taipei, even in the cities, rents are cheap. Decent three-bedroom apartments start at NT$8000. Negotiations are usually possible everywhere. One good approach is to say that you really like the place but can only afford (however much) right now.

Temple & Church Stays

Many cyclists stay at small temples and Catholic churches, though you'll need to speak Chinese if you want to do this. A small donation is appropriate. For proper rooms for pilgrims and visitors, try **Shitoushan** (p150), **Foguangshan** (p256) and **Guangshan Temple** (p258).

Youth Guesthouse Network

This network is a program from the **National Youth Commission** (http://youthtravel.tw) and offers 24 accommodation options for travellers aged 15 to 30 years old. Nightly rates are around NT$500. Many are located in old police hostels, hero houses (for soldiers) or labour recreation centres. The quality really varies and sometimes places are quite far from a bus or train station. See Discount Cards (opposite) for information on picking up a Youth Travel Card. The National Youth Commission also offers free mobile phones (the Digital Tour Buddy program), with a 24-hour service hotline and built-in English-Chinese dictionary (with many set travel phrases) included. To apply see http://youthtravel.tw.

Business Hours

Standard hours are as follows. Reviews won't list hours unless they differ from these standards.

Banks (9am-3.30pm Mon-Fri)

Convenience stores (24hr)

Department stores (11am-9.30pm)

Government offices (8.30am-5.30pm)

Museums (9am-5pm, closed Mon)

Night markets (6pm-2am)

Offices (9am-5pm Mon-Fri)

Post offices (8am-5pm Mon-Fri)

Restaurants (11.30am-2pm and 5-9pm)

Shops (10am-9pm)

Supermarkets (to at least 8pm, sometimes 24hr)

Children

The Taiwanese are very welcoming, and doubly so when it comes to children. If you're travelling with kids, they will probably attract a lot of positive attention. Strangers may want to touch or handle your babies. Some use a sling to help minimise contact as they perform daily business. You can also tell people your child has a cold. If you can't speak Chinese a little sign language will do.

You're not likely to find high chairs or booster seats for kids at lower-end restaurants, but you may well find them at more expensive places. Stands and outdoor markets tend to be very informal. Upper-end restaurants may have set menus for families or even kids. You can generally find Western baby formula and baby foods at supermarkets.

The website www.parentpages.net has forums on children in Taiwan, from birthing and midwifery to raising kids to keeping them amused. The Parenting forum on www.forumosa.com is also helpful. The **Community Services Centre** (www.community.com.tw) in Taipei has lots of information for families relocating to Taiwan.

Lonely Planet's *Travel with Children* prepares you for the joys and pitfalls of travelling with the little ones.

Convenience Stores

Convenience stores are ubiquitous and handy for fresh daily foods, fruit and drinks (especially cheap fresh coffee). Services include bill payment (ie phone, gas, electricity), fax, copy and printing services, and ticket purchases (eg train, HSR, opera). Staff are usually willing to help unless they are very busy. 7-Elevens also offer cheap shipping of goods across Taiwan to other outlets and many online purchases can be paid for and picked up at a convenience store nearest to you. Most stores have ATMs that accept international bankcards.

Customs Regulations

Up to US$5000 in foreign currency may be brought into the country but there is a limit on goods (clothes, furniture, dried goods) brought in from China. Drug trafficking is punishable by death.

Passengers who are 20 years and older can import the following duty free:

» 200 cigarettes, 25 cigars or 450g of tobacco

» one bottle of liquor (up to 1L)

» goods valued at up to NT$20,000 (not including personal effects)

Discount Cards

Student discounts are available for public transport, museums, parks, (some) movie tickets and performances at public theatres. Foreign student cards are not likely to be accepted. However, foreigners studying Chinese can get student cards from their school.

Children's discounts are offered by height rather than age (eg discounts for children under 110cm). Foreign children are usually eligible for this discount

Seniors who are 65 years and older are usually given the same discounts as children. Seniors over 70 often get in free. Foreign seniors usually eligible for this discount.

Government-issued cards **Youth Travel Cards** (www.youthtravel.net.tw) are available to visitors between 15 and 30 years old. Over 800 discounts are on offer, including on admission tickets, accommodations, transportation, food, shopping and Chinese-language courses. You can pick up a Youth Travel Card at the airport or train visitor centres.

Electricity

Embassies & Consulates

Only a handful of countries and the Holy See have full diplomatic relations with Taiwan. It is likely that your country is represented not by an embassy but by a trade office or cultural institute.

Overseas, Taiwan is represented by consular, information and trade offices. Both Taiwanese legations abroad and foreign legations in Taiwan serve the same functions as embassies or consulates would elsewhere: services to their own nationals, visa processing, trade promotion and cultural programs.

See p368, and for a complete list visit the **Ministry of Foreign Affairs** (www.mofa.gov.tw) site.

Gay & Lesbian Travellers

Taiwan's official stance towards gays and lesbians is among the most progressive in Asia. There is no sodomy law to penalise homosexuality, in 2002 the military lifted its ban on homosexuals and in 2003 the Republic of China (ROC) government announced plans to legalise same-sex marriage (though the bill has gone nowhere since). The Chinese-speaking world's best Gay Pride parade is held in Taipei every year. In 2006, then Taipei mayor and now president, Ma Ying-jeou, presided over the opening of the city's annual Gay, Lesbian, Bisexual and Transgender Festival – the first event of its kind to be sponsored by a local government in Taiwan. Taiwanese gays and lesbians have made great strides towards openness and equality, particularly since the end of martial law. In Taiwan's family-oriented society, however, where the propagation of children is considered a duty, there is still a stigma attached to homosexuality for many.

Taipei is an open, vibrant city for gay and lesbian visitors, and has gained a reputation as *the* place for gay nightlife in Asia. Other cities in Taiwan offer far less, if any, gay nightlife, or often any nightlife at all beyond karaoke TV (KTV).

Useful resources include www.utopia-asia.com, www.twpride.info/and *G-spot* magazine. See also the boxed text on p82.

Insurance

A travel-insurance policy to cover theft, loss and medical problems is a good idea. There are a wide variety of policies available, so check the small print.

Some policies specifically exclude 'dangerous activities', which can include scuba diving, motorcycling and even trekking. A locally acquired motorcycle licence is not valid under some policies. Some policies pay doctors or hospitals directly rather than you having to pay on the spot and claim later. If you have to claim later, make

EMBASSIES & CONSULATES

FOREIGN MISSION	CONTACT	ADDRESS (IN TAIPEI)
Australia (Australia Commerce & Industry Office)	www.australia.org.tw	The Presiden International Tower, 27-28th fl, 9-11 Song Gao Rd
Canada (Canadian Trade Office in Taipei)	www.canada.org.tw	13th fl, 365 Fuxing N Rd
France (French Institute; Institut Français de Taipei)	www.fi-taipei.org	Room 1003, 10th fl, 205 Dunhua N Rd
Germany (German Trade Office)	www.dwb-taipei.org.tw	19F, 333 Keelung Rd
Ireland (Institute for Trade & Investment of Ireland)	02-2552 6101	7F, 41 Nanjing W Rd
Japan (Interchange Association)	www.koryu.or.jp	28 Ching Cheng St
Netherlands (Netherlands Trade & Investment Office)	www.ntio.org.tw	5th fl, 133 Minsheng E Rd, Sec 3
New Zealand (New Zealand Commerce & Industry Office)	www.nzcio.com	Room 2501, 25th fl, 333 Keelung Rd, Sec 1
South Africa (Liaison Office of South Africa)	www.southafrica.org.tw	Suite 1301, 13th fl, 205 Dunhua N Rd
South Korea (Korean Mission in Taipei)	http://taiwan.mofat.go.kr	Room 1506, 333 Keelung Rd, Sec 1
Thailand (Thailand Trade & Economic Office)	www.tteo.org.tw	12th fl, 168 Song Jiang Rd
UK (British Trade & Cultural Office)	02-8758 2088	The President International Tower, 26th fl, 9-11 Song Gao Rd
USA (American Institute in Taiwan)	www.ait.org.tw	7 Lane 134, Xinyi Rd, sec.3

sure you keep all documentation. You may be asked to call (reverse charges) a centre in your home country where an immediate assessment of your problem is made. Check whether the policy covers ambulances or an emergency flight home.

For car insurance, see p375. Travel insurance is available at www.lonelyplanet.com/travel_services. Buy, extend and claim online anytime, even on the road.

Internet Access

Taiwan is internet-savvy with the majority owning personal computers and laptops with fast internet. In urban areas wi-fi is widely accessible in cafes, restaurants, libraries, on Mass Rapid Transit (MRT), at visitor information centres and many museums, either free or with a pay-for-time card (*wúxiàn wǎng kǎ*). **Wifly** (www.wifly.com.tw) offers 5000 hot spots in Taiwan. One-day/one-month cards cost NT$100/500. Purchase cards online or at 7-Elevens, which are also common. Wifly hot spots and often have free indoor and outdoor seating.

Many, if not most, hotels, even budget ones, now offer free wi-fi or broadband – homestays mostly do not. Computers with internet access can be found at libraries or visitor information centres and internet cafes (per hour around NT$60), which are not as common as before, though most towns and cities have them. Ask for the *wǎngbā*.

This book denotes internet access, whether broadband cable or a business centre, with the icon @. Wi-fi access is denoted with the icon. For info about Taiwan on the web, see p15 and p371.

Language Courses

Chinese-language programs are widely available at universities and private cram schools. Most offer classes for two to four hours a day, five days a week. Costs vary greatly from NT$7000 a month at a private cram school to over US$1000 a month at a top university program.

To obtain a study visa at the time of writing, you had to enrol at a **Ministry of Education–approved school** (http://english.moe.gov.tw/mp.asp?mp=1).

Some of the better-known programs include **ICLP** (http://homepage.ntu.edu.tw/~iclp/) at National Taiwan University and the **Mandarin Training Program** (www.mtc.ntnu.edu.tw/indexe.html) at National Taiwan Normal University. Both universities are in Taipei but there are programs around the country.

You normally apply for a program in your own country. Once accepted, apply for a multientry extendable visitor visa at a local trade office or ROC mission. You must start classes within the first month upon arrival and after four months of good standing apply for a resident visa at the **Bureau of Consular Affairs** (BOCA; www.boca.gov.tw). After receiving your visa apply for an ARC (Alien Resident Card) at the **National Immigration Agency** (www.immigration.gov.tw), formerly the Foreign Affairs Police. Remember to renew your ARC each year. Note that your school may not do anything to help you through the process.

Having a resident visa without an ARC is the same as not having one at all. You need an ARC to stay legally in Taiwan on your resident visa. Check out the ever-informative www.forumosa.com for the latest from people in the know.

Legal Matters

Smuggling drugs can carry the death penalty; possession can also get you arrested. If caught working illegally, you'll get a fine, a visa suspension and an order to leave the country. You may not ever be allowed back.

Knowingly transmitting HIV to another person is punishable by up to seven years in prison. This law also allows for mandatory testing of members of high-risk groups, namely sexual partners of HIV carriers and intravenous drug users, as well as foreigners who come to work certain jobs and require an ARC. Adultery is also a crime.

If you're detained or arrested, contact your country's legation in Taiwan. Even if it can't provide any direct aid, it can at least offer legal advice and notify your family. You have the right to remain silent and to request an attorney, although authorities are under no obligation to provide an attorney. You also have the right to refuse to sign any document. In most cases, a suspect can't be detained for more than 24 hours without a warrant from a judge – notable exceptions are those with visa violations. Taipei offers pro bono legal service at most district offices.

Legal ages:

» Voting: 20

» Driving: 18

» Military conscription: 18, but most do it after their university studies

» Consumption of alcohol: 18

» Consensual sex (heterosexual or homosexual): 16. Travellers should note that they can be prosecuted under the law of their home country regarding age of consent, even when abroad.

Maps

In most places in Taiwan your Lonely Planet guidebook map will be sufficient. Full city and county maps are available at tourist offices and are useful as they often list more places than we can cover. For driving, the four-part collection of bilingual maps called *Taiwan Tourist Map* is usually sufficient. Pick it up at any visitor information centre. Otherwise, the best road map (in Chinese) is the two-volume *Formosa Complete Road Atlas* by Sunriver Press. A compass can be useful if you're going to be travelling on country roads. For hiking maps see p30.

Be aware that many map boards in Taiwan are the mirror image of what they should be. To understand what this means, consider this example: you are walking north and come to a four-way split in the trail with a map in front of you. On the map, you see the trail to your destination heads to the right. Easy, you think. I should go right at this fork (heading east).

Wrong. If you look at the compass points on the map you'll see that the trail that heads east in reality is heading west on the map.

To solve the problem ignore your immediate environment. Look at the map and discover what direction you should be going in. Then take out your compass and figure out where that direction lies. North and south are usually hard to mix up. East and west are easy to confuse.

Money

Taiwan's currency is the New Taiwanese Dollar (NT$). Bills come in denominations of NT$100, NT$200, NT$500, NT$1000 and NT$2000. Coins come in units of NT$1, NT$5, NT$10, NT$20 (rare) and NT$50. Taiwan uses the local currency exclusively. See p15 for information on exchange rates.

ATMs

ATMs are widely available at banks and convenience stores. 7-Elevens are on the Plus or Cirrus network and have English-language options. ATMs at banks are also on the Plus and Cirrus networks, and are sometimes on Accel, Interlink and Star networks. There may be limits on the amount of cash that can be withdrawn per transaction or per day. Note that banks islandwide charge a NT$7 fee per withdrawal.

Cash

If you have foreign cash to exchange, the most widely accepted currency is US dollars.

Credit Cards

Credit cards are widely accepted – cheap budget hotels, however, won't take them. If rooms cost more than NT$1000 a night, the hotel usually accepts credit cards but most homestays do not accept them. Small stalls or nightmarket food joints never take credit cards. Most midrange to top-end restaurants do but always check before you decide to eat.

Moneychangers

Private moneychangers do not proliferate in Taiwan. Hotels will change money for guests but banks are the most common option.

Tipping

Tipping is not customary in restaurants or taxis (but is still appreciated). It is usual to tip the porter at better hotels (NT$100 is considered courteous). Many foreigners tip at better bars and clubs so staff may expect this. Note that the 10% service charge added to bills at many restaurants is not a tip to be shared with the staff.

Travellers Cheques

As with cash, it is best if your travellers cheques are in US dollars.

Photography

In general people in Taiwan are fine with you photographing them. On Kinmen and Matsu Islands be careful photographing airports or military sites. On Lanyu ask permission before photographing anything (see p305). For photography tips check out Lonely Planet's *Travel Photography*.

Public Holidays

Founding Day/New Year's Day 1 January
Chinese Lunar New Year January or February, usually three to four days
Peace Memorial Day 2-28 Day; 28 February
Tomb Sweeping Day 5 April
Labour Day 1 May
Typhoon holidays possible from May to October
Dragon Boat Festival 5th day 5th lunar month, usually in June
Moon Festival 5th day 8th lunar month, usually September
National Day 10 October

Safe Travel

Taiwan is affected by frequent natural disasters, such as earthquakes, typhoons, floods and landslides. Avoid going out during typhoons and avoid mountainous areas after earthquakes or typhoons. Landmines are still prevalent on Kinmen and Matsu. Mined areas are clearly marked and remaining areas should be cleared in the coming few years.

Bars and clubs are usually safe but especially outside Taipei it's best to get a recommendation. In some areas we specifically avoid listing clubs and bars for this reason.

Telephone

The country code for Taiwan is ☎886. Taiwan's telephone carrier for domestic and international calls is **Chunghwa Telecom** (www.cht.com.tw). For detailed information on rates and services, visit the website.

Area Codes

Do not dial the area code when calling within an area code. Area codes are listed under town headings throughout this book.

The number of digits in telephone numbers varies with the locality: from eight in Taipei to five in the remote Matsu Islands.

Domestic Calls

From public telephones local calls cost NT$2 per two minutes and local long-distance calls cost NT$3 per minute. From private phones local calls cost NT$1.6 every three minutes and local long-distance calls cost NT$2 per minute. Calls to mobile phones (beginning with ☎09XX) cost NT$0.05 to NT$0.11 per second depending on the provider and the time of day. General phone rates are discounted from 11pm to 8am Monday to Friday, from noon on Saturday and all day Sunday.

Fax

Most hotels offer expensive fax services, so almost everyone uses 7-Eleven stores, which transmit local black-and-white faxes for NT$15 per page, local long-distance faxes for NT$20 per page and international faxes for NT$85 per page.

Mobile Phones

In Taiwan, mobile phones are often called *dàgēdà* or just 'cell phone'. Numbers start with the prefix ☎09XX,

GOVERNMENT TRAVEL ADVICE

The following government websites offer travel advisories and information on current hot spots:

Australian Department of Foreign Affairs (www.smarttraveller.gov.au)
British Foreign Office (www.fco.gov.uk/countryadvice)
Canadian Department of Foreign Affairs (www.dfait-maeci.gc.ca)
US State Department (http://travel.state.gov)

followed by six digits. When calling within an area code, you have to use the area code. A Taipei call would look like this: 02-XXXX XXXX. Most foreign mobile phones can use local prepaid SIM cards, which you can purchase at airport arrival terminals. If your mobile phone cannot use local sim cards you can rent mobile phones (per day NT$100) at the airport. If you have an ARC you can apply for a mobile phone in Taiwan. The main carriers are **Chunghwa Telecom** (www.cht.com.tw) and **FarEastone** (www.fareastone.com.tw). In general, rates are about NT$1 a minute for outgoing domestic calls.

Public Phones & Phonecards

Domestic calls from public phones cost NT$2 for local calls of up to two minutes, NT$3 per minute for local long-distance calls and NT$6 per minute for calls to mobile phones. Note that with the proliferation of mobile phones, public phones are not as numerous as they once were. Domestic IC cards cost NT$200 and are available at convenience stores. When your card is about to run out, the display will flash: press the 'change card' button to insert your new card.

For overseas direct-dial calls, dial ☎009 or ☎002 before the country code and number. Chunghwa Telecom's E-call cards are sold in denominations of NT$200, NT$300 and NT$520 and give users up to a 30% discount on standard rates. Note that the quality of connection can be somewhat low. Cards can be purchased at Chunghwa Telecom locations and 7-Eleven stores. To use, dial the access number on the back of the card and then follow the instructions (an English option is available).

Overseas calls are charged per six-second unit, as follows:

COUNTRY	DIRECT DIAL	E-CALL
Australia	NT$1.30	NT$0.96
Canada	NT$0.59	NT$0.40
China	NT$1.22	NT$0.77
France	NT$1.60	NT$1.04
Germany	NT$1.60	NT$1.04
Japan	NT$1.30	NT$0.96
Netherlands	NT$2.00	NT$1.10
New Zealand	NT$1.30	NT$0.96
UK	NT$1.40	NT$0.96
USA	NT$0.59	NT$0.40

A discount of approximately 5% applies on calls made during off-peak hours. For directory assistance in English, dial ☎106 (NT$3 per call).

Time

Taiwan is eight hours ahead of GMT on the same time zone as Beijing, Hong Kong, Singapore and Perth. When it is noon in Taiwan, it is 2pm in Sydney, 1pm in Japan, 4am in London, 11pm the previous day in New York and 8pm the previous day in Los Angeles. Taiwan does not observe daylight-saving time. A 24-hour clock is used for train schedules.

Toilets

Free public toilets are widely available in parks, transport stations, public offices, museums, temples and rest areas. They are usually squat toilets, except for handicapped stalls, and are usually very clean and modern but probably won't have toilet paper. Restaurants and cafes usually have their own bathroom facilities, and Western-style toilets are standard in apartments and hotels. It is handy to remember the characters for men (男; *nán*) and women (女; *nǚ*). Many places ask you not to flush toilet paper but to put it in the wastebasket beside the toilet. It's best to comply when asked.

Tourist Information

Helpful visitor information centres are present in most city train stations, High Speed Rail stations, popular scenic areas and airports. They may have English- and, sometimes, Japanese-speaking staff, plus English- and Japanese-language brochures, maps, train and bus schedules will be available. Major cities usually have a larger visitor centre downtown but they are often not as useful as the train station centres. **Welcome to Taiwan** (www.taiwan.net.tw) is the official site of the Taiwan Tourism Bureau, and the **Tourism hotline** (☎0800 011 765) is a 24-hour service in English, Japanese and Chinese.

Much of Taiwan is organized under National Scenic Areas. Their visitor centres can be hit or miss depending on the staff but their websites are usually very informative:

Alishan National Scenic Area (www.ali-nsa.net/)

East Coast National Scenic Area (www.eastcoast-nsa.gov.tw)

East Rift Valley National Scenic Area (www.erv-nsa.gov.tw)

Maolin National Scenic Area (www.maolin-nsa.gov.tw)

Matsu National Scenic Area (www.matzu-nsa.gov.tw/)

North Coast & Guanyinshan National Scenic Area (www.northguan-nsa.gov.tw)

Northeast Coast & Yilan Coast National Scenic Area (www.necoast-nsa.gov.tw)

Penghu National Scenic Area (www.penghu-nsa.gov.tw)

Sun Moon Lake National Scenic Area (www.sunmoonlake.gov.tw/)

Tri-Mountain National Scenic Area (www.trimt-nsa.gov.tw)

These websites, while not specifically aimed at tourists, are helpful resources:

Forumosa.com (www.forumosa.com)

Information for Foreigners (http://iff.immigration.gov.tw)

TEALIT (Teaching English and Living in Taiwan; www.tealit.com)

Travellers with Disabilities

In general, Taiwan is not a very disabled-friendly environment. Street footpaths are uneven, kerbs are steep, and public transport, other than the MRT and HSRail is not equipped with wheelchair access. Taipei and other cities are slowly modernising disabled facilities. Disabled parking is usually available and respected. **Eden Social Welfare Foundation** (http://engweb.eden.org.tw) provides advice and assistance to disabled travellers.

Visas

At the time of writing, citizens of many countries could enter Taiwan without a visa. The period granted cannot be extended under any circumstances. All travellers need a passport that is valid for six months and an onward ticket with confirmed seat reservation. Countries permitted 30-day stays are Australia, Austria, Belgium, Canada, Czech Republic, Denmark, Estonia, Finland, France, Germany, Greece, Hungary, Iceland, Italy, Republic of Korea, Latvia, Liechtenstein, Lithuania, Luxembourg, Malaysia, Malta, Monaco, the Netherlands, Norway, Poland, Portugal, Singapore, Slovakia, Slovenia, Spain, Sweden, Switzerland and the US. Ninety-day stays apply to citizens of Japan, UK, Ireland and New Zealand.

Those coming to Taiwan to study, work or visit relatives for an extended period of time should apply at an overseas mission of the ROC for a visitor visa, which is good for 60 to 90 days. Visas can be extended up to six months under certain circumstances on the National Immigration Agency website (www.immigration.gov.tv). If you're planning to stay longer than six months, the law requires you to have an ARC. See the Bureau of Consular Affairs website (www.boca.gov.tw) for more information.

Volunteering

Animal groups need volunteers to work shelters, walk dogs, participate in fundraisers and also foster dogs and cats (something you can do even if you are in Taiwan for a short time). Contact **Taiwan SPCA** (台灣防止虐待動物協會; www.spca.org.tw/) and **Animals Taiwan** (社團法人台灣動物協會; www.animalstaiwan.org) in Taipei, **BARK** (www.bark-taiwan.org) in Kaohsiung and **Taichung Universal Animal Protect Association** (寶島動物園; www.lovedog.org.tw) in Taichung. See also the boxed text p115.

You can also volunteer at an organic farm through **WWOOF** (www.wwooftaiwan.com).

Women Travellers

Taiwan (and especially Taipei) is a safe place to travel but women should take normal precautions at night and in uncrowded areas. Apart from the attention normally given to foreign travellers, women travellers should not expect any special attention. If you have to take a taxi home at night alone, call for one as this will be recorded. For additional safety let the driver see a friend write down the taxi licence-plate number. If the driver can also see that you have a mobile phone, trouble is less likely. Women travelling to Taiwan for business should dress modestly and conservatively (as should men). Drinking and smoking are a part of Taiwanese business culture, but Taiwanese women tend to smoke and drink less than Taiwanese men (though this is changing fast among the younger generation).

Work

To work legally in Taiwan you generally need to enter on a visitor visa, have your company apply for a work permit, apply for a resident visa after you receive your work permit, and apply for an ARC after receiving your resident visa. You can apply for a visitor visa at any overseas Taiwan trade office or foreign mission. Your company applies for your work permit from the **Council of Labour Affairs** (www.cla.gov.tw). You can apply for a resident visa through the **Bureau of Consular Affairs** (BOCA; www.boca.gov.tw). An ARC can be applied for at any office of the **National Immigration Agency** (www.immigration.gov.tw). For short-term employment the rules are constantly changing so see the BOCA website and visit your local Taiwan trade office or overseas mission.

Job listings can be found at **104 Job Bank** (www.104.com.tw, in Chinese) and **TEALIT** (www.tealit.com).

Teaching English is not what it once was and there are fewer and fewer openings. Salaries have not risen in 15 years. Jobs are listed on **TEALIT** (www.tealit.com), **Dave's ESL Cafe** (www.eslcafe.com) and **Forumosa** (www.forumosa.com).

Transport

GETTING THERE & AWAY

Entering the Country

Immigration procedures are smooth and hassle free. Most guards speak some English.

Passport

There aren't any countries whose stamps in your passport will cause a problem at immigration. For visa information, see p372.

Air

Airports & Airlines

Main International Airport

Taiwan Taoyuan International Airport (TPE; www.taoyuanairport.gov.tw/) In Dayuan, 40km (40 minutes) west of central Taipei. Formerly known as Chiang Kai-shek International Airport.

Other International Airports

Cing Cyuan Gang Airport (RMQ; www.tca.gov.tw/English/Introduction.htm) In Taichung, mostly for flights from within Asia.

Siaogang Airport (KHH; www.kia.gov.tw) In Kaohsiung, mostly for flights from within Asia.

Taipei International Airport (Songshan Airport; TSA; www.tsa.gov.tw) In Taipei city; handles direct flights from China and Japan.

National Airlines

Taiwan has two major international airlines:

China Airlines (www.china-airlines.com)

Eva Air (www.evaair.com)

Eva Air started operation in 1991 and has had no fatalities to date. China Airlines was somewhat infamous for its safety record in the 1990s. Incidents since the turn of the century have been few. Officials credit this to new training practices (with pilots training at US flight schools) and a new corporate culture.

Tickets

Most people book flights through a travel agent or online at www.eztravel.com.tw. If flying to the outer islands, book directly with the airline. Flights and tours can be booked online at www.lonelyplanet.com/bookings.

Land

Bicycle

You'll have no problems bringing bicycles into the country. See p30 for more about cycling around Taiwan.

Sea

There are no longer ferries to Japan or Macau; however, there are daily ferries from/to Xiamen (Fujian, China) and Kinmen Island. If going from Taiwan to China you must have your Chinese visa prepared.

CLIMATE CHANGE & TRAVEL

Every form of transport that relies on carbon-based fuel generates CO_2, the main cause of human-induced climate change. Modern travel is dependent on aeroplanes, which might use less fuel per kilometre per person than most cars but travel much greater distances. The altitude at which aircraft emit gases (including CO_2) and particles also contributes to their climate change impact. Many websites offer 'carbon calculators' that allow people to estimate the carbon emissions generated by their journey and, for those who wish to do so, to offset the impact of the greenhouse gases emitted with contributions to portfolios of climate-friendly initiatives throughout the world. Lonely Planet offsets the carbon footprint of all staff and author travel.

GETTING AROUND

Air

Airlines in Taiwan

The domestic airline industry is moribund because of competition from the High Speed Rail. There are very few domestic flights now, except to the outer islands.

Daily Air Corporation (☎02-2712 3995; www.dailyair.com.tw) Mostly flies to outer islands from Kaohsiung (to Penghu) or Taitung (to Green Island and Lanyu).

Mandarin Airlines (☎02-2717 1230; www.mandarin-airlines.com) Flies to Hualien, Kaohsiung, Kinmen, Penghu, Taichung, Taipei and Taitung.

TransAsia Airways (☎02-2972 4599; www.tna.com.tw) Flies to Taipei, Hualien, Penghu, Kaohsiung and Kinmen.

UNI Air (☎07-801 0189; www.uniair.com.tw) Flies to Chiayi, Kaohsiung, Kinmen, Penghu, Matsu, Taichung, Tainan, Taipei and Taitung.

Bicycle

Cycling fever has overtaken Taiwan these past three years. See p30 for information on routes, road conditions, safety, rentals, and taking bikes on buses and trains.

Boat

There's a regular ferry service between mainland Taiwan and outer islands. It's a safe but often extremely uncomfortable way to travel, because of rough seas. There are regular predictable routes to Penghu and Green Island in summer, and to Little Liuchiu Island year-round. Sailings to Lanyu and Matsu are subject to weather conditions: cancellations are common and winter schedules change frequently.

Bus

Buses are generally safe, reliable and cheap, and are generally comfortable for a Western-sized frame. Some companies offer very large, cosy airplane-style reclining seats. Reservations are advisable on weekends and holidays.

Intercity Buses

There's an extensive network from Taipei to Kenting National Park. Service from the west coast to the east coast is limited, though good within the east area (from Hualien to Taitung). There are very frequent departures (some 24-hour operations), with midweek and late-evening discounts. All companies serve the same west-coast routes. The main transit points are Taipei, Taichung and Kaohsiung

Intercity Bus Companies

Aloha Bus (☎0800-043 168; www.aloha168.com.tw)

Kuo Kuang Motor Transport (☎0800-010 138; www.kingbus.com.tw)

UBus (☎0800-241 560; www.ubus.com.tw)

Rural Buses

The network is wide, but there are few departures except to major tourist destinations (such as Sun Moon Lake). Note: the government is committed to re-establishing a comprehensive rural network, so we should see big improvements from 2011 onwards.

Tourist Shuttle Buses

These buses go to destinations that are difficult to reach by public transport. The buses usually leave hourly. See www.taiwantrip.com.tw for more information.

Car & Scooter

To be able to access many of the best areas in Taiwan, you need your own vehicle – throughout this guide we've noted where this applies. In general, your motorised renting options will be a car or a scooter.

Driving in Taiwan

By the standards of many countries, driving in Taiwan can be chaotic and dangerous. Accidents are common and almost always the result of carelessness compounded by poor judgment and a 'me first' mentality.

You are not advised to drive in cities or medium-sized towns until you are used to the conditions. On freeways and expressways, on the east coast and in rural and mountainous areas it is usually relatively safe to drive, especially midweek.

Of the big cities, Taipei's traffic is best; Taichung's is worst. Many smaller cities

BUS TRIPS FROM TAIPEI

The following sample trips are from Taipei with Kuo Kuang Motor Transport.

DESTINATION	FARE (NT$)	DURATION (HR)
Kaohsiung	400	5
Sun Moon Lake	460	3½
Taichung	220	4½
Tainan	360	4½

such as Taoyuan, Chiayi and Hualien have horrendous traffic conditions.

See p32 for common driving hazards such as passing on blind corners.

Fuel & Spare Parts

Petrol stations and garages are widely available for parts and repairs for scooters and cars. Check out www.forumosa.com for a thread on reliable and trustworthy mechanics.

Road Conditions

Roads are generally in good shape, though washouts are common in mountain areas, and roads are often closed. Be cautious when driving in such areas during or after heavy rains.

Freeways and expressways are in excellent shape. There are tolls on freeways, at a cost of NT$40 per toll. You can pay with pre-bought tickets or with cash. If paying with cash you must use the cash payment toll booths. Using other booths will result in a fine.

Most road signage is bilingual.

Wikipedia (http://en.wikipedia.org) has an excellent overview of Taiwan's road and highway system. Go to the website and type 'highway system in Taiwan'.

Road Rules

Important rules: Taiwanese drive on the right-hand side of the road; right turns on red lights are illegal; drivers and all passengers must wear seatbelts; and children under the age of four (and 18kg) must be secured in safety seats (rarely done and rarely enforced). Violators face fines of NT$1500 (NT$3000 to NT$6000 on highways). In general, only speeding and turning-on-red-light violations are enforced.

ROAD DISTANCES (KM)

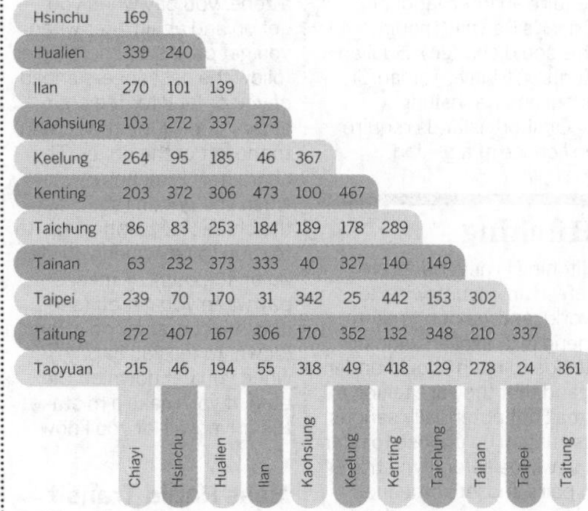

	Chiayi	Hsinchu	Hualien	Ilan	Kaohsiung	Keelung	Kenting	Taichung	Tainan	Taipei	Taitung
Hsinchu	169										
Hualien	339	240									
Ilan	270	101	139								
Kaohsiung	103	272	337	373							
Keelung	264	95	185	46	367						
Kenting	203	372	306	473	100	467					
Taichung	86	83	253	184	189	178	289				
Tainan	63	232	373	333	40	327	140	149			
Taipei	239	70	170	31	342	25	442	153	302		
Taitung	272	407	167	306	170	352	132	348	210	337	
Taoyuan	215	46	194	55	318	49	418	129	278	24	361

Driving Licence

International Driver's Permit (IDP)

This is valid in Taiwan for up to 30 days. With an ARC (Alien Resident Certificate) you can apply to have your permit validated at a local Motor Vehicles Office. This simple procedure validates the IDP for up to one year.

Local Driver's Licence

Driving licences are issued by county, and if you have an ARC you can apply. Tests include a written and driving section – both parts are challenging for their sheer absurdity (such as the infamous backwards 'S' test and questions that refer to national pride). For an example of a test, see the website of the **Taipei Motor Vehicle Office** (www.tmvso.gov.tw).

Reciprocal Licence Agreements

If your country has a reciprocal agreement with Taiwan, you may be able to obtain a Taiwanese licence just by showing your home licence and passport.

Check out the websites of the **Taipei Motor Vehicle Office** (www.tmvso.gov.tw) or **Information for Foreigners** (http://iff.immigration.gov.tw).

Insurance

You'll usually need to take out third-party liability insurance and comprehensive insurance, with a NT$10,000 deduction for damages.

In the case of theft or loss, renters are charged 10% of the value of the car.

Vehicle Hire

Car Hire

Expect to pay NT$800 to NT$1500 for a half-day's hire, and NT$1500 to NT$2600 for a full day, although long-term discounts are available.

All airports, and most High Speed Rail stations, have car-rental agencies (or free delivery).

Car Plus (☎0800-222 568; www.car-plus.com.tw) Good reputation. Island-wide offices.

Central Auto (☎02-2828 0033; www.rentalcar.com.tw) Long-running foreign-managed rental company with Taipei, Taichung and Kaohsiung branches. Good reputation.

Scooter Hire

On average, hire costs NT$300 to NT$600 per day. Some places will allow you to rent with an International Driver's Permit; others require a local scooter licence.

The following areas only require an International Driver's Permit (though this could change): Hualien, Kenting, Chiayi, Tainan, Jiaoshi and Kaohsiung.

Offshore islands require no licence of any kind.

Hitching

Hitching is never entirely safe in any country in the world, and we don't recommend it. Travellers who do decide to hitch should understand that they are taking a small but potentially serious risk. If you do choose to hitch you will be safer if you travel in pairs and let someone know where you are planning to go.

At times, such as getting to or from a mountain trailhead, hitching may be your only option if you don't have a vehicle. Taiwanese are usually more than happy to give you a lift. Money is almost never asked for.

Local Transport

Bus

Outside of Taipei and Kaohsiung, buses are the only public transport option in the big cities. Most city buses have signs in English at the front and many have LED displays inside announcing the next stop.

You can usually find bus-schedule information at the visitor information centre in town (often right inside the train station). In smaller towns and cities it's easier just to walk than to bother with sporadic bus services.

Fares

Fares vary by city. For example, a single zone fare in Taipei is NT$15, while in Kaohsiung it's NT$12. The cost of travelling in two zones is double the price of a one-zone fare.

Sometimes you pay when you get on and sometimes when you get off. If you cross a zone, you pay when you get on and again later when you get off. As a general rule, follow the passengers ahead of you or look for the characters 上 or 下 on the screen to the left of the driver. The character 上 means pay when you get on (see it as the character pointing 'up' to tell you to pay when you step up on the bus); 下 means pay when you get off (see it as the character pointing 'down' to tell you to pay when you get down off the bus). If you make a mistake the driver will let you know (or not).

Mass Rapid Transit

Taipei's and Kaohsiung's Mass Rapid Transit (MRT) metro systems are clean, safe, convenient and reliable. All signs and ticket machines are in English. English signs around stations indicate which exit to take to nearby sights. Posters indicate bus transfer routes.

Check out the stations' websites, which both feature excellent maps of areas around each station.

Kaohsiung MRT (www.krtco.com.tw; fares NT$20-60; ⏲6am-midnight) Two lines, 36 stations, 40km of track. Connects with the international and domestic airports. Trains leave, on average, every six minutes.

Taipei MRT (www.trtc.com.tw; fares NT$20-65; ⏲6am-midnight) Eight lines, 82 stations and 90.5km of track. New lines in the works. Connects with Taipei (Songshan) International Airport (will connect with Taoyuan International Airport by 2013). Trains leave, on average, every three to eight minutes.

Taxi

Hotlines & Language Services

In Taipei, call the taxi hotline on ☎0800-055 850 (wait for the message and press 2). Call ☎02-2799 4818 for English or Japanese drivers. In Kaohsiung call ☎0800-488 888 or ☎07-330 8888.

Within Large Cities

Taxis are everywhere. A ride will cost you NT$70 for the first 1.5km or portion thereof, and then NT$5 per 300m. After midnight, fares are surcharged at an additional NT$20. Surcharges may also apply for things such as luggage and reserving a cab (as opposed to hailing one). You can call for taxis if you have safety concerns (all calls are recorded and saved for one month).

Outside Large Cities

Drivers will either use meters or ask for a flat rate (the smaller the town the more likely the latter). Taxis are not that abundant, so it's a good idea to get your hotel to call first, and then to keep the driver's number for subsequent rides.

Tours

Barking Deer (www.barking-deer.com) Foreign-run company offering complete or partial high-mountain hiking packages as well as day and multiday ecotours with an emphasis on bird- and butterfly-watching.

Green Island Adventures (www.greenislandadventures.com) Diving and scuba tours to Taiwan's outer islands and the mainland.

InMotion Asia (www.inmotionasia.com) Cycling trips around Taiwan, with an emphasis on mountain-biking tours.

Taiwan Tour Bus (www.taiwantourbus.com.tw) Organised by the tourism bureau with easy-to-understand half- and full-day itineraries. Buses depart from train stations, airports and major hotels. Tours range in price from NT$600 to NT$2000.

Whose Travel (www.whosetravel.com) Reliable

SAMPLE TRAIN FARES

FROM	TO	FARE (NT$; TZE-CHIANG/ FU-HSING CLASS)	DURATION (HR; TZE-CHIANG/ FU-HSING CLASS)
Hualien	Taitung	346/222	2½/3½
Kaohsiung	Taitung	364/234	2/3
Taipei	Hualien	441/284	2½/3½
Taipei	Kaohsiung	845/544	4½/7
Taipei	Taichung	375/241	2/3

foreign- and Taiwanese-run travel agency that organises tickets, tours and discount accommodation.

Train

Taiwan Railway Administration (TRA; www.railway.gov.tw) has an extensive system running up both the east and west coasts. There are no services into the Central Mountains, except tourism branch lines.

In the coming years expect travel times to speed up, especially on the east coast as lines become electrified and straightened, new tunnels are added and more tilting trains are brought into operation.

Trains are comfortable, clean, safe and reliable, with few delays. Reserved seating is available on trains, as are food and snacks. All major cities are connected by train. For timetables, see the TRA website.

Classes

Chu-kuang (莒光; Jǔguāng) & **Fu-hsing** (復興; Fùxīng) Slower and more ordinary than Tze-chiang class, with less legroom. The fare is about 20% to 40% cheaper than Tze-chiang.

Local Train (區間車; Qūjiānchē) Cheap, stops at all stations, more like commuter trains, no reserved seating.

Ordinary Train (普通; Pǔtōng) Very cheap, slow, stops at all stations, no air-con (for nostalgia buffs).

Taroko Express (太魯閣號; Tàilǔgé Hào) Special tilting trains that travel from Taipei to Hualien in two hours.

Tze-chiang (自強; Zìqiáng) The fastest and most comfortable class.

At the time of writing, new business and overnight sleeper trains to the east coast were restarting.

Fare Information

At the time of writing there was no English fare information available; however, we were promised that it would be available soon. Try calling the 24-hour **Tourist Hotline** (☎0800-011 765).

Reservations & Fares

For fast trains, especially on weekends or holidays, it is advisable to buy your tickets up to two weeks in advance. You can book online (⌚6am to 9pm) or at 7-Eleven Ibon kiosks (in Chinese only at the time of writing, although this should change). You'll need your passport number to book online. Within three days of booking, collect tickets from 7.30am to 10pm at any train station.

Tourism Branch Lines

Several small branch lines are maintained for tourist purposes:

Alishan (p205)

Jiji (p224)

Neiwan (p148)

Pingxi (p115).

Visitor Information Centres

Most major cities have visitor information centres with English-speaking staff, inside or just outside the train station. The centres are usually open from 9am to 6pm and have local bus, food and accommodation information.

High Speed Rail

Taiwan High Speed Rail (HSR, THSR; www.thsrc.com.tw) started operations in 2007. There is one 345km track between Taipei and Kaohsiung. So far eight stations have opened (Taipei, Banciao, Taoyuan, Hsinchu, Taichung, Chiayi, Tainan and Zuoying). More are expected to open in the coming years. The HSR has a perfect safety record so far.

The trains offer airplane-like comfort, and reserved seating is available. Food and

HIGH SPEED RAIL SCHEDULES FROM TAIPEI

DESTINATION	FARE (NT$)	DURATION
Taichung	700	1hr
Tainan	1350	1hr 40min
Taoyuan	160	20min
Zuoying (Kaohsiung)	1490	1½-2hr

snacks are available (though smelly foods such as stinky tofu are prohibited).

For timetables and fares, see the HSR website. In general, there are three trains per hour. All stations have visitor information centres with English-speaking staff to help with bus transfers, hotel bookings and car rentals.

Most stations are 30 to 40 minutes from downtown areas. Free (or inexpensive) and frequent shuttle buses or commuter trains connect HSR stations and downtown areas.

Classes

There are two classes: standard and business. Business fares are double the price of standard, and offer larger seats and 110V electrical outlets.

Reservations & Fares

On weekends or holidays, it's advisable to buy your tickets in advance (it's possible to purchase these up to 15 days in advance). You can buy tickets at stations (either at machines or counters), online and at 7-Eleven convenience stores. There are small discounts for unreserved seating areas.

Health

BEFORE YOU GO

If you take any regular medication bring double.

In Taiwan it may be difficult to find some newer drugs, particularly the latest antidepressant drugs, blood-pressure medications and contraceptive pills.

Recommended Vaccinations

If you plan to travel from Taiwan to a country with a typhoid problem you should get the vaccination elsewhere as Taiwan does not have typhoid vaccinations anywhere.

Check the World Health Organization (WHO) website (www.who.int/ith) for recommended vaccinations for travellers to Taiwan.

Websites

Centers for Disease Control and Prevention (CDC; www.cdc.gov) Good general information.

Lonely Planet (www.lonelyplanet.com) A good place to visit for starters.

MD Travel Health (www.mdtravelhealth.com) Provides complete travel-health recommendations for every country. Revised daily.

World Health Organization (www.who.int/ith) Publishes a superb book called *International Travel and Health,* revised annually and available free online.

IN TAIWAN

Availability & Cost of Health Care

Taiwan is a developed country with excellent universal medical coverage. Most medical care is cheaper than in Western countries. Many doctors are trained in Western countries and speak at least some English.

In rural areas quality of health care is poorer but Taiwan is small and you should be able to get to a good hospital in a few hours.

Infectious Diseases

Dengue Fever

This mosquito-borne disease is becomingly increasingly problematic in Taiwan in both cities and rural areas (mostly urban areas). Prevent by avoiding mosquito bites – there is no vaccine. Mosquitoes that carry dengue bite day and night. Symptoms include high fever, severe headache and body ache (previously dengue was known as 'breakbone fever').

Hepatitis A & B

All travellers to Taiwan should be vaccinated against hepatitis A and B.

Japanese B Encephalitis

Potentially fatal viral disease transmitted by mosquitoes, but rare in travellers.Transmission season runs June to October. Vaccination is recommended for travellers spending more than one month outside of cities.

Environmental Hazards

Air Pollution

Air pollution, particularly vehicle pollution, is a problem in all major urban areas. Avoid downtown during busy hours. Air is much better in the early morning, at night, and after rain.

REQUIRED VACCINATIONS

Yellow Fever Proof of vaccination is required if entering Taiwan within six days of visiting an infected country. If you are travelling to Taiwan from Africa or South America check with a travel-medicine clinic whether you need the vaccine.

TAP WATER

» Drinkable in Taipei without treatment.

» Filter elsewhere or buy bottled.

» Ice is usually fine at restaurants.

» Shaved ice (with fruit) is usually fine but take a look at the shop.

Insect Bites & Stings

Insects are not a major issue in Taiwan, though there are some insect-borne diseases present.

Ticks can be contracted from walking in rural areas, and are commonly found behind the ears, on the belly and in armpits.

If you have had a tick bite and experience symptoms such as a rash at the site of the bite or elsewhere, or fever or muscle aches, see a doctor.

Women's Health

In most developed areas of Taiwan, supplies of sanitary products are readily available.

Birth-control options may be limited so bring supplies of your own contraception.

Taiwan's heat and humidity can contribute to thrush.

Traditional & Folk Medicine

Traditional Chinese Medicine (TCM) remains very popular in Taiwan. TCM views the human body as an energy system in which the basic substances of *chi (qi;* vital energy), *jing* (essence), blood (the body's nourishing fluids) and body fluids (other organic fluids) function. The concept of Yin and Yang is fundamental to the system. Disharmony between Yin and Yang or within the basic substances may be a result of internal causes (emotions), external causes (climatic conditions) or miscellaneous causes (work, exercise, sex etc). Treatment modalities include acupuncture, massage, herbs, dietary modification and *qijong* (the skill of attracting positive energy) and aim to bring these elements back into balance. These therapies are particularly useful for treating chronic diseases and are gaining interest and respect in the Western medical system. Conditions that can be particularly suitable for traditional methods include chronic fatigue, arthritis, irritable bowel syndrome and some chronic skin conditions.

Be aware that 'natural' doesn't always mean 'safe', and there can be drug interactions between herbal medicines and Western medicines. If you are using both systems, ensure you inform both practitioners what the other has prescribed.

Language

WANT MORE?

For in-depth language information and handy phrases, check out Lonely Planet's *Mandarin Phrasebook*. You'll find it at **shop.lonelyplanet.com**, or you can buy Lonely Planet's iPhone phrasebooks at the Apple App Store.

The official language of Taiwan is referred to in the west as Mandarin Chinese. The Chinese call it Pǔtōnghuà (common speech) and in Taiwan it is known as Guóyǔ (the national language). Taiwanese, often called a 'dialect' of Mandarin, is in fact a separate language and the two are not mutually intelligible. Today at least half the population speaks Taiwanese at home, especially in the south and in rural areas. However, travellers to Taiwan can get by without using any Taiwanese, as virtually all young and middle-aged people speak Mandarin. Hakka, another Chinese language, is also spoken in some areas, and Taiwan's aboriginal tribes have their own languages, which belong to a separate language family from Chinese.

WRITING

Chinese is often referred to as a language of pictographs. Many of the basic Chinese characters are in fact highly stylised pictures of what they represent, but most (around 90%) are compounds of a 'meaning' element and a 'sound' element.

It is estimated that a well-educated, contemporary Chinese person might use between 6000 and 8000 characters. To read a Chinese newspaper you will need to know 2000 to 3000 characters, but 1200 to 1500 would be enough to get the gist.

Theoretically, all Chinese dialects share the same written system. In practice, however, Taiwan doesn't use the system of 'simplified' characters that were introduced in China. Instead, Taiwan has retained the use of traditional characters, which are also found in Hong Kong.

PINYIN & PRONUNCIATION

In 1958 the Chinese adopted a system of writing their language using the Roman alphabet, known as Pinyin. Travellers to Taiwan are unlikely to encounter much Pinyin other than for names of people, places and streets. The new signs tend to be in one of two different systems: Hanyu Pinyin, which is used in China (and has become the international standard for Mandarin), and Tongyong Pinyin, a home-grown alternative created in the late 1990s. Although the central government has declared Tongyong Pinyin to be Taiwan's official Romanisation system for both Hakka and Mandarin (but not for Taiwanese), it left local governments free to make their own choices. Taipei has selected to use Hanyu Pinyin and has applied the system consistently, but in most of the country progress towards standardisation in any form of Pinyin is slow.

In this chapter we've provided Hanyu Pinyin alonside the Mandarin script.

Vowels

a	as in 'father'
ai	as in 'aisle'
ao	as the 'ow' in 'cow'
e	as in 'her', with no 'r' sound
ei	as in 'weigh'
i	as the 'ee' in 'meet' (or like a light 'r' as in 'Grrr!' after c, ch, r, s, sh, z or zh)
ian	as the word 'yen'
ie	as the English word 'yeah'
o	as in 'or', with no 'r' sound

ou	as the 'oa' in 'boat'
u	as in 'flute'
ui	as the word 'way'
uo	like a 'w' followed by 'o'
yu/ü	like 'ee' with lips pursed

Consonants

c	as the 'ts' in 'bits'
ch	as in 'chop', but with the tongue curled up and back
h	as in 'hay', but articulated from farther back in the throat
q	as the 'ch' in 'cheese'
r	as the 's' in 'pleasure'
sh	as in 'ship', but with the tongue curled up and back
x	as in 'ship'
z	as the 'dz' in 'suds'
zh	as the 'j' in 'judge' but with the tongue curled up and back

The only consonants that occur at the end of a syllable are n, ng and r.

In Pinyin, apostrophes are occasionally used to separate syllables in order to prevent ambiguity, eg the word píng'ān can be written with an apostrophe after the 'g' to prevent it being pronounced as pín'gān.

Tones

Chinese is a language with a large number of words with the same pronunciation but a different meaning. What distinguishes these words is their 'tonal' quality – the raising and the lowering of pitch on certain syllables. Mandarin employs four tones – high, rising, falling-rising and falling, plus a fifth 'neutral' tone that you can all but ignore. Tones are important for distinguishing meaning of words – eg the word ma can have four different meanings according to tone, as shown below.

Tones are indicated in Pinyin by the following accent marks on vowels:

high tone	mā (mother)
rising tone	má (hemp, numb)
falling-rising tone	mǎ (horse)
falling tone	mà (scold, swear)

BASICS

When asking a question it is polite to start with qǐng wèn – literally, 'may I ask?'.

Hello.	您好.	Nín hǎo.
Goodbye.	再見.	Zàijiàn.
Yes.	是.	Shì.
No.	不是.	Bùshì.
Please.	請.	Qǐng.
Thank you.	謝謝.	Xièxie.
You're welcome.	不客氣.	Bùkèqì.
Excuse me, ...	請問, ...	Qǐng wèn, ...

What's your name?
請問您貴姓? Qǐngwèn nín guìxìng?

My name is ...
我姓 ... Wǒ xìng ...

Do you speak English?
你會講英文嗎? Nǐ huì jiǎng yīngwén ma?

I don't understand.
我聽不懂. Wǒ tīngbùdǒng.

ACCOMMODATION

I'm looking for a ...	我要找 ...	Wǒ yào zhǎo ...
campsite	露營區	lùyíngqū
guesthouse	賓館	bīnguǎn
hotel	旅館	lǚguǎn
youth hostel	旅社	lǚshè

Do you have a room available?
你們有房間嗎? Nǐmen yǒu fángjiān ma?

Where is the bathroom?
浴室在哪裡? Yùshì zài nǎlǐ?

I'd like (a) ...	我想要 ...	Wǒ xiǎng yào ...
double room	一間雙人房	yījiān shuāngrénfáng
single room	一間單人房	yījiān dānrénfáng
to share a dorm	住宿舍	zhù sùshè
How much is it ...?	... 多少錢?	... duōshǎo qián?
per night	一個晚上	Yīge wǎnshàng
per person	每個人	Měigerén

DIRECTIONS

Where is (the) ...?
... 在哪裡? ... zài nǎlǐ?

What is the address?
地址在哪裡? Dìzhǐ zài nǎlǐ?

Could you write the address, please?
能不能請你把地址寫下來? Néngbùnéng qǐng nǐ bǎ dìzhǐ xiě xiàlái?

Could you show me (on the map)?
你能不能(在地圖上)指給我看? Nǐ néng bùnéng (zài dìtú shàng) zhǐ gěi wǒ kàn?

Go straight ahead.
一直走. Yīzhí zǒu.

Signs

入口	Entrance
出口	Exit
詢問處	Information
開	Open
關	Closed
禁止	Prohibited
厠所	Toilets
男	Men
女	Women

at the next corner
在下一個轉角 zài xià yīge zhuǎnjiǎo

at the traffic lights
在紅綠燈 zài hónglǜdēng

behind	後面	hòumiàn
far	遠	yuǎn
in front of	前面	qiánmiàn
near	近	jìn
opposite	對面	duìmiàn
Turn left.	左轉.	Zuǒ zhuǎn.
Turn right.	右轉.	Yòu zhuǎn.

EATING & DRINKING

I'm vegetarian.
我吃素. Wǒ chī sù.

I don't want MSG.
我不要味精. Wǒ bú yào wèijīng.

Not too spicy.
不要太辣. Bú yào tài là.

Let's eat.
吃飯. Chī fàn.

Cheers!
乾杯! Gānbēi!

Key Words

bill (check)	買單/結帳	mǎidān/jiézhàng
chopsticks	筷子	kuàizi
cold	冰的	bīngde
fork	叉子	chāzi
hot	熱的	rède
knife	刀子	dāozi
menu	菜單	càidān
set meal (no menu)	套餐	tàocān
spoon	調羹/湯匙	tiáogēng/tāngchí

Other

boiled dumplings	水餃	shuǐjiǎo
clams	蛤蠣	gélì
crab	螃蟹	pángxiè
fried rice with vegetables	蔬菜炒飯	shūcài chǎofàn
lobster	龍蝦	lóngxiā
noodles (not in soup)	乾麵	gān miàn
noodles (in soup)	湯麵	tāngmiàn
octopus	章魚	zhāngyú
soup	湯	tāng
squid	魷魚	yóuyú
steamed buns	饅頭	mántóu
steamed white rice	白飯	báifàn
sticky rice	筒仔米糕	tǒngzǎi mǐgāo
tofu	豆腐	dòufu
wonton with noodles	餛飩麵	húntún miàn

Drinks

beer	啤酒	píjiǔ
coconut juice	椰子汁	yézi zhī
coffee	咖啡	kāfēi
Kaoliang liquor	高粱酒	gāoliáng jiǔ
milk	牛奶	niúnǎi
mineral water	礦泉水	kuàngquán shuǐ
orange juice	柳丁汁	liǔdīng zhī
red wine	紅葡萄酒	hóng pútáo jiǔ
rice wine	米酒	mǐjiǔ
soft drink	汽水	qìshuǐ
soybean milk	豆漿	dòujiāng
(oolong) tea	(烏龍)茶	(wūlóng) chá
water	水	shuǐ
white wine	白葡萄酒	bái pútáo jiǔ

EMERGENCIES

Help!	救命啊!	Jiùmìng a!
I'm lost.	我迷路了.	Wǒ mílùle.
Leave me alone!	別煩我!	Bié fán wǒ!
Call ...!	請叫 ...!	Qǐng jiào ...!
a doctor	醫生	yīshēng
the police	警察	jǐngchá

There's been an accident.
發生意外了. Fāshēng yìwài le.

I'm ill.
我生病了. Wǒ shēngbìngle.

It hurts here.
這裡痛. Zhèlǐ tòng.

I'm allergic to (antibiotics).
我對(抗生素)過敏. Wǒ duì (kàngshēngsù) guòmǐn.

SHOPPING & SERVICES

I'd like to buy ...
我想買 ... Wǒ xiǎng mǎi ...

I'm just looking.
我只是看看. Wǒ zhǐshì kànkan.

Can I see it?
能看看嗎? Néng kànkàn ma?

I don't like it.
我不喜歡. Wǒ bù xǐhuān.

How much is it?
多少錢? Duōshǎo qián?

That's too expensive.
太貴了. Tài guìle.

Is there anything cheaper?
有便宜一點的嗎? Yǒu piányí yīdiǎn de ma?

Do you accept credit cards?
收不收信用卡? Shōu bùshōu xìnyòngkǎ?

Where can I get online?
我在哪裡可以上網? Wǒ zài nǎlǐ kěyǐ shàngwǎng?

I'm looking for ...	我在找 ...	Wǎ zài zhǎo ...
an ATM	自動櫃員機/提款機	zìdòng guìyuánjī/tíkuǎnjī
the post office	郵局	yóujú
the tourist office	觀光局	guānguāngjú

TIME & DATES

What's the time?	幾點?	Jǐ diǎn?
... hour	... 點	... diǎn
... minute	... 分	... fēn

Question Words

How?	怎麼?	Zěnme?
What?	什麼?	Shénme?
When?	什麼時候?	Shénme shíhòu?
Where?	在哪裡?	Zài nǎlǐ?
Which?	哪個?	Nǎge?
Who?	誰?	Sheí?

yesterday	昨天	zuótiān
today	今天	jīntiān
tomorrow	明天	míngtiān
in the morning	早上	zǎoshàng
in the afternoon	下午	xiàwǔ
in the evening	晚上	wǎnshàng

Monday	星期一	Xīngqíyī
Tuesday	星期二	Xīngqí'èr
Wednesday	星期三	Xīngqísān
Thursday	星期四	Xīngqísì
Friday	星期五	Xīngqíwǔ
Saturday	星期六	Xīngqíliù
Sunday	星期天	Xīngqítiān

January	一月	Yīyuè
February	二月	Èryuè
March	三月	Sānyuè
April	四月	Sìyuè
May	五月	Wǔyuè
June	六月	Liùyuè
July	七月	Qīyuè
August	八月	Bāyuè
September	九月	Jiǔyuè
October	十月	Shíyuè
November	十一月	Shíyīyuè
December	十二月	Shí'èryuè

TRANSPORT

Public Transport

What time does the ... leave/arrive?	... 幾點開/到?	... jǐdiǎn kāi/dào?
boat	船	chuán
city bus	公車	gōngchē
intercity bus	客運	kèyùn
minibus	小型公車	xiǎoxíng gōngchē
plane	飛機	fēijī
train	火車	huǒchē

I'd like a ... ticket.	我要一張 ... 票.	Wǒ yào yìzhāng ... piào
one-way	單程	dānchéng
platform	月台票	yuètái piào
return	來回	láihuí

Numbers

1	一	yī
2	二, 兩	èr, liǎng
3	三	sān
4	四	sì
5	五	wǔ
6	六	liù
7	七	qī
8	八	bā
9	九	jiǔ
10	十	shí
20	二十	èrshí
30	三十	sānshí
40	四十	sìshí
50	五十	wǔshí
60	六十	liùshí
70	七十	qīshí
80	八十	bāshí
90	九十	jiǔshí
100	一百	yìbǎi
1000	一千	yìqiān

I want to go to ...
我要去 ... Wǒ yào qù ...

The train has been delayed/cancelled.
火車(晚點了/取消了). Huǒchē (wǎndiǎn le/qǔxiāo le).

When's the ... bus?	... 班車什麼時候來?	... bānchē shénme shíhòu lái?
first	頭	tóu
last	末	mò
next	下	xià

airport	機場	jīchǎng
left-luggage room	寄放處	jìfàng chù
long-distance bus station	客運站	kèyùn zhàn
platform number	月台號碼	yuètái hàomǎ
subway (underground)	捷運	jíeyùn
subway station	捷運站	jíeyùn zhàn
ticket office	售票處	shòupiào chù
timetable	時刻表	shíkèbiǎo
train station	火車站	huǒchē zhàn

Driving & Cycling

I'd like to hire a ...	我要租一輛 ...	Wǒ yào zū yíliàng ...
bicycle	腳踏車	jiǎotàchē
car	汽車	qìchē
motorcycle	摩托車	mótuōchē

diesel	柴油	cháiyóu
petrol	汽油	qìyóu

Does this road lead to ...?
這條路到 ... 嗎? Zhè tiáo lù dào ... ma?

Where's the next service station?
下一個加油站在哪裡? Xià yíge jiāyóuzhàn zài nǎlǐ?

Can I park here?
這裡可以停車嗎? Zhèlǐ kěyǐ tíngchē ma?

How long can I park here?
這裡可以停多久? Zhèlǐ kěyǐ tíng duōjiǔ?

I need a mechanic.
我需要汽車維修員. Wǒ xūyào qìchē wéixiūyuán.

The car has broken down (at ...).
車子(在…)拋錨了. Chēzi (zài ...) pāomáo le.

I have a flat tyre.
輪胎破了. Lúntāi pòle.

I've run out of petrol.
没有汽油了. Méiyǒu qìyóu le.

GLOSSARY

aborigines *(yuánzhùmín)* – the original residents of Taiwan, of which there are currently 13 recognised tribes; believed to be the ancestors of all Austronesian people

Amis – Taiwan's largest aboriginal tribe; lives on the coastal plains of eastern Taiwan

ARC – Alien Resident Certificate; foreign visitors must apply for one if planning to stay for long-term work or study

Atayal – Taiwan's second-largest aboriginal tribe; lives in mountainous regions of the north

Bao chung – type of oolong tea grown around Pinglin

Běnshěngrén – Taiwanese people whose ancestors came to Taiwan prior to 1949

black gold *(hēi jīn)* – in Taiwan this refers to political corruption and not oil
Bunun – Taiwan's third-largest aboriginal tribe; lives in Central Mountains

catty – unit of measure (600g)
chá – tea, especially Chinese tea
chi *(qi)* – vital energy
Chu-kuang *(Jǔguāng)* – 2nd-class regular train
cochin pottery (also *koji*) – unique and colourful decorative art for temples
congee – rice porridge
cūn – village

dàgēdà (literally 'big-brother-big') – mobile phone
dǒugǒng – special bracketing system for Chinese architecture
DPP – Democratic Progressive Party; Taiwan's first opposition party

fēnxiāng – spirit division, or the process by which branch temples are founded
Forest Recreation Area – similar to a state or provincial park in the West
Fujianese – people originally from Fujian province in China who migrated to Taiwan; the Taiwanese dialect is derived from that of southern Fujian
Fu-hsing *(fùxīng)* – 2nd-class regular train

gǎng – harbour/port
gōng – Taoist temple

Hakka – nomadic subset of the Han Chinese, the Hakka were among the first Chinese to settle in Taiwan; many prominent Taiwanese are also Hakka people
Hanyu Pinyin – system of Romanisation used in mainland China; though there is some crossover, most signs in Taiwan outside Taipei use the *Tongyong Pinyin* or *Wade-Giles* systems
HSR – High Speed Rail, Taiwan's newly built 'bullet train'

Ilha Formosa – the name Portuguese sailors gave Taiwan, meaning 'beautiful island'

jiǎnniàn – mosaiclike temple decoration
jiǎotàchē zhuānyòng dào – bike path
jié – festival
jiē – street
jīn – unit of measure; see *catty*
jīngjù – see *opera (Taiwanese)*

Kaoliang – liquor made from sorghum; made in Matsu and Kinmen
KMRT – Kaohsiung's MRT system
KMT – Kuomintang; Nationalist Party of the Republic of China

láojiǔ – medicinal rice wine made in Matsu
liǎng – unit of measure (37.5g)
líng – divine efficaciousness; a god's power to grant wishes
Lu Tung Pin – one of the eight immortals of classical Chinese mythology; couples avoid his temples as he likes to break up happy lovers

Matsu *(Mǎzǔ)* – Goddess of the Sea, the most popular deity in Taiwan; one of the Taiwan Strait Islands
miào – general word for temple
Minnan – used to refer to the language, people, architecture etc of southern China (especially Fujian)
mínsù – B&B, homestay
mountain permit – special permit you pick up from local police stations to allow you to enter restricted mountainous areas
MRT – Mass Rapid Transit; Taipei's underground railway system

National Trail System – a system of hiking trails running over the entire island

One China – the idea that mainland China and Taiwan are both part of one country: People's Republic of China
oolong (also *wulong*) – semi-fermented tea, the most popular kind in Taiwan
opera (Taiwanese) – also known as Beijing or Chinese opera, a sophisticated art form that has been an important part of Chinese culture for more than 900 years
Oriental Beauty – type of heavily fermented tea, first grown in Taiwan

Paiwan – small aboriginal tribe; lives south of Pingtung
PFP (People First Party); offshoot of *KMT* started by James Soong
píng – unit of measure for property: land, apartments etc (4 sq metres)
PRC – People's Republic of China
pùbù – waterfall
Puyuma – small aboriginal tribe; lives on Taiwan's southeast coast

qiáo – bridge
qū – district/area

ROC – Republic of China; covered all of China before the *PRC* was established
Rukai – small aboriginal tribe located on Taiwan's southeast coast

Saisiyat – very small aboriginal tribe; lives in mountains of Miaoli County
Sakizaya – very small aboriginal tribe; lives around Hualien
Sediq – small aboriginal tribe; lives in Nantou

sēnlín – forest
shān – mountain
sì – Buddhist temple
Sinicism – Chinese method or customs
suòxī – river tracing; popular sport that involves walking up rivers and streams with the aid of nonslip shoes

tael – unit of measure; see *liǎng*
taichi – graceful but powerful slow-motion martial art commonly practised as the sun rises
Taipeiers – people from Taipei
Taroko – a sub-branch of the aboriginal Atayal tribe, recognised in 2004
Thao – very small aboriginal tribe; lives around Sun Moon Lake
Three Small Links – the opening of cross-Strait trade between China and Taiwan's offshore islands
Tieguanyin (Iron Goddess of Compassion) – type of oolong tea grown in Maokong, south of Taipei Zoo
tongpu – a type of multi-person room with no beds, just blankets and floor mats
Tongyong Pinyin – system of Romanisation used in parts of Taiwan
Truku – small aboriginal Atayal tribe; lives around Hualien
Tsou – small aboriginal tribe; lives around Kaohsiung
Tze-Chiang (*Zìqiáng*) – the fastest and most comfortable regular train

VAT – Value-Added Tax

Wade-Giles – a Romanisation system for Chinese words; widely used until the introduction of *Hanyu Pinyin*
Wàishěngrén – Taiwanese who emigrated from mainland China following the *KMT* defeat in the Chinese civil war
Wang Yeh – a Tang-dynasty scholar, said to watch over the waters of southern China; worshipped all over the south
wēnquán – hot spring
White Terror – a large-scale campaign started by the *KMT* to purge the island of political activists during the 1950s; one of the grimmest times in Taiwan's martial-law period

xiàng – lane

Yami – A small aboriginal tribe inhabiting Lanyu Island
yèshì – night market
Youth Guesthouse Network – program set up by the National Youth Commission to establish cheap hostel accommodation around the island

zhàn – station

behind the scenes

SEND US YOUR FEEDBACK

We love to hear from travellers – your comments keep us on our toes and help make our books better. Our well-travelled team reads every word on what you loved or loathed about this book. Although we cannot reply individually to postal submissions, we always guarantee that your feedback goes straight to the appropriate authors, in time for the next edition. Each person who sends us information is thanked in the next edition – and the most useful submissions are rewarded with a free book.

Visit **lonelyplanet.com/contact** to submit your updates and suggestions or to ask for help. Our award-winning website also features inspirational travel stories, news and discussions.

Note: We may edit, reproduce and incorporate your comments in Lonely Planet products such as guidebooks, websites and digital products, so let us know if you don't want your comments reproduced or your name acknowledged. For a copy of our privacy policy visit lonelyplanet.com/privacy.

OUR READERS

Many thanks to the travellers who used the last edition and wrote to us with helpful hints, useful advice and interesting anecdotes:

Andrew Atkinson, Linda Banks, David Bielamowicz, Sander Bot, Norman Bowe, Cecilia, William Chang, Brian C Chao, Adia Chen, David Chen, Mario Chen, Bill Cox, Taras Czebiniak, John Dankowski, Ariane De Dominicis, Myrtle De Souza, Claire Debenham, Jana Eichel, Gillian Finlay, Matthew Gibson, Jessica Goldblatt, John H, Friederike Haberstroh, Martin Hajek, Alex Horwath, Wayne Hsu, Alice Huang, Seow Hwei Mar, Fan Jack, Patrik Johansson, Michelle Josselyn, David Kendall, Anna Khoo, Mannis Kishon, Marcus Koeman, Justyna Korczynski, Stan Lai, Jill Linderwell, Don Macdonald, Jo Ann Mackenzie, Christoph Mahrenholtz, Rene Meulenbeld, Jens Müller, Luke Perry, Vitus Persson, Philipp, David Porter, Michelle Posadas, David Ragg, Andrea Rau, Irit Reinheimer, Thomas Roth, Erika Skogg, Adrien Stoloff, Gyoergy Szell, Rich Tao, Tim, Graeme Truscott, George Van Den Hove, Frank Van Der Heyden, Sophie Viskich, Grant Volk, David Wagner, Marcel Willems, Yvonne, Ultich Ziefet

AUTHOR THANKS

Robert Kelly

First, a warm thanks to Emily Wolman and Liz Heynes at Lonely Planet. I wish I could also mention by name the myriad surfers, cyclists, scuba divers and hikers whose insights have helped make this book the best it can be. But you know who you are. Little Gabriel, here's to you at least. And as always, deepest thanks to Huei-ming, Kate and Sean for holding down the fort while I was away.

Joshua Samuel Brown

Thanks to all the folks who tagged or got dragged along during my explorations, giving me many fresh eyes through which to view a familiar city: the Brown-Waite clan (Eve, John, Sierra and Jeremiah) and fellow Taipei-based artists and travellers Anna, Leeloo, Dave, Carrie, Phillip, Tammy and Russell. Special thanks to friend and photo-guru, Tobie Openshaw (shooter of my bio portrait), to fellow Asia-based journo Sam Chambers for timely advice, and to Laurie Brown for support mental and material.

ACKNOWLEDGMENTS

Climate map data adapted from Peel MC, Finlayson BL & McMahon TA (2007) 'Updated World Map of the Köppen-Geiger Climate Classification', *Hydrology and Earth System Sciences*, 11, 163344.

Cover photograph: Lantern at entrance to Bao-an Temple, Taipei, Richard l'Anson/ Lonely Planet Images. Many of the images in this guide are available for licensing from Lonely Planet Images: www.lonelyplanetimages.com.

THIS BOOK

This 8th edition of Lonely Planet's *Taiwan* guidebook was researched and written by Robert Kelly and Joshua Samuel Brown. Robert and Joshua also wrote the previous edition. This guidebook was commissioned in Lonely Planet's Oakland office, and produced by the following:

Commissioning Editors Emily K Wolman, Catherine Craddock, Kathleen Munnelly

Coordinating Editor Nigel Chin

Coordinating Cartographer Hunor Csutoros

Coordinating Layout Designer Yvonne Bischofberger

Managing Editor Liz Heynes

Managing Cartographer David Connolly

Managing Layout Designer Indra Kilfoyle

Assisting Editors Kim Hutchins, Joanne Newell, Kristin Odijk, Charlotte Orr, Alison Ridgway, Gabrielle Stefanos

Assisting Cartographers Csanad Csutoros, Xavier Di Toro

Assisting Layout Designers Paul Iacono, Jacqui Saunders

Cover Research Naomi Parker

Internal Image Research Aude Vauconsant

Language Content Branislava Vladisavljevic

Expert Language Advice Betsy Hung

Thanks to

Mark Adams, Imogen Bannister, Melanie Dankel, Stefanie Di Trocchio, Janine Eberle, Joshua Geoghegan, Mark Germanchis, Michelle Glynn, Lauren Hunt, Laura Jane, Evan Jones, David Kemp, Lisa Knights, Rebecca Lalor, Nic Lehman, John Mazzocchi, Annelies Mertens, Wayne Murphy, Katie O'Connell, Susan Paterson, Adrian Persoglia, Piers Pickard, Raphael Richards, Lachlan Ross, Michael Ruff, Simon Sellars, Julie Sheridan, Laura Stansfeld, John Taufa, Angela Tinson, Sam Trafford, Juan Winata, Nick Wood

index

Map Pages **p000**
Photo Pages **p000**

I

J

K

L

M

Map Pages **p000**
Photo Pages **p000**

N

O

P

Q

R

Map Pages **p000**
Photo Pages p000

U

V

W

X

Y

Z

how to use this book

These symbols will help you find the listings you want:

- Sights
- Activities
- Courses
- Tours
- Festivals & Events
- Sleeping
- Eating
- Drinking
- Entertainment
- Shopping
- Information/ Transport

These symbols give you the vital information for each listing:

- Telephone Numbers
- Opening Hours
- Parking
- Nonsmoking
- Air-Conditioning
- Internet Access
- Wi-Fi Access
- Swimming Pool
- Vegetarian Selection
- English-Language Menu
- Family-Friendly
- Pet-Friendly
- Bus
- Ferry
- Metro
- Subway
- London Tube
- Tram
- Train

Reviews are organised by author preference.

Look out for these icons:

- TOP CHOICE — Our author's recommendation
- FREE — No payment required
- A green or sustainable option

Our authors have nominated these places as demonstrating a strong commitment to sustainability – for example by supporting local communities and producers, operating in an environmentally friendly way, or supporting conservation projects.

Map Legend

Sights

- Beach
- Buddhist
- Castle
- Christian
- Hindu
- Islamic
- Jewish
- Monument
- Museum/Gallery
- Ruin
- Winery/Vineyard
- Zoo
- Other Sight

Activities, Courses & Tours

- Diving/Snorkelling
- Canoeing/Kayaking
- Skiing
- Surfing
- Swimming/Pool
- Walking
- Windsurfing
- Other Activity/ Course/Tour

Sleeping

- Sleeping
- Camping

Eating

- Eating

Drinking

- Drinking
- Cafe

Entertainment

- Entertainment

Shopping

- Shopping

Information

- Bank
- Embassy/ Consulate
- Hospital/Medical
- Internet
- Police
- Post Office
- Telephone
- Toilet
- Tourist Information
- Other Information

Transport

- Airport
- Border Crossing
- Bus
- Cable Car/ Funicular
- Cycling
- Ferry
- Metro
- Monorail
- Parking
- Petrol Station
- Taxi
- Train/Railway
- Tram
- Other Transport

Routes

- Tollway
- Freeway
- Primary
- Secondary
- Tertiary
- Lane
- Unsealed Road
- Plaza/Mall
- Steps
- Tunnel
- Pedestrian Overpass
- Walking Tour
- Walking Tour Detour
- Path

Geographic

- Hut/Shelter
- Lighthouse
- Lookout
- Mountain/Volcano
- Oasis
- Park
- Pass
- Picnic Area
- Waterfall

Population

- Capital (National)
- Capital (State/Province)
- City/Large Town
- Town/Village

Boundaries

- International
- State/Province
- Disputed
- Regional/Suburb
- Marine Park
- Cliff
- Wall

Hydrography

- River, Creek
- Intermittent River
- Swamp/Mangrove
- Reef
- Canal
- Water
- Dry/Salt/ Intermittent Lake
- Glacier

Areas

- Beach/Desert
- Cemetery (Christian)
- Cemetery (Other)
- Park/Forest
- Sportsground
- Sight (Building)
- Top Sight (Building)

OUR STORY

A beat-up old car, a few dollars in the pocket and a sense of adventure. In 1972 that's all Tony and Maureen Wheeler needed for the trip of a lifetime – across Europe and Asia overland to Australia. It took several months, and at the end – broke but inspired – they sat at their kitchen table writing and stapling together their first travel guide, *Across Asia on the Cheap*. Within a week they'd sold 1500 copies. Lonely Planet was born.

Today, Lonely Planet has offices in Melbourne, London and Oakland, with more than 600 staff and writers. We share Tony's belief that 'a great guidebook should do three things: inform, educate and amuse'.

OUR WRITERS

Robert Kelly

Coordinating Author; Maokong (Taipei), Northern Taiwan, Taroko National Park & the East Coast, Yushan National Park & Western Taiwan, Southern Taiwan, Taiwan's Islands Ever since he learned that his dad's airline job meant he could fly for peanuts (thanks, Dad), Robert has been travelling. He arrived in Taiwan 15 years ago and quickly found a place he could call home. Though never one to go native, Robert has picked up a few new habits including a deep love of tea, affection for poisonous snakes, an appreciation of the difference between shale and schist mountain slopes, and a love of all things soy. This is Robert's third time writing the *Taiwan* guide for Lonely Planet and once again his final remark remains the same: he has no plans to leave this country now that he's seen yet even more of what it has to offer.

Joshua Samuel Brown

Taipei, Keelung (Northern Taiwan) A 2009 USC Annenberg/Getty Arts Journalism fellow, prolific traveller, writer and photographer, Joshua Samuel Brown (aka Josambro) has written for an eclectic variety of publications around the globe, including the *South China Morning Post*, *Business Traveller Asia*, *Clamor Magazine* and *Cat Fancy*. Joshua's debut book, *Vignettes of Taiwan*, offers tales of betel nut beauties and how to avoid jail time by impersonating a Mormon; it's available through his website www.josambro.com. Still going strong five years on, his blog, *Snarky Tofu*, can be read at http://josambro.blogspot.com. This is Joshua's seventh guide for Lonely Planet.

Published by Lonely Planet Publications Pty Ltd
ABN 36 005 607 983
8th edition – March 2011
ISBN 978 1 74179 043 6

10 9 8 7 6 5 4 3 2
Printed in Singapore